The Labour Party: A Marxist History

Tony Cliff
Donny Gluckstein
&
Charlie Kimber

The Labour Party: A Marxist History
Tony Cliff, Donny Gluckstein & Charlie Kimber

First published October 1988
Second Edition July 1996
This edition December 2018

c/o 1 Bloomsbury Street, London WC1B 3QE

Typeset by Peter Robinson
Cover design Ben Windsor
Printed by Short Run Press Ltd

ISBN 9781910885918 (pbk)
9781910885925 (Kindle)
9781910885932 (ePub)
9781910885949 (PDF)

Contents

Acknowledgements

Several people have helped in the writing and preparation of this book. Many thanks are due to Alex Callinicos, Linsey German, Duncan Hallas, Chris Harman and Gareth Jenkins for their advice and suggestions. We also owe a debt to Lynda Aitken, Sue Cockerill, Geoff Ellen, Nick Howard and Martin Rosier for help in locating material and to Peter Marsden for editing and advice. Chanie Rosenberg deserves a special thanks for work on research materials in the Public Record Office and elsewhere, for typing and for allowing us to borrow freely from her article on the Labour Party and the struggle against fascism.

—Tony Cliff and Donny Gluckstein, 31 March 1988

Donny Gluckstein would also like to acknowledge the invaluable help of Mike Cowley in locating materials for the chapter on New Labour in government.

—Donny Gluckstein and Charlie Kimber, September 2018

Introduction to the third edition

An extraordinary transformation in the image of the Labour Party happened in 2015 with Jeremy Corbyn's election as leader. A party that had acted as an efficient and loyal servant of the capitalist class was suddenly speaking about a challenge to big business, the banks and the super-rich.

Corbyn's success has boosted the whole left, demonstrating how socialist ideas can be popular and can conquer wide backing from working class people. One of the best aspects is that politics has been at least partially raised from a discussion about small managerial alterations within a generally agreed framework of pro-business schemes. Until recently the limit of radicalism was policies such as a cap on energy prices charged by the privatised firms. Now it is possible to discuss nationalisation and what form this should take. Capitalism constantly tries to reduce our horizons to the level of the individual, personal responsibility and detail. This is how the systematic nature of exploitation and oppression is obscured and denied. But now there are debates about structures and overarching patterns.

During the years of Tony Blair's overtly pro-imperialist and neoliberal government many left wing Labour members were shamefaced about their support for their party. After Corbyn's election as leader their hopes soared, and many thousands who had left because they were sickened by Blair returned with new determination to achieve important changes in society through the mechanism of a Labour government.

But at the same time the great majority of Labour MPs remain wholly opposed to Corbyn. A leader who they regard with contempt has been imposed on them by a mass membership (who most MPs despise), and by his ability to crush opponents in leadership elections and drive up the Labour vote in a general election. Yet the MPs and the Labour right are in no way reconciled to this situation. New methods, such as the furore over alleged antisemitism, are regularly used in an effort to demoralise Corbyn and his supporters and force him to make concessions. Regrettably he has frequently compromised with these forces rather than using his mass support to drive them out.

Throughout history Labour's left has prioritised the party's unity over principled support for socialist principles. Far too often they have stifled their criticisms of imperialist war and pro-capitalist policies in order to keep the centre of the party on board, in the hope that it will then ally against the right. But, influenced in its turn by the most backward forces within the party and the trade union leaderships, the centre demands further retreats by the left. The result is a spiral of concessions that becomes stronger the closer Labour seems to entering government.

But disenchantment with the system continues to grow. A City fund manager told a newspaper in 2018, "Capitalism is not working for the under-40s, so they're voting for socialism." Actually it's not working for the over-40s either. In the United States just 45 percent of 18-29 year olds view capitalism positively. "This represents a 12-point decline in young adults' positive views of capitalism in just the past two years and a marked shift since 2010, when 68 percent viewed it positively," notes pollster Gallup. Meanwhile, 51 percent of young people are positive about socialism.

There are reasons to see the potential for a fight for a socialist world, despite the towering threat from the racists and the far right. Yet many of these discussions underplay or recklessly ignore the question of the power of capitalism and the state. Unfortunately neither of these will disregard any attempt at fundamental change that begins to encroach on the wealth and power of the ruling class. The class forcibly separated from the means of production, the working class, has a very big struggle ahead if it is to shape history.

Parliamentary parties such as Labour face the limitations that come from the electoral and constitutional sphere dominating over extra-parliamentary work. Such pressures have always been present, and they still are today. They have been quite well expressed by Francisco Louca, one of the leading figures of the Portuguese Left Bloc. Reflecting on the Bloc's recent experience in parliament he warned of the danger of "resignation to very limited measures in the name of maintaining the positions acquired; refusal to criticise the institutions or their management in the name of possible future agreements; the idea that politics advances in small steps; fear of public opinion, which leads to not presenting a socialist alternative and which leads to other institutional forms; desire to avoid the risk of conflict for fear of losing. All these forms of adaptation distort a left-wing policy based on popular representation".

Corbyn's enemies—big business, the Tories, most of the media, the Labour right—will hit him with huge assaults if he reaches Number 10. There's a real danger for those of us who are revolutionaries to look at this situation and say, "Well I've seen this film before; I know how it ends." What we should say is that we have to ensure we don't go down that same path. A revolutionary's job is certainly to point out the historical experience of Labour governments in Britain who said they were socialist, but then failed the working class. But it's also to say that the key thing that will prevent us simply repeating that experience is the systematic mobilisation of the masses in the workplaces and in the streets.

When Tony Cliff and Donny Gluckstein wrote the original version of this book in the mid-1980s, a generation of former radical socialists had recently entered the Labour Party to support the Benn leadership challenge, only to find themselves trapped in a rightward moving party whose leadership openly attacked its left wing members and retreated from the key class battles against Thatcher such as the miners strike. The book was aimed at providing an historical understanding of these types of betrayals. The second edition was published in 1996, just as Blair's New Labour project, based on the jettisoning of any reference to socialism, was building momentum as a weak and unpopular Tory government staggered to defeat. The circumstances today are different. A new generation and many thousands of older supporters have joined or rejoined the Labour Party inspired by Jeremy Corbyn's leadership. But the sheer enthusiasm for Corbyn's socialist vision and obvious sincerity, after the years of cynicism and betrayal by Blair and Brown, runs the risk of obscuring the actual history of the Labour Party and laying the blame for past failure solely at the feet of individual treacherous leaders. We need a deeper understanding of the nature of the Labour Party, its role in society, as a guide to action in the years ahead.

The experience of a Corbyn-led Labour government will make all these questions clearer. But if that experience is not to demoralise many of those who are now so hopeful, it is essential that as many people as possible learn the lessons from the past and seek to broaden the knowledge of what is fundamental to reformism and Labour beyond any particular leader or grouping in the party. That is what this book sets out to do, to use history and theory as an aid to the debates that are taking place as we unite against the right and capitalism.

We have tried to answer the key questions.

The politics of the Labour Party

- How does its political practice compare to its programme and how have the two developed?
- How have the right and the left fared in shaping Labour policy?

The influence of leadership

— Did Blair change Labour fundamentally, and can Corbyn?

The internal divisions in the Labour Party

— What decides the relative strength of the party's factions?
— What are the limits on the activities of the left and of the right?

The organisation of the Labour Party

— Who controls whom? What are the respective roles of the Parliamentary Labour Party, the National Executive Committee and Conference?
— What influence do the trade union leaders have on the party, and what influence does the Labour Party have on them?
— What is the relationship between Labour's grassroots and Labour in parliament?

The relationship between the Labour Party and struggles in workplaces

— What do the Labour leaders say about such struggle?
— What happens to Labour support during, before and after major periods of class warfare such as 1910–14, 1919–26, 1968–74; 1976–87, 2010–11?
— Does Labour do well in downturns, in resistance or does it benefit from upturns—what is the relationship?

The Labour Left

— Who are they? What do they say? How do they see parliamentary and extra-parliamentary activity?
— How do they operate inside the party—through MPs, through general management committees, the trade unions or local councils?
— How does the Labour left relate to left forces active in workplaces and campaigns? Should revolutionary socialists enter the Labour Party?

The loyalty of workers to the Labour Party in spite of its actions

— Is this loyalty affected by whether Labour is in office or in opposition?
— Is it affected by the state of the economy—whether it is booming or not?
— Is loyalty dependent on the ability of the Labour Party to deliver reforms? Can there be reformism without reforms?

How can revolutionary socialists convince the majority of workers to go beyond Labour's reformism?

— What role does a mass revolutionary party and a big rise in the level of class struggle play in this?

1

The birth of reformism

The precursors: from Chartism to the Independent Labour Party

In 1911 Ramsay MacDonald wrote:

> The Labour Party...is the only political form which evolutionary Socialism can take in a country with the political traditions and methods of Great Britain.[1]

This statement is false. At different times British workers have given mass support to political ideas that are in sharp contrast to reformism. Only in the twentieth century were majority won to the reformist position.

Between 1839 and 1848 workers supported Chartism. Unlike the Labour Party this rejected the legal framework of existing society.* In November 1839, for example, there was an armed rising by several thousand Chartist miners at Newport. Chartism's most prominent demand was for universal suffrage, but to have granted the vote when the working class was in revolutionary mood would have mortally threatened bourgeois society. The ruling class felt that, in the words of Macaulay to the Commons, universal suffrage was 'incompatible with the very existence of civilisation'.[3]

The Labour Party operates a strict division between trade union officials, who take care of wages and conditions, and members of parliament, whose concern is 'politics'. In the Chartist period there was no barrier between political and industrial activity. The Chartist Convention of 1839 made it clear that direct action, not canvassing, was the way forward:

> The Convention continues to be unanimously of the opinion that nothing short of a general strike, or suspension of labour through-out

* The idea of petitioning for the 'Six Points' of the Charter was originally mooted by reformists like William Lovett. But once the movement gained a mass basis the idea of appealing to the goodness of the upper classes disappeared. As Thompson puts it: 'the actual collection of signatures to the petition does not seem to have been a major preoccupation of the new groups... It is also noticeable that none of the recollections of ex-Chartists mentions the collection of signatures as a remembered form of activity'.[2]

> the country, will ever suffice to re-establish the rights and liberties of the industrial classes.[4]

In 1842 the general strike became a reality. This was the first such strike in the world and lasted longer than the 1926 General Strike. Half a million workers initially downed tools because of wage cuts, but soon factory after factory declared itself '"ready to strike for the Charter, but not for wages"... This was the general line'.[5]

Chartism was unashamedly a class movement. Its demands were of revolutionary significance and it saw workers' self-activity as the means to winning these demands. But the movement was extinguished after 1848: In the decades that followed social peace and imperial prosperity prevailed. Britain had become 'the work-shop of the world.' In the boom workers were able to win a rising standard of living.

The militancy and unity of earlier years broke up and the Chartist idea of strikes as a political weapon was absolutely repudiated. In 1856, for example, the engineers' leader declared: 'We do not allow any political matter to be discussed at all nor entertained among us'.[6] Theodore Rothstein shows how this worked in practice:

> the slogan of 'No Politics'...applied only to the organised forms of politics based upon the class struggle. In other words, every individual worker could privately engage in politics... Naturally, by thus atomising himself politically...the English worker fell an easy prey to the organised force of bourgeois party ideology and became a Conservative or a Liberal.[7]

A sign of the collapse of class politics since Chartism was the granting of votes to men living in towns and cities in 1867. By this means Disraeli's Tory government hoped to buy workers' allegiance. Twenty years earlier a similar move would have meant 'the end of civilisation', but now Viscount Halifax reassured the House of Lords of 'the almost universal reasonableness of the working classes...and their vast improvement of late years'.[8] In 1884 rural male workers were also given the vote since it was judged that they too had an unquestioning acceptance of capitalism.

Marx was scathing about British workers at this time:

> The English working-class had been gradually becoming more and more deeply demoralised by the period of corruption since 1848 and had at last got to the point when it was nothing more than the tail of the Great Liberal Party, ie, of its *oppressors*, the capitalists.[9]

In 1874 'the first labour MPs', Thomas Burt and Alexander MacDonald, were elected. Both were mining officials who stood as Liberals. Burt opposed a separate workers' party because: 'Classes they have, and class distinctions they possibly would always have, but they should not accentuate their class differences'.[10] Alexander MacDonald told his union conference: 'he trusted that in their efforts to put down strikes they would accomplish a great work for which posterity would thank them'.[11] These two alone should have been sufficient to expire the myth that the mere fact that workers sit in parliament represents serious progress for the class.

Burt and MacDonald were known as Lib-Labs. This group never grew into a serious force because Liberal voters preferred to elect genuine members of the ruling class rather than union officials who aped them. The Lib-Labs were moved to complain:

> We have ever sought to be allied to the great Liberal Party, to which we, by conviction, belong. They have not reciprocated this feeling... middle-class Liberals preferred voting for the Tories rather than support a working-class candidate.[12]

Nevertheless, a few Lib-Labs were elected from time to time. In 1900 there were 11 of them. There was even a union sponsored Tory-Lab candidate, a cotton union official from Lancashire!

However, such MPs depended on the boom conditions that accompanied Britain's monopoly of world trade. Only in such a situation could workers logically think 'what is good for my boss is good for me', and vote for openly capitalist parties. Engels accurately predicted that 'once America and the joint competition of the other industrial countries make a big enough breach in this monopoly...you will see a lot of things happen here'.[13] Between 1870 and 1913 Britain's share of world trade fell from 30 percent to 15 percent[14], and in 1889 Engels was vindicated by the appearance of new unionism, which led to a break with Lib-Labism.

From New Unionism to reformist politics

The roots of the 1889 strike wave were economic. Yet there had been similar economic fluctuations before without any dramatic new departures. *A crucial factor in the 1889 explosion was the intervention of socialists who, though tiny in number, played a leading role.*[15] Many of them were associated with the Marxist Social Democratic Federation (SDF).

The most famous incident was the 'Great London Dock Strike' led by socialists such as Tom Mann, John Burns and Ben Tillett. Until that time dockers had been, in Engels' words, 'the lowest of the outcasts...a mass of broken-down humanity who are drifting toward total ruination...this host of utterly despondent men'.[16] Now 30,000 dockers had paralysed the largest and wealthiest city in the world, the hub of the biggest Empire, and won!

The new unions were based on unskilled or semi-skilled men and women. It had been thought they could not be organised since they lacked the bargaining power of craftsmen. This was proved wrong for the new 'General Unions', unlike the old ones, looked to organisation across the class embracing all types of worker. Old unions put their faith in negotiation and conciliation; the new turned to direct action with mass pickets and physical resistance to scabbing.

Instead of tailing bourgeois parties, the most advanced new unionists based themselves on the power of the working class: 'our cry is still the vehement and bitter cry of labour against capital. While we are still at war we shall hold out no flag of trace to the capitalist until the product of our labour is ours and not his'.[17] Socialists like Mann coupled the building of union organisation with a demand for the legal eight-hour day, to be forced from the state, thus linking the collective strength of the working class with political demands.

The new unionists thus challenged the institutional separation of politics and economics. It is through this division that the system prevents collective struggle spilling over into a threat to its very survival, because the state faces workers in their capacity as voters only, as atomised individuals. Marx recognised the significance of the campaign for a statutory eight-hour day:

> every movement which the working class comes out as a class against the ruling classes and tries to coerce them by pressure from without is a political movement...the attempt in a particular factory or even in a particular trade to force a shorter working day out of individual capitalists by strikes, etc. is a purely economic movement. On the other hand the movement to force through an eight-hour law is a political movement.[18]

The old unionist leaders fought the new trend bitterly. George Shipton, chairman of the London Trades Council, led the attack. He condemned revolutionary political methods. Instead of mass demonstrations designed to force concessions *from* the state, they should work *through* it: 'When the people were un-enfranchised, were without votes, the only power left to them was the demonstration of numbers. Now, however, the workmen have votes'.[19] Shipton also opposed introducing politics into union struggles: 'The "new trade unionists" look to Governments and legislation; the "old" look to self-reliance'.[20]

Tillett and Mann offered an equally vigorous reply which showed where they differed both from reformist dependence on parliament and the separation of politics and economics. They stressed workers' self-organisation as the key to progress:

> we have been at pains to discredit appeal to the legislature, contending that the political machine will fail into our hands as a matter of course, so soon as the educational work has been done in our labour organisations... The statement that the "new" trade unionists look to governments and legislation is bunkum; the key-note is to ORGANISE first, and take action...[21]

The militant industrial activity of this period had nothing in common with parliamentary reformism, yet within a few years this was what it produced. How was the movement transformed?

The heroic phase of new unionism was short-lived. The ruling class fought back using lockouts and mass scabbing to break the weakest groups. This succeeded because British capitalism's crisis was not so deep that all sections of the working class were stirred up. The hostility of the older unions also obstructed unity. Finally the SDF, the main organisation on the left, was incurably sectarian. It ignored the value of trade union activity and dismissed the dock strike in patronising tones. In September 1889, at the very moment of victory, it published an article entitled 'The Errors of the Strike' which said: 'We congratulate the dockers on the very little modicum of success that has been obtained at so great a cost'.[22]

Between 1890 and 1892 membership of the new unions fell from 320,000 to 130,000, slipping from a peak of one quarter of the Trades Union Congress to 10 percent in 1900. The Gas Workers, the most politically advanced, dropped from 60,000 in 1890 to 24,000 in 1896.[23] Trade unionism in general suffered a serious setback, membership falling by 40 percent in just three years.

With union machines to protect, leaders like Will Thorne and Ben Tillett rapidly adopted some of the conservative attitudes they had criticised in the 'old' union bureaucrats. In 1893 Tillett blocked a national strike against mass scabbing at Hull docks. In 1894 Thorne 'exhorted his members to rely on the advice of their officials, declaring that "a firm stand should be made against men coming out on strike, unless oppressed to such an extent that their position is unbearable."'[24]

At the start new unionist leaders had understood the need for workers' *political action*. Reporting to the Second International in 1891, the Gas-Workers' delegation declared:

> The successful, like the unsuccessful strikes...all of the hundreds of large and small strikes of the last two years, point to the same moral and adorn the same tale—that Trade Unionism and Strikes alone will not emancipate the working class.[25]

It was one thing to understand the need to challenge capitalism politically, but it was possible to draw either revolutionary or reformist conclusions.

One possible direction was to use the fight for reforms, including placing demands on parliament, *as a means of mobilising the working class* and through this experience preparing *the final, revolutionary, struggle for socialism*. But the reformist attitude to parliament was *a means of demobilising the class*, asking it to rely on leaders who avoid confrontation and work within the system. *Their negotiating skills substitute for mass activity*.

Alas, the sectarian attitude of the SDF meant that in the 1890s only the latter alternative was presented, and it triumphed across the board. Even the minority who would have accepted the revolutionary arguments were not organised into a permanent force, and the most advanced ideas of new unionism disappeared without trace.

Tom Mann was one of the last to leave the field. In June 1891 he could still write: 'the belief is quite sincerely held...that parliamentary action is desirable *as a substitute* for unionism...how absurd'.[26] But a new attitude soon emerged. Its most public manifestation was Tillett's parliamentary candidature in Bradford. In 1889 and 1890 he had turned down offers to stand. 'Never mind party politics, to hell with them', was his comment.[27] Yet in September 1891 he accepted the candidature. The tenor of his campaign was significant:

> An avowed socialist, Tillett did not once mention the word 'socialism' during the run-up to the election... He also reprinted in his campaign literature the commendation he had received from the elders of the Congregational Church: 'We have reason devoutly to thank God that our Leader of undisciplined labour is a man like Tillett, a good

> soldier of Jesus Christ, and not a Marat'... He seems to have consciously refrained from envisioning the socialist millennium, remarking on at least three separate occasions that he would not do so.[28]

Tillett's campaign symbolised a general trend among thousands of workers. For Bradford was the clearest example of how industrial defeat led to reformist politics. It was here that the ILP—the Independent Labour Party—held its 1893 founding conference. This city alone provided one sixth of the ILP's affiliation fees, while the West Yorkshire woollen district, of which it was the heart, sent a third of the conference delegates.[29]

Bradford was ideal ground for reformism because it had briefly enjoyed a new unionist upsurge which had been crippled. The turning point was the fight at Manningham Mills against wage cuts of up to 33 percent. It lasted for six months, involved 3,000 workers and included pitched battles in the town centre.[30] Eventually the workers were starved back. After this Bradford became, in the words of Ben Turner, the union organiser, 'the most heart-breaking district for Trade Union organisation that ever I came across'.[31]*

Against this background the Independent Labour Party was founded on 14 January 1893. What had happened since 1889 to make such a reformist party possible? First there were the economic troubles accompanying foreign competition. Secondly there was mass industrial struggle given a coherence by socialist leadership. Without these there could have been no serious break with the politics of Lib-Labism.

If industrial militancy had not been repulsed, a strong political movement based on confidence and self-activity could have emerged. As it was, in 1893 there was the correct combination of circumstances for reformism: workers' struggles had built up organisation but defeats had pushed it into bureaucratic channels. On both the industrial and political fronts leaders had been raised into prominence by the fight, but now they substituted for the movement of the mass. The ILP was not the child of new unionism, but of its defeat. Here in a microcosm was the relationship between reformism and the working class.

* Leeds, just eight miles away from Bradford, provides a fascinating contrast: 'the first authentic ILP councillor in Leeds was not elected until 1906, when Jowett had already done fourteen magnificent years of service on the Bradford Council ... But if we note the social and industrial contrasts, some of the reasons become apparent... The unskilled male workers were in general successful in improving their conditions is a result of new unionism, and some of their discontent was dispersed: the gas strike was short, sharp and victorious where that at Manningham Mills was long, humiliating and a defeat'.[32]

The Independent Labour Party

The ILP marked a limited breach with the 'great Liberal Party'. In Bradford a characteristic debate took place around the party's name. The proposal to call it the 'Socialist Labour Party' was lost to the alternative title of '*Independent* Labour Party' on the grounds that 'they had to appeal to the vast mass of workers outside, and not only to Socialists'.[33]

The issue was fundamental. If the aim was to build an active opposition to capitalism, then what mattered most was not the number of votes, but the number committed to working for socialism. But near unanimous backing for the name Independent Labour Party showed the delegates put electoral success *first*. As Keir Hardie, the ILP's undisputed leader, put it: 'The number of Labour Members in the House of Commons. This, to me, is the question of questions'.[34]

However the title 'Independent' was insufficient to guarantee the party's future. After all, the Lib-Labs, such as miners' MP Charles Fenwick, talked like the ILP about 'the imperative necessity of returning to Parliament...workmen who should be able to speak with authority on all questions affecting the working classes.' They too promoted 'a policy of reform, and not of revolution'.[35] The ILP had to distinguish itself from Lib-Labism and so adopted as its object: 'the collective and communal ownership of the means of production, distribution and exchange.'

This was not a cynical ploy. It reflected the after-glow of new unionist struggles. Later attempts to dilute or deviate from what the ILP rank and file considered the fundamentals of socialism led to massive fights which in 1932 tore the party apart. In this sense the ILP was very different from the Labour Party at its formation. It was formed of individual activists whose ideas had developed through class struggle, even if they retreated into reformist politics. The Labour Party itself began without individual membership, through a process of union affiliation and bureaucratic manipulation.

The myth of the Golden Age

The ILP believed the working class could be freed through the institutions of the capitalist nation state. This has been proved wrong by the failure of successive Labour governments to challenge capitalism. But in 1893 there were no practical examples to refute the reformist argument. The compromises required to get a Labour government had only just begun and would take forty years to work through. Only at the end, in 1932, was the ILP made to face up to the consequences of the position it adopted at Bradford, and the result was its complete collapse.

It is because the logic of reformism unfolded so gradually that there arose the myth of Labour's golden age, a myth as old as Labour itself. In later years those who had descended the parliamentary road, that road upon which workers' interests are exchanged for electoral advantage, would look back on the group who started out from the top of the hill. Inevitably these pioneers appeared to be more elevated and inspired by lofty ideals. As early as 1921 a disillusioned Labour supporter could write:

> between those early days of ardent faith and heroic self-sacrifice, those days of Keir Hardie's cloth cap in the House of Commons, and these days of the political machine with its seeking of votes and place, there is a great gulf fixed.[36]

The gulf was an illusion. Labour's politics have never changed in essentials. The difference between old and new lies in the external conditions in which this reformism operates. Labour has no pure workers' tradition to return to. If we might abuse Shakespeare: some parties are born rotten, some parties achieve rottenness, and some have rottenness thrust upon them. There have been examples of each. *The Russian Communists* had their degeneration thrust upon them by the defeat of the German revolution, the isolation of Russia, its invasion by 16 foreign armies and a civil war. *The German Social Democrats* (SPD) achieved opportunism over a long period and with much effort from people like Kautsky and Bernstein. But *the Labour Party*, even at its origins, has never been anything but reformist.

The Dependent Labour Party

Despite the drawbacks, the foundation of the ILP had a very positive side. In 1886 Engels had pointed to the need for a separate workers' political organisation, whatever its limitations:

> The first great step in a country which enters the movement for the first time is to constitute the workers as an independent Labour party, no matter in what way, so long as it is a distinct Labour party...as long as it is their own movement—[the workers] will be driven forward by their own mistakes, and acquire wisdom by their failures.[37]

Though wisdom through failure has been a long time coming, Engels was right to recognise in the formation of the ILP a genuine step forward for the class.

Yet it is one of the ironies of history that the Independent Labour Party should have been one of the most *dependent* organisations ever created. It was totally reliant on groupings outside the working class for its theory. This was notwithstanding the fact that, as Philip Snowden said: '...the branches were composed almost exclusively of working people.'[38]

Theory is a perennial problem for reformists. *The tradition of bourgeois thought, and that of the working class—which is Marxism—are each based on the lives of the two contending classes of society.* Through philosophers, historians, politicians and economists the capitalists create an intellectual culture to justify their existence. Marxism draws upon the international history of working class struggle. But reformists have *no independent tradition*. They limit themselves to working through established institutions, and so pursue an uneasy theoretical path, seeking to channel working class aspirations *in an ideological framework set by the system*.

None of this can gainsay the dedication of the ILP's membership. As Keir Hardie put it:

> Few of the casual passers-by who halt for a few minutes to listen to a Socialist speaker standing on an upturned soap box under a lamp post at the corner of a noisy street are like to carry away a religious impression... But get to know the man and his work; how he leaves home night after night, undergoing fatigue and inconvenience after a day's laborious toil, how he spends Sunday in visiting some neighbouring town for propaganda purposes, or is hard at work all day in his own town aiding in the arrangements for the two Sunday meetings, and how he continues to do this year in and year out without any hope of fee or reward, and then the truth begins to dawn upon you that the man is at bottom a religious enthusiast lured on by his vision of a Kingdom of God up Earth.[39]

Compare this with a later description of the Conservative temperament from the pen of Lord Hailsham:

> Conservatives do not believe that political struggle is the most important thing in life. In this they differ from...most members of the British Labour Party. The simplest among them prefer fox-hunting—the wisest, religion.[40]

In life-style the gulf between the working class soap-box orator and the fox-hunter could hardly be greater. What they share is religion. The ILP's Nonconformist religious fervour was the clearest proof of its intellectual dependence. True, the Chapel tradition was not, like the Anglican Church, associated with land-owning interests. But its stress on the idea of employer and workman worshipping together emphasised a feeling of common interest and common ideology. To Trotsky this was clear proof that the British bourgeois had 'laid down from above up its proletariat the heavy lid of cultural conservatism'.[41]

The ILP's greatest propagandist was Philip Snowden, who earned his reputation by a recruiting technique known as 'Philip's Come to Jesus'. To a background of singing, converts were ushered forward while Snowden declared in ringing tones:

> there are signs on every hand of a great and righteous power at work in the world. The Sun of Righteousness is rising with healing in its wings. The Christ that is to be appears. A new and brighter social order will arise. It is the promised New Jerusalem.[42]

The importance of religion in the ILP and the early Labour Party was immense. Even Tom Mann, who went on to lead the syndicalist movement of 1911–14 and eventually joined the Communist Party, thought of joining the priesthood at about the same time as he was ILP Secretary. A fascinating survey was conducted into the books that most shaped the ideas of the Labour MPs who sat in the 1906–1910 parliament. Twenty-five of the forty include religious texts (sixteen specified the Bible). Only two mentioned Marx or Engels.[43]*

The ILP consistently talked of smoothing over class conflict, stressing the common interest of employers and workers. Hardie wrote: 'it is a degradation of the Socialist movement to drag it down to the level of a mere struggle for supremacy between two contending factions. We don't want "class conscious" Socialists'.[44] Ramsay MacDonald, whom Hardie acknowledged as the ILP's 'greatest intellectual asset', added: 'I reject what seems to be the crude notion of a class war, because class consciousness leads nowhere… The watchword of socialism is not class consciousness but community consciousness'.[45] Philip Snowden, who

* Other authors mentioned included John Ruskin (sixteen replies), whose critique of capitalism was moulded by a belief in a feudal golden age. Next came Henry George, popular advocate of land taxation, whom Engels described as 'a colossal fraud' (eleven replies). Shakespeare earned five and Robbie Burns and Charles Dickens, not noted for their political insights, each scored twice as many as Marx and Engels.

as the party's economic expert would be expected to know the blunt realities of capitalist society, went even further: 'the rich man...cannot enjoy his riches in the knowledge of the misery of the men and women and children around him... It is to the cultured and leisured class that Socialism makes, perhaps, its strongest appeal.'[46]

If class struggle annoyed the ILP it can be imagined what visions revolution conjured up. In 1895, for example, the *Labour Leader* warned that:

> The shadow of coming Revolution...looms dark and huge over the Continent of Europe. Should an outbreak occur there is nothing save a narrow strip of sea betwixt us and what would then be the theatre of a great human tragedy.[47]

Although the ILP was never revolutionary it was progressive in comparison to the Tories and Liberals. It recognised and indeed owed its existence to working class organisations such as the new unions, but rather than leading a confrontation with capitalism, it demanded that workers be given a place in the national set-up.

The impossibility of formulating an independent reformist theory has already been touched on. For Hardie ignorance was indeed bliss: 'the ILP...has never formulated its theory of Socialism. That is true, and therein lies its strength.'[48] This had devastating effects. It made the ILP incapable of any analysis of society, or even of its own place in history. Listen to Hardie's description of his party's birth: 'How did the ILP originate? Who shall say? Why do buds begin to unfold in spring? I am convinced there are spring tides connected with the affairs of man governed by laws of which we know next to nothing.'[49] The ILP was therefore defenceless against the ideas of capitalism which surrounded it. As ILP Chairman, Bruce Glasier declared: 'I am able to speak and work for Socialism without feeling that I belong to a different cast of beings from that of the ordinary Liberal or Tory.'[50]

This was the nub of the matter. The ILP channelled ideas into the working class that were drawn straight from the well of capitalism, and in particular from the Liberals and the Fabians. Both Hardie and Ramsay MacDonald turned to Labour politics only when they were rejected as Liberal candidates. Even then they repeatedly and publicly paid homage to Liberalism. In later years Keir Hardie claimed that his election as MP for South West Ham in 1892 made him the first socialist MP. It is true his enthusiastic supporters actually carried him to parliament in a carriage complete with trumpeter to announce the dawning of a new age,[51] hut his manifesto declared: 'I have all my life given an independent support to the Liberal Party... *I am in agreement with the present programme of the Liberal Party*.'[52]

Snowden reassured voters that he 'was cradled and nurtured in Liberalism'.[53] Robert Smillie, miners' leader and the ILP's most important industrial figure, claimed to be a better Liberal than the Literal candidate himself when he ran for North East Lanarkshire.[54] When MacDonald became Labour Party Secretary, the flirtation with Liberalism became almost obscene. An important article he and Hardie wrote 1899 twice declared the ILP linked to Liberalism through 'the true line of the progressive apostolic succession'.[55] They hoped to build 'a golden bridge of palliatives' between the two parties.[56]

There were, however, definite limits placed on the ILP's adoption of Liberal politics. An organisation which wanted to be an alternative to the Liberal Party needed to differentiate itself to some extent. To do this, the ILP leaned heavily on the Fabians.

'The worst enemies of social revolution'

These are the words of Beatrice Webb[57], a key figure in the Fabian Society. This organisation shaped both the ILP and later the Labour Party. As one historian put it: 'The Fabians gave modern British socialism its doctrine'.[58] It is surprising that such a tiny organisation could play so large a role. When it affiliated to the Labour Representation Committee in 1900 it had 861 members, after seventeen years. However the theoretical incapacity of the ILP gave the Fabians a pivotal role. Almost from the first two thirds of the ILP's ruling National Administrative Council (NAC), were Fabians, and they included Hardie, MacDonald, Mann—who was the ILP's secretary—, Tillett and Lansbury.[59]*

The Fabians' leaders—the Webb 'Partnership' of Beatrice and Sidney, along with George Bernard Shaw, the playwright, were not afraid to admit: 'we personally belong to the ruling class'.[60] For a long time the society had only one working class member, a house-painter, whom they regarded as an 'exhibit'.[61] The Fabian Society was actually more interested in influencing the upper class by a policy of 'permeating'

* It is evidence of the disregard for theory and looseness of organisation that it was quite possible for activists to retain membership of rival organisations with conflicting politics. Thus Mann moved quickly from the SDF to the Fabians. Without leaving the Fabians, he then led the ILP. Lansbury seems to have held membership of the SDF, Fabians and ILP all at the same time. Thorne while still in the SDF, became a Labour MP five years after the SDF had repudiated the Labour Party. And so on.

the Liberal and Tory Parties and only turned to Labour as a poor third. In 1891 the Liberals' Newcastle conference adopted in entirety a policy which had been drafted by Sidney Webb—whom Beatrice described as 'the chief instigator of policies, the source of Liberal doctrine'.[62] As late as 1910, she confided in her diary that while the Tories had certain attractions, so too did the Liberals: 'So really I don't know from what party we shall get the most. We may have, in the end, to establish a real socialist party if we want rapid progress'.[63]

The Fabians had the utmost contempt for the working class: 'What can we hope from these myriads of deficient minds and deformed bodies that swarm our great cities—what can we hope but brutality, meanness and crime'.[64] A quarter of a century later, the tone remained unchanged. Beatrice talked of 'the colossal stupidity of the trade union rank and file', 'those underbred and undertrained workmen'.[65] There was not even a grain of human sympathy. Beatrice Webb castigated the Liberals' for providing health insurance for workers. In 1911 she wrote that it:

> is wholly bad, and I cannot see how malingering can be staved off... What the government shirk is the extension of treatment and disciplinary supervision—they want merely some mechanical way of increasing the money income of the wage-earning class... No attempt is made to secure an advance in conduct for the increased income.[66]*

The Fabian Tract of 1896 entitled *The Moral Aspects of Socialism* declared:

> The Socialist policy, so far from favouring the weak, favours the strong... it is a process of conscious social selection by which the industrial residuum is naturally sifted and made manageable for some kind of restorative, disciplinary, or it may be, 'surgical treatment'... In this way it not only favours the growth of the fittest within the group, but also the fittest group in the world competition of societies.[68]

Long before Hitler, Bernard Shaw toyed with the breeding of a master race and a 'superman', while advocating 'sterilization of the failures'.

* It might be surprising that with such attitudes, the Webbs were able to write their excellent books on *The History of Trade Unionism* and *Industrial Democracy*. But their meticulous research served a dual purpose—to train the budding union leaders in the arts of behaving responsibly, and to show the ruling class that trade unions were a force to be treated with, rather than to be repressed or given in to. In Beatrice Webb's words, they offered 'a criticism of the trade unions (for the good of the unionists!)...an apology for, or defence of trade unions (for the enlightenment of the middle class and economists)'.[67]

Only if we understand their *thoroughly ruling-class outlook* can we intelligently approach the Fabians' outrageous misuse of the English language when they talked of 'socialism' or more usually 'collectivism'. (The latter had less unpleasant foreign connotations for these rabid racialists).

Two influences formed the background to Fabian politics. The first was Joseph Chamberlain's 'gospel of ransom'. Chamberlain gave the Liberals their national federation and believed that social services and improved working conditions were a necessary 'ransom' to pay to avoid the dangers of social unrest. According to Beatrice: 'We dare not neglect the sullen discontent now spreading...if only for the sake of the rest of the Empire'.[69]

Secondly, the Fabians were conscious of changes in the capitalist economy: For much of the nineteenth century ruling-class policy was known as *laissez-faire*. The French phrase captured the needs of the system well. Units of capital were small and foreign competition minimal. So businessmen demanded free trade and the unrestricted play of market forces. They wanted the minimum of state intervention in the process of capital accumulation. But as Germany and America became commercial threats it seemed to sections of the ruling class that the state should be more interventionist in its support of capitalism. One wing saw imperialism as a means of consolidating markets and sources of raw materials. Another looked to *the state to increase capitalist efficiency at home*. The latter was the policy of the Fabians.

The first complete statement of policy appeared in *Fabian Essays* of December 1889. Though issued three months after the dock strike victory it avoided mentioning trade unions entirely.

Most notable was the idea that state action equals socialism. Sidney Webb, a former high civil servant, had a positively nauseous admiration for government bureaucrats: 'in their every act they worked to bring about the very Socialism they despised'.[70] Therefore 'the Post Office...is now a purely Socialistic institution.' If such was socialism, then, as Shaw proudly boasted, the Fabian programme had:

> not one new item in it. All are applications of principles already admitted, and extensions of practices already in full activity. All have on them that stamp of the vestry which is so congenial to the British mind. None of them compel the use of the words Socialism or Revolution... or anything...un-English.[71]

So it was that Sir William Harcourt, Gladstone's successor in the Liberal leadership, declared: 'We are all socialists nowadays.'

The Fabians set out to be *elitist social engineers*, working entirely within the framework of the system *to increase efficiency and avoid the dangers of revolution*.

The ultimate aim of Fabian collectivism was capitalist production organised on a national scale by the state. In the 1930s many were astounded when the Webbs returned from visiting Stalin's Russia, a state capitalist society, to announce that it 'almost exactly corresponds to our constitution...[the] trade union is placed in exactly the same position of subordination as we suggested'.[72] Commentators should not have been shocked for this had always been the logic of Fabianism. The working class was to play no active role in creating the new society. In 1889, in one of the few essays which deigned to mention workers, the Fabians told them to cease 'fearing [the state] as an actual enemy, [and] come to look to it as a Potential saviour'.[73] Engels rightly described the Fabians as 'a clique...united only by their fear of the threatening rule of the workers and doing all in their power to avert this danger'.[74]

These were the people who 'gave Labour its doctrine'. The ILP and later the Labour Party gave such ideas a working-class veneer and credibility which they would otherwise have lacked. Fabian ideas turned up, for example, in the work of Robert Blatchford, a key figure in the founding of the ILP. His newspaper the *Clarion* and his book *Merrie England*, which sold three quarters of a million copies, popularised Fabian ideas in vulgar form:

> nearly all law is more or less Socialistic, for nearly all law implies the right of the State to control individuals for the benefit of the nation... The abolition of toll bars and bridge tolls was Socialistic action, for it made the roads and bridges common property.[75]

The identification of working class interests with the state also brought with it the idea of nation and nationalism. Blatchford's next masterpiece was entitled *Britain for the British*, and its contents may be imagined. His memoirs recall that at the founding of the ILP: 'we were Britons first and Socialists next'.[76]

Keir Hardie's one attempt at socialist theory, *From Serfdom to Socialism*, also verged on the same nonsense:

> The policeman and the soldier...exist by the will and under the express authority of those same tenants and workmen, who constitute a prepondering majority in the State, and without whose consent neither soldier nor policeman could continue to exist.

Hardie's economic theory bore the pernicious stamp of Fabianism:

> Socialism does not propose to abolish land or capital [only] capitalism and landlordism. The capital would remain; the engineers, architects, organisers, and managers who carry on the businesses would all remain also, and could just as well and as profitably be employed by society as they now are by the private capitalist.[77]

MacDonald probably put this idea best when he said: 'Capitalism is now finding fulfilment, and that fulfilment is this new organisation—Socialism'.[78]*

The ideas that have dominated the Labour Party from the start have not come from the working class. Lenin was absolutely correct when he said that from this point of view 'the Labour Party is a thoroughly bourgeois party'.**

* The Fabians' attitude to their devotees in the ILP was one of disapproval. There was, according to Beatrice Webb, 'no chance of it being more than a wrecking party',[79] for independent workers' politics interfered with permeation of the Liberals and Tories. Furthermore even the mild ILP was too radical for the Fabians. Thus she welcomed its defeat in the 1895 election campaign because: 'No class of Englishmen can long tolerate the simple wrecker'.[80]

** Beatrice Webb described the difference between the Fabians and ILP as a choice between the following propositions: 'To bring about the maximum amount of public control in public administration do we want to organising the unthinking persons into Socialist societies, or to make the thinking persons socialistic? We believe in the latter process'.[81]

2

'Out of the bowels of the TUC'

A background of defeat and passivity

By the late 1890s, the 'socialist boom' fuelled by new unionism was tailing off. The ILP dropped from 11,000 subscription paying members in 1895 to 5,000 in 1901[1] and was bankrupt, its National Administrative Committee having to curtail meetings to a quarterly basis.

In the 1895 general election 28 ILP candidates stood, but all lost, including Hardie, until then the party's only MP. Together they received 25,000 votes, not a discreditable total if the aim was to rally the advanced section of the class. But for a party which muted its principles to gain seats in parliament the result was disastrous.*

So at a time when the Labour Party was in the making, even watered down socialism was narrowly based. The ILP's check on the electoral front was matched by the rout of its new unionist supporters at the TUC. After 1889 the new unions fought regular battles with the old. At first the laurels went the way of the left. In 1890 a motion for the legal eight-hour day, which had been defeated by 88 votes to 63 at the previous year's TUC, passed by 193 to 155.[4]**

But the retreat of the mass movement allowed a counter-attack. The presidential address at the 1895 TUC denounced the ILP as: 'an anti-Labour, anti-trade-unionist movement... The Congress had been in danger of being exploited by men who were really outside the labour movement...'[6]

This old unionist offensive took the form of a rule change. Until then each delegate had a single vote, and political representatives as well as Trades Councils could attend. Now *the card vote system was introduced* and all delegates not directly from unions expelled. Instantly

* This fact did not escape the ILP's rivals on right and left. Jenkins, Lib-Lab president of the 1895 Trades Union Congress, crowed about the election result: 'Was it possible to conceive a greater exhibition of impotence or a smaller justification for the pretension to speak and act in the name of universal labour'.[2] The SDF was pleased too. Being open about its socialism and committed to a definite theory (although posed in sterile sectarian fashion) it survived the difficult years better than its rival. In 1898, the SDF could claimed that in five years it had doubled its number of branches to reach 137, two thirds of the ILP's total.[3]

** The 1893 TUC voted 'for Socialism': 'the principle of collective ownership and control of all the means of production and distribution'.[5] The 1894 Congress added land and mines nationalisation.

control moved to the giant right-wing unions of coal and cotton. The small unions under ILP influence were powerless to prevent this or keep the proponents of a Labour Party at Congress. It is ironic that the same card vote system should turn up later as the chief weapon in controlling Labour Party conferences.

In 1895 all hope of a Labour Party seemed lost. Yet five years later the TUC set one up. What had produced the dramatic turn around? The answer was a ruling-class attack which, in sharp contrast to 1889's mass activity, left the rank and file as passive by-standers to the doings of the bureaucracy. *The ILP had been born of an advanced left wing movement. The Labour Party was born of bureaucratic manoeuvres at the TUC, of a step backward in the class struggle.*

Employers broke unions one by one, starting with 70,000 Scottish miners who were battered into submission in 1894. For most workers such defeats do not encourage the revolutionary idea that class action can succeed where sectional action fails. More common is the reformist conclusion which Hardie (a former miners' union official himself) was quick to draw—that electoral politics are the answer:

> The Scotch coal strike, which to all appearances has ended in the utter rout of the men, has nevertheless been a great victory. For whom?... For the Labour movement... The result of the bitter experiences of the last 18 weeks has been the decision of many miners to abandon [conventional] party politics, and to throw in their lot with the ILP.[7]

Next year saw the defeat of the Boot and Shoe Operatives. Again Hardie chimed in with these comforting words: 'The men have been defeated. That is the long and the short of it... However the lesson of the dispute will not be lost, and the municipal election the other day in Leicester shows that the men have learnt their lesson well'.[8] The railwaymen proposed Labour representation to the TUC after their 'All Grades Movement' was broken. Next it was the turn of the proudest of the old unions, the Amalgamated Society of Engineers, to be locked out.

Within six months the employers had reasserted the right to be 'masters in their own shops.' *Labour Leader*'s comment? 'Failure. And yet in the end it may turn out that the lesson was worth the cost...it would be more in accordance with the traditional principles of English politics and common sense *if the battle was transferred from the poverty stricken homes of the workers to the floor of the House of Commons*'.[9]

Emboldened by successes, employers used the courts ever more frequently. This culminated in the Taff Vale decision, which not only outlawed picketing but compelled unions to refund to their employers every penny lost during a strike. These defeats shook the trade union bureaucracy profoundly. In 1902 one leader declared that: 'Menaced on every hand in workshop, court of law, and press. Trade Unionism has no refuge except the ballot box and Labour Representation.'[10]

However the scale of the employers' offensive must be kept in perspective. In 1898, following the engineers' defeat, the TUC president had warned that:

> For the first time in the history of our movement we had to face a mammoth combination of military-led capital, whose object, as openly stated by its leader, was to cripple, if not crush the forces of trade unionism...[11]

That phrase 'cripple, if not crush' was all-important. The fights at the end of the century had been bitter, but their effect was *to demoralise, to weaken workers' confidence in their own industrial strength*, not to sting them into activity on their own account. Within the Unions themselves, *the influence of the bureaucracy vis à vis the rank and file was immeasurably strengthened*. Their numbers were growing rapidly in spite of the attacks. In 1850 there had been no full-time officials; but in 1892 there were 600. Yet that year alone the number of engineering officials increased fourfold, while the Carpenters' officials grew tenfold. By 1920 there were between three and four thousand full-time officials.[12]

One result of the employers' counter-attack was the partial incorporation of the bureaucracy into working closely with employers through conciliation schemes. The most important was the Brooklands Agreement covering textiles. Such arrangements reduced the number of strikes significantly until a rank and file revolt overturned them after 1910.

Another effect was to jolt the bureaucracy into realising they could neither protect the membership nor defend the union coffers (which were perhaps closer to their hearts). Against their will they were forced to turn from purely economic action towards politics. But they did so in their own interests. The TUC, which in 1895 had totally rejected the idea of a Labour Party, now welcomed it.*

* The ILP's attitude to building a Labour Party also changed during the 1890s. Trades unions and trades councils had been invited to the 1893 Bradford Conference of the ILP, and, with two votes against, the conference had opted for a federal structure into which such groups could be absorbed. As Cole put it: The ILP at Bradford was still dreaming of becoming the Labour Party.[13] After the ILP's rebuttal at the 1895 TUC, Hardie suggested 'that the ILP may open the door for these excluded bodies and such others as cared to join, and so bring about a Socialist Trades Union Congress. He ventured to predict that such a congress may, before the end of the century, become a focus for working class opinion of all shades.'[14]

In the conditions of the late 1890s this idea was a non-sarter. An alliance now had to be on the

The foundation conference creates a 'Labour Alliance'

The resolution that led to the Labour Representation Committee (LRC) was moved by rail union delegates at the 1899 TUC and passed by 546,000 to 434,000. It called for 'a special congress of representatives... to devise ways and means for securing the return of an increased number of labour members to the next parliament'.[16] The Labour Representation Committee was duly founded on 27 February 1900 in London. There were 129 delegates; sixty-five represented 568,000 trade unionists, while the socialist society delegates spoke for 13,000 members of the ILP, 9,000 from the SDF and 861 Fabians. A Labour Representation Committee was elected with seven trade unionists and five socialist society members (two from the ILP, two from the SDF and one Fabian).

Three alternatives were presented to the delegates. The SDF suggested: 'a party organisation separate from the capitalist parties based upon a recognition of the class war...having for its ultimate object the socialisation of the means of production, distribution and exchange'.[17] The right wanted LRC members of parliament to adopt a policy consisting of just 'four or five planks...the said representatives to be left entirely free on all purely political questions'.[18] This meant a continuation of Lib-Labism. Immediate problems such as Taff Vale would have been taken up, but once resolved, the LRC MPs would have sunk back into the Liberal fold.

Keir Hardie defeated both positions. He steered a precise middle course proposing no more and no less than: 'a distinct Labour Group in Parliament, who shall have their own Whips.' So there was to be an organisational break with the old parties, but there was to be no marked political differentiation. The only policy suggested was 'a readiness to co-operate with any party which for the time being may be engaged in promoting legislation in the direct interest of labour'.[19] Though called the LRC until 1906, the Labour Party was launched.

It was built *from the top downwards*. Class struggle played no role at all:

> From 1899 to 1907 was a period of industrial peace unparalleled between 1891 when statistics started, and 1933, when a comparable period began... The annual average of working days lost through disputes was less than 3 million and in no years was the total as

trade unions terms and anything which stood in the way had to be avoided. In 1899 a ballot forced upon the ILP's National Administrative Council Showed 2,397 votes in favour of federation with the SDF and 1,695 for direct fusion. So strong was the feeling in favour of 'socialist unity' that no vote against was taken. Nevertheless the council managed to avoid acting upon the ballot result as it 'would speedily make shipwreck of the ILP' in its delicate negotiations with the union bureaucracy'.[15]

> large as 5 million. By contrast...from 1908 to 1932...the annual average (excluding 1926) was 14 million.[20]

The 1899 TUC which made the fateful decision did not even stir the ILP. *Labour Leader*'s article on the Congress was entitled 'Not worth the Candle': 'It was generally admitted that the congress this year has been exceptionally dull'.[21] The formation of the LRC itself only merited one quarter of a column in *The Times*.[22]

Ordinary workers greeted the LRC with apathy. The engineers and boot and shoe operatives had suffered serious blows and their officials therefore looked eagerly to parliament. But ballots on affiliation produced the following results: out of the 32,000 boot and shoe operatives only 6½ percent bothered to vote, 1,500 for affiliation and 675 against. The ASE result was worse. Out of 85,000, only 4 percent voted, 2897 for and 702 against. Participation was so appalling that even though the engineers vote was positive, the union leadership felt unable to affiliate.[23]

The 1900 general election tells the same tale. The LRC had not yet proved itself to union officials and with just £33 to spend on the entire campaign it was only able to promote three candidates of its own, of whom Keir Hardie and Richard Bell of the rail union were successful.[24] The ILP ran ten candidates without victory. The joint total of some 66,000 votes proved the majority of workers had still to be won to a reformist position.[25]

The establishment of the LRC was bureaucratic in another sense. It involved merely a change of label, but *no* change of politics. For example Clarke's study of Lancashire tells how 'the Ince Liberal Registration Society (Registration Agent, Wm Shaw) ceased to exist and there subsequently appeared the Ince Division Labour Registration Association (Registration Agent Wm Shaw)'.[26] As late as May 1914 the Labour candidate for North East Derbyshire told voters that 'there is no more ardent Liberal in the country than I have been, and there is no more ardent Liberal now'.[27]

Such situations could lead to embarrassment. Until he became LRC MP for Barnard Castle in 1903, Arthur Henderson had for seven years been a Liberal election agent. During his campaign his opponents had the discourtesy to publish his earlier denunciations of the ILP's socialism.[28] Richard Bell had so little adapted his position that he campaigned publicly for the election of a Liberal in Norwich against the LRC candidate, and had to be disciplined![29]

The political expression of the trade union bureaucracy

The major gain made by the formation of the LRC was organisationally to detach the trade unions leaders from the Liberal Party. They now owed political allegiance to their own creation.

Most union officials who affiliated their organisations did so because they wanted to get to parliament. The first affiliations included just three unions which could be said to be socialist through their new unionist background—two dockers' organisations and the Gas Workers. These amounted to only one fifth of the total.[30]

Opposition to the LRC came from coal and cotton, which mustered 351,140 of the 434,000 votes cast against the resolution. Miners' officials, in particular, could expect to become Lib-Lab MPs without outside help because of the membership's geographical concentration. This was therefore the last major union to see the utility of the Labour Party, only affiliating in 1909.

The second wave of affiliation was induced by Taff Vale. *Labour Leader* claimed that from the point of view of the nascent Labour Party 'nothing could have been more fortunate for Trade Unionism than the Taff Vale decision. It has awakened men to a sense of danger'.[31]

From the very outset the trade unions had the preponderant weight in their 'Labour Alliance' with the Socialist societies (ILP and Fabians). The interlocking of union officials and the Labour Party showed itself in a number of ways. Before the First World War union sponsored MPs formed 95 percent of the Parliamentary Labour Party, and of the thirteen members of the TUC's leading committee, nine were Labour MPs.[32]

In one sense this was the *direct entry of trade unions into political affairs.* However it also represented *a retreat from trade unionism—from the belief that collective organisation could defend itself.* Seen from this angle the LRC was precisely that substitute for trade unionism that Mann had found so absurd. O'Grady told the 1898 TUC that: 'their efforts, in his opinion, should be directed towards removing the fight from the industrial to the political field'.[33] There were good reasons for this attitude. Faced with the threat arising from the Taff Vale decision, the union officials had a frightening prospect looming up before them. They might have to fight. Clynes, a prominent union leader, recalled:

> I believe that had there not been a Labour Party in 1901, to which angry workmen could flock, the Taff Vale blow at the justice they claimed might have caused them to strike a counter-blow by proclaiming a state of open revolution throughout the big industrial centres of England.[34]

The creation of the LRC provided a bureaucratic political alternative to industrial activity, a means of separating politics and economics. However, as with all else to do with Labour, there was a contradiction. It was the link which exists in the real world between economics and politics, between the state and the bosses, that brought the LRC into existence. Furthermore the party transposed much of the outlook of the trade union bureaucracy. Thus the LRC's first address to the affiliated members described it as 'Trade Unionism and the Principles of Trade Unionism, applied to national affairs'.[35]

Applying this dictum produced curious results. Just as trade unions recruit people regardless of their politics on the basis of their position in industry, so the Labour Party sought to gather workers' votes regardless of their politics. According to Keir Hardie, Labour must be 'Conservative enough to preserve everything that is good. Liberal enough to reform what is capable of being reformed; and Radical enough to uproot and destroy whatever is altogether wrong'.[36] Elsewhere, Snowden portrayed Labour as 'a neutral meeting ground where Liberal and Tory might meet together'.[37]

The problem of false consciousness

There is no such thing as neutral ground in class society. Take the decision not to include class war in the party programme. This implied a definite political attitude, as one supporter realised in 1921:

> Once you admit 'the class war' you are at once more or less committed to political and industrial tactics of 'war to the knife'. So long as the working class is regarded as an oppressed class yearning for freedom, standing together homogeneously face to face with its oppressors... so long are you committed to a policy of revolution rather than evolution... Deny 'the class war', and [there] will logically follow politics of 'arrangements' of 'reform' of 'understandings' and 'alliances'.[38]

This is correct, but the fact remained that those who supported the Labour Party believed it *could* be politically neutral. We are confronted here with a recurring problem—the difference between Labour's understanding of itself and its actual position, between myth and reality. To comprehend this we must briefly discuss the concept 'false consciousness'.

Marx stated the dichotomy between human understanding of the world and social reality in his *Preface to A Contribution to the Critique of Political Economy*:

> a distinction should always be made between the material transformation of the material conditions of production...and the legal, political, religious, aesthetic or philosophical—in short ideological—forms in which men become conscious of [social] conflict and fight it out.

We can see how this works in the context of Labour. Supporters accepted that Labour rejected class war and believed they could take a neutral, common-sense attitude to politics. They were convinced of the separateness of politics and economics, the existence of a community interest shared by all classes, and the impartiality of the state and the law. But while reformist ideas are sincerely held they are wrong. Historical experience has shown that politics and economics *are* intimately connected, that the state is a weapon of class rule and so on.

Although there is a gap between reality and reformist ideology, the two are connected dialectically. If class struggle had led *automatically* to direct political conclusions we would have seen the irresistible rise of a mass revolutionary, organisation in Britain. This has patently not been the case. If on the other hand there had been no link between the outside world and reformist consciousness then the Labour Party would not have come into existence.

So the reformist view of the world is *false consciousness*, but it has an indirect yet genuine link with the outside world, is influenced by the outside world and in turn influences it.

A technical division of labour

The union bureaucrat is at one remove from the class struggle, stepping between workers and employers when they conflict with each other to negotiate settlements. *The Labour Party is twice removed.* From birth it claimed to embody the 'principle of *trade unionism* applied to *national affairs*', but the two were qualitatively different. *The trade union bureaucracy is weak on political ideas* since its main job is to mediate on wages and conditions. Further, the bureaucracy is divided on sectional grounds—between different industries, crafts and so on, and is subject to collective pressure from the rank and file in workplaces.

However, *parliamentary work requires a different bureaucracy*. They must seek support from workers not as a collective group but as atomised citizens in the polling booths. They must be professional politicians with the appropriate skills and broad electoral attraction. The MPs and full-time Labour intellectuals do this job.*

It was only as *a party standing above trade unionism* that Labour could successfully appeal to an electorate, the majority of whom were not unionised. This was brought home by the notable failure of many trade union candidates to attract the votes even of their own members. The connection between union support and voting in elections is an interesting one, but notoriously difficult to track down, since the bourgeois democratic system deliberately obliterates the idea of class, reducing everyone to the meaningless level of citizen. Only the miners with their large numbers and geographical concentration can be identified with any certainty in the returns. But even here, in the traditionally compact and unionised communities the link between union membership and voting behaviour was weak. As the historian of mining politics records:

> Generally speaking, if a Liberal candidate was also in the field it was rare for the Labour man, even if he himself was a miner or miners' official, to poll as much as half of the mining vote in the constituency.[40]

Thus in 1910 Herbert Smith, president of the Yorkshire Miners' Association, attracted just 2,000 votes in a constituency that included 5,000 miners. He actually came bottom, the Liberal receiving 8,000 votes and the Tory 3,400![41] Because the link between official union recommendations and the vote is so tenuous Labour could claim that as an electoral party it must make a much wider appeal to succeed.

However, trade union officials could retort with equal justice *that without the trade unions, the Labour Party would not exist*. It was in this sense that Bevin said that the Labour Party was 'born out of the bowels of the TUC.'

Denying class in a class society

In structure as well as politics the party therefore consists of the uneasy combination of direct class organisation through the unions and

* The division of labour between union officials and reformist politicians was becoming visible within the ILP even before the formation of the labour Party. In 1898 Tom Mann, dissatisfied with the predominantly political preoccupations of the ILP, resigned. That same year Pete Curran, an organiser of the gas workers, was also forced to choose between his political and industrial roles, quitting the ILP council. As Pelling tells 'The old direct link with New Unionism was severed: the party was now being run, under Hardie's direction, by a new type of Council member—the full-time journalist politician, such as Ramsay McDonald, Snowden or Glasier, who had no trade-union ties and was free to devote all or most of his time if necessary to the activities of the party'.[39]

nationally orientated politics. It voices working class aspirations but only to the extent that they can be fitted into the workings of the national state. Snowden put it like this:

> The Labour Party is not seeking any class triumph. Its object is not to make the manual labour class dominant... It is quite true that the Labour and Socialist Party makes its appeal to the wage-earning classes. It does that because there are the people who need to be aroused to a fuller sense of civic duty...as they are the vast majority of the electorate they must exercise the political influence.[42]

The balance between the two factors is expressed in the split between Labour's left and right—each side articulating one aspect of a common reformist whole. Thus Will Thorne's 1906 election manifesto said a vote for him meant 'encouragement to all who suffer under the heel of Capitalism; a blow struck for the workers in that war between Capitalism and Labour which must be waged relentlessly until the emancipation of the workers is achieved by the abolition of the Capitalist system'.[43] At the other end of the spectrum was the Belfast candidate, William Walker whose manifesto displayed prominently the following words: 'I am, as I have always been, a supporter of the Legislative Union of Great Britain and Ireland, and will do all in my power to maintain unimpaired the supremacy of the Imperial Parliament'.[44]

The LRC, it appeared, had no separate political programme. But this was an illusion. It was all very well to create an independent organisational platform; what speeches were to be made from it? Nine times out of ten the early Labour Party plumped for the Liberal policy. It showed few signs of political self-reliance. In May 1900 an LRC sub-committee suggested:

> that organisations affiliated to us should run their candidates to begin with in such a way as to make it possible for either the local Liberal or Conservative Association to leave an open field for Labour candidates.
>
> We think it would be advisable to write to the Liberal and Conservative Whips stating that...we have no hostility to other political parties, and that...we shall be glad of their cooperation in getting these candidates through.[45]

This proposal jeopardised even the minimal independence enshrined in the decision to create a 'distinct Labour group.' In the event the LRC was evenly split on this motion, but the chairman's casting vote led to its defeat.

Labour's organisation was strengthened in 1903 when unions decided to levy their members at a rate of one penny per person, and a 'Party Pledge' was passed to bind MPs to majority decisions of the parliamentary group. But organisational advance was continually undermined by political dependence on the Liberals.

Without a mass reformism outside to buoy it up, the bureaucratically formed Labour Party led a precarious existence. Its efforts to progress hung between fighting the Liberals to win their voters and fawning upon them for fear of losing 'moderate' support.

Hardie wrote begging letters to Liberal dignitaries, pleading with them to lead Labour (and lend it their electoral influence!) To John Morley whom he had so recently denounced in the strongest terms, he wrote: 'What is wanted...is a man with the brain to dare, the hand to do, and the heart to inspire. Will you be that man?'[46] His 1903 missive to Lloyd George was still more pathetic: 'Here is a leadership sufficient to gratify the loftiest aspirations and it is within your reach; it is yours for the taking.'[47]*

Keir Hardie's appeals fell on stony ground. However he and MacDonald solved Labour's electoral problem in a brilliantly dishonest way. All the while proclaiming the LRC's independence, MacDonald secretly arranged with Herbert Gladstone, the national Liberal election agent, that LRC candidates would have a free run in certain constituencies if they left the Liberals an open field elsewhere. The pact remained concealed for fifty years. Had it been known, Labour's only claim to distinction would have been blown sky high. Its value was demonstrated in the 1906 general election when 19 out of the 27 successful Labour candidates were returned for seats ceded under the arrangement.[51] But secret as it was, *the pact left a dangerous legacy of dependence on the Liberal Party for electoral gains.*

Significance

Keir Hardie claimed the formation of the LRC was a major breakthrough when he addressed the 1903 Labour Conference, but his

* Labour's craven attitude towards Lloyd George as a possible leader had a remarkable sequel. In 1916 Lloyd George 'jocularly remarked' to Ramsay MacDonald, 'that he might have to put him in prison [for his pacifist views]... Discussing Mr Lloyd George's future, Mr MacDonald said that he quite realised the possibility of his coming the leader of the Labour Party'.[48] In the Political Diaries of C P Scott, it is recorded that in December 1917 Sidney Webb agreed with MacDonald that Lloyd George might one day be a suitable leader for the Labour Party.[49] And as late as June 1926 the idea of Lloyd George's joining the Labour Party was canvassed. This time, however, it was MacDonald who put a stop to the idea, declaring that 'the Labour Party was much too sedate and practical' for Lloyd George. He advised him to join the Communists instead.[50]

words raised an important doubt: 'They all, Liberal, Tory and Socialist alike rejoiced at the magnificent conference got together in that hall. What was the principle which enabled them all to come together—Independence'.[52] But if Liberals, Tories and Socialists all agreed, what exactly were they independent of?

Historians sympathetic to the Labour Party give more sober assessments but still assert that the Labour Alliance 'made possible a political, social and economic achievement far beyond...hopes or expectations', or that it was 'the best tool possible under the circumstances'.[53] There are grains of truth in these arguments. The LRC and later the Labour Party were an advance on Lib-Labism.

To rally workers to vote against the established and openly capitalist parties, in favour of one claiming to represent working class interests, *was a forward move in the conditions of 1900*, because it advanced the creation of a mass reformist party if only in an organisational sense. Furthermore, the context of politics was transformed. *The debate between reform and revolution could now be tested in practice.* Also the trade union leaders now looked to their resources and organisation instead of tailing the openly capitalist parties.

But there was a major debit on the balance sheet. Electoral progress was being sought without a corresponding political advance at the base. This could only be achieved *by sacrificing the socialist ideals of the left-wing*. The SDF were not prepared to pay the price and left the LRC in August 1901. Alas, they had no intention of creating a fighting alternative to Labour's politics and returned to the sectarian wilderness from whence they came.

The effect on the ILP was equally serious. These socialists became hostages of the union bureaucracy. An 'Alliance' in which one partner controls between 94 and 99 percent of the votes was hardly even-handed, but the ILP was bound hand and foot to it.

At least the ILP had tempered its scramble to win parliamentary seats with socialist propaganda. The LRC appealed openly and covertly to the Liberals to help it into parliament. As the *Clarion* wrote in 1902:

> the great work of the official section of the ILP at the present seems not so much to push Socialism as to try to intrigue some half a dozen persons into Parliament. There is probably not more than one place in Britain (if there is one) where we can get a Socialist into Parliament without some arrangement with Liberalism, and for such an arrangement Liberalism will demand a terribly heavy price—more than we can possibly afford.[54]

The precarious influence of the ILP was demonstrated by the meteoric rise of David Shackleton, the textile union leader. His United Textile Factory Workers' Association had sponsored a Tory-Labour candidate as recently as 1899. Shackleton himself was no socialist, but a Liberal who had been offered the union's support in an LRC candidacy. He had been Liberal ward secretary in Accrington and was 'a very mild spoken gentleman with ideas very little in advance of the average Liberal'.[55] When a by-election occurred in Clitheroe in 1902 the ILP hungered after the nomination, but stepped aside for Shackleton, who so little offended the main political parties that he was returned unopposed.

Shackleton then came within a hair's breadth of leading the Labour Party when it first became a serious force in 1906. Both he and Keir Hardie stood for chairman of the Parliamentary Labour group. Hardie was 'by every qualification of service and experience...the outstanding candidate for Chairman. He was the senior MP, he was the revered leader of the ILP, and he had done more than any other individual to bring the Labour Party into existence'.[56] A show of hands among the MPs produced a tie. A secret ballot was no different. The deadlock was only broken when a third vote gave Hardie a majority of one. Shackleton returned to his true political home when he took an administrative job in the Liberal government.

The fact that the Labour Party had been created from above meant that *the process of political clarification*, which depended not only on a separate organisation but open criticism of Liberals and Tories alike, *was actually held back*. The compromises of the founding conference therefore could not generate a serious mass critique of capitalism, even on a reformist basis.

For all its shortcomings, the ILP represented some of the most advanced workers in Britain at that time. The hope for socialism depends largely on the ability of the vanguard of the class to lead the mass of workers forward (if not immediately to revolution, at least into fighting for reforms). The Labour Party did not provide leadership in that sense. Indeed, it reversed the equation.

The advanced workers were subordinated to the more backward, not only because of the tendency of the union officials to go at the pace of the slowest workers, but because the ILP was compromised for electoral gain even more extensively than before.

The birth of Labour, like every other aspect of reformism, was a mixed blessing. For the mass of workers, the existence of an organisation linked to the trade unions and different, if only in the vaguest manner, from the openly bourgeois parties, was an improvement. For the minority of advanced workers, who unfortunately accepted the electoralist strategy of Labour, the new organisation was a millstone around their necks. What was gained in breadth was lost in political depth.

The impact of parliament

In 1906 what Herbert Morrison was to call 'the miracle of politics'[57]—the climb of Labour towards government office—began in earnest. The general election sent 29 Labour MPs to parliament with 346,000 votes behind them.*

The capitalist parties felt their long parliamentary monopoly threatened. The Tory leader, Balfour, denounced this 'echo of the same movement which had produced riots at St. Petersburg, riots in London, and Socialist processions in Berlin.'[59] An Anti-Socialist Union was hastily launched to save civilisation and the *Daily Express* carried such horrifying stories as: 'Driven mad by Socialism—suicide of a lad of sixteen' and 'Socialism in the Kitchen Spreading Discontent among Servants.' In a desperate attempt to halt the contagion and prevent a socialist meeting in their town, Cambridge students kidnapped Keir Hardie, or so they thought. But they had only seized a cunningly disguised look-alike.[60]

Red scares are too constant a feature of Labour's history to be dismissed as complete lunacy or propaganda. As Trotsky says, for some members of the ruling class the fear is 'that behind the mock-heroic threats of the Labour Party there lies the real danger from the deeply stirring proletarian masses.'[61] The bosses' press was right to fear the working class but it was stupid to believe that Labour represented that revolutionary potential. As the president of the 1902 Labour Conference had already affirmed: 'Our policy is to take away the food of sedition.'[62]

Indeed the success of 1906 was to take the logic of reformism an important step forwards. *Every advance made the political compromise with capitalism less theoretical and more real.* Nowhere was this better illustrated than in parliament.

---

* Significantly, the vast majority of successful candidates—24 in all—had got through because they had not had to run against Liberals. The precise voting figures were: the LRC received 331,280 votes; the Scottish Worker Representation Committee, soon to merge itself into the national Labour Party, polled 14,878; the SDF and Socialist independents collected 24,473 and the 'Lib-Labs', mainly miners, accounted for another 100,000 or so out of a vote of just under 6 million.[58]

> First we expected 'the best platform in Europe' as is the British House of Commons, to be used in season and out of season. Instead, we found a disinclination to use it and instead an inclination 'to get the tone of the House.' We expected, naively enough, that our MPs would regard themselves not only as leaders and inspirers, but as the interpreters of the movement behind them and the mouthpieces of the dumb masses... Instead we found...the spectacle of forceful speakers...reduced to babbling impotency in their endeavours to ape the statesman.[63]

Snowden, dubbed 'Yorkshire's Robespierre' wrote:

> I remember so well...the early days of this new Parliament... Old members smiled at the impatience of the new members. They reminded us of the time when they first came to parliament full of an earnest enthusiasm to achieve some good purpose; but despair had entered into their hearts, and before the advent of the Labour men, they had resigned all hope of ever being able to move that cumbersome machine at any reasonable rate along the path of reform.[64]

This feeling of impotence was perhaps the most insidious of the Commons' influences.

A second powerful corrupting element was the enticing atmosphere of this 'most exclusive club in Europe'. J H Thomas, the railway union leader quickly fell victim: 'Very early in my experience as an MP I came to appreciate the greatness of the admittedly great, the broadmindedness of the House of Commons as a whole'.[65] In a party which renounced class consciousness, such a 'broadminded' approach favourably compared with workers who, alas, imagined they had some grievance against exploiters. In the Commons:

> There was no snobbery, no side. A man was and is welcomed there for his character and brains and not for the amount of his income.
>
> I remember wishing that grades could be as easily overlooked in the trade union movement as they were in the House of Commons.[66]

Perhaps quoting an arch-right-winger like Thomas is unfair. What about the ferocious Davie Kirkwood, munitions shop steward, leader of the Clyde Workers' Committee, deported from Glasgow for denouncing wartime industrial slavery, and from 1922 one of the dreaded 'Clyde-brigade' which descended like a Jacobite horde on the peaceful environs of Westminster?

> It was a strange House. To me it was full of wonder. I had to shake myself occasionally as I found myself moving about and talking with

> men whose names were household words. More strange was it to find them all so simple and unaffected and friendly. In the House of Commons there is no snobbery.

After Kirkwood launched a violent attack on the unemployment policy of Bonar Law, the latter bearded him in the corridor to say: 'You Clyde boys were pretty hard on me today. But it's fine to hear your Glasgow accent. It's like a sniff of the air of Scotland in the musty atmosphere of this place'... 'What could a man do in the face of such a greeting?' said Kirkwood'.[67] What indeed!

The party was disarmed. Snowden remembered that:

> It was rather amusing to see the Labour members, whose advent to Parliament was expected to outrage all the conventionalities, performing [parliamentary] custom[s] with more correctness than the Tory members.[68]

There was even a apocryphal story about a Liberal member who attended the Commons in a soft hat instead of a topper, because he did not want to be mistaken for a Labour MP.[69]

The degenerative effect of parliament had nothing to do with the nostrum that 'all power corrupts'. On the contrary, *it was the very lack of power in the place for which they had sold so much to reach, that caused such degradation.*

Taming conference

The first act of the MPs was to create the *Parliamentary Labour Party.* The significance of this must be understood. McKenzie explains: 'The term "The Labour Party" is properly applied only to the mass organization of the party *outside* Parliament; it supports in Parliament a distinct and separate organization, "The Parliamentary Labour Party"'.[70]

Much of the history of Labour revolves around *the struggle for dominance between the party leadership centred in the PLP and its supporters outside.* The two poles of class aspiration and the politics of the nation exist side by side in reformism. Nevertheless, from the moment of its birth the PLP asserted its right to ignore the membership.

The reformist loves to deride Marxism as dogmatic. But the logic of reformism is a hard master, and it now dictated that the activists, once they had lifted MPs into the Commons, must become passive spectators of the mighty. *Labour Conference, almost the only arena where the MPs' activities might be questioned, was the first victim of electoral triumph.*

The LRC changed its name to the Labour Party 1906. Its executive decided to present the 1907 Conference with a motion stating that resolutions could do no more than 'register the opinions of the conference without prejudice to any future course of action that may be considered advisable by the Party in Parliament'.[71] But this was too blatant. As someone told Eduard Bernstein, father of German Revisionism: 'My dear Ede, one does not say these things, one simply does them'.[72] In the end the motion was never debated. Pete Curran, an ILP trade unionist, insisted that the executive amend its own resolution.

The final wording deleted the offending phrase, replacing it with this: 'the time and method of giving effect to [conference decisions] are left to the Party in the House in conjunction with the National Executive'.[73] This gave the PLP all it wanted.

The conference debate was remarkable given the short time the Labour Party had had to sell out. The Engine Men's delegate 'said that they found members going to the House of Commons not only disregarding the instructions given them but absolutely voting against the registered wish of conference. He thought they had a right to be suspicious of actions like those.' A Workers' Union representative concurred: 'The Conference and not the Parliamentary Party should decide the Parliamentary business'.[74]But true to form, the union bureaucracy backed their political brothers and the motion passed by 642,000 to 252,000.

The 1907 debates forced the PLP to clarify relations with the extra-parliamentary bodies. Snowden's conclusions were direct:

> My experience of Conferences has taught me to attach very little importance to their resolutions. Of the hundreds of resolutions I have seen passed by Labour conferences outlining a drastic programme of reform, I can hardly call to mind one which has had any practical result. Conferences will talk; let them talk. Governments, including Labour Governments, dispose of Conference resolutions... The rank and file of the Labour Party ought to have learnt the lesson by now. They have had enough experience of the futility of conference resolutions.[75]

Sixty years later the experience of the Labour governments under Harold Wilson and James Callaghan decisively confirmed Snowden's words.

The subordinate position of conference followed remorselessly once the idea was accepted firstly that parliament *is genuinely representative of the masses* and secondly that *it is the only acceptable arena for carrying through change*. MacDonald put it succinctly when he said the important thing is 'not what a Socialist meeting declares itself anxious to do, but what the community [the electorate] is prepared to do'.[76]

Straight after the 1907 Conference Henderson explained that MPs were not responsible to Conference: 'I have the strongest wish to respect the findings of the conference. I must however have some regard to those I directly represent in Parliament. This is an aspect of our position not sufficiently kept in mind...'[77] The idea of a 'constituency interest' is just as spurious as that of the 'national interest'. Since workers can only make serious progress at the expense of the capitalists, and conversely, capitalists live only by the daily sweat and toil of those they exploit, *both cannot be represented at the same time.* If an MP truly wishes to act in the interest of his working class constituents, he can do no more than tell them that parliament is a sham and that real power in society lies with capital and the unelected monopolists of physical violence—the police, army and prisons.

A week after these words from Henderson, Hardie emphasised another point: 'rigidly laying down the lines which the Party must follow...is the road to ruin. If the party in the House of Commons is to succeed it must be free to select its own course...only those on the spot, whose finger is on the pulse of Parliament can decide... No conference meeting at Hull or Belfast or Derby or Newcastle can undertake this task...'[78] Again the logic of reformism dictates; everything bows before the Palace of Westminster.*

The PLP was now firmly embedded in the parliamentary game, but what benefits did all that sacrifice of principle bring? The only notable Labour gain in its first quarter of a century was the reversal of Taff Vale by the 1906 Trades Disputes Act. Labour first thought of amending the law[80] but an outraged TUC excluded people like Webb who proposed this, and insisted that outright abolition was needed. In the end it was the support of the Liberal prime minister that got the measure through.

Poodles of Liberalism

Apart from the Trades Disputes Act, Labour's parliamentary record remained dismal. Between 1907 and 1914, the party appeared to all and

* Trade unionists had by this time become accustomed to the rule of bureaucracy, but its rise in the ILP, as a result of the pressure of parliamentarism, was new and striking. Writing in 1908 Russell Smart and Alfred Salter accused the inner ring of NAC of oligarchy: 'To all intents these few men *are* the party. Conference to them is merely an interlude in which a number of delegates meet together to enjoy an annual holiday, to discuss a vast number of unimportant matters, and go through the unnecessary formality of re-electing them to office year after year... The evil has been accentuated since the general election. Questions of national policy fall more and more into the hands of the Parliamentary members of the council; the divisional members can exercise as little control over the inner ring as the 'inferior' members of a Government exercise control over the cabinet Ministers...'[79]

sundry as the pathetic tail pretending to wag the Liberal dog. In the years 1906 and 1908 Labour MPs backed the government in 86 percent of all divisions.[81]

After 1910 the trickle of opportunism became a flood. That year Labour, boosted by the affiliation of the miners, rose to 42 MPs. But the Liberals lost their commanding majority and only remained in office with Labour support. This should have given the party the whip hand. Hardie saw Labour copying the Irish MPs and forming 'a separate voting bloc prepared to sell its votes to the highest bidder'.[82] But he forgot that the Irish had been a powerful independent pressure group because they wanted Home Rule. The Labour MPs on the other hand wanted to rule from Westminster and so were wedded to parliament and its procedures. So far from the Labour group pressuring the Liberal government, they were consistently blackmailed to back it up.

The second factor was the Osborne Judgement, a legal ruling which prevented unions from paying Labour's political levy, leaving the party short of funds with which to fight any future contests. This was a compelling reason for Labour to vote with the Liberals at any price. The Liberal chief whip reported in 1910: 'Throughout this period I was always able to count on the support of the Labour Party'.[83]

MacDonald drew the political conclusions. If change was gradual and depended on votes, then the fact that the majority voted Liberal surely meant that the best place to be was the Liberal Party itself. By 1910 MacDonald was publicly questioning whether the Labour Party might not do better as a ginger group of the Liberals? He wrote: 'it is impossible to maintain a pure and simple Socialist Party...the Labour Party...will probably fulfil itself by being the creative centre of a much more powerful political movement'.[84] In the same vein he claimed that 'under British conditions, a Socialist Party is the last, not the first form of the Socialist movement in politics'.[85]

The problems were illustrated daily in the Commons. Whether it was the House of Lords blocking Liberal social reforms, unemployment, or the Insurance Act, Labour took a position barely distinguishable from and sometimes to the right of many Liberal MPs. Supporters asked in dismay: 'How can the man in the street, whom we are continually importuning to forsake his old political associations, ever be led to believe that the Labour Party is in any way different to the Liberal Party, when this sort of thing is recurring'.[86]

This behaviour was tragic, but for the bourgeois press it had its comic side:

> The Labour members...talk valiantly on platforms about their independence... But in the House itself they are as obedient as trained poodles... they line into the right lobby with a subservience which is entertaining.
>
> Parliamentarians recall one famous day when the Labour Party led by Mr Ramsay MacDonald proposed what practically amounted to a vote of censure on the Government for not paying fair wages in Government works. But they gasped for breath when...Mr Ramsay MacDonald scuttled. [Fearing a Liberal defeat] he would not support his own motion... It is conduct like this which has caused the working man holding forward political opinions to suspect that the Labour gentlemen at Westminster are bamboozling them.[87]

The farcical state into which Labour had fallen was shown when Labour MPs officially decided they should not vote according to the merits of an issue, but only to keep the Liberals in office!

This was hardly a golden age.

The degradation did not stop there. Labour came within a hair's breadth of entering a coalition with the Liberals. This was raised in 1910 but judged premature. In 1911 MacDonald was in serious discussions with leading Liberals over the possibility.[88] In 1914 Fenner Brockway made these machinations public at the ILP Conference.[89] In fact a coalition including Liberals, Labour and the Tories was just around the comer, but the excuse for this was rather more convincing than the previous ones—the World War.

Left alternatives

Labour's abject position sent a wave of anger across the left. There have always been two very different reactions against the degeneration caused by electoralism. One was a turn towards mass militancy, which involved a practical rejection of parliamentary methods. The other can be called the *eternal Labour left*. It is eternal because reformist politics always involves compromising with capitalism. Ralph Miliband describes the aims of Labour's left thus:

> to push their leaders into accepting more radical policies and programmes, and to press upon them more militant attitudes in response to challenges from labour's opponents. The Labour Left's own acceptance of the categories of the parliamentary system has been distinguished from that of the leadership by a continuous search for means of escape from its inhibitions and constrictions. What the Labour leaders have

> accepted eagerly the Labour Left has accepted with a certain degree of unease and at times with acute misgivings.[90]

Acute misgivings maybe, but *it has always accepted*. It shakes its chains but remains a willing prisoner of the machine.

The organised left presence in the Labour Party dates from the election in 1907 of Victor Grayson who shot like a comet across the horizon of Labour politics and then fizzled out. His eventual disappearance remains an unexplained mystery.[91] Grayson stood as 'Labour and *Socialist*' in the Colne Valley by-election. To the Labour leadership this was a crime. Socialism was acceptable in private but should not obtrude into electoral business.

Grayson was not a revolutionary, but he was militantly reformist. While others saw in parliament the broadmindedness of the 'admittedly great', he saw only an 'ancient Chamber...swaddled in the mediaeval vestments of pompous and now meaningless procedure... The legislative machine is exquisitely devised to prevent, or at least render difficult, any change in stereotyped institutions'.[92] Parliament could only be used as a propaganda platform from which to arouse those outside. In 1908, he was expelled from the Commons for accusing MPs of conniving at murder by allowing poverty to continue.

Grayson lost his seat in 1910 and broke away to form the British Socialist Party (which, though dominated by the former SDF, incorporated dissident ILP branches and Blatchford's *Clarion* movement). But criticisms of Labour continued from within. Tillett wrote a pamphlet whose title, *Is the Parliamentary Labour Party a Failure?* is self-explanatory. A group of ILP members issued the so-called 'Green Manifesto' *Let Us Reform the Labour Party*. Its tone was urgent. The Labour Party was facing 'a crisis touching its very vitals.' This had been brought about by 'the Lazarus-like attitude of many of the members, and the suicidal "Revisionist" policy accepted by all of the members of the Parliamentary Labour Group.' This had 'reduced the whole Movement to acute anaemia or rabid melancholy'.[93] Many senior Labour MPs, including Hardie and Snowden, openly ridiculed the policy prevailing under the MacDonald leadership Snowden declared:

> Unless the Labour Party has a distinct point of view...unless it can show that it is anxious to go farther than, or in a different way to, the Liberals, there is no reason for its existence as a separate party. It would be difficult for the observer to find from the attitude of the PLP wherein its position on questions of taxation differs from that of the Liberal Party.[94]

In the end, however, the campaign by Grayson and those that followed him had minimal impact. It had been fatally flawed from the start, and this was revealed as early as 1909. At that year's ILP Conference the mettle of the left was tested. MacDonald set the stage by suggesting parliamentary procedures were more important than the plight of the unemployed:

> The existence of democratic government is just as essential to the building up of the Socialist State as is the solution of the problem of unemployment... The Party which proposes to strike at the heart of democratic government in order to make a show of earnestness about unemployment will not only not be tolerated by the country, but does not deserve to be.[95]

Hardie nailed his colours to the mast when he leapt up to announce that MacDonald was 'the biggest intellectual asset which the Socialist movement has.'

When a vote went against the leadership and in favour of Grayson the ILP 'Big Four'—Hardie, Macdonald, Snowden and Bruce Glasier dropped a bombshell—they resigned. The response was immediate. Cross describes how one delegate 'moved a resolution so obsequious that even now it takes one's breath away'.[96] Only ten delegates voted against this tearful plea for the leaders to stay on. But the Big Four let their decision stand. They doubted the continuing need for an ILP. Glasier felt: 'We must only save the Party if it is worth saving,' and of this he was not certain.[97]

The ILP had outlived its usefulness. Its enthusiasm had helped create the PLP, but now this body wanted passive obedience, not an organisation telling it how to behave. Russell Smart, an astute left-winger, realised this:

> Is it our part in the fight merely to provide the funds, get recruits, and follow our leaders?... For the last few years the Junta pursued a policy which had steadily and stealthily deprived the branches of their autonomy and increased the power of the centre...we are merely the ladder by which clever, and at a later date self-seeking politicians may climb into office.[98]

There was a fundamental difficulty facing the Labour left. In accepting parliamentary change they had ultimately to bow down before the parliamentarians. Lenin regarded 'direct struggle of the masses... as the highest form of the movement, and parliamentary activity...as the lowest form'.[99] Now this is either true or it is not. If it is true, then *the workers' needs*, their self-confidence and their capacity to fight, *come first, and parliamentary manoeuvres are secondary*. If, on the other hand, Macdonald was right, then *parliamentary influence outweighs everything*. Macdonald put these alternatives in his replies to Grayson:

> We ask you to find money for the establishment and maintenance of a serious and intelligent and determined body of men who use the House of Commons in order that they may work through it, not merely demonstrate through it...[100]

The outside left

Labour's final emergence from the cocoon of Liberalism owed nothing to its own efforts, or even those of the left. It arose from the second, and far more serious alternative to Labourism, the 'Labour Unrest' of 1910–1914. The new unionism of 1889 created a forward movement which, though deflected into reformist channels, gave the impetus for a real break with Lib-Labism. Since then, no mass ideological advance had been made, which partly explained the permanent tendency of the Labour Party to collapse into the arms of the Liberals.

The class struggles that began in 1910 and continued until 1921 provided the springboard for the next major development in Labour politics. We move from an alliance of the reformist ILP minnow with the trade union whale of basically Liberal persuasion, to a *mass reformist party*. Once more the Labour leaders are found tailing the class (where not actually obstructing it) and again the translation of struggle into electoral politics is both indirect and assisted by the weak position of the revolutionary left.

In the 'Labour Unrest' of 1910 to 1914 the working class returned to the stage of history with a ferocity which terrified the Labour Party as much as the ruling class. These years saw the first national strikes of miners, dockers and railwaymen. Within four years trade union membership doubled, and strike days quadrupled. Merseyside's Bloody Sunday, 13 August 1911 captured the spirit of the time. A mass demonstration of 80,000 striking transport workers was attacked by police and military. Driven into the city:

> the residents in many instances took sides with the rioters against the police, throwing bottles, bricks, slates and stones from the houses and from the roofs. The whole area was for a time in a state of siege.[101]

Two days later a couple of strikers were shot dead. The same happened at Llanelli where two more were killed.

These events were precipitated by a continuing decline in British capitalism's competitive position, rising prices and a drop in unemployment. Once again the role of revolutionaries was central. They were inspired by the theory of syndicalism. As one delegate told the 1912 Trades Union Congress: 'Let us be quite clear as to what Syndicalism really is...a protest against the inaction of the Labour Party'.[102]

This was borne out by syndicalist writings. Tom Mann's *Industrial Syndicalist*, *The Miners' Next Step* and other works carried the same rejection of 'politics', understood as Labour's reformism. Leaflets such as this were typical: 'Leaders only want your votes; they will sell you. They lie, Parliament lies and will not help you, but is trying to sell you. Don't touch a tool till you get your minimum. Win, win, win!'[103] And win they did in a number of mighty disputes.

The *Weekly Despatch* explained what had occurred:

> The fact is that the Labour representatives, from their own point of view, become demoralised when they enter Parliament... Their friends in the constituencies who expect so many things from the Labour Party are disappointed. The consequence is that the men outside, the real leaders of labour agitation, are going instead without paying the slightest attention to their parliamentary representatives. They realise, though, rather late, the Labour Party is but an appendage of the Liberal Party.

The truth was that the parliamentary game of the party was irrelevant to the daily needs of the class:

> It has no effect on the matters most important to Labour; wages did not rise, the price of necessities of life increased... It is enough to state that [the Labour Party] has no influence on those vital issues.[104]

A brake on the movement

The reaction of the Labour Party to the unrest was highly informative. First, as has been noted, *it did absolutely nothing to develop the mass militancy*. Although a great number of Labour Party supporters must have been caught up in strike action, on no occasion were they acting *as Labour Party members*, but rather in spite of that fact.

As a force for taking the Labour Unrest forward, or shaping it in a positive direction, the Labour Party was totally and utterly irrelevant.

The President of the Board of Trade, the government's chief conciliation service, told the cabinet of:

> the almost complete collapse of the Labour Party in the House as an effective influence in labour disputes. They were not consulted with regard to and had no share in the Seamen's or Transport Workers' movement last summer. During the railway strike, they attempted to act as a go-between for the men and the Government. But they had very little influence over the actions of the men, or on the result...the Labour Party exercised no influence at all.

And he added a significant rider: 'Their elimination is a distinct loss to industrial peace'.[105]

In the early stages even the union bureaucracy were extremely anxious to exclude the Labour leaders from any involvement. MacDonald complained about the Miners' executive: 'Not only did it hold itself aloof from the Labour Party in parliament, but it sought virtually to interdict the Labour members from expressing on public platforms any views concerning the situation or the government negotiations... This surely was Syndicalism *in excelsis*!'[106]

It is easy to see why Labour should not have been consulted, for if they had been, this was the advice MacDonald proffered:

> If we had been consulted first of all we should have advised the men to begin with Parliamentary action, both on the floor of the House of Commons, and in Ministers' private rooms...whilst the heroics outside are being indulged in, Parliamentary action of a general character is being paralysed and prejudiced.[107]

The party was not ignored because it had nothing to say. It commented in speeches, newspapers and books—with a barrage of abuse beside which Thatcherite attacks on the right to strike begin to pale. The May 1912 issue of the ILP's *Socialist Review* described strikes as 'an apocalypse overspreading the social firmament'.[108] Supporters of direct action formed 'a percentage of the population [which] is mentally defective. [They are] not a subject of discussion but of pathological treatment.' Glasier's pamphlet. *Socialism and Strikes* began by saying that 'among the many curious and, at first sight inexplicable customs of civilisation, that of industrial strikes seems one of the most extraordinary.' To stop work 'is culpable, incomprehensible fatuity'.[109]

However this attitude was not out-and-out reactionary. Labour's leaders did not explicitly side with the bosses. They wished to be neutral and for the state to rise above class warfare. To the belligerents they said 'a plague on both your houses.' Thus during the bitter struggle in 1913 of Jim Larkin and the Dublin workers against a ruthless anti-union boss, Glasier condemned the two sides for showing 'the same wilful anarchistic temperament.' They were 'the upper...and lower jaw of the same clinch'.[110] It might have looked like that from the offices of the ILP; on the ground the impression was startlingly different. Larkin replied that these political leaders had 'sold the cause of Labour, besmirched the flag, dragged it down in the dirt'.[111]

Tillett ridiculed the idea that the capitalist state was neutral. He described the events of 1912 as follows:

> ...strikes...police intimidation, coercion, brutality, riot, imprisonment; Home Secretary intervenes with armed forces, attempts at suppression, Cossack methods of the Home Office forces. Parliament dumb and acquiescent, Labour Party impotent where not indifferent... Parliament is a farce and a sham, the rich man's Duma, the employer's Tammany, the Thieves' Kitchen and the working man's despot... In the 1912 strikes we had to fight Parliament, the forces of the Crown, the judges of the law...[112]

The Labour Unrest showed that in major class struggles Labour *sides with the state and stands for the preservation of capitalist society*. Thus in 1912 the ILP's *Socialist Review* wrote: 'Society is exposed to well nigh mortal injury...the well-being of the whole nation is at the mercy of the workmen...' *Whatever the provocation*, such strikes could never be excused: 'How then is the nation to deal with a menace of such almost incredible coercion—a coercion which is altogether apart...from the question of the justifiability of the claims of the workers'.[113] Macdonald, famed as the 'man who could conceal an ounce of meaning in a ton of verbiage'[114] suddenly managed to speak with crystal clarity. 'Syndicalism is largely a revolt against Socialism [by which he meant the Labour Party]. Socialism must be Parliamentary or it is nothing'. The choice was indeed class or nation: 'There is, therefore, a real unity called a nation, which endows the individual with traditions, with habits, with a system of social conduct. The Syndicalist...lays it down that this national inheritance is unreal, is nothing—can build up no policy upon it'.[115]

However the reaction was not uniform. Some ILP leaders professed sympathy for strikes, *only the more effectively to restrain them*. Witness the byzantine sophistry of Keir Hardie at this time: parliamentary action 'is revolutionary, whereas direct action is but palliative... A general strike against Liberalism and Toryism is the need of the hour. The industrial strike, even when successful settles nothing... The political strike [by which Hardie meant voting Labour] is the only form of strike which is all gain and no loss.[116]The ability of reformists to talk left, when the moment requires, should never be underestimated. In 1912, ignoring the ILP's entire history, Hardie declared:

> The ILP...is not a reform organisation; it is revolutionary in the fullest sense of the word. The ILP does not exist to patch up the present order of society so that it may be made a little more tolerable; it exists to overthrow the present order... Comrades of the working class, we do not want Parliament to give us reforms. We are not asking Parliament to do things for us. We are going to Parliament ourselves to master Parliament.[117]

An interesting pattern was developing. The left wing at the 1900 founding conference—the ILP, *was now to the right*. Most ILP leaders, professionally linked with the concept of 'nation' and distanced from collective pressure outside parliament, were now *far more conservative than their counterparts in the union bureaucracy*.

By 1910 there was a group of professional reformists—the PLP, who had a material interest in resisting strikes. History does not stand still. In the 1890s *reformist politicians were in advance of the class*. From 1910 this was no longer true. The 'Labour Unrest' showed them not only far behind the working class, but a *conscious hindrance* to its advance.

Something else should be noted. Although union leaders ultimately blocked action they had to be *far more sensitive to direct class pressure from the workplaces*. Both left and right-wing officials needed left rhetoric to keep any control and realised that close association with the discredited, passive Labour Party would damage them in the eyes of a rank and file already prepared to act unofficially.

Thus the NUR's *Railway Review*, the paper of the right-wing Jimmy Thomas, denounced a particularly obnoxious Labour attack entitled *Stop the Strike* which described stoppages as 'essentially an abortion':

> How simple the whole matter is... What a magnanimous disregard for the social relations in which this takes place and is conditioned! With a single generalisation the capitalist mode of production is waved out of existence... Landlord, capitalist and wage-labourer have disappeared.'[118]

At this point the interests of the labour bureaucracy—the MPs and the trade union officials—diverged, a fact highlighted by one of the most astounding Bills ever proposed by Labour MPs. It was put forward by a prestigious team including the previous and current party chairmen—Arthur Henderson and George Barnes as well as Will Crooks* and Enoch Edwards. These men, who all had trade union connections, proposed to make it illegal to strike without first going to a Board of Conciliation. Thirty days notice had to be given for any 'intended change affecting conditions of employment with respect to wages or hours.' Any worker who struck in defiance of the law would be fined 'not less than £2 nor more than £10 for every day or part of a day that such employee is on strike.' With average weekly earnings just over £1 the real cost of the fines may be appreciated. The most draconian part of the Bill concerned working class solidarity: 'Any person who incites, encourages or aids in any manner...any employee to go or continue on strike contrary to the provisions of this Act shall be guilty of an offence and liable to a fine of not less than £10 and not more than £200'.[119] An unopposed vote of censure was passed by the TUC on this proposal in 1911, and it had to be dropped.

The events of 1912 reunited the union leaders and PLP once more. The first national miners' strike plus an increasingly articulate syndicalist challenge, led both to discover their community of interest in resisting the workers. Robert Smillie, the veteran ILP member and miners' leader, realised that: 'During our strike...we got to the verge of the horror of revolution'.[120] The shift in emphasis can be seen by comparing Labour Conferences in January 1912 and January 1913. At the first, before the miners' stoppage, conference unanimously approved resolutions congratulating striking unions on their success. But the next year it had become one long diatribe against syndicalism. The Triple Alliance of coal, rail and transport unions was another example of the change. It began as a response to pressure for class unity in action, but Smillie later wanted to use it differently: 'If the three bodies which have now joined hands use their votes wisely at election times they themselves could add 120 Members to those in the House of Commons. That is the place where the future battle is to fought'.[121]

The trade union bureaucracy now recognised, as Lloyd George had done, that Labour politics could act as 'the best policemen for the Syndicalist'.[122] Indeed the party *played an exceptionally important part in controlling the movement*, a part belied by its apparent irrelevance. *It provided the weaponry and the justification for the bureaucrats' holding operation.*

* Crooks was elected in by-election in 1903 and was therefore one of the most senior Labour MPs.

Syndicalism had no answer to the generalised political arguments of Labour, because it rejected 'politics' in principle. Its only policy was a spontaneous general strike. Theoretical weakness did not seem to matter when wages were the issue; but as soon as it was a question of going beyond economic action the syndicalists found themselves unarmed, with Labour occupying the high ground of general ideas. *The syndicalists made the fatal mistake of writing off the politics of reformism.*

For the Labour Party was never simply a reactionary party like the Tories and Liberals. It held out the promise that workers might advance by other means than self-activity. It defended law and order, but bemoaned the 'excesses' of the police and military. *The party may not have been effective in attacking capital, but it proved valuable in defending it.*

In comparison with working-class direct action, Labour's efforts at the polls seemed laughable. Between 1910 and 1914 it lost four seats and came bottom of the poll in the other twelve by-elections. Nevertheless the wider class struggle was shifting many workers to the left, and despite the loss of seats a creeping increase in Labour's vote passively recorded this phenomenon.

However the mass basis for reformism was still restricted. Evidence for this came with the passing of the 1913 Trade Union Act. This amending of the Osborne Judgement required unions to take ballots to ascertain whether to pay the political levy. The levy received just 60 percent of the small numbers of votes cast.*

By 1914 the proportion of trade unionists affiliated to Labour was lower than it had been in 1903.[123]

Even for the most ardent of reformists Labour's first fourteen years must have been a grave disappointment. The working class had rediscovered a type of do-it-yourself reformism—and had achieved in weeks changes such as the miners' statutory minimum wage, which years of lobbying at Westminster had failed to secure. The Labour Party's own efforts, by contrast, were dismal.

* There are precious few measures of the real significance of union affiliation to the Labour Party. During the late 1980s Labour did well in Margaret Thatcher's imposed ballots on the political levy, but we have only one other measure of active union commitment, from 1927. That year the Tories stopped automatic deduction of the levy from dues and individuals had to 'opt in'. Though this cost only a few pence a year Labour's trade union membership dropped by 40 percent overnight.

3

War and reconstruction: Labour adopts socialism

SINCE LABOUR is concerned with winning reforms through the 'ordinary' channels and in 'normal' circumstances, great serial crises such as war seem to have no relevance to a party concerned with the humdrum business of legislative change. The contrary is true. Firstly it is only during crisis that capitalism is weakened and large-scale change in workers' consciousness is possible. Secondly, just as a heart condition may remain hidden until sudden stress brings it out, so periods of crisis test political parties and reveal their inner nature. The 1914–18 war was one such test for Labour.

When the First World War began Labour was a sickly infant. When it ended an extraordinary transformation had occurred. The party was relaunched as the chief opposition force with prospects of office. Most remarkable of all, on its masthead was inscribed Clause Four, the commitment to socialism:

> To secure for the producers by hand or by brain the full fruits of their industry, and the most equitable distribution thereof that may be possible, upon the basis of the common ownership of the means of production and the best obtainable system of popular administration and control of each industry and service.

An early casualty of the fighting

At the outbreak of war the national element in the reformist class/nation mix brutally asserted itself. When MacDonald, as party leader, voiced doubts about the conflict he was deposed by the patriotic trade union bureaucracy and replaced by Arthur Henderson. On 19 May 1915, the party joined Asquith's coalition government.

The ILP leaders who had fought for a separate Labour Party now watched it crumble. MacDonald recorded that Hardie was: 'a crushed man [following] the complete mergence of the labour Party in the war-lusty crowd.[1] MacDonald himself believed that coalition 'jeopardised the existence of the Labour Party' and concluded 'that our Labour Party is finally burst'.[2]

The Labour Party, along with countless workers' lives, had been sacrificed. The figure of one in every ten British men aged under 45 killed or wounded was more than a statistic.[3] Rosa Luxemburg, writing six weeks after the outbreak, counted the cost of abandoning internationalism:

> the cannon fodder that was loaded upon the trains in August and September is rotting on the battlefields of Belgium and the Vosges, while profits are springing like weeds, from the fields of the dead... Shamed, dishonoured, wading in blood and dripping with filth, thus capitalist society stands...as a roaring beast, as an orgy of anarchy, as a pestilential breath devastating culture and humanity.[4]

By the end of four years the beast had devoured some 15 million lives.

In this situation, did labour movement leaders call for workers to die for profits, or did they call on them to destroy the system that made such carnage inevitable? Speaking for the union bureaucrats who now controlled the party, Tillett said: 'In a strike I am for my class, right or wrong; in a war I am for my country, right or wrong'.[5]

The attitude of workers' leaders at this juncture was of tremendous importance. Twentieth century wars have, unlike previous ones, mobilised the entire capitalist economy in their prosecution. Workers were therefore not only required to sacrifice themselves on the battlefields, production at home was central to keeping the conflict going.

Lloyd George, soon to be prime minister and 'architect of victory', well understood the situation:

> Of all the problems which governments had to handle during the Great War, the most delicate and probably the most perilous were those arising on the home front...*industrial unrest spelt a graver menace to our endurance and ultimate victory than even the military strength of Germany.*[6]

The dubious credit for keeping our ruling class secure must go to the Labour Party and union leaders. But it was a close thing. Thus during a rationing crisis the Food Controller told J R Clynes, the ILP member of parliament then attached to his office: 'It might well be, Clynes, that you and I, at this moment, are all that stand between this country and revolution!'[7]

Moralism and Labour politics

War forced Labour to clarify its ideas. Before that, wrote Desmond: 'We were never very clear about anything. We did not say we were for or against country—we simply sidestepped it'.[8]

This was not the full story. The pre-war Labour Party had a position; or rather, the ILP, whose task was to define *general* reformist politics, had a position. This derived from two sources. The first was traditional 'little Englandism' or the Gladstonian idea that Britain should not become embroiled in foreign wars because this disrupted free trade.* The second source was the International,** whose famous resolution of 1907 called for 'the working classes and their parliamentary representatives to exert every effort in order to prevent [the outbreak of war]... In case war should break out anyway...to intervene for its speedy termination.' Keir Hardie even contributed to discussions with the suggestion of a general strike to prevent war.***

Thus there was a strong element of tokenism, of mouthing a slogan rather than intending to carry it out.

Secondly, because the notion of a strike touched the unions directly, their leaders made a rare foray into foreign policy, and defeated the suggestion of a general strike against war.

However when Labour MPs and the Second International leaders referred to internationalism they were not talking as Marxists. The former never had been Marxists, the latter had ceased to be. Marxists see *the world unity of the working class as a fundamental principle without which the socialist goal cannot be reached*. Reformists, however, believe *that it is possible to attain socialism within one country by the control of parliament*. They do not see an indissoluble link between internationalism and workers' power.

---

* The strength of this feeling in the Liberal Party should not be forgotten. John Morley led the anti-war faction in the cabinet. Until put to the test with the actual outbreak of hostilities he believed he had a Cabinet majority of eight or nine, although at the time of his resignation only John Burns joined him.[9]

** When Labour applied for admission to the Second International in 1908 it caused much debate. In the end the party was accepted as an exceptional case. The problem was that there was nothing specifically socialist in the Party programme. Indeed it had no agreed programme! The wording of the resolution was prepared by Kautsky and ran as follows: 'Whereas by previous resolutions of the International Congresses, all organisations adopting the standpoint of the proletarian class struggle and recognising the necessity for political action have been accepted for membership, the International Bureau declares that the British Labour Party is admitted to International Socialist Congresses, because, while not expressly accepting the proletarian class struggle, in practice the Labour Party conducts this struggle and adopts its standpoint, inasmuch as the Party is organised independently of the bourgeois parties.'[10]

In 1912 the International checked up on the Labour Party's pursuance of the class struggle 'in practice' and asked Arthur Henderson to provide it with 'all Socialist Bills [proposed] in the House of Commons.' Henderson did not, nor indeed could not reply.[11]

*** Two qualifications must be made. Firstly Hardie clearly thought that the threat of a general strike would be quite sufficient and never envisioned, or actually prepared for, a real strike: 'I hold the opinion that the organised Labour movement has it in its power to prevent war by simply threatening to strike... Even the threat...would necessitate the keeping of the army at home... Suppose then, an agreement on the part of the workers in all civilised countries to make war upon war by means of the strike, the knowledge that such would take place would make war impossible.'[12]

For reformists, *internationalism was an optional extra*, welcome on moral grounds but expendable. This political moralism had been the norm in Britain with its 'ethical socialist' tradition. In wartime it enabled the ILP pacifists to remain within the Labour Party and to turn the other cheek to the chauvinists knowing that after the war differences would be forgotten in the common scramble for office.

In August 1914 this type of internationalism was tested. On 2 August, as the war clouds gathered, Hardie and Henderson presented this manifesto to a Trafalgar Square demonstration:

> Compel those of the governing class...to respect the decision of the overwhelming majority of the people who will have neither part nor lot in such infamy... Down with class rule! Down with the rule of brute force! Down with war! Up with the peaceful rule of the people![13]

Resolve crumbled at the first challenge. By 5 August MacDonald had resigned and the Party had repudiated the manifesto. Only the ILP stood its ground to the end. It said:

> Out of the darkness and the depth we hail our working-class comrades of every land. Across the roar of guns, we send sympathy and greeting to the German Socialists. They have laboured unceasingly to promote good relations with Britain, as we with Germany. They are no enemies of ours but faithful friends.[14]

The meaning of the split

The party split. On the one side were the trade union leaders (many of whom were MPs) and on the other five ILP MPs who supported the initial anti-war position. The minority included MacDonald—the former party leader, Hardie—its revered elder statesman and Snowden—its financial expert. The trade union bureaucracy had not only split the Labour Alliance, but overthrown the old PLP leadership.

What did this signify? Until 1914 do-it-yourself reformism from below had pushed the union bureaucrats to the left. The ILP leaders, mesmerised by parliament, were on the right. However in war union sectionalism was incapable of withstanding patriotic hysteria. Only the ILP which specialised in general reformist politics, stuck to its ground, and this now placed it on the left. So today, the local Labour MP may oppose strikes, but be more progressive on general questions such as hanging or racism. *Trade unionists can often be militant when it comes to their own workplace, but hold backward ideas in general.*

Finally, the fact that the union bureaucracy had ousted the professional politicians showed the complexity of Party/labour movement relations. *The PLP does not always dictate.*

As Drucker argues, the Labour Party is not 'a parliamentary grouping united by interest or disposition to which a mass party base was added—as is the case in the Tory Party… It was formed to defend in Parliament the interests of already existing institutions'.[15] Thus the trade union bureaucracy can at certain times impose its wishes, and Labour conferences, unlike Tory Party conferences, are not purely rubber stamps for the leadership, although they never control the leadership.

The Tory Party is run entirely from the top downwards. Questions of policy, of who is the leader and so on, are made behind closed doors. It has been described as an 'oligarchy tempered by assassination'.[16] *Labour is tied to an extra-parliamentary movement.* The war crisis showed that the PLP is, in a sense, a superstructure erected on a base, which is the trade union bureaucracy.*

The diverse attitudes to war

Labour gave considerable assistance to the war effort. For example, Henderson arranged the 1915 'Treasury Agreement', by which the unions abandoned many of their defences, including the right to strike. Labour MPs and union officials took an active part in recruiting drives and efforts to raise production. One enthusiast was Lieutenant-Colonel Will Thorne of the West Ham Volunteer Force—a sad contrast to the new unionist fighter of 1889.

Furthermore the bureaucracy took an active part in hounding the pacifist ILP. For the first, but not the last time, members of the Labour Party sent other members to prison for their political views. Arthur Hayday, former SDF councillor, now president of the Nottingham Trades Council and shortly to be a Labour MP, was described by the local press in glowing terms: 'On the [Military] Tribunals no one was more prompt in unmasking any shirker who masqueraded as a "conchie"' (a pejorative term for conscientious objector).[18] When Tillett met anti-war protesters 'he goaded them, he lashed and slashed and

* A further complication arises because the trade union bureaucracy are themselves a superstructure built upon the collective organisation of the working class in the factories and offices.[17]

gashed them with flaying scorn, he mocked them, he reviled them, he laughed at them'.[19] Havelock Wilson, the Seamen's leader, was moved to tears at the ILP's call for a negotiated peace: 'some of you would be content to meet these men! You would take the bloodstained hands of murderers within your own'.[20]

So strong was Havelock Wilson's hatred of pacifism that at the 1916 Trades Union Congress the transport workers' delegation moved a motion which would have dissolved the Labour Alliance: 'This Congress...should take the necessary steps to effectively control and concentrate Trade Union political action through the Trades Union Congress only'.[21] The proposal fell, but other steps were taken.

The 1917 Labour Party conference changed election procedures for its national executive. Instead of the socialist societies choosing their representatives on their own, block votes would elect the entire executive as one body. In other words the unions could dictate which socialist society representatives would get on. Also no affiliated body with a membership less than 50,000 could nominate to the executive. ILP membership was less than this.[22]

The ILP was also attacked elsewhere. Out of 1,191 trials, of objectors, 805 were ILP members[23] and 70 died in detention through mistreatment.[24]

Deep though the division was, the Labour Party did not break up. The German SPD, by contrast, split three ways, forming the 'Majority' Socialists, the Independents and the Spartakists. The majority of Continental 'Socialist' parties went the same way so that after the war there emerged the Second, Third and for a short period the 'Two-and-a Half' Internationals.

The British Labour Party survived partly because the vast bulk of its support came via the trade unions. This gave it *a stability based not on political considerations but on economic ones* since trade unions encompass a range of opinions from reactionary to revolutionary. Another factor was, despite all the furore, the remarkably narrow gulf separating the ILP from the majority.

Only the British Socialist Party,* which affiliated to Labour 1916 and included John Maclean, protested against the war on clear internationalist grounds. But even the BSP did not approach Lenin's extreme position of 'revolutionary defeatism':

> Present-day socialism will remain true to itself only if it joins neither one nor the other imperialist bourgeoisie, only if it says that the two sides

* The British Socialist Party actually split in two when Hyndman broke away with his pro-war minority.

> are 'both worse', and if it wishes the defeat of the imperialist bourgeoisie in every country. Any other decision will, in reality, be national-liberal and have nothing in common with genuine internationalism.

This attitude had no trace of moralism, the idea that war or peace was somehow above the class divisions of capitalist society. Lenin therefore never considered the ILP's idea of conscientious objection. This was an individual not a collective act and therefore ineffective. But more important, Lenin was very much in favour of war—the war of workers against the system:

> Not 'peace without annexations', but peace to the cottages, war on the palaces, peace to the proletariat and working people, war on the bourgeoisie. Socialists cannot, without ceasing to be socialists, be opposed to all war...civil war is just as much a war as any other.[25]

The limits of the ILP position

There were four main currents in the Independent Labour Party. The first was unashamedly pro-war. J R Clynes and James Parker actually took office in the wartime coalition government.* The most important group was centred on the Union of Democratic Control (UDC) which represented a coalition of ILP members and Liberals such as E D Morel and Arthur Ponsonby. Next came the No Conscription Fellowship of Fenner Brockway and Clifford Allen. Finally, there was the Clyde ILP.

The UDC was led by Ramsay MacDonald, whose opposition to war was strangely phrased:

> Victory must therefore be ours. England is not played out, her mission is not accomplished... Well, we cannot go back, nor can we turn to the right or to the left. We must go straight through...the young men of the country must, for the moment settle the immediate issue of victory, let them do it in the spirit of the brave men who have crowned our country with honour in times that have gone. Whoever may be in the wrong, men so inspired will be in the right.[27]

Where, you might ask, is the anti-war position in that? The answer is that MacDonald believed the interests of the British state were ill-served by the war. Diplomatic intrigues and imperial ambitions had created

* In the ILP heartland of Bradford in 1918 the ILP had 429 members in the armed services, nineteen in jail and twenty-nine conscientious objectors who had opted for alternative service.[26]

unnecessary conflict. Where Lenin saw the war as the inevitable result of capitalist competition. MacDonald saw only 'a diplomatist's war... A dozen men brought Europe to the brink of a precipice and Europe fell over it'.[28] As MacDonald told the Commons On 3 August 1914, in his last speech as party leader, if the foreign secretary had proved 'that our country is in danger...we would be with him and behind him. If this is so we will vote him what money he wants. Yes, and we will go further. We will offer him ourselves if the country is in danger. But he has not persuaded me that it is'.[29]

The pacifist and Christian socialist wing of the ILP took a more militantly anti-war position, but their approach had no coherent politics behind it. The No Conscription Fellowship 'was based on the principle of the "sacredness of human life"... In its branches, scattered throughout the country, were Socialists, Anarchists and Quakers, and other religious objectors'.[30]

Clydeside: the legend and the reality

The most fantastic mythology has grown up around the Clyde ILP, suggesting some connection between the Labour MPs elected in 1922 and wartime militancy associated with John Maclean and the Clyde Workers' Committee. Is the claim justified?

The mouthpiece of the Glasgow ILP was *Forward*, which gained notoriety when one issue was banned for alleged 'incitement to strike'. The editors were perplexed:

> Looking through the files of *Forward* we can find no hint of any incitement... The only big industrial strike on the Clyde since war began was the Engineers' Strike in February 1915. Neither before nor during the strike did we publish a single line about it, nor did we even mention that it was taking place...we declared in our issue of 20 March that we should not touch the subject of strikes during the war.[31]

The police raid on *Forward* caused some embarrassment when civil servants discovered that it 'does not appear anywhere as an anti-war paper'.[32]

What of the ILP's leading individuals? Jimmy Maxton was sentenced to 12 months for incitement. In his case, the charge was more appropriate. On hearing of the arrest of leading stewards, Maxton told a meeting: 'It is now time to take action and that action is to strike, to go home and forget to wind up your alarm clocks, and down tools'.[33] To ensure that plain-clothes policemen took down every word, he repeated this. A sympathetic commentator has explained Maxton's motives:

> Maxton had done nothing wilder in the war than voice his militant pacifism, but as a conscientious objector he had already been dismissed by the Glasgow School Board, and, being due shortly to be interned, he felt it better to go down fighting...than to be meekly shut away.[34]

Maxton, like Hardie, had a flair for spectacular gestures, believing in their political efficacy, but even so, he deserves credit as the most daring of all the Clydesiders.

Remarkably, the rest either adopted *Forward*'s approach, or actively worked to prevent strikes. At first sight this is surprising, since Davie Kirkwood of the ILP was a well-known Clyde Workers' Committee activist. His position was ambiguous. Kirkwood's autobiography tells that at the outbreak of war:

> a terrific struggle tore my breast. I could not hate the Germans. They loved their land as I loved mine... Yet I was working in an arsenal making guns and shells for one purpose—to kill men in order to keep them from killing men. What a confusion! What was I to do. I was not a conscientious objector. I was a political objector. I believed that financial and commercial rivalry had led to war.
>
> I resolved that my skill as an engineer must be devoted to my counter. I was too proud of the battles of the past to stand aside and see Scotland conquered.[35]

The Clyde Workers' Committee was a rank and file revolt against the dismantling of trade union defences by Henderson and the officials. When in late 1915 the government wanted to 'dilute' skilled labour by introducing the unskilled to their work, the committee decided to make this a political issue. They would only accept dilution in return for nationalisation and workers' control.

Kirkwood ignored the committee and turned to John Wheatley, an ILP councillor. These two sabotaged the strategy. On the day government commissioners arrived to impose dilution, writes Kirkwood:

> the War news was terrible... We were all scared as the thundering masses of Germans tramped their way towards the coasts... That night I went to John Wheatley... In thirty minutes he drafted the scheme...which became the basis for the whole of Great Britain and worked perfectly until the end of the War... [But] the extremists attacked us for having

agreed to increased production. John Mac made me the theme of innumerable speeches.[36]

The scheme worked perfectly *for reformism.* It accepted dilution as long as the overall wages bill was not reduced, thus detaching the economic agitation from the political issue of war.*

Finally we come to Manny Shinwell who rose to being a Minister in the Attlee administration. He angrily repudiated the suggestion that he was anti-war: 'Nothing could be further from the truth. I was engaged on work of national importance on behalf of shipping'.[37]

None of the Clydeside ILP believed in striking against the war or even using the crisis to challenge the system at home, simply that union organisation should not suffer unduly because of the fighting. This was the limit of their radicalism.**

Lenin discerned three trends in the working class movement, and all three were reproduced in Britain. There were the 'social chauvinists' (represented by the majority of the PLP and the trade union bureaucracy); the 'Centre' (the ILP); and the revolutionaries (Maclean):

> The social chauvinists ie, socialists in words and chauvinists in deed… are our *class* enemies. They have gone over to the bourgeoisie…
>
> The 'Centre' is a realm of honeyed petty-bourgeois phrases, of internationalism in word and cowardly opportunism and fawning on the social chauvinists in deed.
>
> The crux of the matter is that the 'Centre' is not convinced of the necessity for a revolution against one's own Government.[38]

MacDonald illustrated just how far 'the Centre' was prepared to go. Referring to himself and Henderson, he told a Labour Conference that: 'The differences between them were infinitesimal when they came to realities and facts'.[39] A practical illustration of this was the issue of whether there should be a negotiated settlement or 'the knock-out blow'—'the fight to the finish'. MacDonald said in the Commons:

---

* Despite his efforts at moderation, Kirkwood was deported with Gallacher, MacManus and others when the government moved in to smash the Clyde Workers Committee. He was too prominent a figurehead to leave alone, and in any case, the government was in the business of breaking reformist trade union resistance to the war economy not just the revolutionaries. Later on, however, to show there was no bad feeling, MacDonald convinced Winston Churchill, a government minister, that Kirkwood should be 'put in charge' of a munitions factory. He duly obliged.

** Their chief contribution to Glasgow's labour movement lay not in the industrial field but in the fight against rent increases. Wheatley and the ILP were prominent in the rent strike that eventually forced the government to control increases. As we shall see in the case of Poplar, local government can occasionally provide an area for agitation which escapes the crippling logic of the reformism that outlaws industrial action for fear of damaging parliament.

> A fight to the finish! If that is inevitable, it must be done, there need be no quibble about that. I am not trying to evade that issue. If the fight to a military finish is absolutely necessary...then we cannot help it. It must be done. But I do not believe it is.[40]

Many were understandably confused. One delegate explained to the 1916 Labour Conference: 'In Scotland they had a national dance where they laid down two swords and danced all round them. Mr MacDonald had done that to absolute perfection… He was at a loss to know where Mr MacDonald was. He had been at a loss to know, from the very beginning of the war, where the ILP stood'.[41]

Overtures were also made from the other side. The trade unions re-elected MacDonald as Labour Party treasurer throughout the war. Disagreements could not stand in the way of sinecures. As Jimmy Thomas put it: 'after all, the war is but the question of the moment'.[42] Thomas was an astute reformist. Take his refusal to enter the wartime coalition cabinet. As he wrote, this was

> a mystery to many of my friends. My views were best summarised in the answer I gave to King George v… I told him that when the war was over I was certain that the only people who would have any real influence with the masses during the inevitable chaos and difficulties that must arise after the armistice, would be those in a position to say 'I at least made nothing out of the war'.[43]

The political skills of Thomas and Co were soon in great demand; the long patriotic bacchanalia was coming to an end.

The triumph of statism

Reformists believe that the state is above the 'haggling' of classes; it is a means of resolving class division. This attitude is not accidental but reflects the views of the labour bureaucracy and its search for class compromise. The bureaucrat's role is to negotiate and this naturally leads to a view of the state as the institution through which such class collaboration can be organised on the broadest scale.

Given this attitude it was inevitable that Labour politics should be profoundly influenced by the 'national crisis' of war and the development of the wartime state. We have already seen that from the 1800s the Fabians made the state practically their religion. During the war this reached paroxysms of enthusiasm. The result was terrifying.

Sidney Webb wrote: 'If I were in power...I should decree *Universal Submission* to the national need—not young men for the trenches only, but everyone for what he was fitted; and not persons only, but also property and possessions—everything to be placed at the disposal of the Government'.[44]

Only the trade union bureaucracy, with their experience of legal and police attacks on strikers and union rights, had any reservations and these were swept away. For the war brought a revolution in the officials' status. The Treasury Agreement was an example. Led by Arthur Henderson, the union leaders agreed to suspend all rules and customs impeding maximum output. Job demarcation, strikes, refusal of overtime, restrictions on night and Sunday working and a good deal of health and safety legislation went the same way. In return for this paltry sacrifice (after all it was their members not themselves who had to work the new conditions) they received a magnificent prize: 'the capitalist employers were ignored, and the principal Ministers of the Crown negotiated directly with the authorized representatives of the whole trade Union world'.[45] Positions in the government and on official bodies now began to absorb great numbers of officials, making the trade unions and Labour Party virtually organs of state. In his presidential address to the 1917 TUC John Hill of the Boilermakers put it thus: 'the prejudice of trade unionists against politicians has hitherto held us back...but the events of the last three years have taken the scales from our eyes.' 'The man,' he said, 'in our ranks today who is neither a Government official nor a member of some Government Committee is unknown to the movement'.[46]

Principles whose renunciation had previously been inconceivable were freely dispensed with. Conscription was universally abhorred as an infringement of a sacred British freedom. On 6 January 1915 a conference of the chief labour movement bodies not only voted by a majority of 2 to 1 against conscription, but called on Labour to leave the wartime coalition. Henderson was not one to be put off by such things. He told delegates to their faces: 'If this conference considers I must oppose this Bill [for conscription] I shall refuse to accept their decision'.[47] So just two weeks after the conference rejecting conscription a further Labour Conference was induced to swallow it.

The fascination that the state exercised over the bureaucracy was not necessarily the result of cynical personal ambition. It reflected a powerful sentiment that has cropped up every time Labour enters government—that the aim of representatives is to penetrate the 'corridors of power' and stay there, whatever the cost in principle. As Beatrice Webb explained when Labour joined Lloyd George's administration:

> A thorough beating of the Germans may have passed through their minds. But their main motive...is the illusion that the mere presence of Labour men in the Government, apart from anything they may do or prevent being done, is in itself a sign of democratic process.[48]

The corridors of power were made much broader and far-reaching by the war. In 1914 the civil service numbered 57,706 people; after the war 116,241.[49] By 1918 90 percent of the country's imports were purchased directly by the state, while 240 National Factories were established and millions more workers were on government contracts. Two-thirds of all workers and a vast range of social and economic activity, from the food on your table to hours and conditions of work, were now under state regulation.[50] This was clearly a form of centralised state capitalism—the most brutal expression of ruling class war—since everything was subordinated to defend British capital against enemies abroad and at home. *The complete absorption of the upper reaches of the labour movement into the bourgeois state* was clearly a lurch to the right.

However, once more we must remember the fundamental difference between reaction and reform. To the capitalist the state was a valuable adjunct to the process of capital accumulation. In war the most enthusiastic supporters of this concept were the 'social imperialists' around Lord Milner. They even tried to make inroads into the labour movement with a British Workers' league but this failed dismally. As Marwick points out there is a basic 'distinction between the militarist who desires happy and healthy cannon fodder, and the collectivist who desires a better and humane society'.[51]

Reconstructing the party

At the beginning of 1917 the Labour Party was still deep in the mire of class collaboration. Yet by the end of the year Labour had broken free and was poised to bid for power on a socialist programme.

Leopards do not usually change their spots, so what happened in 1917 to bring about the change? It was the revival of working class confidence symbolised by two Russian Revolutions and class struggle at home. Although five million workers were away in the army, Britain's trade union membership rose from four to six and a half a million between 1914 and 1918. The immediate shock of war had reduced strike days per year to almost nil, but by the end of the war the annual figure was six million working days lost through strikes, double what it had been when the Labour Party was founded. This was at a time when strikers risked taking on the bosses, the police, army, trade union officials and Labour Party. The militants who led activity, as in all previous struggles, rejected Labour's passive electoral approach. Many indeed were revolutionaries.

Mining and engineering stood out. In July 1915 two hundred thousand South Wales colliers stopped work over pay. In five days they won. South Wales was influenced by syndicalists who published the famous *Miners' Next Step*. The engineering shop stewards' movement was even more important. It began on Clydeside but soon fanned out into a national network which in May 1917 led a three-week strike of 200,000—the largest of the war. The central figures in the national stewards' movement were revolutionaries such as Willie Gallacher, Arthur McManus and J T Murphy, who joined the Communist Party when it was later established. Behind the revolutionary leaders and the militant industries a growing volume of discontent was piling up.

Labour's reaction to rising struggle was a combination of resistance and adaptation. It did its level best to prevent stoppages but also sought to channel workers' anger. Preventing stoppages had priority even for those supposedly on the left. Thus MacDonald reassured the House of Commons: 'believe me when I say that, rather than [be] an agent to bring men out on strike just now, I would...destroy every particle of influence that ever I had with the working men.'[52] *Labour Leader* wrote: 'Whatever may be one's view about the war...one cannot but regret there should be strikes.'[53] Labour's adaptation to rising struggle, and its own organisational renewal, first showed in the work of the War Emergency Workers' National Committee.

While the Labour Party was riven by internal strife this little committee brought together the diverse elements from Webb to Hyndman, from MacDonald to the trade union leaders. Indeed, 'aside from its sponsorship of [the War Emergency Workers National Committee] the Labour Party hardly existed as a national organisation until late in the war.'[54] The committee was a sort of reformist think-tank, launching initiatives which, by ignoring the war and concentrating on conditions at home, established landmarks for the post-war programme.

One suggestion was the 'conscription of riches.' Since workers could be conscripted to fight for their country, why not take over personal wealth too? When first proposed at the War Emergency Workers National Committee 1916 the suggestion was lost. It was only adopted there in October 1917 and by the Labour Party Executive in November 1917. Surely the fact that it was agreed in the very shadow of the Russian revolution was no coincidence.

Another sign of a political thaw was the Leeds Convention. Held on 3 June 1917 it brought together 1,150 delegates representing all organisations critical of the war. MacDonald described the game played at Leeds in an article written shortly afterwards: 'Before the war I felt that what was called "the spirit of the rebel" was to a great extent a stagey pose. It is now required to save us'.[55]

MacDonald's first gambit was to pay tribute to Russia's February revolution. Addressing the Convention he said: 'When this war broke out organised Labour in this country lost the initiative. It became a mere echo of the old governing classes' opinions. Now the Russian Revolution has once again given you the chance to take the initiative yourselves'.[56]

But the most elaborate 'stagey pose' was struck by W C Anderson, the ILP MP who called for no less than the establishment of 'Councils of Workmen and Soldiers' Delegates for...the complete political and economic emancipation of international labour'.[57] This was stirring stuff! Alas, those present had not heard Anderson expressing his true feelings just before this in the Commons: 'the best way if you wish to deal with extremists is to remove discontent and try to get a better relationship established between the Government and organized labour... unless you are very careful you will bring the country to the very verge of revolution'.[58]

'Uncle Arthur'—apostle of Labour's socialist conversion

The War Emergency Workers National Committee and Leeds Convention heralded great things to come, but produced no lasting results themselves. Labour was eventually led to the promised land of socialism by the most unlikely of prophets—Arthur Henderson. He is a familiar figure in these pages as a Liberal election agent denouncing socialism, as the trade union voice in the Labour Alliance, as sponsor to Will Crooks's anti-union Bill and finally as the first Labour Minister valiantly putting 'country before party' (or rather capitalist state before class).

Yet in 1917 Henderson not only resigned from the coalition,* but went on, with Webb's assistance, to reorganise the Labour Party, giving

* He resigned over the government's refusal to allow participation in the Stockholm conference called by various socialist parties. Labour still continued as a member of the coalition, however.

it a socialist programme. Henderson's 'conversion' was fascinating, not for biographical reasons, but because it sharply summarised changes in the bureaucracy as a whole. The saga began on 30 May 1917 when Lloyd George sent him on a mission to Russia, his task to bolster Russia's flagging military enthusiasm in the wake of the Tsar's downfall.

According to *The Times* Henderson made quite a splash in Petrograd:

> His reference to the unanimous determination of all classes in the British empire to continue the struggle till a victorious peace had been assured evoked tremendous cheering... Men and women, moved to tears, demanded a general mobilization, amid cries of: 'We all are ready to march against the foe'.[59]

The truth was a bit different, for by then the Bolsheviks were rapidly growing in influence. Russian workers must have been bewildered by this man who claimed to speak for labour but was so obviously a tool of the bosses. Indeed, Henderson's apartment was ransacked by 'Leninists [who] stole his papers to ascertain whether he was really a Socialist leader or merely an agent of the British Government'.[60]

Russia both excited and frightened Henderson. He saw reformist socialists lifted into government, but he also saw workers who, he said, wished 'to place Directors and Managers in a subordinate position and the supreme control in the hands of the workpeople themselves...it can only have results that will be disaster'.[61]

Returning to Britain in the late summer Henderson was quick to apply the lessons of Russia. A horror of revolution and belief in the need for pre-emptive reformist measures shines out of every page of his January 1918 booklet *The Aims of Labour*. The chapter on 'Revolution or Compromise?' begins: 'Revolution is a word of evil omen. It calls up a vision of barricades in the streets and blood in the gutters [and] is alien to the British character'.[62] His public confidence in the non-revolutionary nature of British workers was contradicted by a later statement:

> Never before have we had such vast numbers of the population skilled in the use of arms, disciplined, inured to danger... When the war ends this country and every other will be flooded with hardy veterans...if barricades are indeed likely to be erected in our streets they will be manned by men who have learned how to fight... [It] will be veritable civil war.[63]

What conclusion did he draw? 'One good reason for beginning now to build up a strong democratic party in Parliament, with a programme of social and economic reforms carefully thought out [is] to prove that political methods are effective... *The Labour Party can rehabilitate Parliament in the eyes of the people*.'[64]

To assist him in this rehabilitation Henderson dared not turn to the unpopular ILP. Instead he relied on the *guru* of the religion of state socialism—Sidney Webb. Webb fully shared Henderson's fears and willingly embraced his reformist project. In November 1918 Webb published a letter proclaiming: 'The best safeguard against "Bolshevism" is a strong Labour Party in Parliament, voicing the discontent... If you *want* a Bolshevik revolution in this country, the surest way to get it is to succeed in eliminating or discrediting the Labour Party!'[65] How true!

The 1918 constitution: a quest for the 'people's party'

The reorganisation of the Labour Party proposed by Webb and Henderson involved advance on both fronts of class and nation. Union growth and the marginalisation of the ILP endowed the full-time officials with an even greater weight in the party than before. But it was the logic of reformist beliefs that they should deny its class roots and strive to make the party speak for 'the national interest.' Yet there was a difficulty. With 98 percent of the party made up of affiliated trade unionists it was not easy to portray this as a 'classless' organisation. The problem was given added urgency by the 1918 Representation of the People Act which brought many non-unionised women into the electorate.

The party's 1918 Constitution solved this by creating local Labour Parties and a system of individual membership. One victim of the change was the ILP which had in effect been Labour's chief constituency organisation. The union bureaucrats had not forgiven the ILP's pacifism. Trades Councils, which also acted as Labour's local organisation and provided a focus for militants, were cut out too.

At first the idea of calling the reorganised body the 'People's Party' was seriously canvassed.[66] The 1918 Labour Conference made it clear who these 'people' were—middle class non socialists—those without 'the opportunity of joining trade unions on the one hand, or on the other, who are not prepared to associate with the socialist organisations'.[67] This fitted with another motive. The Labour Party had set its sights on government and the social planners who refashioned the party were convinced that 'Labour was not yet intellectually and administratively equal to the responsibility'.[68] Henderson put it less elegantly: 'The Labour Party had been too short of brains'.[69] Individual membership should remedy this.

The Party chairman explained the political consequences. 'We aim in the years to come to be the People's Party—a Party not parochial in its conceptions, but national in its character'.[70] For 'not parochial' read untainted by a trade union orientation.

Socialism at last

Clause Four of the 1918 Constitution—'To secure for the producers by hand or by brain the full fruits of their industry, and the most equitable distribution thereof that may be possible, upon the basis of the common ownership of the means of production'—is perhaps the most intriguing aspect of Labour's history. In a body where symbolism frequently outweighs reality, this is the holy of holies. It is the most pious of Labour's many pious resolutions, yet its words are important. They mark the *conversion of the Labour Party into a 'socialist' organisation, or, to be more exact, a mass reformist party* distinct from the two openly capitalist parties.

So how is Clause Four to be understood? Firstly, it was drafted by Webb and championed by Henderson as a *conscious means of staving off revolution*. It was the fear of mass action which forced them to take this step. Thus the 1922 manifesto finished with the headline 'AGAINST REVOLUTION' and claimed: 'Labour's programme is the best bulwark against violent upheaval and class wars'.[71] There is an important difference between Clause Four in 1918 and Clause Four today. Seventy years ago it registered the high water mark of workers' pressure on the Labour Party. Since then the imminence of revolution has never been so great. But Clause Four remains in the party constitution—a relic of days gone by. In this sense it must now he defended as a sign of Labour's commitment to a minimal anti-capitalist position which some leaders would like to forget.

While its symbolic value is its most important feature, other points should be noticed. The clause talks about 'producers by hand or brain', the latter being a clear reference the social planners, intellectuals and the middle-class baggage of Fabianism so beloved of Webb. 'Common ownership' is clearly intended to come through constitutional means. This is no revolutionary document. But its final call for 'the best obtainable system of popular administration and control of each industry and service' is a concession to the mass demand for workers' control.

Previous attempts to write socialism into the constitution had met a strange fate. The foundation conference rejected the SDF's 'class war' motion. Yet the 1900 LRC manifesto demanded 'the Socialisation of the Means of Production, Distribution and Exchange'.[72] The following year a socialist resolution from Bruce Glasier was defeated. In 1903 another was lost without a debate. Two years later *the very same wording was passed*, again without a debate! In 1907 things became even more bizarre. The previous endorsement of socialism was overturned, at the request of Bruce Glasier and Keir Hardie, by a massive 835,000 to 98,000. In 1908 socialism lost even more heavily. *But*, strange to recount, the same conference voted to set 'as a definite object the socialisation of the means of production, distribution and exchange', and the 1914 conference 'again reaffirmed' this.[73]

There was method in this madness. Conference supported pious declarations of socialism but refused to put them in the constitution. In other words, although the majority of delegates regarded themselves as socialists they thought it would lose votes if socialism was too prominent. The aim of the Labour Party was not to fight for advanced ideas in the working class, but to collect the most votes. As the ILP's *Labour Leader* said in 1908:

> 'We want Socialism' cry the impatients. So did every member of the ILP. [But] we have to make the electors of this county want it, and to persuade the average unimaginative, overworked, and underpaid working-man, the small shopkeeper, and the struggling ratepayer, with all their various religious, political and social prejudices to vote for it. There's the rub![74]

The radicalisation brought by war made it possible for Labour to accept Clause Four without it being an electoral liability. Labour has a definite view of *the relationship between ends and means*. To a Marxist they cannot be separate. The goal of socialism dictates the means—the mass overthrow of capitalism led by a revolutionary party. But as the Labour Party debates on socialism demonstrated, for reformists *the means are more important than the goal. Success in elections came first*.

Labour leaders treated Clause Four more as a useful slogan than a definite plan of action. The distinction was revealed in an interesting exchange at the 1918 Conference. A British Socialist Party delegate pointed out that the resolutions on the order paper were 'not in conformity with the Party objects as set out in the Constitution. The latter was explicitly in favour of the social ownership of the means of production'.[75]

But Webb, the author, thought that one mention somewhere in the Constitution was sufficient: 'they did not want repeatedly, over and over again, to ring the changes on the old shibboleths. [Shibboleths are 'party catch-words'.] The resolutions were not an appeal to the converted but the basis of an appeal to the twenty million electors'.[76]

The ILP was unsure about co-operating with the new Constitution[77] but eventually decided there was no alternative.[78] But the new regime had its compensations, for the ILP *leadership* at least. 'Brains' were now a valued commodity, and through the UDC, the No Conscription Fellowship and the like, the ILP had acquired a lot of grey matter. As a visiting German Social Democrat, Wertheimer, put it:

> The party which before the war had been a definite proletarian organisation in spite of intellectual leadership, became overrun by ex-Liberals, young-men-just-down-from-Oxford guiltless of any socialist tradition, ideologists and typical monomaniacs full of their own projects.[79]

Indeed the notion of the ILP as the left and the union bureaucracy as the right, or *vice versa* ceased to make sense—they became different parts of a technical division of labour. The difficulties of the ILP did illustrate one important fact however. The commitment to socialism was not achieved by the burrowing away of the 'Labour left'. In 1918 the ILP was still despised for its pacifism and treated with contempt. The mass shift to the left came from struggles outside reformist electoral politics and in spite of such politics.

Labour's new social order

The idea of Labour as a 'People's Party' and Clause Four were the right and left faces of the 1918 reconstruction, but the programme *Labour and the New Social Order* was its centrepiece, the place where class and nation met.

This document was written by Sidney Webb and was passed in amended form by the 1918 Labour Conference. Its key points can be divided into those that dealt with *social reforms* and those that concerned *restructuring of the economy*. We shall discuss each in turn.

The Labour Party has always raised the cause of the victims of capitalist society. One early example was an article Keir Hardie wrote in 1894 after a mining disaster. It caused a sensation:

> The Welsh holocaust puts everything into the shade this week. Two hundred and fifty human beings full of strong life in the morning,

> reduced to charred and blackened heaps of clay in the evening. The air rent with the wail of the childless mother, the widowed wife and the orphaned child. Woe, woe unutterable everywhere, all through that fair Welsh valley... Only those who know, as I know, that these things are preventable and solely due to man's cupidity, can understand the bitterness of feeling which they awaken...society places more value on property than it does on human life.[80]

Though the Liberal Party discussed social reform, Labour made protest against poverty its hallmark. *Labour and the New Social Order* called for the 'Maintenance and Protection of the Standard of Life' through a legal minimum wage, for employment or decent welfare provision for discharged soldiers and improvements in education, housing and poor relief.

In 1918 the situation appeared favourable for such a programme. The war economy had temporarily eliminated unemployment. *Labour and the New Social Order* concluded that this could easily be rendered permanent 'by nothing more difficult or more revolutionary than a sensible distribution of public orders for workers and services'.[81]

Even the most radical members of the party always pose human suffering as an *unnecessary* side effect of capitalist society which can be remedied without uprooting the system as a whole. The solution to the problem of poverty is always put *within the framework of the nation state* and is justified *by its beneficial effect on the nation as a whole.*

Nevertheless, Labour's protest against poverty and unemployment expresses the heartfelt aspirations of millions of workers and is not an electoral gimmick. It is foolish to picture the party as a cunning plot to dupe workers by condemning suffering simply to gain a parliamentary salary. Workers are not stupid, and if such had been the case the party would have been seen through long ago. As we know, it still retains the loyalty of the vast majority of the conscious working class.

This loyalty is not dictated by the union bureaucracy either. The bureaucracy cannot determine how citizens vote. *As long as workers wish to create a better world, but lack the confidence to do it themselves, Labour will retain a decisive influence.* Reformism may cease to make sense of reality, just as religion did when Galileo showed that the earth moved or Darwin wrote *The Origin of Species*. But as Marx said of religion, so we can say of reformism: it expresses 'the sigh of the oppressed creature, the heart of a heartless world'.[82] *On a mass scale reformism will never be undermined by appealing for workers to cast out their illusions, it can only be done by helping to raise the confidence of the working class through their own experience of struggle.* As Marx put it in relation to religion:

> To call on them to give up their illusions about their condition is to call on them to give up a condition that requires illusions.[83]

However, to say that Labour genuinely channels workers' hopes for a better life does not mean that it is capable of delivering its promises. Labour in government is ample proof of that. Labour's potential is fatally limited by a reformist outlook that prevents it from harnessing the only force capable of changing conditions radically—the collective power of the working class.

Social reconstruction and nationalisation

The most important aspect of *Labour and the New Social Order* was its treatment of the capitalist economy, the health of which was seen as the foundation for reforms. Labour had its own distinctive method of maintaining the economy—nationalisation. Historically this has been the most important plank of Labour Party policy, and for good reason—*it appears simultaneously to meet the needs of natural interest, working-class aspiration and of the trade union and political bureaucracy!* Thus in 1911 Snowden proposed mines nationalisation because: 'It will be a good thing for the miners; it will benefit the general trade of the country; and the nation as a whole will gain much advantage... being free from the turmoil and inconvenience so often caused now by labour troubles'.[84]

Nationalisation and the 'national interest'

Labour's 'new social order' was to be based on the extension of the wartime state capitalist economy. Jimmy Thomas underlined the point:

> The taking over of railways, mines, munitions factories, and other controlled establishments during the war, really meant that in the considered judgement of the government...a capitalist Government—the private ownership of these things in time of war was a danger to the State. Why? Because they believed that unrestricted competition...was a menace to the State.[85]

State capitalism (though never given that name) was held to be a more efficient system than private ownership. As MacDonald told the conference in the debate on 'Increased Production':

> They could not afford to have any antagonism, or friction in production. They could not afford to have managers who could not manage... They must introduce a conception of cooperation, and regard society from top to bottom—the brain workers, the manual worker, the organiser, the direct producer—regard them all as co-operative factors in one great common life.[86]

In other words, the Labour Party consciously set at the head of its reformist programme *the management of capitalism*. No other solution was possible for a party wishing to run a capitalist state.

Nationalisation and the struggle for workers' control

However we would seriously underestimate the importance of nationalisation if it were regarded as simply a blueprint for capitalist development. In 1918 millions saw it as a means towards controlling their lives and, like the campaign for a statutory eight-hour day in 1889, a way of forcing concessions through collective pressure on the state.

There was nothing specifically socialist about nationalisation itself. The most die-hard Lib-Lab Union had been the Miners' Federation, yet it was the first to adopt nationalisation, long before it joined the Labour Party. The miners and railwaymen were in the forefront of the movement because, unlike the craft unions which enjoyed sectional strength, they depended on centralised bargaining to establish effective negotiating rights. The 1907 rail strike and the 1912 coal strike succeeded by forcing the government to intervene to impose negotiated settlements on obdurate employers. Furthermore both industries were exceptionally dangerous to work in and under national control might be expected to have fewer accidents.

Nationalisation and the union bureaucracy

Nationalisation fitted the trade union bureaucracy like a glove because it was a method of mediation. As the *Labour Leader* wrote just after the 1919 national rail strike: 'To put an end to strikes we must reconcile the interests of Capital and Labour by making the community of workers the owners and directors'.[87] Emil Davies of the Nationalisation Society declared that 'Some sections of the world of labour may at times demand more than conditions justify. This very circumstance is a strong argument in favour of the participation of the workers in the management'.[88]*

* The movement for workers' control found expression in different ways, the most influential being G D H Cole's Guild Socialism. This attempted to produce a sanitised reformist syndicalism and blunt the edge of workers' activity. It institutionalised the struggle for workers' control putting the official machinery at the centre. This ensured that agitation could not spill over into politics.

Nationalisation and reformist politics

The principle of nationalisation also suited the reformist aim of the piecemeal take-over of industries rather than their revolutionary expropriation. Change was constitutional, in parliament, and from the top. The rank and file were to do nothing themselves.

Labour's nationalisation proposals fully accorded with Marx's comments on nineteenth century petty bourgeois democrats who seek:

> a means of softening the antagonism between the two extremes of capital and wage labour and transforming it into harmony, not of superseding both of them. However varied the measures for achieving this goal, however much it may be edged with more or less revolutionary conceptions, its content remains the same. This content is the reformation of society by democratic means, but a reformation within the boundaries set by the petty bourgeoisie.[89]

The Labour Party that emerged at the end of the First World War was very different to its pre-war form. While we have concentrated on the party itself, it must be remembered that *it was pressure from the working class that pushed the labour bureaucracy into a new approach.*

Guilds were unions organised to run industry for themselves. Rather than nationalise from the centre they would gradually supplant foremen and then managers by a creeping process of 'encroaching control', taking over management functions one by one.

This was petty bourgeois fantasy par excellence. Guild Socialism could not endure, its one practical experiment being a builders' guild which lasted for a brief and unhappy moment. However, because of its stress on powerful (but official) union organisation, it exercised a fascination for left-wing bureaucrats and even the ILP, which incorporated Guild Socialist ideas in its 1922 constitution, at the very moment the movement had dropped stone dead. The same illusion in gradually reforming capitalism at factory level reappeared fifty years later in the ill-fated workers' cooperatives of the Bennite era.

4

Riding the post-war storm

Did Labour prevent a British revolution?

The armistice in November 1918 saw simultaneous revolutionary outbreaks in Finland, Germany, Austria, Hungary and Bavaria. Even in victorious imperialist states massive class struggles erupted.

At that moment reformists threw all efforts into strangling the spirit of revolution. Their methods were similar, though in Britain the Labour leaders never had to resort to military repression as did their their counterparts in Germany's SPD. As Rosa Luxemburg put it two weeks before her murder by the German equivalents of Henderson and MacDonald: 'the banner of "socialism" serves merely as a fig leaf for the decent veiling of a counter-revolutionary policy'.[1] In some cases reformists were catapulted into government, in others they were not. But as the newly formed Third—or Communist—International pointed out, 'the Social Democrats obstruct the actual development of the revolution by rendering, *whether as members of the administration* or *as members of the opposition*, all possible assistance in restoring the equilibrium of the bourgeois state'.[2]

The situation in Britain was not essentially different from abroad. If the Labour Party ever really intended to lead the struggle for socialism, this surely was the moment. The capitalist enemy was at its weakest, the workers at their strongest. Army mutinies began to disintegrate the physical force of the state and workers struck in vast numbers. Even the police unionised and stopped work.[3] Unrest peaked in 1919 when, excluding mining, as many days were lost through strike action as during the whole of 1911–14.[4]

Far from taking advantage of the state's weakness. Labour declared its devoted loyalty. Clynes, for example, told MPs he had always opposed police unions[5] and Henderson went so far as to claim:

> if one thing more than another has kept down the revolutionary spirit in recent years in this country it is the fact that Labour has had the power to express its grievances upon the floor of this House. I believe that the coming of a Labour party into this House, even in limited numbers, has done that one thing. It has provided the brake, as it were,

> upon any desire upon the part of the extremists to go lengths industrially that they might have been disposed to go if there had not been this method of giving expression to grievances.[6]*

This assertion of Labour as the chief bulwark against revolution deserves careful consideration. On one level it was false, just as in 1911–14 Labour appeared irrelevant to workers' mass extra-parliamentary activity. The advanced workers were as hostile to Labour's methods as ever. They looked to the traditions of rank and file struggle and to the formation of a revolutionary Communist Party patterned on Bolshevism. As Chanie Rosenberg puts it in the conclusion to her book on 1919: 'There is one permanent feature of the British scene that has hardly been mentioned. That is the Labour Party... [It] was not to be seen'.[8] This seems flatly to contradict Henderson's claim. What was the truth?

The shifting centre of gravity

Not since 1905 had the Labour Party been as impotent in parliamentary terms as it was after the December 1918 'Coupon' Election. Few parliaments have been more out of time with long term trends than the Lloyd George Coalition. Voting was held within days of 'victory' during the last gasp of patriotic hysteria. The characteristic slogans were 'Hang the Kaiser' and 'Make Germany Pay.' This made any taint of pacifism an electoral liability. Nonetheless Labour received 2.2 million votes, or 24 percent of the poll.

The Tories and Lloyd George Liberals who shared the 'Coupon' formed a solid factional block of 535 Coalition MPs. They confronted an opposition of just 60 Labour MPs and 25 Free Liberals, led by Asquith. Labour's best performers were defeated because of their pacifism or through bad luck. With MacDonald, Snowden, and even Henderson out there were only three ILP MPs among fifty trade unionists, half of them miners. In the PLP the stolid Scots miner Willie Adamson took the helm, shortly to be replaced by Clynes, himself no firebrand. As Allen Hutt put it: 'Great things were toward in the country, but they found neither reflection nor inspiration in the activities of the

* Labour politicians were not alone in thinking that in a post-war conditions reformism was the best defence of the existing system. C P Scott, a former Liberal MP, editor of the *Manchester Guardian* and a sharp political commentator had this to say: 'the crude extravagance and injustice of the Bolshevik economic doctrine...seems to be penetrating to some extent our own Labour extremists... It couldn't happen if we have a genuinely progressive Government whom the workers could trust. Possibly we might get that after a General Election when the Labour Party comes back with a force sufficient to determine policy'.[7]

Parliamentary Party'.[9] Clearly Labour did not prevent a revolution by the brilliance of its parliamentary efforts.

Yet it still added its voice to the anti-Bolshevik chorus. For example, H N Brailsford, a leading ILP intellectual, described the October 1917 Revolution as 'reckless and uncalculating folly'.[10] Clynes fulminated about Bolshevism being 'a disease...of this country and other countries as well'.[11] In true Christian fashion Snowden wrote that workers' power was 'a treacherous mirage... Better continue to suffer under domination and oppression than gain economic power through blood and slaughter. For what shall it profit us if we gain the material world and lose our own souls?'[12]

Labour strenuously attacked domestic subversion. Thomas warned the Commons against the 'large and growing body of organised Labour outside which does not believe in political action [by which he meant parliamentary action]... It is a method which I am daily at war against'.[13] Henderson 'deplored' strikes and claimed 'I have done as much as any man alive to prevent strikes'.[14] He was not very effective, as strikes erupted on an un-precedented scale.

This suggests that Labour was not the bulwark against revolution that Henderson claimed. However a closer analysis of events shows reformism must never be discounted. *The labour bureaucracy has two aspects—the Labour Party and the trade union officials.* In 1919 union bureaucrats were the chief obstacle to revolution because of their influence over the heart of the class struggle—workers at the point of production. As Cramp of the NUR wrote in June 1919: 'we find that the centre of gravity is passing from the House of Commons to the Headquarters of the great Trade Unions'.[15] Shinwell was more explicit, telling the 1919 TUC: 'this huge Congress of labour possesses as much capacity and more creative genius than the...mediocrities assembled at Westminster'.[16]

Nevertheless the Labour Party played a tremendously important role as the bureaucracy's political auxiliary and the alibi for their actions. Labour was, as Desmond put it, officialdom's 'hidden hand'.[17] It complemented the efforts of the trade union bureaucracy, just as in periods of Labour government, the bureaucracy assists in the implementation of policies of wage restraint and so on. This is borne out by a study of the key sectors of engineering, mining and the railways.

Three disputes

For a variety of reasons, there was no organised and conscious revolutionary current involved in any of these disputes. Though the potential for revolutionaries was probably greater than in 1889 or 1911-14 they left the field free for reformism.[18]

In the engineers' strike for a 40-hour week on Clydeside, Shinwell, a leading member of the ILP, was the most prominent figure. Was this Labour leading the industrial struggle forward? Alas, no. His involvement as president of the Trades Council consisted of confining the action. Despite his efforts the strike culminated in street fighting, police baton charges and the military occupation of Glasgow. Shinwell paid with a five-month jail sentence. But as Maxton informed the 1919 ILP Conference: 'no doubt readers of the general press would have gathered the impression that the men who took part in this trouble in Glasgow were merely out to create trouble. Shinwell...so far from being an inciting factor in the whole of the forty-hour movement, was there all the time as a restraining element among the strikers'.[19]*

The miners and railwaymen were a still greater threat. Here the state dared not attack directly but depended on reformist officials to disarm the movement. As government ministers admitted: 'Trade Union organisation was the only thing between us and anarchy', the problem being that sometimes the 'trade union was not highly enough developed to make its branch secretaries fall into line with Head Office'.[20]

Robert Smillie was the miners' leader, an ILP member of long standing, an old ally of Keir Hardie and a confirmed reformist. He was proud 'to be the champion defeated Parliamentary candidate of the country... Seven and a half unsuccessful elections stand to my credit—or discredit'.[21]**

The miners demanded a 80 percent wage rise, two hours reduction in the working day *and nationalisation* under joint worker/owner control. Concessions were feasible over wages and conditions (wartime super-profits made sure of that), but the issue of nationalisation was a tremendous political threat. If granted it meant the working class could overcome the express wishes of the coal-owners, who were now desperate to end state interference. Nationalisation that was forced by mass struggle *from below* would not have been the Fabian version but

* *Forward* printed an account of Shinwell's trial which stated that Shinwell addressed a meeting of his own seamen's union to discuss:

'the employment of yellow labour... Somebody in the audience shouted out—"What about the Strike"—and Shinwell replied that...the strike did not concern them.

'Lord Scott Dickson—"There was no 40 hours' movement among the seamen?"

'Answer: "No"'.

** This half arose because he was a prospective candidate for South Ayrshire but never went to the poll. Clegg writes: 'Smillie's undeserved reputation as a militant was due to his habit of making up his own mind and, once he had done so, paying little attention to what others had to say'.[22]

the prelude to open class warfare. At a celebrated meeting with Lloyd George, the officials were told what was at stake:

> if you carry out your threat and strike, then you will defeat us... [But its] very success will precipitate a constitutional crisis of the first importance. For, if a force arises in the state which is stronger than the State itself, then it must be ready to take on the functions of the State... Gentlemen, have you considered, and if you have, are you ready?

After that interview Smillie made this famous comment: 'From that moment on we were beaten and we knew we were'.[23] He was not beaten industrially, he was beaten by his reformist *politics*. As Trotsky put it 'even in the minds of "socialists" the fetishism of bourgeois legality [forms] that ideal inner policeman'.[24] When the real policemen were about to strike, the existence of ideological ones was crucial to the system.

Smillie's acceptance of the bourgeois state did not mean handing over negotiations to the Labour Party. As leader of an organisation which played a direct role in the daily working conditions and earnings of the miners, he assessed more direct influence than the party. The promise of an election five years hence would not silence the militants but a Royal Commission *now* might.

Smillie did not leap at the government offer of a commission chaired by Lord Sankey. As a sincere reformist, he wanted nationalisation and was not sure he could stall his members with a commission. It took all the guile of Sidney Webb to convince him. Beatrice Webb's diary records: 'Sidney found Smillie depressed with a cold and the feeling of responsibility...he wanted the miners to go straight into the fight and win. Sidney reasoned in favour of accepting the commission...but Smillie doubted whether he could get his delegates to go that far in meeting the government'.[25] Webb clinched his arguments by suggesting equal representation for employers and miners (a far better ratio than the 6:1 proportion of Coalition to Labour MPs produced by bourgeois democracy in parliament, though hardly reflecting the true balance of one owner to several hundred miners).

To give the Sankey Commission extra democratic gloss it was for the first time instituted by Act of Parliament. The establishment of the Sankey Coal Commission was one of the great turning points in labour history, for it delayed indefinitely, a supreme opportunity to challenge ruling-class power. Smillie later explained his motives:

> We could have enforced [nationalisation] at that time by our industrial strength... But there is another way, a way that does not need industrial force. It is by putting a Labour Government in power.[26]

The railway strike was the next major crisis, but this time the union leaders was Jimmy Thomas, the epitome of the right-wing bureaucrat. Though a leading minister in the first two Labour governments, he claimed publicly not to be a socialist![27] Thomas could not prevent a railway strike breaking out in September 1919 but he managed to end it within nine days.

For Thomas the primacy of nation over class was much more explicit than with Smillie. In a speech on 'Railwaymen and Citizenship' he echoed Lloyd George's words directly:

> Our union is the strongest in the country. We can demand that unless such and such a thing is done, we can paralyse the community...
>
> [But] however strong and powerful we may be...Citizenship has a stronger claim than any sectional interest.

To complete this hymn to reformism he added the bureaucrat's catechism:

> there were two dangers—people who could not read the signs of the times, reactionaries... Equally was there the danger of those who believed that we could revolutionise by industrial trouble or introduce what was called the Russian method... Both must be fought.[28]

Smillie and Thomas represented opposite viewpoints within the union bureaucracy, but the net effect of their actions was the same—by the autumn of 1919 the revolutionary opportunity had passed.

There is a theory which states that when workers move in a revolutionary direction they will turn to the Labour Party and remake it. 1919 proved this to be arrant nonsense. Even the most left-wing section—the ILP—stood entirely on the sidelines. Its historian writes that the ILP 'displayed only the most casual interest in trade union affairs, neither the *Leicester Pioneer* nor the *Bradford Pioneer* having industrial correspondents, and little better was the *Labour Leader* with a trade union column only once a month.'[29] Indeed, the Labour Party was totally irrelevant *as an organisation*.

However, when we consider the Labour Party *as a body of reformist ideas* the picture is quite different. In 1919 the legacy of a centralised war economy and strong feelings of workers' solidarity combined to make all disputes a state issue. Unlike the normal run of bargaining, union officials could not merely balance the forces of one section of workers against the individual capitalist, because every strike had political repercussions. While the impotent rump of 60 MPs had no authority, *the ideas of reformism were an absolutely invaluable weapon in the hands of the bureaucracy.*

Direct action—threat or opportunity?

By 1920 the revolutionary mood had receded though mass pressure was still very strong. This gave the leaders some limited scope for airing their differences. The 'direct action' debate must be seen in this context. Without a revolutionary current to make the officials turn their rhetoric into deeds, or expose the vacuity of their words, what was said never rose above posturing.

The trouble spots were mines nationalisation and international affairs. Smillie was the chief exponent of the left view. It was impossible to tell whether he made militant speeches merely to contain the movement, or to harness mass action for limited ends. His words contained both tendencies. First came a recognition of opportunities:

> We are the best organised force in the world [and] sufficiently strong with the Government of the day to make it do anything...in justice to the workers.[30]

Then fear of losing control:

> It would be safer for the Labour Movement of this country to meet with the Trade Union movement, and calmly and constitutionally discuss the question and decide upon action, than wait until a revolution breaks out.[31]*

Proposals for union-led direct action gave Labour and parliament a secondary role. John Bromley of the rail drivers explained why:

> Were they going to...wait another four years? They would be sacked... They were told they had not a majority [of voters]. Could any man or

* Robert Williams, leader of the Transport Workers and the most verbally extreme union leader (who went to the extent of joining the Communist Party) echoed these sentiments in his appeal for a national conference of workers' representatives: 'There can be no doubt that until the lead comes from some more or less responsible quarter, matters will reach such a state that open insurrection or revolutionary action may speedily ensue. We must hold the official convention to prevent unofficial strikes, to avoid the growth of anti-officialism among the best of our men and women...'[33]

> woman there point to any progressive movement in the world that had waited for the majority to bring it about? Was there any Trade Union leader who would say that any good movement or reform in Trade Unionism had been brought about by the majority?'[32]

The counter-arguments from Thomas, Clynes, Henderson and the right were based on the idea that 'the nearer we get to power the further we should recede from any advocacy of violent methods'.[34] If direct action were used 'we may as well abolish the Labour Party and the whole political machinery at once... The two things are absolutely irreconcilable'.[35] If they coerced the present government what would happen when Labour won office, 'were they going to concede to every other or any other class the right they were claiming?'[36] They had no right to strike politically: 'You can strike against employers, but on [political] questions the place for action is the ballot-box'.[37] Summing it all up was McGurk, Chairman of the 1919 Labour Conference: 'We are either constitutionalists or we are not constitutionalists...we believe in the efficacy of the political weapon...or why do we have a Labour Party?'[38]

In the set-piece debates of the Triple Alliance, TUC and Labour Party, the direct actionists won majorities more than once, but their bluster proved empty. Thus when the government went back on its promise to honour the Sankey Commission's findings every excuse was invented to delay action. Once the danger of a strike had passed the sop of a 'Mines for the Nation' campaign was offered. It consisted of 'intensive political propaganda in preparation for a General Election'.[39] The party paid little attention, which caused campaign organisers to complain of 'the impossibility of...securing the services of...many of the Party's front-rank platform speakers'.[40]

Prospects for direct action were brighter on international issues. Trotsky wrote:

> In the British labour movement international questions have always been a path of least resistance for the 'leaders'. In regarding international issues as a sort of safety valve for the radical mood of the masses [the] leaders are prepared to bow to a certain degree to revolution [elsewhere] only the more surely to take revenge on the questions of the domestic class struggle.[41]

British repression in Ireland was a possible candidate for direct action. Labour's position, as might be expected from a Liberal-influenced Party, was for Gladstonian Home Rule. But God forbid that the Irish should do anything about their own liberation! *Forward* declared the Easter 1916 Rising: 'a tragedy of unrelieved gloom. Call it madness, or badness or both'.[42] *Socialist Review* was worse: 'We do not approve armed rebellion at all... Nor do we plead the rebels' cause... Nor do we complain against the Government for having opposed and suppressed armed rebellion by armed force'.[43] So much for ILP pacifism!

Yet Labour's position was not purely reactionary. The ability of reformists to mix class and nation is a constant source of wonder. *Socialist Review*'s article quoted above ended by saying: 'what we...protest against is not the suppression of the rebellion by military measures, but the needless harshness and excess.' But this hardly provided the springboard for fighting government use of the Black and Tans in 1920.

Labour's most daring hour

The Russian issue was different. In May 1920, largely through the agitation of revolutionaries such as Harry Pollitt, East London dockers prevented the shipping of munitions on *The Jolly George* to help Poland fight the Bolsheviks.[44] On 4 August 1920 the prime minister, Lloyd George, announced his intention to send British troops to back the Poles. A wave of revulsion stirred the war-weary population, as 'all the middle class pacifists and many middle class taxpayers' and even the City welcomed attempts to prevent conflict.[45]

Confident they had public opinion as well as militant workers behind them, the Parliamentary Labour Party, the party's national executive and the TUC met to form a fifteen-strong Council of Action on 9 August. Four days later a national conference of trade union and Labour branch delegates was held. Some unbelievable speeches were delivered.

Thomas called for a general strike: 'No Parliamentary effort could do what we are asking you to do... If this resolution is to be given effect to, it means a challenge to the whole Constitution of the country (cheers).' The chairman of the Labour executive went on: 'we may be compelled to do things that will cause them to abdicate. (Perhaps) we will be compelled, even against all Constitutions, to chance whether we cannot do something to take the country into our own hands for our own people'.[46]

Even Ramsay MacDonald welcomed direct action because 'confidence in Parliament is forfeited'.[47] This was the same man who had written: 'to degrade in the imagination of the people *even a bad House of Commons* is a crime—a most heinous crime for Socialists'.[48]

In the event the government backed away from war. We cannot know whether a general strike would have been called, but there is no reason to suppose it was absolutely ruled out. Bureaucratically-led mass strikes are not unknown. Thus in 1920 the German Social Democrats and union leaders launched an effective general strike to defeat the Kapp Putsch against the Weimar Republic.

Was direct action ever more than hot air? To answer such a question we must evaluate the motives of the speakers and its effect on the listeners. The ultra-left is concerned only with the first, and the reformist only with the second.

The creation of local Councils of Action provided great opportunities for revolutionaries. The Communist Party, though very new (the first issue of its paper only appeared on 5 August) intervened in many areas and established its credentials. It did so *without being inside the Labour Party* and all the while arguing for workers to resist 'attempts by trade union and Labour leaders to frustrate the wishes of the rank and file...at the critical moment'.[49]

No less than 350 local Councils of Action were set up by September 1920 and some went far beyond what the official leaders intended. Merthyr Tydfil's Central Council of local labour representatives was subject to instant recall and believed itself 'destined to be an important instrument for the emancipation of the workers'.[50] Birmingham wanted a Congress of local councils to force the national body to honour its general strike commitment and so on. Lenin was misinformed when he took the Councils of Action to be 'the same kind of dual power as we had under Kerensky',[51] but they nevertheless had a long-term impact. In 1926 these councils were revived as the organisational backbone of the General Strike.

The motives of the labour bureaucracy presented a very different picture from those of the rank and file. Underlying superficial differences between right and left officials there was a convergence of ideas. Direct action was to *assist* parliamentary action. Reviewing the motive for the Council of Action MacDonald wrote: 'There was as much communism about the Council of Action and the policy that created it, as in taking a breakfast'.[52] Direct action showed *the ability of reformists to move radically to the left and manipulate extra-parliamentary activity when the need arose*. The difference between left and right was never more than whether to offer the carrot or the stick and the years showed that both sides were adept in the use of either.

MacDonald and others claimed they were only defending the constitution, but no bourgeois constitution has ever conceded the right of the population to determine war and peace. The willingness of both right and left Labour and trade union leaders to use extra-parliamentary means proves that the point of reference for reformists is not this or that institution but the function of mediation between classes.*

McGurk's comment, 'We are either constitutionalists, or we are not', had highlighted an important question for socialists. For anyone who takes the emancipation of the working class seriously a choice of priorities must be made. On the one hand we have the classic reformist position as stated by Glasier: 'A thousand votes definitely given for Socialism possesses more promise and potentiality for working class emancipation than 10 million workmen out on strike'.[53] On the other there is Lenin's statement that parliamentary action is 'the lowest form of the movement'.[54]

In the drama of the post-war period only the first of these propositions was tested. Despite all the fire and brimstone the movement for mass struggle had been skilfully defused. In return the British working class has been rewarded by a number of Labour governments. Who was right—Lenin or Glasier?

Black Friday—the transition to a governing party

There is a bitter irony in the history of the British labour movement. The labour bureaucracy has committed gross acts of betrayal, but the weakness of the revolutionary left has meant that far from being punished or overthrown they are frequently strengthened. *Sell-outs can expose reformism.* Alas, under certain conditions *they can have the opposite result*, weakening the rank and file and so raising the status and influence of the bureaucracy.

This happened in 1921 when the colliery owners demanded a wage cut of up to 50 percent in some areas. On Black Friday, 15 April, the Triple Alliance leaders representing the railwaymen, transport workers and miners ran away from their promise to stand together and fight as

* A failure to understand this point is the chief failing of Ralph Miliband's otherwise valuable book *Parliamentary Socialism*. Its analysis, outlined in its first paragraph, is that the chief characteristic of Labour is its parliamentarism. The same weakness afflicts Geoffrey Foote's useful book on *The Labour Party's Political Thought*. Both authors understand the Labour Party's limitations but fail to penetrate beneath the institutional surface, to the class relations beneath. The party is not an independent body but one half of a reformist labour bureaucracy, the other half being the union officials. If either feel that parliamentarism is actually an obstacle to the process of mediation it may be put aside. This happened in 1914 and 1920. In the first case the bureaucracy was willing to see a political truce and the virtual extinction of parliament and the PLP in order to gain access to important positions. In both Miliband and Foote the actual class straggle plays little role in their analysis.

one. They left one million miners to be smashed in a gruelling three month fight. Far from damaging the labour bureaucracy, Black Friday freed it from the spectre of revolution.

In 1919 and 1920 class confidence at the point of production had given trade union matters great weight on the scales of reformism. The capitalist ideology of the 'nation' was relatively light. Black Friday reversed this. The centre of reformism shifted from union officials towards the Labour Party.

The background to this development was the abrupt end of the post-war boom in early 1921. Compared with 1920 exports were down by 48 percent, imports by 44 percent. Between December 1920 and March 1921 unemployment *tripled* (from 5.8 to 17.8 percent of insured workers). Labour had helped prevent major advance when conditions were favourable. Now that the workers were on the defensive, how good was it as a protective shield?

Alas it contributed nothing to the resistance of either the unemployed or the strongly organised workers. MacDonald, for example, denounced the workless for expecting the dole (the system did not exist then): 'It matters not [to them] if the dole is ruinous and soon becomes intolerable...and handicaps a true Socialist policy.' Unemployed agitation would embarrass local Labour authorities or worse, compel them to grant the demands: 'The next thing that happens is that they alienate support, their Labour and Socialist majorities disappear, and the old interests come into possession.' And why should Labour be concerned with these folk anyway: 'how many of the present unemployed supported [us] at the last election?'[55]

Black Friday destroyed the resistance of the organised employed and Labour, though playing second fiddle to the union bureaucrats, contributed its bit to the debacle. Lloyd George, the Prime Minister, was confident that 'J H Thomas wants no revolution. He wants to be Prime Minister... I have complete confidence in Thomas's selfishness [and] the Labour Party will be for moderation. They have nothing to gain politically'.[56]

The consequences of Black Friday became plain as one disaster followed another. Trade union membership suddenly went into reverse, failing from its 1920 peak of eight million to just five million three years later. The Labour leaders fastened like vultures on the weakened body of the movement. It was with ill-concealed pleasure that MacDonald declared: 'We may yet look back upon these dark days with gratitude'.[57] He had good reason: 'The events of this strike ought to settle for a long time the influence of those who preached the doctrine that Labour can emancipate itself by industrial means alone'.[58]

Stripped of rhetoric the Labour left's solution was little different from MacDonald's. *Labour Leader* declared the lesson of Black Friday was the need to attack capitalism in its 'legislative citadel.'

> That citadel can be assaulted and won without a single child losing a meal...without disorder and without fear of starvation... For every insult, for every injury, for every broken promise and shattered illusion, the people can take revenge at the ballot box.[59]

The swing of the pendulum

The sudden decline of industrial militancy had a dramatic effect on Labour's internal life and underlined its parasitic nature. When the body of the labour movement was healthy, Labour's local organisation, as represented by the ILP, was weak. The first great rise in class struggle, 1910–14, cost the ILP a quarter of its membership.[60] The post-war revolutionary ferment left the party 'in a state of confusion and crisis.' In contrast, the period of deep downturn, 1922–5, saw the ILP reaching 'the pinnacle of its success'.[61]*

By October 1922 *Labour Leader* was talking of 'something remarkable in the atmosphere; a sense of relief, of hope, of new impulse to work [because the party is] no longer with one hand tied behind its back, in the conflict with Communism'.[64] That same month John Paton, on the far left of the ILP, explained how militants defeated in class struggle could transfer their hopes to Labour as a *substitute*. He traced the rise and fall of workers' struggle which led to its transformation into 'political' (by which he meant parliamentary) thinking. During the war workers had:

> tasted for the first time a real sense of power. In engineering on the Clyde the shop stewards movement acquired a remarkable power and influence, while in mining areas the men openly boasted that THEY were running the pits... The dazzling prospect of industrial freedom has gone like a dream...sunk in despair, in utter disillusion.

* In the early 1920s local Labour Parties were still in the process of formation and so the ILP continued to reflect what internal organisation there was. Writing of pre-war Britain, Williams wrote that 'Over most of the country indeed *the ILP was the Labour Party*'.[62] This was still true in 1918 when the ILP had 672 branches to Labour's 158. The main growth of local Labour Parties seems to have taken place around 1924.[63]

> Now...men's minds are returning in the direction of building surely and solidly on the will of a politically educated people.[65]

The general election of 1922 confirmed what Paton had sensed. Compared with 1918 Labour's vote doubled to 4.2 million *at the very moment that trade union membership was plummeting*. The quality of the Labour vote changed too. No longer was it an incidental spin-off of mass struggle. It represented an alternative to struggle for an embittered working class.

The transformation also showed itself in a strict separation between the industrial and political wings. The NUR split its chief posts—with Thomas as 'political secretary', and Cramp as 'industrial secretary'. The Miners' Federation decided their president and secretary could not sit in parliament.[66] The TUC replaced its 'Parliamentary Committee' with a General Council because it felt 'that Congress should develop the industrial side of the Movement as against the "deputizing" or "political" conception'.[67] From the other side the first Labour government insisted that trade unionists who became ministers must give up their union positions.[68]

These adjustments altered the balance of power between the hostile brothers—trade union officialdom and the professional politicians. As in the period of Taff Vale, it was the industrial retreat following Black Friday which allowed professional politicians such as MacDonald and Snowden to regain their influence. The unresolvable contradiction in the 1918 Constitution—a 'classless' party dominated by union officials—seemed to be working itself out in favour of the former.

5

Proving Labour 'fit to govern': the 1924 administration

ALTHOUGH THE first Labour Government lasted just nine months, it showed the important qualitative change the Party undergoes when in Government. MacDonald's tenancy of 10 Downing Street was in one way just the completion of 30 years' political work. Yet in another sense it was a sharp break with the past. Labour's mediation between class and nation had to alter dramatically.

Reformist politicians deny the fundamental contradiction between working class interests and capitalism, and *most of the time rank and file workers and the trade union bureaucracy share this belief.* Labourism seems to be sound common sense. But as Engels puts it: 'sound common sense, respectable fellow that he is in the homely realm of his own four walls, has very wonderful adventures directly he ventures out'.[1] Workers' false consciousness can be shaken by contact with the reality of a Labour government if *they are forced to generalise through struggle* and move towards clear class politics. Professional reformists respond differently. *Their attitude is shaped not by working class concerns but the national framework in which they operate.*

Labour government was a necessary experience for the workers' movement. It broke the centuries-long ruling class monopoly. Never before could it be said:

> An engine-driver rose to the rank of Colonial Secretary, a starveling clerk became Great Britain's Premier, a foundry-hand was changed to Foreign Secretary, the son of a Keighley weaver was created Chancellor of the Exchequer, one miner became Secretary for War and another Secretary of State for Scotland.[2]

Only a Labour government could show whether this made any difference. It *was a practical step towards demonstrating the bankruptcy of reformism.* Government office was necessary to put Labour's rhetoric to the test.

In 1924 Labour had a dual task. Firstly, even though it did not fully control the state (thus in October civil servants and secret servicemen helped bring the Tories back), Labour was *responsible* for it. Secondly, its position in 'the executive committee of the ruling class', made Labour the guardian of British capitalism as a whole. We shall deal with each aspect in turn.

Who captures whom?

Labour's supporters thought the new cabinet symbolised a working-class capture of the state. The truth was the other way round.

Take the role of the top civil servant. Thomas declared: 'the country ought to feel everlastingly indebted. His brain capacity is first class. No one can challenge his absolute integrity and desire to serve'.[3] With touching naivety Clynes, the deputy party leader, 'found the permanent officials extraordinarily helpful and kind.' He saw nothing sinister in the fact that: 'They were always beside me, advising, coaching and checking; and in a short time I gained a measure of knowledge necessary in matters where, perhaps, national safety or the spending of millions of money was concerned'.[4]

The remarkable influence of the senior civil servant was illustrated by Thomas Jones of the Cabinet Secretariat. His diaries are a chronicle of manipulation.[5] Jones was 'a passionate Free-Trader, an intimate and trusted friend of Lloyd George [who] voted Liberal'.[6] He himself describes how on 9 October 1924 the King's Speech, the final word of the Labour government, was put together:

> Sidney Webb suddenly entered my room and announced that...he wanted a draft of the King's Speech in twenty minutes... He began writing at once a paragraph on unemployment while I rang up Sir Eyre Crowe [and other Civil Servants]... Sir Otto Niemeyer from the Treasury and Sir John Shuckburgh... Sir Claude Schuster blew in to say that he would like a reference made to the immediacy of the dissolution... Hankey took page by page to the PM, for final approval. I think he saw about half the speech in this way. He made no change of any kind and left the rest to us to finish off as we like.[7]

A few weeks later Jones was giving Baldwin tips on who to include in the newly-elected Tory cabinet and writing anti-Bolshevik speeches for him.

MacDonald well understood the power of the unelected official over the minister. He categorically rejected a Labour Party suggestion that the government appoint its own advisors: 'a Civil Service told quite frankly that we have no confidence in it would never work at all'.[8]*

The army was also a sacrosanct institution. Stephen Walsh at the War Office 'was entirely unable to conceal his reverence for generals', saying 'I know my place. You have commanded Armies in the Field when I was nothing but a private in the ranks'.[10] MacDonald himself dared not place 'a mere commoner and a Socialist' in control of 'the King's Navy' and put a diehard Tory there instead.[11] The intelligence services made clear their contempt for elected persons when they refused to let the premier see his own secret file.[12] Nine months later they helped the Tories return by concocting a famous forgery—'Zinoviev's red letter'—with Conservative Central Office and White Russian *emigres*.

With the army came imperialism. Thomas's first words at the Colonial Office were 'I'm here to see that there is no mucking about with the British Empire'.[13]

Finally we come to the pinnacle of this great establishment heap—the throne. The way in which most Labour ministers literally fell over themselves to conform to pomp and ceremony would have been laughable had it not been so nauseating.** When Labour took office George v wrote in his diary: '23 years ago dear Grandmama died. I wonder what she would have thought of a Labour Government!'[14] He was calmed at his first interview with MacDonald who emphasised 'his earnest desire was to serve his King and Country.' MacDonald assured the king that he would try to break Labour's irritating habit of singing *The Red Flag* and pointed out that he had already used 'all his influence and that of his moderate and immediate friends' to prevent this song being sung in the Commons![15]

Sublime majesty inevitably exuded from the rest of the royal brood. Of the queen, Thomas exclaimed 'with what dignity and charm she will fulfil her great task...the people took to her instantly and instinctively.

---

* This tenderness to the feelings of civil servants did not extend to lower grades who had been agitating for the right to vote and affiliate to political organisations. The TUC was behind their claim, as was Labour and the New Social Order. Whatever the minority position of Labour in the Commons, the government could freely alter civil service regulations and yet, as W J Brown of the Clerical Association told the 1925 Labour Conference: 'while the Labour Government was in office... the Treasury Committee to which the matter had been referred, produced a Report which left Civil Servants in rather a worse position than they were in before'.[9]

** Perhaps pathetic would be the more appropriate epithet. Beatrice Webb's diary records how: 'Uncle Arthur [Henderson] was bursting with childish joy over his Home Office seals in the red leather box which he handed round the company; Sidney was chuckling over a hitch in the solemn ceremony in which he had been right and Hankey [chief of the Cabinet Secretariat] wrong; they were all laughing over Wheatley—the revolutionary—going down on both knees and actually kissing the King's hand'.[16]

The presence, the personality—and the smile, which in itself radiates confidence and affection—are all there and will assuredly be used for the benefit of her people'.[17] It took an outsider like Wertheimer to appreciate how utterly ludicrous was this 'rather Gilbertian vista of a preponderantly Socialist society with a feudal first chamber [consisting of a] hereditary nobility'.[18]

The fact that the state had swallowed the Labour government whole showed itself in innumerable ways. We shall give just two examples, one small, one great. Arthur Henderson, the former lay preacher, found as Home Secretary that, against his beliefs, he was expected to hang criminals. His biographer records that he 'took the line that his immediate duty was to administer the law...and fortunately for him, the murderers he had to hang were such as not to deserve too much public sympathy'.[19]*

Of more political importance was the selection of the cabinet. Labour's internal procedure is no model of proletarian democracy, but at least the indirect methods of block voting and conferences allow a bare minimum of rank and file self-expression. However, following precedent, MacDonald took himself off to his solitary retreat of Lossiemouth and like Moses with the tablets, emerged a fortnight later brandishing the Cabinet list. What an extraordinary document! With the exception of John Wheatley at Health *the entire Labour left was excluded*. But there were *two Tories, an ex-Tory and four ex-Liberals*. Two other Conservatives had been invited to the cabinet.**

In answer to our question—'who captured whom?'—the answer was quite clear. The state had captured the Labour Party. A new relationship between the Labour Party, the ruling class and the workers was about to emerge.

Managing the system

Until 1924 Labour's attitude to many questions could afford to be vague. That changed with the advent of government and responsibility for the economy. As Margaret Bondfield (later to become the first woman

* Clynes, Home Secretary in the second Labour government, overcame his loathing of hanging and flogging by reasoning that however strong my desire to change it may be...it is the right of the public to change the law. It is the duty of the Minister to apply the law'.[20]

** The two Tories were Lord Chelmsford, former colonial governor and Viceroy of India, 'a real aristocrat of the traditional type'[21] and Lord Parmoor, father of Stafford Cripps. He was a lifelong Conservative, Churchman and believer in "Christian methods" in government, who made a reputation...defending employers' rights in relation to Workmen's Compensation'.[22] The most prominent former Liberal was Lord Haldane a vocal supporter of the Taff Vale judgement.

cabinet minister in the 1929-31 Labour government) explained: 'We have taken over a bankrupt machine, and we have got to make that rickety machine work. There are some of us who will lose our reputations before this is done'.[23] How right she was!

The first months of the year saw a spate of strikes principally in transport. Workers wanted to use a partial economic recovery and the government they themselves elected, to advance their position. But the *first ever meeting of a Labour Cabinet* 'without hesitation and without a dissentient voice'[24] *set in motion the blacklegs' charter*—the Emergency Powers Act (EPA).[25] Thomas and Gosling, leaders of the rail and transport unions took the top posts in the government's scabbing body, the Supply and Transport Organisation. They met their own union officials and 'made it perfectly clear that the government was under the obligation to secure the food for the people' and waved a 'Proclamation of Emergency [which] the Government will not hesitate to use'.[26]

In March the cabinet decided that if the tram and bus strike meant 'the protection which the government could offer could not be supplied by the ordinary Police service...it would be necessary to employ Special Constables.' Furthermore it was 'actually arranged with Lord Chelmsford to bring up 800 naval ratings to keep the power stations going (as it was afterwards discovered, going even beyond the law in giving him a Cabinet order)'.[27]

Henderson contributed a new design for the old scab recruitment poster. The only changes were two additions, proudly pro-claiming that 'the Government' had issued the poster and that therefore there was 'No Blacklegging Involved.' According to Henderson's new English dictionary, under Labour strike-breaking was no longer the same as blacklegging. Moreover the government should be complimented for such activities:

> In the past the methods of dealing with an emergency and even the fact that the Government was prepared to take any steps at all, were shrouded in a certain atmosphere of secrecy. That was due to the supposition that a considerable party in the state might be in opposition to the action of the Government...it is obviously incorrect with a Labour Government in office. There is nothing to be ashamed of...[28]

But it was a notable fact that the Labour *never had to use its elaborate strike-breaking provisions*. It had a more effective method of blocking militancy—*the good offices of the union bureaucracy*, which imposed settlements arranged by the government. In the first six months no less than 80 cases were referred to Industrial Courts while there were five full government commissions to resolve the biggest disputes.[29] To the chagrin of the opposition, Bondfield gloated: 'This Government, at any rate has an advantage which many Members on the opposite benches do not share. [It is] in an exceptionally favourable position to deal with industrial disputes.'[30]

Labour was acting *as manager of capitalism* and became increasingly public about it. Some workers could not believe the transformation. During a dock strike, for example, workers in Gloucester called on the prime minister 'to use at once emergency powers to take full control of all shipping and docks *to pay the increases asked for*.'[31] They would not make the same mistake twice.

Labour's new role was a nasty surprise for the union bureaucracy. Loyalty meant they felt compelled to do the government's dirty work, but the fact remained—the party they had created now openly threatened them. A sign of how keen Labour was to prove its independence from the unions was that it ended the established practice of showing the TUC proposed labour legislation before it reached the Commons.[32] Tom Shaw said 'Parliament is the body to which the Government must submit its proposals...it would be wrong to take the line that any other body...has the right to ask consultation.'[33]

The union bureaucracy were angry. Bevin confessed: 'I only wish it had been a Tory Government in office. We would not have been frightened by *their* threats.'[34] Bromley of the engine drivers' union felt that: 'If the success of the Labour Party and of a Labour Government can only be built on such serious losses in wages and conditions by the workers, then I am not sure the workers will very much welcome a Labour Government.'[35] Union officials did not like having to act as government agents in settling strikes because this eroded their authority among the rank and file. Yet grumble as they might, *it was the union bureaucracy that bailed the Labour Government out.*

The true capitalist party?

In August 1924, Leo Chiozza Money, one of Labour's representatives on the Sankey Commission, published an article in the ILP's *Forward*, entitled 'Labour, the True Capitalism.' It argued:

> Labour at least should make it clear that it is, in the true sense of the word, a Capitalist Party—a Party, that is, that intends to wield capital on the large scale to national advantage.[36]

The government came perilously close to proving his point. The prime minister told the opening session of the new parliament:

> We shall concentrate not first of all on the relief of unemployment, but on the restoration of trade...the Government has no intention of drawing off from the normal channels of trade large sums for extemporised measures which can only be palliatives. That is the old, sound Socialist doctrine [!] and the necessity of expenditure...will be judged *in relation to the greater necessity for maintaining undisturbed the ordinary financial facilities* (cheers from Conservative benches).[37]

When class and nation (in the form of British capital) were put in the balance, nation proved 'the greater necessity.'

MacDonald's espousal of an openly capitalist philosophy was only surpassed by Philip Snowden at the Exchequer. In opposition he had seen heavy direct taxation as a means of redistributing wealth to the poor, proposing: 'taxation of the rents of landlords and the profits of the capitalist for the purpose of financing schemes for social betterment'.[38] Now he saw his role in this way:

> It is no part of my job...to put before the House of Commons proposals for the expenditure of public money. The function of the Chancellor of the Exchequer, as I understand it, is to resist all demands for expenditure made by his colleagues and, when he can no longer resist, to limit the concession to the barest point of acceptance.

Clutching the Treasury purse strings, Snowden described his fellow Ministers as 'a pack of ravenous wolves'.[39]

Accordingly the 'first socialist budget' contained no surprises. Concluding his Commons presentation, Snowden remarked that the former Tory Chancellor 'claimed it was a "Tory budget"... Indeed I hear on authority that there is a movement in the City of London to erect a statue to me'.[40]

Wheatley makes his mark

Against this picture must be set the one success story of the government—John Wheatley, the solitary left-winger. His tenure at Health was notable for his handling of Poplarism (which will be dealt with later) and the Housing Act. The latter led to the erection of 521,700 houses before being discontinued in 1933.[41] It slipped through Snowden's penny-pinching grasp because its initial cost was low. To encourage local councils to build new houses, costs were to be subsidised from central funds over a period of 40 years.

Did Wheatley's Act prove that with the right personnel Labour can lead the way to socialism? Alas, Wheatley's success came from skilfully co-ordinating capitalist industry to make it efficient. He had the honesty to say as much himself: 'The Labour Party's programme on housing is not a Socialist programme at all. I wish it were'.[42] During the final passage of his Act through parliament Wheatley asserted:

> I have left private enterprise exactly where I found it...as the protector of the small builder I am the defender of private enterprise and one of its best friends. I am completely frank and honest about it... It requires Labour proposals, Socialist proposals if you like, in order that private enterprise can get going again.[43]

The overall achievement

Given the mildly favourable economic circumstances in which it was operating, even within a capitalist framework Labour could afford to offer certain reforms and, in addition to housing, some were indeed forthcoming.* But these were only marginally different from what the capitalist parties would have done in the circumstances.

We have the word of numerous contemporary politicians for this. The Tory MP Leo Amery wrote that Labour Ministers took 'practically the same view of things as the late Capitalist Government'.[45] Baldwin confided his 'worries of a Party leader in days when there are no deep political convictions to divide men of good will'.[46] He had expected 'some great revolution in method' only to find 'nothing more than a strict adherence to what has been done by the last Government and the Government before that and the Government before that'.[47] Asquith felt that 'most if not all of the [prime minister's] proposals are to be found in the election programme of one or another of the various parties... It is not a new departure'.[48] This was a truth the Labour government was

---

* Clegg gives the following summary of the chief social reforms:

'Trevelyan at the Board of Education, increased the grants to schools starved of money...and set up the Hadow Committee to devise means of providing secondary education for all.

'Shaw at the ministry of Labour, was responsible for two Unemployment Insurance Acts. The first abolished the gap of three weeks between periods of benefit... The second combined a number of administrative improvements with a substantial improvement in benefits—from 75p to 90p a week for men [etc]'.[44]

In addition Labour cut the navy's cruiser-building programme from eight to five (still far higher than its pacifist programme suggested) and ceased work on a naval base at Singapore.

proud to acknowledge, stating 'clearly and definitely that there is no break in the continuity of our policy'.[49]

One can only sympathise with the *New Statesman*'s sad conclusion: 'In the sphere of foreign policy there are no definable party differences, even in home affairs party differences are by no means clear'.[50] MacDonald's eagerness to prove Labour's worth to the ruling class meant, as the historian of the first Labour government puts it, that: 'too often Labour's proposals fell far short of what could reasonably be expected—and publicly demanded of the Liberals'.[51] It was this desire for respectability that brought the government to an ignominious end.

The Red bogey

By the end of the summer of 1924, the opposition parties were getting restless for power. The end came when the government botched the 'Campbell case.' On 25 July the acting editor of the Communist *Workers' Weekly*, J R Campbell, published an open letter calling on soldiers to refuse orders to break strikes. The government began proceedings under the 1795 Incitement to Mutiny Act. No sooner had this started than they discovered a prosecution was unlikely to succeed. When the case was dropped MacDonald came under fire in the Commons and resigned after making this issue one of confidence.

What made things ridiculous was that the government had got itself into the mess because it was so keen to prove its anti-Communist credentials. Thus MacDonald told the king: 'Nothing would have pleased me better than to have appeared in the witness box, when I might have said some things that might have added a month or two to the sentence'.[52]

Labour's anti-Communist paranoia had destroyed the government. It now helped lose the election. The secret service 'discovered' a letter addressed to the British Communist Party and purporting to be from Zinoviev, the Comintern president, shortly before the vote. It called for the creation of Communist military units in the British army. Instead of exposing this document as an obvious forgery, MacDonald gave it credibility by denouncing it more zealously than the Liberals and Tories would have done, and by drafting a formal protest. With Foreign Office connivance the 'red letter' appeared in the *Daily Mail* three days before polling day. Having made so much of the letter itself, Labour was in no position to deny the implication that the country was about to be consumed by civil war unless a strong right-wing government were returned.

The real losers in the October 1924 election were the Liberals. They fell to 42 MPs while the Tories won an outright majority with 413. Labour actually gained 1.1 million votes though they lost forty seats, falling to 151. Despite last-minute bungling, Labour had established itself, not as a party of real socialism (which at that time would not have attracted many millions of votes) but as *the* credible party to form His Majesty's Opposition.

Conclusion: Labour in government

So far we have characterised Labour as a capitalist workers' party whose leaders attempt to mediate between the two main classes of society. *This changed when Labour formed a government.* To understand why, it is useful to compare the differing roles of the union bureaucrat and reformist politician.

The union official is squeezed between workers' collective organisation in production on one side and the need to negotiate deals with the bosses on the other. As Clynes described it: 'He is a man who works for two masters... The men who appoint have the right to demand his loyalty, and the employers with whom he has to deal on behalf of the men expect fairness and reason'.[53] To function at all officials must maintain some relationship with the rank and file or their deals cannot be made to stick. Furthermore, while union leaders may be invited to meet management or even participate in some joint committee, they are never made responsible for the running of the capitalist operation.

There are no such constraints on Labour governments. Their chief link with ordinary workers is not through collective organisation but the passive medium of voting, and even this ceases once the polling booths shut. *It is a mistake to see electoralism as the key determinant of Labour's behaviour*, for it totally fails to explain why Labour governments have indulged in policies which are obviously going to lose votes from the working class—on whom the party's electoral fortunes depend.

From the moment they take office therefore, ministers are freed from any but the most indirect working-class pressure (via the TUC, the party's national executive or perhaps extra-parliamentary action) but are fully responsible for the bourgeois state. What makes their situation worse is that while the cabinet is formally head of the 'management team', its real influence is circumscribed on all sides—by civil servants, army chiefs and above all by the capitalist economy. *Labour is compelled to bow down before the 'national' element in the class/nation equation.* This dictates the degree to which Labour governments can deliver reforms.

6

Revolution or reform: the left in the 1920s

So far we have not discussed how revolutionary socialists should relate to Labour in a practical way. This became an immediate issue when the Communist Party of Great Britain was formed in 1920.* Unlike Labour, the Communist Party did not see workers as a stage army serving parliament. Its central focus was the collective organisation of workers, whether it be the 'Shop Stewards and Workers' Committee Movement', the 'Minority Movement' or the unions generally. But the Communist Party also rejected the syndicalist disregard of politics. It was assisted in its tasks by membership of the Comintern—the Communist International, whose leaders were Lenin and Trotsky. Lenin intervened in the debates which preceded the foundation of the British Communist Party; Trotsky entered the scene in the mid-1920s.

Lenin's starting point was the 1917 Russian revolution, the sole example of working-class power. The Bolsheviks had shown, first, that there is no gradual parliamentary road to socialism, only revolution; second, that this requires the active support of the mass of workers, and, finally, that a mass revolutionary party of the Bolshevik kind must be present to lead the way to victory.

Translated into British terms this meant that to open the road towards socialism, three tasks had to be achieved: it had to be demonstrated that *Labour's reformism inevitably turns it against revolution; Labour's restraining influence over the majority of workers must be broken; and workers must be won to a revolutionary alternative.*

Home-grown attitudes to Labour

Before the foundation of the Communist Party, British revolutionaries had two attitudes towards Labour. On the one hand there was the British Socialist Party (BSP), successor to the SDF. Established in 1912, the BSP merely replaced the SDF's sectarianism with an unprincipled

* The SDF had never posed the important questions for revolutionary socialists confronting the Labour Party because it always had a sectarian concept of Marxism.

accommodation to the Labour Party. The BSP believed Labour was 'nothing other than the political expression of the trade union-organized workers'.[1] It followed that revolutionaries must not split away from the true workers' party, and Labour could be won to revolutionary socialism. As one delegate told the Communist Party's founding conference: 'Let us see that we unceasingly carried out our task, until such time as the Labour Party became a Labour Party with a Communist mind—and this could be done [so that] inscribed on the Labour Party banner were the hammer and sickle'.[2]

An opposite view was put by J T Murphy of the syndicalist Socialist Labour Party (SLP). He countered the BSP by rightly pointing out that: 'The Labour Party is not the working class organized politically as a class but the political reflex of the trade union bureaucracy and the petty bourgeois.' Unfortunately he wrongly assumed Labour to be simply 'an instrument of reaction, a body to be destroyed.'

Murphy had mistaken the trade union bureaucracy and Labour Party for tame servants of reaction, denying their reformist role. By so doing he saw no need to relate to their followers, the ordinary Labour supporters, arguing the immediate aim was 'to destroy the Labour Party as an enemy of the proletarian revolution...by working for disaffiliation of the unions'.[3]

Lenin's analysis

Lenin rejected both BSP and SLP positions. He denied the one-sided claims that Labour was either a workers' political party or purely reactionary . It was a capitalist workers' party with all the contradictions that that involved:

> it is a highly original party, or rather, it is not at all a party in the ordinary sense of the word. It is made up of members of all trade unions... It thus includes a vast number of British workers who follow the lead of the worst bourgeois elements, the social-traitors, who are even worse than Scheidemann, Noske [Social Democrats who butchered the German revolution] and similar people.[4]

Building a Communist alternative required an outright break from the Labour Party 'as an organisation of the bourgeoisie which exists to systematically dupe the workers'.[5] But at the same time revolutionaries needed a relationship with the Labour rank and file. 'If the [advanced] minority is unable to lead the masses and establish close links with them, then it is not a party, and is worthless in general.' 'Cooperation' had to be 'carried on systematically'. Without a connection between Communists and ordinary Labour supporters, 'between the vanguard of the working class and the backward workers...the Communist Party will be worthless and there can be no question of the dictatorship of the proletariat at all'.[6]

Of course the *form* of cooperation between vanguard and mass is subject to change. The Labour Party is not always the central priority, but to imagine, as Murphy did, that revolutionaries can relate to workers without having to address their political ideas was sheer syndicalism.

The affiliation tactic

Having established the *principle* of building a mass revolutionary party in opposition to Labour, Lenin proposed the *tactic* of applying for affiliation to the Labour Party!

Britain was the only place where affiliation to a reformist party was urged in this way. Elsewhere the strategy was only to break away. In Britain the route to a mass Marxist party would be more tortuous. First, *there had to be the split*. The BSP members who wished to become Communists were *already* in the Labour Party, *but had to come out*. They would then reapply to affiliate as the Communist Party, this time on a principled revolutionary basis.

For Lenin the request for affiliation was not the end in itself, simply a means to the end. It would help the young Communist Party 'expose opportunist leaders from a higher tribune, that is in fuller view of the masses'.[7] But what if Labour refused the application? 'If the Hendersons and Snowdens reject a bloc with us...we shall gain still more, for we shall at once have shown the masses...that the Hendersons prefer *their* close relations with the capitalist to the unity of all the workers'.[8]

Lenin saw affiliation as conditional on certain vital factors. First: 'the Party of Communists can join the Labour Party only on condition that it preserves *full freedom of criticism and is able to conduct its own policy*. This is of extreme importance'.[9] No Continental social democratic party conceded freedom of criticism and autonomy, but Lenin believed that the Labour Party's unique alliance between unions and socialist societies would permit such open revolutionary agitation. In evidence he cited the BSP's newspaper *The Call*, which openly attacked Labour leaders with impunity.*

* But the organisation was undergoing a transformation wrought by the 1918 constitution. The closer the Labour Party came to actually holding office, the more a centralised political party with its own distinct and exclusive ideology grew up to impose discipline.

Secondly, the tactic was conceived in the context of the immediate prospect of European revolution. The Comintern thought the battle of revolution versus reform would soon be over. Affiliation was therefore a short-term policy for winning workers to the Communist Party, not a long-term one for becoming an integral part of Labour.

Finally, Lenin's proposal depended on a clearly demarcated Communist Party, able to contrast its politics to those of Labour before the masses. This made Communist Party affiliation very different from that of the BSP. When the BSP had applied to join the Labour Party it made no mention of politics at all, pleading only that its seven prospective parliamentary candidates be permitted to run under Labour colours.[10] Unlike the BSP, Lenin had no intention that the Communist Party should capture the Labour Party, nor that it should dilute its own revolutionary Marxism in order to stay inside. As Duncan Hallas puts it, the Communist Party would go into the Labour Party 'with flags flying and drums beating...to conduct a vigorous and open offensive against the social traitors, ie, against the whole leadership and political tradition of the Labour Party'.[11]*

Tactics have changed with circumstances. Since the anti-Communist witch-hunt of the late 1920s, affiliation on a revolutionary basis has ceased to be credible. Yet Lenin's method retains a permanent validity. Razor-sharp it cut right across the BSP's adaptation to reformism, as it did the SLP's ultra-left dismissal of the Labour rank and file.

Voting Labour

The ultra-left in the SLP and elsewhere thought that voting Labour would compromise their purity and implicate their organisations in Labour's betrayals. They believed opposition to reformism was expressed

---

As long as Communists understood affiliation as just a tactic it did not lead to a compromising of their politics. But if membership of the Labour Party became an end in itself, then pressure to conform would threaten revolutionary principles.

* Tactics appropriate to parties may not be suitable for minuscule groups. Lenin's stress on the 'masses' and the 'class' showed that he was thinking in terms of party, not group, strategy.

There have been occasions when the extreme weakness of the revolutionary left has necessitated different tactics. Thus Trotskyists in the 1930s and 1940s, as well as the Socialist Review Group (the precursor of the Socialist Workers Party) used 'entrism' inside the Labour Party. This did not involve a public declaration of revolutionary intent, or insistence on official recognition of the right to free criticism and organisational autonomy. Such entrism had to be recognised as a tactic imposed by great weakness. As soon as it had served the purpose of helping revolutionaries to stand on their own feet, entrism had to be abandoned. As a long-term policy it could only lead to absorption by the reformist milieu or the abandonment of genuine class struggle (which has always been outside the confines of the Labour Party organisation).[12]

by abstaining or running candidates whose primary purpose was to attack the Labour Party.

Lenin dismissed such ideas, stressing once more the need to win mass support for Communism:

> If we are the party of a revolutionary *class* and not merely a revolutionary group...we must, first, help Henderson or Snowden to beat Lloyd George and Churchill; second, we must help the majority of the working class to be convinced by their own experience that we are right, ie, that the Hendersons and Snowdens are absolutely good for nothing...that their bankruptcy is inevitable; third, we must bring nearer the moment when, *on the basis* of the disappointment of most of the workers in the Hendersons, it will be possible, with serious chances of success, to overthrow the Government of the Hendersons at once.[13]

Though coloured by the rosy prospects of 1920, this approach had very practical advantages over the right-wing BSP ('Vote Labour with illusions') and ultra-left SLP ('Don't vote Labour'). It meant reaching out to a wide audience without abandoning revolutionary politics. As Lenin wrote:

> British Communists very often find it hard even to approach the masses, and even to get a hearing from them. If I come out as a Communist and call upon them to vote for Henderson and against Lloyd George, they will certainly give me a hearing. And I shall be able to explain...why the Soviets are better than Parliament.[14]

The Communist Party could do more, he said. At election times the party leaflet should call for a 'vote for the Labour Party in order to prove that the Hendersons, Thomases, MacDonalds and Snowdens, could not solve the manifold problems confronting society through the Parliamentary machine'.[15]

Lenin did not call for 'Labour to power on a socialist programme' since no socialist programme is possible for a reformist parliamentary party. His position can be summed up as: 'Vote Labour without illusions'; although Lenin had a more colourful description: 'I want to support Henderson in the same way as a rope supports a hanged man'.[16]

The early Communist Party

At its founding convention the Communist Party accepted affiliation by 110 votes to 85. A letter was sent to Labour HQ incorporating just three points: 'a) The Communists in conference assembled declare for the Soviet (or Workers' Council) system; b) The Communist Party repudiates the reformist view that a Social Revolution can be achieved by the ordinary methods of Parliamentary Democracy.' Then came the request for affiliation.[17] This was very much in the spirit of Lenin's arguments, with Tommy Jackson finding an even more blood-curdling metaphor than Lenin's hanged man: 'Let us take the Labour leaders by the hand as a preliminary to taking them by the throat.'

Not surprisingly the 1921 Labour Conference turned down affiliation by 4,115,000 to 224,000, and there were similar votes in 1922, 1923 and 1924.[18] Did this mean the affiliation tactic had failed?

Far from it. Success did not rest on any conference vote. Despite the toughness of the Communist Party's approach there is ample evidence that *it raised its revolutionary political profile* while *at the same time relating to local Labour Party members*.

One example was the Caerphilly by-election in August 1921. Though this was a mining constituency where Labour was sure to win, anger against right-wing Labour movement leaders was still bubbling after Black Friday. The Communist Party decided to use its candidacy to build its organisation and register a left-wing protest. An indication that this was not a sectarian mistake came when the entire Labour Party branch at Bedlinog resigned to campaign for the Communist. He won a respectable protest vote amounting to 20 percent of the successful Labour candidate's total.[19]

There had been fears expressed that standing for parliament would play into the hands of reformists. But because the Caerphilly campaign was clearly related to workers' direct struggle, it successfully used the political interest aroused by elections to get the *revolutionary* argument across.

The question of whether Communists should stand for election where Labour was running (thereby splitting the workers' vote and risking the victory of the openly capitalist candidate) was also addressed. Revolutionaries (unlike reformists) do not make a fetish out of parliament. The decision to stand depends on *whether or not this will assist workers' self-activity and build the revolutionary party*. A campaign which produced a derisory vote could only demoralise the left. One that lined up in sectarian fashion with the openly capitalist Tory or Liberal parties *against* Labour would be equally damaging. Caerphilly avoided both dangers.

Although the Labour leadership was incensed by Communist tactics, many of the rank and file saw it differently. In the 1922 general election six Communist candidates enjoyed local Labour Party support and two were successful, Walton Newbold (Motherwell) and Saklatvala (Battersea North).

Winning two seats in parliament—a minor concern for revolutionaries—was merely the most visible sign of the Communist Party's ability to relate to the advanced sections of the Labour Party without abandoning its opposition to Labourism. Further evidence was provided by the impressive list of local Labour Party branches and unions which repeatedly backed affiliation. In 1923, for example, these included seventeen engineering branches, sixteen miners' lodges and four NUR branches as well as the furniture and shop workers' unions at national level.

The inevitable pressures

Like any genuine intervention of revolutionaries in a hostile environment, the Communist Party's strategy lacked the security of sectarian isolation, exposing Communist Party members to the risk of being influenced by Labour's reformist milieu even as they sought to win its rank and file. An article in *The Communist* of 1922 showed the dangers: 'The Communist Party wants to be able to advocate the working-class programme...and it cannot do this effectively outside the all-embracing working-class organisation—the Labour Party'.[20]

The writer had fallen into every trap. To say revolutionaries could not be effective outside Labour was to forget that Lenin considered rejection of affiliation to be a valuable lesson which would assist Communism. And how could Labour be 'the all-embracing working-class organisation' if it excluded the only people who could point the way to a socialist society?

A pull towards reformism was the price the Communist Party had to pay for intervention, but it was worthwhile *as long as the leadership understood the need to combat such tendencies towards political degeneration*. However, when Lenin died and Stalinism took over the Comintern, the correct orientation on Labour was obscured. The turning point came at the end of 1923 when the Communist Party decided to secretly send its members into the Labour Party in ones and twos so as not to attract attention.[21] This negated the affiliation tactic as a public exposure of Labour's reformism.

The results could be seen during the first Labour government. Palme Dutt, editor of the Communist Party's newspaper, forgot that Communists wanted Labour in office to demonstrate its bankruptcy, not to apologise for it:

> We are not fighting against the Labour Government, which it is our concern to uphold and sustain...we cannot [say] that every folly and weakness of a Labour Government plays into our hands. It is not so.[22]

Palme Dutt implied that Labour in government was somehow 'a lesser evil'. He was mistaken. The Tories, as the open party of capitalism, are relatively straightforward in their defence of the system. In that sense they have *already exposed* their true political tendencies. But although Labour *believes* it can steer a middle course between classes, once in office it is called upon to use the state to break strikes and so on. In *practice* it was not a lesser evil.*

The example of the Mensheviks in Russia illustrates this. Until the middle of 1917 they were a reformist party, to the right of the Bolsheviks, but far more radical than the British Labour Party ever was and apparently miles away from the official parties of the Tsarist state. This changed after October. They then lined up with the most reactionary White generals and the forces of international capitalism attempting to crush the first workers' state.

The Left Wing Movement

Disappointment with the first Labour government created openings for the Communist Party. Disgust with MacDonald was rife. Beatrice Webb wrote: 'The party is certainly in a bad state of mind... Poor MacDonald, what a mess he has made of it'.[23]

The Communists' response was to build a 'Left Wing Movement'. The LWM's newspaper, the *Sunday Worker*, reached a circulation of over 100,000 copies, clear proof that disgruntled Labour activists were looking for answers. But the LWM was actually an obstacle to revolutionary politics. Why was this so?

The LWM described itself as consisting of:

> sympathetic Labour Parties and Left Wing Groups who are pledged to work within the Labour Party for a Left Wing programme. It is not part of the objects of the Left Wing to create splits within the Labour Party, nor is it under the domination of any political party.[24]

* But although it acted as a capitalist party it was not 'a third capitalist party' (as the Communist Party in its ultra-left phase after 1928 called it). For Labour still retained links with the trade unions and was considered to be the workers' political party in the minds of millions. A capitalist workers' party is the only correct description.

Its chief efforts were directed at getting detailed resolutions through Labour Party Conference. The resolution on foreign policy, for example, included opposition to the League of Nations, abandonment of imperialism, diplomatic relations with the USSR and support for the Chinese Nationalists. Then came industrial policy: a minimum wage, a 44-hour week, workers' control, nationalisation of all basic industries without compensation and the formation of a Workers' Defence Corps. This was followed by policy documents on 'Land and Agriculture', 'Unemployment', 'National and Local Finance', 'Health and Housing', 'Local Government' and so on.

The Left Wing Movement was not, as the Communist Party claimed, an application of the Comintern 'united front' tactic. Correctly applied, this involved an attempt 'to force the leaderships of the reformist and centrist organisations into limited co-operation on concrete issues *by winning their followers for unity in action*'.[25] The LWM was neither limited, concrete, nor tied to action. Its vast range of policies, couched in the form of worthy resolutions rather than designed for action, made it a sort of pseudo-revolutionary party in its own right.

Not only did it substitute for the Communist Party, it involved Communists sustaining a reformist left within the Labour Party. Labour lefts were too contradictory in their attitudes to organise coherently for themselves. As the 1925 Communist Party Congress heard: 'We have found the left-wing' elements without the Communist Party entirely lacking in initiative...until our members step in...the others do not move'.[26] The Communist Party gained nothing because there was now a left-sounding home inside the Labour Party for those who, had they had to choose between MacDonald and revolutionary socialism, might have opted for the latter

There are occasions when, as a means of exposing the leaders, revolutionaries put demands on reformist organisations which they expect will be rejected. But this is not always effective as an exposure. It all depends on whether the demand helps *mobilise* the reformist rank and file, or *demobilises* it. To be useful, it must be related to the consciousness of the rank and file.

The demand for affiliation in 1920 was a good example. Labour claimed to be a 'broad church' and during the period of the Council of Action, was spouting its most-left wing rhetoric ever. In such a context the Communist Party's request for affiliation seemed valid to Labour supporters. Whether or not Henderson acceded to it, valuable propaganda opportunities opened up.

But the Left Wing Movement's approach did the reverse. To call, after the MacDonald ministry, for Labour to be returned to power on a semi-revolutionary programme did *not* expose the leadership before its supporters. The distance between the first Labour government and the Left Wing Movement's demand was so great that these demands seemed an impossible fantasy. Even worse, Communist Party sympathisers inside the Labour Party *fell into believing LWM demands could be carried out.*

The emphasis on conference motions played into the hands of Labour leaders adept at the game of resolution-mongering as a substitute for real action. Did anyone, apart from the Left Wing, seriously imagine MacDonald and his cronies would take any notice of motions demanding 'the overthrow of the capitalist class and the establishment of international socialism'.[27]

The Left Wing campaign did not help workers discover the Labour Party was bankrupt. On the contrary. It suggested to the best elements that it was not. As a Communist Party pamphlet declared:

> the workers in the Labour Party must rally to the 'Reds'...and fight for a new programme and a new leadership within the Labour Party, which is the sole guarantee of success in the heavy struggles that are inevitable in the near future.[28]

The theoretical flaw: Labour equals the trade unions

The theories that underpinned the LWM were expounded by Palme Dutt and J T Murphy.

The key argument was put by Palme Dutt: 'Between the mass of the Trade Unions and the mass of the Labour Party there can be no divergence, because the Trade Unions are the Labour Party'.[29] This was the BSP's position all over again, but with a difference. Palme Dutt admitted the reactionary nature of the Labour leadership. He thought that as the mass struggle moved trade unionists leftwards they would drive out the union bureaucracy and, after a delay, convert Labour to revolutionary politics:

> It is natural that the class struggle, revealing itself first in its primitive economic forms without relation to political consciousness, should meet with heavy opposition and obstruction...but must eventually win its way forward, within the ranks of the Labour Party'.[30]

The mistakes here are numerous. Firstly, the British trade union bureaucracy will never lead revolutionary struggle and will not be removed this side of a socialist revolution. Experience has shown that rank and file movements *independent of the trade union machine* are needed to free the rising class movement from bureaucratic control.[31] If this is true of the union bureaucracy, it is even less likely that the Labour Party leadership can be made responsive to a revolutionary working class.*

It is also wrong to suggest that because revolutionaries must be in the unions it follows that they should stay in the Labour Party. Despite formal links, the two are in fact quite different institutions. As we have written elsewhere:

> Despite the...affiliated trade union membership, the party had no direct relationship with the point of production. The [union] bureaucracy signed the cheques and cast the block votes at conference, not the rank and file. Further, the ordinary union member's connection with the party was either totally passive or at best consisted in canvassing... Thus despite the overlap of membership and leaders, the unions and Labour Party were functionally separate and subject to very different influences.
>
> The workplace and the polling booth confront people in different ways, the one as members of the working class in a collective unit, the other as individual citizens of the national state. For these reasons revolutionaries cannot have the same approach to trade unions and the Labour Party. One is the mass organisation *of* the working class, the other claimed to be a mass organisation *acting on behalf* of the working class.[32]

Furthermore, parties and unions are organised on different lines. A party is a *voluntary grouping* united on the basis of *shared political ideas*. Trade unions follow the contours of capitalist industry and are not so concerned with the political beliefs of those who join.

Labour's trade union links made it an exception to the rule. But despite the affiliated trade unions, when Communist Party members said: 'We are going to a Labour Party meeting', they were not referring to their union branches but to the local ward. Apart from Communist Party entrists, this was composed of people whose only motive for meeting was that they shared reformist beliefs.

The content of union meetings necessarily differed from Labour ones, and revolutionaries had to relate differently to each. At the former the agenda concerned collective organisation and industrial or economic resistance. Through their workplaces revolutionaries had

* The soviet type of organisation is the only one which can solve the problem of workers' democratic control of power. It is able to do so because its delegates are elected from workplaces and therefore subject to permanent collective control. The parliamentary constituency offers no such basis.

a common class bond with the membership and so had the right to intervene and offer a lead in collective struggle or perhaps raise wider Marxist positions. It was *a springboard for arguing revolutionary politics*.

What cemented the Labour Party branch together, however, was *general reformist politics*—how parliament or the local council should be used. This gave no common starting point for revolutionaries. Of course, given the absolute freedom that Lenin had demanded when he suggested affiliation, revolutionaries could have attended ward meetings to explain why parliament offered no solutions and that socialism could only come about through smashing the state, not through its reform. But the repeated rejection of affiliation and the beginnings of a witch-hunt meant this was not possible.

In other words both theoretically and practically, while the Labour Party was *connected with the unions* (through the bureaucracy) *it was not the same as the unions*.

From reformist mistakes to ultra-leftism

The flaw in the Communist Party's analysis had damaging consequences. It led Murphy to imagine that the Labour leadership would inevitably fall to the left. In the summer of 1925 he wrote:

> The working class is only at the beginnings of its revolutionary experience and education. The Labour Party will grow in numbers and strength as the working class in increasing numbers awaken to political consciousness. In the process...the bourgeois politics which dominate it to-day [will be] cleansed from its ranks.[33]

Apart from the non-Marxist and mechanical idea of the ineluctable march of history by which the mass of Labour supporters are 'inevitably destined to be driven',[34] Murphy was wrong to see workers' struggles transforming Labour in their own image. We have seen that the great advances in working class struggle—1910–14, the shop stewards' movement and 1919—did not lead advanced workers towards Labour, but *away from it*. Labour's influence over the vanguard grew only when the development of working-class consciousness was blocked by defeat.

Even without such evidence Murphy would have been mistaken. Labour was distanced from workers and not subject to their control. Revolutionary parties may sometimes be out of step with the mass movement and have to be forced back into line—the obvious example being the Bolsheviks at certain stages in the 1917 revolution. But while they can make wrong turnings, these are easily rectified because the aim of the party (its rank and file and its leaders alike) is to develop the workers' struggle to its highest point. In the revolutionary party there is no *bureaucracy* with a vested interest in the preservation of existing society.

Not so with the Labour Party. The leadership always sees the wider movement as *subordinate* to parliament and the state. Labour *responds* to mass pressure (as with the adoption of Clause Four), but it does so only in order to release excess steam and prevent an explosion.

Moreover, to believe that right-wing politics would be automatically cleansed from the ranks was to forget that the only way to unmask fake leftism is by creating *an alternative leadership* free to initiate real action. It is through the test of practice that reformism is dissipated.

The Communist Party's theory led to further errors. If Labour mirrored workers' consciousness, then what did MacDonald and Henderson represent? According to Murphy they were partly middle class 'invaders and partly an historical remnant of Liberalism'.[35] Palme Dutt concurred. Writing at the end of 1924 he described the right-wing leaders as alien usurpers of power. Their days were numbered:

> When, therefore, the ex-trade union parliamentary adventurers and honest middle-class muddleheads in the wake of Mr MacDonald endeavour to fasten a non-working-class formula, such as parliamentary democracy, on the Labour Party, they are only showing their own narrowness and complete unconsciousness of the character of the working-class movement...the working class struggle will press forward beyond them.[36]

Such optimism evaporated with the anti-Communist Party witch-hunt. It was the revolutionary left, not the right, whose days were numbered in the Labour Party. Now the argument changed:

> Either the [right-wing] will destroy the Labour Party and turn it into a Liberal Party and an enemy of the workers, like the German Social Democratic Party, or the Labour Party must destroy them. Either the Labour Party will become a new version of the Liberal Party and share its fate, or else the labour Party must become an open class party.[37]

The bald phrase—'either Liberalism or Socialism'—ignored the permanent contradiction of a capitalist workers' party.

By 1928 the witch-hunt was in full swing and the Comintern was entering its 'third period' insanity. Now the formula 'Labour equals the unions' had completed its journey from reformism to ultra-leftism. If Labour was no longer the workers' political party then it must be an open capitalist party. The 10th Communist Party Congress announced: 'the Labour Party in 1928 has come out unmistakeably as the third capitalist party'.[38] The majority of workers missed this 'unmistakeable' event.

The grotesque sectarian policies which Lenin fought against in 1920 were now wheeled out as fresh ideas. Some Communists wanted union disaffiliation from Labour. Others wanted to tell workers, to stop paying the political levy—at the very time when the Tories were attempting the same thing through the use of the law. The totally unscientific notion of 'social fascism' was hurled at Labour and all its works. The theory of social fascism, peddled by Stalin at the end of the 1920s, suggested that all the parties—from social democracy to the Nazis—were simply different facets of a common reactionary politics, and that Communists should treat them with equal contempt. This entirely overlooked the nature of reformist parties such as Labour and the need to relate to their mass of working-class followers.

The early Communist Party had wrestled courageously against immense difficulties in Britain, the home of reformism. Their failings derived from a faulty analysis and later the baneful influence of Stalinism. It is not a matter of apportioning blame; hindsight confers an advantage which we have no right to squander. The mistakes must not be repeated.

Trotsky's contribution

Trotsky's major contributions to our understanding of the Labour Party are in *Lessons of October* (1924) and *Where is Britain Going?* (1925). He wrote them against Stalin and the Comintern leaders who believed Britain did not require a distinct mass Communist Party.

In 1929 Trotsky discussed the debate in retrospect, quoting his own work as follows:

> 'Without the party, independently of the party, skipping over the party, through a substitute for the party, the proletarian revolution can never triumph... We have paid too dearly for this conclusion as to the role and significance of the party for the proletarian revolution to renounce it so lightly or even to have it weakened.' (*Lessons of October*)
>
> The same problem is posed on a wider scale in my book *Where is Britain Going?* This book, from beginning to end, is devoted to proving the idea that the British revolution, too, cannot avoid the portals of communism and that with a correct, courageous and intransigent policy which steers clear of any illusions with regard to detours, the

> British Communist Party can...be equal in the course of a few years to the tasks before it.[39]

Trotsky's analysis of the Labour leadership elaborated Lenin's main themes and was blistering in its attack:

> These pompous authorities, pedants and haughty, high-falutin' cowards are systematically poisoning the labour movement, clouding the consciousness of the proletariat and paralysing its will. It is only thanks to them that Toryism, Liberalism, the Church, the monarchy, the aristocracy and the bourgeoisie continue to survive... The Fabians, the ILPers and the conservative trade union bureaucrats today represent the most counter-revolutionary force in Great Britain, and possibly in the present stage of development, in the whole world... Workers must at all costs be shown these...liveried footmen of the bourgeoisie in their true colours.[40]

However he did not take an ultra-left line and ignore the link between Labour and the unions. In fact he went beyond Lenin, to locate the specific role of the trade union bureaucracy on the political wing of reformism:

> the Labour Party...is only a political transposition of the trade union bureaucracy...these are not two principles, they are only a technical division of labour. Together they are the fundamental support of the domination of the British bourgeoisie.[41]

Where is Britain Going? was an excellent work which critics derided for its suggestion that Britain was on the eve of gigantic class struggles. Trotsky was vindicated dramatically by the General Strike and miners' lockout just a year afterwards. While the basic propositions in the book were clear and absolutely correct, one important prediction was wrong:

> A certain analogy would appear to arise between the fate of the Communist and Independent [ILP] parties. Both the former and the latter existed as propaganda societies rather than parties of the working class. Then at a profound turning-point in Britain's historical development the Independent party headed the proletariat. After a short interval the Communist Party will, we submit, undergo the same upsurge. [Therefore] the Communist Party will occupy the place in the Labour Party that is at present occupied by the Independents.[42]

In no sense did Trotsky suggest that the Communist Party and ILP shared common politics. The latter was 'in a class sense not worth a rotten egg' while the Communist Party's destiny was to 'prepare itself for the leading role'.[43] The witch-hunt, which took off just after Trotsky wrote the book, soon put paid to any idea that revolutionaries could lead *from inside the party*.

Yet a nagging question remains. Could the mechanism which brought ILP leaders like MacDonald to lead the party be a model for others? To answer this we must pick up the threads of the ILP's story which we left in 1918.

The ILP pays the price of reformist 'success'

For an organisation which by the mid-1920s had reached just 30,000 members, the ILP seemed to have been blessed with astounding good fortune. In 1906 there were 18 ILP members among the 30 Labour MPs, rising to 121 out of 191 during the first Labour government. (Moreover there were six ILP members in the cabinet, three of them from the ILP's ruling National Administrative Council).* The 1924 election raised the proportion to 114 out of 150.

The astute Wertheimer was not deceived. He noticed that although the ILP's 'political influence seemed to reach peak-point', its 'membership was always subservient to Labour Party allegiance whenever the two came into conflict... The responsibilities of statesmanship proved stronger than the party politics'.[44]

That remorseless degeneration which had started the day the ILP spurned the title 'socialist' in order to win a parliamentary foothold had become a gangrene whose spread kept pace with the number of MPs. The putrefaction erupted to the surface during the first Labour government:

> the ILP appeared at the very pinnacle of its power, when its members were in a Cabinet and Government whose leader they had helped to select... The failure to win even the active sympathy of a Front Bench which, in principle, was dominated by the ILP suggests a lack of commitment in ILP allegiance which was remarkable. Throughout the period it is *almost impossible to detect what MacDonald would have called 'the ILP spirit' in anything the Labour Government achieved*.[45]

Leaders who had used ILP membership as a ladder to success now kicked it away. MacDonald told the ILP to: 'mind its own business and regard Socialism, not as a creed of a lot of blethering easie-oozie asses

* In comparison, the massive trade unions battalions, which controlled conference and financed 101 MPs, were rewarded with only seven cabinet members.

who are prepared to pass any resolution without knowing its meaning.'[46] Snowden proposed the ILP's disbandment, MacDonald its castration. (They resigned from the ILP in 1927 and 1930 respectively). Clifford Allen's rather pathetic defence of the ILP's existence was that 'there was a necessity for a Left Wing organisation in the larger Party; otherwise there would be a tendency of certain elements to drift towards the Communist Party.'[47]*

Thirty years of hard work, the achievement of parliamentary influence beyond their wildest imaginings, had brought the rank and file ILP members exactly nothing. There are two common explanations for left-wing failure. Reformists and centrists blame *individual weakness of character*—the next leader must 'try harder'. To the ultra-left, failure proves that *all intervention must be shunned*. The real reason was that the ILP attempted the impossible—to satisfy workers' aspirations through capitalist institutions.

ILP socialists were like industrial militants who suppose that by winning top union posts they gain control. In the end they invariably wake to find that one remote bureaucrat is simply replaced by another.

The Clydesiders

The 'Clyde Brigade' valiantly tried to break this impasse. In 1925 and 1926, they drove MacDonald's supporters from the ILP leadership. The change was symbolised by Jimmy Maxton replacing Clifford Allen as party chairman.

The Clydesiders did not contribute a new politics, but a certain *style*. They attempted by sheer will-power to bridge the widening gap between working-class aspirations and the MPs in parliament, a gap that was imposed by the Parliamentary game. The famous procession to St Enoch's Station in Glasgow on 19 November 1922 captured the mood. Kirkwood wrote:

> We were going to do big things. The people believed that. We believed that. At our onslaught, the grinding poverty which existed in the midst of plenty was to be wiped out. We were going to scare away the grim spectre of unemployment which stands grinning behind the chair of every artizan.[49]

---

* Maxton was not averse to using the Communist bogey as a justification for ILP style reformism, as his parliamentary speech on How to Avoid a Communist Crash shows: 'We on these benches...think that the crash...may be avoided if all sections of this House rise to a sense of that ideal and are able to say not merely that they have sympathy, but that they can produce each year tangible evidence... We want to join with every well-disposed person in the House who is prepared to avoid this crash.'[48]

In parliament they resolved by personal example* to galvanise the sagging ranks of Labour Party and frighten the government benches. Johnny Muir, ex-revolutionary, leader of the Clyde stewards began the attack: 'Muir asked for no palliatives...the system was wrong and the system must go. When he sat down, Sir John Simon stepped across, wrung him by the hand, and cordially congratulated him on a brilliant maiden effort'.[50] The experience must have broken Muir, for he became a lame MacDonald supporter. Something stronger was needed. They decided to *create scenes*, sometimes on the floor of the Commons and occasionally outside.

The first occasion was 27 June 1923. Despite an 11 percent rise in tuberculosis deaths among children, the Tory spokesman, Walter Elliott was cutting health expenditure. Maxton rose to describe how his own wife died nursing their sick child back to life. He castigated Elliott's party policy: 'I call it murder. I call the men who initiated the policy murderers'.[53] Uproar followed and Maxton was suspended. Wheatley jumped to his feet and repeated the accusation, followed by Campbell Stephen and Buchanan. They were all thrown out. Later Maxton was removed for uttering such dreadful words as 'blackguard', 'liar' and 'damned unfair'! The House of Commons has presided over the forcible subjugation of a third of the planet and its policies have, whether deliberately or not, shortened the lives of millions. But so to accuse a Right Honourable Member is unforgivable!

The Clyde comrades' outburst was totally sincere and fully justified. Their personal incorruptibility was absolute. But the value of their strategy must be evaluated. Although appearing rebellious, it operated within strict limits. *The Parliamentary outburst was designed to shake up the House of Commons, not to smash it.*

'Socialism in our time'

The Clydesiders' weakness has been common to 'official' Labour lefts. Like the right they combine class and nation, though the left gives extra emphasis to class. This sharing of a common ideological ground between left and right was evident in the ILP's acceptance of 'Hobsonism'—a

* John Wheatley, the intellectual leader of the group, impressed many contemporaries. Mosley (at that time a left-wing Labour MP) described him as 'the only man of Lenin quality the English Left has ever produced'.[51] Wheatley believed that setting an example of simple living and moral rectitude could prevent degeneration. Thus he moved a motion at the 1923 ILP Conference to ban MPs from attending social dinners. It was passed by 93 votes to 90 (although dinners with the king were excluded from the resolution since he was above politics and therefore no political risk).[52]

theory which inspired the ILP under the MacDonald supporter Clifford Allen *and* under Maxton.

J A Hobson was a Liberal economist who sought an alternative to socialism. He wrote: 'Talk about "the abolition of the wage system" is commonly as vague as it is heroic. What is feasible is the gradual enforcement of the principle of a living wage, embodied in a minimum standard of comfort for a class'.[54] Later he added the notion that capitalist crises were due to underconsumption. Workers could not buy back everything they produced and over-production was the result. By stimulating demand through a minimum wage or providing family allowances, the boom/slump cycle could be abolished.

There was nothing socialist about Hobsonism. Keynes, a Liberal, adopted similar ideas while Henry Ford, viciously anti-union and champion of an aggressive modem capitalism, argued the same thing: 'an underpaid man is a customer reduced in purchasing power. He cannot buy... The cure for business depression is through purchasing power'.[55]

Hobson's idea that the interests of workers and bosses could be made compatible through the planning of demand was ideal for all sorts of reformists. The right-wing TUC leaders after the General Strike took it to justify collaboration between employers and unions. Hobsonism served Oswald Mosley as a Labour minister in the 1920s and as a fascist in the early 1930s.

In the mid-1920s Hobson and other 'experts' joined ILP Commissions to develop a range of new policies. The result was 'The Living Wage' or 'Socialism in Our Time'. Proponents like H N Brailsford made it clear that 'the New Socialist Policy' was quite feasible '*even with privately-owned industries*'.[56] Like Fabianism, this was ruling class ideology masquerading in socialist clothing. An attempt to plan capitalism rationally and stimulate demand appeared to benefit workers, but did so *only to the degree that their enemy, the capitalist system, was strengthened even more.*

Yet when the Clydesiders took over the ILP leadership they swallowed the bait—hook, line and sinker. Of course they gave it a left-wing colouring. A living wage and family allowances would help workers, and the bosses' refusal to pay up could have been an excuse to expropriate them with or without compensation, as the ILP argued. Yet all this only seemed plausible if the entire structure of capitalism and the state were overlooked. Vagueness suited Maxton's temperament, but Wheatley, the intellectual power-house of the group, felt a duty to think the policy through and draw conclusions. The result was terrifying nonsense.

The state must organise capitalism within the national framework: 'Socialists recognised that if Britain is to be saved from submersion... our aim [must be] to link up our essential industries as departments of one great national British industry working in cooperation with other parts of the Empire'.[57] And why not use the British Empire? Until the first Labour government only rabid right-wingers slobbered over the Empire. Now the left discovered it was part of a state whose power they wished to increase and they competed with each other in extolling its virtues. Thomas Johnston, editor of the ILP's paper, *Forward*, modestly described the empire as 'the greatest lever of human emancipation the world has ever known'.[58] Maxton wanted 'a great Empire that shall house and develop a free people... Our only objection is that it is too limited'.[59]

Rebutting Communist Party criticisms, Wheatley wrote: 'It may be very nice to list a series of idealistic abstractions, but these cut no ice... Whatever we think of [Empire], our duty as members of the Labour Movement is to see how we can utilise it to serve our purposes'.[60] International solidarity was replaced by fear of foreign imports. He wrote: 'I would use the navy, were I in power, to sink the ship that brought from abroad the product of sweated labour to reduce the standard of life here'.[61] The end of this reformist odyssey was racism: 'It was necessary to end that state of affairs where "the Coolies are busy, the Britishers are at the Buroo [the dole office]"'.[62]

Wheatley represented the most extreme of the 'official' Labour left. He simply pressed the extraordinary contradictions of capitalist/worker ideology to their limit when trying to think his way through to socialism.

Needless to say MacDonald was going to have nothing to do with 'flashy futilities' like *Socialism in Our Time*. 'These tactics will never be pursued...and that's that'.[63] The wordy Reports, the carefully thought-out pamphlets, the Commissions—all crumbled into dust.

In 1928, with the labour movement in precipitate decline after the General Strike and MacDonald riding high, Maxton took a desperate step, going over the head of the ILP National Administrative Council to issue *Our Case for a Socialist Revival* with A J Cook of the miners. This manifesto was the prelude to a national campaign. It was Maxton's grandest gesture, also his most disastrous. Not only did the independent action of its chairman threaten to rip the ILP apart, but the packed launch meeting in Glasgow flopped. For Willie Gallacher it was 'The saddest meeting I ever saw',[64] while on the platform John Wheatley, 'with a face eloquent of disgust, drew from his waistcoat pocket the substantial cheque he'd written for the campaign funds and carefully tore it into little pieces'.[65]

The deflating effect of the meeting was due to the manifesto's lack of realism. It called for rapid and substantial change, but the campaign was clearly directed at gingering up the existing Labour Party rather than providing any alternative:

> It was on the one hand far too soft and centrist to have a long-term survival, and on the other hand it was far too little to have an immediate impact. One can make use of a little axe that is sharp, or a massive axe that is blunt. But what can one do with a little axe that is blunt?[66]

Poplarism

Poplarism was the one glimmer of light in the gloom of the left inside the Labour Party during the 1920s. It showed the difference between *the struggle for reforms* and *reformism.*

Poplarism was dominated by George Lansbury. He was active in London's East End from the turn of the century, and as early as 1905 Poplar was 'notorious' for unemployment schemes. Soon Lansbury and his associates gained an influence on the council and on the boards of guardians that administered unemployment relief.

Mass post-war activity had an impact on this part of London. In 1919 this combined with the grassroots involvement of Poplar leaders in the unions to help give Labour its first majority in the Borough Council elections.* The councillors' aim was summed up by Lansbury: 'The workers must be given tangible proof that Labour administration means something different from Capitalist administration, and in a nutshell this means diverting wealth from wealthy ratepayers to the poor'.[67] To this end the councillors raised unemployment allowances as well as council employees' wages. Casual employment in the docks meant Poplar was already a deprived area, and so that the cost of raising allowances and wages did not fall on the workers locally, the councillors demanded 'equalisation' of rates across London. Rich boroughs would have to assist their poorer brethren. To force this policy on Lloyd George's unwilling government, the councillors withheld their contribution to police, asylum and county council funds.

In September 1921 thirty councillors were jailed for their action. They were freed after a six-week campaign which revealed what was unique about Poplarism:

* Of the 30 councillors who later went to jail, nearly half were or had been lay officials in their unions.

> the day after their release, 2,000 enthusiastic supporters crowded into Bow Baths to cheer their councillors, while an overflow meeting of another 2,000 had to be held outside in Roman Road. That weekend there was a 'monster demonstration' in Victoria Park to welcome them home.[68]

This mass support had been built by consistent work. Noreen Branson's excellent history shows how the original proposal to break the law was thrashed out at a conference of local trade union branch representatives. There followed a series of 'well-filled public meetings'. The final Council meeting before the arrests saw the town hall besieged by supporters 'packing the alleyways and [standing] on the window sills. Outside [were] some 6,000 people who could not get in.'

Ten thousand people followed the women councillors to their jail. A rent and rate strike was prepared by a many-thousand-strong Tenants' Defence League. Two other left-wing councils decided to follow Poplar into illegality and action spread: 'marches by the unemployed demanding "work or maintenance", deputations to boards of guardians and clashes with the police were reported from many areas.' The TUC Conference gave support.

Herbert Morrison, who led London's Labour Party, did his best to isolate and destroy Poplarism, but even he was forced to plead with the prime minister to do something:

> a sheer lack of faith in the whole of the institutions of State...is growing among those bands of hungry desperate men... Sir. I say there is a distinct tendency in that direction which is dangerous to National Government and to Local Government.[69]

In the end the government had to give way, freeing the councillors and equalising London's rates. The tangible result was a fall in Poplar's death rate. In 1918 it had stood at 22.7 per 1,000 people; in 1923 this had halved to 11.3. Over the same period infant mortality fell from 106 to 60, which despite Poplar's social deprivation was the lowest rate for the 95 largest towns in Britain.[70]

The councillors' determination to withstand prison until victorious, marked these events as exceptional in Labour's history. Local government could be more than just a platform. There is a potential contradiction between the *national* state, whose prime function lies in the deployment of 'armed bodies of men' to defend the ruling class, and *local government* which has a service function. The Comintern had recognised this when it passed a resolution which, though clearly designed for different circumstances, had a bearing on Poplar:

> Should the Communists receive a majority in the local government, institutions, it is their duty to take the following measures:
> a. form a revolutionary opposition to fight the bourgeois central authority;
> b. aid the poorer sections of the population in every possible way (economic measures, the organization or attempted organization of armed workers' militias etc.);
> c. expose, at every opportunity, the obstacles which the bourgeois state power places in the way of fundamental social change;
> d. launch a determined campaign to spread revolutionary propaganda, even if it leads to conflict with the state power;
> e. under certain circumstances, replace the local government bodies with Soviets of workers' deputies.[71]

Poplarism was very different from the long tradition of 'gas and water socialism' practised by many Labour Parties under Fabian guidance. This had envisaged the creation of 'municipalised' industries—public transport and so on, as a step towards 'nationalisation'. The emancipation of the working class or local government as a base to attack central government played no part. The key concern was efficiency in the provision of services.

Poplar's councillors did not substitute themselves for action, they *led* it. Between 1919 and 1923 the masses were not used as a means to win council seats and then protect them. The councillors saw their role as serving the workers' movement. They had, unfortunately, an Achilles heel.

Until 1924 the *activities* of the Poplar Labour Party were not hindered by the general *reformist beliefs* they undoubtedly held. But the first Labour government presented Poplar with a dilemma. This should have been the opportunity Poplar needed to consolidate its gains and extend its methods nationally through legislation. Naturally the councillors expected John Wheatley's assistance—for not only was he the most left-wing member of the cabinet but as minister of health, responsible for local government. Alas, Wheatley did no more than cancel a surcharge which his Tory predecessor had imposed but never dared enforce. *That was all.* He assured his cabinet colleagues:

> I have expressed no opinion whatever in regard...to Poplar... I explicitly decline to do so and carefully avoided any indication of either

> sympathy or the reverse... The motion tabled by the Liberal Party suggested that the rescission of the Poplar order is calculated to encourage illegality and extravagance. My answer is that you are much more likely to encourage illegality by keeping alive a statutory order which you cannot enforce... The Government means to carry out the law as they find it...and has no intention whatever of encouraging or allowing lax administration.[72]*

The Poplar activists had to admit that Wheatley had done nothing positively to assist them: 'Mr Wheatley's action did not give fresh powers to Guardians or...afford new opportunities for the exploitation of public funds by the Socialists. Guardians all over the country are still liable to surcharge'.[74] As a final humiliation it was stated: 'The Poplar Board...know that in Mr Wheatley they have a Health Minister who...will understand and sympathise with them in the horrible problem of poverty'.[75]

The Labour government prepared the downfall of Poplarism. In April 1925, during the very week Labour won *every* seat on the Poplar Board of Guardians, Poplarism collapsed. Its £4 minimum wage policy caved in to a ruling in the House of Lords and the council agreed to introduce pay cuts.

What happened in Poplar in 1925 was a sorry contrast to 1921. When the courts had been used previously the local mass movement had been involved in direct defiance and wider sections were drawn in. But in 1925 Lansbury put his hopes in parliamentary action. He addressed MacDonald and Thomas, avowed enemies of Poplarism, begging them for help, to no avail. The municipal workers eventually decided to strike to defend their wages. As the local press reported, all departments came out, but 'at 3pm George Lansbury accompanied by Councillors and Trade Union officials arrived and as a result the strike was called off some three hours later'.[76] In Lansbury's *Labour Weekly* we read that after hearing their MP: 'They realized that a strike in Poplar would be a strike against themselves, and only their own flesh and blood would suffer.' Presumably their flesh and blood were unaffected by wage cuts.

The parliamentary graveyard had claimed its latest victim. *Reformism* had killed the *struggle for reforms*.

---

* Naturally Wheatley's explicit refusal to express sympathy evaporated as soon as he was in opposition and he was no longer in a position to do anything. Opening a block of flats in the area in 1925 he said that 'The Poplar Borough Council in many respects was a great pioneer in the work of social emancipation, and it was only as the policy of Poplar permeated the country that they would march towards a different order of society'.[73]

The balance sheet

If we try to draw up a balance sheet for Labour's official left at the end of the 1920s the result is depressing. Apart from the local episode of Poplarism, which the Labour government ended, there had been a lot of 'sound and fury signifying nothing'.

First there were the Clydesiders and their ILP. In 1919 Clydeside workers had indeed struck terror in the hearts of the upper class during the forty-hours' strike and put the king in 'a funk about the labour situation'.[77] But Wheatley and the other MPs elected in 1922 were but the palest reflection of that earlier militancy. Wertheimer noticed that scenes in the Commons had little effect:

> Both Conservatives and Liberals refused to recognise these foibles as expressions of the class war and regarded them as nothing more than a rather sympathetic eccentricity. In the same way James Maxton enjoys a popularity on the 'other side of the House' and in the capitalist dailies that stands in striking contrast to his fanatical extremism.[78]

A recent history concludes:

> It all made for colourful Press Coverage. Red Clydeside had left the streets and sat in Parliament. But the Press of 1919 had registered genuine panic at the Bolsheviks of George Square; the Press from 1922 offered no more than condescending indulgence to Maxton and Kirkwood. From the beginning the Scottish rebels were treated as colourful curiosities and not as threats to public order.[79]

The Clydesiders were just part of the picture. Could not a united left wing have done better? There had in fact been a left wing formed in 1925, which included all the prominent figures, partly to counter the challenge from the Communist Party. As well as the Clydesiders, there were important people such as Marion Phillips, Susan Lawrence, George Lansbury and John Scurr. The last two were heroes of Poplarism. The evolution of this left wing was described by John Scanlon, a Clydeside socialist writing just after the collapse of the 1929–31 Labour government:

> Dr Phillips is one of the staunchest defenders of the Labour Government's Anomalies Bill [to disqualify certain unemployed claimants]. Miss Susan Lawrence...was the first person to 'tick off' Mr Wheatley when he dared to criticise the Government. Mr George Lansbury...framed the rules which finally expelled Mr Maxton...

> Mr John Scurr...was the first judge appointed to try Mr Maxton each time Mr Maxton tried to carry out...the programme approved by Mr Scurr in 1925. That was the rebel group of 1925.

Scanlon then added the epitaph which should be inscribed on the tombstones of successive generations of Labour left-wingers: 'Was it not that nature sometimes tempers a keenness of politics with a sense of humour, suicide would be the only alternative of the disillusioned Socialists'.[80]

A contrast: the revolutionary struggle for reforms

Our criticism of the Labour Party is not solely that Labour can never bring socialism, but that for most of the time *it is an obstacle to the struggle for reforms.*The Labour Party sets out to work *within* an enemy institution, the capitalist state. This is a hostile environment. But the path it chooses is not the only one available: there is another way of fighting within enemy institutions which contrasts strongly with the British experience. This was demonstrated by the Bolsheviks in Russia before the revolution of 1917.

Under Tsarism the Bolsheviks had only the most limited opportunities for legal activity, yet made expert use of them. Elections themselves became occasions for mass action. When, in 1912, the authorities disqualified some of the electorate a strike movement immediately began which involved 70,000 people, forcing the government to back down and organise new elections.[81]

The Clydesiders treated the Glasgow electorate as a stage army whose task was completed once their MPs boarded the train at St Enoch's Station. Parliamentary scenes were supposed to be the *real* force for change. The Bolshevik deputies saw scenes in the Russian parliament, the Duma, as a catalyst for struggle outside. When a deputy was prosecuted for sedition, the entire Social Democratic group (Mensheviks and Bolsheviks) protested and were suspended; 72,000 workers in St Petersburg and 25,000 in Moscow came out on strike. A reactionary newspaper gave the deputies the following magnificent compliment:

> very close connections have been established between the deputies and the workers...every speech in the Duma arouses a response among 200,000 workers. All live questions in working-class circles are immediately re-echoed from the Duma rostrum, whence the Social-Democrats censure the government and still farther excite the ignorant masses.

> At the same time all utterances of the Social-Democratic deputies are taken up by the workers. The objectionable obstruction in the Duma organised by the Social-Democrats as a protest against their arrogance being curbed, entailed a mass strike.[82]

The Tsarist Duma, packed by reactionaries elected through a rigged voting system and deprived of any power by an autocratic state, became a powerful weapon, not to change Russia, to be sure, but to raise the combativity of the working class.

Labour's official left in the 1920s made virtually no impact within parliament or the party. Its belief that Labour was *the* instrument to achieve socialism also precluded it from serious work outside. The far tinier forces of the Communist Party, which lacked decades of history and hundreds of MPs, were not bound by the same limitations. Through its agitation in the collective organisations of the class it made a real contribution to the crucial event of the 1920s, the General Strike.

7

General Strike and aftermath

You must understand that the Labour Party and its Parliamentary leaders or representatives had *nothing to do with it*.'
—Secret letter of Sidney Webb to George Bernard Shaw, 13 May 1926[1]

WHEN THE Labour Party was first mooted in 1892 the promise was for: 'something more than a mere Electoral Club... It is an organisation formed to rouse, to educate, to unite the vast inert masses of the workers and to give the strength of sympathy and cohesion. It will do more than bring out Labour candidates... It will give assistance to the workers in all trade disputes and crises'.[2] Better than any other single event, the General Strike showed whether that vision matched reality.

In the General Strike the Party had to choose between a movement which was in form, if not in intention, *a direct challenge to the state*. Secondly, it clarified *Labour's relationship to the workers' mass activity*. Next the strike demonstrated the underlying *unity of the union bureaucracy with the party* and their interest in separating politics and economics. Finally, the results of the strike proved conclusively that *Labour's political fortunes are linked to the working-class movement, but that the connection is wholly parasitic.*

Background

Just as the Labour Party has a number of reformist currents within it, so the union bureaucracy is not homogeneous either. Union officials are under varying pressures from below and above. Although they ultimately defend their common group interest, they may choose different methods to the same end.

In the period after the first Labour government (and partially because of disappointment with that administration) the TUC was dominated by left-wingers like George Hicks, Alfred Purcell and Alonzo Swales. They were apparently determined to keep Labour's nose out of their affairs, 'erecting impenetrable barriers between 33 and 32 Eccleston Square' (the respective headquarters of the two organisations).[3] In reality the semi-revolutionary speeches of Hicks and Co were designed not to overthrow the system but to ginger up the unions.

Events seemed to be going the way of the TUC lefts when, on 'Red Friday', 31 August 1925, the threat of united strike action compelled Baldwin's government to subsidise miners' wages for nine months. In general, workers took Red Friday to be a great victory, a triumph for their collective strength.

Naturally the Labour leadership were appalled. MacDonald's reaction to Red Friday was astounding in its frankness:

> The Government has simply handed over the appearance, at any rate, of victory, to the very forces that some well-considered thoroughly well-examined socialist feels to be probably the greatest enemy... If the Government had fought their policy out, we would have respected it. It just suddenly doubled up... The consequence has been to increase the power and the prestige of those who do not believe in political action.[4]

Labour's objection to Red Friday went beyond the fear of strikes. Government aid for wages was 'madness' and 'sheer waste'. MacDonald wrote: 'To think of a subsidy as a means of taking from the rich something they ought never to have in order to give it to the workmen who ought to have had it all the time, is not a policy that will bear examination'.[5]*

As the General Strike approached, the gap between the Labour Party and the TUC narrowed, for the fundamental similarity of their interests became apparent. On 30 April 1926, with full government approval, the miners were locked out. At the Conference of Union Executives to launch the General Strike, MacDonald made a 'hypnotic' speech[7]: 'we will be by the miners' side, because it is a just side, an honourable side. It is the life of the toiling masses that we have been striving for, not to make enemies of society, but to make the very best friends that society has'.[8]

MacDonald's speech could never have been made by a Tory or Liberal. His identification with the working class, even the demand for 'the toiling masses' to be accepted into the bosom of society rather than remaining outcasts, embodied aspirations common to millions of workers. This aspect must not be forgotten. But what was special about the General Strike was that it revealed just how incompatible workers'

* When the issue was discussed in parliament Labour's efforts to embarrass the government were remarkably feeble, which was not surprising since Baldwin's speech, and that of Thomas, who concluded for Labour, were both written by that ubiquitous civil servant, Thomas Jones![6]

aspirations and capitalist society really were. When concern for miners had to be weighed against the need 'not to make enemies of society' it was obvious which would be the loser. A sell-out was inevitable.

Solidarity, treachery and irrelevance

The story of the nine-day General Strike and its tragic betrayal by the TUC has been told elsewhere.[9] What concerns us here is the Labour Party's role. This had three totally different aspects. Firstly, the mass of trade unionists affiliated to Labour gave a show of solidarity without equal. There were more out the day after the strike was called off than before. Secondly, the Labour Party itself did absolutely nothing to direct them forward. *No-one struck as a Labour Party member, only as a trade unionist*. The claim of Sidney Webb that heads this chapter—'You must understand that the Labour Party and its Parliamentary leaders or representatives *had nothing to do with it*'—was deadly accurate. The outstanding support the miners received was *in spite* of the whole thrust of Labour's policy. Any local assistance the strike received from Labour was independent of the national organisation.

The third aspect of Labour's role was that while the parliamentary leaders did nothing to advance the strike, they were tremendously active in selling it out. Baldwin tried to embarrass MacDonald by quoting his earlier anti-strike speeches. He misjudged his man. MacDonald answered:

> If I have a grievance against the Prime Minister for having read out a statement of mine, it is that he selected a very poor condemnation. I have gone far more into detail than that... With the discussion of general strikes and Bolshevism and all that kind of thing, I have nothing to do at all. I respect the Constitution.[10]

Sometimes the Labour leaders went too far even for the TUC.

In the middle of the strike MacDonald and Thomas were reported as being 'in hourly conference...regarding a settlement', and the TUC was forced categorically to deny this.[11]

Such open activity was nothing compared to the frenetic efforts in secret. When the strike began, wrote Sidney Webb:

> we had all to make the best of it, and we started, individually, straight away to contrive some way of resuming negotiations... MacDonald and Henderson (with Thomas)...have been all the week almost

> continuously at work, from early morn to past midnight, tying one proposal after another, wrestling with stupidity, and obstinacy and jealously, seeking fresh avenues of negotiation and bringing to bear all possible influences.[12]

By 'stupidity, obstinacy and jealousy' Webb meant the miners fighting for survival.

This hyper-activity contrasted strangely with the party's national executive, which Beatrice Webb called 'the Cabinet of the British Labour Movement'.[13] The minutes noted the mining crisis no earlier than 28 April when local parties wrote in asking for guidance. The executive's reply was that 'propaganda literature had been published.' During the strike itself, there is no evidence of executive activity or even that it met. Thus *the very first mention* the minutes make of the General Strike is *3 June 1926* when the finance and general purposes sub-committee remarked: 'The effect of the General Strike upon the finances of the unions appeared to be such as would adversely affect the income arising from the current affiliation fees.'

On 21 June the organisation sub-committee remitted that a joint TUC/Labour Propaganda Committee had organised public meetings on 8 and 9 May. At last on 23 June, just five weeks late, the executive itself considered this momentous event, though much against its will. With trade unionism in tatters after the TUC's treachery it was assailed by the demand for 'the National Labour Party [to give] a definite lead in dissipating the feeling of distrust and despair.' The executive's helpful conclusion? 'That a reply be sent explaining the propaganda work in which the Party has been and is engaged; and stating that the Trade Union Congress are the custodians of the industrial side of the matter.'

Paton of the ILP witnessed these events: 'the gigantic machine of the Labour Party, with its organisation in every constituency in the country [was] in the house adjoining that of the General Council in Eccleston Square. On the first day [of the General Strike] the entire machine, with its perfectly functioning staff was placed at the disposal of the General Council; apparently they'd as little use for this machine as for ours'.[14]

Further down the ladder of organisation the picture is repeated. The party's best-organised section was the London Labour Party led by Herbert Morrison. According to its 1926 Report, its main contribution was to put 'two members of our clerical staff,' at the General Council's disposal. But this was not all. 'Particulars of Choral, Dramatic and Orchestral organisations...were communicated' to the TUC.[15] Yet more followed! Morrison reorganised the TUC courier system, but 'the first job that my revised despatch service had to discharge was to deliver the notice terminating the General Strike'.[16]

What of the ILP, 'easily the most efficient and widespread socialist organisation in Great Britain'?[17] Wheatley, at least, had recognised that the bureaucracy would probably sell-out. After Red Friday he caused a mild sensation with an article which said 'Prepare for the great struggle nine months hence... Refuse to enter Coolieland... The workers' army of defence can be increased by one million a month. A Labour army of 10 million can preserve industrial peace. Now to the recruitment office'.[18] What an incredible combination–racism, class war rhetoric and a ten million strong workers' army devoted to...industrial peace. This was a centrist extravaganza that confused even Wheatley's friends. The idea was not repeated. Instead the ILP retreated back into its ivory tower of '*Socialism in Our Time*'.*

The day the miners were locked out the ILP re-awoke. Its newspaper warned workers to watch the TUC carefully. But did the ILP go beyond the abstentionism of the Labour Party national executive? Not in the least. In the last *Labour Leader* before strike Maxton wrote: 'It is not part of the duty of those outside the miners' ranks to attempt to make their decision for them... The duties of the Labour movement begin when the miners have made their decision'.[20] In other words, Maxton was saying that socialist politics have nothing to do with leading actual workers' struggles since they are really directed at winning seats in parliament.

Paton, the ILP's organising secretary, recounts what happened during the strike:

> I wrote at once to the General Council, putting at their disposal the entire resources of the ILP, lock, stock and barrel, for the duration of the strike... I returned to my office to make feverish preparations for the call that must soon come...we were certain we'd an invaluable contribution to make in a struggle of this magnitude... We transported mattresses and blankets to the office where we'd decided to camp for the duration of the strike and await the call to action with confidence. A week later we were still waiting.[21]

* Maxton, Stephen and Kirkwood spent much of the time between Red Friday and the strike on a tour of the Western Isles, hardly the best recruiting ground for the proletarian army. However the ILP did play an auxiliary role in the continuing miners' lockout by helping produce *The Miner* newspaper for the Miners' Federation (MFGB), collecting money and evacuating miners' children to ILP homes.[19]

Labour—the alibi for a sell-out

The TUC had been pushed unwillingly into a strike and was determined to head it off as soon as possible. Again, as in 1919, *reformist politics were the chief ingredient of bureaucratic sell out*. The General Strike, like any other war, could only be won if the enemy stronghold was attacked. That stronghold was the state. The bureaucracy was terrified by this prospect and used the existence of the Labour Party as an excuse to keep politics out of the strike.

MacDonald did not overstate the case when he said: 'Never for a single moment, never for a solitary hour, did the men responsible for the strike toy or play with political issues... I never heard a single member of the Trade Union Congress Committee whisper an idea, give a piece of advice, suggest a move or policy that was aimed at a political issue'.[22] Four of the seven issues of the General Council's paper, *British Worker*, carried an identical declaration that the strike did

> not challenge the Constitution. It is not seeking to substitute unconstitutional government. Nor is it desirous of undermining our parliamentary institutions. The sole aim of the council is to secure for the miners a decent standard of life. The council is engaged in an industrial dispute. In any settlement the only issue to be decided will be an industrial issue, not political and constitutional. There is no constitutional crisis.[23]

Now any organisation that was even remotely 'a party of the working class' would not have sat in its offices waiting official sanction but would have been drawn in inexorably, debating, arguing, suggesting lines of action and attempting to provide a socialist lead to the rank and file. The fact that *even the best Labour activists abstained politically* was extremely significant. Labour's national organisation (the ILP included) had precisely nothing to say to the working class. What earthly use is the best way to wheedle votes or make telling points at prime minister's question time when the destiny of the working class is at stake? As we have written elsewhere:

> The Labour Party is purely electoral. Hence it relates to its supporters as a multitude of individuals. The trade union bureaucracy must relate to groups of workers as collectives. With this separation of politics and economics, the Labour Party leadership is always an outsider to the industrial struggle. In contrast to this, the trade union bureaucracy can never completely avoid heading the industrial struggle, even if only in order to restrain it.[24]

Electoralism denies even the best Labour activists any independent role. It is the secret of their irrelevance whenever real class struggle breaks out.

Even the best reformists see a Chinese Wall separating struggle at the point of production from the question of state power. This attitude has a material basis. Under 'normal' capitalist conditions there *does* seem to be a division between politics and economics. Struggles at the point of production rarely generalise to the point where the state is seen to be involved politically. Conversely 'high politics' appears to have little relation to day-to-day events in the workplace. This separation is vital to the preservation of the bourgeois democratic *status quo*. Being thoroughly adapted to capitalist conditions, *Labour strives to perpetuate the separation of politics and economics, even when a revolutionary opportunity is to hand.* It leaves collective action to the unions (or more usually, to the union bureaucracy).

However, to win socialism the working class must overcome the division between politics and economics, using its industrial power as the base for building its *political* domination. This takes the form of the workers' state which grows from *soviets* or workers' councils of factory and office delegates. The working class *is* capable of this leap. Workers can make sense of their own experience and draw revolutionary conclusions, but for this to happen a party committed to workers' power must gain leadership.

The only political organisation to come near to advancing the General Strike was the Communist Party. Alas it was already distorted by Stalinism, as shown by its slogan 'All Power to the General Council', the very body which killed the strike. But even while carrying this awful burden, the Communist Party's 6,000 members contributed infinitely more than the ILP or Labour Party. *All* the forward initiatives—Councils of Action, Workers' Defence Corps and the movements for the control of food—had already been argued for and were now set up by activists in and around the Communist Party. With a different leadership these might have been a basis from which to challenge the sell-out. The Communist Party played a prominent role in running the strike and picketing. Of the 5,000 arrested during the strike, fully 1,200 were Communist Party members. A Communist striker was 200 times more likely to be arrested than a Labour one.

The contrast between Labour's immense forces and the tiny Communist Party makes nonsense of the frequent claim that revolutionaries are irrelevant to the working-class movement while Labour is somehow relevant. When the class is really *in motion* the Labour Party has nothing to offer but sabotage. Only in periods of relative passivity can it appear that the make-believe world of parliamentary socialism embodies the working-class movement.

The post-mortem

On 12 May the TUC unconditionally surrendered. At least the union leaders showed some contrition for their scandalous behaviour or pretended the outcome was not a total disaster; across the space of fifty years we can almost hear the Labour leaders gleefully rubbing their hands at the defeat.

The Webbs considered the strike to be

> a monstrous irrelevance...the noxious futility of this mild edition of the 'dictatorship of the proletariat' will be apparent to everyone... The failure of the General Strike of 1926 will be one of the most significant landmarks in the history of the British working class [because it is] the death gasp of that pernicious doctrine of 'workers' control.[25]

Best of all for them was that

> the only organisation that comes out the stronger for this disaster is the Parliamentary Labour Party—for the simple reason that the...strike as a weapon has been discredited. Indeed the agony of the Miners' Federation *might* mean a Labour government after the General Election of 1928.[26]

Ramsey MacDonald considered the strike to be 'one of the most lamentable adventures in crowd self-leadership of our labour history'.[27] but its defeat made it 'a glowing point in the history of British Labour'.[28]

Snowden agreed: 'the experiment provided lessons of the greatest value to Trade Unionism... I was not sorry that this experiment had been tried. The Trade Unions needed a lesson of the futility and foolishness of such a trial of strength'.[29]

Thomas extracted the most enjoyment from this crushing blow. He revelled in the strike-breaking activities:

> When the strike came...the working-class had to take back the bitter things they had said about the pampered upper classes... These fellows—clerks, dandies, even—tackled any sort of job; they drove trains, piloted motor buses, and even unloaded ships in harbour. That is how England tackled her first General Strike.[30]

And the lesson? 'The only real and lasting remedy against social injustice is the ballot box'.[31]

This joyous dancing on the grave of the workers' movement was well-founded. Shopfloor confidence was in ruins. Between 1927 and 1929 'the number of recorded strikes and the number of working days lost through strikes fell to the lowest figures since systematic recording had begun nearly 40 years earlier'.[32]

MacDonald and company were not jubilant just because revolution was prevented; trade union action was also discredited. There is a fundamental difference between reforms won from below and those granted from above. The former strengthen class organisation and this creates the possibility of future advance. Those from above encourage passivity, tend to integrate the workers into the system, and so may hold back the struggle for socialism. The Labour Party stands for change from above and requires a tame workers' movement that patiently awaits parliamentary action. Reforms must come from this source, or they should not come at all. Thus the humiliation of the TUC (although not its destruction) was a major boost for the Labour leaders.

The TUC was indeed brought to heel. Alongside the Mond-Turner talks about employer/union collaboration, it was ready to substitute electoralism for collective action. At its Bournemouth Congress the TUC president, Arthur Pugh, thanked Labour for pointing out the reformist alternative to revolution: 'The supreme lesson of the national strike is the clear evidence it adduced as showing that the Trade Union Movement retains belief in the essential rightness of democratic methods... We have had a Labour Government, the symbol of our victory'.[33]

The following year that former left-winger George Hicks sang a new tune at the TUC: 'I say that it is now an imperative duty to use every atom of organised strength we possess, and every scrap of time and energy for the return of the Labour Government at the next General Election'.[34] The *Daily Herald*, run by the official leaderships of the Labour Party and the TUC, led the chorus. Two weeks after the sell-out its editorial declared:

> When we said the gains of the nine unforgettable days were far larger than the losses we were asked by a number of correspondents what these gains were. [The by-election victory at] Hammersmith is one of them. There will be many more. Gone is the notion, sedulously put about by Communist organs, that the ranks of Labour are split, that there is a feeling of 'betrayal', that the strike left workers bewildered and resentful.

> We see now that the Strike and the battle for the Miners...has brought into the movement large numbers who never voted Labour before.[35]

If there had been no General Strike, the smashing of the miners—one quarter of all trade unionists—might have so devastated the class that Labour itself would have suffered. But the magnificent display of solidarity sent a rush of new blood into the workers' movement. The terrible defeat that followed allowed the Labour Party to feed on this. The vampire needs living victims, and these victims grow to love their predator. Workers did not feel strong enough to fight independently but were sufficiently stirred up after the defeat to hope MacDonald would fight for them.

So *the most important effect of the Strike was to establish the absolute dominance of electoralist strategy* right across the workers' movement.*

A horrific postscript

The most disgraceful episode of 1926 was Labour's treatment of the miners, who contributed more financially and electorally to the party than any section of the labour movement. Whatever might be the failings of the Communists or ILP during the General Strike, they did their best to support the miners in their lone fight after 13 May. The Labour Party blocked their way. Appeals by the Communists for an embargo on the movement of coal fell on deaf ears, with even the ILP objecting. Then when the ILP suggested levying Labour Party members to provide funds for the locked-out miners and their families, the motion was carved out of the 1926 Labour Party Conference agenda at Margate. Kirkwood pleaded with the delegates: 'a levy should be made on all the organisations of the Labour Party. Was that too much to ask?... Why not give an actual demonstration that they were in earnest?'[36]

There were sound reasons why Labour supplemented treachery with callousness. The 'agony of the miners' was a vote winner; a victory for strikers was a threat. So Labour backed the TUC when it refused £300,000 collected by Russian trade unionists for the miners. Morrison considered this 'about the only thing he could find to praise the unions for'.[37] MacDonald lauded the Margate TUC's refusal to lift a finger for the miners: 'The proper and helpful thing to do was done. The Conference declared emphatically that the solution was political'.[38]

* In addition Labour did consistently well at the polls. On 3 November *The Times* announced outstanding victories at the municipal elections. Significantly it was the very section that had been stabbed in the back—the miners, who now voted most heavily for Labour. Beatrice Webb's prediction was one year out, but it came true. In 1929 the agony of the miners brought Labour to office.

Labour's delay in providing the miners with *any* form of assistance was scandalous. The timing of events was as follows. On 28 September, *four months after the lockout began*, the Parliamentary Labour Party suggested a party whip-round might be appropriate. On 13 October 1926 the national executive got around to agreeing. Alas, things went badly 'owing to the fact that the campaign was inaugurated in the closing stages of the Municipal Contests.' So it was that in the fifth month of the lock-out it managed some 'social meetings' in which 'the desired resolutions were passed'.[39]

The last word should go to the Webbs. As MP for Seaham, County Durham, Sidney owed his parliamentary salary to the votes of miners and their families. But he was most displeased to have to make a donation to the locked out miners! What terrible heart-searching he and his wife suffered over that £10. Beatrice wrote:

> Ought we or ought we not to give, and ask others to give, to the fund for the miners' wives and children? Neither Sidney nor I would have given a penny to it if no one would have been the wiser. I gave my name to the Committee and sent a cheque for £10 simply because I conformed to the loudly expressed opinion of the world of labour—with which I secretly disagreed.[40]

How sickening!

A capitalist workers' party is under stress in two directions. There is the tension between left and right. In the 1920s the chief protagonists were on the one hand the ILP and TUC lefts and on the other MacDonald and the TUC right. But there is also a division between the working class and the leadership. The General Strike showed that the latter is the more fundamental. During the nine days a massive split opened between the reformist organisations and union bureaucracy on the one hand, and the rank and file on the other. The inability of the revolutionary left to challenge the labour bureaucracy ensured that it was MacDonald who triumphed.

The fruits of defeat: the anti-communist witch-hunt

Witch-hunts date from Labour's earliest days. They began when the party was officially just two years old with Hardie attacking Grayson's supporters thus: 'In almost every branch there is this snarling disruptive element. You have got to fight it down and fight it out'.[41]

Given Labour's consistent right-wing leadership there can be little doubt it has relished the idea of banishing its opponents permanently.

But the leadership's actions are limited. Public infighting can be electorally damaging and the process of elimination is not simple. Finally, the very nature of the Labour Party encourages diversity. The affiliated trade unions, for example, recruit around economic questions, not shared political ideas. Moreover, electoralism—which requires votes rather than a definite political commitment—means that Labour will recruit racists, multi-millionaires or red revolutionaries so long as each is worth an extra ballot paper. This is the basis of the very real claim that Labour is 'a broad church'.

So while witch-hunts extend throughout Labour's history, they are not a constant feature and only occur in specific circumstances. They have *not* been launched when the leadership feared losing control to the left. When the class is on the offensive the leaders don left clothing themselves to preserve their position. The action of arch-right-wingers Arthur Henderson and Sidney Webb in proposing Clause Four was an example. So expulsions are not a sign of right-wing weakness or collapse, but of its *strength*. They are associated with a passive or retreating workers' movement.

This has a number of effects. Firstly, as the political climate shifts to the right, a vocal left-wing is seen as an electoral liability. At the same time a *downturn in workers' confidence leaves a wide gap between the majority and the advanced section* of the working class, who are then easily isolated and attacked.

This pattern was confirmed by the hounding of the Communist Party in the 1920s, Labour's most important, vicious and thorough witch-hunt. The Labour leadership had been keen to destroy revolutionary influence from the October 1917 revolution onwards. In the 'direct action' period, however, there had been little that the leaders could do in terms of witch-hunts.

The first phase

The tide turned after Black Friday, 15 April 1921. The 1922 Labour Party Conference in Edinburgh passed a resolution by two to one stating that 'No person shall be eligible as a delegate who supports candidates other than such as have been endorsed by the Labour Party'.[42] This was directed at the Communists who, as revolutionaries, reserved the right to stand separately, and if need be, in opposition to reformists.

However the resolution proved inoperable. Communists were not only returned as delegates, they were selected to run for parliament by local parties without hiding either their principles or the fact that they belonged to a separate organisation. For example Walton Newbold, the Communist who stood for parliament with Labour sponsorship in 1922, had written to the local party in these terms:

> I begged them to realize what they were doing and to understand that I would only fight as a Bolshevik, and if they did not want a Bolshevik they should choose someone else... They chose me with their eyes open-prised wide open.[43]

A year after the resolution was passed Henderson had to admit that 'the new rule was somewhat difficult to administer' and withdrew it.[44]

The first attack failed for two reasons—one political, the other technical. The spirit that brought Britain to the brink of revolution in 1919 was not dead. It had been dampened down in 1921, but activists were still not prepared to sacrifice the Communists, and the fighting policies they stood for, to please the right wing.

The second problem flowed from the unusual structure of Labour itself. At *national level* the PLP had tremendous power because of the reformist idea that change comes through parliament. At conference the trade union bureaucracy exercised a decisive influence through its block votes. Together the Labour leaders and the officials could ram through anything they jointly agreed.

However this picture of right-wing domination at the centre was not mirrored *at the base*. Indeed the structure worked in the opposite direction. The rank and file of the unions and constituencies elected delegates to local Labour Parties independently of party HQ and conference. This gave the left a local basis from which to resist the centre. They found it possible to ignore orders from national bodies.

This local situation might encourage, a belief in the possibility of transforming the whole party, but it was pure illusion. *The very structure that allowed for a degree of local autonomy meant it was impossible for the rank and file to control the leadership.*

Revolutionaries are sometimes criticised for their adherence to 'democratic centralism' which demands discipline in action combined with full discussion amongst an informed membership. The apparent freedom of opinion in the Labour Party is merely a disguise for the untrammelled power of the centre.

The 1923 general election and first Labour government made the leadership hanker after respectability even more. Now Labour was in the political big league. What could be tolerated in a party striving for entry to the corridors of power was unacceptable once access was granted.

Pressure to renew the witch-hunt developed after the May 1924 Kelvingrove by-election in which a Communist standing under Labour auspices lost by 1,000 votes. The Labour executive put up with MacDonald breaking election pledges and threatening to smash strikes with troops, but losing a seat was unpardonable.[45] An inquiry into Communist activities was set up and reported that the chief obstacle to destroying their influence was their strength in the unions.

The Communist Party did not see socialism coming through parliament but by the activity of the working class itself. So it concentrated its efforts in industry, where it established its credibility as a fighting organisation. As the inquiry complained: 'It is doubtful whether the unions are prepared to enforce a ruling that individual Communists shall not be eligible to serve as delegates to local Labour Parties.'[46]

When the government fell in 1924 the right-wing wanted scapegoats, and who better than the Communists? Was it not Labour's efforts to prove its hatred of subversion that had led to the bungled prosecution of a Communist newspaper and forced an early election? And the 'Zinoviev letter' added a further excuse.[47]

The 1924 party conference, held just before polling, was keen to show voters that Labour hated Communism. MacDonald set the tone, declaring: 'We have as much to do with Bolshevism as the man in the moon—except that we regard it as an enemy... We have not a thousandth-millionth part of sympathy with the Bolshevik point of view.'[48] Morrison said that 'if there was any fundamental difference' between the Communist Party 'and the Fascist army of Signor Mussolini he would like to know what it was.'[49] The conference was convinced. Affiliation received its lowest vote yet and passed a resolution that Communists could not be candidates for local or national government. Even individual membership was proscribed.

Electoral defeat only served to whet the leaders' appetite for more blood. Clynes was sure that Labour would not win power 'until the public mind is purged of the mistaken impression that the party entertains a measure of approval with Communist objects and policy.' But if the Communists were ditched 'we may fairly hope to change the one third of the sixteen million who have just voted into the two thirds or more required.'[50] MacDonald said: 'I firmly believe the attitude of the Labour Party in turning down the Communist proposals...will bring the party hundreds of thousands of votes.'[51]

The situation inside the Labour Party was clearly ripe for a witch-hunt; but the mood of the movement outside was not.

Just two months after the crushing conference majorities for a witch-hunt, a national executive sub-committee on Communist activity ruefully admitted defeat. No action could be taken. The reasons for failure had long been understood. As one executive member put it:

> I fail to see how any member of a Trade Union, who is put forward by his TU, can be disallowed, so long as he pays for political efforts as laid down in his particular society rules. The mere fact that he agreed to pay for Labour representation entitles him to full opportunity to exercise the right he pays for in his TU contribution. The fact that an individual is a Communist, who does so, is of no more consideration than if he were a Spiritualist.[52]

The 1925 Labour Conference in Liverpool tried a new tack. It pleaded with the unions to be 'consistent' and 'appeal' for branches to 'refrain' from selecting Communist delegates.[53] Once more the power of the block vote gave these proposals a massive majority—2,870,000 to 321,000. But still the localities resisted. Regular reports of defiant branches reached the executive. Disaffiliation became the only alternative, but until May 1926 only three local parties had been dealt with.

The final battle begins

The right's efforts had been baulked for four years, but the General Strike finally cleared the way for them. The very executive meeting after the strike expelled Springburn Labour Party and the next added fully five more.[54] By the end of 1926 13 out of an eventual total of 27 labour Parties had been dissolved. An indication of the executive's double standard was its treatment of G A Spencer, the Nottinghamshire Labour MP and leader of the scab miners' union. Despite calls for him to be disciplined for organising scabbing, the executive refused, claiming 'this is primarily a matter for the Miners' Federation'.[55] No such diplomatic niceties were reserved for the Communists.

By this time the Communist Party had decided to promote the Left Wing Movement. As we have seen, this was a mistake. Nevertheless the LWM did not trim its sails to stay inside the party, because, unlike the Labour and trade union lefts, it was based on an independent political organisation with roots in the collective organisation of workers. The

LWM's immediate response to the witch-hunt was 'we will fight it without mercy'.[56]

J J Vaughan, chairman of the LWM, put its priorities in this way:

> We have been asked by several people why we do not propagate our ideas inside the Labour Party without organising a Left Wing Movement on a national scale which carries on a constant struggle... The Left Wing would easily be crushed and with it the spread of working-class ideas in the Labour Movement if the Left Wing did not organise and prepare to fight for its point of view.[57]

The first outbreak of hand-to-hand fighting was in Manchester, where the Borough Labour Party announced it would eject Communist Party members who acted as delegates to Labour Party bodies. In response the Trades Council ostentatiously picked two Communists as its representatives. NUR members instructed their Communist delegate to 'sit tight and refuse to leave the meeting.' The engineers withdrew their non-Communist delegate solely in order to send a Communist Party member.[58]

Similar tactics were repeated all over the country. Expelled Communists were re-elected to responsible positions, dozens of Labour Parties stood in open defiance and were disaffiliated. The official record mentions a total of 27[59], but this covers only borough and divisional parties which were dealt with by party headquarters. Countless individuals, wards and affiliated organisations were involved in the fight.

In October 1926 came the Margate conference. Discussion was stitched up by excluding local Labour Parties which had put forward awkward resolutions. Eleven Communist Party members were either banned from attending or 'discovered' and chucked out. Only two Communists, both union representatives, survived the purge.[60] 1927 raised the struggle to a new intensity.

Dissolved local parties fought a rearguard action to the point of running candidates against 'official Labour'. In the 1928 municipal elections the Bethnal Green rebel polled twice as many votes as his official rival, and across London they received one third.[61]

But in reality the war was almost over. Labour determined to smash the last pockets of resistance at its 1928 conference. This was an extraordinary affair. All resolutions and amendments from branches were ignored. The executive alone could present items for discussion. Even emergency motions could only be brought by the executive. A 'Loyalty Clause' was introduced barring association with Communists and excluded them from attending meetings or appearing on the same platform as Labour Party members. At the end of the year the tally of disaffiliations stood at 24. The Third Left Wing Conference heard its chairperson declare that 'from 10 percent to 15 percent of the entire movement...has been sacrificed'.[62]

The LWM closed down in March 1929. It has been wrongly argued that the Communist Party threw away great opportunities to convert Labour to Communism. Of course, the idea of a Left Wing Movement did not accord with its new line that Labour was 'social fascist', but by the time this was adopted the movement was already in ruins. It had fought as hard as possible, but in post 1926 conditions the witch-hunt was unstoppable.

The constitutional left

One feature of the witch-hunt was the position of those on the Labour left who disliked the expulsion of the Communists but refused to fight it as the LWM had done. The Clydesiders said little, apart from even-handedly rejecting MacDonald's gradualism and the Communist Party's 'catastrophic' revolutionism. Maxton 'stood for toleration of both left and right wings', adding he would do nothing which 'would lead to his own expulsion'.[63] *Forward* carried headlines such as 'Communists, biggest asset of Capitalists'.[64]

The most prominent figure to deal with the question in detail was Lansbury. He began by stoutly denouncing anti-Communist measures. But when the witch-hunt gathered pace Lansbury found he could no longer have it both ways; either he backed the party or he backed socialist policies. The choice was quickly made. In December 1925 he wrote:

> One or two Labour Parties have defied the [anti-Communist] resolutions and have been faced with the consequences. The official Headquarters did its duty in carrying out the official policy. The result is: the dissidents find their local party faced with disaffiliation and expulsion... If they fight on, they know they must face splitting the Party. *They and their instigators are the wreckers of the movement.* It is hard saying, but true.[65]

How dare the Communist Party defend itself!

Perhaps Lansbury hoped, by keeping his head down, to fight another day. Nothing could have been more wrong. *The smashing of the Communists meant the gagging of everyone else.*

The contrast between the Communist Party and the constitutional left was significant. When a period of working-class defeat leads to a rightward drift, and Labour moves with it, only an organisation which *puts socialism above the electoral game* and builds its own base *independent of the Labour machine* can resist the pressure to conform.

8

Reformists and the slump: the second Labour government

IF THE General Strike is the recurring nightmare of the trade union bureaucracy, the 1929–31 Labour Government holds terrors for the Party leadership. For the first time a reformist administration had to cope with full-scale capitalist crisis. The result was a disaster which Sidney Webb said 'finds no parallel in anything in the Parliamentary annals of this or any other county'.[1] Clement Attlee, saw it as 'the greatest political betrayal in the political history of this country'.[2]

The main outlines of the story can be briefly told. Elected in the year of the Wall Street crash, the government limped on aimlessly until the summer of 1931 when it was hit by the full force of what prime minister MacDonald called 'the economic blizzard'. In August he proposed a 10 percent cut in unemployment benefit. A majority of the cabinet agreed, but MacDonald, Snowden and Thomas broke with Labour anyway to form a National Government with Tories and Liberals. At the 1931 Election which followed. Labour plummeted from 289 to 46 MPs. With the sole exception of Lansbury, all those cabinet ministers who remained faithful to Labour lost their seats.

The road to 1931

After the General Strike the new-found dominance of the Labour right wing was not confined to witch-hunting Communists. Labour acquired a new programme, scrapping *Labour and the New Social Order*, which it had held since 1918, to make way in 1927 for *Labour and the Nation*. The change of name was significant. Although the earlier document was by no means revolutionary, the later version was so vague that, in Maxton's words, it meant 'giving a free hand to the next Labour Government to define any programme it pleases'.[3] No doubt MacDonald saw as a virtue the very point criticised by Wheatley: 'No-one suggests we are doing anything more than undertaking to run capitalism successfully where other people equally qualified have failed to run capitalism in the past'.[4]*

* A sign of Labour's attitude was the fact that only 6 percent of its 1929 election addresses mentioned

When Labour won in May 1929 MacDonald prophesied: 'I have reason to believe that this Government will go down into history as the Government of Employment.'(!)[6] Labour was the biggest party in the Commons with 289 MPs, though it still lacked an absolute majority, the Tories having 260 and the Liberals 58.

The government made its intentions plain with a king's speech which 'chilled the Parliamentary Labour Party'[7]. One perceptive Tory remarked:

> It may be one of fate's little ironies that the principal tasks confronting the present so-called Socialist administration should be to make Great Britain safe for the capitalist.[8]

Before considering the central issue of unemployment, we will quickly deal with some other items of policy. Labour began by refusing Leon Trotsky political asylum because he 'would inevitably be the centre of mischief-making and intrigue'.[9] This was too much for even some Liberals and Tories, who valued the British tradition of sheltering political refugees.

In revenge for the General Strike Baldwin had passed the hated 1927 Trades Disputes Act to make certain strikes illegal and attack the political levy. *Labour and the Nation* vowed: 'Among the *first* tasks of the Labour Party will be the repeal of the cynical measures of class legislation by which the Conservatives have sought to cripple the strength of trade unionism'.[10]* Yet months passed without action and Ernest Bevin accused the government of backdoor manoeuvres designed to avoid repeal.[11] Grudgingly a weak Bill was introduced in 1931, but according to Mowat the Cabinet secretly arranged for a Liberal amendment to wreck it.[12]

Many local Labour authorities had accumulated debts when helping the miners in 1926. They naturally expected a Labour Government to bail them out. Instead they were threatened with a surcharge if they did not settle their accounts. The miners themselves did no better. Labour's election promise to restore the seven-hour day was forgotten.

Conference had committed Labour to 'full self-government and self-determination [for India] at the earliest possible moment and by her consent'.[14] Alas, many Indians took Labour at its word, with the result that after nine months 54,000 were in jail for civil disobedience. One MP said his government was 'responsible for a repressive movement in

---

socialism, while 43 percent of the Conservatives did so (to attack it of course).[5]

* It was ironic that the very first justification the Tory Government found in 1926 for the Trades Disputes Act came from a book by Henry Slesser, Labour's legal counsel.[13]

India sterner and severer than any repressive movement since the time of the Indian Mutiny'.[15]

But there was one thing the government was not allowed to forget. Month after month, the capitalist crisis announced its grim presence through the rising toll of unemployment. When Labour came into office this stood at 1.3 million, or 10 percent of the workforce. After a year this had risen to two million. At the end of Labour's tenure of office the figure was 2.7 million or a staggering 22 percent of all workers.[16]

Of course Labour could blame the economic system for unemployment. The president of the 1930 Labour Conference said in her address: 'it is not within the power of any single country to deal with the roots of these evils by means of any purely national policy'.[17] But the crux of Labour's argument was that the results of capitalism *could* be removed within a 'single country' by using parliament to carry out a 'purely national policy'.

Jimmy Thomas was picked to tackle unemployment because of special qualifications—an intimate acquaintance with leading bankers and industrialists! He inevitably failed. In a private capitalist economy government job creation projects alone, however massive, could never turn the tide of unemployment. His schemes were in any case limited, because the Cabinet had decided:

> we must not be rushed into shovelling out public money merely for the purpose of taking...people off the unemployed register... Both for political and financial reasons, we must do all we can to combat the present feeling of insecurity in our financial prospects, and we must, therefore, avoid all schemes involving heavy additions to Budget charges or grandiose loan expenditure.[18]

By the end of 1929 the government was arguing that unemployment 'must continue until the nation assent to conditions wherein production would enlist the services of all who are capable of work, instead of... compelling large groups of people to remain idle'.[19] Brilliant! For some it was becoming just too much. Wheatley, already a dying man, looked back on a life of reformist politics and concluded:

> In election after election, [workers] are asked not to adopt strike or industrial action, or adopt revolutionary methods, and not to listen to agitators who create confusion in society, but to settle matters reasonably and constitutionally and moderately by the Parliamentary machine...now they are reaping the reward of their innocence.[20]

Labour had settled down to the business of curing capitalism and freely admitted *this must be at the expense of the unemployed.* Thomas, who was supposed to *reduce* unemployment, said: 'I have deliberately, and will continue deliberately, to proceed [*sic*] on the basis of a process of rationalisation in industry, which must for weeks increase unemployment figures. I have got to do this in the interests of the country'.[21] However, curing capitalism was not straightforward. The debate about how best to do this occupied the rest of the government's term in office.

Economic alternatives

There were many policies considered, but not one of them included socialism. Attlee explained why: 'We do not believe in the capitalist system. We feel it has failed to deliver the goods and we should like to see it ended. But the country has not yet said that we shall end it. We have no mandate for that'.[22]

The Tories argued for 'protecting' industry by imposing duty on foreign goods. *Both Liberals and Labour had a simple and undoubtedly correct reply to their critics.* In an economy dependent on importing raw materials and exporting finished articles, that meant suicide. Apart from jacking up prices, reprisals would bring a collapse in international trade. This is exactly what happened in the 1930s.

In their 1928 *Yellow Book* John Maynard Keynes and the Liberals argued for a massive programme of public works financed by government borrowing. During the 1929 campaign Labour lifted these ideas (reproducing them in a form vague enough to commit it to nothing definite). Once in power Labour changed its tune. Now, *both Tories and Labour had a simple and undoubtedly correct reply to their critics.* Government borrowing would frighten the banks and decrease the already dismally low sums going to investment.

The first Labour government had hinted at the fact that under the pressure of office the leadership abandons its balancing act between class and nation. 1929-31 confirmed the suspicion absolutely. Labour behaved exactly like any other capitalist government. Snowden clung to tried and tested Gladstonian principles—balanced budgets, maintaining sterling's value and free trade. Winston Churchill described Snowden's appointment as Chancellor in this way:

> We must imagine with what joy Mr Snowden was welcomed at the Treasury by the permanent officials... Here was the High Priest entering

> the Sanctuary. The Treasury mind and the Snowden mind embraced... with the fervour of two long-separated lizards.[23]

Ultimately the most important economic alternative was put by the TUC leaders who toyed with the ideas put forward by Keynes and Hobson. Despite the rhetoric this was yet another ruling-class theory. The TUC blamed problems not on the inevitable results of capitalist accumulation but the disruptive influence of banks and finance. In line with the Mond-Turner talks, the TUC thought that a partnership of labour and capital could modernise industry and save the system.

Other policies were discussed. Sir Oswald Mosley proposed dramatic surgery. A former Tory MP, he was Chancellor of the Duchy of Lancaster in the 1929–31 administration and tipped to succeed MacDonald. Mosley believed the economy could be insulated from a hostile world, using the British Empire for cheap raw materials. At home the government should undertake a grand programme of rationalisation and public works. He later realised that the degree of state planning required would necessitate massive coercion and turned to fascism to provide it. But in 1930 he still hoped Labour would carry out this programme. Finding little support in the cabinet, he took his campaign to the 1930 Labour Conference, losing by the narrow margin of 1,046,000 to 1,251,000. It is indicative of the Labour left who supported him (such as John Strachey and Aneurin Bevan) that they imagined that Mosley's concept of planning had something to do with socialism.

The ILP offered an 'alternative economic strategy' based on *Socialism in Our Time* and the minimum wage. This has already been discussed. It could not work in conditions of slump. Just as the cutting of wages cannot ultimately cure crisis, nor can the raising of wages, for this reduces the employers' rate of profit, the mainspring of capitalism. The only socialist solution to crisis was to smash the system based on capital accumulation. The ILP never thought in such terms. Their left reformism was just one more way of saving capitalism, as Fenner Brockway showed:

> To increase the mass purchasing power of the people will result in a growing demand for goods, and...for labour; and it is only by that method that any hope of an industrial recovery is possible.[24]

But even the most left-wing plans lacked a solution, because all thought in terms of reform within a national framework. The cure for the system's unemployment (though temporary) came when *all* major capitalist states were forced to re-arm in the late 1930s to fight each other.

It seems remarkable that this minority government, paralysed by indecision and slump was not thrown out of office long before it collapsed in 1931. So desperate was its situation that when, in June 1930, the Liberals threatened to vote against the government, MacDonald told the cabinet: 'We could not be better employed...than going down on our knees and praying to the good God that this may happen.'[25]

Labour was tolerated because the Opposition parties wanted it to lead the fight to make workers pay for the crisis. As the Liberal leader Herbert Samuel put it: 'in view of the fact that the necessary economies would prove most unpalatable to the working class, it would be to the general interest if they could be imposed by a Labour Government.'[26]

Labour's aptitude to the unemployed had been fixed since the days of Keir Hardie. The principle was 'work or maintenance'. If there were no jobs, then the workless were to have some level of comfort. The tiny reforms enacted in 1929 fell, far short of the party's manifesto and by the summer of 1930 the minister of labour, Margaret Bondfield, was putting forward proposals for the benefit system which ministers found: 'so disgusting...that rather than allowing any danger of their publication, the PM insisted that each copy should be handed in and...destroyed.'[27] Nevertheless Bondfield, the first woman cabinet minister, went on to introduce the spiteful 'Anomalies Act' specifically designed to disqualify married women who dared claim dole. The government thus 'saved' £5 million.

On 11 February 1931 Snowden decided to go beyond threats to action. He told the House of Commons:

> the national position is so grave that drastic and disagreeable measures will have to be taken... An expenditure which may be easy and tolerable in prosperous times becomes intolerable in a time of grave industrial depression.[28]

Snowden was fully backed by Willie Graham of the Board of Trade, who later denounced his former ally as a traitor for suggesting economies. The following morning the *Daily Herald* carried the headline: 'Britain faces a Crisis... There must be Sacrifices! But Further Taxation on Industry the Last Straw'. Bourgeois papers announced that the government now favoured cuts in unemployment benefit and wages. A few days later the *Daily Herald* reported without comment that the prime minister was to meet unions and employers to discuss the employers' demand for a one-third cut in unemployment benefit, as well as reductions in civil service pay and social services.[29]

However, Snowden had acted prematurely. The Labour leaders needed a bigger panic to bounce the PLP and Labour movement into submission. Luckily for them, the Liberals came to the rescue with a proposal for an inquiry into government finances. The people chosen for this 'impartial' investigation were Sir George May of the Prudential Assurance Company (as president), two Labour MPs and four businessmen (including the heads of the Hudson Bay and Cunard Steamship Companies and Lord Plender).[30]

Snowden had to bide his time and use the May Committee report to force workers into accepting the unacceptable. Therefore the April budget made no important changes, but Snowden warned: 'I definitely contemplate that any gap which occurs in the finance of the year should be met by economy'.[31] Again Willie Graham echoed his master in the parliamentary debates.[32]

Since the precise details surrounding the fall of the government have been so overlaid with charge and counter-charge we will have to follow its development in some detail. The May Committee reported on 31 July that government finances were tottering on the brink of disaster. £120 million had to found by, among other things, reducing the dole by 20 percent. On 12 August MacDonald created an emergency Cabinet Economic Committee. It consisted of Henderson, Graham, MacDonald, Snowden and Thomas. The first two were to emerge as heroes of the Labour Party. The last three became the villains of the piece. The committee's first decision was to pursue consultations with the Tories and Liberals.

Certain ideas were then put to the full cabinet. On 19 August it accepted economies on things like teachers' pay. £22 million was to come from unemployment spending. The idea that the Labour government was against attacking the unemployed is thus a myth. Savings would come through the means test (which meant that benefits would be withheld until claimants provided proof that they had literally *nothing* on which to live) through raised National Insurance contributions from workers, and other measures. From the point of view of what followed, however, it must be noted that they had not *yet* agreed to cut the unemployment benefit rate.

Until this point there was no great disagreement. Even Arthur Henderson, soon to be leader of the anti-MacDonald revolt, had participated in the Economy Committee. As Lord Sankey noted: 'he and I agreed to equality of sacrifice and cut in the dole'.[33]

It was the TUC alone that prevented complete capitulation to the economy measures. Sidney Webb's reaction was expressed in the sort of elegant phrase that made him the foremost Labour intellectual: 'The General Council are pigs...they won't agree to any "cuts" of unemployment insurance benefits or salaries or wages'.[34] The TUC General Council entered the scene on 20 August at a joint meeting between Labour's national executive and government representatives.

The Labour executive's *unanimous* message to the government was summed up by the *Daily Herald* headline: '"We leave it all to you" say leaders'.[35]* But the TUC resisted government pressure, partly because it retained links with workers' collective organisation and because it believed in an alternative means of curing capitalism.

The constituency parties, the Labour executive and the PLP, which existed merely as the means to winning government office, were impotent spectators throughout. The TUC and cabinet were the sole protagonists because they alone had independent bases.

In the battle for the allegiance of the party, the TUC proved the strongest. Its influence derived in part from its financial contributions to the party (three-quarters of receipts in 1930) and sponsorship of MPs. When these factors combined with MacDonald's desertion, the national executive and parliamentary party were persuaded almost unanimously to follow the General Council line. But we are running ahead.

On Friday, 21 August, the TUC suggested economies based on 'equality of sacrifice':

1. Unemployment insurance to be paid for by a graduated levy on profits, incomes and earnings;
2. Securities and other unearned income to be taxed;
3. Payments on the 'Sinking Fund' by which the National Debt was paid off should be suspended.

The cabinet answered that 'no Government worthy of the name could for one instance submit to dictation from an outside body'.[36] It did not see the run on the pound as financial dictation, only the TUC's defence of the millions who had elected Labour in the first place. So the cabinet threw out the whole TUC package. The third

* Indeed the executive did not meet again until 26 August, after the National Government was formed. Nor did it hold meetings to cope with the approaching crisis. Thus the only previous discussion on rising unemployment and possible problems was on 25 November 1930, when the executive took steps to discipline W J Brown, an MP who had publicly stated that unemployment was losing Labour votes. Just as in 1926 the party's national executive, as distinct from the PLP, was stone dead in the midst of major events.

point alone—the suspension of Sinking Fund payments of £50 million a year to moneylenders—was worth more than twice the government's intended savings on dole payments.

At this stage extraordinary events began to unfold which showed where real power lies in bourgeois democracy. The cabinet first went cap in hand to the parliamentary representatives of big business—the Tories and Liberals—to ask whether a 10 percent dole cut would satisfy them. The reply was that the bankers were the ones to see. So Labour humbly turned to the Bank of England. According to the cabinet minute:

> It was in the Deputy Governor's view essential, particularly from the point of view of the foreign interests concerned, that very substantial economies should be effected on the Unemployment Insurance...and he reported the view of a distinguished and very friendly foreign financier [!] on the vital need for securing budget equilibrium.[37]

However the deputy governor of the Bank of England would not make a final decision. Mr Harrison of the American Federal Reserve Bank had to be consulted. When his turn came in this merry-go-round he said he would have to consult New York financial interests. And so it went on.

One cabinet minister described the situation in this way:

> One of the memories that abides with me, and I hope I shall never forget it, is that of twenty men and one woman, representing the government of this country, standing one black Sunday evening in the Downing Street garden awaiting a cable from New York as to whether the pound was to be saved or not, and whether the condition would be insisted upon that the unemployed would be cut 10 percent.[38]

At last the replies came in. World capitalism used its various mouthpieces to say that big business did not care a damn about elections, manifesto promises or the unemployed, since it had the power to make or break governments at will. As a token of good intent towards the wealthy it demanded an immediate and swingeing attack on the most underprivileged section of society. If Labour could pull it off without any opposition then all well and good, but if there should be any hint of dissent that might encourage mass resistance, then harder-line politicians would have to move in.

On Sunday night Beatrice Webb reported in her diary: 'So it is the financiers, British and American, who will settle the personnel and the policy of the British government. Sidney hopes that they will decide against the Labour Cabinet remaining in office... The dictatorship of the capitalist with a vengeance!'[39]

The actual outcome was unexpected. That night the cabinet voted by some eleven or twelve votes to eight or nine (the size of the majority is disputed) *in favour of a 10 percent cut in unemployment benefit*. This was made in the full knowledge that, as MacDonald told the meeting: 'the proposals as a whole represented the negation of everything that the Labour Party stood for'.[40] A narrow majority was not enough, however. The bankers had made it clear that the government *in its entirety* must join in or, as MacDonald warned: 'If on this question there were any important resignations, the Government as a whole must resign.' Having failed to secure unanimity MacDonald ended the Labour government there and then.

Aftermath

Since 1931 a myth has been sedulously fostered according to which Labour fought the cuts and left office rather than carry them out. The truth was not that Labour drove out MacDonald, but that he evicted them from the cabinet even though the majority accepted his programme. This can be substantiated in two ways. Firstly, it was MacDonald who decided that the government was resigning. As the king's private secretary recorded:

> The Prime Minister...told the King that all was up and that at the Cabinet eleven had voted for accepting the terms of the Bankers and eight against... In these circumstances the Prime Minister had no alternative than to tender the resignation of the Cabinet.[41]

Secondly, a number of different writers corroborate Kirkwood's assessment that if MacDonald had wished to do so he might have taken the Labour Party with him in imposing cuts:

> Of one thing, however, I feel certain. If Ramsay MacDonald had come to a meeting of his Party and told them his views and invited them to join him in creating a National Government most of them would have agreed...[42]

Instead, out of the four renegade ministers only the least important—Sankey—attended this meeting of the Parliamentary Labour Party and put up a lame defence.

There is one farther method to establish the truth about Labour's attitude to the dole cut—by measuring its resistance to the economy package when this was introduced. The justification for a campaign of mass extra-Parliamentary activity was obvious. As Miliband puts it:

> Given the fact that Britain was in 1931 one of the richest countries in the world, and blessed with one of the richest ruling classes the world, it is surely amazing that there were actually found rational men to argue that the saving of a few million pounds a year on the miserable pittances allowed to unemployed men and women and their children was the essential condition of British solvency.[43]

Needless to say Labour did nothing positive to fight back, even though the unemployed were themselves far from passive. On 7 October 50,000 rioted in Glasgow; the next day 30,000 did likewise did in Manchester, and the day after 60,000 in Glasgow.[44] The *Daily Herald* was pathetic. In 1930 it had attacked the Communists for organising the unemployed movement:

> Only the reckless and heartless would accept responsibility dragging through the streets crowds of men and women, many of them badly clothed and fed and the great majority totally unfit to march... And it becomes essentially objectionable since no useful end can be attained.[45]

In spite of all that had happened 1931, the paper's line remained unchanged: 'The remedy is in [the unemployed's] hands. Not in rioting and futile demonstrations, not in pointless collisions with the police (who are also victims) but in a determined effort to win the election for Labour'.[46] Even the mildest action was condemned. Teachers resisting a 15 percent pay cut were criticised for a ban on 'out-of-school oversight of children's games'. The *Daily Herald* urged them: 'to rescind the resolution and...rely on the polls...to help them secure justice'.[47]

Fortunately, there were better ways than waiting fourteen years for the next Labour administration. The best opportunity to roll back the ruling-class offensive came with the Invergordon mutiny of 15 September 1931. 12,000 seamen, some of them threatened with a 25 percent cut in pay, refused to obey orders. When the issue was raised in parliament the official Labour spokesman said the mutiny was: 'a matter of extreme regret [and] created a dangerous precedent'.[48] The mutiny proceeded nonetheless, with instant success. Within days the financial panic it caused demolished the Gold Standard, the measure which had caused deflation and on whose altar the miners had been sacrificed in 1926. And on 21 September the National Government' 'discovered' that there were 'just' grievances to be answered. The wage cuts for teachers, police and the armed services were greatly reduced.[49]

Labour's resistance to economies was not helped by Snowden rightly claiming that 'nine-tenths of the [National Government's] economies... were adopted and approved by the late government'.[50] The October election brought further humiliation:

Labour votes in elections 1900–1929

1900	60,000
1906	300,000
1910	450,000 (the average of two elections)
1918	2.2 million
1922	4.2 million
1923	4.3 million
1924	5.5 million
1929	8.4 million
1931	6.6 million*

What felt worse than the loss of almost a quarter of the Labour vote was reduction to 46 seats in parliament and the ignominious end of the first generation of Labour leaders. Not just the renegades to the right, but Henderson, Clynes, Webb and many more were finished politically. The Second Labour government broke *thirty years of reformist continuity* and the pattern of relentless growth. Sidney Webb's phrase—'*the inevitability of gradualness*'—suddenly rang hollow.

The Labour Party did its best to cover up the degree to which Henderson, Graham and the other ministers had gone along with the cuts. At the party conference in October 1931 the chairman begged for all present to 'refrain from recriminations'.[51] The executive's conference report spent just half a page dealing with the collapse of the government. Some delegates pleaded in vain for a proper account of this most momentous event. But so derisory was support for a reference back that a card vote was deemed unnecessary.

There were a number of explanations for the extraordinary turn of events. The official Labour version had it that everything was plotted,

* It is important to note that this drop was not simply the result of the August 1931 crisis or the smear tactics of Snowden, who viciously turned on the party which had brought him to prominence. By-elections in March and June had already shown a catastrophic decline in the Labour vote. In May for example, the majority in St Rollox (Glasgow) fell from 8,000 to 1,382, in Rutherglen from 5,000 to 683 and in Gateshead from 16,000 to 1,392!

perhaps months or years in advance, by Ramsay MacDonald. Sidney Webb described the collapse as 'a single drama, in all its developments foreseen in advance-only by the statesman who was at once its author, its producer, and its principal actor'.[52]

It was true that thirty years of playing the parliamentary game had turned MacDonald and his National Government cronies into renegades. At the height of the crisis MacDonald told his daughter that 'all this sentimentality about workers is trash [and] the unemployed must sacrifice too',[53] and boasted: 'tomorrow every Duchess in London will be wanting to kiss me!'[54] Snowden may have been influenced by his wife who said 'she needs no friends because she is so intimate with the royal family',[55] and so on. Yet that was hardly an adequate analysis of the crisis, nor could it show how such characters could rule the party for years.

In reality, the collapse resulted from capitalist pressure and the failure of reformism. Labour had always told voters that the interests of workers could be advanced within the framework of capitalism. As the economic crisis grew deeper the appeals to keep that framework going grew louder. In 1931 the latent conflict between the needs of capital and workers became open.

The demise of the second Labour government proved beyond any doubt that *reformism cannot work when capitalism is in crisis.* No national capitalist state can long defy the power of capitalism: any reformist administration that tries to is doomed to be torn apart by the contradictions of its situation. The synthesis of class and nation, which reformism represents, simply cracks under the strain.

The political beliefs that led inexorably to 1931 were expressed by Snowden the year before:

> Some people call themselves Socialists and talk about the overthrow of the capitalist system. Arrant nonsense! What we had to do is not to overthrow the capitalist system, but to transform the capitalist system.[56]

The *starting point* for reformism was a healthy capitalist system.

One Labour MP grasped the full import of what happened in 1931. While Labour was still in office, W J Brown warned that the leadership's policy:

> struck at the very root of the whole philosophy of constitutional and peaceful progression... The essence of the idea upon which this party has been built is the idea that, if you could acquire sufficient political

> power in this House, you could...gradually transform our state of society into a new state... The Chancellor's speech today represents the complete destruction of that aim.[57]

Marx had looked to the workers' movement as 'the gravedigger of capitalism'. It was obvious that *Labour saw itself as the doctor whose duty was to cure capitalism.*

The contradictions of reformism which wrecked the second Labour government are linked to contradictions in capitalism. Reformism grew from a specific set of circumstances—a degree of balance between the working class and capitalists which allowed a relative truce in the class war. Through this there emerged the labour bureaucracy, to negotiate, politically and industrially, the terms of armistice. In 1931 the balancing act came to an end. But this did not mean the end of reformist consciousness.

In a crisis, neither the bureaucracy nor reformist ideas simply evaporated. Both endured so long as workers lacked confidence in their own power. Labour retained strong working class support, even when no reforms could be delivered.

Nevertheless, the crisis had profound effects. For those on the periphery of the Labour Party, reformism lost its attraction—since it was unable to counter the arguments of the outright defenders of capitalism. Outside its core support the Labour vote declined.

In 1931 there were three avenues open to Labour. One was to abandon reformism and shift to the right, as MacDonald and Co did when they formed the National Government. Another was to abandon reformism by shifting to the left and adopting a revolutionary outlook. There was no automatic swing in this direction since the general mood of the class was defensive and the Communist Party was on an ultra-left binge. The third was to hold on to reformism in its decaying, unstable form. This course was adopted by the majority of the working class, who now clung more desperately to Labour as the solution to their problems.

9

From socialist dictatorship to National Unity: Labour in the 1930s

IT IS a common feature of Labour's history that it swings leftwards after severe electoral setbacks, only to 'recover its senses' and return to its traditional stance in time for the next election This was true of Bevanism which grew up after the 1951 defeat, and of Bennism, which was stimulated by Tory victories in 1970 and 1979. But both movements seem pale in comparison with the radical images conjured up by the left in the 1930s.

The circumstances of the time powerfully contributed to this mood. The collapse of the second Labour government and disastrous election result had been engineered by international finance and clearly put into question the notion of a peaceful constitutional transition to socialism. Doubts were reinforced by the destruction of German bourgeois democracy by the Nazis, and by the slump. As Frank Wise, a leading left-winger, told the 1933 Labour conference: 'we are at the parting of the ways. We have either to go forward to Socialism or acquiesce in Fascism'.[1]

Unlike earlier radical postures, the leftism of the 1930s was not adopted to contain mass pressure from without. Even the right which had for years supported MacDonald, felt suddenly robbed of the old certainties, and toyed with new ideas. Although for the mainstream the political spasm was short-lived, it produced language far stronger than anything uttered since.

Thus Clem Attlee promised to deliver a death blow to capitalism:

> The moment to strike is the moment of taking power when the Government is freshly elected and assured of its support. The blow struck must be a fatal one and not merely designed to wound and to turn a sullen and obstructive opponent into an active and deadly enemy.[2]

He even moved towards the concept of a revolutionary party: 'The most urgent job of every socialist now is to...create advance guards of the revolution, and to create them *now*. For when the revolution comes it will be too late'.[3] He suggested they 'should train people to take over the commanding positions in the army and navy in the event of a revolution'.[4]

Herbert Morrison, a right-winger whose first reaction to the collapse of the second Labour government was to seek a place in the new National Government[5] swung sharply to the left. His initial reaction to the 1931 election result was:

> Labour must move to the Left in the true sense of the term—to the real Socialist Left. Not the spurious left policy of handing out public money under the impression that we are achieving a redistribution of wealth under the capitalist system. That is one of the illusions of reformism... The brain and manual workers...must be organized for the mutual service of the Commonwealth and not merely to collar the crumbs from the rich man's table.[6]

The most Christian R H Tawney now argued that capitalism could not be abolished gradually: 'onions can be eaten leaf by leaf, but you cannot skin a live tiger paw by paw; vivisection is its trade and it does the skinning first'.[7] Drunk with rhetoric, Hugh Gaitskell wanted to:

> smash the economic power of the upper class. When they had the power he believed they would be in a position to carry into action measures which were essentially revolutionary...[8]

Exit the ILP

The collapse of the second Labour government produced a new alignment on the Labour left. An opening for new forces had appeared because the ILP had broken away.

During 1929–31 the ILP had had 142 members among Labour MPs 37 of whom were financially sponsored by the ILP. Each was asked to accept 'the policy of the ILP as laid down by of the Annual Conference'[9]—apparently a modest and reasonable request. *Only eleven ILP-sponsored MPs agreed*, along with seven others! When the government collapsed in 1931 the ILP tore itself apart. Its conference voted to quit Labour in despair, while the majority of MPs left to stay with the Labour Party.

From this point on the ILP was in serious decline. It had not split in order to build a new movement on the basis of separate politics, but chiefly to preserve the independence of its left reformist parliamentarians. With shallow roots in the working class, the ILP found itself living off past accumulated capital that dwindled quickly. Membership plummeted—from 16,773 in 1931 to 11,092 in 1932 and just 4,392 in 1935.[10]

Cripps—a Jacobin in the ranks?

The collapse of the 1929–31 government had its strongest impact on Stafford Cripps, who became the most prominent front bencher after George Lansbury. Cripps was a very new recruit to the Labour Party, having joined it as recently as May 1929. He became an MP straight away, his path being smoothed by Morrison and his uncle and aunt—the Webbs. Cripps was offered a place in the National Government by MacDonald, and because of admiration for the man, it took him some time to make up his mind to reject the offer.[11]

But after the 1931 election he became a new person, turning the famous Fabian statement on its head: 'It is not now a question of the inevitability of gradualness. The one thing which is not inevitable now is gradualness'.[12] Reformists did not understand how false was the old belief 'that the capitalists will permit the change to be made within capitalism. The whole history of the Social Democratic movement in Europe negates any such idea'.[13]

Cripps predicted the need to thwart the opposition not only of international capitalism, but 'Buckingham Palace' and the army! He wrote of the first: 'I cannot imagine the Labour Party coming into power without a first rate financial crisis. That is why we ask for full emergency powers'.[14] On the second he said: 'When the Labour Party comes into power we shall have to overcome opposition from Buckingham Palace and other places as well'.[15] He finished by arguing: 'We have to face the problem of dealing with the armed forces of the Crown. The Labour Party has to be prepared to take steps more forceful than the steps taken at the time of the Ulster rebellion'.[16]

His position was summarised in his essay *Can Socialism Come by Constitutional Means?*, where he argued that to defeat its enemies a future Labour government would have to resort to draconian measures:

> The Government's first step will be to call Parliament together at the earliest moment and place before it an Emergency Powers Bill to be passed through all its stages on the first day. This Bill will be wide enough in its terms to allow all that will be immediately necessary to be done by ministerial orders. These orders must be incapable of challenge in the Courts or in any way except in the House of Commons...the Socialist Government would make itself temporarily into a dictatorship until the matter could again be put to the test at the polls.[17]

We have no more challenging statement from Labour leaders than this. However it is essential to separate oratory from serious intent. There is a simple test. Is the politician ready *to will the means as well as say the words?* Cripps never dreamt of going beyond parliamentarism, which meant his statements remained little more than daring oratory.

Thus when the National Government, the Labour leadership and the press attacked Cripps for his slur on the monarchy, his defence was that he was 'most certainly not referring to the Crown.' He had used the words Buckingham Palace as 'a well-known expression used to describe Court Circles and the officials and other people who surround the King.' Anyway, he wanted the monarchy retained![18]

On another occasion Cripps was attacked by the attorney-general who accused him of advocating violent revolution. This was too much for Cripps, who replied: 'I have always condemned revolutionary means and the Communist movement which relies on such means. I have stated that I believed in a very rapid change in the system by the method of Parliamentary Democracy'.[19]

In Cripps' writings and speeches at the time there was never a hint that workers' industrial power should be mobilised for political ends. His radical suggestion for the next Labour government to introduce Emergency Powers was encased within Labour's parliamentary tradition.

Rise and fall of the Socialist League

In October 1932 the Socialist League was founded to fight for the sort of radical policies Cripps advocated. It was a small organisation which at its peak in March 1934 claimed 74 branches and about 3,000 members.* It brought together a number of left MPs and intellectuals, including Frank Wise, Aneurin Bevan, George Strauss, Clem Attlee, Sir Charles Trevelyan, William Mellor, Ellen Wilkinson, D N Pritt, Harold Laski and H N Brailsford. Cripps was chairman while J T Murphy, who quit the Communist Party in 1931, was its secretary. Murphy saw the League as 'the organisation of revolutionary socialists who are an integral part of the Labour movement for the purpose of winning it completely for revolutionary socialism'.[20]

* The agenda of the important 1937 Socialist League conference contained twelve motions and nineteen amendments, only one of which was moved by a branch from outside London. The historian of the League, Patrick Seyd, drew the conclusion: 'the Socialist League, notwithstanding its national structure, followed a pattern which has since prevailed for most Labour left factions, namely, of being London-based with little organisation elsewhere.'[21]

As long as the Labour leadership was stunned by 'MacDonald's betrayal' the League was an effective ginger group. For a couple of years—1932 and 1933—it was given free rein and enjoyed an influence out of proportion to its size.

At the 1932 Labour Conference Frank Wise defeated the platform with his proposal to go beyond nationalisation of the Bank of England to take other banks into public ownership on the grounds that control of them would be essential for real socialist planning.[22] Another successful League resolution laid down 'that the leaders of the next Labour Government and the Parliamentary Labour Party be instructed by the National Conference that, on assuming office...definite Socialist legislation must be immediately promulgated...we must have Socialism in deed as well as in words.'[23]

Henderson warned conference against tying the Parliamentary Labour Party's hands. But Attlee supported the resolution, on these grounds:

> we are bound in duty to those whom we represent to tell them quite clearly that they cannot get Socialism without tears, that whenever we try to do anything we will be opposed by every vested interest, financial, political, and social, and I think we have got to face the fact that, even if we are returned with a majority, we shall have to fight all the way.[24]

So clear was the sentiment of the delegates for the resolution that it was carried without a card vote.*

At the 1933 conference, the left resumed its offensive. Cripps wanted an assurance that the next Labour government would immediately abolish the House of Lords, and pass an Emergency Act 'to take over or regulate the financial machine, and to put into force any measure that the situation may require for the immediate control or socialisation of industry and for safeguarding the supply of food and other necessaries.'[25]

However this important motion was not voted on. Despite all its verbal radicalism, the left had an Achilles heel, which showed when Cripps announced his willingness to grant the executive a year to consider the problems raised by their resolution. He thus avoided a vote and direct confrontation.

The victories of the left at the 1932 and 1933 Labour Party Conferences were victories on paper. It remained to be seen whether the millions of

* The policy decisions of the 1932 conference favoured the left. Few noticed that the elections to the national executive failed to reflect this trend. The right-wingers Dalton and Morrison were easily returned for the constituency section, while Frank Wise and Clem Attlee trailed far behind. (Until 1937 the whole conference, including the trade unions, voted for the constituency section).

votes cast for the League at conferences represented any genuine shift of opinion among the working class.

The panic engendered in 1931 began to subside by the middle of the decade. The empire cushioned British capitalism from the worst rigours of the slump: Britain did not have 33 percent unemployment, like the US, or six million out of work, as Germany did when Hitler took power. Bourgeois democracy survived and the Labour leadership discovered that reformist business could go on. The blood and thunder of the Socialist League need be tolerated no longer.

The right reasserted its dominance at the 1934 Labour Conference. The political perspective and language of the Socialist League still had great influence, but once the official juggernaut began moving even the most brilliant arguments on the conference floor could not stop it. The Socialist League was thrashed.

The main debates centred around the general document *For Socialism and Peace*. Subtitled 'The Labour Party's Programme for Action', the executive described it as 'a comprehensive and concise statement of policy.' *For Socialism and Peace* was far more incisive and definite than *Labour and the Nation* (1928). But it was vague about the time scale for public takeovers and emphasised 'the achievement of change by the process of consent.' The Labour Party 'sees no reason why a people who, first in the world, advanced through Parliamentary institutions their political and religious freedoms should not, by the same means, achieve their economic emancipation.'[26]

For Socialism and Peace challenged the idea of drastic emergency powers against capitalist obstruction. The Socialist League was not about to let such statements go, and it put down no fewer than twenty-two amendments to the draft—but lost all along the line.

The Communist Party moulds the Labour left

By 1934 disastrous defeats at Labour conference had cruelly exposed how shallow the League's base really was. To discover new sources of influence, it therefore turned to the Communist Party. Although both bodies shared common characteristics the contrast between them is instructive.

The fundamental weakness of the Labour left was lack of real links with the working class. It could mobilise constituency support, but when it came to the union block vote at conferences, the Labour left could only act indirectly, through the medium of the Communist Party. Cripps, Bevan or Pritt did not derive their political influence as representatives of workers in collective struggle, but from their standing in parliamentary politics; from oratorical brilliance, not the ability to lead activity. They occupied roles which gave them much more publicity than influence. So they were ready to quarrel with the leadership of the Labour Party, but not to break decisively with Labourism, as that would have meant undermining the element in the situation that gave them prominence.

The Labour Left was very heterogeneous, since left-wing criticism of the leadership could reflect a multitude of varied motives. Thus the National Council of the Socialist League, included D N Pritt, the most ardent Stalinist, and the ex-Liberal Sir Charles Trevelyan, an enthusiastic supporter of the League of Nations.

The Communist Party was quite different. It was a tightly organised body, but alas no longer the revolutionary party Lenin had helped to establish. After 1926 it uncritically followed every twist and turn made by the Comintern, itself a tool of the new Russian bureaucracy. However the Communist Party had one great advantage over the Socialist League. It still rejected Labour parliamentary cretinism and stressed workers' collective organisation, even if this was ultimately subordinated to the *diktat* of Stalinism. It had direct roots in the working class. This was demonstrated when the labour movement, practically dormant since 1926, re-awoke.

A low point had been reached when, from 1929 to 1933, the slump had dealt a further blow to trade union organisation, workers' confidence and the ability to fight. However from 1934 onwards things started changing. The number of trade unionists rose from 4,392,000 in 1933 to 6,298,000 in 1939. The number of strikes also rose from 359 in 1933 to a pre-war peak of 1,129 in 1937.[27]

This owed nothing to the Labour left, and still less the Labour Party as a whole. Labour can reflect the movement in distorted form but it never initiates.

Richard Croucher's book, *Engineers at War*, explains some reasons for the revival:

> From about the beginning of 1934 there was a real change in the nature and tone of industrial relations in the engineering industry… The effect of seeing old mates, even in ones and twos, coming back into the shops, was out of all proportion to the numbers involved.[28]

The aircraft industry led the way, the number of workers leaping from 17,600 in 1930 to 140,000 in spring 1939.[29] Within the industry militant strikes were organised by a Communist-led shop stewards' movement—the Aircraft Shop Stewards' National Council and its paper, *The Propellor*.

1937 witnessed two strike waves of engineering apprentices which spread through the north and down to London.[30] Croucher writes that the movement 'for sheer enthusiasm and organisation invites comparison with the industrial upsurges in France and America in the same year'.[31] Once more the Communist Party was in the lead, the chairman of the central strike committee being in the Young Communist League.

The same pattern was repeated in mining. To resist both the breakaway scab union run by George Spencer and the pressure towards 'non-political' unionism, the rank and file developed a new weapon, a stay-down strike. The main battle came in 1937 when miners at Harworth, who had overwhelmingly voted to join the Miners Federation, were compelled by the company to continue to subscribe to the Spencer union. Six miners were sentenced to terms of hard labour for picketing offences under the 1927 Trades Disputes Act and strikers were threatened with eviction from company-owned houses. The Miners' Federation voted for national strike action in Harworth's defence and management backed down. The Spencer union and its officials were then absorbed into the Federation, which now became the negotiating body for the industry. Once more Communists were in the forefront of the fight.[32] Indeed in practically all the significant strikes of these years Communist Party members played a prominent part.

Besides its own organisation in industry, the Communist Party relied on some ancillary organisations. First there was the National Unemployed Workers' Movement, which had considerable support. In contrast, throughout the 1930s the Labour Party did nothing practical about unemployment. It approved only of moves that assisted parliamentary opposition, believing little could be done until it was itself returned to office.

To fight the evil of unemployment 'the TUC promoted only the one demonstration, in February 1933, while the Labour Party remained opposed to demonstrations because of the threat to public order'.[33] The TUC demonstration was organised in complete collaboration with the police. This passive approach was significant. It presented the unemployed as helpless victims pleading for charity from society. A serious campaign against unemployment, for which the only solution was the abolition of capitalism, was bound to challenge law and order. That was why mass marches supported by the Communist Party were regularly met with brutality by the police.

The attitude of the Labour Party to the active unemployed movement was summed up well by John Saville:

> What was not lacking in vigour was the denunciation by the Labour leadership of bodies outside the Labour Party who were engaged in agitation on behalf of the unemployed. The most important was the National Unemployed Workers' Movement, who organised national hunger marches to London on four occasions: 1930, 1932, 1934 and 1936. Not one of these marches was officially supported, and in the first two the local Labour parties and trades council were specifically instructed to offer no help. The reason was that the NUWM was led by Communists. Only in 1936—and to a lesser extent in 1934—were the bans imposed widely disregarded. In the 1936 reception in Hyde Park Attlee was among a number of leading Labour personalities who spoke from one of the platforms.[34]

Saville chooses the Jarrow march as the best example of Labour's 'stupid, reactionary and politically self-destructive' attitudes.[35] Though one of the smallest hunger marches during the 1930s, it became legendary because it tamely obeyed the rules and did not seek to challenge the authorities. This self-styled 'non-political' march excluded known Communists and set off after every church and chapel in Jarrow had said prayers for it and the Suffragan Bishop had blessed it.[36] It sent the respective Tory and Labour agents for the constituency ahead to make arrangements.

In London, instead of the usual welcome for the unemployed—the end of a police truncheon, the Commons provided tea for the marchers and they were given the opportunity of 'cheering lustily' as the king passed their vantage point in the Mall.[37]

Ellen Wilkinson, MP for Jarrow, takes up the story. When she reached the 1936 Labour Party Conference things changed:

> I went from the warm comradeship of the road to an atmosphere of official disapproval. The Trades Union Congress had frowned on the marches, and the Labour Party Executive followed the lead... The Labour Party drew out, and the TUC circularized the Trades Council advising them against giving help. So in places like Chesterfield, where the Trades and Labour Council obeyed the circular, the Conservative Party weighed in with hot meals and a place to sleep. Mostly, of course, the comradeship of the trade unions and the Labour Movement was circular-proof on such an occasion...[38]

She was denounced from the conference platform for 'sending hungry and ill-clad men across the country on a march to London.' Her reply:

> You cannot expect men, trapped in these distressed areas, to stay there and starve because it is not convenient to have them coming to London.

> What has the National Council done? It disapproved of it. What has gone from the General Council? Letters to the local areas in fact saying, in the politest language, 'Do not help these men.' Why? Because some of these marchers might be Communists. I hope when Sir Walter Citrine gets to the pearly gates St Paul will be able to assure him there is no Communist inside.

The executive 'would not even let us take a collection for these men'.[39]

Another striking contrast between the attitudes of the Communist Party and the Labour Party to the primary issues of the 1930s was the question of Mosley's fascists. The Labour leaders may genuinely detest fascism and all its works. They have good reason, for fascism tries to annihilate all workers' organisations, upon which the reformists rely. However it is one thing to hate an enemy, it is another to know how to fight him. Precisely because fascists do not accept the rules of the parliamentary game, using terrorism and intimidation on the streets rather than the ballot box, the Labour Party finds it difficult to offer any practical resistance.

Thus in the 1930s the Labour Party was neither active nor effective, doing nothing to stop the march of the fascists, and not daring to go beyond passive protest against fascism.

When the Communist Party and ILP issued a call to demonstrate against the supporters of Mosley gathering at a mass rally in Hyde Park on 9 September 1934, the Labour Party executive declared that the counter-demonstration 'would almost inevitably lead to widespread disorder,' and Labour supporters should 'refrain from having anything whatever to do with the proposal'.[40]

Labour leaders' cynicism reached its height over the Battle of Cable Street of 4 October 1936. Mosley's Blackshirts decided to march through Stepney, at the time the centre of London's Jewish population. The Communist Party and ILP called for a mass demonstration to stop them and called on the local union branches, trades councils and Labour Party to support a counter march. Between 100,000 and 150,000 people took to the streets to stop 3,000 fascists. Notwithstanding the protection of 6,000 policemen plus all London's mounted police, the fascists could not pass through Cable Street.

What was the reaction of the Labour Party leaders? George Lansbury, whose pleas to the Home Secretary to divert the march failed, issued a statement urging people to stay away; the *Daily Herald* and the *News Chronicle* on 1 October implored readers to follow this advice, the latter saying 'The Communist has no more right to break up a Fascist meeting than the fascist has to break up a Communist demonstration.'[41]

The day after the Battle of Cable Street Morrison declared at the Labour Party Conference: 'I have no more sympathy with those who desire to stimulate disorder from one side as I have with those who desire to stimulate disorder from the other...' All he did was move an executive resolution to prohibit the wearing of political uniforms. This was approved unanimously.[42]

John Saville summed up the role of the Labour Party thus:

> All the major political initiatives and campaigns for which the 1930s are remembered were conducted either against the expressed wishes of the Labour leadership or without their approval.[43]

Given the contrast between the complete passivity of the Labour Party and the energy of the Communist Party it was no surprise that Cripps and Co should become increasingly dependent upon the latter. This was notwithstanding the tiny membership of the Communist Party, which, though it rose from 6,500 in 1935 to 12,250 in 1937, was dwarfed by the Labour Party.

Political dependence

The Labour left in the 1930s was dependent on the Communist Party both for links with extra-parliamentary activity and for its ideas.

Keir Hardie's ILP had been an amalgam of ethical arguments, Liberalism and above all Fabianism—all three originating from within the ruling class. Maxton's ILP leant heavily on the ideas of the former Liberal J A Hobson. Soon the Liberals Keynes and Beveridge would gain ascendancy. It might appear that the Socialist League was an exception, since it rejected all of these trends, as symbolised by Cripps' repudiation of 'the inevitability of gradualness'. Its close relations with the Communist Party led it to talk about Marxism.

But the Communist Party was now a thoroughly Stalinist organisation. Was Stalinism based on a different social class from Fabianism or Liberalism?* Although Stalinism had completely different origins—in the strangulation of the spirit of 1917, in the physical elimination of Bolsheviks and in the breakneck accumulation of capital through the exploitation of

* It should be remembered that the Webbs themselves renounced the 'inevitability of gradualness' in the wake of the 1931 crisis and became ardent supporters of Stalin and all his works.

the peasantry and workers—in fact it represented just another ruling-class theory, that of the state capitalist bureaucracy. It still employed the rhetoric of Marxism but only to cloak its intentions. So the 'dictatorship of the proletariat' had been transformed into the dictatorship of the bureaucracy, the socialist planned economy had been changed into five year plans for the forced industrialisation of a new capitalist state.

Of course when Cripps and the Socialist League talked of the need for a period of Labour government dictatorship and centralised economic planning they believed the Russian model represented a real socialist alternative to the chaos and looming fascism they saw in Western Europe. Nor was the Socialist League alone. The belief that planning and other Stalinist measures in themselves equal socialism was only seriously resisted by tiny groups of Trotskyists. Nevertheless, whether consciously or not, the League fell into the familiar trap of even the most extreme left reformists, and by relying on a ruling-class theory paid the political price.

So long as the marriage held, it was the Communist Party that overwhelmingly dictated terms. This becomes crystal clear if one reads *Left News* and above all *Tribune*, the weekly paper launched by Cripps on 1 January 1937. Many Socialist Leaguers practically became mouthpieces of Stalinism. Harold Laski, for example, relished the vile prosecution of Trotsky, whose supporters he described as 'strong allies of Nazi Germany in her militarist plans'.[44] John Strachey had no doubt that the Moscow Trials were absolutely fair. He was:

> wholly convinced of the authenticity of the confessions. I can only say that no man can advance his political education more than by studying this supreme historical document of our time.[45]

The solid wall of support for the Moscow Trials was breached for a time only when Marshal Tukhachevsky and other top officers of the Russian army were executed. The outcry in the Labour movement was far too great for *Tribune* to remain untouched. A number of trade unions that had supported the Socialist League-Communist Party alliance in 1936 now reversed their position including the engineers and the miners.

Until that time practically every issue of *Tribune* was adorned with pictures of smiling Russian children. Seven consecutive issues of the paper had a whole page on 'Women in the Soviet Union', by Barbara Betts, later better known as Barbara Castle. An entire page of the paper was devoted to Stalin's unscrupulous *History of the Communist Party of the Soviet Union (Bolsheviks)*, the superlative 'book of the hour'.[46]

When Russian foreign policy made a sharp turn with the signing of the Hitler-Stalin pact in the summer of 1939 the marriage was put in jeopardy. Even then *Tribune*'s initial reaction was to praise the Russians:

> A pact of non-aggression between Russia and Germany, if it is signed, will be a great reinforcement for peace in Eastern Europe. At the same time it is a lie to suggest that it leaves Germany a free hand against Poland or anyone else.[47]

Even after the Russian invasion of Poland on 17 September, articles appeared in *Tribune* justifying Russian foreign policy. This only stopped in November with the outbreak of Russia's war on Finland. From then onwards only the Communist Party slavishly followed the Moscow *diktat*, while the Labour left adopted a policy of the defence of Britain.

Foreign policy

This brings us on to the dominant issues of the 1930s: foreign affairs and the approach of war. The mainstream of the Labour Party soon settled into its customary position—supporting the traditional policies of the capitalist state and perhaps putting a vague reformist gloss upon them. For the most part Labour's slogan was 'collective security under the League of Nations'. However there were some who disagreed, including Lansbury, who was party leader after MacDonald's desertion and the defeat of his heir, Arthur Henderson, in the 1931 election.

The issue of foreign policy came to a head at the 1935 party conference, which coincided with Mussolini's attack on Abyssinia. The conference had before it an executive resolution pledging 'firm support of any action consistent with the principles and statutes of the League [of Nations], to restrain the Italian Government and to uphold the authority of the League in enforcing peace'.[48]

As a Christian pacifist, Lansbury's opposition to fascism took the form of turning the other cheek. Abyssinia was wrong to resist the Italians. 'If mine was the only voice in the conference, I would say in the name of the faith I hold, the belief I have that God intended us to live peaceably and quietly with one another—if some people do not allow us to do so, I am ready to stand as the early Christians did and say, "This is our fate, this is where we stand and if necessary, this is where we will die"'.[49]

This was followed by Ernest Bevin, who attacked Lansbury savagely. He accused him of 'hawking your conscience around from body to body asking to be told what you ought to do with it.' The resolution was carried overwhelmingly, by 2,168,000 votes to 102,000.[50] Since the alternative to the traditional policy of supporting the capitalist state was Lansbury's impractical pacifism, there was no real contest. Lansbury resigned from the leadership and was replaced by Attlee.

Lansbury's Christian pacifism was symptomatic of the intellectual dependence of Labour leaders on conservative ideas, and is therefore worth expanding on. His solution to the approaching war was:

> An international conference of the Heads of States...to provide funds for investment in backward areas, to stabilise currencies, to lower tariffs, and so set going again the wheels of industry all over the world. The sacrifices would be almost nil; the reward would be such a prosperity that no nation would be driven by despair into war-like preparations.

Lansbury decided to act on this suggestion. He visited the conventional statesmen and the unconventional ones, his travels including a meeting with Hitler which he described as 'a triumph'. 'He *will* not go to war unless pushed by others,' wrote Lansbury, describing Hitler publicly as 'one of the greatest men of our time'. Privately he described him as a distressed and lonely man. Lansbury believed quite honestly that if he had been able to speak German and could have stayed with the Fuhrer a short while at his country retreat in Berchtesgaden he could have calmed him and perhaps converted him to 'Christianity in its purest sense'. After this the warm reception he got from Mussolini caused no sensation.

Lansbury's later visits included Dr Schushnigg, the dictator of Austria, King Carol and his 'patriarch-premier', Myron Christen in Romania, and the butcher of Hungary, Admiral Horthy. All these dictators enthusiastically desired a Christian peace. At the time of the Munich Agreement, when Chamberlain returned from his meeting with Hitler waving a piece of paper and declaring it meant 'peace in our time', Lansbury was one of his ardent supporters.[51]

It is difficult to think of any other working-class party in the world that could produce a leader with the muddleheadedness and reactionary ideas of Lansbury.

After Abyssinia another crisis in foreign affairs faced the Labour leaders—the civil war in Spain. Franco launched this in June 1936 against the recently elected Popular Front government. It became at once a central issue facing the working class movement.

The British government, in association with other leading powers, advocated 'non-intervention', which was supposed to mean an agreement not to supply arms to the combatants on either side. In fact behind the screen of 'non-intervention' the Germans and Italians sent planes and supplies to help Franco. Later the Italians even sent whole armies to Spain.

At the Labour Party Conference in October 1936 the main argument used by the supporters of 'non-intervention' was the fact that it was advocated by the French Popular Front government. There was not a word about the pressure the British government exerted on the French to adopt non-intervention; not a word of criticism of the spinelessness of the French Socialist prime minister Leon Blum in the face of British pressure.

In the conference debate Aneurin Bevan exposed the fraud of non-intervention:

> Is it not obvious to everyone that if the arms continue to pour in to the rebels in Spain, our Spanish comrades will be slaughtered by hundreds of thousands? Has Mr Bevin and the National Council considered the fate of the Blum Government if a Fascist Government is established in Spain? How long will French democracy stand against Fascism in Germany, Fascism in Italy, Fascism in Spain and Fascism in Portugal?[52]

Support for non-intervention was carried by 1,836,000 votes to 519,000.

Although doubts about the wisdom of this policy grew, the Labour Party did not go beyond passive protest. True, the following year's Labour Conference decided unanimously to oppose non-intervention,[53] but this led to nothing more than a few speeches in parliament, not the organisation of mass movements in the streets, factories or mines.

To salve their consciences the Labour leaders organised relief measures and Red Cross services for the Spanish Republicans. But even this was done on a miserable scale. Thus the 1937 Labour Party conference was informed that from 1 August 1936 to mid-July 1937 £126,000 was collected for the International Solidarity Fund. The British trade unions contributed £37,000 of this.[54] Two years later the 1939 conference was told by the national executive that 'approximately £53,000 had been raised by the National Council of Labour in the country for the International Fund'.[55]

The left alternative

If the Labour leadership's record on foreign policy was summed up by its appalling abandonment of Republican Spain, the left at least began with quite a distinct and radical policy. Thus Cripps' *Can Socialism come by Constitutional Means?* included a chapter entitled: 'Permanent Peace Impossible with Capitalism'. In 1933 the Socialist League won executive acceptance of discussions as to 'what steps, including a general strike, are to be taken to organise the opposition of the organised working-class movements in the event of war or threat of war'.[56]

Once the tide turned against the League, however, this decision became meaningless and within a year the Labour Party openly and completely repudiated the resolution on the general strike and war.

Argument also raged over the League of Nations. A 1934 Labour statement on *War and Peace* took a strong line in support of the League of Nations and proposed a 'Peace Pact' to embody the obligations derived from the League Covenant. *War and Peace* wanted 'to abolish all national armed forces maintained for the purpose of self-defence against other nations', and to substitute 'the international police force under the League's authority.'

At the 1934 conference the Socialist League had denounced the League of Nations as indissolubly bound up with the Treaty of Versailles, which had concluded the First World War, and as a defender of the *status quo*. 'The League of Nations inevitably reflects the economic conflicts of the capitalist system [and] cannot end war.' Instead a Labour Government should 'seek to establish the closest political and economic relations with the Soviet Union and with all other countries where Socialist Governments are in control.' In 1933 this might have passed. In 1934 it stood no chance, gaining 269,000 against the right's 1,953,000.[57]

Another issue was a united front against fascism. In January 1933 Hitler came to power. In February 1934 the executive of the Second (Socialist) International declared the need for united working-class resistance to fascism and its readiness for common action with the Comintern. The latter responded with a call to Communist Parties in each country to seek to convene a conference to form a united front. The Communist Party of Great Britain there upon approached the Labour Party, the TUC and the Co-operative Party on the question. The ILP also issued an appeal for a united front, and in March arrived at general agreement with the Communist Party to bring it about.

What was the reaction of the Labour leaders? The Labour National Joint Council declined the proposal of the Communist Party and ILP, and issued a manifesto, *Democracy versus Dictatorship*, in which it coupled a denunciation of Nazi dictatorship in Germany with Communist dictatorship in the Soviet Union, and argued that Nazism was a reaction to the dictatorial 'reaction of the Left'. It said in effect that Nazism and Communism were much the same, and so rejected any notion of a united front.

The Labour Party executive adopted strong measures against bodies influenced by the Communist Party's call for a united front and issued a general circular urging its affiliates to have no dealings with such bodies. It also published a pamphlet, *The Communist Solar System*, which aimed to expose the tactics of the Communist Party in working through front organisations.

At the 1934 Labour Party conference Ernest Bevin argued that the activities of the Communists had brought about the fascist menace: '...if you do not keep down the Communists you cannot keep down the Fascists.'[58] The Left was badly routed. The vote was 1,820,000 against the united front, and 89,000 for.[59]

Although the united front was far better than the Labour leadership's do-nothing attitude, there were difficulties with it. The Labour left sought the united front as a means of utilising the Communist Party's connections with workers. The Communist Party, on the other hand, wanted the Labour left leaders for its own purposes. For a time the marriage of convenience held. It was helped by the fact that the two parties shared a common view of the united front, seeing it as largely parliamentary. This was miles away from the concept of the united front put forward by Lenin and Trotsky. Trotsky's words on the united front were a book closed with seven seals to them, when he wrote: 'The united front opens up numerous but nothing more. In itself, the united front decides nothing. Only the struggle of the masses decides.'[60]

At the 1936 Labour Conference the proposal for a united front was lost by 1,805,000 to 435,000.[61] A few months later, in January 1937 the Communist Party, ILP and Socialist League signed a *Unity Manifesto* calling for 'Unity in the struggle against Fascism, Reaction and War, and against the National Government...in the struggle for immediate demands and the return of a Labour Government, as the next stage in the advance to working-class power.' The Labour Party executive reacted at once with a statement on 'Party Loyalty' which reiterated conference's decision making united action with the Communist Party 'incompatible with membership of the Labour Party.'

In January the executive disaffiliated the Socialist League, after attempts at delaying action had been lost by fourteen votes to nine. Ernest Bevin was in a nasty mood: 'I saw Mosley come into the Labour Movement and I see no difference in the tactics of Mosley and Cripps.'[62] Soon membership of the Socialist League was made incompatible with membership of the Labour Party.[63]

The Socialist League faced an impossible position. First, not all its members solidly supported the *Unity Manifesto*. Its specially convened conference had voted by 56 delegates for, 38 against, with 23 abstentions.[64] Secondly, and above all, the *raison d'etre* of the League was its being part and parcel of the Labour Party. Membership of the League was confined to Labour Party members; its first rule stated that 'all members are expected to become individual members of their Constituency Labour Parties.'

So the League had little alternative but to disband, doing so at its Whitsun conference in 1937. It decided:

> This conference...having determined to do its utmost to prevent any splits or breakaways from the Labour movement, is prepared to sacrifice its own organisation rather than allow its continued separate existence to be made an excuse for further disunity in the ranks of the workers.[65]

In the meantime, the Unity Campaign Committee continued an active propaganda campaign of meetings throughout the country, first under the auspices of the three bodies, the Communist Party, ILP and Socialist League, and then of only the first two, with the participation of some ex-Leaguers as individuals. In addition, ex-Leaguers formed a 'Committee of Party Members Sympathetic to Unity' which carried on a separate campaign of its own. Michael Foot remembers the meetings organised were 'on a scale that dwarfed anything known for years'.[66]

The Labour Party executive duly banned the 'Committee of Party Members Sympathetic to Unity', and prohibited any members from campaigning for the cause of unity with the Communists and the ILP. A number of affiliated organisations sent in resolutions for annual conference on the united front and the position of the Socialist League, but the executive used its power to disallow all of them.

The only way to get round this was by reference back of the executive report. Cripps, who moved the reference back, pointed out that the ban imposed on association with the Communist Party and ILP was 'not extended to those who associated themselves with members of opposing capitalist parties.' Harold Laski, seconding, said that if he had to choose between appearing on the same platform with Winston Churchill or Harry Pollitt, he had no doubt at all that his proper place was with Pollitt. In the debate Herbert Morrison used the disarray between the Communist Party, ILP and Labour Left most effectively:

> I understand Sir Stafford to say that you must never appear with well-to-do persons on a platform, or a person of another Party, and that you

> ought to appear on a platform only with working class representatives... Would Mr Pollitt appear on a platform with Socialist, working-class Trotsky? He would not. If some of the leaders of the POUM in Spain and a working-class Party came to London and the ILP wanted another united front platform with them and Mr Pollitt, Mr Pollitt would not appear. But Mr Pollitt will appear with the Duchess of Atholl.[67]

Two votes were taken, one on the issue of banning the Socialist League, the other on the executive's action on the united front. In both cases the reference back was heavily defeated.[68] Even among constituency delegates no more than one vote in three was cast for the united front.[69] But the left was still not completely on its back. In the elections to the executive Pritt, Laski and Cripps were among the seven elected for the constituencies, while Ellen Wilkinson secured her place in the women's section.

Sliding towards the Popular Front

Although the demand for an 'Anti-Fascist Front' had its problems, at least it called for working-class unity. Despite the movements parliamentary emphasis, its class character still had some role. However, the Labour left abandoned even this position. Events were precipitated by the foreign minister, Anthony Eden, who resigned over government appeasement of Germany after Hitler's annexation of Austria.

In the same month that Austria was occupied, March 1938, the Communist Party's *Daily Worker* called for the formation of a 'Peace Bloc' headed by Winston Churchill. The party was slavishly following orders from Moscow.

Cripps, who at that time still opposed co-operation with capitalist elements, executed a complete somersault. Within three weeks he was preaching the Popular Front. It was 'necessary to reconsider one's opinions and decisions in the light of changing events,' he said.[70] An example of his 'reconsidered opinion' was his presiding over a rally for Spain which included speakers such as the Duchess of Atholl, a Conservative MP, Harry Pollitt of the Communist Party and D N Pritt.

The new line consisted of calling for a Popular Front. This meant workers allying with openly capitalist forces in the widest possible coalition of anti-government organisations. The object was to topple prime minister Chamberlain, stop appeasement and curb the expansionism of Hitler and Mussolini.

The 'anti-government' elements which were supposed to combat fascism included people like Winston Churchill, the arch reactionary of 1926 and a man who uttered admiring statements about Mussolini's Italy. Popular Front supporters ignored the fact that politicians like Churchill or Eden opposed appeasement not because they stood for the rights of small nations or workers' freedom to organise, but solely because they were concerned with a militant defence of British imperialism.

The new policy had catastrophic implications. Fascism had no respect for passive paper alliances. If the working class was to defeat fascism, it had to mobilise its economic, political and physical might. This was precisely what the Popular Front prevented. The price of the alliance with the 'democratic bourgeoisie' was the undermining of independent working-class struggle. The politicians who had stood by and watched the Spanish workers defeated by Franco were now expected to take the helm in the anti-fascist struggle.

The transition from the united front to the Popular Front was rapid but not always smooth. The ILP repudiated the turn towards the Popular Front and broke with the Communist Party and Labour left. But the ILP was a wasting force, both in numbers and political direction. Though it had left the Labour Party in 1932 it wanted to remain a left reformist organisation. This did not fit the situation at all. It was neither a serious alternative to Labour, nor did it have the authority of Russia behind it as the Communist Party did. In the face of the crisis posed by fascism it was crushed between these two millstones.

William Mellor, editor of *Tribune*, was shocked by the fact that with practically no internal discussion, Cripps and his friends on the Labour left could move from the united front to the Popular Front, from advocating the overthrow of capitalism as a prerequisite for peace to favouring class collaboration in order to oppose fascism. When Mellor, refused to swallow the new line he was removed unceremoniously from the editor's chair without one word of explanation. The change from united front to Popular Front was settled behind the scenes. Suddenly *Tribune* announced: 'Today we have a Government of national capitulation. We must replace it with a Government of national regeneration'.[71]

In the Labour Party the right-wing foreign policy of the Popular Front had no more success than the united front, a left-wing foreign policy. The labour bureaucracy was at this stage no more willing to sink its independence into an alliance with the capitalist class than it was prepared to stimulate grassroots activity against it. The issue of class and nation had still not been posed sharply enough. It was the war that led the labour bureaucracy to make its usual response to crisis—rushing to the defence of the capitalist *status quo*.

In January 1939 Cripps sent a memorandum to the secretary of the Labour Party, calling for a Popular Front open to every opposition group. At the executive Cripps' proposal was defeated by 17 votes to 3. (The three who voted for the memorandum were Cripps, Wilkinson and Pritt).[72]

Cripps' boomerang from class politics to an all-class alliance was ridiculed by Attlee. He was bemused by the 'remarkable' turn from 'the advocacy of a rigid and exclusive unity of the working classes to a demand for an alliance with capitalists, and from insistence on the need for a Government carrying out a Socialist policy to an appeal to put Socialism in cold storage for the duration of the international crisis.' Attlee penned this scurrilous verse:

The people's flag is palest pink.
It is not red blood but only ink.
It is supported now by Douglas Cole
Who plays each year a different role.
Now raise our palace standard high
Wash out each trace of purple dye,
Let Liberals join and Tories too
And Socialists of every hue.[73]

After the executive rejected Cripps' memorandum he circulated it widely under the auspices of an *ad hoc* National Petition Committee. The executive took strong objection to his action, and demanded that Cripps withdraw the memorandum. He refused and the executive expelled him by 13 votes to 11.[74]

Despite protest in the Labour ranks the May 1939 Labour Conference confirmed Cripps' expulsion by 2,100,000 votes to 402,000[75] and rejected the Popular Front by 2,360,000 to 248,000.[76] Cripps had not even rallied the constituency vote. More than three-fifths of the constituency delegates apparently voted against him on the expulsion issue, and fewer than one in six backed the Popular Front.[77]*

Expulsion did not stop with Cripps. At the end of March the executive expelled Bevan, Strauss, Trevelyan and a number of others

* Outside the Labour Party Cripps indulged in general politicking: he tried to convince individual Tory leaders to join forces against Chamberlain and establish a government of all parties. On 28 June 1939 he wrote in his diary: 'I had an hour with Oliver Stanley [a Conservative MP] and completely convinced him of the urgent need of an all-in Government. I told him who I had already seen and begged him to start doing something.'[78] Cripps approached Churchill, Baldwin and Halifax, who was at the time foreign secretary in the Chamberlain government.

who refused to withdraw their support from Cripps' campaign.[79] Bevan came under pressure from the executive of the Miners' Federation to accept the conditions laid down by the Labour Party executive and seek readmission. This he did in December 1939, and was accepted.

The extraordinary contortions that the Labour left achieved showed how completely disoriented and fuzzy was their thought. Lacking any theoretical foundations, revolutionary traditions or clear programme, the Labour left disintegrated in the fever of the threatening war.

Yet another acrobatic feat was performed by the Labour left when Britain entered the war in late 1939. The Hitler-Stalin pact in August completed the political transition to support for a war which not so long before it had vowed to oppose. Once more *Tribune*'s editor was the sacrificial lamb. H J Hartshorn, who stuck closely to the Communist Party line, and had got his job just for that reason in 1938, was unceremoniously kicked out. Again *Tribune* did not explain. With the Russian attack on Finland in November, the paper abruptly became a vociferous opponent of Russia and the Communist Party. Thus an editorial on the attack stated: 'It is useless to conceal from ourselves that this action of the Soviet Union has profoundly shocked Socialist opinion throughout the world. The diplomatic preparation for the invasion smelt more of *Mein Kampf* than of the *Communist Manifesto*'.[80] In the stampede towards nationalism, former principles were trampled underfoot. In 1933 the Socialist League had resolved:

> that war between nations arises directly from the necessities of capitalism and imperialism, [we] pledge ourselves neither to fight nor in any way actively to help in such a war, nor to support any policies or actions that put the interests of a miscalled patriotism before those of the workers throughout the world.[81]

The League's 1935 conference reiterated: 'the Movement must declare that under no circumstances will it assist in a war waged under capitalist rule'.[82]

But for the Labour left the four years that separated 1935 from 1939 were 'a very long time in politics'. Trotsky said that the revolutionary party is the memory of the class. Cripps and his friends suffered from amnesia and were now beating the war drum as enthusiastically as anyone.

Disciplining the youth

Time and again, the Labour Party leadership has conflicted with its various youth movements. Labour's youth movements are classic examples of activism without power. Youthful energy is handy when canvassing, but since young people do not have the vote, and tend anyway to 'extremism', they should 'be seen but not heard'.

In the 1930s the Labour Party League of Youth was officially described as

> an integral section of the Labour Party organisation [but] it does not deal with questions of Party policy. The Annual Conference of the Party alone deals with these. The League of Youth activities should be mainly recreational and educational.[83]

It was an impressive organisation with more than 15,000 members. Its conferences repeatedly asked for the right to discuss party policies. The executive consistently refused. The 1936 Conference of the League of Youth

> demanded complete freedom for *The New Nation* [the Youth monthly], including the right to use the paper to criticise Party policy; demanded the right to reach decisions upon policy matters and to give full publicity to decisions reached without any regard to decisions already reached by Party Conference; asked that the Advisory Committee should be given Executive powers and not be responsible to the National Executive Committee; and passed a resolution in support of a 'United Front' of all working-class Youth Organisations.[84]

Only one delegate in the League of Youth Conference supported the stance of the party executive.[85]

The reaction of the executive was swift and harsh:

> The National Executive Committee have...decided to:
> a. disband the National Advisory Committee of the League of Youth;
> b. not to convene the Annual Conference of the League next Easter;
> c. suspend publication of *The New Nation*.[86]

But the resistance continued, so the 1937 party conference decided to remove the youth representative from the executive.[87]

In 1939 trouble started all over again. The executive alleged that the League of Youth's National Advisory Committee was again exceeding its function. Its secretary, Ted Willis, had committed the heinous crime of 'condemning the National Executive Committee and supporting Sir Stafford Cripps's Popular Front Campaign...'[88]

If the youth demanded they be heard, Labour decided they would not be seen. In March the party executive wound up the League's

National Advisory Committee, disbanded its local committees, cancelled its conference and closed down its paper, now renamed *Advance*, even though—or perhaps because—its circulation had recently risen from 9,000 to 15,000.[89] It is not accidental that the same meeting of the executive which passed these draconian measures was the same one that expelled Cripps from the Labour Party.

Right-wing Labour repels the youth. The conservative bureaucracy of the Labour Party always tries to stifle its youth movement, which reflects the hopes, aspirations and impatience of the young. As it was in the 1930s, so it has been in the 1980s, when the crushing of the left includes the breaking of Labour's youth organisations.

Conclusion

The change that the Labour Party underwent in the immediate aftermath of the 1931 debacle and the radicalisation of the Labour Left in the following years were practically restricted to resolutions and speeches. Fine oratory at Westminster and in conferences was accompanied by no action outside at all. The left leaders shone as public speakers, but not as organisers of workers in struggle. Ultimately they proved unable to break with Labour's right-wing leadership, because that would have meant rejecting precisely those elements in the situation that gave them personal prominence. So they were unwilling, even resentful prisoners of the parliamentary right which in a bloc with the trade union bureaucracy, controlled the Labour Party.

On the face of it. Labour seems capable of great transformations. Because it is based on a combination of two incompatible elements, class and nation, it can dramatically switch emphasis from one to the other. An important factor in this is whether Labour is in office or not. Thus as a governing party from 1929–31 it acted as the loyal manager of capitalism; when it was hurled into opposition it was for a couple of years intoxicated with revolutionary rhetoric. This apparent instability, however, conceals a rock-hard and consistent trend which is impervious to change because it is bound up with the fixed social interests of a particular group—the labour bureaucracy. It might seem that there was nothing in common between MacDonald and Bevan, or indeed between Cripps in 1932 and Cripps the 'Chancellor of Austerity' in the 1945 Labour government after the war, but surface appearances are in these cases highly misleading.

10

The Labour Party during the Second World War

It is a commonly held myth that the Second World War was a 'People's War' against fascism, which rose above class interests. Like the First World War, however, it was an imperialist conflict. Although fascism was just one particular form of capitalism, this did not mean that socialists could afford to be indifferent to its threats to bourgeois democracy. That would have been dangerously ultra-left.*

Many of the freedoms which bourgeois democracy allows are the fruits of past workers' struggle. Such things as the right to organise in trade unions, hold demonstrations or publish and sell newspapers, weigh little when set against the economic enslavement of the working class, but they can be invaluable weapons in building the mass movement towards the point where capitalism can be overthrown.

However the Second World War was not a struggle of bourgeois democracy versus fascism. The ruthless suppression of movements for colonial liberation by the rulers of France and Britain, the policy of non-intervention which had allowed unrestricted fascist supplies to Franco, and the cold-blooded carving up of Europe after the war, all pointed in the same direction.

This war was indeed an imperialist one. The threat to the workers' movement and to the human race represented by modern capitalist militarism—of which fascism was but one guise—would in no way be ended by the victory of the Allies. Then, as now, the only real solution was successful workers' revolution. It was the task of socialists to build towards this revolution and *against* their capitalist rulers.

Needless to say, such considerations never entered the minds of the labour bureaucrats. In May 1940 the Labour Party joined a coalition government led by Winston Churchill. The party executive agreed to this with only one dissenting voice. The Labour Party Conference endorsed it by 2,413,000 votes to 170,000. Opposition came only from pacifists, a few Trotskyists and some fellow-travellers of the Communist

* This has been the criminal policy imposed by Stalin on the German Communist Party, it had cleared a path for Hitler's rise to power in 1933.

Party, which at that time declared the war to be an imperialist war. In the Commons only two ILP MPs, Jimmy Maxton and Campbell Stephen, opposed a vote of confidence in the new government.

There was a clear division of tasks in the coalition. When it concerned fighting for the interests of capitalism abroad, the choice was Churchill, the Tory leader. But when it came to containing the class struggle at home, Labour had the advantage. That was why Ernest Bevin was made minister of labour and Herbert Morrison, home secretary. (Of course Labour was not entrusted with control of the purse-strings. A Tory, Kingsley Wood, was chancellor of the exchequer.)

The value of this arrangement was soon obvious. One of Bevin's first acts as minister was the passing of the Emergency Powers Act of May 1940, endowing his office with virtually dictatorial powers to conscript labour. Attlee explained:

> The Minister of Labour will be given power to direct any person to perform any services required of him... The Minister will be able to prescribe the terms of remuneration, the hours of labour, the conditions of service.[1]

Had the Tories attempted this alone the resistance might have been extensive. Instead only a handful of Labour MPs raised any queries. One was David Kirkwood who probably remembered his jail experience in the last 'war to end all wars' of 1914–18: 'Am I in a position to say that if Labour is conscripted, so will wealth be conscripted?' The Bill passed unanimously without any amendments.

On 4 June 1940, a joint consultative committee composed equally of employers and TUC representatives agreed that for the duration of the war strikes and lockouts would be banned and arbitration would be binding in their place. This agreement was embodied in Bevin's Order 1305 which regulated industrial relations until 1945.

Order 1305 did not aim to arrest recalcitrant workers, since this was impossible on a mass scale. The effect of declaring a strike illegal was largely to strengthen the power of union officials over the members. Nevertheless, during the war 2,200 breaches of Order 1305 were reported leading to the prosecution of 6,281 people, of whom 5,100 were convicted. (Proceedings were taken against groups of workers 109 times, against employers just twice.)[2]

With the rising wave of strikes at the end of 1943 and beginning of 1944, Bevin wanted a much harsher measure than Order 1305. His speech of 4 April 1944 startled his audience when he said that the whole conciliation machinery was in danger of being wrecked by striking miners:

> What has happened this week in Yorkshire is worse than if Hitler had bombed Sheffield and cut our communications. It is the most tragic thing that in Britain you can do more harm by thoughtless action and lack of discipline than your enemy can do to you.[3]

Bevin received full support from the TUC General Council in driving the miners back to work. It was as a result of this crisis that Regulation 1AA emerged to strengthen the authorities against 'anyone who attempted to foment or exploit a strike in an essential service. The penalty for incitement was raised to a maximum of five years' penal servitude or a fine of £500 or both'.[4]

Despite the support of the General Council, there was resistance to Regulation 1AA at the TUC Congress itself. Reference back of the General Council statement was only defeated by 3,686,000 to 2,802,000.[5] The law would in fact have been powerless against a united workforce, but the new Regulation was used mainly as a psychological threat. It was never used in practice before its withdrawal in May 1945.

The government shows its true colours

Another area in which the government showed its real nature was that of the repeal, or at least amendment, of that notorious act of revenge for the General Strike—the Trades Disputes Act. From early 1940 the TUC pleaded in vain for its repeal. Eventually Churchill wrote stating that this was impossible during the war.

> I am convinced that to propose to Parliament repeal or even modification of this Act would start a controversial discussion which might well develop into difficulties which will hamper our war effort.[6]

A TUC delegation discovered 'that the decision which had been come to was a decision of the whole Cabinet—which rather startled us'.[7] The 1943 Labour Conference added its voice for repeal. But when it appeared that Attlee, Bevin and Morrison were willing to enforce the punitive provisions of the Act against the civil servants the campaign folded. Other issues that aroused anger were the detested means test and miserly pensions.*

The reactionary character of the government showed itself not only in home policy, but in foreign policy.

* It was against Bevin's defence of the paltry pensions increase of 1942 (2s 6d per week, or 12½p in today's currency) that 63 MPs voted against the government, the biggest vote against since Churchill became prime minister.[8]

Let us start with Britain's attitude to India. With the entry of Japan into the war on 7 December 1941, the question of winning the support of Indian political parties for the British war against the advancing Japanese became very important. For a long time Churchill made it clear that he was against the independence of India. In 1941 he declared that the Atlantic Charter, with its promise of self-determination of peoples, applied primarily to Europe.[9] On 22 March 1942, Cripps was sent to India to pacify Indian Congress Party leaders who refused to support the war unless India was granted independence.

> It was transparently a mere manoeuvre, prompted by the new danger to the subcontinent from the Japanese. Cripps offered the Cabinet's promise of full independence after the war. Mahatma Gandhi, with justice, refused to accept what he called a 'post-dated cheque'.[10]

In August 1942 the Indian Congress Party began civil disobedience to force the British to quit India. Gandhi, Nehru and other Congress leaders were arrested, with Cripps' approval. Attlee chaired the cabinet meeting which approved the detention of these leaders. When this was revealed in the Commons, Aneurin Bevan shouted, 'Then they ought to be ashamed of themselves. They do not represent us'.[11] British repression led to nearly 1,000 people being killed by November 1942. This was followed by a famine in Bengal that cost the lives of as many as one and a half million. On 20 November Churchill restated his aim to preserve the empire. 'I have not become the King's First Minister in order to preside over the liquidation of the British Empire'.[12]

Another example of reactionary foreign policy was the affair of Admiral Darlan who, after Petain and Laval, was the most notorious collaborator with the Nazis in the French Vichy government, formed under German occupation. On 8 November 1942 US and British troops landed in Morocco and Algeria and prepared to move towards Tunisia. There was opposition from the Vichy French, but suddenly, when it was clear that the Allies were winning in North Africa, Admiral Darlan, who was visiting the area, turned round and joined the Allies. He was welcomed with open arms, as though there was nothing to forgive.

> As the allies moved forward to victory, such cases would often arise, and with them renewed suspicion that Churchill wanted, not a New Order in Europe, based on the Resistance movements, but a return to the Old Order presided over by monarchs, industrialists and military men, whether or not they had collaborated. Even on the right, many

were sickened by the respect now shown for a man who had associated so closely with Petain and Laval.[13]

Nye Bevan led the protest, writing:

> What kind of Europe have we in mind? One built by rats for rats? It may appear to some people a very clever idea to seduce and beguile these men who owe their power to hurt us to their having been the jackals of our enemies; but it does not bear that appearance to the millions of oppressed men and women in Europe to whom we look for help in our offensive against Germany. Are they to be expected to face torture, imprisonment and death so that the authors of their calamities may be feted by us?[14]

A new chapter of infamy started with the entry of US and British troops into Italy. On 25 July 1943, a coup overthrew the Italian fascist dictator Mussolini. He was replaced by the former Italian Commander in Chief in Ethiopia, Marshal Badoglio, who soon turned towards the Allies. The coup against Mussolini took place against the background of a huge strike wave, which swept Milan, Turin and other parts of Northern Italy.

Bevan won a parliamentary debate against government resistance and managed to touch a raw nerve, coming close to exposing the imperialist character of the war. Bevan began by reciting, amidst ever angrier interruptions, the speech which Churchill had delivered on a visit to Rome in 1927:

> I could not help being charmed, like so many other people have been, by Signor Mussolini's gentle and simple bearing and by his calm, detached pose, in spite of so many burdens and dangers... Anyone could see that he thought of nothing but the lasting good, as he understood it, of the Italian people, and that no lesser interest was of the slightest consequence to him.
>
> If I had been an Italian, I am sure that I should have been wholeheartedly with you from start to finish in your triumphant struggle against the bestial appetites and passions of Leninism...

Bevan went on:

> Let us make no mistake about this... There are many Members in the House who have no complaint against Fascism, except when it is strong enough to threaten them... There was no complaint either against Italy or against all her sins and vices. The whole Fascist setup was supported by a majority of this House...[15]

Another disgusting chapter in British foreign policy occurred when, in October 1944, the Germans withdrew from Greece. Churchill sent the British army to fill the vacuum and prevent a takeover by the Communist-dominated resistance movement, EAM. Churchill went to Moscow to clear the issue with Stalin. They discussed the division of spheres of influence among the Allies. Churchill jotted down on a half sheet of paper his ideas for the relative degree of control by the Great Powers in the Balkans as follows:

> Rumania: Russia 90%, others 10%.
> Greece: Great Britain (in accord with USA) 90%, Russia 10%.
> Yugoslavia: 50–50.
> Hungary: 50–50.
> Bulgaria: Russia 75%, others 25%.

Stalin took his blue pencil and made a large tick upon it.[16] Churchill's instruction to the British army was to 'treat Athens like a conquered city' and within a month it was fighting the EAM, which had carried the main burden of the struggle against the Nazis in Greece. Stalin, as good as his word, stood by while 60,000 British troops turned on the Communists. In the House of Commons a motion of censure was moved by Seymour Cox of the *Tribune* group but was lost by 279 to 30, with the official Parliamentary Labour Party abstaining.[17]

At the Labour Party Conference the following week, many agreed with the left's outrage at the Greek events. But the leadership had put its prestige on the line over this issue. Wielding the union block vote given 'out of loyalty rather than conviction' the party executive won by 2,455,000 votes to 137,000[18]

As a gauge of the constituency delegates' mood, one could point to the result of the elections for constituency party members on the executive. Harold Laski, a strong critic of the party leaders but not an MP, came top; Emmanuel Shinwell, a strong critic inside the House of Commons, came second; and most significant of all, Nye Bevan, standing for the first time, secured the fifth place out of seven.

The Labour left's illusions in the coalition government

When the coalition government was formed the Tories had an overwhelming majority in parliament and took the lion's share of cabinet posts. In view of this it seems amazing that the left of the Labour Party should imagine the government would implement numerous progressive measures. How could anyone believe that prime minister Winston Churchill with a 30-year record as ruling-class bloodhound, was the modern saviour? He had been responsible for the repression of miners at Tonypandy before the First World War, organiser of intervention against Bolshevik Russia, and most vicious opponent of the 1926 General Strike.

No Tory politician had illusions that the Churchill government would introduce measures of a socialist nature, but Nye Bevan, Laski and Co were full of this idea; the logic of the war, the need for victory, would lead Churchill to see the light. Utopian irrationalism took the place of a rational explanation of class interests and motivation. George Orwell noted in his diary on 20 June 1940:

> I don't think he [Churchill] would jib at any step (eg, equalisation of incomes, independence for India) which he thought necessary for winning the war.
>
> Well, if only we could hold for a few months, in a year's time we shall see red militia billeted in the Ritz, and it would not particularly surprise me to see Churchill or Lloyd George at the head of them.[19]

On 1 June 1940 Laski declared the democratic revolution had begun: 'We cannot actually achieve socialism during the war, but we can institute a whole series of Government controls which after the war may be used for Socialist ends'.[20]

John Strachey, his biographer tells us, regarded criticism of Churchill as 'scarcely conceivable'[21], and Bevan said: 'I yield to no one in my personal admiration of the Prime Minister's qualities'.[22]

The most extreme case of adoration was the book *Guilty Men* by Cato, published in 1940. Cato was the pseudonym for several authors, including Frank Owen and Michael Foot.* To bring into relief the strength of Churchill, the book exposes the pacifism of Ramsay MacDonald. MacDonald neglected the equipment of the armed forces. 'He had been a pacifist in 1914–19 and therefore felt no anxieties about the strength of the Air Force'.[23] MacDonald and Baldwin

> found us at the end of a great war, wounded indeed and weary, but victorious, confident of solving our manifold problems and capable of doing so. MacDonald and Baldwin took over a great empire, supreme in arms and secure in liberty. They conducted it to the edge of national annihilation.[24]

But now salvation was at hand:

* Incidentally, Michael Foot, as well as Aneurin Bevan, were very much at home in the Beaverbrook circle in the 1930s. Foot even became editor of Beaverbrook's *Evening Standard*.

> In Mr Churchill as premier, and in his three service supply chiefs, Ernest Bevin, Herbert Morrison, and Lord Beaverbrook (to name only four) we have an assurance that all that is within the range of human achievement will be done to make this island 'a fortress'.[25]

In the Popular Front vice

If the leadership of the Labour Party during the war was the complete prisoner of social patriotism, the Labour Left was the prisoner of Popular Frontism. Its arguments for reforms, for social change, were always in terms of the national interest. In the pages of *Tribune* for example, Nye Bevan wrote: 'If the Tory members of the Government carry their defence of private property rights to the extent of refusing the public ownership [of land, mines and railways] then we shall lose the war'.[26] The class-nation synthesis, which is the essence of reformism, applied to the Left as much as to the right.

A central theme in *Tribune* from 1941 onwards was that the profit system impeded the war effort, that national needs called for the power of capital to be restricted. Again and again the call for nationalisation, of mines or railways, was put forward in the name not of working-class interests, but of the national interest. Thus Bevan's argument for raising the old age pension was:

> It is most important for maintaining national unity and morale at the present time.
>
> We are very anxious to preserve *the façade of national unity* for a year or so because we are still going to face great military adventures. Why do Hon Members not help us to preserve it?[27]

Even when Bevan was most critical of the coalition government he still did not see its policy as an *inevitable* outcome of the class which dominated it. For instance he wrote:

> Labour has brought about no change of importance on the economic front... Why is this? There is no reason why it should be so... If Labour insisted upon it, if Labour demands, that the railways shall be nationalised as an essential step towards the successful prosecution of the war, no vested interest would dare raise any objection.[28]

The main crime of the ruling class, it seemed, was not exploitation but incompetence. Bevan criticised Churchill, not as a defender of ruling-class power, but for his failure to agree that: '*There is one dominant consideration and that is to win the war*. Property as well as men should be commandeered by the state.'[29]

While the *Tribune* Group was still following the Popular Front policy it adopted before the war, there were some crucial differences.

In the 1930s the Socialist League and the *Tribune* Group shadowed the Communist Party. Those links were gone. Mixed with Laski's references to Russia as a 'socialist commonwealth,'[29a] and G D H Cole's suggestion that 'the best solution for Germany might be in co-operation in an enlarged USSR,'[30] were other statements very critical of Russia. Thus Raymond Postgate, editor of *Tribune*, could write a few months before the Nazi invasion of Russia:

> Just as I would have nothing to do with Himmler, Ley or the Commandant of Dachau Camp, nor believe a word they say, so I will have nothing personally or politically to do with Communist Party chiefs, nor sit on Committees, nor attend meetings where I might have to meet them, nor pay any attention to propaganda that they start.[31]

A few months before the end of the war an editorial in *Tribune* stated: 'The Soviet Union wishes to carve up Eastern Germany in order to have her own Quisling Government in Poland. That, of course, is naked power politics.'[32]

Although *Tribune* opposed the Communist Party's extreme anti-German chauvinism it did not advocate a policy of 'neither Washington nor Moscow' but 'both Washington and Moscow': the bridge between the two powers could be strengthened by small nations and the United Nations.

Thus an editorial in *Tribune* welcomed the 'Yalta conference of Britain, Russia and the USA.' This met on 11 February 1945. It was the last blaze of mutual harmony among the Allies. It was also one of the most coldly calculated imperialist meetings since the Versailles Conference in 1919.[33]

But despite its illusions, the Labour left became differentiated from the mainstream. When reality obviously failed to match the Popular Front icon, doubts surfaced. Failures on the military front in 1942 led *Tribune* to print the headline, 'War Office: Architect of Defeat.'[34] The impact of the fall of Tobruk, when Rommel captured 33,000 prisoners, was so great that in a parliamentary by-election the solid Tory seat of Malden was lost to Tom Driberg, a left-wing socialist standing as an Independent.

Even arch-right-wingers like Lord Beaverbrook began intriguing to get rid of Churchill.[35] In July Sir John Wardlow Milne, an influential backbench Conservative and chairman of the All-Party Select Committee on National Expenditure, moved censure on the Government and 'no confidence in the central direction of the war.' The seconder was a Tory Admiral of the Fleet.

The second morning of the debate was opened by Bevan with a massive attack on the government, on the War Office, on the generals: the main strategy of the war was wrong. The wrong weapons had been produced, and those weapons were managed by men not properly trained in their use.[36] The cross-party opposition, however, mustered only 25 votes against 475 for the government.

A few weeks after this debate Bevan launched an even more vigorous attack on Churchill: '...the Prime Minister's continuation in office is a major national disaster. He is no longer able to summon the spirit of the British people, because he represents policies that they deeply distrust'.[37]

Bevan and the *Tribune* Group did question the effectiveness of Labour's parliamentary strategy, yet they did so from within a shared premise about the centrality of parliamentary politics and the need for national unity and defence. The Popular Front policy in the 1930s strengthened the reformism of the Labour Left. Even after the Communist Party ceased to influence it, the politics of Stalinism, the muddledness and crudity of its 'Marxism' continued to mould left Labour thinking. This continued in different forms throughout the 1950s and beyond.

It was impossible for the Labour left to be consistent. Support of the 'war for democracy' did not square with Britain allying itself with semi-fascist and reactionary regimes. Labour was a member of the coalition government that allowed a most reactionary home as well as foreign policy. This implicated the party in the brutal suppression of the Indian people, and collaboration with the likes of Admiral Darlan and Marshal Badoglio. Such a policy made a mockery of progressive aims. The Labour left never resolved its conflict of loyalty between principles and being inside a party that is not in opposition but in government.

The extraordinary contrasts and shifts of the left during the war years stemmed from a desire to defeat fascism which sometimes led them to suggest ways of waging the war which would only have been possible for a revolutionary workers' government. But their attempt to fit workers' demands within the framework of the national capitalist state continually led them to fall back on talk of cross-class alliances, and therefore into a position where workers were subordinated to the needs of British imperialism.

Towards the summit of reformism

Under capitalism crisis can take many forms. The slump of the 1930s was one form. The Second World War was another. It is through capitalist crisis, when 'normal' society is dislocated and classes are forced to rethink their positions, that fundamental change can occur. The result is by no means automatic—change can mean descent into fascism, but it can mean many other things too.

The Second World War, like the first, created full employment. It also showed that unlike the parasitic capitalists, the working class are the real productive force in society. In the late 1930s workers had already begun to flex their collective muscles after the long sleep. Now the war, through its multitude of large and small transformations in daily life, gave them a new confidence and militancy.

One aspect was particularly galling. Although Labour participation in government was supposed to show that all classes were in the war effort on an equal footing, workers could not help noticing that, in Rosa Luxemburg's phrase: 'profits are springing, like weeds, from the fields of the dead'.[38] There was profiteering and the black market. Fortunes were made. One author recounted

> that he had been auditing the accounts of a builders' merchant who had earned a thousand pounds a year from his business before the war, but in the last year had drawn over fifteen thousand pounds in director's fees—this for a small firm employing half a dozen people. The same accountant spoke of two war factories where the auditors had insisted on paying out the wages themselves, and had found that hundreds of pounds were reaching the firms in respect of non-existent workers.
>
> These tales were not the carefully selected ammunition of a lonely red revolutionary. The buses, and even the newspapers, were noisy with such anecdotes.[39]

The profiteering was of course a symptom. The wartime government policies meant an increase in the rate at which workers were being exploited, and while their so-called leaders were willing to turn a blind eye to this, workers were not. One aspect of their response was increasing organisation. Trade union membership, which had been in the region of four and a half million before the war, approached seven million by its end. Even more significant were the strikes, which all involved unofficial, rank and file action, independent of the union bureaucracy:

Year	*1938*	*1939*	*1940*	*1941*	*1942*	*1943*	*1944*	*1945*
Disputes[40]	875	940	922	1251	1303	1785	2194	2293
of which mining	374	417	386	482	555	862	1275	1319
engineering	138	181	229	472	476	612	610	591

The 3,714,000 strike days of 1944 were not only higher than the decade preceding the war, they were only surpassed again in 1955. Two-thirds of the strike days came from the coal industry, the highest figure since 1932, while the number of strikes, 2,194, was the highest since records began.

A historian of the period compared the strike levels in the Second World War with those of the first:

> Taking the yearly average for the two periods 1939–1945 and 1914–1918 the number of stoppages. was 1,527 as compared to 814—in both wars the greatest number occurring during the last year of hostilities. On the other hand, the number of workers directly or indirectly involved in stoppages. of work was smaller in the Second World War—480,000 as compared with 632,000 in the earlier war. Secondly, the aggregate number of days lost was only 1,900,000 by contrast with 5,360,000 between 1914 and 1918, as most of the stoppages. were of relatively short duration.[41]

The Second World War, unlike the first, had not interrupted a period of titanic class conflict or been influenced by Bolshevism. It followed years of working-class passivity. It claimed to be conquering the evils of fascism. And from 1941 the Communist Party, now at the height of its influence, put its efforts into preventing strikes. Crucially, the Second World War produced nothing like the onslaught on working-class standards that had been experienced in the first.

Nevertheless there were important disputes, including engineering apprentices, shipyard workers and many others. One important struggle was against the conscription of young men into the mines—the 'Bevin boys'.* In another 30,000 Belfast workers struck against the imprisonment of five of their shop stewards.

But the most strike-prone industry was undoubtedly mining, the outstanding stoppage being at Betteshanger colliery in Kent. In January 1942 its 1,620 miners went on strike over a wage claim. Three branch officials were sentenced to imprisonment because of the strike, and

* The conscription of young men into the mines was one of the most unpopular measures the government took during the war. Up to October 1944, out of 16,000 called to the mines, 500 had been prosecuted for refusal to obey the National Service Officers' Order, or for leaving their employment. Of this total, 143 were sentenced to prison.[42]

others were fined but refused to pay. It was soon obvious that there was no way to imprison a thousand miners. The home secretary decided to recommend remission of the sentences on the three officials, so they were freed. By May 1942 only nine of the miners had paid their fines. The miners won their wage claim. Spectacular though it was, Betteshanger was just one miners' strike among many even larger affairs:

> in the whole year 1944 the number involved in mining disputes were no less than 568,000. The duration in working days of all disputes that year was 2,480,000, a figure that had only once been exceeded in the previous seventeen years. But a still more significant figure is the number of disputes, big and small. There were no less than 1,253 disputes in 1944, half as many again as in the preceding year, 1943, which year had the highest total of disputes since the beginning of the century.[43]

The impact of class struggle on the left

The role of the Labour left, which had only recently conflicted so seriously with the leadership, is interesting. One instance during 1944 was Nye Bevan's trip to a miners' strike in South Wales:

> to urge the men first to accept the original award, whatever the anomalies, and later to call off their unofficial strike action. He went to the second round of meetings following a pressing private appeal from Ernest Bevin himself. Other MPs from the mining areas had done the same.[44]

Although the Labour left were not prepared to advance working class self-activity, they did try to halt government intervention against it. Thus Labour backbenchers stormily rebelled against Regulation 1AA. Spearheading the attack, Bevan accused Bevin of working up a campaign of calumny against the miners through the press, and trying to cover up the failure of the government's industrial policy, especially in the mines, by starting a witch-hunt against agitators:

> Cartoons in the public press and articles written by highly-paid propagandists in the millionaire newspapers made our task almost impossible when we went to address meetings in the coalfields. The miners came out on strike because of real grievances, he said.
>
> He went on:
>
> Do not let anybody on this side of the House think that [Ernest Bevin] is defending the trade unions; he is defending the trade union official,

> who has arterial sclerosis, and who cannot readjust himself to his membership. He is defending an official who has become so unpopular among his own membership that the only way he can keep them in order is to threaten them with five years in gaol.[45]

The strength of feeling among the Labour backbenchers was shown by the voting on Regulation 1AA. The government majority was convincing enough: 314 to 23 with about 70 abstentions. But only 56 out of 165 Labour MPs voted in support of Bevin, and that with a three-line whip.[46]

Bevan's behaviour enraged the Labour leadership and Arthur Greenwood proposed his expulsion from the party. He described Bevan's speech as 'a speech of anti-trade union character the like of which I have never heard from the most diehard Tory in the House or outside the House'.[47] However, at the first meeting of the PLP no decision was reached. The next meeting was the best attended for years. Attlee spoke for expulsion, but the leaders could not get their way. By 71 to 60 an amendment moved by Shinwell was carried which was against immediate action 'in view of the probability of a general election in the next twelve months'.[48]

However an ultimatum was given to Bevan demanding a loyalty pledge from him to avoid expulsion. Next day Bevan gave it.[49] But the Labour right wing and the TUC refused to be satisfied with the compromise achieved. Bevan was reported to the Miners' Federation, which sponsored him as an MP, and the union's executive added its censure to that already passed by the General Council, and adopted a resolution supporting the TUC and Labour Party in their stand on Regulation 1AA.[50]

However Bevan had considerable backing within individual unions. South Wales, Scotland and Cumberland Areas of the Miners' Federation, the engineering workers (AEU), the train drivers (ASLEF), the shopworkers (NUDAW), the Chemical Workers' Union, the Civil Service Clerical Union and the Tobacco Workers' Union, all strongly opposed Regulation 1AA.[51]

In fact the Labour left now, as in the 1930s, had little contact with workers' struggles. In *Tribune* one finds hardly an echo of the strikes that took place, with the exception of the miners (after all, Bevan was a miners' MP). But even then the paper was not *agitating* for strikes, but only reporting them as a sad fact of life. *Tribune* protested against Regulation 1AA, but never agitated for the workers' demands which spurred the government on to introduce this regulation. *Tribune* argued for joint production committees, for increasing effort by workers to raise productivity, for opposition to the use of the strike weapon; it never agitated for strike action to raise wages.

Yet once more it was the forward thrust of the working class itself that had opened the way to new reformist advance, just like in the First World War. It was in the summer of 1943, as struggle moved towards the point at which Bevin felt compelled to institute Regulation 1AA, that Nye Bevan called for a new political realignment—a coalition of the left. Thus on 18 June he called for the affiliation to the Labour Party of the Communist Party, Common Wealth (a left-wing party formed during the war), the ILP and a Radical Liberal Group formed of left-wing Liberals.[52] A few months later *Tribune* called for an 'Alliance of the Left' of Liberals, Labour, Common Wealth, ILP and Communists[53], and this was repeated in one issue after another.

There were other signs that the old politics were breaking up and a new current was being created under the impact of world events and the rise of working-class pressure. One was increasing tension in the parliamentary field.

In 1939 the Labour Party had accepted a by-election truce. By this agreement, the party that had previously won the seat would have the right, when it fell vacant, to nominate a candidate approved by the other two parties. The truce held until the autumn of 1941 when it became apparent that a sizeable proportion of the electorate were ready to support Independents against official Conservative candidates where no Labour or Liberal candidates were put forward.

ILP candidates in 1941 had polled a steady 20–30 percent of the vote in various constituencies, presumably because Labour supporters saw this as a way of protesting. In 1942 four Independents were victorious, all against Conservative nominees. That July the Common Wealth Party was established, very much as a protest against the electoral truce. At its peak Common Wealth had 15,000 members, mainly from the liberal professions.

> Between the spring of 1941 and the end of 1942, nineteen Labour seats fell vacant and two of them were contested. Twenty-eight Conservative seats fell vacant, nineteen were contested, and three lost. In other words, the by-election independent knew his trade—blame the Tories—and the voters responded.[54]

In April 1943 Common Wealth won its first seat in a rural constituency in Cheshire. Others followed at Skipton and West Derbyshire.

Brighton was one of the safest Tory seats in the country, yet the Tory majority of 40,000 was reduced to less than 2,000 by an Independent challenge. A fortnight later, in West Derbyshire, a Conservative majority of 5,500 turned into an independent socialist majority of 4,500. In April 1945 a Common Wealth candidate swept the Conservative out of the hitherto safe seat of Chelmsford with a phenomenal turnover of 23,000 votes.

These defeats occurred notwithstanding the fact that Churchill, Attlee, Ernest Brown (for the National Liberals) and Sinclair (for the Liberals) sent a joint letter to all constituents saying:

> The verdict recorded by a single constituency is flashed around the world as though it were the voice of Britain that had spoken...it has the responsibility at this moment of indicating to the United Nations, and to neutral countries, that we are united among ourselves in our unflinching determination to organize our total resources for victory.[55]

Local Labour Parties were under orders to co-operate in the return of Conservatives or at least take no part against them. The rank and file found this infuriating. Even so, not one of the leaders of the Labour Party, not even Nye Bevan, suggested that Labour should withdraw from the government. However Bevan urged a clear declaration by the Labour Party that it would fight independently of the Tories at the first post-war election. Further, from 1942 onwards he called on the Labour Party to break the by-election truce agreed upon at the beginning of the war.

That year the party executive put a motion to conference committing the party not merely to abstain from putting up candidates in by-elections, but to give active support to government candidates in by-elections, whatever party they came from. Resistance was massive: the resolution passed by a narrow majority—1,275,000 to 1,209,000 votes. The miners, engineers and railwaymen voted against it.

At the next Labour Party Conference, Attlee won the extension of the electoral truce on the grounds that to break it would mean an end of the coalition and the death of any chance of Labour's influencing post-war planning. The majority was convincing: 2,243,000 to 374,000.

Part of the left's weakness arose from its extremely equivocal attitude to the government. It veered wildly from supporting the coalition to wanting to end it. A few examples will illustrate. On 11 December 1942 Bevan wrote a *Tribune* article which said that the presence of Labour ministers

> in the government is no protection against the most reactionary Tory policies being adopted. Nor can it now be said that the Labour members of the Government are doing anything which could not be done at least equally well by a Tory Minister... Has not the time come for Labour to regain its freedom and set itself at the head of the British people in their march to the new world?[56]

In October 1944 he argued the opposite: 'it would be foolish to break up the National Government now. I think our representatives are entitled to say that, having gone so far, they must complete the journey and remain in the Government until Germany is defeated'.[57] Just two months later this line was reversed once more, as Bevan called for the dissolution of the coalition government.[58]

Tribune was equally hard to track. In March 1943 it favoured preservation of the Coalition: 'The dilemma for labour is a painful one, for it involves the question of whether Labour should leave the National Government. This...would be a mistake... If great British and American armies are sent into battle, they must do so as far as possible with united nations behind'.[59] Some months later the opposite was argued: 'The Coalition is dead. Let us bury it quickly'.[60] Within a year the paper reverted to its original stance: 'Having persisted so far, it is reasonable for the parties forming the Government to hold together until the task which brought them into coalition is performed; the defeat of Nazi Germany'.[61]

The Labour left could not make up its own mind, because it could not decide its true allegiance—to the class collaborationist policies of Attlee and Co, or to the workers. So it always fell between two stools. It opposed the electoral truce but supported the coalition. It called on the Labour Party to end the truce, but did not take part in the electoral activities that would force it to do this.

A growing workers' movement and the ripples of discontent it generated within the Labour Party were only a part of the profound changes that were taking place. The ruling class was also re-shaping its ideas. For a party which seeks to mediate between the upper and nether millstones of capitalist society, this had far-reaching consequences.

'We are all Keynesians now'

When the Second World War began it ended the more or less uninterrupted economic decline that stretched back to 1920. Wartime expedients seemed to solve problems that had baffled the conventional economic wisdom, itself little changed since Gladstone's day.

The most obvious difference was the level of state involvement in the general management of the economy. This got a massive fillip as a result of the war. By 1941 about 49 percent of the total occupied population was engaged in some type of employment for the government.[62] With full employment for the first time for two decades, the idea that this could be maintained by state demand management became very widespread. For leading politicians of all parties the doctrine put forward by J M Keynes had been fully vindicated. According to Keynes, the prime responsibility of government was to use fiscal and monetary policy to ensure that there was enough effective demand in the economy to maintain full employment, but not so much as to cause 'demand-pull' inflation.

Before the war there were already a number of politicians who accepted Keynes's doctrine. Among the Labour people by far the most prominent early convert was Ernest Bevin. From the mid-1930s a number of Labour Party intellectuals were Keynesian converts: Douglas Jay, Evan Durbin, Anthony Crosland, and Hugh Gaitskell. These were on the right wing of the party. However some left-wingers moved towards Keynes, the most prominent being Strachey.

In 1932–5 Strachey wrote three books, *The Coming Struggle for Power*, *The Menace of Fascism* and *The Nature of the Capitalist Crisis*, in which he claimed to be an orthodox Marxist (even though he was in fact much influenced by Stalinism). But in 1938 he wrote to the barrister and hard-line Stalinist Palme Dutt: 'If, for good or evil, we have adopted People's Front politics, we must have a People's Front economics also'.[63] On the eve of the war the need for class collaboration strengthened further Strachey's search for a solution of the crisis of capitalism without overthrowing it. He wrote on 2 October 1938:

> the British people must be made to feel that those who ask them to, at least, risk fighting and dying for their country are determined to preserve their country and to improve those features which make it worth living in, and therefore dying for, eg, its democracy, in the widest sense of that term...[and] a determination just as great as that shown by the fascists to deal with unemployment *no doubt on Keynesist lines*. In two words, a 'progressive patriotism' must be the positive note struck.[64]

In 1940 Strachey published a new book, *A Programme for Progress*. This argued that while in the long run socialism was the only remedy for the breakdown of capitalism, in the short run what was needed was an interim programme for reforming capitalism similar to that of Roosevelt's New Deal. His programme included six main points: the extension of public enterprise, low interest rates on loan capital, increased social services, including monetary allowances to individuals, and a redistributory taxation. There would also be a state controlled banking system and strict public control over the balance of payments.[65]

This programme was so minimalist that Crosland could say: 'It was incomparably more modest than the programme the Labour Party adopted in 1937.'[66]

There were a number of converts to Keynesianism among the Tories. Harold Macmillan, a Conservative MP, published *Reconstruction: A Plea for a National Policy*, and *The Middle Way* in 1938. Thirty-six Tory MPs in 1943 formally constituted themselves into the Tory Reform Committee under the chairmanship of Lord Hinchingbrooke, who wrote:

> True Conservative opinion is horrified at the damage done to this country since the last war by 'individualist' business-men, financiers, and speculators ranging freely in a *laissez-faire* economy and creeping unnoticed into the fold of Conservatism to insult the Party with their vote at elections... I would wish nothing better than that these men should collect their baggage and depart.[67]

It was one of the members of the Reform Committee, Quintin Hogg, who told the House of Commons: 'If you do not give the people social reforms they are going to give you social revolution.' Harold Macmillan, R A Butler and Anthony Eden, being in the government, could not belong to the Tory Reform Committee, but had sympathy with it.

Capitalism must be preserved, said the Reform Committee, but the state could play a positive role in promoting its efficiency, and this might include nationalisation measures. Thus the committee argued for the nationalisation of electricity, gas and water, while excluding coal mining. Similar ideas regarding the mixed economy were put forward by Labour politicians from as diverse backgrounds as Morrison and Cripps.

Labour's shift from verbal opposition to capitalism to consciously trying to run it in its best interests involved a dramatic break with its past. As late as 1937 Attlee's book, *The Labour Party in Perspective*, had argued that socialism equalled nationalisation and this would lead to the abolition of classes. Such ideas were sprinkled throughout the book:

> The evils that Capitalism brings differ in intensity in different countries, but, the root cause of the trouble once discerned, the remedy is seen to

> be the same by thoughtful men and women. The cause is the private ownership of the means of life; the remedy is public ownership.[68]
>
> The aim of socialism is the nationalisation of all industries. All the major industries will be owned and controlled by the community...[69]
>
> The abolition of classes is fundamental to the Socialist conception of society.[70]

Whatever reservations might be held about Labour's ability to carry these through, such positions summed up the long-held beliefs that first inspired the socialists of the ILP, and once enshrined in Clause Four were held to be the property of the entire Labour Party.

Now, during the war, the Labour leaders started rewriting the political dictionary. The aim of Labour became the 'Mixed Economy'. In the words of Herbert Morrison:

> a practical mixture of genuine socialism and genuinely free enterprise, the whole resting upon and in turn supporting national policies of social and industrial welfare... Public ownership where it is appropriate, stimulating public control elsewhere.[71]

Nationalisation had once been held to be the cornerstone of a socialist society and to be the policy that separated Labour fundamentally from capitalism. Now Cripps argued that control of industry did not require its nationalisation. On 12 October 1944 he wrote to Richard Acland: 'Oh, no, my dear Richard. We have learnt in the war that we *can* control industry'.[72] Attlee himself pointed to the increasing consensus between Labour and Tory leaders about State intervention in industry: 'It colours all our discussions on home economic policy'.[73]

One expression of the way Keynesian ideas had come to dominate political thinking was the government *White Paper on Employment Policy*, of May 1944. This marked the Treasury's conversion to the use of fiscal means to avoid cyclical unemployment. When Bevin introduced the White Paper to the Commons he explained that the passive acceptance of deflation and unemployment would be replaced by active, conscious direction of the economy for the first time. Government would confront 'any depression at an early stage by expanding and not contracting capital expenditure, and by raising consumption expenditure and not reducing it'.[74]

Keynes seemed to promise a prosperous capitalism in which state intervention was to play a stabilising role. Nationalisation was irrelevant to this. As he put it:

> It is not the ownership of the instruments of production which it is important for the State to assume. If the State is able to determine the aggregate amount of resources directed to augmenting the instruments and the basic rate of reward to those who own them, it will have accomplished all that is necessary.[75]

Thus Keynes' ideas were attractive to right-wing Labour leaders, who were attached to gradualism, hence to the mixed economy.

Of course not all Labour leaders accepted Keynes' panacea. Bevan argued in the House of Commons that such ideas were incompatible with socialism. He did not believe Labour should accept the White Paper, for if it did so, he argued, there would not

> ...be any argument for Socialism and no reason for it... The subjects dealt with by the White Paper represent all the matters which distinguish that side of the House from this. The question of how the work of society is to be organised, how the income of society is to be distributed, to what extent the State is to intervene in the direction of economic affairs—all these are questions which first called this party into existence... Indeed, I will go so far as to say that, if the implications of the White Paper are sound, there is no longer any justification for this party existing at all.[76]

The debate between the moderate Labour leaders' policy of administering the capitalist economy and Bevan's critique of them was to dominate Labour thinking for a generation.

One should not suppose that since both centrist Tory and Labour leaders accepted Keynes, this consensus meant the *identity* of the two camps. Both accepted the objectives of full employment, reasonably rapid growth, stable prices and a satisfactory balance of payments. But Tory leaders put a different emphasis on the various objectives. Keynesians accepted that there was a trade-off between unemployment and inflation: the lower the level of unemployment the more intense the pressure of demand for labour, the faster will be the rate of inflation. For the Tory Party, as an open capitalist party depending very much on middle-class voters, people who have some savings, the emphasis would be on preventing inflation. For the Labour Party, whose voters are overwhelmingly workers without any financial cushion against unemployment, the emphasis was far more on jobs.

Labour Keynesians also emphasised greater economic equality. They believed that raising wages and improving welfare would themselves tend to increase demand, thus stimulating production and reducing unemployment.

Keynsianism was the most important new economic orthodoxy. But there were other new trends at work in the area of industrial relations and social reform.

One important development during the Second World War was the close cooperation between government and trade unions. This was a continuation of the 'Mondism' of the late 1920s. The 1928 Mond-Turner talks had been abortive, since the conditions of the slump of 1929 made it superfluous for management to take union leaders into their confidence, but in the partial recovery after 1932 such cooperation did produce some results. Trade unions, especially the two general unions—the Transport and General (TGWU) and the General and Municipal (GMWU)—established cosy relationships with a number of major employers and became involved in a growing number of state-sponsored bodies. This cooperation was symbolised by the granting of knighthoods to three prominent figures—Walter Citrine, TUC Secretary, Arthur Pugh of the Iron and Steel Trades Confederation, and the Labour Chief Whip Charles Edwards—in the Silver Jubilee Honours List of 1935.

During the war, with Ernest Bevin, a former general secretary of the TGWU, running the ministry of labour, and with the government in urgent need of trade union cooperation to preserve industrial peace at a critical period, the trade union leaders were incorporated into state activity: '...trade union leaders became members of the large number of wartime committees which took over functions previously fulfilled by private industry and tackled new ones arising out of war needs'.[77] As TUC general secretary, Sir Walter Citrine found himself serving on some 30 public or semi-public bodies.[78] At the end of the war he could tell Congress: 'We have passed from the era of propaganda to one of responsibility'.[79]

The Beveridge Report

In December 1942 the *Beveridge Report* was published. This proposed a comprehensive scheme for social insurance against illness, poverty and unemployment, plus proposals for a national health service, family allowances and the maintenance of full employment.

The report's assumptions about social reform fully accorded with the new Keynesian economics. Beveridge took for granted that the government would secure a high level of employment after the war, that it would introduce family allowances, and that it would devise a comprehensive health service for all. The Plan for Social Security which Beveridge drew up in the main body of the report was a rationalisation of existing financial arrangements, so that in return for a single weekly contribution, wage earners, the self-employed, and their families would receive old age pensions and sickness benefit. Former wage earners would receive unemployment pay.

Yet the scheme was not as radical as Beveridge claimed.* For example it considered the principle of a national minimum for old age pensioners to be so expensive that it could not be fully implemented for twenty years. Nevertheless, no official report has ever aroused greater popular interest and enthusiasm.

> The public welcome given to the report was well-nigh universal. The national press, with the exception of the *Daily Telegraph*, behaved as though it fell only slightly short of the millennium. A total of 635,000 copies were sold. A survey of opinion...showed that 86 percent believed that the report should be adopted, as against 6 percent who though it should be dropped.[81]

This is not to say the report was received uncritically.

> Nearly three out of five people thought the proposed pension rates too low. But the overall popularity of the report was established beyond a doubt, and the idea of free doctors and hospital services for all was approved by 88 percent, including 81 percent of the wealthier.[82]

Beveridge, however, had put the Tories' backs up. 'Churchill is reported to have taken strong exception to the Report, to have refused to see its author and forbidden any government department to allow him inside its doors'.[83] The government did all in its power to stifle publicity for the report and make plain that its contents were disapproved of.[84]

The National Council of Labour, representing both the Labour Party and TUC, endorsed the *Beveridge Report*, as did the Liberal Party (Beveridge was, after all, a Liberal himself). Soon the British Council of Churches followed suit. A good many Conservatives also welcomed it enthusiastically.

---

* Beveridge was a true Liberal. His contempt for working-class people can be gleaned from this letter sent to Tawney:

'The well-to-do represent on the whole a higher level of character and ability than the working classes, because in the course of time the better stocks have come to the top. A good stock is not permanently kept down; it forces its way up in the course of generations of social change, and so the upper classes are on the whole the better classes'.[80]

A three-day debate on the *Beveridge Report* took place in the House of Commons on 16–18 February 1943. Hardline Tories were for full implementation at some date no closer than Doomsday. Labour, tied by its coalition commitments, took an official position of no more than lukewarm approval and for very gradual implementation.

But a Labour MP, James Griffiths, put down an amendment calling for prompt legislation: the House 'expresses its dissatisfaction with the now declared policy of His Majesty's Government towards the Report of Sir William Beveridge on Social Insurance and Allied Services and urges the reconsideration of that policy with a view to the early implementation of the plan.' Attlee, Morrison and Bevin tried to counter the revolt at a private meeting of the PLP. A three-line whip was hurriedly organised by both Tories and Labour.

But the Labour backbenchers rebelled. Notwithstanding a very conciliatory and clever speech by Morrison for the coalition, the whole PLP turned on the government. In the division on 18 February, 121 votes were cast against the government: ninety-seven Labour, three ILP, one Communist, eleven Independents and nine Liberals. About thirty Labour MPs abstained. Of the twenty-three Labour members who voted for the government, twenty-two were ministers.

Towards the first majority Labour government

The Second World War ended in different circumstances to the First. Above all in 1945 the world entered the longest boom in capitalist history. Naturally its benefits were unequally shared, but it did help defuse the inevitable demands that workers were to make after the heavy sacrifices of the war years.

On the economic front the First World War had ended with a 'bonfire of controls' as bosses sought to return to the palmy days of Queen Victoria and *laissez-faire* success. Their efforts had ended in slump. In 1945 capitalists knew that there could be no going back to the 1930s.

In the general election of July 1945 Attlee's party raised its share of the vote by one-third to twelve million votes. With 393 Labour MPs, it now had a crushing majority over the 210 Conservatives and twelve Liberals in parliament. The election was just one symptom of a massive change in workers' attitudes that had been brought by the experience of war. The ideas of people like Nye Bevan now fitted the mood of the millions who had seen full employment in wartime, and the potential to use full employment in peacetime to banish poverty, misery and victimisation. Even the armed forces, still swollen to massive proportions, began to mutiny in Egypt, India and Malaya, demanding to be released from service. The rank and file soldiers could not have been used to halt major social change.

In these circumstances MacDonald's old excuse of being 'in office but not in power' was of no avail, and Labour faced a tremendous opportunity to achieve that constitutional transition to socialism that it had talked about so ardently. But the Labour Party too had changed during the war. Its synthesis of class and nation remained, but it had a new twist: 'what was good for the workers—fair wages, better housing, better pensions—was good for the nation.' The criticism of capitalism, and the acceptance of capitalism, were combined in a new form.

11

The Attlee government: zenith of reformism

The apotheosis

The Attlee administration of 1945 was not only the first majority Labour government, it represented the high point of Labour Party history. From 1951 we are on the other side of the mountain.

The memory of this government has become sacrosanct for both the right and the left of the Labour Party. Thus Bevan's political testament *In Place of Fear*, published in 1952, contains not a hint of criticism of the government in which he served for nearly six years. On 23 April 1951 Bevan declared:

> Ever since 1945 we have been engaged in this country in the most remarkable feat of social reconstruction the world has ever seen. By the end of 1950 we had...assumed the moral leadership of the world. There is only one hope for mankind, and that hope still remains in this little island.[1]

Similarly Tony Benn, in his book *Arguments for Socialism* makes numerous admiring references to the heritage of the Attlee government. The right-wing Labour leaders, from Morrison to Crosland, from Dalton to Hattersley, say the same.

Whatever the myths regarding the Labour government of 1945–51, there is no doubt that it was the most effective reformist Labour government of them all. The task of political analysis, however, is not simply to describe appearances, but to ask more fundamental questions. How much continuity was there with past Labour governments which had performed as the managers of capitalism? If Labour policies did develop in new directions, as it would appear, were these a vindication of the way gradualism and reformism were taking 'practical steps towards socialism?'

Nationalisation

The 1945–51 government is remembered for two positive policies: nationalisation and the welfare state.

In 1919 the miners' demand for nationalisation had brought Britain closer to revolution than at any other time this century. The same demand in 1947 had no such implications. Why was this? Two things had changed and as a capitalist workers' party Labour was deeply affected by both: first the attitude of the ruling class; second the logic of reformism, which had progressed to a new stage.

When Marx summarised the aim of capitalism he described it as 'Accumulate, accumulate—that is Moses and the prophets'. Capitalism, therefore, is not a 'juridical relationship'; it is not based on legal notions of ownership. Historically forms of ownership have been extremely flexible, ranging from the small individual entrepreneur through the joint stock company to giant multinationals; from almost 100 percent private ownership on the American model to 100 percent state ownership on Stalinist lines.

Therefore state ownership in no way implies socialism. Socialism means the economic and social liberation of the working class by subordinating the creation of wealth to the fulfilment of human needs. This can be achieved only when workers themselves take political power directly, through institutions such as *soviets* or workers councils.

Labour's approach to nationalisation was set out in its 1945 Manifesto, *Let us Face the Future*. This argued for the state takeover of certain branches of the economy—the Bank of England, coal mines, electricity and gas, railways, and iron and steel. Nationalisation measures were justified on grounds of economic efficiency, not as a means of shifting the balance between labour and capital. Each case was argued empirically. Thus 'public ownership of gas and electricity undertakings would lower charges, prevent competitive wastage, open the way for coordinated research and development.' By arguing for piecemeal nationalisation Labour accepted the mixed economy; by no means a socialist society, but a variant of the consensus achieved in rough outline during the war.

Thus it was that when the election results became known, employers accepted the Labour programme of a mixed economy with good grace. They had reasons.

Given British capitalism's previous history, one might have expected it to yearn for *laissez-faire*, as it did in 1919. However after the Second World War this option had grave drawbacks. In 1945 nobody could predict with certainty that a long boom lay ahead instead of a return to depression.

Secondly, modem capitalism required a well-developed infrastructure, including transport and power supplies, in order to function efficiently. Now this 'social overhead capital' tended to be costly, requiring long-term investment, and its benefits accrued to industry as a whole rather than to the individual entrepreneur. For these reasons the infrastructure in most countries was developed and controlled by governments. In 1945 British capital was ready to break with tradition. It was unwilling to tie up large sums in rebuilding necessary but largely unprofitable areas of industry after the ravages of war. So the bulk of Attlee's nationalisation programme did not worry capital in the least.

The coal industry was a prime example. It suffered from obsolescence, which, unless remedied, would act as a brake on the rest of the economy.

> The Mining Association now declared its willingness to withdraw its opposition to nationalisation of coalmining, 'because of the result of the General Election'. This lamb-like utterance from the former lions of 'excessively tenacious individualism' was not unconnected with the fact that the antiquated equipment of industry had been worked to its limit during the war and now needed drastic renewal, that manpower would soon be scarce enough to win concessions, and that oil looked like undercutting the monopoly value of coal. It was not a bad time to sell out.[2]

Thus it was that leading Tories did not oppose the nationalisation of the mines. Even Churchill, the uncompromising class warrior, did not resist. Nor did he fight nationalisation of the Bank of England, which in this era of Keynesian planning was a logical step. He said in parliament that the nationalisation of the Bank of England 'does not, in my opinion, raise any issue of principle'.[3] Both the retiring governor of the Bank, Lord Catto, and the retiring deputy governor, Cameron Cobbold, were reappointed.

The actual process of takeover was easy. In the case of the Bank of England, coal, gas, electricity and transport, a close relationship with the government was already well established in 1945. Between October 1945 and January 1948 the government introduced legislation to nationalise all of these. The measures evoked little Commons opposition.

To sum up, nationalisation of these industries was vital for the expansion of the profitable industries that remained private. It strengthened the private sector by freeing it of the burden of industries which demanded heavy investment and were essential to the running of all industry.

So the employers cooperated. They readily continued to staff the system of wartime controls, which was operated largely by representatives of private industry and prolonged by the government.[4] In the words of Ralph Miliband, the government enjoyed the cooperation of private industry. Or more accurately, private industry enjoyed the cooperation of the Government'.[5]

The government ensured that the management structure of nationalised industries served the general needs of capitalism and did not offer any element of workers' control that others might want to emulate. There were joyful mass demonstrations on vesting day—1 January 1947, when the coal mines were taken over and the ensign of the National Coal Board replaced that of the old discredited private owners. But the rejoicing soon stopped; for the NCB, like other nationalised industries, took the form of a public corporation, a copy of the structure of private industry with the same hierarchical relationship between managers and workers. Managers were recruited from former management. Thus the head of the National Coal Board had previously been involved with one of the largest private colliery companies. No wonder there were so many unofficial strikes in the mines.

Summing up the Attlee government, one historian wrote:

> Whatever aspect of the Labour program one considers, one always returns to the same theme: a similar policy was advocated, perhaps even before Labour advocated it, by non-socialists. Central economic planning under the post-war Labour Governments...involved little more than the application of Keynesian nostrums...one of the most remarkable things about Labour's nationalization measures is that most of them were enacted in response to the reports of Conservative-dominated investigating committees: the Bank of England measure as a result of the Macmillan Report, coal because of the Reid Report, gas because of the Hayworth Report, electricity because of the McGowan report. Moreover, nationalization, as carried out by Labour, made use of an administrative device first worked out by Liberal and Conservative governments—the 'public corporation'.[6]

The nationalisation programme eventually affected between two and three million workers and involved roughly one-fifth of total economic activity.[7] *But there it stopped.*

This was of the greatest significance. All Labour leaders accepted the idea of the mixed economy, even Nye Bevan, who chaired the sub-committee of the Labour Party executive on privately-owned industry. He was anxious to reassure private capitalists that their interests were being looked after, so as to gain financial stability for the economy as a whole. Bevan made the mixed economy a question of principle—not a transition to the total nationalisation of the economy, but an aim in itself. To quote the words of Jennie Lee, his wife:

> Hence Nye's much quoted phrase, 'the commanding heights of the economy'. Let the State bring order out of the anarchy of unrestrained private enterprise by taking over industries essential for a planned economy, such as coal, steel, transport and such like, but leave ample margins for private individuals and groups of individuals to make their contribution. Total nationalisation is not compatible with a democratic, constitutional, parliamentary system.[8]

This attitude represented a landmark in Labour's history. True, the government's nationalisation schemes surpassed all previous measures, but the voluntary acceptance of a mixed economy was a departure from previous beliefs. For all that the Fabians represented a ruling class current, their 'state socialism' had never intended to leave 80 percent of the economy in the hands of private profit-makers. Clause Four's 'social ownership' was clearly understood to apply to as much of industry as administratively possible. Of course the two previous minority Labour governments could plausibly argue they could do little to carry it out. In 1945 no such excuse existed, so the Labour leadership simply re-wrote the political textbook.

The synthesis of class and nation now meant a mixture of nationalised and private enterprise. Capitalism would not be overthrown, but made more efficient and more humane by laying the foundations of a mixed economy and welfare state. The logic of reformism was on a new plane when Labour not only *acted* as manager of capitalism, but *justified* it without shame. To buy 20 percent of the economy it sold its political soul.

Welfare

If Labour's policies were designed chiefly to benefit the ruling class, in conditions of boom crumbs could still be thrown to workers. Under Attlee, workers and their families fared much better than before the war. The government

> kept up a high level of expenditure on the social services; while food subsidies were pegged in the April 1949 budget at £465 million, they still represented a formidable sum and did much to keep down the cost of living for working people... And of course, full employment

> and relatively mild inflation were immeasurable boons to workers everywhere, for which much else would be forgiven.[9]

The flagship of the welfare state was the National Health Service, which seemed for once to rise above the sordid calculations of profit and loss that blight the industrial world, nationalised corporations included. Nye Bevan was the minister of health who introduced the scheme. He explained: 'The field in which the claims of individual commercialism come into most immediate conflict with reputable notions of social value is that of health'.[10]

However, the origins of the welfare state date as far back as the Workmen's Compensation Act of 1893 and Liberal schemes of old age pensions, unemployment and health insurance, which were introduced after 1906. These were certainly not socialist in motivation. Nor could the shortlived Conservative caretaker administration which began family allowances in 1945 be described as socialist.

As Marx and Engels showed, there is a basic contradiction within capitalism: 'The essential condition for the existence, and for the sway of the bourgeois class, is the formation and augmentation of capital; the condition for capital is wage labour'.[11] Labour power is the most important productive force in capitalism.

The ruling class regards workers not as human beings, but as providers of labour power, a simple factor of production. Just as efficient transport and energy supplies are vital, so a productive, educated and healthy workforce is necessary. This is particularly true in periods of expansion when bosses require new skills and are unable to pick the 'best' workers from a pool of unemployed. Therefore welfare provision fully accorded with a planned Keynesian economy. The state would help sustain the physical and human infrastructure. Thus the head of Courtaulds, the textile giant, predicted Beveridge's plans would 'be about the most profitable long-term investment the country could make'.[12]

Expansion of the welfare state was based on three Acts in 1946 (the National Health Service Act and two National Insurance Acts) and the National Assistance Act of 1948. They were effective. Take the NHS. It tackled an appalling situation. Of two and a half million men surveyed during the First World War, only three in every nine were fully 'fit and healthy', three were in reasonable condition, two were 'incapable of undergoing more than a very moderate degree of physical exertion' and one was 'a chronic invalid with a precarious hold on life.' In the 1930s 83 percent of Durham children were found to be suffering from rickets.[13]

Today, partly as a result of the NHS, formerly common diseases such as tuberculosis and rickets are a rarity and general health is greatly improved.

In introducing the NHS Bevan met bitter opposition from the British Medical Association (BMA), the main doctors' pressure group, which was supported by the Tory Party and their press run rampant. Bevan made a whole series of concessions to them, which left the door ajar for the future erosion of the service. Hospital consultants could retain private beds as well as receiving a salary for cooperating with the state scheme. As John Campbell, Bevan's biographer, rightly says:

> Bevan arguably paid too high a price for the consultants' support... Since they were now to be paid for the work they had previously done (in the voluntary hospitals) for nothing, they achieved the best of both worlds—the regular pay of the municipal hospitals with the prestige of the voluntary, plus private fees. No wonder Bevan was reported to have said 'I stuffed their mouths with gold.' And as well as gold he gave them power, the predominant power to shape the new service.[14]

The medical journal *The Lancet* said in November 1946 that the NHS was 'much less socialistic than was predicted a year ago'.[15]

The Socialist Medical Association and Labour backbenchers were disappointed to find the 1945 manifesto promise of a national, full-time salaried service had been lost through concessions to the BMA. Bevan knew how much had been conceded: as he told MPs in 1948, private patients, private beds and private fees put the ideal of a free and equal health service for all in 'a very grave danger and it was a very serious and substantial concession made to the medical profession...that was repugnant to many of my hon. Friends'.[16]

The net result, in Campbell's words, was:

> to contrive the appearance of a political triumph for his party when in fact he had enacted virtually none of the cherished nostrums of those in the Labour Party who had cared about health. 'His outstanding success', one of his critics wryly noted, 'was the way he applied the anaesthetic to supporters on his own side, making them believe in things they had opposed almost all their lives'.[17]

Just as with nationalisation, employers and the working class had different reasons for welcoming the welfare state. From the workers' point of view, they and their families do not exist merely to reproduce and sell labour power. Good health, decent education and housing are valued for improving the quality of life, not the employer's bank balance.

A capitalist workers' party tries to get the best of both worlds, but in a clash has to choose sides. The meaning of nationalisation was exposed by the struggle over profitable industries like road haulage and steel. Was welfare there to make British industry more productive, or did social spending (financed largely through direct taxes on income), represent the thin end of a wedge which would ultimately bring the redistribution of wealth from rich to poor?

The issue became a live one at the end of Labour's term of office. The deteriorating balance of payments, higher taxation and cuts in the already meagre food rations had already disillusioned many socialists. The question then arose: was it more important to sustain the Health Service or back American imperialism in Korea, where war broke out in 1950? The defence budget, much expanded during the Korean war, led to Bevan's resignation from the government in April 1951. When Gaitskell, chancellor of the exchequer after Cripps fell critically ill, imposed prescription, denture and spectacle charges, Bevan had had enough.

The Health Service was mauled, but it survived. How exceptional was it? In Britain modem health provision was introduced by a reformist government. Yet in countries without social democratic governments the proportion of social product going to health has been far higher. Until 1969 NHS spending never exceeded 4.5 percent of Britain's GNP, whereas in that year the Netherlands spent 5.9 percent, the US 6.8 percent and Canada 7.3 percent.[18] However it would be a mistake to assume that Britain's low proportion of GNP going to health meant the NHS lagged behind other countries: the *universal and free* nature of the NHS meant that low income groups benefitted greatly. Also in places like the US, doctors take a far greater proportion of the money spent on health than they do in Britain.

Nevertheless social spending is not a peculiarly Labour policy. Between 1945 and the election of Tory prime minister Margaret Thatcher in 1979 the Labour Party was in government roughly half the time. But spending on welfare benefits in Britain compared unfavourably with other European countries which have not had social democratic rule. West Germany, France, and even Spain, offered in a number of fields welfare benefits more generous than those in Britain. 'Among the eighteen advanced industrial democracies included in the OECD sample, Britain devotes 12.6 percent of the gross domestic product to [welfare], but is surpassed by ten countries in this group, and is below the average (13.25)'.[19]

To conclude, Labour supporters often presume that major reforms must have originated from their party. This is too simplistic. Historically there are two types of legislative reform, that wrested from below, and that handed down from above.

Lenin described the situation in Tsarist Russia in which reforms were 'merely a by-product of revolutionary class struggle' and 'possible only as a by-product of a movement that is completely free of all narrowness of reformism...'[20] Labour can certainly never be accused of fighting for reforms by such revolutionary methods.

The question arising about Attlee's reforms is whether they were achieved because Labour was in office, or would the capitalist class have conceded them anyway, whatever party was in government? The welfare state is a case in point.

The Labour government did not transform the state from 'the executive committee of the ruling class' into some classless benefactor. It brought in a set of changes that the employing class intended to be a 'profitable long-term investment'. They were not and never could be, a serious inroad to the power of the system itself. The Labour Party, depending on reforms from above, and discouraging mass movements from below, can do exceedingly little to shape what happens. By holding back the working class—the real force for socialist change—they are left in a situation in which their ability to improve the lives of their working-class supporters depends almost entirely on the vigour of the national capitalism.

The Tories would not necessarily have acted in precisely the same fashion. A reformist party in government may achieve changes that are different *in form* from those of a reactionary party, but only within strict limits determined by the system. The NHS could not rise above these constraints. From the point of view of capitalism the NHS was an efficient method of maintaining a fit and able workforce at minimum cost, so the principle behind the system was not seriously attacked until the 1980s, even by the Tories. Nevertheless, even before this the health of workers was subordinated to the health of capitalism. Whenever things became tight the NHS was attacked. And the first cuts came from Attlee's Labour government; later, as the sickness of British capitalism grew, both Labour and Tory governments would attack the NHS with increasing ferocity.

The turning point: 1947, '*annus horrendus*'

Until the start of 1947, the Labour government's reforming programme seemed to advance without a hitch. It had established an impressive record of legislative achievement, with more than seventy Bills carried through parliament in the 1945–6 session, including the introduction of widespread public ownership, the National Health and National Insurance Bills and the reform of the law on trade unions. Within the Labour Party itself there was immense enthusiasm. Outside, popular support for the government was solid.

One factor ensuring mass support for the government was full employment. Throughout Labour's tenure of office, unemployment was extremely low (except during the fuel crisis of winter 1947 when it reached 3 percent). There were three and a half million more workers employed in June 1951 than six years previously. In Labour Party mythology this was entirely due to government policy. However, Sir Alec Cairncross, an economic adviser to the Attlee government, saw behind the appearances:

> The maintenance of a high level of employment was only to a limited extent the government's doing. It was made easy because world markets remained in a state of boom... What can be claimed for the Labour government is that the one thing that it had to plan, and did plan—the balance of payments—was effectively planned.[21]

The dominant figure in the first period of Labour policy was the chancellor of the exchequer, Hugh Dalton. Dalton's policy of 'cheap money' symbolised the new era, in total contrast to the deflation and retrenchment that had dominated the policy of the Treasury after 1918. Dalton's financial policy underlay the social reforms, the industrial reconstruction, and the public investment projects of the first two years.

However, social reforms financed by expansionist policies were only part, and a lesser part, of the government's aims. It was also the manager of capitalism, both at home, and defending Britain's imperial role. Until 1947 reforms and the needs of capitalism did not conflict. But the foundations of British capitalism, upon which the reforms depended, were shaky.

During the war the British ruling class lost a massive portion of its foreign assets. Income from these was now no longer available to pay for imports of food and raw materials. Additionally the war itself had given Britain accumulated debts of £2,723 million around the world. In 1945 estimates held that exports would have to increase by between 50 and 70 percent just to finance imports on the same scale as before the war.[22] Furthermore, Britain's imperialist commitments added to the burden on its economy. In March 1948 there were still 937,000 in the armed forces.

The underlying weaknesses were suddenly brought to the surface in 1947. The previous year had been a very successful one for the government. According to a leading article in the *News Chronicle*:

> Industrially the year has been marked by steady progress. Unemployment (apart from a few areas in Scotland and Wales) has been almost negligible. Britain, too, is almost the only democratic country in the world which has survived 1946 without a major industrial dispute.[23]

In total contrast, 1947 was a year of almost unmitigated disaster. It began with terrible weather. The winter of early 1947 was, as the Annual Register recorded, the 'most severe since 1880–1.'

> The result was calamitous. Coal stocks, already failing, slumped to below the four million tons level, which was regarded as the minimum for national survival. Coal could not be transported by rail or road; collier vessels from Newcastle, bringing coal to power stations in London and the south-east, could not put to sea. Shinwell told a stunned House of Commons on 7 February that many power stations had run out of coal, that much of industry would therefore have to close down, and that many domestic consumers would have to do without electricity for large parts of the day… Factories were closed down; villages were cut off; livestock died in thousands; people froze in their homes without even the radio as a solace since that, too, was a victim of the power crisis. Unemployment reached over two millions by the start of February. Not until March was there any visible improvement in fuel supplies; in the end, the government was rescued only by an improvement in the climate in late March.[24]

Dalton described 1947 as the '*annus horrendus*'[25], and the laying off of more than two million workers certainly did not assist the financial crisis that followed. In the first quarter of 1947 Britain's reserves of dollars were heavily depleted as a result of a world-wide shortage of food and raw materials which left the USA as virtually the sole supplier. The 'dollar drain' was associated with very negative terms of trade for Britain. The British fuel crisis of January-February 1947 made things even worse.

> Indeed, the dollar drain in the first six months of 1947 swept away some $1,890 million, more than half the original US loan of $3,750 million. At that rate, the loan, intended to last Britain until 1951, would run out by 1948, or even earlier.[26]

Since Britain was committed, by the terms of the July 1946 American loan, to allow the pound to be freely convertible into dollars on the foreign exchanges by July 1947, the country faced financial catastrophe.

The government was not responsible for the weather. But this natural event had uncovered what was to become the perennial problem of the postwar British economy—the tendency for rising domestic demand to encourage imports as much as home production. Moreover this became progressively worse as time went on. There were sterling crises in 1947, 1949, 1951, 1955, 1957, 1961, and between 1963 and 1967. Hence the 'stop-go' cycle: the chancellor stimulated demand, which led to increased imports and caused a balance of payments deficit, and hence a speculative attack on the pound. Restoring confidence was achieved by raising the interest rate, imposing cuts and increasing taxes in order to lower the level of demand in the economy. In the short run this deflation worked, but in the long run it delayed investment, slowed technical change, caused low productivity and weakened Britain's competitive position in the world. The periods of 'go' got shorter, while the periods of 'stop' got longer.

The first postwar financial crisis, of August 1947, was the gravest Britain had experienced since August 1931. The Attlee government panicked. A new financial policy was put forward, with dire implications for the entire thrust of Labour's reforming strategy. Deflation, cuts in basic rations of meat, fat, sugar and other foodstuffs—these were the essential ingredients of Dalton's November 1947 budget. On 13 November Dalton resigned the chancellorship (having carelessly leaked some items of his budget to a newspaper reporter). Cripps took his place, to continue the austerity programme with a vengeance.

The entire direction of government had been dramatically altered, and the limits of reformism revealed with startling clarity. While socialists would have hoped Labour would thrust the burden of the crisis on to those most capable of bearing it, the opposite was true. The man in charge of government economic policy from August 1947 until 1950 was Stafford Cripps, the *enfant terrible* of the 1930s. His first move was to reassure business and the city.

Cripps' penchant for draconian measures found a new target. He began with the imposition of a series of austerity measures: a sharp reduction of consumer purchasing power, new indirect purchase taxes and heavy cuts in imports which had to be paid for in dollars. Consumers faced reductions in living standards after the cabinet decision to cut food imports by £66m and basic rations. This would cut the average calorie intake per person per day to between 2,650 and 2,725 in the first half of 1948, compared with 3,000 in the last year of the war.[27] When Cripps announced these measures in the Commons, he was highly praised by *The Times* 'before he had ended his 100-minute speech Sir Stafford Cripps had sounded a note which stirred the pulses of the House'.[28]

Plans were made to increase exports further, to restrict consumer spending and to cut public investment, especially the housing programme. While the capitalists got financial inducements from the Treasury, the workers had to pay higher taxes, with a shift in the balance from direct to indirect taxes.

One of the key elements in Cripps' policy was the encouragement of an export drive by diverting manpower to the export trade as never before. From the summer of 1948 further help came with the injection of dollars through Marshall Aid, the US postwar aid programme for Western Europe.

> The obverse of this concentration on exports was the remorseless cutting down of resources for the consumer at home. Rationing of food, clothing, petrol, and other commodities had continued since the end of the war. In the Cripps era, the system reached new extremes of severity. By 1948, the average citizen had to make do with a weekly ration of thirteen ounces of meat, one and a half ounces of cheese, six ounces of butter and margarine, one ounce of cooking fat, eight ounces of sugar, two pints of milk, and a solitary egg.[29]

Side by side with this rationing there was the 'black market', which would supply all the luxuries you required—as long, of course, as you could afford to pay the price.

Wage restraint

The corollary of control of consumption through rationing and other austerity measures was the attempt to control wages. In a situation of full employment, with a confident working class, it would take more than political wiles to pull this off. Above all, Labour's trump card—the loyalty of the trade unions—would have to be played.

On 4 February 1948 Attlee announced a White Paper titled *Statement on Personal Incomes, Costs and Prices*. It demanded that there should be no increase in wages, salaries or dividends, save in exceptional circumstances. Trade union leaders at once went to Downing Street in a body and demanded the withdrawal of this 'unacceptable attempt to interfere with free collective bargaining'. They had, after all, created the Labour Representation Committee in 1900 with the express intention of removing such government interference after Taff Vale.

The TUC's Economic Committee expressed concern at the White Paper and especially at Cripps' call for a wage freeze. Cripps' negotiations with the TUC did not go well, especially since he was unwilling to tax profits or dividends any further. But the all-too-familiar spell of 'don't rock the boat' wrought its magic for the Labour government. A conference of trade union executive delegates on 24 March voted by the comfortable majority of 5,421,000 to 2,012,000 to accept the policy of wage freeze for the foreseeable future. The opposition was made up of the engineers', electricians', shopworkers' and other unions, especially those representing the low-paid. The same policy was endorsed by the TUC Congress later in the year.

The call for working-class sacrifice rang hollow against the impressive achievements of British industry at the time. The volume of industrial production in the first half of 1949 was 30 percent above that of 1938; exports had risen from 50 percent below pre-war level to nearly 55 percent above; and earnings from exports covered 85 percent of the cost of imports—the best performance in Europe. But financial pressures still forced the government to devalue the pound in September 1949. This led to a significant rise in the cost of living, as the prices of imported goods soared.

Cripps was also demanding a reduction in public expenditure of some £700 million. The foreign secretary, Ernest Bevin, and the minister of defence, Albert Alexander, were threatening to resign if the full weight of the cuts fell on defence; Nye Bevan was threatening to resign if social expenditure suffered unduly; Cripps was threatening to resign unless all agreed with him.

Finally, on 21 October 1949, the cabinet put forward a package of cuts with a total deflationary effect of £280 million. Attlee announced these measures to a completely silent House of Commons, and sat down in front of benches of openly dispirited supporters.[30]

After the devaluation of the pound, it became far more difficult for the union leaders to hold the line for the government on the wages front. A special conference of trade union executives in January 1950 endorsed the policy of wage restraint by only a very narrow margin—4,263,000 votes to 3,606,000. When the Korean war pushed the rate of inflation even higher, the 1950 TUC Congress voted down the wage freeze by 3,949,000 to 3,727,000. Both the Confederation of Shipbuilding and

Engineering Unions and the rail unions took tentative steps which might have led to official national strikes.[31]

Nonetheless the government wages policy had been successful. As Cairncross explains:

> The White Paper policy undoubtedly slowed down the rise in wages and prices. In the first two post-war years from June 1945 to June 1947 hourly wage rates had increased, first by 9 percent, then by 8.5 percent. In the next nine months to March 1948 the rise continued at nearly 9 percent per annum. From then until the devaluation eighteen months later, the annual rate of increase fell to 2.8 percent... [After inflation was accounted for] real wages were stationary or falling... That money wages rose so little when real wages were stationary or falling and unemployment was down to 300,000 is striking testimony to the influence of the trade-union leaders. Hourly wage rates after March 1948 rose no faster than in the mid-1930s, between 1934 and 1938, when unemployment was around two million.[32]

As a reward for sacrificing their members' living standards, union officials were welcomed on to an increasing number of government committees: in 1931 there had been union representatives on only one such committee; by 1939 they had been on twelve, and by 1948–49 they were on sixty.[33]

The strike-breaking government

One sign of how the union bureaucracy successfully imposed Labour's wage restraint was the lack of industrial resistance. Compare this to the level after the First World War when Labour was in opposition. During 1945–50 fewer than ten million man-days were lost through strikes, compared with 170 million in the five years 1918–1923, an average of less than two million days per year as against more than 35 million.

Nevertheless those few workers who did strike were not treated with kid gloves. Order 1305, which had made wartime strikes illegal and had been justified as necessary to defeat fascism, was continued. In 1950 and 1951 the government used the order to prosecute ten gas workers and seven dockers. These decisions enraged the whole trade union movement, and the order had to be terminated in August 1951. The minister of labour regularly attributed strikes to Communist agitation. An enormous weight of vilification was heaped on the heads of shop stewards who during the war had been described as loyal patriots, but were now 'extremists' and 'subversives'. Labour set the tone for what was to be a long-running media witch-hunt of industrial militants.

Throughout the lifetime of the Attlee government the military were used again and again to break strikes. Thus, cabinet minutes of 5 July 1950 included the following:

> **List of recent industrial disputes involving the Services**[34]
>
> *April 1949: London dock strike:*
> All preparations including assembly of troops, for use of 6,100 troops and 1,200 vehicles in all three Services, but not actually used
> *May/June: Avonmouth dock strike:*
> 800 Army, 100 RN and 400 RAF employed for nearly three weeks
> *June: Liverpool dock strike:*
> All preparations including assembly of troops, for use of 700 Army, 120 RN and 800 RAF but not actually used
> *June: Newport dock strike:*
> All preparations for 2,100 Army, 1,400 RAF and 500 vehicles but not used. No movement of troops
> *June: Threatened railway strike:*
> Preparations did not go further than preliminary planning
> *July: Threatened London electricity strike:*
> Preparatory action but no actual movement of troops
> *July: London dock strike:*
> Services worked docks for just under three weeks. Total numbers employed 17,000 men and 1,200 vehicles
> *September: Belfast electricity power strike:*
> Services operated power stations for a week. About 250 men
> *September: Smithfield strike:*
> Preparatory action only for use of 600 vehicles
> *October: Threatened Belfast electricity strike:*
> Preparatory action only
> *December: London power strike:*
> Four power stations operated for just under a week.
> 420 men in all three services employed
> *April 1950: London dock strike:*
> Services worked docks for just under three weeks.
> 20,000 men and 645 vehicles
> *June: Smithfield drivers' strike:*
> 1,500 men and 660 vehicles of Army and RAF at work.
> Expected to build-up to 5,000 men and 1,000 vehicles

Historians report that when the government used troops to break strikes 'there was no hesitation about it and no reservation around the cabinet table'.[35] Nye Bevan concurred!

The Attlee government evoked the Emergency Powers Act of 1920—the first time it had been used since the general strike of 1926. The government revived the Supply and Transport Organisation, which had been used to help crush the general strike, and it did so with the complete agreement of Nye Bevan and Stafford Cripps. 'It would be prudent to have wide powers in order to deal with any trouble that might arise', Bevan told the cabinet's industrial emergency committee on 28 June 1948.[36]

In May 1947 Bevan urged the use of legal steps by the attorney-general against dockworkers responsible for 'the instigation of illegal strikes'.[37] When busmen in the Midlands and the North went on strike, Bevan argued for the use of military vehicles to transport miners. Miners, of all people!

> The Minister of Health felt that there would be great advantage in stating publicly that in view of the overriding importance of maintaining coal production the Government had decided to make military vehicles available for carrying miners to and from their work.[38]

When workers in the power stations in London went on strike, it was Bevan, as minister responsible for labour, who, on 24 January 1950, argued for civil proceedings as these had 'worked as an effective deterrent in the mining industry'.[39] Bevan was minister of labour during January–April 1951 when seven London dockers were prosecuted under Order 1305. He rounded on a group of heckling dockers at Bermondsey: 'Shut up... Do you think the government should do nothing about it?' There was more shouting and Bevan declared: 'You are a lot of skulking cowards hiding behind your own anonymity...'[40]

Bevan's old comrade from the Socialist League, Cripps, was still more original. At a meeting of the cabinet's industrial emergency committee on 15 January 1947, when 20,000 London dockers were on strike, he suggested that the large number of Polish ex-servicemen in the country might be used as blacklegs for the maintenance of essential supplies.[41]

The cabinet's discussion in 1947 of equal pay for women, which had been unequivocally adopted as policy by party conference, was one of the most nauseating performances. The quibbling went on and on. Eventually 'The Cabinet accepted the principle but not the implementation'.[42] Three years later George Isaacs, then minister of labour, still argued in a memorandum to the cabinet that equal pay should not be introduced in government employment.[43]

Geoff Ellen summed up the Labour government's strike-breaking activity thus:

> Striking dockers, gas workers, miners and lorry drivers were denounced, spied upon and prosecuted. Two States of Emergency were proclaimed against them and two more were narrowly averted. Above all, the government used blacklegs against these strikes, often with the connivance of the strikers' own trade union leaders. On 18 different occasions between 1945 and 1951, the government sent troops, sometimes 20,000 of them, across picket lines to take over strikers' jobs. By 1948, it has been argued, 'strike-breaking had become almost second nature to the Cabinet'.[44]

Reforming zeal gives way to the consensus of 'Butskellism'

In the 1950s *The Economist* introduced a new term to the English language—Butskellism. This was the name given to the growing similarity between Labour and Conservative Party practices. Butskellism was a legacy of the postwar Labour government and its policies.

In December 1946 an unofficial Industrial Policy Committee was formed, made up of a number of Tory MPs and chaired by R A Butler, the author of the 1944 Education Act. It produced an Industrial Charter, which was enthusiastically received by a Tory conference in October 1947. The charter accepted state intervention to ensure full employment. Although nationalisation was forsworn as a principle of government, the cases of coal, the railways and the Bank of England were accepted in practice. Labour's welfare legislation was also accepted. Above all Butler described the charter as 'an assurance that, in the interests of efficiency, full employment and social security, modern Conservatism would maintain strong central guidance over the operation of the economy'.[45]

Of course not all Conservatives welcomed the Industrial Charter. Thus Sir Waldron Smithers called it 'milk and water' socialism.[46] On the other hand, Harold Macmillan later said that the Industrial Charter 'proclaimed the theme which inspired thirteen years of Conservative government which followed the final overthrow of the Socialists in 1951'.[47]

When the Conservatives won the general election of October 1951, Churchill appointed Butler chancellor of the exchequer in succession to Hugh Gaitskell. The break between the policies of the two was so minuscule that *The Economist* invented this new word, Butskellism, to describe it.[48] Richard Crossman, an MP and supporter of Nye Bevan, saw the new Conservative cabinet as 'only very slightly to the right of the most recent Attlee Cabinet', and commented that 'just as Attlee was running what was virtually a coalition policy on a Party basis, so Churchill may well do the same'.[49]

A consensus on economic and social policy had been forged.

However the Tories accepted only those measures which were unequivocally of benefit to their class. Nationalisation could be tolerated where the infrastructure was run-down and unprofitable. But even here there were pockets of industry where money could be made. Real resistance developed as soon as it looked as though going concerns such as road haulage and electricity, but above all during 1950–1 the steel industry, were to be nationalised.

One of the sticks used to beat supporters of further nationalisation was the inevitably low profitability of the dilapidated industries that were taken over. The fact was that coal was sold to private industry with a hidden subsidy. This helped make the NCB unprofitable, but it was a godsend for anti-nationalisation propaganda. A Gallup poll in November 1948 found only 24 percent of the population supported the proposed nationalisation of steel while 44 percent opposed it.[50]

In the altered political climate that prevailed after 1947 this could not but influence the more hesitant reformists, whose confidence was already dented. The effect on Labour was double-edged. On the right there were those who were satisfied that Nationalisation had completed its job of assisting private profit-making. They therefore opposed its extension to steel. However some on the left still saw the programme so far as merely the first step towards socialism.

A long period of dispute was beginning for Labour. Even in the conditions of economic expansion following the war, the consensus, the compromise achieved, was bound to be pulled in different directions. Mixed economy? All right. But what exact mixture between nationalised and private industry? A welfare state—but at what level should welfare benefits be pitched? And if there was a worsening in the economic situation and cuts became the order of the day, how much to cut and in what areas? In foreign policy NATO, the Atlantic alliance set up after the end of the war, was accepted as written on tablets of stone. But how far should Britain go in supporting the United States?

In move of the Tories towards Butskellism also affected the discussion. Right-wing Labour leaders argued that electoral success depended on winning the voters in the middle by having moderate policies. The left argued that Labour had to sharpen its differentiation from the Tories by adopting more distinct socialist policies.

With the economic crisis of 1947 as its background, a bitter argument took place in the cabinet between April and July over steel nationalisation. This was the first time that clear differences of opinion appeared in the cabinet. On the one side Herbert Morrison and John Wilmot, minister of supply, opposed steel nationalisation; on the other were Nye Bevan and Hugh Dalton. Although the cabinet did go ahead with legislation in 1948, the conflict over the issue continued right down to the end of 1949.

In 1947 the Labour Party adopted a document, *Industry and Society*, which in practice froze the borders of the public sector. The time had arrived for 'consolidation', it said, going on to praise private industry: 'under increasingly professional management, large firms are, on the whole, serving the nation well.' Both the left and right in the leadership supported this document although it did raise some resentment in the party.

Morrison told the 1948 Labour conference:

> do not ignore the need, not merely for considering further public ownership, but for allowing Ministers adequate time to consolidate, to develop, to make efficient the industries which have been socialized in the present Parliament... We must make the programme as attractive as we can to ourselves, but we must make it attractive also to public opinion...[51]

The constituency delegate who followed Morrison clearly expressed the unhappiness of the rank and file:

> the programme will be attractive to the public, not if it is something very wishy-washy and watered down but if it is bold and challenging I want to see in the forefront of our General Election programme a declaration of faith in Socialism—not the approach the Liberal has to nationalization, that when two or three Royal Commissions have decided that in a particular case, for empirical reasons, an industry ought to be nationalized, then we will nationalize it. I want us to say we believe, as economic scientists and on the grounds of social justice, that the large resources of production in this country ought to belong to the common people... When the present programme of the Labour Government has been completed some twenty percent of the industrial and economic life of this country will be publicly owned. At this speed it will take us 25 years to get to the stage when Socialism predominates...we are going too slow...

The delegate went on to reject the mixed economy:

> I do not believe that it is feasible, as a permanent basis, for a Socialist Government to control privately-owned industry. Ownership gives control. The only way in which we can get control is by getting ownership.[52]

He was to be disappointed. In April 1949 the party executive published a draft programme for the next election, *Labour Believes in Britain*. It was accepted by conference the same year. The list of industries proposed for nationalisation was water, cement, sugar, meat-wholesale and Industrial Assurance. This last proposal was later watered down under pressure from Morrison and Cripps. One delegate in the 1949 conference could rightly say: '*Labour Believes in Britain* reads like a White Paper... It is certainly not a Red Paper...'[53]

Bevan did his best in his summing-up to reassure the doubters.

In the name of party unity he was quite ecstatic about the 'wonderful opening speech of Herbert Morrison'.[54]

Many on the left did not follow Bevan's support for *Labour Believes in Britain*. Ian Mikardo, in a pamphlet titled *The Second Five Years*, urged the need to nationalise the joint stock banks and industrial assurance companies, shipbuilding, aircraft, construction, aero-engines, machine tools, and the assembly branch of mass produced motor vehicles. Then in January 1950 twelve MPs published a pamphlet entitled *Keeping Left*, in which they advocated the public ownership of road haulage, steel, insurance, cement, sugar and cotton.

Labour won the general election of 1950, but with a very small majority. None of the measures outlined in *Labour Believes in Britain* were implemented, save for the commitment to nationalise steel. Otherwise the whole issue of public ownership was shelved. In the run-up to the general election of October 1951, the new party manifesto, *Labour and the New Society*, for the first time since the war included no candidates for nationalisation save for steel, as Morrison wanted. The manifesto acceded to Bevan's wish, however, that the possibility of further takeovers be left open, calling in vague terms for new public enterprises when this would 'serve the national interest'. Morrison's opposition to further Nationalisation had won the day. When Bevan spoke in favour of *Labour and the New Society* at the 1950 annual conference the left was mute.

Morrison was strongly influenced by his estimate that nationalisation was an electoral albatross for the Labour Party. From 1948 onwards, and especially after the 1950 general election, he argued that future

Labour victories depended on an appeal to moderate voters who opposed nationalisation. Even the language of the first three years of government, itself a retreat from long-held Labour beliefs, was being abandoned.

A reactionary foreign and defence policy

Before coming to office, Labour leaders spoke of a foreign policy which was radically different to that of the Tories. As Attlee put it in 1937: 'there is no agreement on foreign policy between a Labour Opposition and a capitalist government'.[55]

The most extreme expression of the need for a real socialist foreign policy was the speech by Denis Healey, then a delegate at the May 1945 Labour Party Conference, in which he called on Labour to support the socialist revolution in Western and Central Europe:

> the Labour Party should have a clear foreign policy of its own, which is completely distinct from that of the Tory Party.
>
> The socialist revolution had already begun in Europe and was already firmly established in many countries in Eastern and Southern Europe. The crucial principle of our foreign policy should be to protect, assist, encourage and aid in every way the Socialist revolution wherever it appears... The upper class in every country are selfish, depraved, dissolute and decadent. These upper classes look to the British Army and the British people to protect them against the just wrath of the people who have been fighting underground against them for the first four years. We must see that that does not happen. The penalty for entertaining any hesitation about the support for the revolution would be that Labour would wake one day to find itself 'running with the Red Flag in front of the armoured car of Tory imperialism and counter-revolution'.[56]

Once Labour took office, socialist euphoria evaporated. On the day the election results were received, Ernest Bevin announced: 'British foreign policy will not be altered in any way under the Labour Government'.[57] On becoming foreign secretary he told the House of Commons: 'The basis of our policy is in keeping with that worked out by the Coalition Government, in which I worked in close collaboration with the Right Hon Member for Warwick and Leamington [Anthony Eden].' Eden reciprocated: '"I cannot recall one single occasion when there was a difference between us. I hope I do not embarrass the Foreign Secretary by saying that"... Mr Bevin: "No"'.[58]

Eden's memoirs note:

> I was in agreement with the aims of [Bevin's] foreign policy and with most that he did, and we met quite frequently. He would invite me to his room in the House of Commons where we discussed events informally. In Parliament I usually followed him in debate and I would have agreed with him more, if I had not been anxious to embarrass him less.[59]

James F Byrnes, the US secretary of state, wrote that 'Britain's stand...was not altered in the slightest'.[60]

Notwithstanding the economic plight of Britain, Attlee's government devoted a greater proportion of the GNP to defence than any other non-Communist nation in the period before the Korean war.

> In 1947 British defense expenditures amounted to 9.5 percent of GNP, and American expenditures to 6.5 percent; in 1950 they amounted to 7.7 percent, American to 5.9 percent, and French to 5.0 percent. Where defense manpower was concerned, it was the same story: in 1948 Britain had double the percentage of men under arms as the United States, and in 1950 still more than 50 percent as much.[61]

The Attlee government tried to salvage Britain's dwindling world imperialist role, notwithstanding its decline during the Second World War. Imperialism had bolstered British capitalism during the latter decades of the nineteenth century and during the 1930s, but history could not be repeated. Massive spending on armaments, started by Attlee and continued by the Tories during the 1950s, only accelerated the relative decline of British capitalism compared to other countries. Germany spent very little on armaments, and Japan even today spends only about 1 percent of its GNP. While both these countries were engaged in a high level productive investment in new factories and new technology, British capitalism wasted resources.

The linchpin of Labour's policy was the 'special relationship' with the USA. This was the means by which Britain's world role was preserved—by accepting the position of junior partner to the Americans in the new world economic and political order. Britain ceded the job of world policeman to the US, but still maintained extensive military commitments in certain areas—including Greece, Palestine, the Middle East, Singapore and Malaysia. The new relationship was cemented by Bevin's creation of NATO, which was established in April 1949.

Britain also accepted a subordinate position to the USA in the world financial field. Sterling was restored as an international currency—not, however, as powerful as the dollar.

In March 1946 Attlee became the first prime minister in British history to implement military conscription in peacetime with the setting up of National Service. Pressure from the PLP at first reduced the period of service from the intended eighteen months to twelve. The brass hats did not like it. As Lord Montgomery, Chief of the Imperial General Staff, recalled:

> In October 1948, we assembled the Military Members of the Army Council...and asked them if they were all prepared to resign in a body, led by me, if anything less than eighteen months National Service with the Colours was decided upon by the Government. They all agreed.[62]

The government capitulated. Like the Curragh mutiny this was a demonstration that the state machine was not neutral, to be used by any party that happened to be in office, but was an instrument of the ruling class.

When the Korean War broke out conscription was increased to two years. Korea had been partitioned at the end of the Second World War. The war between north and south began on 25 June 1950. Two days later the cabinet agreed unanimously to endorse US intervention in support of the south.[63] British troops were immediately sent to assist. When the issue eventually reached the House of Commons on 5 July, only three Labour MPs voted against the government action.

The Labour Government also helped to crush risings in Greece, Malaya and Vietnam.

Indian independence: a shining exception?

The granting of independence to India seems to run against the right-wing trend of Attlee's foreign policy. Labour leaders depicted it as a magnanimous gesture. In fact it was brought about by the revolt of the Indian navy in February 1946, alongside movements in the military and air services and massive civil disturbances which led to the deaths of 223 people in Bombay.[64] This made nonsense of what one historian calls 'the legend of magnanimity':

> [In February 1946] the whole of the Navy in India was immobilized for five days... In Bombay and Karachi British forces actually engaged in battle with Indian sailors. It is hardly conceivable that such a crisis did not have a direct impact on the attitude of the Labour Party towards independence... Nehru's biographer...notes that 'it seems more than a mere coincidence that the announcement about the British Cabinet Mission was made one day after the outbreak of the Bombay mutiny'.[65]

It was the threat of a revolution that forced the hands of the government. In the words of P J Griffiths, leader of the European Group in the Indian Central Legislative Assembly during 1946: 'India in the opinion of many was on the verge of a revolution before the British Cabinet Mission arrived. The Cabinet Mission has at least postponed if not eliminated the danger'.[66] The respite was brief. Lord Ismay, chief of staff to Mountbatten, the Viceroy charged with the transfer of power, described the situation a year later:

> India in March, 1947, was a ship on fire in mid-ocean with ammunition in the hold. By then it was a question of putting out the fire before it reached the ammunition. There was, in fact, no option before us but to do what we did.[67]

Even the editor of the *Daily Mail* admitted that to stay in India 'it would have needed an occupation force of 500,000 men'—and no such force was could have been made available given Britain's other commitments.[68]

Forced out unwillingly from India, Attlee nevertheless made sure that British capital would not suffer unduly. The 1947 settlement negotiated by Lord Mountbatten with the leaders of the Indian Congress Party and the Moslem League was both a retreat for Britain and a compromise for British imperialism with the capitalists and landlords of the subcontinent. This included the partition of India into two states, India and Pakistan, with extremely artificial boundaries, leading to mass shifts of population, communal bloodbaths and the wholesale flight of refugees. There were many massacres, especially in the Punjab, with Sikhs and Moslems primarily involved. Perhaps half a million lost their lives.[69]

Despite the massive human suffering not a penny of British investment had been sacrificed. Thus the Attlee government was far more effective in defending British interests in India than the French were with their prolonged colonial struggle in Indochina and Algeria, the Dutch in Indonesia, the Belgians in the Congo, or the Portuguese in Angola and Mozambique.

South Africa

Until this point India had been the touchstone for Labour's attitude to imperialism. Since 1947, however, South Africa has taken its place. Attlee set the tone for what has been one of the ugliest features of Labour's foreign policy in government.

Richard Ovendale has described Labour's reaction to the Nationalist Party election victory and establishment of apartheid in 1948. In the growing atmosphere of Cold War elsewhere in the world, the Nationalists in South Africa could be useful allies, being 'terrified of communism' and 'in "complete sympathy" with the aims of British foreign policy.' Admiration was mutual. A cabinet paper of September 1950 wished to cultivate South Africa's goodwill 'from the general strategic and defence points of view.' In addition uranium for the nuclear programme, gold for the sterling area and the hundreds of millions of pounds worth of British investments in South Africa were powerful inducements towards friendship.

In 1951 Patrick Gordon Walker, Labour secretary of state for Commonwealth relations reported on South Africa:

> Those who argue that because we dislike the Union's Native policy we should ostracise her and have nothing to do with her completely fail to understand the realities of the situation. Such a policy would not only gravely harm us in the defence and economic fields it would also weaken our power to deter South Africa from foolhardy acts from fear of breaking with us.

Ovendale concludes:

> it was Attlee's Labour governments that perceived South Africa's strategic and economic importance for Britain, and the need to maintain contact to ameliorate the policy of apartheid. They laid down the fundamentals of British policy towards South Africa that were, with fluctuations, pursued for the following 30 years.[70]

Labour and the bomb

One of the most remarkable events in the 1945–51 period must be the production of the atom bomb. Not only did Attlee introduce the nuclear arms programme, but he kept it secret from the public, the trade unions, the party executive, the Parliamentary Labour Party and most of the cabinet! It seems that only those cabinet ministers on the secret committee Gen 75, which since 1945 had dealt with decision-making on atomic energy, had any inkling of the existence of Britain's atomic bomb.[71]*

---

* A key role in Gen 75 was played by Sir John Anderson, an Independent Conservative sitting on the opposition front bench. In January 1947 Gen 75 was converted into Gen 163, a secret cabinet committee consisting of Attlee, Bevin, Morrison, A V Alexander (minister of defence), J Wilmot (minister of supply, later replaced by Strauss), and Lord Addison, the Dominions secretary. It was this committee that decided, in the month it was established, to make the bomb. Expenditure on atomic research and development was concealed under other items.

During the whole period of the 1945–51 Labour government there was not a single Commons debate devoted to atomic energy. In the same six years the subject figured less than ten times on the cabinet agenda and seven of these were concerned with the two visits Attlee made to US President Harry Truman in November 1945 and December 1950. Apart from these:

> the Cabinet as a body was completely excluded from all the major decisions on atomic policy in these years. It took no part in the decisions to establish a research establishment, to build piles to produce plutonium, or, later, to build gaseous diffusion plants to separate uranium 235; no part in the decisions to make and then test in atomic bomb...and about the planned place of atomic bombs in British strategy.[72]

Not until October 1952, when Britain first publicly tested her own atomic weapons on the Montebello Islands off the North West Australian coast, did the decision of the Attlee government become general knowledge.

Remarkable complacency in the ranks

By and large Labour MPs were very placid. In very few cases did a number of MPs vote against the government. The opposition of the left inside the Parliamentary Labour Party was sporadic and dominated by issues of foreign policy and defence.* This passivity extended to the party outside parliament.

Throughout the six years of the Attlee government the Labour Party executive was completely tame. In the words of Bob McKenzie:

* Here some of the few examples in which this occurred:

On 13 December 1945, twenty-three Labour MPs voted against the government's acceptance of a US loan.

On 18 November 1946, forty-five Labour MPs voted against the introduction of peacetime conscription.

On 7 May 1947 an amendment to the Conscription Bill stating that no person subject in the Act 'shall be required to take duty in aid of the civil power in connection with a trade dispute' got the support of eleven Labour MPs.

On 12 March 1949, four Labour MPs voted against the ratification of NATO (and about 100 abstained).

On 16 May 1949, forty-five Labour MPs voted against the Ireland Bill.

On 13 July 1949, when emergency powers were introduced to deal with the London dock strike, four Labour MPs voted against.

On 25 March 1959, when Seretse Khama, Chief of Botswana, was banished from his country by the government for marrying a white woman and thus antagonising the South African government, seven Labour MPs voted against.

On 2 May 1951, five Labour MPs voted against the imposition of dental and optical charges.

> not once in the lifetime of the Labour Government of 1945 and 1950 did the NEC give any public indication that it disagreed with any item of Government... At each of the conferences during the period 1946 to 1951 the NEC invariably acted as a watchdog for the Government; they never once advocated, or were even prepared to tolerate, a proposal which differed in any significant particular from the policies of the Labour Government.

One reason for this was that:

> The Executive of the Party...is impotent during a Labour Government, since constitutionally Cabinet Ministers, although themselves members of the Executive, must not discuss in their secondary capacity details of what they have done as Privy Councillors.[73]

The party executive actually withered through disuse. Whereas in the 1930s it met on average thirty-five times a year, after 1945 it managed fewer than twelve meetings a year.[74] The idea that the national Labour Party can really control the parliamentary leaders has always been a nonsense. It is doubly so when they are in government.

Critics of government policies on the executive probably never numbered more than four or five of its twenty-seven members. Its docility led Harold Laski to refuse further membership in 1948, on the ground that he could operate more effectively as an individual party member.[75]

The executive was matched by conferences. In *Tribune* Ian Mikardo pronounced them to be 'as dead as the dodo'.[76] McKenzie furnishes the proof: 'On a total of only nine occasions during the six party conferences (1946–51) was the advice of the NEC rejected by the conference...[77]* On the whole, the Attlee Governments were as nearly immune as any Conservative Government can expect to be from outright condemnation by its annual conference'.[78]

Strains did eventually appear over foreign policy and the dislocation caused by the Korean War. Nonetheless the 1950 conference endorsed

* McKenzie records, 'in 1946 the conference passed four resolutions which were opposed by the NEC... The 1947 conference overrode the advice of Aneurin Bevan, the Minister of Health and a member of the NEC, by passing a resolution favouring the abolition of tied cottages. The same conference overwhelmingly insisted on adopting a resolution favouring equal pay for equal work for women despite a plea from the NEC that the resolution should be withdrawn. The 1948 conference renewed the demand for the abolition of tied cottages, again overriding Aneurin Bevan and the NEC; and the same conference passed a resolution opposing "any reduction or withdrawal of food or clothing subsidies..." During the conferences held in the three year 1949–51 inclusive, the Executive's advice was rejected on only one issue involving...food distribution... This...apart, the NEC had not the slightest difficulty in restraining the conference from taking action which would in any way embarrass the Labour Government'.[77]

Britain's involvement in Korea by a huge majority. The star of the conference was Nye Bevan, who made a passionate plea for the conference to rally behind the government. Bevan said that that conference showed a 'greater degree of unity than I have ever known before in my experience in the Labour Party'.[79]

This was remarkable in view of the constant skirmishing during the first MacDonald government and the deep split of the second. Later Harold Wilson's administration would experience great turbulence at conferences between 1964 and 1970, and there was to be a yawning gulf between left and right under the Labour governments of 1974–9.

Because Labour combines class and nation, it is inevitable that individuals should synthesise them in different ways. Usually the left emphasises the immediate aspirations of workers, while the right stresses that a healthy national system is necessary *before* workers' demands can be attended to. There is an in-built tension. The 1945–51 government showed that despite this habitual animosity between left and right, together they form a fundamental unity. Since Keynesian economics appeared to gratify the claims of the left, Attlee and the cabinet were able to pursue a very right-wing reformism without opposition. This was shown by the fate of the *Keep Left* manifesto and *Tribune*.

A feeble opposition: *Keep Left*

In May 1947 *Keep Left* was published by Richard Crossman, Michael Foot and Ian Mikardo. Another twelve MPs put their names to this manifesto. Though covering domestic policy, its sharpest criticism was directed at foreign and defence policy. As always, reformists are far more radical on issues far from home since these relate less directly to real domestic class struggle.

The core of the pamphlet was that 'Britain has been driven into a dangerous dependence on the United States.' It called for the abandonment of the 'Tory idea of bolstering up the British Empire with American dollars and fighting America's battle with British soldiers.' Britain should 'regain her independence.' Not strong enough to do this on her own, she should create a 'third force' in the shape of a European Socialist alliance based on Britain and France. More socialism was needed at home to assist the economy and avoid dependence on the United States. This demanded more planning to cut costs of production and thus encourage the export drive. A synthesis of the national interest and socialism were at the heart of *Keep Left*.

At little over a year, *Keep Left* holds the record as the shortest lived left rebellion in the history of Labour: Marshall Aid from America killed it stone dead. This aid, designed to restore stable capitalism to war-tom Western Europe, was very popular indeed. Cripps described it as 'an act of grand immediate generosity and enlightenment'.[80] He later stated: 'Without Marshall Aid something like one and a half million men might have been thrown out of work for lack of raw materials'.[81]

Reformists dare not bite the hand that pays for reforms, whatever its source. The American cash injections of 1946 and 1948 helped pay for the welfare state and tied Labour Britain firmly to US imperialist objectives. The price of Labour's reformism was an alliance with international capitalism, and the Cold War.

Crossman, one of the authors of *Keep Left*, explained the impact of the Marshall Plan on his thinking:

> I will be frank. My own views about America have changed a great deal in the last six months. Many members have had a similar experience. I could not have believed six months ago that a plan of this sort would have been worked out in detail with as few conditions.[82]

Thus an amendment to the Marshall Plan got short shrift at the 1948 Labour Party conference.[83]

Crossman now wrote *Keep Left*'s obituary. He put its demise down to two factors: first the economic austerity policy of Cripps with which *Keep Left agreed*; second, the announcement of Marshall Aid. 'Once Cripps took over the economic front and began serious Socialist planning, and once Ernest Bevin adopted Western Union [NATO] and began to make it work, it was my view that the *Keep Left* group had fulfilled its purpose'.[84]

Tribune, loyal guard of the government

Tribune was for many years the mouthpiece of the Labour left, or more precisely, of the left in the Parliamentary Labour Party. Let us see what its attitude was to various planks of the government's policy.

Tribune was enthusiastic about Stafford Cripps' austerity policy and his wage freeze. If anything the measures did not go far enough. An editorial on the 1948 budget stated: 'So far both the Government and the TUC have failed to make an adequately bold approach towards a wages policy... Sir Stafford Cripps should have done more'.[85]

When in October 1949 the government announced massive spending cuts, *Tribune* asked in an editorial 'Do the Cuts Make Sense? answered unequivocally, 'Yes': 'They have one immediate aim, and one only—to enable the country to get the central advantage of devaluation'. The government was however criticised' 'for not presenting the cuts in a more understandable and stimulating way'.[86]

Strikes did not find favour with *Tribune*. An editorial in June 1948 declared:

> *Tribune* believes that the dock strike is an unmitigated calamity. We think that the dockers were wrong to strike and that they could only do injury to themselves by persistence in this course. We dearly hope that by the time we go to press the men will have returned to work'.[87]

When a State of Emergency was declared in July 1949 with the aim of breaking a national dock strike, *Tribune* had this to say:

> the Government has now staked its authority on the success of the emergency powers, and we must hope that the dockers will quickly accept the verdict and return to work... We hope they will quickly realise that it is only the Communist and Tory enemies of trade union rights who stand to profit by their action.[88]

Many other examples could be cited.

If once you mistake economic planning under capitalism for socialism, such confusion is inevitable. As *Tribune* showed, ultimately such reformist delusions lead those who hold them to turn against the workers.

Tribune again and again commended union leaders for supporting wage restraint, complaining only that the policy was too loose. What was necessary was a legally binding incomes policy. Writing on the White Paper on Personal Incomes it stated: '...the White Paper sits precariously on the fence between free wage bargaining and Government intervention in wage regulations'.[89] The latter should be imposed against what Mikardo called the prevailing 'wage anarchy'[90]: 'It really is idle to talk about planned economy with an unplanned wages sector... That revolution won't be easy to accomplish, but without it we have no real hope of Socialism in our time'.[91]

Together with government ministers and trade union bureaucrats, *Tribune* indulged in the witch-hunting of Communists for 'inciting' strikes. Attlee's decision to remove Communists (and fascists) from certain civil service posts in the spring of 1948 was endorsed:

> [Communists] owe allegiance to another State... They do not accept the premises of democracy... To ask that Ministers should be prepared to trust Communist Party members with security secrets seems absurd.[92]

In similar vein *Tribune* supported the ban on Communists holding office in the TGWU in 1949.

Tribune could stand reality on its head to defend the government. When Ernest Bevin's maiden speech as foreign secretary emphasised the continuity of his policy with that of the war time coalition, *Tribune* wrote: 'Ernest Bevin's speech in the Commons last week marked a turning point which future historians might well describe as the moment at which Britain broke the continuity of her foreign policy'.[93]

Tribune criticised only details. On the main issues—NATO, Marshall Aid, National Service, the response to the Russian blockade of Berlin, the Korean war—it was in complete agreement with the government.

On NATO, for example, *Tribune* said: 'it certainly improves the chance [of peace] because it makes aggression against any of the member states more dangerous for the aggressor'.[94] This was too much for Ian Mikardo, who resigned from the editorial board. He could not stand the transformation of the paper from a fellow-travelling broadsheet of Moscow in the 1930s to being a shadow of Washington. In contrast Nye Bevan backed NATO fully: 'I never have had any doubt—that Western Europe is perfectly entitled to form whatever alignments and coalitions, and take whatever measures it wishes for its own defence'.[95]

When the House of Commons voted on the establishment of NATO on 12 May 1949, Churchill had a field day. Not one *Tribune* stalwart had voted against. He recalled that immediately after his famous Cold War speech, in which he had coined the phrase 'iron curtain', 105 MPs moved a motion of censure against him. Where were they now? 'I do not see them all here today...we have got about a hundred [converts] in a bunch, so far as I can make out'.[96]

Tribune not only supported the introduction of National Service but with little disagreement wanted its selective extension to two and a half years.[97] When it came to the Berlin blockade, Bevan urged the cabinet to send tanks across the Russian zone of Germany to back up the Western airlift.[98] When Harry Truman, who had ordered the bombing of Hiroshima and Nagasaki, was re-elected president of the USA at the end of 1948, *Tribune* was ecstatic 'Salute to America!... We have no hesitation in hailing the sensational Democratic triumph at the polls as a victory for the common people all over the world'.[99]

At the outbreak of the Korean War, *Tribune* came out firmly on the side of the United States, whose action:

> demonstrated that there is no possibility of Communist aggression succeeding by reason of Western appeasement. The West has shown that it has preferred to fight, if need be, and that is a lesson that will not be lost on the Russians.[100]

When the American army was doing well in the field, *Tribune* argued that it should not stop at the 38th Parallel, the border of North and South Korea, but should go on to unite the whole country.[101]

At the same time *Tribune* waxed enthusiastic about the British Empire:

> We want to stay in Africa both for our own purposes and in the interests of the African peoples... Africa offers huge natural resources which can be exploited for the benefit of Britain and the world... We do not need to apologize for our mission in Africa. Whatever the reason which took our forebears there, we must stay.[102]

In fact one of the charges *Tribune* laid at the door of the Tories was that they 'neglected the Empire'.[103] Nationalism was the paper's dominant obsession.

Michael Foot chooses as Bevan's outstanding feature that he spoke about Great Britain: 'he always used the "Great" long after most others had abandoned it'.[104] For example, in a speech on 4 July 1948 Bevan said:

> The eyes of the world are turning to Great Britain. We now have the moral leadership of the world, and before many years we shall have people coming here as to a modem Mecca, learning from us in the twentieth century as they learnt from us in the seventeenth century.[105]

In his speech of resignation from the government Bevan stated: 'There is only one hope for mankind, and that hope remains in this little island'.[106] Foot, quoting these words, adds: 'He would never allow the Tories to purloin the patriotic argument'.[107] Marx's words that 'workers have no country' were a sealed book for Bevan and Foot.

Conclusion

History has been kind to Attlee. In the midst of today's mass unemployment, privatisation and welfare cuts, his tenure in office seems a paradise by comparison.*

* It has not always been the case. When memories were still fresh, both right and left found things they objected to, although this never amounted to a full-scale attack. The right blamed the government for its cloth-cap image and too close identification with obsolete shibboleths such as nationalisation. The left pointed to its failure to capture the commanding heights of the economy,

Yet the real legacy of 1945–51, like so much in Labour's history, is deeply paradoxical. After only twenty months in office, the weakness of British capitalism, its dependence on the US and the massive burden of imperialism put an end to the government aggressive reformism. Its final collapse in 1951 was rooted in the same causes, this time sharpened by the impact of the Korean War On foreign affairs, nuclear issues, and the suppression of strikes Labour had behaved like its capitalist rivals, and sometimes with more effect.

On the other hand the party kept its popularity with workers high. In forty-three by-elections it lost only one seat! Furthermore the October 1951 general election gave Labour the highest poll ever achieved by one party—13,948,605 votes—48.8 percent of the total votes cast. Only the vagaries of the electoral system gave the Tories a majority in parliament. Notwithstanding austerity and rationing at home, and wars overseas, Labour kept its support. How can we explain this?

First of all the economic difficulties were viewed by the mass of the people as a consequence of war rather than government mismanagement. Secondly, the existence of full employment, contrasting so strongly with the 1930s, served as proof that the government kept its promises. Finally, as the level of industrial militancy was low compared with the period after the First World War, the Labour government demonstrated success in making the transition from war to peace. And to many, the reforms granted to workers were the main reason for the social peace.

Another striking feature of the time was that although Labour had acted as it always does in government—as the manager of capitalism—the left were applauding this loudly. Again, how was this done?

MacDonald had had the excuse that he led only minority governments to explain his behaviour as prime minister. Attlee had no such alibi. Instead he grasped the nettle, and dispensed with even a verbal commitment to the ending of capitalism. He got away without trouble because of the world boom. This was one of those increasingly rare moments during which British capitalism was not in crisis. So Attlee could perform what is usually an impossible feat of magic—to satisfy the ruling class without alienating working-class supporters. For once the reformist project worked. So great was expansion that the bosses' desire to accumulate could be satisfied while something was left over to sweeten the system for the workers. *This was not a situation likely to be*

and its capitulation to big business and the cold war.

repeated. Attlee's government is likely to remain the highest pinnacle of reformist practice.

This brings us to the question of how many reforms were gained by having Labour rather than the Tories in office.

The Tories would not have nationalised steel. But in any case, Labour ignored its 1945 manifesto commitment to do so until January 1951, and steel was returned to private hands after the Tory election victory in October. Apart from this, as later developments showed, the Tories understood the need to maintain an infrastructure and a productive, well-educated workforce. If we give Labour the benefit of the doubt we can say that their reforms went a *bit* further. But that is all. As comparisons with countries without reformist governments show, not too much can be made of the difference between Labour and Tory welfare.

Indeed, it can be argued that in many ways the Labour government of 1945–51 was an obstacle to any but the most limited reforms. Under Attlee capitalists conceded as much and no more than they felt like. We know that they were not afraid of Labour's parliamentary majority. Neither 600 people sitting on benches and emitting hot air, nor 'popular opinion' has ever prevented capitalists from fighting tooth and nail to defend their interests. Bosses are, however, afraid of the power of the working class. By 1944 workers had been showing a capacity for action and self-activity not seen since before the General Strike. Yet it was precisely this force that Labour successfully shackled through the union bureaucracy and, where that failed, by using troops as strikebreakers.

The political results of Attlee's government lasted beyond 1951. The Labour leadership had tied itself more closely to the ruling class than ever before. Worse still, it had led many of its most active supporters more or less to renounce the idea of overcoming capitalism (even by gradual stages) and to accept not only that the system was here to stay, but that it should be consciously nurtured. For the minority who considered themselves socialists, the result was disastrous. The Labour left was reduced to a pathetic rump and the space for revolutionary socialist ideas was cut to a minimum. Looked at in this way, the ruling class got the best of the deal

However the picture was not so simple.

Because Labour was in office, *the language of consensus came to be expressed in reformist terms*. This was of long-term importance. Many of the gains of 1945–51 were not especially due to Labours efforts, yet the period planted the idea in the working class that workers had *a right* to a job, *a right* to decent housing, and *a right* to health. It was society's duty to provide them. Other countries, such as Germany and the US, may have delivered a similar level of reforms since 1945, but, because they lacked the veneer of reformist ideology provided by a Labour Party, they were not seen as a *social duty* in the same way. British workers gained only the crumbs from the rich pickings of the booming world economy, but they did not see them as crumbs, but as theirs *as of right*—and this stored up a potential for resistance when those crumbs were withdrawn. Even today this potential, around issues such as the health service, is a long way from being exhausted.

Therefore the assault on the post-war consensus mounted since the mid-1970s (first by Wilson and Callaghan and more radically by Thatcher) is a reactionary attack on reformist consciousness, which, because it partially represents working-class aspirations, must be resisted.

Even during the Attlee government, the reformist consensus was shown to be built on unstable foundations. The reforming zeal of the government had more or less run out by 1948, and still the mole of history went on working. The increasing suppression of unofficial strikes, the bouts of inflation especially following the devaluation of the pound in 1949, the outbreak of the Korean War, the cuts, all caused a degree of disaffection among politically advanced workers that was reflected in the Labour Party.

The growing threat that the Korean War could escalate into a far wider conflict, and rising witch-hunts against Communists, jolted the constituency parties to revolt against the national executive from 1952 onwards, and spurred wide rank and file support for Bevan in the unions.

Attlee's government had not ushered in socialism. Its real triumph lay in its steering of British capitalism through a period of stress in the aftermath of the Second World War, and in assisting the USA to stabilise capitalism the world over.

12

'Thirteen wasted years'

LABOUR WENT into the October 1951 election exhausted by six years of hard work but euphoric about the future. Supporters were convinced that even if the Tory Party won, it would not last long. It would be unable to maintain the two great assets that made the Attlee government better than the 1930s: full employment and the welfare state. So after a short time Labour would return to office. Labour's 1951 election slogan was 'Ask your Dad!'

Prophecies of doom if the Tories won were many and varied. Arthur Deakin, general secretary of the TGWU, told the 1951 Labour Conference, held three weeks before the election: 'I know how desirous the Tories are of reimposing those restrictions that will enable them to bring us to our knees'.[1] Alice Bacon, in her presidential address to the TUC, insisted:

> All in Britain who suffered unemployment and poverty between the wars look to us with hope. They dread, and they are right to dread, the return of a Tory Government. They dread the re-emergence of unemployment, reductions in social services and the catastrophic price increases which would surely follow a Tory victory.[2]

Predictions about the Tories proved wildly inaccurate. Contrary to reformist beliefs, full employment and the welfare state were not the single-handed achievements of Attlee, but the result of a booming capitalist system that the Tories were happy to live with. So it was that Labour remained out of office for thirteen years—the longest period spent in opposition by a major political party since the Reform Bill of 1832.

The long boom—which was to last until the 1960s—was a by product of the high level of spending on arms, extended by the escalating cold war and the development of nuclear weapons. The tendency in capitalism for profit rates to fall and for society to lurch from boom to overproduction and slump was allayed by massive state spending on armaments, particularly in the US and Britain. So the prosperity of these years was built on the cone of a bomb. Capitalism was not more rational and harmonious, but less so, and equally subject to the *diktat* of competition, now taking really deadly forms in the nuclear arms race. From 1951 to 1964 productivity in Britain increased faster than in any other period of comparable length in the twentieth century. By 1964 total production measured at constant prices was 40 percent higher than in 1951. The economy grew faster than at any time since the peak of the Victorian era. Unemployment averaged less than 2.5 percent of the labour force in all but one of the thirteen years of Tory rule. This was radically different, of course, from the years between the two world wars. From 1921 to 1938 there was no year in which less than 9 percent of the labour force was unemployed. In the slump of 1931–2 the figure exceeded 22 percent. But even in the relatively prosperous mid- and late 1930s, the figure was usually well above 10 percent.

Inflation too stayed low in the 1950s. Retail prices rose by about 3.25 percent per year from 1952 to 1964, less than half the rate of 1946–1952 (and also a good deal slower than in 1964–70, not to speak of 1974–79, the two periods Labour was again in office).

Real wages of workers rose by over 25 percent in those thirteen years. Social provisions were not slashed. For example, house building ran at over 300,000 a year, as against some 200,000 when Labour left office.

The political commentator Andrew Gamble wrote:

> The 1950s were the golden years for the Conservatives...the contrast between the years of 'austerity' under Labour and the years of 'affluence' under the Conservatives was apparent enough to seem a vindication of the Conservatives' claim that they could run a welfare capitalist system better than Labour'.[3]

The Tories did not attack on the trade union front; on the contrary they appeased. The union bureaucracy must function whether Labour is in government or not, so when the Conservatives were returned to office, the TUC General Council announced:

> It is our long standing practice to seek to work amicably with whatever Government is in power and through consultation jointly with Ministers and with the other side of industry to find practical solutions to the social and economic problems facing this country.[4]

Despite expectations, the Tory government reciprocated:

> Indeed, the stage was reached under the Government when hardly any Government committee was formed without someone in authority asking for the trade union view to be represented on it.[5]

In some respects the Tories treated the unions even better than Labour. As one writer put it, whereas the Labour government frequently resorted to emergency measures against strikes, the Tories were 'almost nonchalant in their treatment of strikes... They have been less disposed to use emergency powers or troops'.[6]

The Tory boom threw the Labour Party into disarray. It was more and more obvious that Labour was not the only party that could produce full employment and welfare services.

The revisionists

With the continuation of the boom, a group of leading Labour intellectuals declared themselves Revisionists. They took their name from the German Social Democrat Eduard Bernstein, who had attempted to revise Marxism at the turn of the century. He had redefined the fundamental character of the labour movement as a 'democratic socialist reform party' and not a party of social revolution. Opposing Marx, he argued that the contradictions in capitalism do not get sharper but, on the contrary, are continuously being alleviated. Capitalism is steadily being tamed, becoming more adaptable, and there is a tendency towards permanent prosperity. Social contradictions are also weakened by the expansion of the middle class and the more democratic distribution of capital ownership through shares. Bernstein's trump card in support of his arguments was that for two decades, since 1873, capitalism had not suffered a major slump.

The extent to which the British Revisionists of the 1950 were a copy of the German Revisionists half a century earlier was uncanny. Equally extraordinary is the way they overlooked the fact that Bernstein had been discredited first by the brilliant arguments of Rosa Luxemburg in her book *Reform or Revolution* and then by the First World War, the revolutionary crises that followed it and the Nazi regime. These confounded all his surmises.

The most important intellectual in Labour's new current was Anthony Crosland. His book, *The Future of Socialism*, published in 1956, was to become the Bible of the Revisionists. According to Crosland, the anarchy of capitalism was withering away and with it class conflicts. The system was becoming more and more rational and democratic. Capitalism itself would peacefully dissolve, helped along by the increasing role of the state in the economy and developments inside the private firm that undermined the profit motive.

With the growing separation of shareholders from managers in the large companies, the latter would pursue goals other than maximum profits.

> Business leaders are now, in the main, paid by salary and not by profit, and owe their power to their position in the managerial structure, and not to ownership. Meanwhile, the nominal owners have largely lost even the residue of control which they retained before the war.
>
> And top management today is independent not only of the firm's own shareholders, but increasingly of the capitalist or property-owning class as a whole, including the financial institutions... The economic power of the capital market and the finance houses, and hence *capitalist* financial control over industry (in the strict sense of the word), are thus much weaker. This change alone makes it rather absurd to speak now of a capitalist ruling-class...

If capital accumulation was no longer the prime goal, what was?

> The business leader can also acquire prestige by gaining a reputation as a progressive employer, who introduces co-partnership or profit-sharing schemes: or by being known to possess a high standing in Whitehall, and to have the ear of Ministers, an obvious candidate, perhaps, for Royal Commissions and National Advisory Councils; or by enjoying an outstanding local and civic reputation, as a benefactor, a helpful friend to the City Council, a member of the Court of the civic University; or by displaying obvious patriotism, and devoting a lot of time to the British Productivity Council; or simply being an intellectual, who broadcasts and writes in Bank Reviews, or makes speeches at the British Institute of Management or Nuffield conferences at Oxford.[7]

All the talk about production being dedicated to making profits rather than meeting human need was, according to Crosland, sheer nonsense.

> Production for use and production for profit may be taken as broadly coinciding now that working-class purchasing power is so high. What is profitable is what the consumer finds useful; and the firm and the consumer desire broadly the same allocation of resources.[8]

What an ideal picture of capitalism and its workings! A golden age was born.

> Private industry is at last becoming humanised. I do not mean that all businessmen now behave as though they were *manqué* philanthropists

> or social reformers...most businessmen are at least tinged by these more social attitudes and motives.[9]

A 'peaceful revolution' had begun in which class conflict would be unthinkable: 'One cannot imagine today a deliberate offensive alliance between Government and employers against the Unions,' wrote Crosland.[10]

As the ownership of industry became less important so too did the demand for nationalisation:[11]

> there is now no insuperable *economic* difficulty about the Government imposing its will, provided it has one, on either public or private industry. Indeed, post-1945 experience in the planning field strongly underlines [the argument] that ownership is not now an important determinant of economic power.[12]

The land would flow with milk and honey from here on in: 'We stand, in Britain, on the threshold of mass abundance'.[13] Now that Keynesianism guaranteed uninhibited growth the state could look forward to high tax revenues which could finance social reforms and social welfare plans. Socialists should divert their attention away from economic issues. To what?

> we shall turn our attention increasingly to other, and in the long run more important, spheres—of personal freedom, happiness, and cultural endeavour; the cultivation of leisure, beauty, grace, gaiety, excitement... more open-air cafes, brighter and gayer streets at night, later closing-hours for public houses, more local repertory theatres, better and more hospitable hoteliers and restauranteurs...more murals and pictures in public places, better designs for furniture and pottery and women's clothes, statues in the centre of new housing-estates, better-designed street-lamps and telephone kiosks, and so on *ad infinitum*.[14]

Crosland was like the scientist who measures the growth of a puppy and predicts that in fifty years it will be an elephant. As a 'realist', therefore, he now found Marx's analysis completely useless. The old man had 'little or nothing to offer the contemporary socialist' since, 'His prophecies have been almost without exception falsified'.[15]

Crosland concluded that Britain had ceased to be a capitalist country:

> the proper definition of the word capitalism is a society with the essential social, economic, and ideological characteristics of Great Britain from the 1830s to the 1930s; and this, assuredly, the Britain of

> 1956 is not. And so, to the question 'Is this still Capitalism?', I would answer 'No'.[16]

The Revisionists bore the hallmarks of Fabianism. Like the old Fabians, they believed in the neutrality of the state, they were committed to gradualism and consensus. But they strayed away from their forefathers by passing a positive judgment on the present system and by rejecting the need to transform society. Thus the Revisionists moved from Fabian 'Socialism' to a position indistinguishable from the main progressive branch of Liberalism. Hugh Gaitskell, the most important Revisionist and leader of the Labour Party from 1955 to 1963, accepted this logic.

We have already described the Labour Party as a form of organised amnesia. The Revisionists were its greatest exponents. Crosland behaved as though the sort of society that could produce the Second World War, or the horrors of fascism and mass unemployment that preceded it, had disappeared entirely. This inability to understand the inner processes of capitalism, to comprehend its past or predict its future, but to paint a completely impressionistic picture based on today's events is deep-rooted in the Labour Party.

Labour's avoidance of theory stems from its refusal to take a class standpoint from which to analyse society. As we see with Crosland, the net result is that they capitulate to the most superficial ruling class ideas available at the time. The boss would have you believe he is not an exploiter, but a kind-hearted and charitable fellow, Crosland duly obliges with what passes as an intellectual theory to support this.

This shallowness of ideas, alas, is not confined to the Labour right.

Bevanism

Aneurin Bevan led the biggest, although not the most left wing, rebellion in the history of the Labour Party. The context of this revolt was the increasing consensus between the Tories in office and the Labour Revisionists. Because of this, political conflict developed not so much between the two parties, as within the Labour Party. Bevanism was a reaction to the radical move to the right by the Labour leadership.

Unfortunately Bevan was afflicted with a poverty of ideas. While the Revisionists wandered around the new post-capitalist Wonderland, the Bevanites, like the dormouse at the Mad Hatter's tea party, kept their eyes tight shut. They tried simply to deny the boom would last, saying that mass unemployment was only just around the comer. But facts are stubborn things.

Bevan and his supporters were not Marxists. Like the Revisionists they accepted gradualism and the mixed economy, even if they wanted the mix tilted towards the state sector. Both the right and the left in the Labour Party considered nationalisation as an addendum to private enterprise, not destined to be its replacement. Accepting the mixed economy meant agreeing to the subordination of the public sector to the rule of the market and the much larger and more prosperous private sector. Both the right and left accepted that economic efficiency should be the criterion in deciding which industries to nationalise. They argued only over how the criterion should be applied.

Bevan's politics could be summed up as 'dynamic parliamentarism'. But given the electoral success of the Tories under the conditions of the boom, the outlook for radical reformists looked bleak.

The pursuit of dynamic parliamentarism had further consequences. To succeed in parliament the Bevanites had to stay in the Labour Party. To be outside the party would have meant the end of their electoral prospects. The wartime successes of independent candidates were long gone. The heavy defeat of five Labour MPs who had been expelled from the party during the Attlee government, and had then stood as 'Independent Labour', was a warning.*

Bevanism was a symptom of the tensions created inside the party as a result of consensus with the Tories. It offered no alternative vision of the future; it was more a defence of the reforms of 1945-51 against the Tories, which was in fact not needed, since the Tories did not intend to overthrow the achievements of the Attlee government.

Throughout the thirteen years of Tory rule, the Labour left practically avoided domestic issues, and concentrated instead on foreign policy and defence. This can be seen clearly from the revolts of Labour MPs in the House of Commons against official party policy.

Revolts in the PLP[18]	*1951–55*	*1955–59*	*1959–64*
Domestic policy	1	1	0
Foreign policy and defence	14	8	13

* Labour rebel elections in 1950:[17]

Candidate	*Rebel Vote %*	*Official Labour Vote %*
H L Hutchinson	2	60
J Platts-Mills	18	53
D N Pritt	25	40
L J Solley	10	40
K Zilliacus	1	45

As a leading Bevanite, Richard Crossman wrote in his diaries on 1 December 1952: 'It's fairly clear that, on the strict economic level, there is literally no difference between the Left and the Right of the Party... The real disagreements are not about economic policy but about relations with America, military commitments, etc'.[19]

In the years 1951–4, the main issues on which battle was joined were the British defence programme and the rearmament of Germany. With the Korean war and the deep winter of the Cold War, the US and allies decided in 1951 to rearm West Germany (which had been completely disarmed since the defeat of Hitler). This move could only increase tension between West and East and the left therefore opposed it. The Bevanites also put up resistance to Britains's own high arms spending. A sign of discontent in the ranks was that on both issues the party leadership had a narrow escape.[20]

Despite these arguments, in all essentials the Bevanites and the right shared the basic assumptions of Labour's foreign policy: acceptance of NATO and of the need for Britain to rearm in order to defend British interests abroad. Thus while the 1952 party conference saw Bevan launch his bitterest attack on the Labour leadership, it also witnessed his endorsement of NATO and the executive's statement 'Labour's Foreign Policy', which said that 'close cooperation with the United States of America is vital to Britain and to the Commonwealth as a whole'.[21] This reduced the impact of Bevan's Commons speech of April 1953 against SEATO, the South East Asia Treaty Organisation. It was difficult to be an opponent of SEATO while supporting its elder brother, NATO.

However inconsistent it might seem, this was just what Bevan did. While supporting NATO, he immediately resigned from the shadow cabinet over the SEATO issue. Harold Wilson, a Bevanite who had been a runner-up in the 1953 election to the shadow cabinet, did not turn down the vacant seat Bevan's protest had created. This was neither the first nor last example of one left-winger stabbing another in the back in order to climb into a position of influence. Neil Kinnock was to do the same to Tony Benn in the 1980s.

The Bevanites did not condemn US policy as a whole, but the Labour leadership's uncritical acceptance of it. Dislike of specific US policies was quite compatible, the Bevanites argued, with general support of the Western Alliance.[22]*

* Together with the Labour right (and the Tories), the Bevanites showed continued enthusiasm for summit talks of the Great Powers. In reality it was hard to outwit Eden and Macmillan in Summitry, and the latter being in office, they had quite an advantage over Labour in this field. Eden's 1955

Bevanism found a powerful echo in the Labour Party. Although a loose and heterogeneous group, the Bevanites' connection with the rank and file was maintained chiefly through the organisation of Brains Trusts, consisting of MPs, 150 of which were held throughout the country up to 1954. Peggy Duff, secretary of *Tribune* from 1949 to 1955, recalled:

> The fifty or so MPs more or less meant the Brains Trust worked as a group in the House and met regularly at least for a time...were the front line, the upper strata of the Bevanite movement, the First Eleven. But there was also a lower strata, people outside the House who were either parliamentary candidates or aimed to become so. This was the Second Eleven.[24]

However the influence of the Bevanites did not stop there. They dominated the constituencies. With the exception of the Communists in the 1920s, who had a base in the industrial rank and file, left opposition within the Labour Party has always been concentrated in the constituencies. Constituency Labour Parties differ from other components of the party. The parliamentary party is directly dependent on electoral success and even in opposition is under pressure to prove itself 'fit to govern'. It shows the least willingness to stand out against the prevailing ideas of capitalism. The trade union bureaucracy has on occasion made significant protests against the Labour leadership. But it is limited from rocking the boat too much by its mediating role between capital and labour. As for the mass affiliated membership of the unions, they have only the most tenuous links with Labour, either through general elections every five years or indirectly through the trade union bureaucrats.

The constituency parties, on the other hand, are not so thoroughly subordinated to immediate electoral needs; nor do they mediate like the bureaucracy. They are a self-selected group whose ardent reformism leads them to rise at least one step (and in some cases more) above passivity. It is ironic and not entirely accidental that the constituency parties are also by far the most powerless of all the groups that make up the party.

In a way the unhappy fate of the Bevanites shows clearly the impotence of the constituency parties. After all, their membership reached its zenith in 1952:

---

election campaign leaned heavily on his claim to have badgered the Americans into considering meeting the Russians. One historian argued that America's willingness to negotiate was directly related to the 'necessity of winning an election for the British Conservatives'.[23]

Labour Party membership (excluding affiliated trade unions)[25]

1901	13,861 (Socialist Societies plus Coop Societies)
1910	31,377 (Socialist Societies plus Coop Societies)
1918	52,720 (Socialist Societies plus Coop Societies)
1928	214,970
1938	428,826
1945	487,097
1952	1,014,524
1963	830,346
1970	680,656
1974	691,888
1976	659,058

The later figures are distorted, especially since 1963 when a rule was introduced that made it obligatory for every constituency party to affiliate with at least 1,000 members. This rule was abolished at the 1979 Labour conference, when party membership was estimated at 284,000.[26]

In 1952 at the Morecambe conference, Morrison, Dalton and Shinwell were defeated in the elections to the constituency section of the party executive, so that of the seven members of this section, six were Bevanites. Gaitskell, who had stood for the constituency section, achieved a vote little more than half that of the lowest successful candidate. *Tribune* was overjoyed. Under a front-page headline 'Oh! What a Beautiful Morning!' Michael Foot celebrated not merely 'the most significant shift in British politics since 1951', but 'the happiest political occasion I can remember' since 1945.[27]

Unlike the Bennites thirty years later, Bevanism seemed a lesser threat to the right-wing leadership because, despite its base in the constituency parties, the majority of union officials felt little need to support it. The officials of a minority of unions, such as the engineers, the railworkers, the shopworkers and some smaller ones, did however back Bevan.[28]

Like the rest of the Labour leadership, Bevan had no link with rank and file workers' struggles. He showed hardly any interest in them. The only time Bevanites intervened was in the 1954 docks dispute between the National Amalgamated Stevedores and Dockers (NASD), known as 'the Blue Union', and the TGWU, 'the White Union'. *Tribune* backed the Blue Union and the right of dockers to join a union of their choice. This was motivated largely by the hatred of the Bevanites for Arthur Deakin, who had used the massive force of the TGWU to squash the Labour left. The fall-out from the dockers' dispute was that *Tribune* briefly reflected the struggles of other workers and for a year or so even had an industrial correspondent.

Lacking deep roots in the working class, hazy in their ideas, the Bevanites were a very loose organisation, in fact hardly an organisation at all. According to Crossman:

> *5 December 1951*: The fact is that Bevanism and the Bevanites seem much more important, well-organized and Machiavellian to the rest of the Labour Party, and indeed to the USA, than they do to us who are in it, who know that we are not organized...we have not even got the beginnings of a coherent constructive policy.
> *17 December*: ...So far from being a great strategist and organizer of cabals, Nye is an individualist, who, however, is an extraordinarily pleasant member of a group. But the last thing he does is to lead it.[29]

Jennie Lee commented: 'It should have been plain for all in see that the so-called Bevanites were at sixes and sevens. It was the right wing that had successfully organised "a party within a party".'[30]

Labour lefts dare not organise as effectively as the right. They define themselves *first* as members of the Labour Party and *second* of a radical wing gingering up the main body. Unlike entrists who can for a time keep the organisation they bring with them, ordinary Labour lefts cannot become 'a party within a party'. They fear copying the right's aggressive methods because witch-hunts have only ever been mounted against the left. Prominent right-wing individuals have been excluded from the party, such as MacDonald, and always with much soul-searching, but never a whole tendency.

The disintegration of Bevanism

The bloc of right-wing union leaders—Arthur Deakin, general secretary of the TGWU, Sir William Lawther, president of the NUM, and Sir Tom Williamson, general secretary of the General and Municipal Workers—guaranteed that Labour Party conferences would reject Bevanism. The six Bevanites on the executive were a small minority among its twenty-seven members and not more than a quarter of the PLP were Bevanites. And despite the caution of the left, the right could easily find pretexts for witch-hunting.*

* It was ironic that the attack should be lead by Sir William Lawther who thirty years before, as plain Will Lawther, had defended the Communists. He wrote in the *Daily Telegraph* in 1953: 'The opinion of the Trades Unions is that the Bevanite activities are a deliberate attempt to undermine the

An example of the risk they ran was shown on 3 March 1955, when Bevan challenged Attlee in the Commons on whether the Labour leadership supported the Tory government statements that Britain would use thermo-nuclear weapons to repel an attack by conventional arms. He then led sixty-one MPs in abstaining from voting on a Labour amendment. The following day the shadow cabinet decided to recommend to the PLP that the party whip be withdrawn from Bevan, with the clear inference that once the matter passed to the executive, Bevan would be expelled from the party altogether.

Fortunately for Bevan, the PLP was not united in favour of such an extreme measure. The motion passed by 141 to 112, but such a narrow majority was not enough for a proper killing. However the warning to Bevan was clear, and he must have taken it to heart.

When Gaitskell succeeded Attlee as leader of the party in December 1955, Bevan decided that the time had arrived to call a halt to his oppositional activity. He was convinced that to be effective you had to be inside the party's leading circles. Once he made it clear that he was not going to challenge Gaitskell, he was elected to the shadow cabinet and became shadow foreign secretary.

In 1956, the war over Suez gave Bevan his opportunity to prove his reliability. The Suez Canal was still jointly controlled by Britain and France—a relic of the days when it was a vital link with India and the rest of the British Empire. When President Nasser of Egypt nationalised the canal, Britain and France collaborated with Israel in sending troops to seize the area. Labour, almost in spite of itself, ended up opposing this intervention and organised a massive 'Law not War' demonstration in Trafalgar Square. But the weakness and confusion of the left was quick to appear. Gaitskell compared Nasser to Hitler and Mussolini. Bevan agreed that the nationalisation of Suez was an act of robbery and added: 'If the sending of one's police and soldiers into the darkness of the night to seize somebody else's property is nationalisation, then Ali Baba used the wrong terminology'.[32]

Although Bevan thought the invasion of Egypt by Britain and France a mistake, as it would mean 'the dismantling of NATO and the destruction of the United Nations,' he still received an accolade from *The Economist* for his Trafalgar Square speech on the subject: 'It was for Mr Aneurin Bevan—the new Mr Bevan. who is at the moment trying so hard to sound moderate—to feel the mood, and he made an undeniably brilliant speech'.[33]

---

leadership in the same way as Hitler and the Communists did. There is no difference between them'.[31]

The 1957 Labour Party conference at Brighton gave Bevan another chance to prove he had made peace with Gaitskell. The new executive document, *Industry and Society*, was thoroughly revisionist. Apart from the inevitable renationalisation of steel and road haulage it suggested no other targets for nationalisation, but rather the state purchase of a share of large firms. Many in the Labour Party saw this less as increasing public ownership, than as creating a situation whereby 'a future Labour Government is going to be a hostage bound hand and foot to the capitalist system'.[34]

The NUR opposed *Industry and Society*, reaffirming 'its belief in the common ownership of all the basic industries and means of production'.[35] Even Morrison complained that it 'appears to me to be somewhat biased against nationalisation', and called for its rejection.[36] Shinwell urged this too: 'If we endorse this document... the *Daily Herald* will no longer be the Party newspaper, it will be the *Financial Times*'.[37] Jennie Lee, Bevan's wife, also attacked *Industry and Society* as 'Too Pink, Too Blue and Too Yellow'.[38] But sitting on the platform, Bevan did not stir. It was the Bevanite Harold Wilson who moved *Industry and Society*, and Hugh Gaitskell, for the executive, who summed up. The document was adopted by an overwhelming majority.

However, Bevan's greatest service for the right wing was in the debate on the H-Bomb. A composite resolution called on the British government to take the following measures:

> an end to H-Bomb tests;
> a ban on nuclear weapons and the destruction of existing stocks with international control and inspection;
> progressive disarmament with adequate supervision by the United Nations.[39]

Bevan, for the executive, spoke against. If the resolution was passed, he said, it would be tantamount to sending the next Foreign Secretary 'naked into the conference chamber...to preach sermons...you call that statesmanship? I call it an emotional spasm'.[40] Former followers of Bevan first kept a stunned silence. But this was the last straw. Now they heckled him vehemently. There were cries of 'Shame!' 'Nonsense!' 'Rubbish!' One delegate called out: 'You have sold the pass!' Bevan stood clasping Gaitskell's hand demonstratively. The *Daily Telegraph* gleefully announced: 'Bevan into Bevin'. The *New Statesman*, in an article entitled 'The End of Bevanism', wondered:

> Has Bevan, one is bound to ask after Brighton, sold himself too cheap? Unity has been achieved entirely on Mr Gaitskell's terms and Mr Bevan has surrendered unconditionally... He enters the Cabinet Room naked, a complete prisoner of his former opponents.[41]

Michael Foot's explanation of Bevan's behaviour is quite revealing of the policies of both Bevan and Foot. 'So why *did* he do it?' asks Foot, and answers:

> it was true that Party considerations influenced his conduct, and why not?...he saw more clearly than ever before the divisions which might occur if he refused to speak, if a new split developed. He saw the chasm opening at his feet, he saw the renewal of the old battles as the months went by, he saw the destruction of any hope for a new Labour government, he saw the accusations of his opponents—and perhaps of history—that he could have forestalled the catastrophe but that he had preferred the ease of his own conscience and the comfort of his friends. He saw the long trek back for the Bevanites and himself into the wilderness and the endless sojourn there, and he never had the taste, despite all the taunts, for martyrdom, for the locusts and wild honey. He was interested in power to achieve great objectives.[42]

After the 1957 conference Bevan went on a tour of the United States, so that, as Jennie Lee records:

> he could begin to undo the bogey-man image of him depicted in their press as well as our own. Afterwards Adlai Stevenson wrote to him saying, 'I can report with fair accuracy that your visit was an unqualified success. I gather it may even have been helpful in Washington.' Leading banking and business associations he had addressed wrote letters of thanks to him which went beyond the demands of mere politeness.[43]

The disintegration of Bevan as a leader of the left was complete. He had travelled a long political distance to end this way. He had begun as an industrial syndicalist associated with *The Miners' Next Step* before the First World War. But according to his own account, defeats in the 1920s turned him in a new direction:

> The defeat of the miners ended a phase, and from then on the pendulum swung sharply to political action. It seemed to us that we must try to regain in Parliament what we had lost on the industrial battlefield.[44]

Having lost faith in the ability of the working class to change society directly, Bevan spent the rest of his life searching for the power to do so through state channels:

> When I got older I said to myself: 'The place to get to is the Council. That's where the power is'. So I worked very hard and...I got on the Council. I discovered when I got there that the power *had* been there, but it had just gone. So I made some enquiries, being an earnest student of social affairs, and I learned that the power had slipped down to the County Council. That was where it was and where it had gone to. So I worked very hard again and I got there and it had gone from there too.'[45]

Bevan reached the cabinet and still found that the power was elsewhere, in the company boardrooms and officers' clubs. He once described parliament as 'the most formidable weapon of all'. Alas it has proved formidable indeed, by breaking generations of socialists upon its wheel.

The attack on Clause Four

In the 1955 general election Labour lost one and a half million votes compared with the 1951 election, while the Tories dropped by only 400,000. This was the first time in ninety years that a peacetime government, after a normal period of office, was returned with an increased majority in parliament. The number of Conservative seats increased from 319 at dissolution to 345. Labour fell from 293 seats to 277.

The general election of 1959 was even worse. Labour's vote went down by a further 190,000 votes, while the Tory vote rose by 448,000. The government was returned with an even greater majority, 366 MPs to Labour's 258.

This humiliating third defeat in a row had a traumatic impact. Douglas Jay, one of the most prominent Revisionists, wrote: 'The better-off wage earners and numerous salary earners are tending to regard the Labour Party as associated with a class to which they themselves do not belong...we are in danger of fighting under the label of a class which no longer exists.' He argued too that the word 'nationalisation' had been a liability, and that 'we must destroy this myth decisively; otherwise we may never win again.' The Labour Party should change its name to 'Labour and Radical' or 'Labour and Reform'.[46]

Depression permeated the Labour Party. Decline seemed inevitable. One historian remembers:

> It is difficult now to recapture the atmosphere of the years 1959 and 1961, when so many political commentators were arguing that the Labour Party in its present form, would never again win a General Election... Professor Mackintosh in a book written in 1961 argued that 'it is hard to escape the conclusion that the Labour Party is unlikely to return to power and that the Government of the country will remain in the hands of the Conservatives for the foreseeable future'.[47]*

After the defeat of 1959 Gaitskell decided radical changes must be made in party policy. At the two-day post-mortem conference in Blackpool, he made a tough presentation of the Revisionist case. He began by suggesting that the party's defeat could not be attributed to the election campaign:

> What has caused this adverse trend?... First, there is the changing character of the labour force. There are fewer miners, more engineers; fewer farm workers, more shop assistants; fewer manual workers, more clerical workers; fewer railwaymen, more research workers... The second general change is the absence of serious unemployment or even the fear of it.
>
> In my opinion, capitalism has significantly changed, largely as a result of our own effort.

The party should modernize itself by ceasing to be a doctrinally pure class party. 'Our object must be broaden our base...to avoid becoming small cliques of isolated doctrine-ridden fanatics, out of touch with the main stream of social life in our time.'

Above all the party had lost votes, he said, through its identification with public ownership. Gaitskell saw Clause Four of the party constitution, advocating 'common ownership of the means of production, distribution and exchange', as the root of the problem:

> [Since] our goal is not 100 percent state ownership...we should clear our minds on these fundamental issues and then try to express in the most simple and comprehensive fashion what we stand for in the world today. The only official document which embodies such an attempt is the Party Constitution, written over forty years ago. It seems to me that this needs to be brought up to date.

* After the 1966 victory, many of the same commentators said that Labour was the natural 'majority party' and was in for a generation. One of the funniest explanations of why Labour was bound to win in the future was a reference to the fact that the birth rate among working-class people who vote Labour is higher than among Conservative votes, while the death rate among Conservatives was higher than for Labour.[48]

The conference was mute as Gaitskell continued, but there were cries of dissent at the end of the following passage:

> Standing as it does on its own, this [clause] cannot possibly be regarded as adequate... It implies that the only precise object we have is nationalization, whereas in fact we have many other Socialist objectives. It implies that we propose to nationalize everything, but do we? Everything?—the whole of light industry, the whole of agriculture, all the shops—every little pub and garage? Of course not. We have long ago come to accept, we know very well, for the foreseeable future, at least in some form, a mixed economy...had we better not say so instead of going out of our way to court misrepresentation?

Fury greeted Gaitskell's assault on Clause Four. It fell to Bevan to pour oil on the troubled waters. He tried to produce a unifying formula which would keep the party's divergent tendencies together. He pointed out that both Hugh Gaitskell and Barbara Castle, the chairperson of the conference, had quoted his own phrase about the commanding heights of the economy:

> If Euclid's deduction is correct they are both equal to me and therefore must be equal to each other... I agree with Barbara, I agree with Hugh and I agree with myself... I am a Socialist: I believe in public ownership. But I agreed with Hugh Gaitskell yesterday... I do not believe that public ownership should reach down into every piece of economic activity, because that would be asking for a monolithic society.[49]

Gaitskell's attack on Clause Four was in reality an attack on the working-class nature of the Labour Party. In 1918 Clause Four had been put forward to stave off a possible revolution. In 1959 it survived as a symbol of Labour's commitment to a minimal anti-capitalist position.

Gaitskell's insult to Clause Four was too much even for those trade union officials who had helped him become party leader. They, plus the left of the constituency parties and a substantial portion of the PLP, united in its defence. Drucker explains why:

> As long as Labour retains Clause Four, the Tories can never assimilate all of Labour's achievements or demands. The national health service can be assimilated by a Conservative government, and so, too, in prosperous days can strong trade unions, but 'the common ownership of the means of production, distribution and exchange' cannot. Thus, Clause Four's continuance as the sole statement of principle in Labour's

> constitution holds Labour true to its past, true to what its originators wanted it to be: *for* labour and *against* capital.[50]

Labour is a *reformist* party, not a reactionary one. It has obvious limits to its leftward movement, but as the debate showed, there were also limits to the right, and Gaitskell had gone too far.

Clause Four was a potent symbol. The rhetoric of Labourism was precious to practically everyone in the party: its whole history is one of moderate policies wearing radical clothing. The traditionalists did not think the argument Gaitskell was raising over Clause Four was worth having. It was misconceived to raise the question of whether or not more common ownership was desired. They loved the ambiguity that dominated Labour. To repeat what Eduard Auer wrote to Eduard Bernstein: 'one does not say these things, one simply *does* them.'

The struggle around Clause Four was shadow boxing. Win or lose, the Labour Party would continue with the policy of mixed economy.

Labour and CND—a resolutionary road to socialism?

The Campaign for Nuclear Disarmament (CND) grew out of disappointment with the failure of summit meetings between the great powers in the 1950s. It was spurred on in 1956 by the Hungarian uprising and the Suez war. At a time when politics appeared to be one drab consensus, when people talked of 'the death of ideology' and when Gaitskell and the right were presiding over the demise of Bevanism, the growth of CND caused tremendous excitement on the left.

One sign was the 100,000-strong CND demonstration of Easter 1960. Hopes were high among the 10,000 CND supporters who converged on the Labour Party conference at Scarborough later the same year. The election of Frank Cousins, an enthusiastic supporter of CND, as general secretary of the TGWU, was another fillip for unilateralists at the conference. The conference adopted, by 3,303,000 to 2,896,000, a resolution demanding the 'unilateral renunciation of the testing, manufacturing, stockpiling, and basing of all nuclear weapons in Great Britain.' The TGWU, AEU, NUR, USDAW and electricians voted for the resolution. This was the high point of the first CND campaign.

It hardly seemed to matter that Gaitskell reacted aggressively, making a provocative speech: 'There are some of us...who will fight and fight and fight again to save the Party we love.' Three million votes for disarmament, said the card vote! Not for the last time were the left to mistake conference decisions for political reality. The joyful celebrations overlooked fundamental weaknesses. In no way did it connect with the day-to-day bread and butter issues facing working people. As an editorial in *International Socialism* during Winter 1960–1 put it:

> Our strongest weapon would be to link the issue of defence with the stuff of ordinary life on which workers have shown unshakeable convictions to the point of heroism... It is obvious that progress for the Left lies in breaking down the high stakes of nuclear diplomacy into the small chips of class struggle.
>
> It is here that the Left might show its greatest weakness. There is nothing in the record of its accepted leadership to suggest that it will organise around a program of argument by action rather than by word, or indeed, that it sees any connection between Boss and Bomb. On the contrary, to date it has remained a prisoner to the basic Gaitskellite assumption: that defence is a national issue, not a class one.[51]

It was excellent that the Labour conference had passed a unilateralist motion, because this gave the opportunity to carry the CND argument further. But to defend this gain and build on it, it was essential that the limitations of Labour conference votes should be clearly understood. Alas, the Labour left set too much store on block vote arithmetic, as if it reflected the views of the majority of rank and file workers and was sure to remain true to those views. This was wrong on both counts. Opinion polls suggested that only 16 percent of trade unionists favoured unilateralism and that the figure for Labour voters was never much more than 24 percent.[52]

If support was so low, why did the union leaders throw their block votes behind unilateralism in 1960? To a great extent it was in protest against Gaitskells insult to the holy of holies—Clause Four. This was not to be the only occasion on which the union bureaucracy, angered by a quite separate issue, decided to slap the wrists of the Labour leadership.

However the union leaders never intended to upset the whole apple cart. They were shocked by the implications of unilateralism and the jubilation of the left. Immediately after the conference the major union leaders closed ranks around Gaitskell. The following year's Labour conference rejected unilateralism by a massive 4,526,000 to 1,756,000.

The fact that the party rank and file did not in the main support unilateralism helped the bureaucrats to turn tail. Added to this was the cowardly behaviour of the leaders of the left. Straight after the Scarborough conference Barbara Castle argued that the row had been caused by 'confusion over words, rather than by policies'.[53] By February 1961 the *New Statesman* was advocating compromise.[54] The same month leading CND supporters produced a flurry of documents fudging the issue and preparing the way for retreat.

CND leaders had assumed a simple step by step advance. First Labour Party conference should adopt unilateralism. Then Labour would win the next general election, and unilateralism would be home and dry. The 1961 Labour Party conference in Blackpool was a shocking blow to CND, and led many Labour MPs to withdraw from the campaign. In August 1963 *Tribune* dropped its front-page banner claiming that it led the campaign against the H-Bomb.

The paper victory of 1960 and its quick reversal had left a shambles. The left was in a terrible state. Crossman's diary entry for 23 November 1960 described the situation: 'We are all...fragmented, at sixes and sevens, actuated by personal motives, without any coherent policy'.[55]

The changing locus of reform

The years 1951–64 were an unsatisfactory and insubstantial period in Labour history. There were reasons for this. Labour lives to win office—and a long period of opposition gives debates and decisions an air of unreality. But there were other reasons for unease. The attention of the working class was mostly elsewhere. Parliamentary reformists may think the working class should bestir itself only once every five years, but the battle between the classes goes on day in, day out. Even in booms the struggle to gain the new hilltop or defend an old trench continued in open or hidden form.

In these years the workers' struggle for improvements met with tangible practical results, but it was focused not in parliament but in the workplace. Roger Cox describes the situation:

> The long post-war boom meant that workers were very much in the driving seat... That was especially true in the engineering industry. Engineers were absolutely essential to the post-war economy. The bosses would give them almost anything they wanted, and the workers knew it.[56]

All Labour governments, even when they had a large majority, have felt powerless to challenge the capitalist class. But workers collectively have this power, and in the 1950s and 1960s they used it, if only at factory level:

> There were dozens of instances where groups of militants quite ruthlessly went after a particular manager who had treated them like shit in the thirties.
>
> Workers would compete to see who could give the foreman the hardest time, who could drive him to a nervous breakdown, or at least out of the factory first... Management really had to be careful. They needed production to go smoothly.

Rank and file action brought higher wages, better conditions and a confidence that gains came through self-activity, not by looking to someone to act *on your behalf*. This left the union bureaucracy with little control, and even less to do:

> The role of the fulltime bureaucracy was totally different. The only function they had really was to get the rank and file workers out of trouble. If militants had cocked up a strike for example, they would call in the officials to call off the strike. But [the officials] wouldn't play any role while things were going well. In those situations they were more or less irrelevant.

If that were true of the bureaucracy who at least had some connection with collective organisation, how much more irrelevant was the Labour Party to day-to-day activity!

This rank and file activity, although sharply differentiated from the party, was in the 1950s and 1960s but another kind of reformism, of the 'do-it-yourself variety. Aspirations were met without challenging the framework of the system. As Roger Cox puts it:

> Although it was very easy to build strong shop organisation it was almost impossible to argue socialist politics at work...workers were getting a lot out of the system as it was... Everything was terribly sectionalised. What happened in the next town or even the next factory didn't seem to matter, let alone what happened in the rest of the world.

It would be extremely foolish to make the syndicalist error of seeing even the most militant do-it-yourself reformism as sufficient to win socialism. At the same time it must not be equated with Labour Party reformism. Generations of good socialists have sunk their efforts into making the Labour Party a vehicle for winning working-class advance. They have been watering the desert. Nothing has grown except illusions in an organisation which defends capitalism, *if necessary against the working class*.

Militant workers have also sacrificed much to develop the collective organisations of the working class, particularly at the grassroots level of union branch and shop stewards' organisation. The vast bulk of this activity may be contained within a reformist framework and to think anything else would be self-deception. But these efforts have not been wasted. They have consistently born fruit.

Do-it-yourself reformism differs in three main ways from Labour reformism. Firstly, in Luxemburg's words:

> [through union action] the worker succeeds in obtaining for himself the rate of wages due to him in accordance with the situation of the labor-power market...the capitalist law of wages is applied and the effect of the depressing tendency of economic development is paralyzed, or to be more exact, is attenuated.[57]

Secondly, the daily struggles that sustain the trade unions are in the main not revolutionary—but they can challenge the prevailing ideas of capitalism in practice, if only partially or for a limited period. By contrast, Labour always accommodates to prevailing ideas in order to win votes.

Finally, because rank and file struggle is necessarily collective and this is where the strength of the class lies, it sustains and develops the sinews of workers' organised resistance to capitalism. Labour's electoralism leads away from such grassroots resistance and towards the bosses' state.

Do-it-yourself reformism is not socialism, but it is the necessary process by which the working class maintains its basic collective organisation. Luxemburg compared it to the labours of Sisyphus, condemned in Greek mythology forever to push a boulder to the top of a hill, watch it roll down, and then begin again. This activity 'is, nevertheless, indispensable'.

The difference between shopfloor struggles and the Labour Party's approach was about to be thrown into sharp relief, for the strength of the shop floor was about to be tested by an offensive from the party. In 1964 Harold Wilson became the third man to lead a Labour government.

13

The Wilson government 1964–69

Revisionism's crowing victory: the 'scientific revolution'

The early 1960s saw British capitalism expanding at a slower rate and suffering increasingly from 'stop-go'. The economy was trapped in a vicious circle. Crises in the balance of payments led to deflation. Deflation meant cuts and delays in investment, and under-use of resources. This curtailed growth and thereby precipitated future balance-of-payments crises. As a result Britain lagged more and more behind its rivals.

Capitalists must not only expand, they must compete. While British industrial production rose by 40 percent between 1951 and 1962, France's doubled, that of West Germany and Italy went up by two and a half times, and that of Japan quadrupled. Britain's exports rose 29 percent, France's by 86 percent, Germany's 247 percent, Italy's 259 percent, and Japan's by 378 percent. British national income fell below that of Germany and France for the first time.

Now Revisionism took a new form. Hope of bright cafes, fashions and murals evaporated, along with major social reform and redistribution of wealth and income. Emphasis went on a high growth economy with the state encouraging private industry. This meant a partnership between both sides of industry under a Labour government.

In 1961 the Labour Party executive published *Signposts for the Sixties*. It was drafted by a subcommittee of two Revisionists, Gaitskell and George Brown, and two former Bevanites, Crossman and Wilson. Unlike earlier Labour Party propaganda, *Signposts for the Sixties* did not attack the Conservatives for their private enterprise philosophy or for their business interests, but rather for their staleness, incompetence and archaic attitudes. Apart from one specific commitment to public ownership—the renationalisation of steel—document said that Labour's aim was to make the economy more dynamic. All would be solved 'If the dead wood were cut out of Britain's boardrooms and replaced by the keen young executives, production engineers and scientists'.[1]

Wilson, who led the party after Gaitskell's unexpected death on 18 January 1963, said that party political debate was defined in a new way:

'The argument will be this: can the Conservatives or Labour best galvanize our sluggish and fitful economy into steady and purposive expansion?'[2]

Wilson acted as if the debate on Clause Four had never taken place. He was completely pragmatic, offering not a vision of socialism, but a rejuvenated, modem capitalism under dynamic management. Under Wilson Labour would fight the 1964 election as a people's party, a classless party, with special appeal to the new middle class.

Wilson's central theme was the Tories' scientific failure. In *Labour and the Scientific Revolution*, published in 1963, he summed up the measures necessary: 'a new deal for the scientists and technologists in higher education, a new status for scientists in Government, and a new role for Government-sponsored science in industrial development are three essential requirements for reviving the economy.'

At the 1963 Labour Party conference he waxed lyrical about the new 'revolution': 'We must harness Socialism to science, and science to Socialism' and spoke about a 'Britain that is going to be forged in the white heat of [the scientific] revolution'.[3]

Crossman, one of the main authors of the 'scientific revolution', concluded aptly: 'In fact, of course, [Wilson] had provided the revision of Socialism and its application to modem times which Gaitskell and Crosland had tried and completely failed to do. Harold had achieved it'.[4]

From the planning utopia to massive deflation

As noted, Britain's growth rate was far below that of its competitors. Again and again governments tried to hasten expansion. In 1954 Butler, then chancellor of the exchequer, had set a long-term target of an annual increase in GDP of about 3.75 percent. In 1961 Selwyn Lloyd, another Tory chancellor, had raised the target to 4 percent. Wilson wanted to go still faster. His panacea was *economic planning*: 'A comprehensive plan of national development can recreate a dynamic sense of national purpose and restore our place in the world'.[5]

Labour's 1964 election manifesto was largely about this wonderful new scheme to transform the economy, shaking it out of the miserable stop-go and stagnation policies of the thirteen years of 'Tory misrule'. Straight after the election victory the Department of Economic Affairs was established, headed by George Brown. In September 1965 he published the National Plan, which he claimed was 'a major advance in economic policy-making in the United Kingdom [and is] prepared in the fullest consultation with industry...'[6]

Since the economy was overwhelmingly in private hands, the plan could not be obligatory, but only indicative. It tried to coordinate the activities of different industries within a total economic perspective.

Nationalisation does not necessarily equal socialism; *nor does planning*. Under the present system production is for profit and not for need. Fierce competition leads to anarchy in the market place and periodic booms and slumps. Socialists have naturally seen rational planning of wealth production and distribution as an essential component of the society they want to create. You cannot have socialism without planning. But you can have planning without socialism. Long ago Engels pointed out that capitalism created rational 'organisation of production in the individual factory' alongside 'the anarchy of production in society as a whole'.[7]

Labour's plan had nothing to do with socialism. It provided a state overview and assistance in British capital's struggle to compete. It remained to be seen whether even this strategy could be successfully applied; whether the governmental machine could restrain the wildness of capitalist anarchy *in its own interest*.

The plan was composed by assembling replies to a questionnaire sent to firms and trade associations. The labour movement was not shown so much consideration. Not even the PLP was consulted. The first time the MPs discussed it was on the morning of 3 November, the eve of parliament's re-assembly and six weeks after the plan had been published.

'Industries were asked what 25 percent national growth from 1964 to 1970 would mean for them'.[8] None dreamt of telling the world that they would fail to raise production swiftly or that their export performance would be inadequate. Thus the bosses' estimates used in the plan were not forecasts of what they expected to achieve, but hypothetical statements of what they might achieve given certain assumptions.

To shape business, the government had to use the carrot rather than the stick. If industry was to be encouraged there was no point coercing it, so the plan relied on changing the environment in which big business worked, on persuasion. This meant giving financial inducement to business—to big business above all. The aim was to ensure that profits and investment would rise more quickly than wages (and hence consumption).

This central theme was only too clear: 'Investment lies at the heart of the Plan'.[9] Fixed investment in manufacturing rose by 2.4 percent a year from 1960 to 1964. The plan set out by the Tory government in 1961 had wanted to raise this to 4 percent, for the years 1961–66. But George Brown's plan lifted the target to 7 percent a year, or 38 percent between 1964 and 1970! This would open the way to other impressive targets. Over the same period the plan projected a 25 percent increase in national output.

Even if *British* capital were prepared to play ball, it formed only a small corner of the world system. The plan did not take into account the impact of international capitalism through the balance of payments, nor did it solve the declining rate of profit that affected world capitalism in general and British capital in particular.

To increase investment one must of course have increasing profits. In fact, despite Labour's efforts, between 1964–70 the rate of profit fell more rapidly than in the past. Pre-tax profits fell from an average of 18.8 percent in the 1950s to 12.3 percent in 1966–8, and finally to 10.9 percent in 1969.[10] The result was that productive investment in the private sector grew at only half the intended rate—3.6 percent per year instead of 7 percent.

However, the greatest immediate threat to the plan's realisation was the deterioration in the balance of payments.

Deflation and devaluation

Wilson understood the dangers. In a speech to the 1962 TUC Congress he declared: 'If you borrow from some of the world's bankers you will quickly [lose] independence.' The same theme was repeated twelve days before polling in 1964:

> You cannot go cap in hand to the central bankers as [the Tories] have now been forced to do, and maintain your freedom of action... The central bankers will before long be demanding that Britain puts her house in order and their ideal of an orderly house usually comes to mean vicious inroads into the Welfare State and a one-sided pay pause. The Government would then launch into savage cuts. The brunt will fall again on wages, on salaries, on the ordinary family struggling to make ends meet.[11]

He was absolutely correct. Within weeks of becoming prime minister he was up against the governor of the Bank of England, Lord Cromer, who demanded 'immediate cuts in Government expenditure, and particularly in those parts of Government expenditure which related to the social services'.[12]

The background to this was Jim Callaghan's budget of 11 November 1964, whose prime features were 20 percent increases in old age pensions and other social security benefits by the following March, and abolition of prescription charges. This was less radical than appeared because the increases were going to be more than paid for by higher National Insurance and petrol tax. 'The net result of the changes was to increase revenue in a full year by £100 million more than expenditure, so that the measures, taken as a whole, were mildly deflationary'.[13]

Unlike the Tories, Labour governments must win the confidence of the ruling class. After 13 years of opposition rhetoric, this wooing had only just begun. The budget combined with the already weak state of the economy to precipitate a run on the pound.

Wilson's later apology for failure says a lot about the reality of bourgeois politics:

> Not for the first time, I said that we had now reached the situation where a newly elected Government with a mandate from the people was being told, not so much by the Governor of the Bank of England but by international speculators, that the policies on which we had fought the election could not be implemented; that the Government was to be forced into the adoption of Tory policies to which it was fundamentally opposed. The Governor confirmed that that was, in fact, the case.[14]*

Wilson met the challenge head-on by threatening to float the pound, dissolve parliament and hold an election on the theme of 'the People *versus* the Bankers'. Cromer backed down, and within 24 hours had organised three billion dollars of support from the central banks of the United States and the EEC.

Nevertheless pressure on the pound continued, and in May 1965 the British government borrowed a further 1.4 billion dollars. The price paid was a package of measures which included the delaying of various public and private sector investment projects. But foreign opinion was not particularly impressed, and foreign exchange markets remained in a highly jittery condition. So the Bank of England and the City came back for more. To defend the currency and ward off devaluation, they insisted that the Labour government undertake further drastic deflation.

---

* This reminds one of the following words attributed to Ramsay MacDonald:

'The power of the financier is to be that by which Labour Parties and Labour governments are likely to be brought to grief... The class which is the creditor class can bring to its knees any public movement with which it disagrees, because by refusing to continue credits, by unsettling confidence, by raising the price of money, it can always create panic and crisis, and thereby turn the people back upon the paths upon which they have entered'.[15]

After the 1966 general election, Wilson unveiled a package reducing demand in the economy by £500 million. All indirect taxes were increased by 10 percent. Hire purchase and building controls were tightened, public investment cut by £150 million, and overseas expenditure, both civil and military, reduced by at least £100 million and so on. Most dramatic of all—there was to be a six-month standstill on wages, salaries and dividends, to be followed by a further six-month period of 'severe restraint.' Wilson 'had introduced the biggest deflationary package ever'.[16]

These measures destroyed economic growth and full employment. Numbers out of work rose from 1.1 percent in July to 2.3 percent in November and to a height of 2.6 percent in February 1967. As one economist put it, the National Plan was: 'conceived October 1964, born September 1965, died (possibly murdered) July 1966'.[17] In fact annual economic growth was not the planned 3.8 percent but merely 2 percent—lower than the last five years of the previous Tory government, and well below that of the six countries then in the EEC.

These attempts to improve the balance of payments in the short term, and thus protect the pound, failed. The situation was not helped by the 'Six Day War' between Israel and Egypt in June 1967 which closed the Suez Canal and significantly increased the cost of imports. In November the government was forced to devalue the pound. Thus the economy had to suffer deflation followed by devaluation. The Labour government got the worst of both worlds.

1968 saw three rounds of deflation. In January came social spending cuts. The prescription charges abolished in March 1965 were now restored and at 2s 6d were higher than those imposed by successive Tory governments over thirteen years. The March budget aimed to convert an expected 2 percent rise in private consumption during the next year and a half into a 1 percent fall. Taxes increased and a 3.5 percent ceiling on pay increases was announced, with some exceptions. In November indirect taxes rose while hire purchase and bank lending were tightened. Finally came the budget of 1969. Mild compared with the earlier measures, it nevertheless reduced demand by between a further £200 million and £250 million.[18] The only success of Wilson's economic policy was the rise in exports: by 42 percent over the years 1964-70 as against the projected rise of 36 percent.

A deep-seated crisis of profitability continued to dominate British (as well as world) capitalism from the late 1960s onward. Profitability dipped to a very low level in 1972 and 1973, rose a bit in the late 1970s, and tumbled again in the early 1980s. It subsequently recovered, only, however, to the kind of level it held in 1973, the level that helped to precipitate the world crisis in the first place.

The economic history of the Wilson government of 1964–70 is one of continuing 'stop-go', with longer and longer periods of stop interspersed with shorter periods of go. The economist Sam Brittan could rightly note that Wilson was the 'best Conservative Prime Minister the Party did not have'.[19]

The Labour government was a pawn in the hands of world bankers. Its promises were sacrificed to reassure them. The anarchy of competitive capitalism and the tyranny of its laws invade every unit of the economy.*

Incomes policy

Whatever Labour's rhetoric, it knew that profit drives the system. Still smarting from the mistrust capitalism had shown in 1964, Harold Lever, the PLP's leading economics expert, pleaded for business confidence:

> Clause Four or no Clause Four, Labour's leadership...knows as well as any businessman that an engine which runs on profit cannot be made to run faster without extra fuel... [Profits, then] must and will, over a longer period, increase significantly... For their part businessmen should show less sensitivity and more sense. It is time they realised that a ringing political slogan is often used as a sop to party diehards or as an anaesthetic while doctrinal surgery is being carried out.[21]

With international competition putting pressure on profit margins in Britain's semi-stagnant economy, workers' bargaining power became a greater problem for bosses and government. Labour's solution was incomes policy.

This was not new. In its last couple of years Harold Macmillan's Tory administration had moved towards it. In 1961 the government had frozen public sector wages and asked the private sector to follow suit. This was supplanted in 1962 by a 'guiding light' wage norm of between 2 and 2.5 percent as the upper limit for increases. In June that year the National Incomes Commission was established to look into pay claims

* It is funny to see Labour leaders clutching at straws in face of the bankruptcy of their economic policies. Crossman wrote on 31 July 1966:

'When I told Anne over lunch today that the World Cup could be a decisive factor in strengthening sterling she couldn't believe it. But I am sure it is. It was a tremendous, gallant fight that England won. Our men showed real guts and the bankers, I suspect, will be influenced by this, and the position of the Government correspondingly strengthened'.[20]

referred to it by the government. It was linked with another new body, the National Economic Development Council, which the government envisaged as involving the unions in an incomes policy.

But the Tories faced a serious obstacle in the trade union movement. In *principle* the TUC accepted that it was 'a condition of price stability that increases in income should keep in step with the growth of real output'.[22] However, it was not ready to collaborate with a *Tory* incomes policy. So it was that TUC participation in voluntary incomes policy had to await the election of a Labour government.

Labour could not plan the bosses' system for them, but its working class links meant it stood a better chance of planning wages. By a massive 6,090,000 to 40,000 Labour's 1963 Conference adopted 'an incomes policy to include salaries, wages, dividends and profits (including speculative profits) and social security benefits'.[23] With Frank Cousins, leader of the powerful TGWU, behind it, acceptance was guaranteed. Indeed it was this left-wing bureaucrat who coined the slogan 'planned growth of incomes', included in the 1964 Labour Party manifesto, *The New Britain*.

Incomes policy, or a variation of it, became a hallmark of the Labour approach to industrial relations. When in government Labour, like the Tories, acts as manager of capitalism. *But it does not always adopt the same methods*. Incomes policy fitted Labour's synthesis of class and nation—the belief that there is a community of interests within existing society. Labour's incomes policy was the main reason why the Conservative weekly paper *The Economist* supported 'profit conscious and profit seeking' Labour in the 1964 election.[24] The Tory economist Sam Brittan also recommended a Labour vote because: 'Paradoxically, one of the strongest arguments for a Labour Government is that, beneath layers of velvet it might be more prepared to face a showdown in dealing with the unions'.[25]

In December 1964 representatives of government, the Trades Union Congress and the employers' organisations signed a *Joint Statement of Intent on Productivity, Prices and Incomes* and a National Board for Prices and Incomes (PIB) was set up, under the chairmanship of former Tory MP Aubrey Jones. After this the Labour government's incomes policy went through a number of stages.

The first stage lasted from December 1964 to July 1966, when restraint was 'voluntary'. Then the government imposed a standstill on all wage rises for six months, followed by six months of severe restraint. Few exceptions were permitted. This was state two.

Stage three ran from July 1967 to March 1968, with a 'norm' of between 3 and 3.5 percent for pay rises, while the government had the power to delay any rises for six months. Finally, the fourth stage last from April 1968 until the end of 1969, during which time the government loosened its power to delay pay rises but the 3.5 percent ceiling was imposed except where there were also rises in productivity. The government retained the power to delay any rises that were above this level by up to eleven months.

Bashing the unions: *In Place of Strife*

For incomes policy to be effective, Wilson had to diminish the unions' power to strike. As *The Economist* wrote on 15 January 1966: 'The only way to achieve an incomes policy in 1966 is going to be by out-facing the trade unions in some big national wage struggle'.

The opportunity came with the seamen's strike, which started on 16 May 1966. The minister of labour, Ray Gunter, met the shipowners and persuaded them to oppose the seamen's demands. Crossman noted:

> we could have a settlement at any time, since the owners were ready to put up the cash: it was the Government that was preventing the settlement because of the prices and incomes policy... We are trying to smash the seamen although we have just given huge concessions to the doctors, the judges and the higher civil servants. It is an ironical interpretation of a socialist incomes policy.[26]

Speaking on television the night the stoppage began, Wilson described it as a 'strike against the State, against the community' with the main issue being the credibility of the incomes policy.[27] A week later a state of emergency was declared. On 20 June Wilson read the Commons a thinly disguised MI5 Report about Communist infiltration. Among the seamen, he said, there was a 'tightly knit group of politically motivated men who [are] endangering the security of the industry and the economic welfare of the nation'.[28] This notwithstanding the fact that there was not one member of the Communist Party on the seamen's union executive!

Having seen doctors given a 30 percent pay rise over two years, the mass of trade unionists were unshaken by Wilson's remarks and remained sympathetic to the seamen: 'the Gallup poll showed that 50 percent of Labour Party supporters and 51 percent of trade unionists took the strikers' side, while only 13 percent and 17 percent respectively sympathized with the employers'.[29] However, out of loyalty to the Labour government, the TUC did nothing to aid the seamen. The TGWU refused to bring out the dockers. This did not prevent MI5 from bugging Jack Jones, its assistant general secretary, during the strike. (He was elected TGWU general secretary in 1968).[30] On 29 June the seamen's executive called the strike off in defeat.

While union bureaucrats were easily called to heel, the *unofficial* strike—the wellspring of do-it-yourself reformism, had to be capped.

Workers do not knuckle under

The shackles imposed on workers did not stop them fighting back. Throughout the 1960s the number of strikes continued to rise significantly, Labour government or no Labour government, incomes policy or no incomes policy[31]:

1957	640	1964	1,456
1958	670	1965	1,496
1959	780	1966	1,937
1960	1,180	1967	2,116
1961	1,220	1968	2,350
1962	1,244	1969	3,116
1963	1,082	1970	3,906

The rise of strikes in the motor industry was especially steep.

In the last months of 1969 militant wage demands and strikes by dustmen, local government workers, teachers, firemen, miners, car workers and nurses initiated what has come to be known as the 'wage and strike explosion' which characterised Britain in the early 1970s.

The working class was not in government (despite the rhetoric of Labourism), nor was it tied to curing the system's ills as the Labour Party was. The crisis had the effect of *encouraging militancy*. There are some on the left who mechanically predict working-class activity according to the economic cycle. They say that booms *always* lead to passivity and right-wing ideas, while slumps *always* create class struggle and stimulate the left. As Trotsky showed in the 1930s, while boom and slump are as natural to capitalism as breathing, the working class response can never be calculated from economic developments alone. Much depends on the attitude of workers, which is the result of many different influences—one of which is Labour politics, a major but not all-powerful component. This time crisis did indeed lead to militancy. The next time it would not.

When incomes policy was launched, ministers claimed it would help the low-paid above all, since collective bargaining had failed to win them adequate improvements. Ironically the groups hardest hit by incomes policy were low paid public sector workers. It was largely these workers who spearheaded much of the action in 1969, when the issue of equal pay for women also came to the fore because a big proportion of the lowest paid were women. This involved large numbers of women workers in union activity and industrial conflict, the majority of them for the first time.

We have already contrasted the shop stewards' do-it-yourself reformism with Labour's 'reformism from above.' It was common for the same individual to support Labour on a range of general issues but fight its incomes policy tooth and nail at work. After all, parliamentary politics and industrial struggle were traditionally separate. Just because a Labour government, assisted by union bureaucrats, acted as manager of capitalism, this did not automatically dispel workers' determination to defend their living standards.

Furthermore, the situation was not static. Because bosses were less willing and able to deliver concessions, stoppages had to take broader and more determined forms to succeed. Do-it-yourself reformism has a potential far greater than reformism from above. Collective struggle may begin as a fight for better wages and conditions, but it also opened up:

> the possibility of the rebirth of a revolutionary working-class movement. For wherever workers are fighting *for themselves*, fighting for better wages, fighting in defence of their shop stewards and fighting for their right to control the conditions of their work, wherever they are doing things for themselves and not leaving it to their leaders, they are growing in self-confidence and growing in their ability to run things for themselves.[32]

One factor which showed the most advanced trade unionists the need to generalise the struggle was the legislative attack on trade union rights which Labour attempted to launch in 1979. Legal shackles on rank and file union action were a natural corollary of incomes policy.

As early as 1963 a Fabian Tract explained: 'Acceptance of an incomes policy will also have implications for the right to strike. Clearly, to be operable, such a policy cannot have hanging over it the threat of a strike by a dissatisfied union'.[33] Two years later *The Economist* said the same: 'The price of securing an incomes policy in Britain will be a willingness to stand up to strikes',[34] adding 'quite bluntly, blacklegging must become respectable again'.[35]

On 17 January 1969 Barbara Castle, the employment secretary, produced the White Paper *In Place of Strife*. It contained three proposals: that the government could demand a compulsory cooling-off period of 28 days, a compulsory ballot before official strikes and the imposition of a solution in intractable inter-union disputes. In each case the penalty could be a fine, with presumably imprisonment for non-payment. A Register of Trade Unions and Employers' Associations would be formed and fines imposed on unions whose rules conflicted with its regulations. New kinds of industrial courts were also suggested.

Labour was taking up the anti-union stand first tentatively proposed back in 1912, but which only openly reactionary governments had dared to enact in peacetime. Wilson's Guildhall speech in November 1969 explained the need for this legislation: 'We face the problem of an assertion of the power of the factory floor'.[36]

Despite the threat posed by *In Place of Strife*, in 1969 the number of strike days was 6,800,000, an increase of two million over 1968 and four million over 1967. A new movement was rising, the like of which had not been seen since 1919. Its basis was not only existing shopfloor organisation but also a massive extension of trade unionism to an increasing number of white-collar unions.

The shop stewards were 'the potential builders of the mightiest socialist movement yet in the history of Britain'.[37] This evaluation was founded on the dynamic forces of class struggle that were stirring the shop stewards to go beyond the narrow horizon of the individual shop floor.*

Unlike MPs, shop stewards were not corrupted by being divorced from those they represented. They suffered the same wages, conditions and exploitation. They could be called to account for their actions by the shopfloor and, most important of all, they could, under the right circumstances, draw upon collective strength in a real fight against capitalism.

But for this potential to be realised they had to go beyond 'the narrow horizon of economic, trade union demands'[39] and overcome their other main weakness—the fragmentation of workplace organisation. The fact that workers had won gains in small groups—in an individual shop or factory—meant that these were not seen as victories for the class as a whole, and that solidarity between different sections of workers was weak.

* These years saw a great upsurge in the working class struggle internationally, of which the general strike of May 1968 in France and the Prague Spring in Czechoslovakia are but two examples.[38]

This helped to explain, for example, the strength of racism among workers. Nevertheless the effect of the employers' offensive would force many workers to generalise, and to link together their struggles. This analysis was broadly confirmed by the events of 1970–74.

Before describing the stand the Labour Party and trade unions took towards Wilson's government policies, let us deal with a couple of other aspects of government policy.

Immigration and race

Back in the 1920s Wertheimer noted the:

> close affinity of the Labour Party with traditions of national culture... Separated by no class barriers from the mental and spiritual concepts of capitalism, which would otherwise have given birth to an exclusively proletarian way of life and morality, and deep-rooted in national religious tradition, the Labour Party has never been able to make a clean breakaway from capitalist culture.[40]

Nowhere is this more true than in the area of race. When economic expansion demanded more workers, immigrants had been welcome. But the first sign of economic decay saw a racist Tory offensive before which the Labour government capitulated shamelessly.

Since the war Labour leaders had publicly opposed immigration control. Thus Arthur Bottomley, Labour spokesman on Commonwealth affairs, told the Commons in 1958: 'We on this side are clear in our attitude towards restricted immigration. We are categorically against it'.[41] Gaitskell had strongly opposed controls because 'every Commonwealth citizen has the right as a British subject to enter this country at will. This has been the right of subjects of the Crown for many centuries and the Labour Party has always maintained it should be unconditional'.[42]

When Wilson took over from Gaitskell he adopted a different line: 'We do not contest the need for control of Commonwealth immigration into this country'.[43] Indeed, he argued for tightening the provisions of the Tory Immigration Act to secure 'effective' health checks and extended powers of deportation.[44] The 1964 Labour manifesto stated:

> Labour accepts that the number of immigrants entering the United Kingdom must be limited. Until a satisfactory agreement covering this can be negotiated with the Commonwealth, a Labour government will retain immigration control.[45]

In the general election an extreme Tory racist won Smethwick, with a swing against the national trend. This shook the Labour leaders. Although Wilson referred to the Tory victor of Smethwick as a 'parliamentary leper', he and the rest of the government decided to cave in to the racist pressure. Entries in Crossman's diaries prove the point:

> Ever since the Smethwick election it has been quite clear that immigration can be the greatest potential vote-loser for the Labour Party if we are seen to be permitting a flood of immigrants to come in and blight the central areas in all our cities.[46]

Elsewhere he wrote: 'We felt we had to out-trump the Tories by doing what they would have done and so transforming their policy into a bipartisan policy'.[47]

On 5 August 1965 Labour proposed cutting work vouchers for Commonwealth immigrants from 208,000 to 8,500. The new measures succeeded in reducing voucher holders from 30,000 in 1963 to 4,000 by 1970.[48] If capitalism was to be nursed back to health, Labour was not about to accuse the system or its own policies of causing unemployment or housing difficulties. Scapegoats were needed, and Labour willingly embraced Enoch Powell's suggestion that the most exploited and oppressed victims of capitalism shoulder the blame.

On 9 February 1968, at a Conservative dinner, Powell made a diatribe against Kenyan Asians who held British passports. A month later the Labour government introduced a new Immigration Act withdrawing rights of entry for British passport holders lacking a 'close connection' with Britain. In future, such people had to obtain special vouchers, which were to be severely restricted in number.

Just to show that Labour could play the racist game as well as the Tories, the Act included a clause preserving free entry for those, almost all whites, who had a grandparent born in the UK.

In 1969 Labour made it obligatory for dependants of Commonwealth immigrants to obtain an entry certificate before coming to Britain, thereby ensuring lengthy delays and increased hardship while people queued to join their families.

As always, concessions to the racists do not quell their appetites but increase them. On 20 April 1968 Enoch Powell made his most inflammatory speech: 'Like the Romans, I seem to see the River Tiber foaming with much blood...'

British foreign policy under Wilson

Wilson was the most loyal supporter of America's Vietnam war.

Without hesitation he applauded bombing the North and 'made absolutely plain our support for the American stand against Communist infiltration into South Vietnam'.[49] Wilson held US President Lyndon Johnson ('LBJ') in tremendous esteem and swallowed his phoney protestations of peaceful intent: 'I am absolutely convinced about the sincerity of the President in this matter. I could not be more convinced about anything'.[50]

Wilson's position was shaped by the interdependence of British and US imperialisms and the fate of sterling which relied on President Johnson's goodwill. Crossman describes a cabinet meeting in February 1966 where Wilson explained that US 'financial support is not unrelated to the way we behave in the Far East: any direct announcement of our withdrawal, for example, could not fail to have a profound effect on my personal relations with LBJ and the way the Americans treat us'.[51]

When it came to dealing with Ian Smith's racist regime in Rhodesia (today Zimbabwe), Wilson limited himself to denouncing it as illegal, applied ineffectual economic sanctions, and made it clear that he opposed the 'using of force' against 'our kith and kin'. He showed no comparable hesitation about employing violence in Aden or Cyprus. Crossman wrote in his diary:

> the last thing the British public wants is the use of force or sanctions in Rhodesia... Harold Wilson's policy is designed not to unseat Smith but to carry the Tories with him.[52]

One of the most shameful chapters during the 1964–70 government was the supplying of arms to South Africa. Shortly after being elected leader of the Labour Party, Wilson told a mass rally organised by Anti-Apartheid in Trafalgar Square:

> Under Hugh Gaitskell's leadership we condemned the supply of arms to South Africa as long as apartheid continues. That is the policy of the Labour Party today. It will be the policy of the Labour Party when we are called upon to form the Government.[53]

However, soon after taking office Wilson announced that the arms embargo to South Africa was not total. 'Existing contracts will be honoured—sixteen low-flying Buccaneer strike bombers on order by the South African Government would be delivered' as well as spares. In 1965 permission was given for Vauxhall Motors to supply the South African army. No mention was made of what Harold Wilson earlier described as 'the role of British armoured cars in the brutality we condemn today'. A host of other more subtle ruses were also employed.[54]

In 1967 the cabinet majority was for lifting the arms embargo altogether. Crossman described how the cabinet's defence and overseas policy committee approached the issue:

> George Brown began the attack saying that though he realized it was very painful one couldn't really go on being so unrealistic about the sale of arms. He was then supported by Denis Healey, who said one must surely make a distinction between arms which could be used for suppressing insurrection (such as Crusader tanks or Saracen cars) and strategic arms—that is to say, the Air Force and the Navy which are needed for our own Commonwealth interests.[55]

And Crossman added:

> My own view is that Rhodesia and South Africa between them are costing us an enormous amount in our balance of payments. We are completely immobilized because of the moral blackmail exerted by the left-wing of the Party and Harold Wilson's personal commitments.[56]

However, the government could not get away with openly lifting the embargo. On 12 December 1967, some 140 Labour MPs signed a motion demanding its retention.[57]* Wilson gave way. The PLP had actually blocked the government. The Labour left makes much of these rare occasions, rather like a gambler who knows he will lose a fortune because the system is stacked against him, but plays on because once upon a time he made a killing.

In 1953 Harold Wilson's book *The War on World Poverty* had called on the advanced countries to contribute 3 percent of their national income in aid to poorer countries. In fact the Wilson government gave even less foreign aid than the Tory governments preceding it. It fell from

* Nonetheless, when it came to economic sanctions against South Africa Wilson was not ready to give an inch, and his arguments were much the same as Thatcher used some 20 years later. On 13 April 1964 Wilson told West European Socialist leaders that an effective trade embargo 'would harm the people we are most concerned about, the Africans and those whites fighting to maintain some standard of decency'. Despite the unanimous call of African leaders for economic sanctions, the following day he declared: 'Sanctions which hit at the people of South Africa, without influencing its Government, would be futile and tragic.' Three years after the Labour government came to power, the minister of state at the Board of Trade 'could proudly tell a businessman's dinner that trade with South Africa had grown at a remarkable speed. In two years South Africa had jumped from fourth to second in the table of Britain's largest customers'.[58]

0.53 percent of gross national product in 1964 to 0.39 percent in 1969, and 0.37 percent in 1970.[59] In Labour's synthesis of class and nation, it is always 'nation' which comes out on top, at the expense of the working class, not just in Britain, but internationally.

Deep rifts between Labour government and Labour Party

Under the Attlee government the party conference, the executive and the parliamentary party had almost solidly supported the government. The Wilson government of 1964–70 could hardly be further from this picture.

There were few disagreements so long as the government had only a wafer thin majority, as it did between the general elections of October 1964 and March 1966. But once it had a secure majority after the 1966 election, bitter wrangles erupted, principally over incomes policy and deflation. At conference 'between 1966 and 1969 "the floor" defeated "the platform" with a regularity unparalleled in the Party's history... defeats for "the platform" changed from being a rarity'.[60]

The national executive, and by implication the government, were defeated fourteen times in conferences between 1966 and 1969, and as Lewis Minkin puts it: 'No Labour Government (indeed no British Government of any complexion) had been so extensively rebuffed by its own Party Conference. It was not just a range of reverses. It was the depth of opposition. '[61]

The rift between the conference and the executive was duplicated in a rift between the executive and the government, even though ministers made up about half the executive's membership:

> Under all previous Labour Governments the NEC had behaved with a devoted loyalty, publicly mute and privately circumspect in its criticisms. [But] it was prepared now, for the first time in Party history, to be publicly identified with critics and criticism of Labour Government policy.[62]

The PLP was also far from being united behind the government. The measures introduced in July 1966, which included the wage freeze and increases in indirect taxes, found a significant minority of the PLP repeatedly voting in opposition to the government. In March 1967 60 MPs abstained in protest against a refusal to make further defence cuts. Wilson rounded on the left at the PLP meeting, warning them that 'a dog is only allowed one bite', and threatening them with a general election unless they came to heel. The following month Norman Atkinson moved a private member's motion in the Commons calling for the 'cessation of the bombing of North Vietnam'. Fifty-nine Labour MPs and three Liberals, supported the motion.*

The limits of PLP opposition, however, were shown by how few left-wing resignations there were from the government, and the fact that those who did resign (such as Frank Cousins) were soon replaced by others from the left (Tony Benn and Judith Hart). Nevertheless the PLP was discontented as never before.

Undoubtedly the issue that caused the greatest strife was the White Paper *In Place of Strife*. When it was debated in parliament on 3 March 1969, fifty-five Labour MPs voted against and approximately forty abstained. Three weeks later the party executive adopted, by sixteen votes to five, a resolution saying 'it could not accept legislation based on all the proposals of the White Paper'.[63] Among the majority were James Callaghan (home secretary and party treasurer), Jennie Lee (minister for the arts), and Tom Bradley (parliamentary private secretary to Roy Jenkins, the chancellor of the exchequer). Two other ministers are believed to have abstained.[64]

Opposition continued to mount. On 7 May 1969 Douglas Houghton, the chairman of the PLP, denounced *In Place of Strife*: 'No good that any contentious Bill of this kind can do to industrial relations or the economy will redeem the harm we can do to our Government by the disintegration or defeat of the Labour Party'.[65] In the cabinet meeting on 17 June, the chief whip, Robert Mellish, claimed that there was no chance of any penal legislation passing the Commons. According to one source this precipitated a dramatic shift in ministerial alignments and 'at the end, Wilson and Castle were virtually isolated'.[66]

The struggle around *In Place of Strife* is instructive. First, the federal structure of the party, where there is no precise chain of command, makes for contradictory positions and tendencies in different branches of the labour movement—the trade unions, the constituency parties, the PLP and the executive. *In Place of Strife* tried formally to integrate working-class organisations—the unions—and their activity into the British state. Unions accept Labour's political synthesis of class and

* At the second reading of the Commonwealth Immigrants Bill, 35 Labour MPs voted against the government. Although the government whips were out for the third reading, only 109 Labour MPs voted in support, sixteen voted against and some 200 abstained. At the second raiding of the Prices and Incomes Bill (1968), one Labour MP voted against and thirty-four abstained. Forth-nine voted against NHS prescription charges. In June 1968 twenty-three Labour MPs opposed the Prices and Incomes Bill, and about twenty abstained. In December 1969 forty-nine Labour MPs entered the lobbies against the government's Vietnam policy. Six months later this had risen to 61, with nearly a hundred abstaining.

nation. That is why they are federated to the party. Yet they still resist complete state integration. The Labour government's desire to put nation before class came into conflict with the actual foundation of the Labour Party in the organised working class. As Panitch put it:

> while Labour's structural ties with the unions were the condition of its success as an integrative party in the quasi-corporatist state, the defeat which Labour suffered on the penal clauses was indicative of the extent to which Labour's ties with the unions can also act as a structural constraint on its ability to act out its integrative role.[67]

However, we must be precise when we say the unions defeated *In Place of Strife*. It was not the trade union bureaucracy but the activity of the rank and file that shattered it. Of course union leaders protested against Labour Government policies—from the wage freeze to trade union legislation—but they did nothing. When the wage freeze was made statutory in 1967 the TUC expressed regret, but considered any attempt to evade the freeze was against the interests of the unions which accepted it. Frank Cousins told the 1967 TGWU conference why he opposed striking against the freeze: 'We did not do so because we do not want to destroy the Government; we wanted to persuade them'.[68] And this was the man who had recently resigned from the government in protest at the 1966 statutory incomes policy.

The 1967 Prices and Incomes Bill was not formally endorsed by the TUC because of rank and file resentment but the General Council continued to counsel wage restraint...the only public demonstrations were mobilized by the newly-organised and Communist-led Liaison Committee for the Defence of Trade Unions.[69]

At the 1968 TUC Congress the vote against pay policy was carried by a majority of seven to one. But this did not mean the General Council was ready to campaign. Instead it would 'watch how the Government used its power after it was passed'.[70] The passivity of the trade union leaders also showed itself over *In Place of Strife*. Thus the General Council almost unanimously rejected a one-day protest strike against the Bill.[71] This was notwithstanding the emergence of a new generation of union leaders, such as Hugh Scanlon, who won top union positions through the support of Broad Left organisations comprising Communist Party and left Labour activists. Although the rhetoric of such leaders showed the influence of the prevailing militancy, Scanlon convinced his union, the AEU, to refuse official backing for the May Day strikes against *In Place of Strife*.

It was the pressure of rank and file do-it-yourself reformism that generated the effective opposition to *In Place of Strife*. This led to the Ford strike of February–March 1969 and widespread strikes on May Day. Any resistance that came from the union bureaucracy stemmed from the pressure of workers below.

The contradictory nature of the Labour Party, being the political expression of the trade union bureaucracy, but still separate from it, revealed itself clearly in the antagonism between the labour movement and the Labour government. The government, committed to the management of capitalism, was unwilling and unable to bow to the wishes of the Labour Party conferences, the executive or the PLP. To use Wilson's expression, the dog had barked, but could it or would it bite?

There has been an ebb and flow in conference authority throughout Labour's history. The formula established in 1907 gave conference the right to propose, but left the parliamentary wing to dispose. This could be interpreted in widely different ways. The shock of MacDonald's treachery in 1931 dramatically raised the status of conference. The effect lasted into Attlee's reign. In the few cases where he went against the wishes of the Labour Party conference, a verbal formula was produced to paper the cracks. But Wilson did not give a damn. Throughout 1966–70 he ran roughshod over the wishes of the different bodies of the movement, going further than anyone before in openly flouting conference decisions. Minkin records:

> Harold Wilson's response to the 1966 Party Conference marked a clear break from the practice of the Attlee Government. In the assertion that 'the Government must govern' there was none of the deferential formulae of the past. Nor was there the use of any of the procedural loopholes which might have been forthcoming. It was now clearly a matter of rejecting the authority of the Party conference over the policy of a Labour Government... The authority of the Conference sunk to a new low as the Government carried out a range of policies diametrically opposed to Conference decisions. Defeats for Government policy at Conference became as repetitive as they were ineffectual.[72]

This contempt for conference and the executive showed itself graphically in the drafting of the 1970 election manifesto. Wilson, aided by Peter Shore and Tony Benn, drafted the manifesto behind the back of the executive and then presented it as a *fait accompli*. At the executive's final meeting before the election campaign, Douglas Houghton is reported to have said: 'Look, if the Government doesn't want to carry out any of your promises it won't.'[73] The result was:

> the controversial policy items were all either smoothed over with vague or ambiguous formulae, stated in non-committal terms or simply avoided entirely...important Conference commitments disappeared behind innocuous phraseology. Thus the Conference policy of dissociation from United States' policy in Vietnam became opposition to a 'purely military solution' and support for 'the Geneva agreements and the withdrawal of all foreign troops.' The specific commitments to Wealth and Gift Taxes, faced with unremitting opposition from succeeding Chancellors, were obscured by a vague promise to ensure 'a greater contribution to the National Revenue from the rich'.
>
> What emerged, therefore, was cautious, complacent and of uninspiring generality. The *Manifesto* defined the Party's purposes in terms acceptable to almost any person of goodwill, 'a steadily growing economy, a 'better society for all the people of Britain; a strong, just and compassionate society'... Thus by the time of the General Election, the Labour Party Conference appeared to have moved into irreversible decline as a political institution. Its authority over a Labour Government was openly defied. Its immediate decisions had minimal impact upon the Government policy.[74]

The rift between the government on the one hand and the executive and even a great proportion of the PLP on the other, was a reflection of the estrangement of the trade unions from the government, and this was, at one remove, a reflection of the massive rise of workers' industrial struggle and its conflict with government policies.

Labour was certainly not under the control of the labour movement. If it had been, *In Place of Strife* would never have been published. But neither was it completely independent of the movement.

Wilson and the Labour left

On being elected leader of the Labour Party Wilson had been greatly praised by spokesmen of the left. Frank Allaun, the hardy socialist warrior, went so far as to say 'Harold Wilson is the best Labour leader since Keir Hardie'.[75] Perry Anderson of the *New Left Review* believed 'Wilsonism has made the Labour Party into the dynamic left-wing of European Social Democracy' and that Labour had 'at last, after fifty years of failure, produced a dynamic and capable leader'.[76]

The most uncritical accolade was found in Michael Foot's *Harold Wilson: A Pictorial Biography*, which describes Wilson as:

> a *dedicated* person, dedicated to politics, to the Labour Party, to his own interpretation of Socialism which he believes can contribute so much to the well-being of the British people. The word, be it noted, means *sacredly, solemnly or formally devoted, wholly given up. Zestfully devoted* might be the final, more accurate definition in this case.[77]

Elsewhere Foot emphasised Wilson's 'political acumen, political skill and survival power...a coherence of ideas, a readiness to follow unorthodox courses, a respect for democracy...above all a deep and genuine love of the Labour movement'.[78]

But *Realpolitik*, the need to adapt socialist ideals to ruling-class needs, lurked close to the surface. Foot wrote:

> Like it or not, the Labour Party programme on which we fought the election was one in which we envisaged working a mixed economy in a country involved in the Western alliance and in the predominantly capitalist Western world. The operation is extremely difficult, but, as Jimmy Maxton once said, if we thought we couldn't ride two horses we should never have joined the bloody circus'.[79]

Maxton's aphorism might suit circuses, but it became increasingly difficult to ride the capitalist horse *and* the workers' horse when they galloped in opposite directions!

Thus when it came to incomes policy *Tribune* faced two ways. At first it published a number of articles in support. Michael Barrett Brown and Royden Harrison described George Brown's incomes policy with words borrowed from Marx: 'The scene is once again set for a decisive victory for the political economy of Labour'.[80] In 1965 an article welcomed wage controls, complaining only that the government should have 'accepted the need for "teeth" earlier'.[81]

However, the government's handling of the seamen's strike abruptly ended the honeymoon. 'Support the Seamen!' was *Tribune*'s front-page slogan. Now the paper turned sharply against the government's incomes policy: 'The Labour movement is being asked to accept the prospect of wage control and the operation of an unfair incomes policy in the context of a rampantly capitalist economy,' wrote Foot.[82] A week later he wrote: 'The latest trick in the Government pantomime leads all that has gone before. They have dressed up one of the Ugly Sisters as Cinderella'.[83]

Still the left Labour MPs suffered moral torture when it came to voting on the wage freeze in parliament. Ian Mikardo, in an article entitled 'Why we Abstained', said they 'were naturally unhappy about adding to the considerable difficulties which the Prime Minister and the economics Ministers already have on their plate. This is no contumacious defiance: there never was a sadder or more regretful revolt'.[84]

At least *Tribune* was prepared to criticise openly. When health charges were reimposed it shouted: 'The Shame of it All!' *Tribune* campaigned consistently against Wilson's policy in Vietnam and against *In Place of Strife* but was conspicuously silent on the question of industrial action against the Bill. A letter from Peggy Duff, Nigel Harris and others, entitled, '*Tribune*'s Sham War?' complained: 'Last week's *Tribune* did not even mention, let alone support or encourage, the strikes against the Government's anti-strikes legislation, which were planned to take place on May Day'.[85]

Although more in sympathy with working-class demands than the right, the Labour left was just as distant from the actual struggle. In this period it was in practical terms irrelevant. Its difficulties were compounded by the fact that, like Voltaire's Dr Pangloss, the left wanted to believe that in the Labour Party 'all was for the best in the best of all possible worlds.' Only when harsh reality slapped it in the face did this change. But even then the commitment to Labour and its electoral progress prevented the left from giving a real lead to the movement fighting back against Wilson's policies.

Alienation of workers from the Labour Party

Wilson's plea at the 1966 election—that Labour could only be effective with a strong majority in the Commons—produced the best result for Labour since 1945. This made the electoral decline that followed all the more striking. As the thrust of Labour's policies became clear after 1966, it created massive disillusion among the party's traditional supporters. This showed in huge losses at parliamentary by-elections:

> Until 1966, it had for many years been a rare exception for a seat to change hands in a by-election. The Labour Governments of 1945–51 lost only one seat... In the whole of their thirteen years the Conservatives lost only ten seats—eight to Labour, two to the Liberals.
>
> The astonishing thing about the by-elections of the 1966 Parliament was that, far from being an exception, the loss of seats by the government

> became for a time the almost invariable rule... By the time they lost office in June 1970 they had shed sixteen seats out of the thirty-one they defended in just under six years of office—more than in their whole previous parliamentary history (fifteen were lost between 1900 and 1964). Swings which had once seemed disastrous now came as a relative relief. No government in thirty years had experienced anything remotely like it.[86]

Elections do not control capitalism, but they allow a protest vote when promises are betrayed. These by-elections showed the growing contradiction between expectations of full employment and rising living standards and the growing inability of governments to meet these expectations. A pattern of see-saw between the parties was established in 1966 and would continue for more than a decade.*

At local elections Labour fared no better. In April 1967 a Tory landslide ended thirty-three years' control of the Greater London Council, leaving Labour just eighteen seats out of a hundred. The May 1968 local elections cost Labour 919 seats. In London Labour lost fifteen of its eighteen boroughs. A nearly equivalent disaster took place at the 1969 local elections when some 917 seats were lost.

In the 1970 general election, Labour received 1,800,000 fewer votes than in 1951, notwithstanding the six million people who had been added to the electorate register, mainly because the voting age had been reduced from twenty-one to eighteen.

Widespread cynicism prevailed at the time. This was reflected in a National Opinion Poll Survey conducted in February 1968.[88] Although too much reliance should not be placed on surveys of this sort, the extreme figures are particularly illuminating.

Attitude	*Percent agreeing*
Most politicians promise anything to get votes	78
Most politicians care more about party than country	66
Politicians are all talk and no action	59
Most politicians are in it for what they can get	57
Once MPs are elected, they forget about the voters	55

One cause of disillusionment was that the majority of the electors could see no real differences between the parties, nor any connection between their own vote and their daily lives. As one book puts it:

* Proportion of by-elections showing falls in the government vote amounting to over 20 percent of the total poll: 1945–51, 3 percent; 1951–55, 2 percent; 1955–59, 10 percent; 1959–64, 18 percent; 1964–66, zero; 1966–70, 34 percent.[87]

> The leaders of both parties...steered towards the middle. The real clashes of principle in 1966–70 and in the [1970 General Election] campaign seemed extraordinarily few.[89]

This became, in turn, one of the main reasons put forward to explain Labour's defeat in 1970. Colin Crouch wrote:

> there is little purpose...in a social democratic party seeking to become the party of the national consensus simply by adopting the policies of its opponents. Not only does this involve a complete loss of purpose in the party itself, it is also likely to fail. An electorate may well decide that a Conservative Party is a better party to head a conservative consensus.[90]

This seemed to be confirmed by the turnout at the 1970 election, which, at 72 percent, was the lowest since 1935. The result was determined by 'the reluctant decision of just enough electors that the Conservatives were, marginally, the lesser of two evils'.[91] The Tories won 46.4 percent of the votes cast, to Labour's 43 percent.

The greatest demoralisation was inflicted on Labour activists. According to Minkin: 'the roots of the Party shrivelled'.[92] Thus a third of constituency parties did not bother to send delegates to the Labour Party conference which followed the 1970 election[93]

> too much had been sacrificed for many to stomach. The monument to it all could be seen in the empty committee room, the lapsed membership, the tireless activist of former years now nodding gently before the television screen.[94]

Ken Coates wondered: 'How many thousands of good socialists have withdrawn in disgust?... How many local Parties have been, to all apparent signs, demobilised? Certainly there have been heavy losses'.[95] The prevailing gloom dominated the conference. One delegate described the state of the local parties:

> Party morale collapsed. Membership fell dramatically and in some constituencies, like mine, became non-existent... Ask...how lonely they felt, and then tell them about political loneliness.[96]

We know that the official figure for individual Labour Party membership grossly overestimates the real membership (and overstates still further the active membership). But still it is indicative that the individual membership dropped from 830,116 in 1964 to 690,191 in 1970. In 1964 when Wilson came to office, there were sixty-six constituency parties with a membership of more than 2,000, but when he lost the 1970 general election the number had fallen to twenty-two. Some local parties underwent a traumatic decline, such as Brixton Labour Party, which in 1965 had 1,212 members and in 1970 only 292.[97]

The end of the reformist era

The permanent arms economy had slowed the decline in the rate of profit, it had not halted it. Furthermore the uneven burden of arms spending created unique problems for Britain—a second rate capitalist economy with a first rate imperialist role. Since the Second World War there had been a clear inverse relation between the level of wages and the level of unemployment: a high wage economy seemed to mean low unemployment. But after 1965 both moved in the same direction. Inflation, fuelled by US spending on the Vietnam war, spread throughout international capitalism. This added in Britain to the problems of recurring balance-of-payments crises, pushed back priority given in government circles to the reduction of unemployment and encouraged attacks on wages.

Keynesianism fitted Labour's synthesis of class and nation so well because it suggested what was good for the workers was good for the nation. But now that fear of balance-of-payments crises and inflation dominated government thinking. Trade unionists, and shop steward militants in particular, were blamed for the country's economic failings. High wages were declared to be *the enemy* of the national interest.

Labour's politics faced a dilemma. The foundation of gradualism is the belief that the government controls the national situation and can build reform upon reform. But under Wilson the truth slipped out. The capitalist economy dictated to the government. Reforms gained in the Attlee era had not been a springboard to future progress but had been due to exceptional circumstances—and these had now disappeared.

Take nationalisation. It was assumed that one takeover would lead to another, in cumulative fashion. As a matter of fact state ownership of unprofitable industry under Attlee became an impediment to further nationalisation under Wilson. Not only did it give the press an opportunity to discredit the whole notion of nationalisation, but it also meant that those industries taken into public ownership could not contribute financially to the buying of further enterprises. In the 1960s, siphoning money from the private sector in order to nationalise further industries became economically difficult if not impossible. Attlee's government had nationalised some 20 percent of all industry. Apart from steel, which the Wilson government renationalised after the Tories had privatised it, the basic ownership pattern of British industry hardly changed between 1951 and 1970.

The post-war boom had imposed a relative symmetry on state policies which was labelled Butskellism. The new policies imposed by crisis were also symmetrical: by 1970 there was little qualitative distinction between Labour and Tory programmes. As Reginald Maudling, deputy leader of the Conservative Party, said in 1967, the Labour government had 'inherited our problems. They seem also to have inherited many of our remedies.'[98]

Although Attlee's administration lost the 1951 election, it ended on a note of optimism and confidence. When Labour fell from office in 1970 its supporters looked back on the Wilson governments with a feeling of bitterness, anger and disillusion.

14

The Labour Party under the Heath government

The industrial scene

Union militancy had mushroomed in face of the economic difficulties and the failures of the Wilson government. It was given further impetus by the policies of the new Tory government led by Edward Heath. Legislation on industrial relations and a determination to control public sector wages produced a series of strike explosions.

An Industrial Relations Bill was introduced in December 1970 which had affinities with *In Place of Strife*. Again there was to be a register of unions, exclusion from which would mean the loss of legal immunities, and a cooling-off period (in this case sixty days). Secret ballots reappeared, along with an industrial court—the National Industrial Relations Court (NIRC). The closed shop was to be banned and collective agreements would be legally binding unless they included a written statement to the contrary.

The union leadership reacted far more sharply against the Tories. The TUC held a series of national, regional and local meetings, a rally in the Albert Hall and many open air demonstrations, including a 140,000-strong march on 21 February 1971. The TUC called on the unions not to register under the Act, and practically all sizeable unions responded. All unions employed the draft clause suggested by the TUC for collective agreements, stating: 'This is not a legally enforceable agreement.'

However, when Labour is out of office, union bureaucrats do not change their spots entirely. The TUC still rejected industrial action. In spite of this, one-day protest strikes did take place, organised by the rank and file, involving 600,000 workers on 8 December 1970, 180,000 on 12 January 1971 and about 1,250,000 on both 1 March and 18 March 1971.

One high point in workers' struggle was over sackings at Upper Clyde Shipbuilders (UCS). On the afternoon of 24 June 1971 more than 100,000 workers in Glasgow stopped work. Half of them demonstrated through the city. This was the largest Clydeside protest demonstration since the General Strike. A month later John Davies, the secretary for industry, announced that employment in the UCS yards would be cut from 8,500 to 2,500. Next day the workers of UCS took control of the four yards.

On 10 August a meeting of more than 1,200 shop stewards from all over Scotland and the north of England unanimously endorsed the plan for a work-in, and appealed for financial support for the workers of UCS. On 18 August, some 200,000 Scottish workers downed tools, and about 80,000 of them went on a demonstration. The shock to the government was immense. David McNee, head of Strathclyde police, phoned Downing Street and made it clear he would not take responsibility for civil order unless the government kept UCS open. Heath obliged by making a U-turn.

In July 1972 five London dockers were imprisoned in Pentonville for breaking the industrial relations law. All 44,000 dockers struck unofficially. Fleet Street followed suit and a number of engineering workers also came out. It seemed even the union bureaucracy might lose control unless it acted. On 26 July the General Council called a one-day strike for 31 July. The government took fright, and on the very day the General Council issued the call, the House of Lords took the dramatic step of altering the law to get Heath off the hook. The men were freed immediately; the TUC dropped the call for a strike.

There were more than 200 occupations of shipyards, factories, offices and workshops between 1972 and 1974. Workers also won important battles on the wages front. The most significant were the magnificent miners' strikes of 1972 and 1974.

The first of these involved a great deal of rank and file activity and industrial solidarity which culminated in the 'battle of Saltley gates'. Thousands of miners, assisted by some 20,000 striking engineers, shut a strategic Midlands coke depot and thereby insured the success of the strike. The second miners' strike, during the winter of 1973-4, though more passive than its predecessor, finally precipitated the downfall of the Tories and forced the general election which returned Labour to office.

The total of strike days reached 10,980,000 in 1970 and 1,551,000 in 1971, climbing to 23,909,000 in 1972—the highest figures since the 1920s. The average number of strike days in 1945–54 had been 2,073,000, in 1955–64 3,889,000, and 1965–9 1,951,000.

The political strike reappeared in Britain for the first time in over half a century. As political strikes are not officially counted, one has to rely on estimates for their size. One estimate suggests that official and unofficial strikes against the Industrial Relations Act in 1970–71 involved twice as many workers as the entire year's industrial disputes.[1]

Circumstances had forced both Labour and Tory governments to conduct a general attack on the workers on behalf of the ruling class. But government intervention—incomes policy, industrial relations legislation, pressure towards productivity deals—forced workers to generalise their own struggles too. Ingrained sectionalism began to be overcome. In the words of Colin Crouch:

> In part it has been the very reforms designed to re-institutionalise local action—incomes policy, reforms to bargaining structures and payment systems, productivity bargaining, and industrial relations reform—which have broken the local isolation of militant action and given it wider repercussions both economically and politically. The growth of shop-floor militancy initially produced a government response which forced industrial relations to become intensely politicised.[2]

One labour historian, Royden Harrison, called the struggle during Heath's government

> the most extraordinary triumph of trade unionism in its long conflict with government... The Labour Unrest of 1970–74 was far more massive and incomparably more successful than its predecessor of 1910 to 1914. Millions of workers became involved... Some of them began to exhibit an ominous concern with the conditions of *distribution* as well as production... But it was the coal miners, through their victories in the two Februaries of 1972 and 1974 who gave to this Labour Unrest a structure, a final roundness and completeness which their contribution of 1912 had failed to supply to the earlier experience. First, they blew the Government 'off course'; then they landed it on the rocks. First, they compelled the Prime Minister to receive them in 10 Downing Street—which he had sworn he would never do—and forced him to concede more in 24 hours than had been conceded in the last 24 years. Then two years later their strike led him to introduce the three day week—a novel system of Government by catastrophe—for which he was rewarded with defeat at the General Election.
>
> Nothing like this had ever been heard of before![3]

Under Heath the government was compelled to declare a State of Emergency no less than five times! What was the positive, active role of the Labour Party in these massive struggles? The same as during the Labour Unrest of 1910–14: *none*.

Who led the massive industrial struggles?

Trotsky wrote of the apparently unplanned February 1917 revolution that: 'The mystic doctrine of spontaneousness explains nothing'.[4] This is true of all mass action. There was a leadership in 1970–74, but it did not come from the Labour Party.

Industrial militants traditionally looked to the Communist Party. In 1966 this had founded the Liaison Committee for the Defence of Trade Unions (LCDTU). Although the Communist Party had the direct allegiance of only a minority of the country's 300,000 or so stewards, it had the ability to lead the shop stewards' movement as a whole. The left Labour stewards, by contrast, had no similar organisation, and Labour's politics led away from any idea of such a body as the LCDTU. It was the Liaison Committee which organised the one-day strike involving half a million workers against Labour's *In Place of Strife* in 1969 and the massive unofficial strikes against the Industrial Relations legislation. Communist Party militants led the Upper Clyde Shipbuilders' struggle, and the solidarity action to back it. The work-in adopted by UCS shop stewards popularised factory occupations throughout Britain.

Like the New Unionist leaders of 1889, the syndicalists and the wartime shop stewards, the leadership of the rank and file struggle of the 1970s was a small organisation standing outside the constraints of parliamentarism. Indeed it was only to the degree that the Communist Party was independent of the trade union bureaucracy and electoral methods, that it was able to channel the militant resistance to capitalism.

But that independent position was already gravely compromised by the Communist Party's leadership. They had long abandoned revolutionary socialism for a policy of changing British society through achieving 'a majority of Left Labour and Communist MPs'. This logic had not yet nullified the membership's fighting ability, but it sapped it inexorably. The effect was to water down criticism of the Labour left and left union bureaucrats. Stress was put on a bureaucratic alliance with these forces in opposition to the right.

Since the 1960s the main form of Communist Party intervention in industry has been the creation of 'Broad Lefts'—alliances with Labour left-wingers in the trade unions, whose main task was organising resolutions and electing left officials. The same approach affected the alliance of Broad Lefts across the unions—the LCDTU.

The contradiction between rank-and-file militancy and the cultivation of left union officials blunted the impact of the LCDTU. The crunch came in 1972. On 10 June 1,200 LCDTU delegates met to call for industrial action against the Tory Industrial Relations Act. But when the Pentonville five were jailed the following month, the LCDTU took no action because the Communist Party was desperate to accommodate Jack Jones, leader of the TGWU, who opposed industrial action. Four docks shop stewards wrote to *Socialist Worker*: 'If the average docker who took part in this struggle was asked what the LCDTU did, they would not even know who they were'.[5] Thereafter the LCDTU was little more than a rump, calling conferences to pass resolutions but not leading any action.

Because the Communist Party's politics were stifling the ability of its rank and file militants to lead, this gave others an opportunity to occupy a little of the space vacated. The once minuscule International Socialists (IS), predecessor of the Socialist Workers Party, was able to launch new initiatives, because, unlike the Labour Party and to an increasing extent the Communist Party, the IS stressed the importance that socialist politics should have a firm base among workers at the point of production, in the workplaces. As Alex Callinicos records:

> Between 1971 and 1974 IS was transformed from being a predominantly student to a predominantly working-class organization. Crucial in this process was the decision by the IS conference of May 1973 to build factory branches. By the next conference, in September 1974, IS had nearly 4,000 members and some forty factory branches. At the same time, IS members in various industries and unions had launched rank-and-file papers whose aim was to group around them militants who did not fully share their ideas but who were prepared to work with them around concrete issues such as higher wages...these papers had by 1973 achieved a small but nonetheless significant circulation.
>
> In the light of the LCDTU's paralysis and its own growing workplace base, IS took the first step towards building a national rank-and-file movement by calling a delegate conference to discuss the prospects of such a movement on 30 March 1974. 500 delegates representing 270 trade union bodies attended, and set up the National Rank and File Organising Committee. A second conference in November of the same year attracted delegates from a larger number of bodies, including 49 shop stewards' committees. Despite Communist Party attempts at a witch-hunt, a new, albeit small movement had, it seemed, been born.[6]

There could hardly be a greater contrast between these efforts by a tiny group of revolutionaries to relate to working-class activity and what even the most left-wing of the Labour Party were doing at the time. To underline this one needs but read Eric Heffer's book, *The Class Struggle in Parliament: A Socialist View of Industrial Relations*, published in 1973. Its theme was the struggle against the Tory Industrial Relations Act. Heffer was not only on the left of the party, but had been a trade union militant before being elected to parliament. Yet out of 339 pages, the UCS occupation, it seems, deserved only six lines; the miners' strike, one page; Pentonville and the national dock strike, again, one page. As against this, the 'brilliant' [Heffer's word] speech of the right-wing Labour MP Brian Walden against the Tory Industrial Relations Bill takes three whole pages! Heffer explains in his book that he did his best not to antagonise the official leadership of the TUC or Harold Wilson. He says he favoured a one-day strike against the Bill but did not speak openly for it 'because I was tied by Front Bench responsibilities',[7] [and] 'I did not want to get at cross purposes with what Harold Wilson had said'.[8]

The Labour Party as such *did nothing to develop mass militancy*, although a great number of Labour Party supporters were involved in the action. Once more they were not acting as members of the party.

The echo of the battle: Labour's customary leftward swing

Labour does not positively lead the working class, but it tails the class in certain circumstances. The two factors that always pushed Labour leftwards—pressure from without, and falling from office—now combined. Spurred on by the tremendous industrial militancy of the time, and in reaction to the Wilson government's miserable performance and the right-wing policy of the Tories, the party swung sharply to the left. At the core of the Labour left was the alliance of the TGWU and the AEU, led respectively by Jack Jones and Hugh Scanlon. At the 1973 Conference their combined strength accounted for 1,971,000 votes out of a total trade union vote of 5,449,000, and a total conference vote of 6,197,000. This block vote provided the base for a powerful left-wing thrust.

Now the Labour leadership used radical rhetoric. Tony Benn staked his claim as the spokesman of the Left and appeared at the UCS occupation chatting to stewards. But even traditional right-wingers like Denis Healey became political chameleons. Healey told the 1973 conference:

> Our job is to get power, and we join battle armed with the most radical and comprehensive programme we have had since 1945. Its aim is

> honestly stated, to bring about a fundamental and irreversible shift in the balance of power and wealth in favour of working people and their families. (*Applause*)... We are going to introduce a tax on wealth. We are going to turn the estate duty into a real tax... I warn you, there are going to be howls of anguish from the 80,000 rich people.[9]

Successive Labour Party conferences passed resolutions for more public ownership. Between 1971 and 1973 they supported nationalisation of banking, insurance and building societies, the building industry, finance houses, road haulage, shipbuilding and repair. *Labour's Programme for Britain* (1972) proposed to take back undertakings denationalised since 1970, without compensation. It advocated extending public ownership to North Sea oil, ports, pharmaceuticals, financial institutions, banking, shipbuilding and repairing, and building land.

Labour adopted extreme unilateral nuclear disarmament policies, the 1973 conference deciding:

> it is opposed to any British defence policy which is based on the use or threatened use of nuclear weapons, either by this country or its allies, demands the closing down of all nuclear bases, British and American on British soil or in British waters, and demands that this pledge be included in the General Election manifesto.[10]

Even the party's national executive showed growing left influence and a degree of independence from the actions of the parliamentary leadership.

After the previous Labour government's cavalier attitude towards conference resolutions, party democracy and the supremacy of conference were all the rage. At the 1970 Labour conference Jack Jones powerfully attacked elitism in government:

> For too many Members of Parliament the constituency Labour Party is a bit of a nuisance, a device for giving him a free hand as the mood takes him...we need greater influence from below, not less.[11]

In the spirit of his speech the following resolution was carried by 3,085,000 votes to 2,801,000, against the executive:

> This Conference believes that the Parliamentary Labour Party leaders, whether in government or opposition, should reflect the views and aspirations of the Labour and Trade Union Movement, by framing their policies on Annual Conference decisions...it deplores the Parliamentary Labour Party's refusal to act on Conference decisions'.[12]

In 1971 Scanlon demanded 'a definite decision that decisions of the Party Conference are binding on us all, and that includes every MP in this Party',[13] while the 1973 party programme promised that 'Policy in the Labour Party is made by the members. The long-term programme of the Party is determined by Annual Conference.' The party had embarked on a struggle which would culminate in the constitutional changes made at the 1981 Wembley Special Conference.

The birth of the Alternative Economic Strategy

The Labour Party conference of 1973 adopted what was to become known as the Alternative Economic Strategy. It was prompted by the failure of traditional Keynesianism under the Wilson government. Wilson had sacrificed expansion to maintain the confidence of the financial markets and improve the balance of payments. To do so he held down wages and raised taxes on working people, ending with the fiasco of *In Place of Strife*.

Labour's 1973 programme concluded that Britain must break the chains that tied the country to world capitalism, and with massive national reconstruction restore its position as a major industrial power. The programme rested 'on three major pillars...new public enterprise... the planning agreements system...[and] a new Industry Act'.

New public enterprise was necessary to break complete 'domination of the economy by a few leading firms.' Therefore,

> only direct control, through ownership, of a substantial and vital sector of the growth industries, mainly in manufacturing, which hold the key to investment performance, will allow a Labour Government of the future to achieve its essential planning objectives in the national interest. [An] expanded public sector is a key element of the planning process...

Public ownership would be exercised through a National Enterprise Board (NEB) based on 'existing State shareholdings...with a substantial addition of...*some twenty-five of our largest [private] manufacturers*.' This would be required '*very early in the life of the Board*'.[14]

Apparently George Brown's National Plan had not failed because *planning capitalism is impossible*. It had just not been ambitious enough. So the programme called for a Planning Agreements system, to include:

> all the major companies in this country...certainly the largest 100 or so manufacturing firms—and all the major public enterprises. Its role

> will include the following: to get up-to-date information [which] will concern both past performance and *advance* programmes...investment, prices, product development, marketing, exports and import requirements.

Labour would use this to:

> provide a systematic basis for making large companies accountable for their behaviour, and for bringing into line those which refuse to co-operate.

To make international capital accountable, special measures were suggested:

> We shall seek to ensure, for example, that the Government has the right to appoint public directors to the resident subsidiary companies of non-resident multi-nationals and to the main boards of resident multi-nationals; that the state—possibly through the NEB—is able to acquire shares in the parent company of multi-nationals and place a director in the board...

This was nothing if ambitious. Judith Hart said on 24 June 1973 that the NEB would be used radically to transform the structure of the economy:

> at the end of a five-year term *one-third of the turnover of the top 100 manufacturers,* who account for about half of our net manufacturing output and *two-fifths of their profits and about half their employment, should be invested with the board.*[15]

To do this all that was needed was for the six hundred or so individuals reclining on the benches of the Palace of Westminster to pass a New Industry Act. Instantly the government would have real powers to intervene. All the above measures, the programme claimed, would remedy the comparatively low rates of investment in the British economy, hence rebuilding British industrial capacity and raising its productivity to world levels. To reduce the influence of international capitalism, Britain should leave the EEC. Only then could economic sovereignty be regained, only then could the British state plan the national economy.

As the Alternative Economic Strategy was developed, new elements were introduced such as stringent control over the export of capital. Sterling would cease to be an international currency and would no longer be freely convertible. Foreign exchange controls would aim not only to halt runs on the pound, but also to prevent the expansion of British firms abroad rather than in the domestic economy. While the bulk of the economy would still be privately owned, the state would be the dominant force.

Safeguarded by import quotas from balance-of-payments problems, the government would make the achievement of full employment and economic growth its top priorities. This would be achieved by expanding demand; in this way Keynesian policy would come back into its own. In essence the Alternative Economic Strategy was nothing but revamped nationalist Keynesianism.

To strengthen the popular support for the Alternative Economic Strategy, *Labour's Programme 1973* offered a few extra goodies. After all if you are writing a cheque that will bounce, why not enter some astronomic figure?:

> *Economic Equality*:
> ...We are therefore now determined to launch a fundamental attack on the principle of the hereditary transmission of great wealth, with its associated power and privilege, and the accumulation of unearned gains...
> *Industrial Democracy*:
> ...we are considering the provision of direct representation for workers—with this representation being based firmly upon trade union channels, and being directly accountable to the workers in the company concerned. We are also considering with the TUC introducing the 'Supervisory Board' to British company structure. Such a Board would then be responsible for overall company policy and practice...

The Alternative Economic Strategy was completely unrealistic, utopian. With the bulk of industry remaining in private hands, with profit as the main spur of economic activity, would the most powerful sector of British capital—the multi-nationals and the banks—meekly accept the nationalisation of 25 leading companies and the *diktat* of the state and its planning agreements? Would the multi-nationals acquiesce with the appointment of directors by the government without a fight? Would they accept democratic control of industry? Would the present state machine—the civil service, judiciary, police and army—break the 'strike of capital' if big business resisted?

The Alternative Economic Strategy, it seemed, would be good for the workers—achieving full employment—and for the nation—restoring the international competitiveness of the British economy. It was the old, tired Labour synthesis of class and nation, reworked.

The picketing of Saltley gates, which led to the closing of a coke depot in the Midlands, seems pale in comparison to these world-shattering proposals. Yet the battle of Saltley gates had one important advantage, it advanced the *real* workers' movement to a position of confidence and power it had not held for half a century. The Alternative Economic Strategy, on the other hand, *was totally stillborn.*

The Social Contract

An integral part of *Labour's Programme 1973* was 'a far reaching *social contract* between workers and the Government—a contract which can be renewed each year as circumstances and as new opportunities present themselves.' The way for such an agreement had been prepared by the establishment, in January 1972, of a joint 'Liaison Committee' of the Parliamentary Labour Party, party executive and the TUC. In February 1973 this produced a compact, titled *Economic Policy and the Cost of Living*, which became part of the 1973 programme of the party.

The compact included the repeal of the Industrial Relations Act, extension of industrial democracy, a Royal Commission on incomes distribution, and the establishment of a Conciliation and Arbitration Service. It also mentioned new public enterprises, effective public supervision of the investment policies of large private corporations, new taxes on wealth, a redistribution of wealth and income, and direct statutory control of prices, particularly of food, housing and rent. Finally there were commitments on pensions, housing, health service charges and withdrawal from the EEC.

Through the influence of Jones, Scanlon, Benn and the Communist Party's network of supporters, the idea of Social Contracts and Alternative Economic Strategies filtered down to a substantial number of militants.

In the 1974 election the Social Contract proved invaluable to Labour. Its campaign, far from reflecting the fighting minority, stressed that the Social Contract proved that Labour could handle the unions when Heath could not. But its greatest role was to come. As we shall see, after 1974 it was the Social Contract—in support of which the left union leaders Jones and Scanlon played a crucial role—which strangled the rank and file militancy which had gripped Britain under Heath.

Parasite lost

Given the radical policies adopted by Labour conferences during the years of the Heath government, it is surprising to find that the organised Labour left was weak. The *Tribune* Group was the only serious force, and for such influence as it had, it depended on a number of big unions which, for the moment, went along with it. Despite *Tribune*'s vocal denunciation of past Labour government policies, there were close links between its former editor Michael Foot, the party leader Harold Wilson, and the TGWU general secretary Jack Jones. It was this triumvirate that acted as a reconciling force between the party executive and the leadership of the PLP. Who of the three was paramount became obvious after Wilson was returned to Downing Street in 1974. He dragged the big unions along, and they in turn pulled the Tribunite left.

Indeed despite the mighty industrial struggles and the left rhetoric, the Labour Party did not do well at all. *Individual membership of the party actually went down.* It was 690,191 in 1970, and 665,379 in 1973. As pointed out elsewhere, membership figures were distorted by the rule that every constituency party must affiliate on the basis of at least 1,000 members. Nevertheless the figures make the general trend clear.

Things were also bad electorally. In the four years of the second Wilson government, 1966–1970, Labour lost 15 seats in parliamentary by-elections and won none. Under Heath, between 1970 and 1974, Labour had made only one gain from the Tories, while in 1973 it lost Lincoln to Dick Taverne, the Labour renegade who became a Social Democrat, Rochdale to the Liberals, and Govan to the Scottish Nationalists. The memory of the 1966–70 Labour government was still fresh in the minds of the voters. The experience of the Wilson government had lowered the threshold of Labour's electoral support on a long-term basis.

The Labour vote did not benefit from the radicalising effect of class struggle. This was a serious sign for the future. Since the birth of the Labour Party, there had been a link, albeit indirect and tenuous but real nevertheless, between the class struggle and voting Labour. Now the aspirations aroused by victories of workers' struggle at Pentonville, Saltley and many other places seemed so divorced from the known record of what Labour could offer that for a growing number of workers, the link had snapped.

Thus only a minority of workers drew general political conclusions from the great struggles of the early 1970s. As a result, although Labour won the general election of February 1974, its vote was lower than in 1970 by 531,904, or 6 percent. Compared to 1966, there had been a loss of 1,418,560—or 10 percent. The 1974 election added a new twist to the see-saw effect described earlier. Having tried both Labour and Tories under conditions of crisis, many voters abandoned the two major parties in the elusive search for a better parliamentary alternative. The growth of nationalist parties was one sign of this, but the main beneficiaries were the Liberals. Their share of the vote, which had been 8.5 percent in 1966, now stood at 19.3 percent. It was this that allowed Labour to defeat the Tories.*

Nevertheless, Labour had come to office with an extremely radical left-wing programme and during the greatest wave of working-class struggle for half a century. How would the party respond?

* A sign of the disillusionment with both main parties was that together Tories and Labour had received 96.8 percent of the votes in 1951; in 1974 this dropped to only 74.9 percent.

15

The Labour government of 1974–79

HEATH CALLED the general election of February 1974 in desperate circumstances. He had lost the 1972 miners' strike and tried his best to defeat their second strike, which began earlier that month. The country was plunged into black-outs and a three-day working week. The Tories put a simple question to the electorate: 'Who rules Britain?' When the lights went out it was obvious that the working class had the potential to rule, but the parliamentary system does not work that way. In the polling booths the choice was whether to put a cross against the Labour or Tory candidates.

The Tory offensive had brought a political generalisation among workers. What the workers were against was clear: against incomes policy, against anti-union legislation, against the Tories. But what were the majority of them *for*? The answer was still Labour. Not that they were enthusiastic about it. Many illusions had evaporated under the 1964–70 Labour government. But the only positive answer that most workers were conscious of was the election of another Labour Government. Workers had blunted and driven off the Tory attack *without breaking with their predominantly reformist politics.*

The resultant Labour government disrupted the pattern of growing workers' struggle:

> In the years 1968–74 there was an unstable balance between the political generalisation on the employers' side—incomes policy and industrial relations legislation—and the industrial militancy on the workers' side. Such a situation cannot last for long. The unstable equilibrium can lead to one of two outcomes: to political generalisation of the industrial militancy, or to the decline of sectional militancy.
>
> In fact the unstable equilibrium in the following few years was destroyed by the policies dominating the British working class—Labourism—the nature of which is summed up in the banner of the Kent NUM: a miner outlined against a pithead and looking towards the Houses of Parliament. This is the essence of what Labourism represents in the relations between industrial action and politics. The

> logic of this dichotomy between economics and politics is that if workers have a claim that brings them up against a Tory government, there is the alternative of a Labour government. But if the claim brings them headlong against a Labour government they have no alternative but to retreat.[1]

When the Attlee government dampened postwar militancy, at least this was bought off with reforms. The 1974–79 government did not even have these to offer.

The bankruptcy of Keynesianism

Keynes had formulated his theories in the 1930s, at a time of high unemployment and falling prices. He and his followers assumed a trade-off between inflation and unemployment: that cutting unemployment might to some extent push the level of prices upwards, while rising unemployment would push prices down again. The modest price rises associated with the thirty years of full employment between 1939 and 1969 seemed to justify this analysis. (This is not the place to discuss whether the post-war boom was mainly the result of the massive arms expenditure).

The trade-off between unemployment and inflation had been formulated arithmetically by Professors Phillips and Paish: when the unemployment rate was 2.5 percent, wages would rise at about the same annual rate as productivity—3 percent or so—and the price level would therefore be stable. But the 1970s exploded the Phillips-Paish theorem. In the 1950s unemployment had been generally 1 percent or lower. It began climbing in the 1960s and for most of the next two decades was far above the 2.5 percent Phillips and Paish believed to be the level at which inflationary pressure would cease. Instead inflation *accelerated* from an average of only between 2 and 3 percent in the 1950s to between 3 and 4 percent m the 1960s and to annual rates of 10 percent and often more in the 1970s.

Taking the general level of prices in January 1974 as 100, then by December 1974 it had risen to 117.4; by December 1975 it had jumped to 146.1; and by December 1976 to 166.8. From the beginning of the 1970s there were short inflationary booms in which unemployment fell slightly, followed by deep, more protracted slumps in which inflation dropped only marginally, and unemployment hit the roof. This is what the economists call 'stagflation'. A reflation of the economy will feed inflation more than it will cut unemployment.

Stagflation was generated by the massive arms spending of the Vietnam War, the ability of multinationals to offset the falling rate of profit by raising their prices, and the bailing out of large bankrupt companies by the national state for fear of economic and social instability.

This combination of recession and reflation swept the Labour leaders off their feet. Keynesianism gave way to monetarism. Butskellism was replaced—to use Stuart Holland's word—by 'Howleyism': a combination of the monetarist policy common to the Labour chancellor Denis Healey and the Tory chancellor Geoffrey Howe. *Thatcher's policies took shape before she was elected*, for, in the words of Peter Riddell, political editor of the *Financial Times*: 'If there has been a Thatcher experiment, it was launched by Denis Healey'.[2]

Now Keynesianism was put on its head: the way to cut unemployment was to cut inflation. Prime minister Harold Wilson told the 1975 conference of the National Union of Mineworkers:

> Inflation is causing unemployment... The more inflation we have the more unemployment we have. And if we were to tolerate the rates of inflation reached in recent months, then no industry would be secure, no job safe... Lose the battle against inflation and the battle for full employment is lost before you begin.[3]

Economic history had to be re-written. This is what Callaghan told the 1976 Labour Party conference just after he took over from Wilson as prime minister:

> We used to think you could spend your way out of a recession, and increase employment by cutting taxes and boosting government spending. I tell you in all candour that that option no longer exists, and that in so far as it ever did exist, it only worked on each occasion since the war by injecting a bigger dose of inflation into the economy, followed by a higher level of unemployment as the next step.[4]

Little freedom of manoeuvre for Labour government

The massive development of the multinationals, the enormous volume of mobile capital that can be switched from one country to another at the press of a button, has made nonsense of attempts by reformist governments to pursue national policies in isolation. 'Keynesianism—or reformed capitalism—in one country' is no more practical than socialism in one country.

Furthermore, British capitalism has been declining steadily relative to other capitalisms for a century. No government has managed to arrest the decline in Britain's share of world trade which stood at 33.2 percent in 1899, 22.9 percent in 1929, 21.3 percent in 1937, 25.5 percent in 1950, 16.5 percent in 1960, 10.8 percent in 1970 and 9.7 percent in 1979.

As these figures demonstrate, the decline accelerated in the three decades after 1945, a time of the longest and most rapid period of continuous expansion of world capitalism. True, at this time, in 'absolute terms the British economy has never been so prosperous, nor has it ever expanded so fast',[5] but its growth was significantly below all other major capitalist countries:

> In terms of Gross Domestic Product per head Britain slipped from ninth in 1961 to thirteenth in 1966 and fifteenth in 1971. By 1976 Britain was eighteenth, having fallen behind not just the United States, Canada and Sweden, but Iceland, France, Finland, Austria and Japan as well.[6]

The underlying cause lay in 'persistently low levels of investment' which ran at half the levels in competing countries. In 1978 it was estimated:

> that the fixed assets per worker in manufacturing in the United Kingdom were only £7,500, compared with £23,000 in West Germany and £30,000 in Japan. Whereas in 1870 Britain enjoyed the highest productivity level amongst the major capitalist economies, by 1970 Britain had one of the lowest.[7]

Labour took office at a time of world economic crisis in which unemployment and accelerated inflation went hand in hand. In Britain the rate of inflation rose from 10.2 percent in 1973 to 24.6 percent in 1975. The balance of payments deteriorated from a deficit of £923 million in 1973 to £3,565 million in 1974 on the current account. Unemployment, which had been half a million in 1974, reached a million in mid-1975 and 1.6 million a year later. Internally, British capitalism was weak. Externally it was constrained by those who controlled international credit—the Arab governments with massive petro-dollar surpluses, the central banks and the IMF.

To improve Britain's competitiveness the government increased the exploitation of the workers. As Healey told the annual dinner of the CBI in 1974: 'I can assure you that the Government has no intention of destroying the private sector or encouraging its decay.' It was not the rich, after all, who were going to be squeezed 'till the pips squeak', to use Healey's own oft-quoted phrase. On the contrary, the government wanted 'a private sector which is vigorous, alert, imaginative and profitable'.[8]

Promises of radical measures ditched

In this situation, even if the right-wingers who controlled the government had been enthusiastic about the bold policies of the Alternative Economic Strategy, their implementation would have been blocked by the massive pressure of international capitalism. Big business and the City clamoured for the economy to be deflated. The Treasury collaborated with the International Monetary Fund to reshape the policies of the elected but 'profligate Labour Government'. As Joel Barnett, chief secretary to the Treasury remembers:

> there were some senior Treasury officials who felt more strongly than others that the IMF was needed to keep a check on this profligate Labour government... There are some who suspect sabotage by at least one official, senior official...

US Treasury secretary William Simon got the message—'be tough':

> The people in the Bank of England and the people in the UK Treasury knew what had to be done. While they would never say it, because they were fiercely loyal, I think that they were secretly rooting for us, that we would hold fast our ground.[9]

That fierce loyalty of civil servants was in the service of one master—the interests of capital.

The CBI intervened directly in government affairs on behalf of big business. Campbell Adamson, director-general of the Confederation of British Industry, the CBI, recounts:

> I remember going through with the council at one meeting a whole list of actions that our side might have to take if Benn really got his way in a White Paper... We certainly discussed an investment strike...the possibility of industry withholding its investment. But we also discussed various things about not paying various taxes, and a list—I don't know that I want to be very specific—but a list of things which in themselves would not have been legal.[10]

The CBI never had to act on its threat. What nationalisation measures were undertaken were few and not part of an overall nationalisation strategy. When British Leyland faced bankruptcy, the National Enterprise Board (NEB) took it over. The same happened to Ferranti, the machine tool company Alfred Herbert, and International Computers (ICL). Once Ferranti's profitability had been restored it was handed back to private enterprise in 1978. To use Bernard Donoghue's words: 'The NEB became a convenient casualty ward for firms the Government wished to rescue from bankruptcy'.[11]

Labour also bailed out the shipyards:

> to the great relief of the private owners who, while remaining the staunchest supporters of the Tory party and denouncing public ownership in all its forms, were in nearly every case ready to take the Labour Government's cash for their near bankrupt yards.[12]

What happened to the 'planning agreements'? Draconian government measures by compulsory means were replaced by a voluntary system. In fact 'system' is an exaggeration. Just one company—Chrysler—actually signed a planning agreement. The insult was that the government gave Chrysler £162.5 million when the company threatened to close its factory. As Wilson said: 'the Labour Government [had] been presented with a pistol at its head'.[13] This did not prevent Chrysler pursuing the traditional business practice of 'take the money and run'. It sacked 8,000 workers, and at the end, in July 1978, sold Chrysler UK to the Peugeot-Citroen motor company, without even telling the government until the deal was signed. Some planning agreement!

Farce gave way to tragedy. Instead of economic reflation we got cuts in government spending, cuts and more cuts; cuts in the November 1975 budget; further cuts in April 1975, February 1976, and the most swingeing axe-blows in July and December 1976. Public spending levels were reduced in 1976-8 by an incredible 9.5 percent in real terms after allowing for inflation.[14] No area of welfare was safe. Tens of hospitals closed and schools, houses and roads suffered. Nothing Thatcher did later matched the carnage wrought by Labour in 1977.

Incomes policy once more

Capitalist pressure did not cease with Labour's spending cuts. These could only tamper with the economic problems facing Britain. A more important task for capitalism was the reduction of wages. Since the war this had been Labour's special talent. The Tories were not nearly so adept, as the following graph shows:

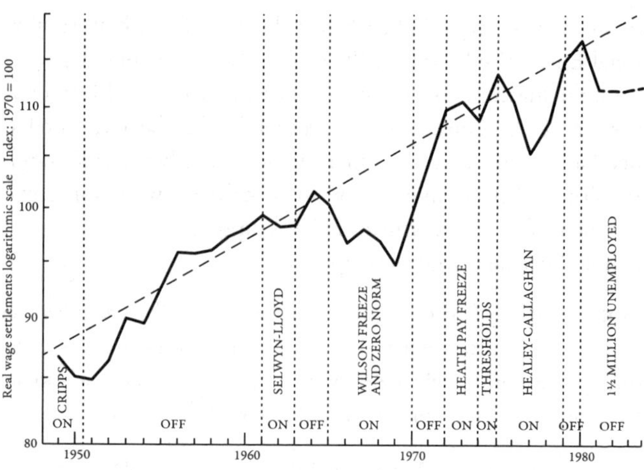

Real wage settlements and incomes policies 1949–1981[15]

Now the Social Contract came into its own, not only as a means of attacking wages, but also of stabilising British capitalism in its most dangerous period since the 1920s. The policy of collaboration between the union bureaucrats and the government was effective in restraining workers. All the union leaders' talk about 'the national interest' could mean only one thing—if Britain was to catch up in the international race, it would have to do so *at the expense of the workers*. Even when speeches were at their most radical, *Labour's Programme 1973* had left the door open to such a move.

> The choice is either for a great contract between government, industry and the trade unions, with all three parties prepared to make sacrifices to achieve agreement on a strategy to deal with the problems of rising prices; or else an interminable debilitating inflation which will help nobody...

Once more the idea that a Labour government could be a neutral agency straddling the class/nation divide was proved nonsense. Labour could not control the CBI, the IMF or even its own Treasury officials, but the Social Contrick (as it was called) gave it control over the workers.

On 1 July 1975 a fixed flat-rate wage increase of £6 (for those on incomes up to £8,500) was introduced, with a statutory twelve-month interval between awards. The £6 amounted to about 10 percent of average wages at the time, while the rate of inflation was 24.2 percent. The TUC General Council complied, and Healey gave it high praise:

> the most impressive thing has been the speed with which members of the General Council have themselves reached a voluntary agreement on a limit to pay...which will mean some reduction in real take home pay for the majority, though by no means all of its members.
>
> I do not think there has been any previous occasion in the history of this country, nor maybe any other country, in which the trade union movement of its own will has not only agreed to such a policy but has agreed it in very great detail.[16]

Not a single union challenged this phase of the incomes policy. On 1 August 1976 stage two of the incomes policy was introduced: a 4.5 percent increase in wages—at a time that the rate of inflation was 16.5 percent. Again this meant a serious cut in real wages. Yet again not a single union officially challenged it.

But there were limits to how much the rank and file would endure. By stage three, crucial union conferences—those of the AEU, TGWU, NUM and many others—decided to oppose any third year of wage restraint. From the summer of 1977 the government was obliged to police this phase on its own. However, the union leaders still tacitly collaborated. Only one union resisted stage three with strike action—the Fire Brigades Union, which began an eight-week strike for a 30 percent pay claim in November 1977. The Labour government mobilised all its forces against them—including the use of troops. Despite wide public support the firemen were defeated.

When the government tried to impose stage four in August 1978—a 5 percent pay limit—the floodgates broke. The result was the 'winter of discontent'. Nevertheless, Wilson and Callaghan could still pat themselves on the back. They had achieved de facto union cooperation in incomes policy over a long and tough period, 1975–78.

Blunting workers' militancy

To carry its policies, the government had above all to blunt the militancy that the working class had shown in 1968–74. By using the trade union bureaucracy it regained by stealth what the Heath government had lost in open battle.

Already under the Wilson government of 1964–70 a whole number of steps had been taken to undermine shop stewards' organisation. The final fruits were garnered under the Labour government of 1974–79.

In 1964, Wilson had appointed the Donovan Commission to look into union affairs. In 1968 it delivered its report. The main target was clear: shop-floor organisation. To overcome this, Donovan suggested productivity deals, which would replace piecework, deprive the shop stewards of their basic role of negotiating bonus rates, make more convenors and senior stewards full-time so as to distance them from the shop floor, and tighten the links between the senior stewards of the factory and the union bureaucracy. By 1980 69 percent of workplaces employing over 1,000 manual workers had full-time convenors. The speediest growth in the number of full-time senior stewards was in the years 1975–77.[17]

The pernicious effect of the rhetoric of 'national interest' in the mouths of Labour and trade union leaders can be seen if we look at three core sections of the organised working class which had shaken the Heath government to its foundations: Govan on the Clyde, British Leyland and mining.

The advantages of Labour's carrot over the Tory stick were shown graphically with the introduction of the 'workers' participation' which Donovan had argued for. Govan, the new name for three of the four former UCS yards (the fourth becoming Marathon) had been pioneers in the field. Stewards sat on a joint union-management committee monitoring a harsh productivity deal. They signed a 31-point agreement which contained elaborate no-strike pledges and massive concessions on work practices which gave management the right to impose compulsory overtime.

When shipyard workers at Swan Hunter on the Tyne refused a tough management package tied to a large Polish ship order, Govan scabbed on them. Jimmy Airlie, Govan's Communist convenor, had led the UCS occupation in 1971 and asked at that time, 'Are the other shipyards going to accept our orders and let my men starve?' But in 1978 he sang a new song. 'If Newcastle are losing six ships through disputes, we will build them. If not us, then the Japs will.'

Participation also became the rage in the car industry. It led to blacklegging becoming respectable at Longbridge, British Leyland's biggest factory, and for decades by far the most militant plant in the car industry.

In 1975 senior stewards accepted a three-tier system of participation accompanied by an announcement that 12,000 jobs had to go. Now, instead of seven full-time senior stewards, Longbridge had more than fifty. A gap was created between them and the members. The *Financial Times* gave fulsome praise of the Longbridge senior stewards.[18]

Derek Robinson, the Longbridge convenor, chairman of the British Leyland combine committee and a leading member of the Communist Party, was more profuse in his praise of 'participation' than anyone else. More and more he spoke as the partner of management: '*we* still haven't won the conception amongst the broad masses of people on the shop floor that *they*'ve got a vested interest in efficiency no less than *we* have. It is one of *our* problems...if we are able to...make Leyland successful as a publicly-owned company, then it is self-evident that that will be a major political victory'.[19]

Under Robinson the Longbridge works committee, instead of serving as a transmission belt for channelling workers' demands upwards, came to serve the interests of the employers, transferring their orders downwards.

Participation weakened shop-floor organisation, increased sectionalism, and, finally, made scabbing an official tactic. In February 1977 2,365 toolmakers throughout British Leyland went on a one-month strike for separate bargaining rights and restoration of differentials. When the government threatened to sack them, AUEW president Hugh Scanlon declared that this decision 'has the full backing of all the unions'. Robinson agreed and encouraged all workers to cross the toolroom workers' picket. In August 1978 the toolroom in the company's SU Carburettor plant came out on strike. Again both union officials and the leadership of the combine lined up with management.*

The years of participation did terrible damage. The government appointed a tough new manager at British Leyland, Michael Edwardes, who proposed 12,500 redundancies in January 1978. Mass meetings were held in protest, but soon the majority of senior stewards and union officials decided to accept. In November a strike called by the Longbridge shop stewards' committee against the government's 5 percent limit on wage rises petered out without a murmur. On 10 September 1979 Edwardes, with the support of the leadership of the Confederation of Shipbuilding and Engineering Unions, exploited the gap between the shop stewards and their members, and initiated a ballot over the heads of the stewards. This simply asked workers: 'Are you in favour of the

* Two other examples of official scabbing by unions during the 1974–79 Labour government deserve mention. During the March 1977 strike for higher pay by 535 electricians, members of the EETPU in BSC's Port Talbot steel plant, the other 6,500 trade unionists in the plant, members of the AUEW, TGWU and other unions, were instructed by their leadership to cross the picket line. This strike went on for more than two months. The second example is the strike of 5,000 maintenance engineers at London's Heathrow Airport (1 April to 27 April 1977) when 54,000 other trade unionists, members of the TGWU, GMWU, EETPU, among others, were instructed to cross the picket line.

Leyland survival plan?' without even pretending to spell out what that meant. The vote was 'yes' by 7 to 1.

Now Edwardes no longer needed participation. On 19 October he sacked Robinson. In spite of everything, Longbridge was solid, and 57,000 workers came out on strike in BL as a whole. But the picket was small, and little effort was made to spread the strike elsewhere. On 27 October the AUEW called it off, and Robinson himself backed down, leaving the shop floor terribly demoralised.

In short, the strength of the Longbridge workers' organisation, which had played a key role in supporting the miners in 1972, had atrophied disastrously.

In the case of the miners, the measure used to undermine their ability to struggle was the incentive scheme, a sort of productivity deal giving widely differing incomes between coalfields, and even between individual pits. In September 1974 the National Coal Board and representatives of the miners' union executive submitted details of a draft agreement. In a ballot 61.53 percent of the NUM members rejected this.

But the government, represented by energy secretary Tony Benn, and the Coal Board kept the pressure up. NUM president Joe Gormley obliged them by breaking the union's constitution and balloting again. He hoped to overrule the previous decision but once more the majority (55.6 percent) rejected the scheme. Now the NUM executive allowed separate areas to negotiate their own local incentive schemes, which Nottinghamshire and others rapidly proceeded to do. This, more than anything, created the deep divisions that were to take such a heavy toll in 1984–85. The needs of the scabbing in that strike were sown by the Labour government in 1977.

The Callaghan government went further than just encouraging scabbing. When the Glasgow dustcart drivers came out on strike in March 1975, the government sent in troops to break the strike—and the army was used again against the firemen in the winter of 1977–78.

The differing roles of the political and trade union wings of the labour bureaucracy were underlined by these events. When *In Place of Strife* had been proposed back in 1969, mass pressure had forced the TUC to lean on the Labour Party. Now, however, Labour exploited the Achilles heel of do-it-yourself reformism—its openness to generalised reformist politics in the shape of appeals on behalf of the 'national interest'. Labour's link with the trade unions now meant that it could *use the union bureaucracy to police the working class* far more effectively than could Heath's industrial relations courts and all the paraphernalia of the state.

A Chamber of Horrors: the Labour government's economic record

Despite its efforts, the five years of the 1974–79 Labour government saw the lowest economic growth since the war. The sickness of capital was beyond the cure of its doctors. Britain's industrial output in 1978 barely recovered to the 1973 level. Between 1953–66 the average annual real growth was 2.9 percent. In the years 1967–73 it was 3.4 percent; during 1974–78 it was only 0.9 percent.[20]

While in office, the government turned the average 2 percent annual wage rises between 1948 and 1973 into a 1.6 percent average annual fall.[21] Even after the breakdown of incomes policy in 1978, real wages were still below 1973.[22]

When in the winter of 1971–72 unemployment had mounted to nearly a million—at that time an unprecedented post-war figure, panic had gripped the Tory government and it quickly resorted to a whole number of reflationary measures. Under Labour the loyalty of the trade unions and their members abated the outcry. In January 1975 there were 678,000 people out of work; by December 1975, this figure had risen to 1,129,000, by December 1976 to 1,273,000, and by September 1977 to 1,609,000. Despite a moderate fall 1,300,000 people were still unemployed in December 1978.

The February 1974 Labour manifesto had promised to 'strike at the roots of the worst poverty.' Actually the numbers living below the official poverty line rose from 1,410,000 in 1974 to 2,280,000 in 1976. There were 5,260,000 people with income levels no more than 40 percent above the Supplementary Benefit poverty line in 1974. Two years later there were 8,500,000.[23]

An economist wrote in *The Observer* of Labour's wage restraint:

> The past twelve months have almost certainly seen the sharpest fall in the real living standards of Britain's working population in any year for at least a century, including the wars. Indeed, to find a comparable fall, it will probably be necessary to go back to the eighteenth and early nineteenth centuries.[24]

And a *Financial Times* columnist commented:

> I cannot for the life of me think of any reason why anyone should consider voting Conservative at the next general election...we are already served by about as good a conservative government as we are likely to get. For a start Mr Callaghan's government has sat out a level of unemployment that no Conservative government would have dared to accept.[25]

Reformism is the product of left ideas generated by class struggle but contained. Upon this soil the labour bureaucracy grows up. But the crisis forced the bureaucracy to go much further than before. It moved from *containment* to actually *attacking the very basis of the movement upon which it rested.*

Fortunately, as we shall see in the next chapter, basic workers' organisation proved more resilient than pessimists such as Eric Hobsbawm believe. Nevertheless, in the five years between 1974 and 1979 Labour turned the greatest advance in workers' struggle for fifty years *into a retreat*. By demoralising the working class Labour *positively assisted* an ideological advance of the right.

One example will demonstrate.

The National Front: ugly child of government policies[26]

Mass unemployment, government spending cuts, a decline in real wages and increasing general social deprivation in the years 1975–78 created conditions for the neo-fascist National Front to nourish. Spring 1976 saw a set of unfortunate Asians kicked out of Malawi, a tragic legacy of British imperialism in Africa. Media hysteria mounted, with *The Sun* screaming: 'Scandal of £600 a week immigrants' (the money went to a racketeering hotelier), the *Daily Mirror*: 'New Flood of Asians to Britain', and the *Daily Telegraph*: 'Invasion of Asians Forces Borough to Call for Help'.[27]

The National Front made substantial electoral gains in 1976. In local elections at Blackburn the National Front and National Party together got an average of 38 percent of the vote; in Leicester the NF got 18.5 percent. In Deptford (Lewisham) in a council by-election in July 1976 the two parties together won 44 percent (possibly over half the white vote)—more than the winning Labour candidate, who got 43 percent.[28]

Instead of campaigning against racism, the Labour Party leadership at the time was pandering to it. On 18 May 1976 Bob Mellish, Labour's chief whip and MP for Bermondsey, spoke on the 'influx' of Malawi Asians: 'This nation has done all it should have done. Its record is one of great honour and integrity, but I say "enough is enough"'. It was perfectly natural that the very next speaker should be Enoch Powell, who whipped up further hysteria round Mellish's catchphrase: 'Measures were needed: the first was that they should terminate net immigration and say "Enough is enough"'.[29] The chorus was then taken up by the press and racists far and wide. With Labour spouting racism the cockroaches began emerging from under the stones. They had plenty to feed on.

1977 saw a massive deterioration in working people's living standards. It is no wonder that the year saw even greater electoral successes for the NF. In the May elections for the Greater London Council (GLC) they stood candidates in 85 out of the 92 constituencies, getting 119,063 votes or 5 percent of the poll, and beating the Liberals into third place in 33 constituencies. In 1973 they had received only 0.5 percent.

The Labour Party was paralysed before the fascist menace which by its nature stood outside the rules of the parliamentary game. By contrast, the Socialist Workers Party organised repeated demonstrations against the National Front. The most important was in Lewisham on 13 August 1977, when 5,000 anti-fascists broke through police lines twice and dispersed an NF march. The police then violently attacked the anti-fascists in a battle that raged for hours.

Afterwards, just as had happened in the 1930s, the Labour Party and press treated the fascists and anti-fascists to exactly equal abuse.

Michael Foot, then deputy prime minister, said: 'The most ineffective way of fighting the Fascists is to behave like them.'[30] Ron Hayward, general secretary of the Labour Party, 'saw little difference between the violent demonstrators [by whom he meant the Socialist Workers Party members] and "NF Fascists"'[31] The Labour Party West Midland organiser went on in the same vein about the Socialist Workers Party: 'They are just red Fascists. They besmirch the good name of democratic socialism.'[32]

At the 1977 Labour Party Conference Sid Bidwell MP described the anti-fascists as 'hooligans...who have yet to take their part in responsibility in the real Labour movement.'[33] At the same conference, the delegate from Lewisham East Constituency Labour Party declared: 'Certainly the answer is not in violent confrontation with the National Front. Who won on 13 August in Lewisham? Only the National Front.'[34]

On the contrary. The battle of Lewisham was a springboard for launching the immensely popular Anti Nazi League (ANL) in November 1977, in which the Socialist Workers Party played an important role.

Mainly to give a focus for youth against the National Front—the age group where they drew most of their support—the ANL organised its first Carnival in London at the end of April 1978. Its success was beyond everyone's expectations, bringing 100,000 on a march from Trafalgar Square to a music festival six miles away.

Rock Against Racism (RAR) then grew up alongside the ANL. Huge Carnivals took place in Manchester (35,000), Cardiff (5,000),

Edinburgh (8,000), Harwich (2,000), Southampton (5,000), Bradford (2,000) and London again (80,000). In the ensuing weeks and months there was a rash of ANL groups springing up all over the country.*

The NF vote in subsequent elections collapsed. In Leeds it declined by 54 percent, in Bradford by 77 percent, even in its East End heartland it dropped by 40 percent. The ANL did this by taking a hard-hitting campaign on to the streets, into the factories and council estates, and undid some of the political damage wrought by government policies.

Despite all the taunts about 'red fascists' and that the ANL was outside the labour movement, it was in fact rooted there. As early as mid-April 1978, before the Carnival, it was sponsored by thirty AUEW branches and districts, twenty-five trades councils, eleven NUM areas and lodges, more than five branches from each of the unions TGWU, CPSA, TASS, NUJ, NUT and NUPE, and thirteen shop stewards' committees in major factories.[35]

The Labour leadership played no role in the ANL. However, the ANL did not ignore the value of winning the support of individual MPs where this was possible. Thus Neil Kinnock, Audrey Wise and Martin Flannery were asked to sponsor and did so. They were joined by fifty local Labour Parties.

In a small way, the SWP was applying the Comintern tactic of the united front. In fighting the NF the SWP did not fall into the ultra-left trap of writing off reformist organisations. As a revolutionary body its starting point was absolute political and organisational independence from the reformist Labour Party. Membership or commitment to the latter would have strangled the ANL at birth with the cord of electoralism. But this was not enough. As Trotsky put it in relation to revolutionaries in the 1920s:

> If the Communist Party did not seek for organizational avenues [to] coordinated action between Communist and non-Communist (including Social-Democratic) working masses...it would have thereby laid bare its own incapacity to win over—on the basis of mass action—the majority of the working class. It would degenerate into a Communist propaganda society but never develop into a party for the conquest of power.[36]

* From 22 April to 9 December 1978 the following ANL groups declared themselves: School Kids, Students, Fordworkers, Longbridge, Civil Servants, Rail (ten branches), Firemen, Busworkers, Teachers—which held a rally of 1,000, Miners—which held a conference of 200 delegates, Engineers, NUPE, Two Halifax Night Spots, Football, Spurs, Everton, Women on one housing estate, Christians, Bikers, Vegetarians, Skateboarders, Skins, Disabled Students, and Art Against Racism and Fascism.

Obviously fighting the NF was a long way from conquering power, and calling on certain Labour MPs to make a stand would not change the world. Nevertheless it bore out the truth of Trotsky's assertion that:

> The reformists dread the revolutionary potential of the mass movement; their beloved arena is the parliamentary tribune, the trade-union bureaus, the arbitration boards, the ministerial ante-chambers.
>
> [But] we are, apart from all other considerations, interested in dragging the reformists from their asylums and placing them alongside ourselves before the eyes of the struggling masses.[37]

The ANL was one bright spark in a gloomy period. Alas there were precious few others.

The Labour government and the bomb

In the case of unilateral disarmament the Labour government did not 'fight, fight and fight again' as Gaitskell had done to win the party conference away from its unilateralism. It simply ignored it.

The 1972 Labour Party conference had carried a unilateralist motion demanding 'the removal of all nuclear bases in this country'.[38] The resolution was passed on a show of hands with support from the party executive. The executive's spokesman was right-winger Joe Gormley!

The 1973 conference had gone further, insisting that the unilateralist pledge 'be included in the general election manifesto…' This time, perhaps with a view to the approaching election, the executive had opposed the motion. Nevertheless it was carried on a card vote by 3,166,000 to 2,462,000.[39]

But on coming to office, Wilson, and later Callaghan, went behind the back of the Commons and spent £1,000 million on the Polaris submarine nuclear missile improvement programme, code-named Chevaline. The Labour Government also entered into an agreement with NATO to increase defence spending by 3 percent in real terms for the six years from 1979.

Labour and Northern Ireland

As Britain's oldest imperialist possession, the question of Northern Ireland is an important touchstone for socialists. Labour's commitment to the British state has meant that since the Attlee government, the three tenets of Labour policy on Ireland had been: support for partition;

bipartisanship at Westminster—in other words the mutual support by Labour and the Tories of each other's policies towards Northern Ireland whichever is in government; and the upholding of the right of the Unionists in Northern Ireland to veto any constitutional change. It was Attlee who, in May 1949, enacted the Ireland Act, which stated 'that in no event will Northern Ireland or any part thereof cease to be part of His Majesty's Dominions and of the United Kingdom without the consent of the Parliament of Northern Ireland'.[40]

Wilson was the prime minister who, in August 1969, had sent the troops into Northern Ireland. When the internment of Republicans without trial had been introduced by Stormont (the Northern Ireland parliament) in August 1971, an emergency debate took place in the House of Commons. By now the Tories were back in office, and Labour officially abstained, although numbers of Labour MPs voted against the government.

On 30 January 1972 in Derry, the British army shot and killed 13 anti-internment demonstrators in what became known as 'Bloody Sunday'. When Lord Widgery, the high court judge, whitewashed the army's action, Jim Callaghan, for the Labour opposition, declared: 'The Prime Minister asks for the combined support of the House. He has it'.[41]

In 1974 it was the Labour government which rushed through the Prevention of Terrorism Act, allowing arrest without charge, as well as deportation and exclusion of suspects from Britain without trial.

In 1976 the political 'special category status' for Republican prisoners, which had been won from the Tory administration in 1972, was taken away by Merlyn Rees, Labour's Northern Ireland secretary. Republican hunger strikes followed in the H-blocks of Long Kesh. This culminated with the death in prison of Bobby Sands in 1981. When news of his death reached the Commons:

> There were loud cheers from all parts of the Commons yesterday as Mr Michael Foot, leader of the Labour Party, placed himself squarely behind Mrs Margaret Thatcher in her firm rejection of the demands of the IRA hunger strikers'.[42]

Nine other hunger strikers died without any change of position by Labour.

In the meantime, the Labour leadership was not even ashamed to forge a parliamentary alliance with the Official Unionists in July 1977. Its pact with the Liberals had ended and Labour no longer had an overall Commons majority. In payment for the Orange vote, six extra parliamentary seats were given to Northern Ireland.

Deep divisions between government and party

Relations between the Labour government and the rest of the party had been strained between 1966 and 1970; likewise under the Labour government of 1974–79, but on a much grander scale. During these years Labour Party Conference was to overrule the executive no less than twenty-three times.*

The executive's policy recommendations were often critical of the government. Geoff Bish, secretary of the Labour Party Research Department, reviewing relations between the executive and the government, described the vast input of the executive into Labour's policy process:

> Over the past five years, working through a network of subcommittees and study groups, the Home Policy Committee has been responsible for the publication of no less than 70 major NEC statements of one kind or another, including statements to Conference, the 60,000 word *Labour's Programme 1976*, evidence to Royal Commissions and direct submissions to the Labour Government itself. Over 2,000 research papers have been prepared, either within the Research Department or by outside experts.[44]

The result? *Nil.* The government paid scant attention to resolutions from the executive or conference. By a majority of two to one the Labour Party Special Conference in April 1975 strongly endorsed a 'No' vote in the referendum to be held on whether Britain should remain a member of the Common Market. No matter. Prime minister Jim Callaghan went his own way, joining Tories and Liberals in campaigning for Britain to stay in.

The 1977 conference decided by 6,248,000 votes to 91,000 to include abolition of the House of Lords in Labour's election manifesto. Constitutionally any conference resolution that received two-thirds of the vote had to be included in the manifesto. But

* In 1974 there was one defeat over the Common Market. 1975 saw seven, on issues ranging from housing, new towns, import controls, education and NHS to pensions. 1976 saw seven more, on things such as cars for the disabled, housing, the NHS, child benefit and public spending. There were three defeats in 1977 on housing, Zimbabwe and the disqualified Clay Cross councillors. 1978's four defeats were on the NHS, incomes policy, economic strategy and education. 1979 saw the executive overruled on the election of the party leader.[43]

Callaghan didn't give a damn: abolition of the Lords did not go into the manifesto.

The same conference deplored 'the continuing disqualification from public office of the twenty-one Clay Cross Labour Party members* and demands that the Government introduce a Bill to remove the disqualifications forthwith.[45] This resolution had no more impact on the government than water off a duck's back.

In 1978 the Labour Party conference rejected the government's 5 percent pay rise guideline by 4,077,000 votes to 194,000—to no avail. The sort of methods used were described by Wilson's press secretary: 'His tactic for dealing with the NEC was simply not to turn up at its meetings, and ignoring any decisions it took with which he disagreed'.[46]

Innumerable times Labour Party conferences went against government policy. While the Attlee government suffered only a few defeats, and on largely marginal issues, in 1974-79 defeat was common.

An unprecedented number of rebellions also took place in the parliamentary party against the government, and this at a time when the government had little or no majority. Although the rebellions could do little to change the course of events, the betrayals had at last become too disgusting for even the most cast-iron reformist constitution to stomach. As P Norton writes: 'the Parliamentary Labour Party witnessed the most serious division lobby dissent of its post-war history, indeed of its whole history.'

Divisions Witnessing Dissenting Votes of Labour MPs[47]

1945–50	79	1955–59	10	1970–74	34
1950–51	5	1959–64	26	1974	8
1951–55	17	1966–70	109	1974–79	309

Under the Attlee government, in only one case did fifty or more Labour MPs vote against the government; in 1964–66 there were no such votes and in 1966–70 it happened six times; but in 1974-79 it happened *forty-five times*.[48] The situation deteriorated as each year passed. In the 1974–75 parliamentary session, Labour MPs dissented in 14.5 percent of all divisions. This rose steadily to reach 45 percent in 1978.[49] The average number of Labour MPs voting against the 1974–79 government was three times that of 1964–70 and four times the level under Attlee.[50] Norton concludes:

* The Clay Cross councillors had carried out Labour's policy of refusing to implement the Tory government's Housing Finance Act, which forced councils to raise council house rents, and had been surcharged and debarred from holding public office.

> there were more divisions witnessing dissenting votes in the one Parliament returned in October 1974 than there were in the whole of the period, covering seven Parliaments, from 1945 to 1970.[51]

The Labour dissidents were largely organised in the *Tribune* Group. This met once and sometimes twice a week, principally to debate current parliamentary business. In Neil Kinnock's words:

> ideals must, like any other motive force, be organized if they are to be effective and the *Tribune* Group's most frequent and telling activity is to give an organized lead to opinion in the PLP.[52]

Kinnock consistently opposed the 1974–79 government's right-wing policies, voting 84 times in dissent. The total ineffectiveness of this activity can be measured by the government's appalling record in all spheres.

The impression may be gathered that even if the PLP, the party executive or conference could not control events, at least the cabinet, perhaps, had some influence. Nothing could be further from the truth. One need only read the cabinet diaries of Richard Crossman and Barbara Castle to see that the prime minister and the chancellor of the exchequer, who hold the key posts in any government, paid little heed to the rest.

Joe Haines, Wilson's press secretary, was amazed by what he learnt of the way government actually functions:

> I find it astonishing that a Labour Cabinet can still tolerate a situation where the Chancellor of the Exchequer only acquaints them with the content of his Budget some twenty-eight hours before he presents it to Parliament.[53]

This could lead to the sort of farcical situation that occurred with the budget of 6 April 1976. The previous day Callaghan had been chosen as the new prime minister. He had no clue as to the budget's contents! Even more pathetic is this story from the same year:

> When the announcement about further cuts in public expenditure were [*sic*] made on Thursday, July 22, the Cabinet were only told on the previous day… The Secretary of State for Employment, Albert Booth, was forced to do his own calculations, on the back of an envelope while the Cabinet meeting progressed, about its likely effect upon jobs.[54]

The apparent freedom of the chancellor is illusory. The very secrecy of the budget disguises the real influence of outside forces. This secrecy is, in Haines' words:

> not only absurd and anti-democratic, it is a powerful buttress to the supremacy of the Treasury mind over that of the elected Government's.[55]

The Treasury for its part reflects the power of capital: business, finance, industry, foreign exchange and commodity markets, economists, monetarists, shareholders, stockbrokers, the City of London and the Governor of the Bank of England, not to mention the speculative pressure of the financiers, whose ability to engineer a sterling crisis always puts Labour government on the defensive. From the inside Haines witnessed what outsiders had suspected all along, that top civil servants were willing to sabotage or cripple a government that did not comply in every detail with the needs of capital as they understood it.

> At times the determination of the Treasury to compel the Government of the day to accept the policies in which it honestly believes is ruthless, even to the point where it seeks to create the conditions which make it impossible for the Government to spurn its advice...
>
> The fall in the sterling exchange rate to below two dollars, which occurred in March 1976, was welcomed by the Treasury and the Bank of England though it came to the surprise and dismay of the politicians. The cuts in public expenditure of over £1,000 million...following upon cuts of more than £3,000 million which had been decided upon only five months earlier, were a direct consequence... The pattern then, you can be certain, was exactly the same as it was on countless previous occasions.[56]

Imagine for a moment that the impossible happened—that MPs really controlled the cabinet which in turn controlled the chancellor of the exchequer and the prime minister. This still would not mean that the House of Commons had the power to initiate real changes in the economy and society. Much larger forces than the House of Commons face any government. The fate of every Labour government has shown that any reform which the establishment disliked came up against the undemocratic House of Lords and the monarchy, as well as the top layers of the Civil Service. Behind these are the forces of the police, army and judiciary, the 'bodies of armed men' which guarantee the power of the state whichever government is nominally in office.

The contortions of Tony Benn

The position of Tony Benn under the Wilson/Callaghan administration was awkward. He wanted to be the star of the left on the executive and at party conferences, while retaining membership of the most right-wing cabinet Labour has ever had. Even his talents as a political acrobat could not stave off an occasional fall from the tightrope. A couple of cases will illustrate this.

On 30 October 1974 the party executive censured the government for the Royal Navy's joint exercises with the South African navy at Simonstown, which were 'directly contrary both to party policy and to clear assurances given by the government itself'.[57] Benn was one of three ministers on the executive who voted for the censure. Wilson wrote to each saying they had broken collective cabinet responsibility and demanded a promise it would not happen again. If this was not forthcoming, he would interpret this as resignation from the cabinet.[58] Barbara Castle tells the rest of the story:

> The three Ministers concerned in the row had got together to draft a letter which Harold had not found satisfactory. Then, before they could meet again, Wedgie [Benn] had written to Harold again off his own bat, capitulating and leaving the other two high and dry. Joan Lestor was furious with him. 'He's a very odd chap', said Mike [Foot] in his typically tolerant way.[59]

Wilson commented with glee: 'I insisted on the exact words of my demand, which in each of the three cases was finally met'.[60]

Benn's behaviour was no more heroic when it came to the 1976 government spending cuts. Donoghue records a phone conversation in the prime minister's study. Benn rang to say he was under pressure from his constituency activists in Bristol over the cuts. The prime minister replied:

> 'Tony, why don't you make up your own mind? And if you do stay in the Cabinet but continued campaigning against a collective Cabinet decision, you will be sacked immediately.' I do not know what the small elite group of Bristol activists advised, but Tony Benn remained, and relatively quietly.[61]

Benn was the energy minister who, while speaking left in support of the miners, did not baulk at imposing the incentive scheme—even though it was repeatedly rejected in miners' ballots. Moreover, between October 1976 and March 1977, in the biggest ever closure programme, Benn totally or partially shut forty-eight power stations, thirty-nine of which were coal-fired. This contrasted with his eager support for the nuclear industry. In his former role as minister of technology he encouraged the processing and reprocessing of nuclear fuels and later went as far as arming the police at the Windscale nuclear reprocessing plant.[62] He also shut his eyes to the fact that Windscale ran on uranium from South African-ruled Namibia—despite Labour's official opposition to trade with South Africa and the United Nations ban on the importing of Namibian uranium.

Throughout the years 1974–79 Benn was torn between his executive and government roles, but let the second dominate. He had been a member of every Labour government since 1964 despite their anti-working class actions.

Benn's equivocation followed not only from his position as leader of the left on the executive and also a 'responsible' minister, but also from the moderate political stance he took in the 1950s and 1960s. Only during the Heath government did he move politically to the left. Thus he had not been a member of the *Tribune* Group, the *Keep Left* Group or the Victory for Socialism Group, he was not a Bevanite nor a supporter of CND.

At the 1959 Labour conference, Benn followed Gaitskell's muck on Clause Four and, mounting the platform, declared: 'You cannot attract and keep the loyalty of younger people, if the majority of the movement are still thinking too much about the past as they seem to be'.[63]

When Frank Cousins resigned from Wilson's cabinet in 1966 as minister of technology in protest at incomes policy, it was Benn who took over his office.

The denouement

The Callaghan government collapsed under the massive pressure of industrial discontent in the winter of 1978–79. In September 1978 the TUC opposed the 5 percent pay norm; in October the Labour Party rejected it by 4,017,000 votes to 1,924,000. Strikes swept through Fords, the bakeries and provincial journalism. In January it was the turn of railwaymen followed by a two-week strike of petrol tanker and road haulage drivers. The transport and public sectors were drawn into a vast range of disputes.

Disruption was compounded by widespread secondary picketing and an extremely severe winter exacerbated by a local authority dispute which meant roads were not gritted. On 22 January 1,250,000 local authority workers engaged in a one-day national strike, followed by widespread disruption. The tanker drivers settled for a 15 percent pay rise and the haulage drivers for between 15 and 20 percent; the local authority workers accepted 9 percent.[64]

Labour's pay policies had once more broken down under pressure from below. Labour had failed to fulfil its promises to those who had elected it. *But for the ruling class it had achieved a great deal.*

Unlike 1969, the 'winter of discontent' of 1979 was not part of a rising tide of struggle or class consciousness, but a receding one. The Labour Party had broken the tendency which had been growing under the Heath government, when workers were beginning to challenge capitalist society in action. Though this had been insufficient in 1974 to pose an alternative to electoral politics, it had been a developing force. The high level of strikes in 1979, however, did not break out of the cycle of sectionalism and scabbing which Labour had helped make respectable. The element of growing political generalisation had been lost.

Labour's success in holding back the workers' movement provided the background to the general election of May 1979, which the party lost badly.

16

Labour under Thatcher

Downturn on the industrial front

In 1974 many capitalists welcomed Labour's election victory. Five years later they rejoiced at its defeat. The Labour Government had successfully protected the employers from workers' militancy. Now the employers wanted a government less beholden to the trade unions. They no longer needed a defensive shield to shelter behind, but a sword to carry their offensive forward against the workers.

The downturn in the industrial struggle started by the Wilson-Callaghan government accelerated. Compared with 1970–74 the anti-working class policies of the newly-elected government led by Margaret Thatcher met little resistance: rank and file organisation had been undermined through the Social Contract, productivity deals and the creation of a layer of full-time convenors acting as a crucial adjunct to the trade union bureaucracy. Added to this crisis of organisation was one of leadership. The reformist ideology of most union militants could not cope with a situation in which there was little room to win significant concessions from the system.

Rising unemployment added to the downturn. Workers generally lost the confidence to take on their employers. When they did so the disputes were defensive, fragmented, long, bitter and demoralising. The early 1970s had been a period of victories punctuated by defeats; ten years later saw defeats punctuated by only partial, short-term victories.

This increased the domination of the union bureaucracy over the rank and file. Union leaders moved to the right throughout the period after Thatcher came to office. Nevertheless, when forced into a situation where they felt they were not being taken seriously by employers and government, they on occasion mobilised their members for action—while keeping a firm grip all the way.

A series of such bureaucratic strikes began in 1980 when the steel union, ISTC, came out for fourteen weeks in its first national stoppage since 1926. Alas, sectionalism meant scab steel streamed out of the non-striking private firms and was carried through the gates of factories by TGWU lorry drivers. In the years that followed the workforce of the industry was cut by two thirds.

During the national strike in 1982 by train drivers in ASLEF, the NUR scabbed and the TUC General Council unanimously ordered the stoppage ended. Health workers were defeated despite one-day and selective strikes supported by hundreds of thousands of ancillary workers and nurses. The wholesale privatisation of hospital services such as catering and cleaning followed. Only the February 1983 national water workers' strike resulted in a partial victory.

In 1983 the Trade Union Congress adopted the policy of 'New Realism'. The TUC's initial reaction to the Tory offensive had been, if not resistance, at least turning their back on Thatcher. Now Len Murray, general secretary of the TUC, grovelled: 'We have to put our members' case wherever we can, and that means talking with Government... Arguing the trade union case with anybody does not make us an instrument, a tool, of Government or of any political party'.[1]

However, a short time later the advance of New Realism was delayed by three disputes. In November 1983 the printers' union, NGA, one of the strongest unions in the country, was taken on by a small employer in Warrington who was using the Tories' anti-union laws to undermine the union. The TUC General Council ruled against the NGA when it defied the Tory laws and, faced with the police and the courts, the union was beaten at the end of February 1984. Five weeks later the government banned civil service unions at its secret communications centre, GCHQ. The TUC called a one-day national strike. Despite the short notice and bureaucratic method of calling it, there was some support. But still the government triumphed.

The day after the GCHQ strike, on 1 March, the Coal Board announced Yorkshire's Cortonwood Colliery was to close in five weeks' time. Answering protests, the chairman of the Coal Board, Ian MacGregor, announced his intention to shut twenty pits and destroy 20,000 jobs within a year. The Thatcherites were obviously staging a deliberate provocative action.

The struggles round the NGA, GCHQ and the miners delayed the march towards New Realism. Unfortunately this was merely the hiatus in its progress. After the miners' defeat it pushed forward with greater vigour.

Despite the defensive nature of the strike, there were times when the miners could have broken through and inflicted a major defeat on the Tories. That they did not do so was in large part due to the attitude of the TUC and Labour Party leadership. There was no lack of sympathy for the miners' cause among great numbers of trade unionists. But the potential for industrial solidarity was deliberately undercut so as not to justify militant tactics such as the flying picket, or provide an alternative to electoralism. This was why the Labour leadership's attacks on 'violent picketing', which they described as no better than the brutal tactics used by the police, were so invidious.

As a result, the national miners' strike was both a break in the downturn and at the same time had all the characteristics of strikes in the downturn. It was the longest ever mass strike in Europe. But it was radically different from the 1972 miners' strike. Rank and file activity was lower, and, crucially, the miners showed less willingness to act independently of the bureaucracy. The sectionalism which had been encouraged by the Labour government's incentive scheme of 1977 tore the miners apart and isolated them from other workers. In 1984–5 at most 10 percent of the miners were active on picket duty, and, in contrast to 1972, they had to spend much of their time picketing out other miners.

This time there was little industrial solidarity from other workers. The damage had been done. For example, in 1972 power workers had been organised in a rank-and-file combine throughout the industry; they were involved in a pay campaign of their own, so all power stations strongly supported the miners. Within a couple of weeks twelve power stations had been closed completely, and 1,400,000 workers had to be laid off in industry. In 1984–5, on the other hand:

> No meetings were organised by the TGWU and GMBATU between shop stewards in the power stations and miners' representatives. The first meeting between Arthur Scargill and shop stewards in the power stations in Yorkshire did not take place until the strike had been going for ten and a half months—on 16 January 1985![2]

And on 11 April 1984 the unions in the power industry signed a 13-month agreement for a 5.2 percent wage increase. Not one worker was laid off for lack of electricity in the twelve months of the miners' strike.

The Orgreave coke depot near Sheffield should have been the Saltley of the 1980s, but miners' leader Arthur Scargill's call to repeat the 1972 victory here was not heeded. In 1972 Birmingham engineering workers had come to the aid of the miners. But in 1984 the engineering workers of Sheffield (which is much nearer to the coalfields than Birmingham) did not. At Saltley the engineers joined the picket line en masse on its fifth day. At Orgreave picketing started on Thursday 24 May with about 1,000 miners. The nation's television screens showed several thousand miners on the picket line being hammered on 27 May, 29 May, 31 May, and 18 June. On 30 May Scargill was arrested, and on 18 June he was wounded and had to be taken to hospital.[3]

But there was still no sign of the Sheffield engineers turning up to picket. Why?

To answer this one must look at the state of the Sheffield engineers. *The Department of Employment Gazette* reported that in Sheffield there had been no major stoppages in 1981, one in 1982 (against redundancies), and again *only one* in 1983 (over redundancies).[4] Workers who lack the confidence to stand up to their own bosses cannot be relied upon to come out in support of other workers. This was the basic cause of the Orgreave tragedy.

It would be a case of tunnel vision, a concession to sectionalism, to see the roots of the miners' defeat as in the mining industry alone. They were part of a much wider picture. To explain the industrial explosion of 1972 we have to look at the changes in the situation of the working class in the period since the Second World War. To explain the state of the working class during the 1984-5 miners' strike we need to look to the years since Labour came to office in 1974.[5]

Political upturn: Bennism

The sorry state of the working-class movement had both a short-term and a long-term impact on the Labour Party. At first the industrial downturn went hand in hand with a political upturn expressed in the rise of a new and powerful Labour left-wing current—Bennism. Since workers did not have the confidence to lake on their employers *in the workplace*, many of the activists looked for a political solution *outside the workplace* from a saviour on high: the Labour Party.

After Labour's 1979 election defeat the party experienced its biggest swing to the left for a generation. During 1970–74 Labour conferences had moved sharply to the left, but the activists found their focus in industrial struggle. Now their struggles were largely resolutionary, against the right-wing inside the Labour Party.

The Labour left was convinced that there was no point in having a re-run of the Wilson-Callaghan government. In November 1980 the parliamentary party elected Michael Foot as Labour leader. This far from satisfied the call of party activists for change. Nor was it sufficient simply to pass left-wing resolutions at conference, as they had done for years past. What the party needed, the left believed, was a package of *constitutional* changes.

First, Labour MPs should stand for reselection by the local party before every election. Secondly, the party leader and deputy leader should be chosen by an electoral college of representatives of local parties, trade unions and MPs, in other words by representatives of the whole party, not just the MPs, as hitherto. These issues dominated the Labour conferences of 1979, 1980 and the Special Conference held at Wembley in January 1981 where they were eventually won.

Wembley put the Labour left into ecstasy. To quote some of their papers:

> *Tribune*: A watershed for Labour Party democracy.[6]

> *Militant*: Wembley was a great victory for Labour's ranks... The block vote of the union delegations at Labour Party conference will become a vital transmission belt for the demands of an aroused and mobilised working class.[7]

> *Socialist Challenge*: What a day at Wembley...a famous victory for the workers' movement.[8]

> *Morning Star*: It is a momentous decision in the struggle not only for the return of a Labour government at the next election, but also to ensure a Labour government which carries out the policies of the labour movement.[9]

The left advance hinged on an alliance between constituency party activists and parts of the trade union bureaucracy. Many union leaders were livid with the Callaghan government whose 5 percent pay norm had forced them into the 'Winter of Discontent'. The zenith of the resulting alliance was Benn's contest with Healey for the deputy leadership of the party in September 1981. Benn only lost by a hair's breadth. He received 49.6 percent of the electoral college votes to Healey's 50.4 percent. Benn attracted 81.1 percent of the Constituency Labour Party vote, 37.5 percent of the trade union vote and 34.1 percent of the PLP vote. The left was euphoric but self-deluded. The block vote system massively exaggerated Benn's real support.

This is not to say that Benn lacked enthusiastic support from union activists. Throughout the spring and summer of 1981 he spoke to packed fringe meetings at union conferences. However, the activists were not in tune with the millions of union members who were retreating before the employers' offensive, and becoming more open to the media's anti-socialist hysteria against its new *bête noir*, Tony Benn.

Healey beat Benn hands down in those few unions—NUPE, COHSE, FBU and NATSOPA—which balloted all their members instead of leaving it to the political activists at conference. The only exception was the NUM, where votes at branch meetings supported Benn. He got the block vote of 1,200,000 members of the TGWU, but the union's executive had not asked its rank and file for a mandate.

In the constituencies the real support for Benn was measured not in millions, but perhaps tens of thousands. In recent years the total membership of the Labour Party has been in the region of 300,000, of whom about 10 percent were activists. The definition of activist is one who turns up regularly to his or her Labour Party branch. How small this group was emerges from the circulation of the party's paper, *Labour Weekly*, which at this time was 17,000, much of it bought in bulk orders by unions.

The wide gap between the activists and the majority of individual members was demonstrated by a survey in Newcastle-under-Lyme during 1960–61. This showed that 54 percent of the members had never heard of Clause Four of the party constitution, even though it was printed on the back of every party card and though the survey was made immediately after bitter public debate roused by Gaitskell's effort to drop this clause.[10] Notwithstanding all the excitement in the early 1980s, party membership actually fell from 348,156 in 1981 to 273,803 in 1982. Benn's support on the ground was limited.

In September 1981 the Gallup Poll posed the following question:[11] 'If the choice for the Deputy Leader of the Labour Party was between Denis Healey and Tony Benn, who would you choose?' The result was:

	General public	*Labour supporters*
Healey	72	60
Benn	20	34

The internal party battles of 1979–81 were largely fought out before a small audience: the players thought they spoke for millions, but evoked a response from very few.

The character of the Labour left was another limiting factor. Many of the activists fought their way into positions against people from working class backgrounds who had risen to hold council positions and had become the backbone of backward, corrupt right-wing Labourism. However, this new layer of Labour left-wingers were overwhelmingly middle class products of the 1968 generation. Larry Whitty, Labour's general secretary, has described the current social composition:

> 60 percent of party members have a degree or equivalent higher educational qualification, compared to a national average of just 11 percent. Labour Party members are twice as likely to be employed in the public sector as in the private. Sixty-two percent of them read *The Guardian*, and only 25 percent the *Daily Mirror*.[12]

The chief stronghold of the left in recent years has been local councils. Here, by tradition, the middle-class element of the Labour Party always played an important role. Thus the Fabians, the architects of 'municipal socialism', drew their members from the middle class. In the 1920s medical officers of health and district health workers were typical members, and played a crucial role in shaping Labour's welfare policies.

More important still, the constituency left has no real links with workers in struggle. Despite the great talk about extra-parliamentary activity, the constituencies have remained essentially what they have always been—small groups overwhelmingly geared to elections. To millions of workers the continuous discussion of 'reselection' and 'electoral colleges' meant very little indeed.

Bennism's constituency base was numerically far smaller than that of Bevan in the early 1950s (because the individual party membership had shrunk by some three-quarters). Yet it succeeded in making quite an inroad into the party machine. In the 1950s the Bevanites faced a Revisionist right arguing with confidence from the basis of full employment and rising living standards. In the 1980s the right had witnessed the worst economic crisis for some half a century and the utter bankruptcy of Labour government in the face of this. It had temporarily lost confidence in itself. A sign of this was the splitting off of a number of MPs to form the Social Democrats.

The Bevanites lacked the support of any major union bureaucrats. Benn's successes in the years 1979–81 depended entirely on the goodwill of a whole layer of union officials in the TGWU, NUPE, NUM, TASS, FBU, among others. Their support was shortlived. Having expressed their anger against Callaghan's economic policies by going along with a certain leftism in the party, they decided criticism had gone far enough. Already in 1982 the left union officials started distancing themselves from Benn, as is shown by the 'Peace of Bishops Stortford', which they encouraged him to agree to.

Total dependence on union block votes had never worried the constituency activists and the left MPs. Nor did they ever dream of challenging the union bureaucracy. Accepting the traditional separation of the political and industrial wings of the movement, they discussed 'political' issues in Labour Party meetings, while leaving the struggle in the workplaces to the union bodies. Yet it is in the workplace that workers can win confidence, can have their minds opened to new ideas. It is here that the conservative union bureaucracy can be effectively challenged.

The constitutional changes of Bennism never touched the basic arrangement of power within the party. Thus of the twenty-nine members of the party executive, twelve are in the union section and five are in the women's section—which is elected by the whole conference, in which trade unions have some 90 percent of the vote.

Union influence is carved up in executive elections according to 'preordained patterns in which representation by size and traditional position were the dominant consideration.' Thus, if the post of party treasurer is held by a politician then 'eight positions out of the twelve on the [union] section were automatically allotted through customary understandings'.[13] What did this 'understanding' consist of?

> Each union had a regular custom of deciding who filled the position on the NEC, and one of trade unionism's oldest customs, that of "Buggins' turn" ensured that the next in line formally followed in succession.[14]

Bureaucratic arrangement rather than politics decides the majority influence on the executive.

Leaving the union bureaucracy's power intact made the left's constitutional changes *toothless*. They did not touch the bureaucratic structure of the party and its actual power relations.

Labour Party structure makes it easy for the participants to deceive themselves. A handful sitting in a ward pass a resolution. This is adopted by the constituency general management committee (CMC) and then moved at the national conference. Hundreds of thousands of votes, or even millions, are cast for it. It reminds one of a distorting mirror in which a pygmy may look like a giant. This does not actually turn the pygmy into a giant.

Constituency activists have a lot of leeway to express radical views, but when it comes to important decisions the bureaucrats have the final say. Richard Crossman precisely and cruelly depicted the relation between the two:

> the Labour Party required militants, politically conscious socialists to do the work of organizing the constituencies. But since these militants tended to be 'extremists', a constitution was needed which maintained their enthusiasm by apparently creating a full party democracy while excluding them from effective power. Hence the concession in principle of sovereign powers to the delegates at the Annual Conferences, and the removal in practice of most of this sovereignty through the Trade Union block vote on the one hand, and the complete independence of the Parliamentary Labour Party on the other.[15]

Such considerations were far from the minds of the Labour left as they celebrated the outcome of the January 1981 Wembley special conference. The day after the conference, the right-wing 'Gang of Four' inaugurated the Council for Social Democracy, forerunner of the SDP. Their formal break with the Labour Party came when the SDP was launched in March. It radically cut Labour's support. The following Gallup poll[16] tracks this impact. It shows answers to the question 'Are you satisfied or dissatisfied with the way: Mrs Thatcher is doing her job as Prime Minister? Mr Foot is doing his job as Leader of the Opposition':

	Thatcher		*Foot*	
Percentages:	*satisfied*	*dissatisfied*	*satisfied*	*dissatisfied*
1980	37.4	55.3	35.3	35.5
1981 (first half)	32.4	61.75	25.05	46.25
1981 (second half)	28.45	64.3	21.6	55.65

In December 1980 Gallup estimated that Labour had the support of 47.5 percent of the electorate. By December 1981, after the split of the SDP and a year of internecine warfare, support was down to 23.5 percent, a uniquely low level for the main opposition party.[17]

The creation of the SDP had a major influence on Labour's internal struggles. The Labour left were delighted by developments. Their capacity for self-deception seemed limitless. They believed the exit of the Gang of Four would tilt the balance to the left. In the very short term this was the case. But it soon became obvious that the general impact was in exactly the opposite direction. The electoral success of the SDP-Liberal Alliance put pressure on the Labour leaders to move rightwards in order to compete for the 'middle ground'. This was especially so after the 1983 general election, when Labour beat the Alliance to third position only by a tiny margin (27.6 percent of the votes to 25.4 percent).

Still Benn managed to continue to fool himself. He saw the general election as a triumph:

> ...for the first time since 1945 a political party with an openly socialist policy had received the support of over eight million people...socialism has reappeared once more upon the national agenda... The 1983 Labour manifesto commanded the loyalty of millions of voters and a democratic socialist bridgehead had been established from which further advance in public understanding and support can be made.[18]

Benn's words did not cut any ice even with his own supporters. Labour had received its lowest proportion of votes since 1918. Because there had been fewer Labour candidates in 1918, the number of votes per candidate in 1983 was the lowest ever. And these results followed four years of increasing mass unemployment and attacks on the welfare state!

The moment of truth for the Bennite left could not be postponed for long. The industrial downturn had engineered a political upturn, but it would not be long before the political level of the movement was adversely affected by the low level of class struggle. The Bennites, who fell into the substitutionist trap of claiming to speak for workers they had not brought into active agreement with themselves, were open to the hammerings of the media and the right-wing. In fact their obsession with resolutions, with constitutionalism, played into the hands of the right. The political activists found it a waste of time and effort to relate to the mass of the workers who did not attend the meetings where the resolutions were passed.

Labour and the Thatcherite consensus

The working-class movement is not the only factor shaping the Labour Party. The other element for a capitalist workers' party is the ruling class. We saw how Labour's electoral landslide of 1945 led to a political consensus in the reformist mould. Butskellism was born when the Tories came to terms with the changes introduced by the Attlee Government, the essence of which were policies of full employment, a mixed economy and expanding welfare.

Let us see what happened to these three elements under Thatcher. When world capitalism entered the prolonged crisis of the 1970s full employment perished. Mass unemployment remained. The crisis also overtook welfare. With national production generally stagnant—in 1987 manufacturing output in Britain reached only the 1979 level and was still 4 percent below that of 1973—the likelihood of business sanctioning any expansion of welfare was small indeed, especially with £12,000 million being spent on dole payments.

The clearest sign of the changing consensus was nationalisation, always a sensitive barometer of the progress of reformist politics. Three broad phases emerge. First, there was the period before 1945 when practically no nationalisation was carried out anywhere in Western Europe. As Przeworski explains:

> Although social democrats formed or entered governments in several countries, the global result of these first attempts at socialization was null: with the exception of the French armament industry in 1936, not a single company was nationalized in Western Europe by a social democratic government during the entire inter-war period...while social democrats held power in Austria, Belgium, Denmark, Finland, France, Germany, Great Britain, Norway, and Sweden.[19]

Things changed after the Second World War. In Britain and France there was a wave of nationalisation, while in Italy, Spain and Austria important public sectors emerged through a variety of other government measures:

> Characteristically, state enterprises are limited to credit institutions, coal, iron and steel, energy production and distribution, transport, and communication. Outside these sectors only those companies which are threatened with bankruptcy and hence a reduction of employment pass into public hands.[20]

The post-war economic expansion not only generated full employment and funds for welfare, it paid the cost of buying out private capitalists.

Once the crisis began, however, the chance of new nationalisations, or of re-nationalising privatised industries, became practically nil.*

This has facilitated the privatisation of industry by right-wing governments throughout the world in recent years. In France twenty-three companies, worth around a hundred billion francs (£10 billion), had been sold by early 1988. In Spain, Italy, West Germany, Austria, Australia, New Zealand and elsewhere, the process of privatisation has also taken place. In Britain, 'in the past eight years, sixteen major publicly

* There can be isolated exceptions to this. François Mitterrand attempted extensive nationalisation in France in the early 1980s but was quickly forced to beat a retreat. On the other hand, in crisis situations even right-wing governments may feel constrained to nationalise collapsing businesses—as has been the case in Pinochet's Chile.

owned UK companies, employing 650,000 people and accounting for 40 percent of the state sector, have been wholly or partially privatised, raising total proceeds of £17.5 billion'.[21]

Had the stock market not crashed in late 1987, the privatisation of the oil company BP had been expected to bring the government some £7 billion, the water industry £8 billion and the electricity supply industry £18 billion. Throw in the British Steel Corporation, Land Rover and a few other odds and ends, and the Treasury agenda had obviously pencilled in receipts of over £40 billion.[22] No future Labour government could spend sums like this buying back privatised industries.

Labour's Programme 1982 was the basis for the 1983 election manifesto. It claimed that public ownership of industry would be expanded. The following year, the party conference passed a resolution, 'carried overwhelmingly on a show of hands', which reaffirmed 'that Clause IV Part 4 of the Labour Party Constitution is the central aim of the Labour Party' and called for 'repossession of all parts of the public sector privatised by the Tories'.[23]

As late as 1985 Roy Hattersley, as Labour's deputy leader, still asked for, and expected, unanimous support for a resolution on 'the need to extend social ownership and democratic planning into a significant number of key organisations in the banking, manufacturing, new technology and service sectors'.[24] Conference obliged.[25] It also passed a resolution which called on the next Labour government 'to return all privatised services to direct labour and all privatised industries to public ownership, and to repeal any privatisation legislation'.[26]

The slide began once Labour geared itself for the 1987 election. The ambiguous concept of 'social ownership' was used to downgrade nationalisation and blur the distinction between common ownership and Liberal-SDP schemes for employees' share ownership. At the 1987 election Labour pledged to take back only British Telecom and British Gas under 'social ownership'. Neither company would be renationalised: instead existing shares would be converted into new bonds, including varieties of deep discount bonds designed to win favour with institutional shareholders. The growth in the underlying assets of British Telecom and Gas would in accrue to their shareholders. The fact that shares would be exchanged for non-voting bonds, and that safeguards would be introduced against short-term speculative gains, does not alter this.

At the 1987 Labour Conference the NUM moved a resolution to renationalise all industries privatised by the Tories. But this was now rejected by 3,869,000 to 2,397,000. Alan Tuffin of the Communication Workers Union told conference: 'By the time we get back to power, we will not want to spend something like £15 billion in today's prices getting these industries back. We are going to have lugger priorities like the National Health Service and low pay'.[27]

Another nail in the coffin of public ownership was the support for wider share ownership. On Channel 4 television Bryan Gould, Labour's campaign manager in the 1987 election and one of the pacemakers in the shift to the right, argued: 'The idea of owning shares is catching on, and as socialists we should support as one means of taking power from the hands of the few and spreading it more widely.' Gould did not shy from using the language of self-interest: 'Why should we leave all the advantages of capital gains to people who already have plenty?'[28] (By the way, Gould overlooked the fact that Thatcher's privatisation share sales were popular because the buyers were able to make a fast profit by selling. Gould's support for share ownership offered no such easy vote-catching appeal).

Partnership with private industry

In the mid-1980s Labour policy moved from public ownership towards state encouragement of private industry. Thus in 1986 an article in *The Observer* on 'Labour's Plan for Recovery' by Neil Kinnock—who had become party leader in 1983—said: 'It is a matter of learning from the success of the French, the Germans and the Japanese, who have forceful governmental agencies and use them to great economic advantage'.[29] His book *Making Our Way* was rhapsodic about the achievements of the Japanese.[30] In conscious imitation, Labour would establish a British Industrial Investment Bank, and a new state investment vehicle, British Enterprise, which would be empowered to take equity stakes in high tech and other industries.

To reassure private capital, Hattersley went out of the way to promise that future Labour governments would not impose high level of taxation on the rich. In September 1986 he was flown to New York by Greenwell Montagu, the City stockbroking firm to address institutional investors. He promised them a new Labour government would not return to 'the very high marginal rates of taxation' levied on the highest paid before 1979.[31]

Hattersley also underlined Labour's financial prudence. Writing in July 1986, he criticised past Labour governments for their levels of public spending: 'We have almost always committed ourselves to more public spending than the electorate thought credible and the economy could reasonably bear'.[32]

To encourage private industry, even Labour's moderate call for exchange controls was thrown out. The capitalists would find a way round them, Hattersley told the 1986 Labour conference, so we won't bother trying to institute them.

The party leadership wanted to avoid the *Mitterrand syndrome*. On becoming French president in 1981 Mitterrand had attempted to increase demand in the economy by large-scale nationalisations by increasing social welfare. Within a year this ran into disaster: French capital refused to cooperate and fled the country. Inflation rose and the franc collapsed. International bankers demanded that the government put its house in order, and Mitterrand complied.

With this in mind, Hattersley told the 1984 Labour conference: 'I don't want to see the next Labour government start one or two years of unreality and end with another two years of deflation for the economy and despair for our party members'.[33] Kinnock and Hattersley did their best to push down the expectations among their supporters that a Labour government would bring quick economic expansion. They knew well that British industry and banking are so integrated into the world economic system as to limit government influence on exchange rates, interest rates and the flow of capital.

Accepting these constraints, Kinnock became a purveyor of 'Thatcherism with a human face'—a term first coined by the *Financial Times* to describe David Owen.

Keeping inflation down became a top priority. In a speech to the London Bureau School on 30 January 1986 Hattersley said:

> We will only proceed as quickly as the inflation constraints allow.
>
> If we have not constructed a mechanism which allows us to expand at maximum speed with minimum inflation then the speed of our reflation will have to be reduced.[34]

New Jobs for Britain, published by Labour in March 1987, made it clear that Labour's plans for increased public spending took second place to incentives to private capitalists to invest. Above all, to advance economic success a 'national consensus' was needed, wrote Kinnock.[35]

> We need a workforce that wants to be on the winning side, but we also need those who can manage—and manage to make it all work...the

> days of 'Them' and 'Us' are gone now. We are all in this together, and it is only together that Britain will make its way in the world.[36]

To cure capitalism Labour was even willing to embrace some Tory anti-union laws. The Labour Party and TUC document of September 1986, *People at Work: New Rights, New Responsibilities*, accepted the Tory-imposed ballots before strikes and to elect union executives. With justice the *Financial Times* noted this break with Labour's own history:

> Never before has the Labour Party, created by the unions, attempted to bring in controls of trade union activities on the scale proposed in the document. Never before has Labour tried to make that control statutory, backing it up—albeit now in a modified form—with the involvement of the courts, traditionally seen within the Labour movement as its enemy.[37]

In August 1986 John Prescott, Labour's shadow employment spokesman and a leading figure on the 'soft' left, wrote: 'I do not believe it is possible or even desirable to attempt to exclude the law from industrial relations.'[38]

The Tories made secret pre-strike ballots central to their laws because they detest strikes being discussed at workers' mass meetings. A meeting can give workers the confidence to fight. They can see the strength of their workmates all round them. The secret ballot atomises the workers and leaves them prey to the capitalist media. This is what the Labour Party now acceded to.

What about full employment? In 1983 the aim of Labour's economic strategy was 'to reduce unemployment to below a million within five years of taking office.' The 1987 manifesto promised only to reduce unemployment by one million over two years. Since unemployment at the time was around four million, the target was to cut it to three million!

Thatcher's consensus had its genesis not with Thatcher but with the Labour government of Jim Callaghan, with its monetarism, massive cuts in welfare, hospital closures and cuts in housing programmes. The consensus rising from the 1945 Labour election victory was coined as Butskellism. What would combine Thatcher and Kinnock?

Consensus does not mean unanimity. Tories and Labour put different emphases on the reformist consensus during 1945–1970. Labour put priority on full employment as against keeping down prices. It was more favourably inclined to the nationalised element in the mixed economy and more enthusiastic about welfare than the Tories. Throughout the period differences rose between the two parties and within the parties. Similarly with the new consensus the parameters of the debate were determined by Thatcher, but there were conflicts within those parameters.

In 1988 the Thatcherite consensus was far less stable than Butskellism, which was based on expanding capitalism. In a situation of extreme economic and financial uncertainty, with the problems of massive unemployment, inflation, and threats to the balance of payments, there were bitter disagreements between the Tory and Labour Parties about the level of spending cuts, the scale of the attack on real living standards, and the level of unemployment to be tolerated.

Underlying the conflict between the Tory Party and Labour Party was the deepening conflict between workers and employers. This situation drove workers to strain at the leash of the Labour leadership which, as always, used workers' loyalty to itself as a restraint. At the same time capitalists were pressing the Tory Party and any future Labour government for further attacks on workers living standards. All this was bound to lead to conflicts within the Tory Party and even more so within Labour.

The Labour Party will always represent a synthesis of class and nation. The balance in this synthesis will shift from time to time, above all according to the conditions of the class struggle, whether or not the party is in office and whether capitalism is prosperous and thus open to give more reforms or not. Labour is and always will be a capitalist workers' party.

Bennism in retreat and the witch-hunt against Militant

It was just a matter of time before the retreat of the workers' movement and crisis of capitalism caught up with the internal life of Labour. Indeed in 1981 the Labour Party conference elected a centre-right majority to the executive, ending ten years of left-wing control. Within weeks the new executive decided to block left-winger Peter Tatchell's endorsement as parliamentary candidate for Bermondsey and to institute inquiries into the Militant, an organisation within the party which published its own newspaper of the same name. Then at a meeting in Bishops Stortford during January 1982 Benn, under pressure from top party and union lenders, agreed not to stand again as deputy leader. By withdrawing his challenge he abandoned the central thrust of the left's previous case—that there is no point in having left conference resolutions if the party has a leadership unwilling to implement them.

1982 saw no campaign around the union conferences to compare with the previous year. Instead there was the miserable spectacle of Labour leader Michael Foot wrapping himself in the Union Jack over the Falklands. On 3 April 1982 the Argentinians took control of the Falklands Islands in the South Atlantic and Foot made a jingoistic speech to the Commons which had Tory speakers practically falling over themselves to congratulate him for 'speaking for Britain'. Only one Labour MP—George Foulkes, a right-winger—dissented! On 14 April Foot again pledged his support for the sending of a British Task Force. Just a handful of union-sponsored MPs refused to support Thatcher's imperialist war.

Only on 28 April did Tony Benn distance himself marginally from Foot. Even so he was careful to emphasise his agreement with the basic assumptions on which the war was conducted:

> The reality is that there is unanimity in the House on the question of opposing the aggression of the [Argentinian] Junta. There is also unanimity on the right of self-defence against aggression… I support my right Honourable Friend the Member for Ebbw Vale [Michael Foot].[39]

At last, on 20 May, after six major parliamentary debates on the war, a vote was forced. Thirty-three Labour MPs voted against—less than half the number of MPs who had supported Benn for the position of deputy leader in 1981. Benn himself had been touring union conferences in 1981 addressing packed meetings over the deputy leadership issue. He did not campaign against the Falklands war, although he did address a small anti-war rally in London's Hyde Park.[40]

The rightwards movement continued. The 1982 Labour Party conference discussed the setting up of a register of organisations within the party—its intention was to witch-hunt the Militant group. At first many thought that the conference might actually reject this. On the week of the conference *Militant* itself carried the headline: 'TGWU Executive rejects register.' But the union's leaders, Moss Evans and Alex Kitson, easily persuaded their TGWU delegation to vote for the register, which passed by a massive 5,173,000 to 1,565,000.

The attack on Militant was the Trojan horse which opened the way for the defeat of Bennism. Like the ILP in the 1920s Benn's supporters could not decide whether to resist the witch-hunt or not, so they sat on their hands. The Labour Coordinating Committee, which had campaigned for Benn's election, refused to defend Militant on the grounds it was sectarian. The same tack was taken by other left groups in the party.

Witch-hunts are associated with retreat in the wider working-class movement and strengthened power of the right. They are not, as Militant leaders believed, a sign that the right fears losing control to the left, but that the left is weak. As the political climate lulls to the right, a vocal left-wing is seen as an electoral liability. At the same time a downturn in workers' confidence leaves a wide gap between the majority and the advanced section who are easily isolated and attacked.

The witch-hunt of Militant in the 1980s had elements in common with that against the Communist Party in the mid-1920s, but the differences were stark. The Communist Party and Left Wing Movement had had far more power inside the Labour Party than Militant. *Sunday Worker* had a stable circulation of 85,000.[41] *Militant*'s circulation never surpassed 12,000. The Communist Party had controlled dozens of constituency parties. Militant had a decisive influence only in Liverpool district.

In the 1920s the Labour leadership had to dissolve twenty-seven constituency parties to get rid of the Communists' supporters. In the 1980s only Liverpool District Labour Party and Broad Green constituency Party were dissolved (up to the time of writing), while St Helens, Southwark and Bradford North constituencies and the Merseyside district were suspended.

The Communist Party had had great influence in many unions—the Miners' Federation, NUR, AEU, Amalgamated Society of Woodworkers, Shopworkers, Furniture Workers Union, and the tailoring unions. The Militant had influence in only one fairly weak union—the CPSA.*

The Left Wing Movement had been associated with the Communist Party—an organisation with an independent existence outside the Labour Party and rooted in workers' collective organisation. Militant had no supporting organisation outside the Labour Party. Last but not least, the Communists and their fellow-travellers in the Labour Party in the 1920s were centrists but did not act as a sect. They were involved in

* This is a union of low-paid civil servants whose membership is young. A survey published m May 1986 showed that 44 per cent were under the age of 26.[42] Figures for job turnover are management data and not released, but much has been made by the CPSA of the fact that some DHSS offices in London have had a turnover of more than 100 per cent per year.

every field of activity of the labour movement. Militant was a centrist sect. It did not support any campaign unless this was organised through the Labour Party or by itself.

Three examples. *Militant* made no reference to the 100,000-strong demonstration against the American war in Vietnam in October 1968. The National Abortion Campaign suffered a similar fate. During 1975, there is not one single article about abortion or the campaign in *Militant*. The 50,000-strong demonstration in June 1975 warranted neither photo nor report. The same applied to the Anti Nazi League.[43]

Militant's sectarianism was combined with fantastic triumphalism. Again and again *The Militant* praised the labour-controlled Liverpool Council's housing record to the sky. What were the facts?

Annual Average Council House Building in Liverpool

Administration	*Years*	*Houses*
Labour	1955–61	1,650
Tory	1961–63	1,594
Labour	1963–67	2,993
Tory-Liberal	1967–70	2,204
Tory	1970–72	2,638
Labour	1972–73	4,297
Liberal	1973–79	1,728
Labour (in hung council)	1979–83	127
Labour (under Militant influence)	1983–86	951

The main conclusion from these figures is that, compared with the previous administration, the record of the Militant-influenced council is impressive, but compared to the record since 1955 it was very poor indeed.

From 1981 Militant was continuously witch-hunted. Conference votes for expulsion of leading supporters of Militant show graphically the retreat of the Labour left. The average votes confirming the expulsion from the party of the five members of the *Militant* editorial board in 1983 were 5,091,000 to 1,651,000. By 1986, the expulsion of eight leading Liverpool Militant supporters, including Derek Hatton and Tony Mulheam, was carried by 6,146,000 votes to 325,000.

In 1983 support for the *Militant* editorial board came from unions as large as NUPE. In 1986, only the tiny bakers' and furniture makers' unions voted against the expulsion of the Militant Eight. The same conference, in 1986, saw Eric Heffer pushed off the executive, his vote halved two years after he was chairman of the party. He was being punished for protesting demonstratively the year before against Kinnock's attack on the Liverpool Militants.*

The axe also fell on the Militant-controlled Labour Party Young Socialists. This paralleled the 1930s, when the squashing of the Socialist League was accompanied by attacks on the Labour League of Youth. The LPYS paper *Socialist Youth* was closed, regional LPYS committees and conferences shut down and its national conference cancelled. The age limit for LPYS membership was reduced from twenty-six to twenty-three, thus excluding half the membership. Finally, Andy Bevan, the Labour Party youth officer, who was also a Militant supporter, was sacked.

The confidence shown by Ted Grant, the political editor of *Militant*, at the 1983 Labour Party conference was entirely misplaced. He said then: 'There is no way you will succeed with these expulsions. We will be back. We will be restored, if not in one year, in two or three years. We will be back'.[44]

The Labour left ignored the witch-hunt in favour of fantasy. After the 1985 Labour Party conference, *Tribune* declared: 'the Left has never been stronger and the prospect of a radical, left-wing Labour Government has never been greater'.[45] Militant wrote: 'The conference, made up of delegates representing nearly ten million workers, remained firmly behind radical socialist policies'.[46]

The Labour left consistently fails to come to grips with reality. It lives in a dream-world in which block vote millions take the place of the flesh and blood millions outside the conference chamber and committee room, in which the radical policy resolution substitutes for the real struggle of class against class.** One only had to juggle the constitution a bit, pass a few resolutions, get the right candidates elected, and the road to socialism would then be open.

To the Labour left, struggle in the real world seemed irrelevant to its forward march. If it was doing well at Labour conferences, the weakening of shopfloor organisation or defeats of strikes could be ignored. In

* Heffer's vote in the election for the executive in 1983 was 538,000, in 1984 520,000, in 1985 414,000, in 1986 251,000, and in 1987 187,000.

** The Socialist Workers Party tried to come to terms with the changing situation by constantly reassessing the actual balance of class forces and adapting its activity to this. Recognising the downturn after 1974 was not a simple process and the debate was long and difficult. Only experience can prove whether a sneeze is the prelude to pneumonia or only a light cold. The same applies with still more force to the molecular process linking shopfloor developments, general politics and working class consciousness. With hindsight it is clear that the correct judgement of the situation after 1974 provided the basis for the SWP to continue as an autonomous revolutionary socialist force. Alas, many independent socialist groups evaded the harsh reality of the period and escaped into the Labour Party only to face the onslaught of Kinnockism.

1988, after the witch-hunt and Labour's third election defeat, we saw the obverse of the same coin. All was gloom and despondency. As a result the underlying resilience of class organisation and its potential was ignored in its turn.

The 'dream ticket': Neil Kinnock becomes leader

When Michael Foot retired in disgrace after Labour lost the 1983 general election, the Bennites suffered one of their greatest defeats—the selection of Neil Kinnock as Labour leader. He had become the Bennites' number one hate-figure when he urged left-wing MPs to abstain in the 1981 deputy leadership election crucially affecting the outcome. The bulk of Benn's 1981 constituency vote now, two years later, swung to Kinnock with scarcely a murmur of protest, as did the unions. The hard left candidates Eric Heffer and Michael Meacher did very badly. Only thirty-six constituency parties, less than one in fifteen, voted for Heffer.

Percentage of votes in 1983 leadership election

	Kinnock	*Hattersley*	*Heffer*
Constituencies	91.5	1.6	6.6
Trade unions	72.6	27.2	1.0
PLP	49.3	26.1	17.0
Overall result	71.3	19.3	6.3

Percentage of votes in 1983 deputy leadership election

	Hattersley	*Meacher*
Constituencies	51.5	47.8
Trade unions	88.1	11.8
PLP	55.7	29.3
Overall result	67.3	27.9

Where union leaderships declared for Meacher as deputy leader (as they did in the POEU, NUM, and NUPE) the unions' rank and file overturned this. The TGWU delegation did likewise at the party conference itself. The death agony of the Labour left battalions was tragic. Two years after the general election defeat of 1983 the Labour left campaign had crumbled to nothing. People like Michael Meacher, David Blunkett and Tom Sawyer, former standard bearers for Benn, ended up as allies of Kinnock and the right against their former comrades.

Kinnock's dominance over Labour after 1983 repeated a familiar pattern. Practically all Labour Party leaders come from the left (the two exceptions were Gaitskell and Callaghan). Kinnock's proletarian credentials were exemplary. His biographer Robert Harris explains: 'His father, Gordon Kinnock, was a miner, as were both of baby Neil's grandfathers, three of his uncles on his father's side of the family and his two uncles on his mother's side'.[47]

In 1972 it came naturally to Kinnock to defend miners' mass pickets in parliament, violence and all:

> Honourable gentlemen opposite have bemoaned picketing. If they had been on strike for five weeks, if their families' total income was £7 a week social security benefit, if they were worried about smoking their next cigarette, if they were worried about paying the rent, and they saw some cowboy coming along, driving a bald-tyred wagon without a road-fund licence, what would their reaction be? What would be the instinct of any red-blooded man in this House, having put his family to all that inconvenience and near misery if he saw someone riding roughshod over his picket line? I know what my attitude would be. In fact, I should be worried if it were not the case.[48]

This quotation is especially telling if one compares it to his attack on miners' violence on the picket lines of the 1984–5 strike, when he even-handedly denounced both police and pickets.

From his election as an MP in 1970, Kinnock stood out as a rebel. Robert Harris writes:

> If one thing can be said to have been the making of Neil Kinnock, it was his repeated and documented opposition to the policies of that period. It won him popularity in the Party. It gave him a power base.[49]

Kinnock was especially cutting in opposition to the Wilson-Callaghan leadership. He was going to fight to defend his party from such people because: 'This mass movement is too important and too valuable to be abandoned to careerist pimps'.[50] In a debate on public expenditure, in March 1977, Kinnock pilloried Healey and his team of Treasury ministers.

> They treat the City of London as if it were some kind of winnable Tory marginal constituency... They think, generation in and generation out, as their predecessors have done, that somehow there is some deal, some kind of understanding, that can be reached with people who are sworn ideological enemies. The sooner my right hon and hon Friends understand that, the sooner we shall have the policies that we need if we are to have a Labour Government that we can be proud of.[51]

During the five years of the Wilson-Callaghan government Kinnock voted 84 times against the government, at a time when Labour did not have a majority in the House. He voted against the defence budget, twice, against the Prevention of Terrorism Act, against the Civil List increase in the money paid to the Queen, and he launched a tremendous attack on her wealth.[52] This was a far better record than Benn's, who voted against the government just twice, and that only when MPs had been given a free vote on issues concerning the Common Market. Kinnock had the ideal left credentials necessary to lead the Labour party to the right.

His determination to do so became clear in 1984-5, with his denunciation of both police and pickets during the miners' strike. He underlined his insistence that the labour movement should respect the Tory law by denouncing both miners' leader Arthur Scargill and the Militant-influenced Labour-controlled council in Liverpool at the party conference in October 1985. The conference was followed by an acceleration of the witch-hunt against Militant which included the suspension of Liverpool District Labour Party and the expulsion of the leading Militant supporters in the city. Under Kinnock Labour moved further to the right than it had been since Gaitskell.

The collapse of 'municipal socialism'

With Labour in a minority in parliament and the right-wing offensive at national level, the lefts seemed marginalised. Local government seemed to offer an opportunity to hold power and find a haven from the onslaught of Thatcher and the supporters of Kinnock.

There were more than 150 cities, towns and boroughs under Labour control in the early 1980s, with more than 9,000 councillors. This included virtually all the major towns and cities—London, Glasgow, Manchester, Liverpool, Birmingham, Sheffield, Newcastle, Leeds, Edinburgh and Bradford. Although some authorities were controlled by right-wing Labour, an influential left wing emerged in places such as Liverpool, Manchester, Sheffield and Edinburgh. However, the jewel in the crown of 'Socialist Town Halls' was the Greater London Council (GLC) where the party won control in 1981 and elected Ken Livingstone as leader of the Labour group.

Tory determination to cut public spending meant that the Government's grant to councils—the Rate Support Grant—was being constantly slashed. The government then imposed rate-capping—limiting the ability of specific councils (overwhelmingly those controlled by Labour), to raise money by means of the rates.

The Labour councils had the policy of 'Three Noes'—no cuts, no rent rises, no rate rises. But as the government tightened the screw, the Labour councils failed to match their radical words with deeds. They *did* raise the rates, they *did* raise the rents *and* carried out cuts.

For a number of years the Labour councils declared their intention to fight on, even if it led to breaking the law. The 1983 Labour Conference called 'on all Labour-controlled local authorities to collectively resist all curbs on local authority spending...using the political and industrial strength of the labour movement'.[53] The July 1984 Labour Local Government conference added further resolutions to defy rate-capping.

But Kinnock did not intend to be bound by this. He advocated that Labour councils should stay in office and act within the law to protect services—'better a dented shield than no shield at all', he said. None other than Ken Livingstone pledged support for Kinnock's position at a local government conference in February 1985, then the following month engineered the collapse of the GLC policy of defying the Tory rate-capping law. It was no accident that this coincided with the defeat of the miners' strike. The week the miners went back the left councils' fightback also collapsed. The GLC gave up the struggle. Others soon followed within weeks, leaving only Lambeth and Liverpool to fight on. Eventually they too caved in. Every single council pledged not to set a rate did so. There was no repetition of the Poplarism of the 1920s. Why was this?

Firstly not many councillors were ready to risk bankruptcy, surcharge and disqualification from public office. Unlike at Poplar, the left's faith in conference votes had meant there were few links between councillors and the local workers' movement to give them courage and act as a conscience against betrayal. Secondly there was the belief that an all-out fight now was unnecessary since over the electoral horizon was the white charger of a Kinnock government to rout the Tory attack. Finally, there was never any understanding *that local government is impotent in the face of central government unless the collective power of workers could be marshalled behind it*. Instead the move to the right justified surrender—laws should not be defied but changed in parliament.

Local councils could not even maintain reformist gains from the past in the face of Tory attacks. Thus from 244,916 houses built in 1953, the number fell to 151,824 in 1976, 86,194 in 1979 and 17,200 in 1986. At the same time local authorities sold a million dwellings to sitting tenants under the Tory 'Right to Buy' legislation. So in 1986 one million people were listed as waiting for a council house, plus a further 600,000 waiting for transfers. The number of homeless families had doubled since 1979.

Rent and rate rises accompanied cuts. In Walthamstow in March 1987 the rates were raised by 62 percent, fuelling large demonstrations and the defeat of the sitting Labour MP in the 1987 general election. Ealing's 65 percent rate rise led to a swing of 10 percent against Labour in the election.

While some Labour councils cooperated with the privatising of services, cutting jobs and selling council houses without so much as a whimper of protest, others tried to find ways round the problem. *They did not face up to the need to break the law* but turned to 'creative accounting'—borrowing money for services now and paying it back later. Liverpool, for example, took on debts of £92 million to Swiss and Japanese banks, to be repaid by 1992. 'Creative accounting' produced a yawning gulf between what the councils actually spent and what they declared in the returns to the government. The result, *The Guardian* predicted, was that some local authorities faced future financial catastrophe unless about £2 billion was found to unscramble 'creative accounting' measures.[54]

Everything hinged on a Labour victory in the 1987 general election. The defeat put the councils in a grim situation. In September 1987 the Controller of the Audit Commission forecast that council spending could fall by a third and their workforces be reduced by 700,000 over the next five years.[55] Eight London boroughs were left with a staggering £300 million shortfall on their budgets. In Sheffield the shortfall was £50 million. Straight after the election Manchester implemented a cuts package of £40 million and Liverpool £45 million.

Could the cowardice of the Labour councils be justified because no power could stop the Tories? Some two million workers were employed by local councils, about 20 percent of all trade-unionists in the country. Their mobilisation would be crucial if the councils set out to fight central government. The Comintern considered that local councils could be a springboard of opposition to central government. But this is not the view of reformists, who see the process as dependent upon the action of government—central and local—and not on workers' activity. They see their main task as to win 'public opinion.' So in the 1980s they turned to clever advertising campaigns instead of leading a real struggle and relying on the collective strength of the council workers.

The 'dented shield', far from protecting working people from the Tories, turned out to be *a shield protecting the Tories from the anger of working people*. The reformist logic of taking responsibility for managing capitalism, although trying to reform it, had run its course. The experience of Labour councils completely, although negatively, confirmed Rosa Luxemburg's statement that this side of the revolution socialists should be the party of intransigent opposition. Reformism, otherwise, becomes the agent of capitalism inside the working-class movement.

Not ready to defy the government, and unable to deliver much in real terms, left-wing councillors concentrated their efforts on presentation and on tokenism. Instead of more houses, jobs and services, there was a plethora of committees—ethnic monitoring committees, police monitoring committees and women's committees among others. These token gestures did virtually nothing to improve the lot of women or blacks.

Of special interest were the economic policy units. The best known was the Greater London Enterprise Board (GLEB). Despite the fanfares it was a complete fiasco. Claims that its activities had created 208 new companies and 4,000 new jobs were false.

> In most cases GLEB's 'investment' offered a temporary reprieve before commercial pressures took their toll and the companies were forced into liquidation... On a number of occasions it found itself supporting atrocious employers and business people of dubious financial integrity.[56]

The cost of GLEB over three years was £60 million with little to show for it. Even if 4,000 jobs had been created, this would mean that every job cost GLEB £15,000, while London's 400,000 unemployed were barely touched! At the outset Hilary Wainwright described GLEB as a force which would 'haunt capital in London for years to come'.[57] It was a joke!

If someone attacks you with a stick, brandishing a picture of a revolver will not protect you much. Posturing and tokenism disappoints everyone, and opens the door to smears about the 'loony Left' in the town halls. Failure really to fight the Tories led Labour to become identified with the very slum housing and decaying social services that their enemy's policies had produced.

The collapse of municipal socialism was one added factor in the marginalisation of the Labour left.

Feminism: a broken reed

One influence on the Labour left was feminism. Many women who came into political activity around 1968 turned to the Labour Party in the late 1970s and early 1980s, a time of industrial downturn and the disappearance of popular movements. A vast political gulf separated the women's movement of the early period from the later one.

In the first phase *the woman's movement coincided with huge struggles of working-class women*—the Ford women machinists' strike for equal pay, the London night cleaners' fight for union recognition, the 20,000 Leeds clothing workers (85 percent of them women) on strike using flying pickets, the tens of thousands of teachers striking for the first time in half a century and many others. Thus in the ten years 1968–78 the female membership of NUPE more than trebled, NALGO's more than doubled, COHSE's quadrupled, and that of ASTMS rose seven times. Women gained important reforms—the Abortion Act of 1967, free contraception on the NHS in 1973, free contraception for under-16s in 1974. Counter-attacks against abortion rights in 1975, 1977 and 1979 were rebuffed with demonstrations of up to 80,000 women and men. At this time the demands of the women's movement were collective: for equal pay, abortion rights and nurseries, and the claims were against government and employers.

The influx of middle-class feminists into the Labour Party came later, when the women's movement was in rapid decline and industrial defeats were shifting the labour movement to the right. If the general argument for New Realism was that strikes do not pay, it took a special form among feminists. To people like the Euro-Communist Bea Campbell, strikes and pickets were macho and typified the 'anti-woman', 'male-dominated' working-class movement. The focus was no longer collective, but on the individual woman as a victim of men: on rape and other violence against women. The theory of patriarchy—that the enemy of woman is man, that men benefit from women's subordination—came to dominate. Now the women's movement concentrated on personal solutions, on alternative relationships and lifestyles. This naturally appealed to middle-class women: working-class women could not afford the luxury.

The search for individual solutions led to fragmentation and collapse of the women's movement, so that its remnants shifted away from the politics of movements towards institutional politics, largely towards the Labour Party. Protesting against women's oppression, the product of capitalism, without challenging capitalism *in toto*, they fitted very well into Labourism, which both expresses workers' opposition to the *status quo*, and at the same time blunts this opposition.

There is an affinity between the women's movement and the Labour left. First, in terms of social composition they are white-collar and professional.

> Secondly, for the socialist members of the women's liberation movement and the Labour left, ideas are not moulded by the collective class struggle of workers, but are seen simply as a debate between individuals. Thirdly, unlike the revolutionary socialist organisations, which would demand from anyone in the women's movement that she breaks with both the analysis of the movement and its style of work, the Labour Party, being a 'broad church', makes no demands. Fourthly, even in terms of structure there is far more in common between the structurelessness and loose federalism of the women's movement and the bureaucratic swamp of labourism, than between either of them and the democratic centralism of a revolutionary socialist party. There is no party discipline, except where the bureaucratic right find it necessary.[58]

Women who joined the Labour Party in the early 1980s concentrated on setting up women's caucuses within the party. Some became councillors and leaders of local government: such as Margaret Hodge in Islington, Merle Amery in Brent, and Linda Bellos in Lambeth. Though committed to women's rights, they had to contend with the government offensive against working people, which especially hurt working women. Against this they threw not an organised fightback but committees! More pathetic tokenism. To give a couple of examples: the chairperson of the GLC women's unit had a salary of £18,000 in 1982. That is impressive; it gives equality to women. Alas, many working women were lucky to earn a quarter of this. In 1983–4 the Stirling District Council women's committee had a budget of £16,000, of which £11,000 was the salary of the Women's Officer, leaving the magnificent sum of £5,000 for everything else.[59]

Instead of real services women were offered 'participation in the decision-making structure', in other words the opportunity for a handful of middle-class women to climb socially. Initiatives on blacks and gays, equally worthy in intention, were equally hopeless in application. They too failed to address the social roots of the problem or mobilise those forces that could resist the right-wing ideological attack of press and Tory hysteria.

New realism: Exploiting political advantage from electoral defeats

Losing three elections in a row—1979, 1983 and 1987—seems disastrous to a party dedicated to office. The only comparable period in Labour's history was the defeats in 1951, 1955 and 1959, but these were by comparison far less severe. In the elections of the 1950s the percentage lead of Tory votes over Labour was 0.8, 3.3 and 5.6. In 1979 and the 1980s the corresponding figures were 6.9, 14.8 and 11.8. In 1983 the Tories polled 4.5 million votes more than Labour, in 1987 3.75 million. Such majorities are larger than any British party has enjoyed over its main rival since 1945.

The 1959 defeat led Gaitskell and the right-wing to blame failure on Labour's loss of the vote of the affluent worker. The working class was undergoing 'embourgeoisment', they said, it was becoming middle class. According to the famous pamphlet *Must Labour Lose?* Labour's class appeal was outdated: new industries and full employment meant workers' attitudes were shaped by consumer needs—the washing machine, the television and the car.

The catastrophes of 1983 and 1987 also produced an extremely sharp reaction. Gaitskell's thesis was resurrected in a grotesque new shape—the old theory of 'embourgeoisment in affluence' now returned as 'embourgeoisment in recession'. According to this Labour needs to woo the share-owing credit card holder, the 1980s equivalent of the proverbial affluent worker. This somersault requires every traditional policy that is presumed unpopular to be jettisoned. And Labour's New Realism found its prophet in Eric Hobsbawm, the Euro-Communist.[60]

Let us take the arguments in turn. One thesis was that the traditional working class was in decline, while the white-collar middle class was expanding massively. In fact there were still more workers in many core 'traditional' industries in 1988, such as engineering und road transport, than at the time of the 1926 General Strike.

Hobsbawm falsely labelled white-collar workers as middle-class, yet some three-quarters of them earned the same or less than traditional manual workers, worked under similar forms of discipline and came from similar home, educational and cultural backgrounds.[61]

For the Labour leadership, 'yuppies' were the symbol of the direction society was heading. Add to this the supposed affluence of workers (especially in the south of England) and we arrive at the most memorable phrases of the 1987 Labour Party conference—Kinnock quoting TGWU leader Ron Todd:

> 'What,' Ron Todd had asked, 'do you say to a docker who earns £400 a week, owns his own house, a new car, microwave and video, as well as a small place near Marbella?
>
> 'You do not say—let me take you out of your misery, brother'.[62]

But did this docker really exist? Grade One dockers at Tilbury, the best-paid, earned a basic rate of £181 in 1987.[63]

Could it be that living standards were rising significantly elsewhere than the docks? In 1985 only 3.8 percent of the heads of all households earned more than £400 a week. Manual male workers earned on average £163.60 a week.[64]

The Tories wanted us to believe, and Labour echoed them, that a new popular capitalism had won the masses through wider share ownership. There were, we were told, nine million shareholders. This was a phoney statistic. It referred to the number of shareholdings, so that if one person owned shares in British Gas, British Aerospace, British Telecom and Britoil this was reported as four. The Tories claimed that their privatisation share issues had widened share ownership, but many of these shares were quickly resold for profit. By August 1987 British Airways shareholders had fallen from 1,200,000 to 420,056, British Telecom from 2,300,000 to 1,417,905, and Jaguar from 125,000 to 35,749.[65] In 1986 only 13 percent of adults owned shares, and among the semi-skilled and unskilled workers just 4 percent.[66] One survey found that these shares made so little difference to people's outlook that around half the respondents could not remember if they had shares. The group of employees among whom share ownership was most widespread, British Telecom workers, took little heed of their 'investments' during their bitter strike in early 1987.

All in all the picture of widespread affluence was a sick joke. The number of people below the official poverty line was six million in 1979, 8.8 million in 1983, and 11.7 million in 1986.[67]

Hobsbawm argued that traditional working-class loyalty to Labour was in irreversible decline, and so therefore was socialist politics. Such nostrums were exploded by a study of the 1983 general election,[68] a particularly bad one for Labour. The party still got 51 percent of the skilled workers' votes and 48 percent of the semi-skilled and unskilled workers' votes. 'Labour is...obviously a working-class party'.[69]

Why did commentators think skilled workers were far more Conservative than semi-skilled and unskilled, and were turning their backs on Labour? It is because the psephologists include among 'skilled workers' the manual self-employed and small businessmen, together with 'foremen and technicians'.

Changed patterns of consumption and house ownership have less effect on workers' attitudes than Hobsbawm assumed when he wrote: 'the manual working-class core of traditional socialist labour parties has been transformed...by the decades in which living reached levels undreamt of even by the well-paid in the 1930s'. The study *How Britain Votes* shows that the purchase of council houses did not change people's voting habits at the 1983 election. Those who bought 'did not swing to the Conservatives at all. And while some did abandon the Labour Party for the Alliance, so of course did many council tenants'.[70]

Similarly the absolute improvement in living standards is less decisive in shaping workers' views than how far they advance relative to the rest of society:

> conflicts of interest are as much, or more, about relativities as they are about absolutes. The cake may grow in size, but rising expectations will mean that conflicts over the size of the shares will continue unabated.
>
> In this context what is important is that, although average real incomes have increased, income relativities have diminished only slightly. Similarly, while there have been great increases in educational provision in sixth forms and universities, class inequalities in access have remained unchanged. Absolute rates of upward social mobility have increased, but relative class chances have stayed the same.[71]

The *subordination of workers to capitalist exploitation is the key factor* affecting their voting habits:

> employment conditions are more fundamental determinants of values and political allegiance than is life-style...manual wage-labourers have relatively little security of employment and relatively poor fringe benefits such as sick pay and pension schemes. They have little control over their own working conditions and little discretion, being subject to managerial authority, over what they do at work. They also have relatively poor chances (despite some social mobility) of gaining promotion to the better paid and secure managerial positions. As a result manual wage-earners cannot be sure to improve their lot through individual action. Instead they must look to collective action.[72]

The working class has changed throughout its history, as the accumulation of capital leads to new industries and the contraction of others. Still workers continue to bear the weight of exploitation and make up the overwhelming majority of the population—in Alex Callinicos's calculation at least 75 percent of all those employed.[73]

Hobsbawm saw in the shift from manual to white-collar jobs the cause of Labour's loss of social base. But the greatest rise in white-collar employment took place in the 1960s, a time of Labour success, while economic recession slowed the process in the 1970s, the period leading to Labour's electoral disasters.[74]

Workers' votes reflect, though indirectly and imperfectly, the class struggle on the ground. Chris Harman analysed the recent changes:

> The working class was won to 'collective' values and Labour voting by three waves of industrial struggle—that of the late 1880s and the 1890s, that of 1910–26, and that of the late 1930s and the wartime years. It was the experience of these struggles which led first the 'old' manual working class of heavy industry and textiles to turn to Labour, and then the newer working class of light engineering, motors and so on to do so.

Yet white-collar workers, who were 'won to the collective' values of organised trade unionism, did not turn to the Labour Party in the same way:

> this process, by which new layers of workers were pulled behind others into support for Labour, stopped in the 1950s and 1960s—just as the massive growth of 'routine' white-collar employment began.
>
> This was not because the conditions of work in such white-collar employment ruled out 'collective' attitudes… But this industrial 'collectivism' did not translate itself into political collectivism… Why?
>
> You can't begin to answer that question without remembering that Labour was in power for eleven of the years between 1964 and 1979—the very years in which white-collar industrial militancy blossomed. Much of the militancy was, in fact, generated in reaction to the pro-capitalist policies of Labour in power. It is hardly surprising, therefore, that most routine white-collar workers and lower grade 'semi-professionals' did not see any reason to identify politically with the Labour Party.[75]

Workers' organisations intact

The future for socialism in Britain did not lie with Neil Kinnock or any other saviour, however glossy their advertisements. It lay with the working class. To fit in with the consensus set by a ruling class in crisis, the New Realists had to write the workers out of the picture. They therefore stressed not only the decline of the working class as a class, but its organisations, above all the trade unions.

However, the Thatcher period uncovered a tremendous resilience in workers' basic organisation. Unemployment reduced union membership, but far less than in previous slumps: 'between 1890 and 1893 the trade unions lost almost 40 percent of their membership, and between 1920 and 1923 they lost 35 percent. In the three years 1979–1982, trade unions lost 14 percent of their members'.[76]

Among employed workers, 48 percent were in unions in 1988, compared with 49 percent at the height of the struggle in 1974. Indeed, the Thatcher period saw a slight rise in the proportion of workplaces recognising unions: from 66 percent in 1980 to 68 percent in 1984.[77] The number of shop stewards and office and school reps, rose from 317,000 in 1980 to 335,000 in 1984.[78] One commentator wrote: 'at workplace level, especially in the primary sector of the labour market, Thatcherism often meant "business as usual" [with] surprisingly little evidence of a dramatic halt of bargaining power away from the unions'.[79]

Thus average wages did not decline. Indeed between 1979 and 1986 workers' resilience meant they rose by 13.8 percent for full-time male workers; 21.1 percent for female full-time workers and 8.1 percent for female part-time workers.[80]

Workers were often beaten in Thatcher's war of attrition, but their organisation was not smashed. Confidence inside the working class declined for ten years, a process reinforced with every major defeat. Defeats breed sectionalism, and sectionalism feeds defeat. Yet it is one thing to say that the class army lacks self-confidence, but quite another to suggest that it has dispersed and joined the other side. There was no place for the doom and gloom scenario so beloved of the TUC, Kinnock and Co.

Did Thatcher win the ideological battle?

New Realists suggest that Thatcher's populist ideas carried all before her. Nothing was further from the truth. One has but to read *British Social Attitudes: The 1987 Report* to see the beliefs of Thatcher *were not popular at all.* John Curtice marshals the evidence and concludes: 'The Thatcher policy revolution has simply not so far been accompanied by an equivalent revolution in public altitudes'.[81]

Class interest rips Thatcher's propaganda apart. 'Within the working class there is a large majority with radical or egalitarian views.' The following figures about workers' attitudes[82] are indicative:

Nation's wealth shared unfairly	76%
One law for rich, one for poor	71%
Management and workers on opposite sides	65%

Bolshie attitudes prevail! What is true of workers applies to the population as a whole[83]:

Percentages:	*Agree*	*Disagree*	*Neither*
Ordinary working people do not get their fair share of the nation's wealth	65	14	19
There is one law for the rich and one for the poor	59	22	17
Full cooperation in firms is impossible because workers and management are on opposite sides	57	23	19
Big business benefits owners at the of workers	54	19	26
Management will always try to get the better of employees if it gets the chance	52	27	20

The same picture was repeated when it came to the need for government provision of social services and the solving of unemployment. Few people prefer tax cuts to reductions in health, education and social spending.

Percentages:	*1983*	*1984*	*1985*	1986
Reduce taxes and spend *less* on health, education and social benefits	9	6	6	5
Keep taxes and spending on these services *at the same level* as now	54	50	43	44
Increase taxes and spend *more* on health, education and social benefits	32	39	45	46

Margaret Thatcher has misjudged the public mood on welfare spending and cuts in services...[84]

The fact is that, contrary to conventional wisdom, more people accept the values traditionally associated with the Labour Party than those of the Tory Party.

Of course, despite the above evidence the majority are not socialists. In the contradictory fashion typical of the reformist consciousness that prevails in the working class, protest against exploitation is combined largely with acceptance of the capitalist system as natural and inevitable. This can be seen from the attitude to profits: 57 percent of the population believe we would all be better off if industry made bigger profits, and only 18 percent believe that profits are already too high.[85] But at the same time 91 percent think owners, shareholders, directors and managers would benefit most from the profits earned, while only 5 percent and 2 percent respectively think the general public or employees would be the main beneficiaries.[86]

Just how far many of the people who favour economic equality are far from being socialists is clear in the attitudes towards civil liberty or law and order:

Percentages:	*Agree*	*Disagree*	*Neither*
Schools should teach children to obey authority	83	7	10
People who break the law should be given stiffer sentences	72	7	20
Censorship of films and magazines is necessary to uphold moral standards	66	18	15
Young people today don't have enough respect for traditional British values	66	13	20
The law should always be obeyed, even if a particular law is wrong	45	31	22

Simultaneously, then, we have economic radicalism *and* moral 'traditionalism'.[87]

Full of contradictions it may be, but the combined acceptance and rejection of the economic order and social *status quo* fits Labour much more than it does straightforwardly reactionary Thatcherite 'populism'.

Kinnock may not like it, but the Labour Party has always appealed most to the working class. David Butler and Donald Stokes quote many interviews like this one in which a Stirling worker's wife explains her support for Labour: 'I always vote for them, it's a working man's place to vote Labour'. Their research 'makes it clear how very much more salient to the working class are the ideas of class interests and class conflict. Seven in eight of our working-class Labour supporters gave evidence of seeing politics as the representation of class interests, and almost half regarded such interests as opposed'.[88]

Kinnock is embarrassed by any reference to class interest. Instead, by promoting Thatcher's values he makes the fightback more difficult.

So why did Thatcher win three elections in a row?

If the majority have attitudes that conform more closely to the Labour Party than the Conservatives, how could the latter have won in 1979, 1983 and 1987?

First one must avoid exaggerating Thatcher's electoral success. Her big Commons majority is sustained by a percentage of the electorate smaller than the Conservatives obtained in the 1950 or 1964 elections, when Labour won. In ten of the nineteen elections since 1922 the Tories won a larger share of the votes than Thatcher managed to do in 1983 and 1987.

The electoral balance between Tories and Labour is rooted, in the final analysis, in the class struggle:

> [Labour] cannot live at the expense of the mass movement indefinitely. Though hated and feared by the Labour leadership which craves respectability and wishes to run the system harmoniously, its long-term electoral support lies ultimately in the radicalism generated by workers' struggles.
>
> Since Labour contributes nothing to these by its own activity, an absence of struggle brings only temporary electoral success. In the long run a serious setback for the class eventually saps the source of Labour votes.
>
> This happened in 1931 and the same seems to be occurring today. On both occasions a long period of class collaboration had been the rule among trade union leaders. Then came economic crisis which caused mass unemployment and a loss of shopfloor confidence.
>
> In 1931 the unions seemed inadequate in the face of global economic problems. But the Labour Party had no solution either, and while many of the best militants clung to Labour for want of a belief in any other alternative, millions of voters drifted away.[89]

The same story repeats itself in recent years.

Industrial downturn was the prologue to the electoral debacles of 1983 and 1987. The clearest evidence of this can be found in shifts of mood during the 1984–85 miners' strike. In February 1984, one month before the beginning of the strike, the MORI poll found Labour ten points behind the Tories (at 33 percent and 43 percent respectively). In August, when picketing was at its height and workers' self-confidence in the face of the Tories was returning, Labour edged 3 percent ahead at 39 percent. When it became clear that the strike was heading for defeat, the position of the two parties changed again: in October Tory support went up to 44.5 percent, while Labour went down to 32 percent.

The elections of the 1980s have as their background the damage to working-class organisation inflicted by the policies of the Wilson/Callaghan governments. Labour was in office for eleven out of the fifteen years between 1964 and 1979. The experience of those years was decisive in lowering the threshold of support for Labour.

Labour's general election results 1900–1987

Election	*Percentage Labour vote*	*Total vote in millions*	*MPs*
1900	2	0.06	2
1906	6	0.3	29
1910 (1)	8	0.5	40
1910 (2)	7	0.4	42
1918	22	2.2	61
1922	30	4.2	142
1923	31	4.3	191
1924	33	5.5	151
1929	37	8.4	288
1931	31	6.6	52
1935	38	8.5	154
1945	48	12.0	393
1950	46	13.3	315
1951	49	13.9	296
1955	46	12.4	277
1959	44	12.2	258
1964	44	12.2	317
1966	48	13.0	364
1970	43	12.2	288
1974 (1)	37	11.6	301
1974 (2)	39	11.5	319
1979	27	11.5	268
1983	28	8.5	209
1987	31	10.0	227

Between 1945 and 1966 Labour's share of the total vote was relatively stable. Then the imposition of incomes policy, cuts, and other measures which sacrificed reforms to save the system, lowered the threshold of Labour support radically. Particularly damaging was the impact of the Wilson-Callaghan government on Labour's support among trade unionists.

Labour's percentage share of the trade union vote (MORI)

1964	73	February 1974	55	1983	39
1966	71	October 1974	55	1987	42
1970	66	1979	51		

The memory of the Wilson-Callaghan governments meant that during the 1987 election campaign, 30 percent of Labour supporters no longer believed the party's promises, according to opinion polls. As the crisis made all governments turn on the majority of voters, so over the past two decades there has been disenchantment with both major parties: 'the proportion of the electorate claiming an attachment to any of the political parties has fallen remarkably from 44 percent in 1964 to around 20 percent in the mid-1980s'.[90] Millions of votes are cast, but with less and less conviction.

An extra nail in Labour's electoral coffin is its remarkable skill at *snatching defeats from the jaws of victory*. Thatcher has slid on banana skins time and again, but each time Kinnock has managed to prevent her from falling.

For example, in April 1986 the US launched an air attack on Libya from British bases. About ten days later the disaster at the Russian Chernobyl nuclear plant showered parts of Britain with radioactivity. The Tory government handled both events badly. Polls showed these two events badly dented the popular support for Thatcher. That month MORI found Tory support was at 28 percent, while Labour was at 38.5 percent.

What was Kinnock's reaction to these opportunities? On Libya he declared: 'Gadafi is without doubt a malignancy who is sponsoring and financing terrorism throughout the world', and called for 'imposition of economic sanctions and the denial of credits and subsidised foodstuffs from the EEC to Libya'.[91] On the nuclear industry Kinnock wanted a 'pause before any further decisions are taken about the future of nuclear power in Britain'.[92] How radical!

When Labour tried to look more imposing it was sabotaged by its own record in government. On 19 June 1986, when Kinnock called for economic sanctions against South Africa, Thatcher quoted the statement of the Labour government's UN representative, who had voted against full mandatory economic sanctions in 1978 'because... we do not agree that the far-reaching economic measures which the resolution calls for would produce the changes in South Africa which we would like to see'.[93] When Hattersley tried again Thatcher quoted his statement as minister of state at the Foreign Office on 7 July 1976: 'I do not believe that the policy of general economic sanctions would be in the interests either of the British people or of South Africa'.[94] Whatever the issue, a battery of damning quotations lies to hand.

This combines with Labour's attempt to chase respectability, to make Kinnock a mighty gladiator when smashing his own left wing, but a meek little mouse when facing Thatcher. Labour MPs may complain here and there about her actions but the leadership is wretchedly defensive and apologetic.

With all the slick election broadcasts, with all the razzamatazz in 1987, 'Neil' added only 3.2 percent to the election vote achieved by Michael Foot. But instead of Kinnock being blamed by his party for the defeat, he became its chief beneficiary.

The Labour Party in 1987

Kinnock used the 1987 election result to consolidate his position over the left, introducing 'one member one vote' in the election of parliamentary candidates. This was portrayed as an extension of democracy, but in fact it was designed to undermine the left wing of constituency activists (a term of abuse in recent years). The party leadership will appeal to the passive membership over the heads of the activists; in reality they will allow the Tory media decisive influence in setting the terms of the debate.

The contrast between the active and overwhelming majority of passive members in the Labour Party is staggering. The party paper *Labour Weekly* could raise a circulation of only 17,000 from an official membership of 300,000 individuals. In 1987 only 8.4 percent of members had attended the last round of selection meetings (in London only 5.8 percent) to choose election candidates. 'In 205 constituency Labour Parties, almost a third of the constituencies in Great Britain, less than thirty people attended to select the parliamentary candidate. In eleven, there were ten or less people in attendance'.[95] These figures refer not only to delegates from Labour Party branches, to the General Management Committees, but also to the trade union branches!

At the 1987 party conference Kinnock's straightforward one-member-one-vote selection of parliamentary candidates was rejected by the TGWU general secretary Ron Todd and other union leaders, who warned against weakening traditional links with the unions. So a compromise was reached establishing an electoral college in each constituency designed to retain the union voice in constituency politics.

The right's easy victory was facilitated by the character of the Labour left. The politics of conference resolutions and vying for position failed to involve workers in struggle, it also failed to activate even the bulk of Party members. Reformist parties breed passivity, and passive members do not give their leaders much trouble.

Kinnock laid the 1987 election defeat at the door of the hard left, gays and blacks. The last group in particular had organised independent caucuses within the party to combat the prevailing prejudice-ideas of capitalism—which Labour inevitably includes as a capitalist workers' party. But in blaming the caucuses for the party's electoral problems the right wing forgets that minority viewpoints have always existed in the Labour Party (though with little hope of success). In the past they did not prevent elections being won, just so long as Labour could deliver popular reforms.

After the 1987 election Kinnock initiated a comprehensive review of all Labour's policies in an attempt to increase its appeal to voters—a rightward shift proposed by 'a leader who fought the recent election on the least socialist programme since the war'(!), as the *Financial Times* put it.[96]

At the 1987 Labour Party conference Kinnock did nothing to renew the delegates' battered enthusiasm. Kinnock and his blue-eyed boy, Bryan Gould, argued that the only way to beat the Tories is to copy the policy that gave Thatcher three election successes. It is not much fun to be told that the only hope is to imitate the hated enemy. Norman Tebbit boasted to the Tory conference a week later that Labour was already 'half intent on half-heartedly adopting our policies.' The *Independent* reported from the Tory conference:

> The office-seeking wing of the Labour Party was now anxious to let it be known that they accepted what the Conservatives had done and that they were willing to live with it in 'the post-Thatcher era'. The sale of council houses, reform of the trade union movement, denationalisation and wider share ownership had all become firmly entrenched.
>
> Mr Tebbit mocked Neil Kinnock, struggling into Mrs Thatcher's 1983 outfit only to see her wearing an even more radical and appealing style.[97]

Gould suggested that Labour should 'leapfrog Thatcherism' by advocating 'shares for all' to 'appeal to the self-interest of those whose vote we need'. Kinnock spelt out the new line thus: 'an appeal to electors as individuals rather than as members of a class or other collective interest'; in other words, Labour should attract votes on much the same individualistic basis as the Tories do when appealing to workers.

In conference debates on foreign policy and defence Kinnock extolled the peace-loving efforts of US president Reagan (and drew cheers!) He signalled a retreat from unilateralism, the most holy tenet of Labour's creed. Next time Labour would have a defence policy that would do no more than 'enhance the prospect of removing reliance on nuclear weapons'.[98] He was greatly assisted by Joan Ruddock, the new

Deptford MP and former chair of CND. (CND was another movement that thought Labour would be a convenient bed to lie on, but when it got there discovered itself in a coffin). During the defence debate, she stated that Britain should use Trident as a bargaining-counter to persuade the Russians to scale down their nuclear weapons. This was a move to multi-lateral nuclear disarmament.

In a radio interview Kinnock repeated the idea. Asked whether this was not a multilateralist approach, he said: 'I don't think anybody should get hung up about the words. I'd be delighted to be part of a multi-lateral move'.[99] What, asked a later interviewer, if multilateralism failed? 'We must be part of NATO. By definition, because it is a nuclear pact, we will be part of a nuclear pact'.[100]

Kinnock met with hardly any resistance to his moving Labour rightwards. Indeed the main threat to his position was that the Labour right wing might apply his own electoral logic to Kinnock himself, replacing him with a more 'effective' leader chosen from their own ranks.

The climate of defeat which pervades the working class movement explains the 'don't rock the boat' atmosphere which has allowed Kinnock to ride roughshod over the Labour left. The defeats of workers in struggle, the climax of which was the miners' strike, *were not inevitable*. The defeats reflect the *cowardice and treachery of the trade union officials and Labour Party*, the people who at present lead, or rather mislead, the working class movement. But these defeats helped to undermine the base and morale of the left. Kinnock could plausibly argue that Labour should follow the centre of political gravity rightwards. Even those who dislike the new direction have smothered their doubts in the hope that voters will respond *next time*.

Full circle

The Labour Party has always argued that politics is about elections and which party forms the government. However, history shows that reforms depend less on the colour of the government than the state of the economy and the strength of the working class. In the 1950s the Tories expanded the welfare state. In the 1970s Labour introduced monetarism. Governments made a difference but were not decisive. In the 1940s, 1950s and 1960s there seemed to be clear alternatives to the slump: reflation through Keynesian demand management, supported by nationalisation and matched by welfare policies. In the crisis of the 1970s and 1980s all this has changed. In the 1980s there is no room for reform. Labour or Tory governments will try to make workers pay for the economic crisis.

The Labour Party, like all other social democratic parties, finds itself without a distinctive alternative of its own as it faces the crisis of international capitalism. If it came to office, it would be forced to behave like the Tories. Neither nationalisation nor radical wealth redistribution policy would be feasible. Even to attempt major reflation as a means of ensuring profits and encouraging investment would be fraught with dangers. The Mitterrand syndrome hangs like a cloud over Labour's head.

The Labour Party has come full circle. It started as hardly different in terms of policies and ideology from the open bourgeois party predominant at that time—the Liberals, and it ends as an imitation of the predominant capitalist party of the present—the Tories. The verbosity, vacuity and woolliness of Ramsay MacDonald and of Neil Kinnock are uncannily similar. This is not a simple return to its past. The infant and the geriatric have a lot in common, but what distinguishes them is that one has a future, and for the other the best times are behind.

Notwithstanding the Labour Party's weakness in its infancy, its birth was a step forward, part of the forward march of the British working class. Now the Labour Party is a complete and absolute impediment on the further development of this class. The ideological and political shapelessness of the Labour Party was the by-product of a rising workers' struggle and its partial defeat. The conservative nature of the Labour Party under Thatcher is the by-product of the defeat inflicted on workers' struggle by the Labour Government itself, under Wilson and Callaghan.

17

New Labour

WHEN THIS book first appeared in 1988 it was generally accepted that 'Popular capitalism' had triumphed. The working class was disappearing and socialist politics were irrelevant. Moreover, many argued that Labour was unlikely ever to get into office. The British Communist Party's now defunct *Marxism Today* talked of 'the development of the Conservative Party into the single dominant party'.[1] The *New Statesman* added, 'Socialism died with the Russian Empire [and] the Labour Party has been brain dead; it is time someone switched off the life support system'.[2] But the 1990s turned out somewhat differently.

The fall of Thatcher and the poll tax

Until the moment she fell in 1990 Margaret Thatcher was regarded as 'one of the most astute and powerful of contemporary political leaders'.[3] Five years later Blair was still attempting to follow her by making 'New Labour' 'the true expression of the radical "anti-Establishment" spirit of the Reagan/Thatcher administrations'.[4] Labour had given Thatcherism a free run and, as the Observer's editor Will Hutton says: 'While individual countries may have at least one horror story of radical marketisation similar to Britain's, only Britain can tell them all... No Western industrialised country in the twentieth century has been subjected to such fast and excessive marketisation'.[5] How successful was this for British capitalism?

> The economic miracle of a country ranking bottom of the OECD turns out, upon cursory inspection of the mandate reality, to be a 'gigantic con-trick'... They touted the startling improvement in the productivity of manufacturing industry, delivered by the destruction of 2.5 million jobs, and a radical legislative reduction of union power. This improvement, however, amounted to the capacity to produce the same output with one third fewer workers... Meanwhile Britain's competitors increased their output by more than half (Japan), one third (USA), or a quarter (Germany)... From 1979 to 1992 UK GDP had grown by a

mere 1.75 percent per annum...an unparalleled post war disaster in half a century spoilt for choice.[6]

The key long term impact of Thatcher and her successors meant that between 1994 and 1995 Britain's standing in 'world competitiveness' was 18th out of 48, well below Singapore, Hong Kong and Taiwan, while it was 21st for 'domestic economic strength'.[7]

Thatcher was not brought down by British capitalism or Labour,[8] but by an anti poll tax campaign which saw some 11 million people breaking the law to withhold payment of the tax and a huge riot in Trafalgar Square.

The poll tax symbolised a Thatcherism bloated by easy election victories. Replacing local rates with a tax that had dukes paying the same as cleaners was immensely unpopular. Labour's response was to review its own policies. Kinnock said this was the 'precondition for defeating Thatcherism', requiring 'socialists to face up to the realities... To recognise it is not defeatism, accommodation of Thatcherism or collaboration with Thatcherism, it is the opposite'.[9] Anything else was anathema. So even before poll tax forms were issued in 1988, Kinnock 'warned that frustration should not explode into futile illegality and so play into the Tories' hands'.[10] David Blunkett, then Labour's local government spokesman, insisted 'we will be successful in removing the poll tax [only] by removing the Government which imposed it'.[11]

When anti poll tax unions flourished anyway, the Party joined union leaders in the 'Stop-It' campaign. This was more concerned with containing non-payment than with overturning the Tories' legislation. Labour's stance was tested in the Glasgow Govan by-election where its candidate had pledged non-payment but was rapidly brought to heel by Party HQ. The Scottish Nationalist stood on an anti poll tax ticket increasing the SNP's vote an astonishing five fold to win from a previous fourth place.[12]

Labour concluded that in future candidates must tow the official line more closely. Changes were made helping Headquarters impose candidates over locally selected ones.[13] By early 1990 Labour was threatening to discipline Tower Hamlets councillors who refused to prosecute poll tax non payers and withdrawing the whip from 16 Liverpool councillors over the issue.[14]

As protests erupted outside town halls Labour 'launched the second...phase of its poll tax campaign'. Bryan Gould declared people should protest by joining the Party while the planned 1 April national demonstration was 'cancelled due to lack of money'.[15] Involvement in anti poll tax unions by Labour's own membership was minimal reaching just 4 percent.[16]

On 31 March 1990 an enormous anti poll tax demonstration in Trafalgar Square was attacked by police and turned into a riot in which 340 were arrested. The Home Secretary blamed Labour. Hattersley, Shadow Home Secretary was outraged: 'The Labour Party condemns, without reservation or qualification, the violence which took place... no cause can justify such conduct. It is literally intolerable. May I offer the sympathy of Opposition Members to those police officers who were injured [and call] for exemplary sentences for those who were convicted'.[17] Nevertheless, the result was 'the most spectacular reversal of a flagship policy ever seen in Britain'.[18]

Incredibly, Blunkett now claimed: 'It was our campaign and it was our belief in the policies that we were putting forward that ensured that the poll tax eventually met its doom'.[19] The Party turned on those who really beat the tax, arguing: 'The biggest threat to Labour losing the advantage we currently hold comes from those in our ranks who publicly advocate non payment... Warrant sales cannot be avoided'.[20] Hackney, where Labour had 58 out of 70 council seats, issued 40,000 court summonses. Labour even criticised the government for being 'lazy' in closing loopholes in rules for prosecution of non-payers.[21] Meanwhile Cherie Booth, £200,000 per annum lawyer wife of the future Party leader Tony Blair (and former Labour candidate herself), demanded a penniless poll tax defaulter should stay in prison.[22] Two thirds of all those jailed had a Labour council to thank.[23]

However, the Glasgow Govan experience was not repeated south of the border. There was no electoral alternative to Labour, so it benefited from the protest vote. The mid-Staffordshire by-election (March 1990) saw Labour's biggest swing since 1935. In May the Tories suffered their worst local government results ever.[24] The opinion polls between the 1987 and 1992 elections showed rising non-payment and demonstrations boosting Labour's popularity and destroying the Tories'. This was thrown away partly because Labour collected the tax as viciously as the Tories.

Labour's Gulf War syndrome

John Major succeeded Thatcher in November 1990, a political lightweight chosen as a compromise leader to keep out Michael Heseltine. Major had been closely involved with the hated poll tax and was suspected of being Thatcher's puppet. When he took office in November 1990, he and Kinnock were close in popularity ratings. By the spring of 1991 Major's personal rating was almost double that of Kinnock's. One reason was the way Kinnock aped the Tories, as was shown clearly in the Gulf War.

War began with Iraq's invasion of Kuwait in August 1991. The US seized the opportunity to tighten its grip on world oil supplies and assert its position as the world's leading superpower. The US government coordinated an invasion of Kuwait and Iraq by thousands of American and European troops. Anywhere between 100,000 and 250,000 Iraqi troops and civilians were killed, many in the infamous 'turkey shoot' of soldiers trapped on the Basra road. Kurds and Marsh Arabs, duped by Allied statements, rose up against the Iraqi regime only to be abandoned. Many died and 2 million Kurds fled into the mountains.

Liberal and even not so liberal opinion was worried by US President Bush's hectic rush towards military conflict. But the Labour leadership matched every jingoistic statement of the Tory government point for point. Yet an early survey of backbench Labour MPs showed 80 percent against immediate military action, with 25 percent rejecting war outright.[25] Slavish obedience to the leadership outweighed conscience for all but a minority. Labour failed to argue for delaying war. It even avoided calling a Parliamentary debate on policy during the entire conflict. This was unique in British history.[26]

As war approached Labour MPs asked incredulously why the Party was not setting out its own position. Kinnock replied: 'In the variety of discussions that have taken place some say that I should, as they put it, "distance" myself from the Government. I will not distance myself'.[27] Once the war began Major was subjected to a torrent of Kinnock's sustained grovelling:

> I join the PM in his thoughts for the families... May I take this opportunity of supporting the feeling expressed by the Prime Minister... The Prime Minister has been right, both today and on previous occasions... The Prime Minister gave fair notice to Saddam Hussein.[28]

Kinnock's position was to the right of Edward Heath, much of the US Congress, and even the Pope. When the Parliamentary Party now discussed the issue, the vote was 5 to 1 in favour of prolonging the slaughter as against a ceasefire.[29] An NEC meeting took the same position but 'twelve hours after [it] rejected a ceasefire in the Gulf, Bush and his allies declared one'.[30]

Some left MPs did protest[31] and five resigned Labour's front bench. One said, 'The vast majority of us are deeply depressed. We feel this is horrendous, the beginning of something dreadful', while a backbencher described his colleagues' feeling of 'guilt and shame'.[32] Largely because of Labour's position, the British anti-war movement was small, whereas elsewhere vast demonstrations took place, with 400,000 in Algeria, 100,000 in San Francisco and 300,000 in Washington.[33] Bernie Grant blamed the weakness on 'Labour MPs who lurked in supper clubs and bars mumbling their disagreement, afraid of damaging their political careers'.[34] The 'supper club' was a rallying point for left MPs but when a *Daily Mail* reporter crashed a meeting, 'at least three of these brave souls dived under tables in an attempt to hide their identities from the public and, presumably, the leader's private office'.[35]

The leadership's connivance in mass murder was justified by electoralism. Kinnock said: 'We must save the Party [and] make clear we are not pacifists'.[36] Yet before the war Labour was 15 points ahead in the polls, after it was 5 points behind. The poll tax dividend had been squandered and the next election probably decided.

The 1992 election

For the 1992 general election policies were comprehensively overhauled. Kinnock scorned 'those who say they do not want victory at such a price'.[37] Thirst for office gripped the Party membership: 'The new generation of younger members was much more self disciplined, business-like and single minded in its ambition for power'.[38] Labour's left and right spoke with one voice as never before. As Livingstone put it: 'If the chief aim is to fight [the Tories] it is absolutely necessary to unite with those who support the general policies of the party leadership in order to do so'.[39]

The 1992 General Election should have been a gift for Labour. Instead it was:

> a remarkable victory for the Conservatives. To win by such a margin of votes over Labour (7.6 percent) was totally unexpected. It was achieved in the trough of the longest depression since the 1930s and at the end of a campaign that had been much derided. It went against the trend elsewhere in Europe, where established government parties were meeting electoral rebuffs. The fourth successive election victory meant that by the end of the new parliament the Conservatives would have been

> in office continuously for 18 years—the longest period of one party rule since the Great Reform Act of 1832.[40]

The road to defeat in 1992 was laid by Peter Mandelson and Philip Gould's Shadow Communications Agency (SCA). It began with a presentation to the Shadow Cabinet and NEC by pollsters which 'exploded on some of those present like a grenade'.[41] Henceforth, opinion polls were accorded the mysterious power for prediction given to astrologers. The SCA forged 'an approach to political strategy which has never before been seen—certainly in the Labour Party, and arguably, even in British politics. They wielded policy, politics and image creation into one weapon'.[42] Now, Labour's values and the people's values were—abracadabra—identical'.[43] Supporters were told that image was the key and indeed, in 1992:

> Labour gained good marks for its campaign. Since 1987 it had dropped virtually all left wing policies and embraced modern campaigning methods even more fully. With the exception of the promise of higher rates of taxation for the better off, it had accepted most of Mrs Thatcher's achievements in the 1980s.[44]

Even after the event 'all the surveys...reported that Labour fought a better campaign than the Conservatives'.[45]

Labour's approach foundered for three reasons. First, as Hugo Young admitted ruefully: 'The opinion poll business has proved to rest on fantasy'.[46] Second, even if they had been accurate, Labour leaders read polls selectively. On 24 March Labour's Party Political Broadcast told the true story of two girls, one who received prompt private treatment for 'glue ear' while another suffered awaiting treatment under the Tories' reformed NHS. 'Even opponents acknowledged that it was superbly done; members of the panel on which it was tested before transmission were said to have been moved to tears'.[47] The three polls preceding the broadcast put Labour 2.7 percent behind. The three polls after showed Labour gained an average 8.3 percent.[48] So the Party dropped health! 'Labour's leaders were themselves scared of the message in the broadcast, nervous of what one insider called its "class war propaganda"'.[49] Unbelievably they switched, in what was the final week, to promoting Proportional Representation. While pollsters reported the NHS the single most important issue with 93 percent of voters backing higher NHS expenditure,[50] Labour concentrated on policies which could hardly have been weaker. This brings us to the third point.

Labour policies are not primarily shaped by public opinion. The dictates of capitalism are far more important.

Labour's vote did rise—by 3.5 percent—during the election. Given the poll tax fiasco and recession this was not surprising. Labour's 11.5 million votes were 3 million fewer than the number of summonses and warrants issued to poll tax non-payers, a group the Party assiduously avoided courting. The social composition of its vote also changed. Amongst the unemployed Labour's share actually fell as compared to 1987, and its share of the poorest and most numerous social grouping (D/E) remained completely static. With the *Financial Times*, of all papers, calling for the Tories' defeat, Labour's greatest gains were made at the top end—the smallest and wealthiest group A/B.[51]

Until 1974 supporters strongly identifying with Labour always exceeded those of the Tories. The Wilson/Callaghan government broke the bonds of loyalty and Kinnock had done nothing to restore them.[52] Yet the leadership blamed defeat on its tax proposals. An authoritative study shows 'there is very little evidence' for this. Those who intended to vote Labour but changed their mind were not 'particularly adverse to high taxation, rather they seemed to be people who had relatively little faith in Labour's ability to improve services like health and education... taxation may actually have lost the Conservatives some votes between 1987 and 1992'.[53]

In the fourteen general elections since 1945 Labour had only done worse in 1983 and 1987. The abandonment of one principle after another, its Gulf War policy and so much more had been designed to win this election. The interests of millions of workers were, win or lose, being betrayed by the Party they hoped would help them. This was not the conclusion the Labour leadership drew. After the election it rounded on the trade unions.

The mines tragedy

Electoral defeat brought a leadership contest. Rule changes in 1988[54] meant no left-wing candidate was able to stand for the first time since the 1930s. The choice was John Smith or Brian Gould. In a *Financial Times* poll of businessmen Smith was a more popular choice for Chancellor than the Tories' Norman Lamont. Gould was famous for his 'leapfrog over Thatcherism' speech.[55] Smith won with 91 percent.

Labour had based its strategy on the disappearance of class as a political issue. In October 1992 this non existent force suddenly reappeared at centre stage and from that point, in opinion poll terms, Labour never looked back. Michael Heseltine's plan to shut 31 pits created a massive protest. Two enormous demonstrations on Wednesday 20 and Sunday 25 October, numbering nearly a quarter of a million between them, marched through London. *The Sun*'s headline was 'Is Major a goner?'[56]

The labour movement had slowly recovered confidence since the defeats of the mid 1980s. There had been no comparable setbacks since then, while the poll tax movement's spectacular demolition of Thatcher showed Tory vulnerability. However, the mines movement differed from the anti poll tax movement. Labour had not been able to derail non payment since this had in large part been organised on a localised basis at a grass roots level. Defending the pits, however, demanded a collective centralised leadership. Demonstrations, important as they were, would not be enough. Mass strike action was necessary.

Two months before the threatened closures Labour's energy spokesperson told the NUM 'in a speech ringing of defeatism' that 'the cards are heavily stacked against keeping coal in the public sector'.[57] Still, the TUC and the Labour Party had the potential to force the government into a headlong retreat. Tories and Labour alike realised this. Ex-Tory Minister, Cecil Parkinson, admitted on TV 'The government seems to have lost control',[58] while David Blunkett for Labour boasted: 'I could have asked for a general election. Maybe we'd have got one as well'.[59]

At first Labour treated the issue as a TUC matter while the TUC insisted that, with the support of dissident Tory MPs, the Parliamentary Labour Party would save the day for the miners in parliament. When protests grew:

> John Smith did turn up at the big rally in Hyde Park. His absence would have been embarrassing...he urged the 'public' to keep up the pressure. As mining communities were attacked during the winter and spring he said nothing. He did not even reply to the NUM's appeal for support for a one day strike. He addressed the Confederation of British Industry conference and...caused his audience to laugh nine times.[60]

No further national demonstrations were countenanced and the movement dissipated into regional events.

Labour says Parliament is the proper place to achieve progress yet its performance here was pathetic. It weakly accepted vague promises from Heseltine that if the Labour chaired Select Committee on Trade and Industry produced a unanimous report on the pits, he would adopt it. Such compliance would have been unique in select committee history.[61]

In February 1993 the eagerly awaited report appeared. Twenty of the 31 pits were still to close. After months of prevarication Labour MPs were too demoralised even to vote against Heseltine when he ignored the committee's findings. In the NEC report to Labour's 1993 conference the mines merited half a page, the witch-hunt against the Labour left filled three. The *New Statesman* concluded: 'Here, out of the blue, was an opportunity not given to oppositions even once in a decade: a monumental gaffe by government, which had the burghers of Cheltenham marching in the streets and Catholic priests pronouncing anathema in the pulpits.' The Party's failure showed 'inertia, amounting to almost intellectual and political paralysis that appears to have seized Labour'.[62]

In the months afterwards there were a spate of industrial struggles on the railways, at Fords, amongst firefighters and at the Timex factory in Dundee. The period after saw a continuing slow and patchy revival in the working class movement, the victory of the railway signal workers in 1994 being a prominent example.

However, the pattern seen in the pit closures was repeated a number of times. Though Labour sought to distance itself from unions, the symbolic relationship between the Labour and union bureaucracies continued. One sign of continued Labour influence on the levels of class struggle was shown in a survey showing that in a sample of 500 strike ballots two thirds produced 'yes' votes but in only 82 did action occur. In 1995 massive votes for industrial action in the NHS, which saw even the Royal College of Nurses abandoning its no strike status, were side-tracked by hope that a Labour government would repair the damage inflicted by the Tories. As the next election neared the union bureaucrats resisted action ever more strongly. In early 1996 an important strike of Liverpool dockers sacked for refusing to cross picket lines was shamelessly abandoned by the Transport union. Blair stood aloof from the trade unions yet used his links with the union leaders to quell discontent. A direct example was when 'Senior Shadow Cabinet members' warned train drivers against striking on the day of the Littleborough and Saddleworth election.[63]

One Member One Vote (OMOV)—weakening the union link

The links between trade unions and the Labour Party continue to be an important issue for socialists. Together, the trade union bureaucracy and the Labour Party weave reformism out of a blend of working class and capitalist class influence.

Union class consciousness is very durable. Despite the pressure of capitalist ideas, the daily experience of exploitation, the permanent trench warfare over conditions and pay provides a social reality at odds with the dominant ideology. Even at times of defeat like the 1980s, when many felt impotent in the face of the bosses and their legal system, class distinctions between boss and worker were self-evident. Despite all the bureaucratic obstacles in the way of its expression, this consciousness does influence the Labour Party via its union connection.

Apart from this connection the PLP is far removed from working class influence. The ballot box has no connection with the workplace while MPs work within the constraints of Parliament, an institution deeply imbued with capitalist tradition. Thus, in the battle between working class and ruling class ideas the PLP is influenced more by capitalist pressure than unions.

The individual membership of the Party is both numerically smaller than the unions and less rooted in immediate class experience. It is therefore more volatile. For much of Labour's history it has been mostly left of the unions. In the 1990s, with a membership which lacked roots in key areas of class organisation, much of the membership generalised from electoral defeat to draw right wing conclusions. Falling levels of activism further this process. Activists may be involved in debate, demonstrations and campaigns. Passive members, by contrast, are more easily influenced by right wing ideas, a rightward shift that moving away from links with trade unions is likely to accentuate.

The process of weakening union links began in earnest after the 1987 defeat. Kinnock clearly outlined the intentions of the strategy when he said Labour governments 'have to go against the unions in the national interest, so why shouldn't the Labour leader in normal party matters?'[64]

By the early 1990s, policy making, which used to take place in Labour's NEC (which includes members elected by union votes at conference) had been informally transferred to policy review committees and then to the Shadow Cabinet. The unions also agreed to reduce their share of votes in leadership elections from 90 to 50 percent.

Defeat in the 1992 election brought a carefully prepared ambush of the unions. Tom Sawyer of NUPE (forerunner of Unison) writes: 'I was immediately overwhelmed with requests to offer my opinions on Labour's links with the trade unions—an issue which had hardly featured in the election. This was puzzling at first... I now understand that there were influential people in the party who are prepared in the event of defeat, for a concerted attack on the trade union link'.[65]

One 'influential' person was Blair. Without consultation, he had already withdrawn Labour support for the union closed shop on the grounds that the European Social Charter gives the right to 'join or not to join a union'.[66] Blair allowed the Tories to sweep away the closed shop, but there was still no right to join a union. 'Blair's coup' targeted something which one biographer says: 'inevitably appeals to the party's instinct for archaic forms of solidarity'.[67] This action led some to see Blair as a future contender for the leadership.[68]

After the election Blair was determined 'to strike instantly'[69] believing that 'if Labour loses the next election it will be the fault of Bill Morris' and the other union leaders.[70] This was quite simply wrong. In 1992 only 4 percent of voters gave unions as a reason for not voting Labour, while 20 percent mentioned Kinnock.[71] Opinion polls showed rising support for trade unions. Those opposing further anti union legislation easily outstripped Labour's share of the vote, while a massive 79 percent in 1992 supported giving workers more say in running their work.[72] Popular opinion was not driving the campaign against union links forward. Again it was the pressure on the Labour leaders to appease the ruling class.

The union/Labour link was maintained principally through union leaders and some resisted the erosion of their influence. Ron Todd of the Transport Union lambasted Labour's 'modernisers and reformers with sharp suits and cordless telephones', reporting 'a certain middle class embarrassment in some circles at the idea of belonging to a movement which remains dominated by working-class organisations. They need our money and our strength, but they resent our power'.[73] As the offensive intensified after the 1992 election an exasperated Morris, Todd's successor, asked, 'Has Labour got a death wish?...the whole issue of Labour's future has been reduced in a few short weeks to the trade union problem'.[74]

It was at Labour's 1993 Conference that key decisions were taken. The Party leadership wanted parliamentary candidates selected by individual members only (one member, one vote—OMOV). Local trade unions would lose their 40 percent vote. In selecting the Labour leader union participation would be cut to one third. The debate lasted throughout the spring and summer of 1993. The media warned that Labour was unelectable without OMOV and then conducted polls designed to show that people were more likely to vote Labour if OMOV were adopted. As *Tribune* pointed out: 'One might as well ask if people are in favour of free ice cream and chocolate'.[75] The label 'one man one vote' was a misnomer. John Edmonds of the GMB pointed out it meant 'denying union levy payers any say... OMOV means a narrower franchise. Fewer people will be consulted and fewer people will vote'.[76] Morris added that the proposals for electing the leader 'would make each MP's vote equivalent to that of more than two constituency parties. Less than 300 Labour MPs would have the same share of the vote as more than 200,000 individual members... What the modernisers really want is: one MP loads of votes'. Their decision would carry as much force as that of 4 million trade unionists.[77]

In the end Conference approved OMOV (along with a special membership rate for trade unionists to join locally) by the narrowest of margins. To win this Smith was forced to announce his conversion to 'the goal of full employment—at the heart of Labour's vision'.[78] John Prescott cashed in his left-wing credentials calling on delegates to 'give us a bit of trust'.[79] Still it required strenuous arm twisting and sharp practice to get OMOV through. For example, 750 delegates at the postal workers' union conference voted by a majority to reject Smith's scheme but at Labour's Conference the 19 delegates voted in favour. The MSF was committed to opposition, but a secret meeting from which a left-wing delegate was excluded, chose to withdraw its 4.5 percent from the anti OMOV camp. OMOV passed by a 3.1 percent margin.

The union leaders could have sunk Smith's plan, but they had an Achilles heel. They needed the goodwill of the Party leadership in the event of a Labour government. That is why 80 percent of them supported OMOV.[80]

How did OMOV affect the union/Labour link? Trade unions still had connections via affiliation to CLPs, individual membership, NEC elections (12 seats), Labour conference and other channels. The Party was financially dependent on union support (£4.7m out of the £8.8m total in 1993). Blair hoped to mirror Bill Clinton's Democrats, but Clinton raised more corporate cash than the Republicans. Despite its efforts, Labour's leaders did not manage to win major sponsorship from big business and as one union leader nicely put it—'No say, no pay'.[81]

So OMOV did not represent a final break with the unions, though the link was weakening. For example, in 1985 Labour had 98 workplace branches. By the mid-1990s they had all but disappeared.[82] The decline of channels for working class influence encouraged further capitulation to ruling class ideas making it easier to cut influence again, and so on. The stampede to the right was less restrained as a result.

New Labour's new members

OMOV raised the issue of Labour's dwindling membership, which was 261,000 in 1992, just 60,000 more than the Liberals. The fiction of OMOV democracy required constituency members. There was also convincing academic evidence, after yet another election defeat, that local canvassing actually wins votes, up to 5 percent more.[83]

The problem for Labour Party leaders was their political volunteers, working without the lure of expense claims and Parliamentary salaries might actually be socialists. If the membership were expanded it must be tamed and neutralised. So the witch hunt against left-wingers in the party was stepped up. In 1990 the Socialist Organiser grouping was exiled followed by the Militant organisation in Liverpool, including 29 sitting councillors. At the 1991 Conference 200 more were suspended and threatened with expulsion. Meantime, 'Young Labour' was being 'sanitised to death'.[84] Ken Livingstone described the tactics as 'completely Stalinist'.[85]

Within local Parties debate and discussion involving activists were replaced by ballots of the whole membership. Since half the membership hardly attended meetings and less than a third attended frequently,[86] this abolished informed collective debate.

> The passive, depoliticised individual membership now adumbrated would not be obliged to do anything quite so heavy as attend branch meetings, participate in debates, and resolve to support candidate Y or policy Z in the light of collective discussion. Rather, drawing a residue of political activists, they would ratify by postal ballot, in the privacy of their own homes, the will of a more centralised leadership which had already arrogated powers to screen parliamentary candidates. Under the guise of extending democracy, the leadership was further circumscribing it... Apparent decentralisation of power concealed actual centralisation of sovereignty.[87]

OMOV was presented as bringing Labour closer to its supporters. In fact its membership had drifted away from the voters. As a study by Seyd and Whiteley showed, though once composed largely of ordinary workers, it was now dominated by well intentioned professionals. Whereas 57 percent of Labour voters were industrial workers, only 26 percent of members were in this category. The 'salariat' gives Labour 14 percent of its total vote but formed 49 percent of its membership.[88] Household incomes revealed the same pattern. In 1990, 6 percent of

Labour voters earned more than £20,000 per annum, among members it was 30 percent.[89] It was claimed Labour's activists were unrepresentative extremists while right-wing policies matched the general membership's views. In fact, even in the 'new model party' members' views were left of the leadership. A full 68 percent were for unilateral disarmament; a massive 92 percent thought taxes should be increased to spend more on services[90] and 71 percent favoured more nationalisation. The remoulding of the membership did not eliminate left-wing ideas but ensured passivity. In 1990, 20 percent reported being more active over the previous five years; 43 percent were less active.[91]

In this context it was now safe for the leadership to expand Party membership to undercut union influence. By April 1995 the figure reached 320,000, having grown 93,000 in a year.[92] Although one quarter of the intake were trade unionists,[93] the head of Labour's membership team called them 'non-political people'.[94] One activist remarked: 'There are people becoming members who would actively dislike the idea of socialism'.[95] The *Financial Times* concurred: 'The types of people who have joined the Labour Party, self employed, small business people, young men and women, are not interested in that old Labour message'.[96] Interestingly very few of the new members paid the full £18 annual subscription, the proportion of all members doing so falling from 48 percent in 1993 to 40 percent in 1995. Since the party spent more in servicing the passive members than they contributed, the unions were subsidising the reduction of their own influence.[97] Even given all of this it was still probable that many new members joined because their hatred of the Tory government outweighed the effects of Labour's shift to the right.

The Labour left's manic depression

These changes in the composition of the party affected the Labour left. In 1981 Tony Benn received 81.1 percent of the constituency vote in the campaign for party leader. In 1988 it was 18.8 percent.[98] In 1989 Ken Livingstone lost his seat on the NEC, and in 1993 Benn was ousted after three and a half decades on that body. Until then 'constituency parties' representatives on the NEC, first elected by constituency delegates in 1937, [were] consistently and overwhelmingly on the party's left'.[99] By the 1990s the left were a minority, though the right had not succeeded in wiping it out, with Dennis Skinner and Diane Abbott retaining seats in 1995 while 'moderniser' Jack Straw lost his. Labour's left proved relatively powerless against the leadership's right-wing authoritarianism.

A sign of the reformist left's disintegration was the closure of much of its press: *News on Sunday* (June 1987); *New Socialist* and *Labour Weekly* (Oct 1987); *Marxism Today* (December 1991); the *Socialist* (June 1992); *Spare Rib* (February 1993). This left the newly launched *Red Pepper* and *Tribune*, its circulation down to 5,000 from a high of 40,000. The fate of the *Tribune* Group exemplified the trend:

> Its once passionate and well attended weekly meetings had dwindled to directionless once-a-month gatherings attended sometimes by as few as four or five MPs... Only a few years before it had been touted as the new powerhouse of the PLP but it was now an irrelevance, without ideology or purpose, eviscerated by the disease of leadership loyalty.[100]

At times the situation was acknowledged. Skinner said: 'The elimination of alternative viewpoints within the Labour Party is now more thorough than it has ever been... We have a small group of people at the top of the party controlling everything and putting a firm stop to any dissent'.[101] Benn thought 'Socialism has been explicitly repudiated... People who have given their life to the party are wondering whether it actually is in terminal decline'.[102]

When Smith was elected in 1992, Livingstone wrote: 'The triumph of the right is now complete. They control every lever of power in the party',[103] while the election of Tony Blair topped even this as 'the most extreme right-wing leader' the Party had ever had.[104] Hain described power as 'centralised to an unprecedented extent'.[105] Finally, in 1993 Clare Short predicted: 'We have two years at most to flush out the modernisers... If we do not achieve this, then the electorate will have a choice between the new Labour SDP and the Liberal Democrat's, with little difference between the two. But time is running out and the prospects do not look good'.[106]

Yet tied to reformism, for the Labour left hope springs eternal. In 1994 'the best Labour Conference for some years' was held, according to Livingstone.[107] (This was the one preceding abolition of Clause Four.) Although the left were a beleaguered minority on the NEC 'the votes for the left candidates increased'.[108] Hain said the challenge to Clause Four, 'has clearly put the cat among the ideological pigeons and, not before time, injected new vigour into the debate about the nature of socialism... This should be welcomed.' The left should be 'engaged constructively with Blair'.[109] Hain's 'engagement' took the form of a book which starts with the libertarian tradition dating back through Kropotkin, the Russian anarchist, to the Diggers and Levellers, and ends saying 'Governments have to save capitalism from itself'.[110] Thus, Labour 'will need the backing of the unions, especially when carrying through economic policies which require a switch from consumption to investment and from real wage increases to job creation'.[111] Short, her two year deadline of flushing out modernisers due, wrote; 'Tony Blair has a remarkable ability... Anyone who indulges in split and public rows... should never be forgiven... We now have a duty that all of us must rise to. Blair cannot do it without us and we cannot do it without him'.[112]

The evolution of Labour policies

We have already shown that Thatcher had failed to win the ideological argument by 1987.[113] By the early 1990s, far from the trend of public opinion following the Labour leadership to the right, it was clearly going in the opposite direction, as the following survey shows:

Views on major political issues since 1979[114]

Percentages in:	*1979*	*1987*	*1992*
Are you in favour of:			
Spending more money to get rid of poverty?	80	86	93
Nationalisation?	16	16	24
Privatisation?	38	31	13
Having no stricter laws against trade unions?	16	33	40
More money being spent on the NHS?	87	90	93

The 1992 election study concluded: 'There has been a considerable amount of evidence in recent years suggesting that, rather than being converted to the tenets of Thatcherism, many of the electorate have actually been moving to the left.' The issues included unemployment, nuclear weapons and privatisation where 'there were modest but statistically significant moves to the left'.[115]

Labour's policies went from being based on genuine reformist principles (such as unilateralism, universal welfare), through Kinnock's Policy Review to consciously occupying right-wing Tory territory. Below are a few examples. As far as possible we let Labour speak for itself:

Unilateral disarmament

In 1988 we noted Kinnock making 'a move to multi-lateral nuclear disarmament'.[116] By the mid-1990s Labour appeared to have abandoned disarmament altogether. Financial prudence was demanded for social spending, but the £22 billion Trident project was not questioned:

> We stand four-square by the notion that, whatever is required to defend Britain, Labour will provide... Obviously it doesn't make sense for us to give up a capability that we are unique in NATO in providing... I would not scrap [Trident, though] it is difficult to argue out a particular role for [it]. We just need it there as a standing reminder.[117]

Blair complained the Tories spent too little on arms. 'It would be an abdication of Labour's duty if we did not point out that these cuts will weaken Britain's operational capabilities'.[118]

Along with this went a disgusting nationalism. Straw was 'reclaiming the flag' from 'the grotesque caricature of England that is the National Front.' How? 'English patriotism has for too long been corralled. We should stop apologising for being English. Feeling pride in one's country should not make one into a jingo.' The Union Jack flew over the first concentration camps, over the slave ships and the violent conquests of the largest Empire in world history.[119]

Education

In 1991 Labour condemned Tory policies of selection, testing and school opt outs as fostering:

> a privatised divided education system, in which a few get the cash, while for the rest it is second best. The Tories are creating a system so offensive to the values of justice and fairness that they have been condemned by the heads of both the Anglican and Catholic churches.[120]

Blair sought to change these labour opinions. The 'old' (1991) Labour attitude to education, he said, 'typifies the reasons why the left has been losing general elections for the last 16 years instead of winning them'.[121] In December 1994 Blair, who set so much store by the local community, applied to send his son eight miles to London Oratory, a non-union opt out school, headed by a former advisor to the Tory Education Minister, which has been criticised by the Catholic education service for its over rigorous selection of pupils.[122] Blair was 'aghast' when he discovered Labour's General Secretary relaxed about sending his children to a local school: 'The Blairs were apparently asking [him] the sort of incredulous questions about life in an inner city "comp" that used to face nineteenth century explorers when they came back from overseas with tales of the strange things that the natives did in the jungle'.[123]

To cover the Blair family's tracks Labour's Diversity and Excellence document invented 'foundation schools' (opt out schools by another name) operating with 'a fair admissions policy'.[124] 'On tests one MP declared: 'It's not good enough to bang on about socio-economic background... By measuring outcomes we can define which schools are performing well and which are performing badly'.[125] With this in mind Blunkett encouraged the NUT to abandon opposition to tests and league tables because 'a Labour government would keep the tests and continue to publish results'.[126]

Roy Hattersley, hardly a man of the Labour left, concluded:

> The Labour Party will, in effect, repudiate the principle of comprehensive education [and] cannibalise one of the most discredited policies of the Government... The grant maintained idea is one of the Government's major policy failures. Despite escalating bribes, less than one school in 20 has chosen to leave the maintained system. Yet Labour has chosen to breath life into the corpse.[127]

Even in opposition these policy somersaults had a direct impact. When, in 1995, almost half the secondary school governors were considering whether to set illegal budgets, Labour rushed to oppose this. By 1996 the Tories planned to expand selection by schools because Labour had taken over so many other Tory education policies like closing failing schools.[128] Two weeks later Harriet Harman sent her child to one of the most selective schools in the country.

Law and order

Numerous revelations about miscarriages of justice surfaced during Tory rule—the Guildford Four, Maguire family, Birmingham Six, Broadwater Farm Three, SAS executions in Gibraltar, the murder of Joy Gardner and more. Police largely stood by as racist attacks doubled between 1989 and 1994. Labour should have lambasted the Tories, pointing out the social deterioration behind the crime figures.

Yet Blair made his reputation outflanking the Tory right. 'The Tories have given up on crime'[129] he argued and went on 'Labour is the Party of law and order in Britain today'. He added: 'We need to be tough on crime and tough on the causes of crime'.[130] While the first phrase obviously was the Tory agenda, the second appears to criticise a society where, it had been clearly demonstrated, increases in unemployment lead to rising crime rates.

But Blair meant something else. He was stealing Major's 'back to basics' campaign. Blair's 'causes of crime' were 'our disintegration as a community, with standards to sustain a community.'[131] According to Blair this was not caused by mass unemployment or a slashed welfare state, but a failure to 'demand responsibilities'.[132] His 'cure'—stop and search powers to the police, prosecuting parents for truanting children, custodial sentences for youngsters, and condemning single parents because 'it is best for kids to be brought up in a normal, stable family.' When Major said, 'we should forgive a little less', Blair told the police, 'We do not excuse and we do not ignore…speak the language of punishment'.[133]

What did the Tories make of this? Chris Patten, former Conservative Chairman, said: 'I find myself in complete agreement with somebody like Tony Blair'.[134] Norman Tebbit added: 'you have to approach from a direction which some might say is almost Labour Party direction'.[135]

As with education, Labour's right-wing policy statements allowed the Tories to move much further than they had dared before. The Criminal Justice Bill was 'designed to be so unpalatable to Labour that it would force Blair to oppose the Bill at the very time he was trying to convince people that Labour was now tougher on law and order than the Conservatives.[136] This Bill, said the *Observer*, 'will cause more miscarriages of justice, the jailing of harmless demonstrators and, in tenser parts of the country, the transformation of the police into something like an occupying army'.[137] Save the Children Fund said that jailing young children contravened the UN Convention on the Rights of the Child. Michael Mansfield, QC, warned: 'The police are to be given another weapon with which metaphorically to beat even more confessions out of people'.[138]Labour quibbled over parts of the Bill and then abstained.

Labour's Frank Field called for identity cards and 'a core SAS style anti-fraud officers'.[139]

The National Health Service

In 1991 Kinnock slammed Tory health policies:

> Their hospital opt outs will create, and are intended to create, a health service consisting of trading units. Their GP contract system will create and is intended to create, a market place of haggling doctors 'buying and selling patients'… This process is called privatisation. At the next election the British people will be deciding whether they keep the National Health Service… Those who vote Labour will be voting to build up the NHS.[140]

In reality there was no such choice. The Tories had closed one third of beds since 1979 and one in eight hospitals,[141] but in 1995 Blunkett said there were 'too many beds'. Launching *Renewing the NHS* Blair added, 'We are not reversing all the Conservative reforms'. Labour will merely 'discourage the signing' of long term contracts for private run hospitals. The 'buying and selling' purchaser-provider split at the core of marketisation was virtually retained and there was 'no absolute commitment' to abolish GP fundholding, merely a plan to phase it out.[142] Patricia Hewitt, Blair's adviser, was a member of the Healthcare 2000 committee whose report favoured ending the universal health service free at the point of delivery.[143]

Poverty and the Welfare State

In 1990 Michael Meacher criticised Thatcher's claim that 'all people on all incomes have increased their standard of living': 'Tell that to the 150,000 homeless people in London and the beggars'.[144] He continued that with the 'scrounger myth [the Tories] hope to turn attention away from the fact that benefit levels themselves have hit an all time low'.[145] Between 1979 and 1992 the real income of the wealthiest 10 percent (including housing costs) rose 62 percent. The poorest 10 percent saw an 18 percent fall.[146] A 1995 report showed wealth inequality in Britain to be the second worst among the developed countries. Only New Zealand was worse.

Labour's response? A Commission for Social Justice headed by Sir Gordon Borrie, QC, who said: 'I have a substantial house in the country and a rented flat in the Temple. I belong to a couple of clubs where the subscriptions are quite high and have enjoyed a high public salary'.[147] He cited his qualification for the Commission as 'being uncommitted to either side of the universality or means testing debate.' Others on the Commission included two founders of the SDP and Liberal Democrat advisers.[148] The results of the Commission were described in the following terms:

> The extent of the common ground between the Tory left and 'New Labour' is remarkable. The Commission argues that people should be able to use the money spent on their benefits as a subsidy with which to attract potential employers; the government is already running a pilot scheme. The Commission urges that unemployment benefit, income support and family credit be reformed to encourage part time work and to encourage people off welfare into work; the Chancellor has already signalled that this will be a key theme in next month's budget. And the Commission argues that the married couple's tax allowance and mortgage interest tax relief should be phased out gradually; this is already happening.[149]

Labour dropped its 1992 pledge to restore income support to 16–17-year-olds. With the Party adopting US workfare schemes these 250,000 young unemployed would no longer be entitled to full benefits but earn them.[150] This threat was extended, with plans to cut 40 percent of benefit from other 'work-shy' young people.[151]

Major caused outrage saying beggars were 'an eye-sore which must be swept from the streets'.[152] So Straw followed: 'Aggressive begging, along with graffiti' and, in some cities 'squeegee merchants' are responsible for 'intimidation and bullying on the streets'.[153] This earned him the nickname 'Jackboots Straw' at the 1995 TUC where an FBU delegate declared 'I'm not saying Straw is a fascist—yet—but he is heading down a road with very dangerous company'.[154]

Minimum wage

This was 'one of the few distinctive policies' Labour had, said the *Financial Times*.[155] The 1992 manifesto pledged a rate of half median male earnings, at that time £3.40, by the mid-1990s the figure was nearer £4.15. In 1995 Blair would not set a rate until 'after the election'[156] to be calculated by a committee including businessmen, on the basis of 'economic...as well as social justice considerations'.[157] Bill Morris of the Transport and General Workers' Union likened the involvement of business in setting the minimum wage to 'putting Dracula in charge of the blood bank.' Harriet Harman subsequently promised the CBI that 18–24 year olds would get a lower rate minimum wage and 'very young workers' wouldn't be covered at all.[158]

Full employment

Although full employment was destroyed under Labour, it was axiomatic that this was its policy. Then Kinnock's review document *Opportunity Britain* made it 'an objective'. By 1993 Gordon Brown was going 'beyond traditional notions of full employment. In the new world our aspiration must be full and fulfilling employment through work and training'. What the party had in mind was to 'Replace redundancy with the prospect of new work through training'.[159] Blair put 'the notion of full employment within a bigger notion, that of a cohesive and united society.' 'Focus on the quality of the jobs created', he pleaded.[160] What a disgraceful end to a policy.

Taxation

Reformism has always sought to redistribute crumbs from the capitalist table. In 1990 Labour changed, but Smith, no left winger, still told Conference:

> we do insist that the minority who received an enormous bounty from Mrs Thatcher should pay their fair share. [*Applause*] [And] because of

> the vital importance of our public services we cannot promise cuts in income tax...or cut back on education and training, on research, [on] our health service.[161]

In 1993 the richest 10 percent of the population paid 34 percent of income in taxes, the bottom 10 percent paid 46 percent.[162] The share of national output taken by tax put the UK low down at 17th out of 24 major economies according to the OECD.

Labour's 1992 manifesto called for top rate tax at 59 percent. The following year this was dropped. 'Labour is not against wealth, nor will we seek to penalise it,' said Brown. As for public spending commitments—'There are none'.[163] Blair felt 'there are top rate tax payers now who are hardly in the super rich bracket and I think we've got to be extremely sensitive to them'.[164] In his *News of the World* column Blair wrote: 'if someone goes on to be wealthy, then good luck to them'. He went on to commiserate with 'Middle England' who 'have suffered the real burden of tax increases'.[165] Labour outflanked Tory income tax cuts in the November 1995 budget. Unlike them Labour's tax cuts 'would apply to all taxpayers'.[166] A lower starting rate for income tax was Brown's 'main ingredient in efforts to cut welfare costs and persuade claimants to take low paid jobs'.[167]

Labour's economic strategy

In the 1970s Dennis Healey ended Keynesian policies and set the scene for Thatcherism. Over the next few years the overlap between Tory and Labour strategies was extraordinary:

> In the run up to the 1992 election, the Tories forecast a PSBR [Public Sector Borrowing Requirement] of £28,000 million. We said that, by an amazing coincidence, that was exactly the PSBR we would have as well...[168] Well, said the Tories after the election, it might have to be a bit higher—perhaps £37,000 million. That's exactly the figure we have arrived at too, we said... Hang on a minute, said the Tories, it will have to rise to perhaps £50,000 million. Just what we thought, we said.[169]

Is this really the voice of an effective opposition?

Labour's only disagreement with the Tories (or rather one wing of the Tories) was 'Labour's total endorsement of European monetary union, the exchange rate mechanism [ERM] and the concept of a single central bank.' Alas, 'they were being more Thatcherite than the Thatcherites.' It was a 'me too, only more so' approach.[170] Labour got its fingers burnt when the pound crashed out of the ERM in September 1992.

Labour became so cautious that Ken Clarke, Tory Chancellor mused: 'I must be the first Chancellor who has a shadow chancellor who is not criticising what I am doing. Gordon Brown's problem is he thinks what I am doing is working. He has not, for some time, opposed anything I have done'.[171] What could Brown say? 'If the Tories take on our agenda, it's a recognition that the political argument is moving in our direction.' And what is that direction? (Readers might like to swap the words 'Conservative' and 'Labour' in the next Brown quote). The result was a typical speech used by Tory politicians against Labour for the last 90 years.

> Labour will be tougher on the causes of inflation than the Conservatives... And it's right that we should be tough. The war against inflation is a Labour war. It affects pensions and those with savings, it damages investment and therefore jobs.[172]

So Labour refused to solve the poverty, homelessness and welfare cuts the Tories had created, either through taxing the rich or by borrowing.

Tory anti union laws

While Blair praised the insight of Thatcher's ideology, as one writer put it: 'none of this ramshackle ragbag of half-cock theories and accidental wheezes, could possibly have "seen off socialism" on their own...we may be getting closer to the true murder weapon when we turn to Lady Thatcher's onslaught on the trade unions'.[173] The anti union laws were flouted on many occasions, but they remained simultaneously a shackle and an alibi for the inaction of union leaders. Even Blair once recognised that restriction of 'secondary' (ie solidarity) action was 'a draconian limitation on effective industrial action'.[174] Prescott expressed the general viewpoint in 1989: 'It all has to go'.[175]

What was the situation by the mid-1990s? The 1995 TUC Conference defeated a motion for repeal of 'all anti trade union laws'. Blair told the TUC: 'We are not going back to the old battles. I will say now that there's going to be no repeal of all Tory union laws... Ballots before strikes are here to stay. No mass or flying pickets. All those ghosts of times past, they are exorcised'.[176] When the Tories, following Blair's 'stakeholder' speech, wondered if it meant more union power, Brown rushed to deny Labour would 'extend union rights' beyond the minimal ones in the European Social Chapter. A perplexed commentator concluded that 'Labour would prefer to upset the unions rather than the CBI'.[177]

Racism, immigration and asylum

The unpopularity of the Tory government meant that whipping up racism to try and win votes was an option they seriously entertained. Yet Shadow Home Secretary Jack Straw asserted that 'it should not be possible to insert a cigarette paper between the government and the Labour front benches over immigration'.[178] The Labour left's response to rising racism, attacks and murders was to support an organisation called the Anti Racist Alliance (ARA). Much time was spent denouncing the other much larger anti racist organisation, the Anti Nazi League, as an SWP front. The election of a BNP councillor in Tower Hamlets in September 1993 raised the profile of racism and racists everywhere. The turning point in the fortunes of the Nazis came on 16 October 1993 when 60,000 demonstrators marched on the BNP's headquarters in Welling, south east London. That day ARA also held a demonstration, many miles away in Trafalgar Square, attended by 2,000 people and Labour's high dignitaries. Not long afterwards ARA imploded in disarray.

The Tory government then turned its attacks on to refugees, introducing a spiteful Bill. The furthest Labour dared go was to suggest, respectfully, that a Committee be appointed to look into the question. When the Tories decided to deport a Saudi Arabian democrat who sought asylum, in order that the government could secure lucrative arms contracts with the Saudis, Jack Straw was asked if he would have done the same thing. He answered: 'That's not a decision which I can take'. On the moral question of deportation to win arms sales, Straw commented, 'You've obviously got to take account of that consideration in the world in which we live'.[179]

Tony Blair and Labour

This book began with a quote from Lenin noting that workers support Labour but it is 'led by reactionaries and the worst kind of reactionaries at that, who are quite in the spirit of the bourgeoisie'.[180] As Labour leader Blair was the purest expression of this. No other leader matches his career: son of a Tory councillor, educated at Edinburgh's premier public school, then Oxford; first links with top Labour echelons made as legal adviser for witch hunting Militant; becomes 'leadership material' when he dumps the closed shop; becomes publicly known when calling for children to be jailed; first act as Labour leader—abolition of Clause Four.

Commentators of all types agreed that there was something incongruous about Blair heading a movement composed largely of working class people. John Sopel wrote: 'As he stands before an audience of Labour activists and union fixers, the pre-eminent feeling is that he is not one of them'.[181] Lawson said: 'I was always slightly surprised that he was in the Labour Party at all. He is quite definitely the least socialist leader the Labour Party has ever had'.[182] Ken Coates, Labour MEP felt Blair 'does not begin to understand the mentality of the party which he has been elected to lead'.[183] According to Rentoul his modernising trend 'did not arise from a social movement outside the party, or from the grass roots or the unions within it. It was synthesised by the Parliamentary leadership'.[184] So Blair didn't fit, yet he was perfectly appropriate in a 'capitalist workers' party'.

Blair had many admirers. Thatcher was one: 'He is probably the most formidable leader...since Hugh Gaitskell. I [do not] see a lot of socialism in Mr Blair'.[185] To the *Daily Telegraph*'s editor he was a 'proper Tory Prime Minister in waiting'.[186] Alan Clark, far-right ex-Minister, said 'virtually single handed [Blair] has transformed the Labour Party into a credible political party'.[187] The *Sunday Times*' Martin Jacques praised his 'deep hostility towards labourism—towards the culture of class'.[188] *The Economist* appreciated this 'presidential style candidate: nice man, nice wife, nice kids, good on telly'.[189] It added that 'Scrapping Clause Four is the start...but what a good start'.[190] Murdoch 'could even imagine supporting' him and Roy Jenkins thought he was 'the best hope for social democracy'.[191]

Blair was a great admirer of then US president Bill Clinton, whose disastrous administration nourished the rabid right of Newt Gingrich's Republicans. Clinton stood as a 'New Democrat', Blair as 'New Labour'. Clinton appealed to 'the forgotten middle class, who work hard and play by the rules', Blair appealed to 'middle income Britain, who work hard and do well'.[192] Clinton would 'offer more opportunity to all and demand more responsibility for all'.[193] Blair: 'We give opportunity, we demand responsibility'.[194] But if Blair was 'Clinton with his flies done up'[195], he did learn from the American's failures. An *Independent* editorial entitled 'Tony Blair's Newt Labour' concluded 'he has anticipated many of the popular themes that have characterised the recent success of Newt Gingrich and the US Republicans, and is now seeking to capture them'.[196]

Blair's also idolised Thatcher, who, his 'Chief of Staff' confirmed, 'is his model. And she once said that her single greatest success was the change she had brought about in the Labour Party. That's also Tony Blair's job—in reverse, of course'.[197] Blair said 'The new right had struck a chord. There was a perception that there was too much collective power [ie, union influence], too much state intervention and too many vested interests' [unions, again!][198] 'I believe Mrs Thatcher's emphasis on enterprise was right. She was thoroughly determined and that is admirable'.[199] He was nostalgic about 'the Thatcher administration [which had] a very strong sense of what they wanted to do with the country and that's what we've got to communicate.' But isn't Labour left wing and the Tories right wing? 'The terms left and right had become, in many ways, meaningless within the Labour Party'.[200] New Labour's objectives 'should and will cross the old boundaries between left and right, progressive and conservative'.[201]

Obviously Blair's popularity was not confined to the right. After all the Labour Party elected him over Margaret Beckett and John Prescott in July 1994. But caution needs to be exercised here. Though Blair campaigned with the entire press behind him, his share of the vote—57 percent—was not remarkable, especially compared with his predecessor's 91 percent. The comparative distribution of Blair's votes was notable—61 percent of MPs, 58 percent from the constituencies, just 52 percent from the trade unionists.[202]

There were periodic murmurings against Blair. For example, Richard Burden, MP, not noted as hard left, protested at Labour's Littleborough by-election leaflet which said: 'The choice is therefore between the Liberal Democrat and his views on drugs and hefty tax increases and Labour's local candidate...raised here in the Pennines and committed to Tony Blair's New Labour.' Burden condemned such 'political amorality in which anything goes.' Labour was 'a ruthlessly effective electoral machine...rather than a radical party with a definable ideological base... with immense pressure on everyone to fall into line in the interests of unity and not jeopardising electoral chances'.[203] Blair had to fight hard to avoid commitment to a specific minimum wage rate. Jack Dromey, Blairite challenger to Bill Morris in the T&G leadership election, was defeated and Blair had to tell the T&G conference that they would not have 'an armlock on Labour or its policies.' For his part, Morris warned that unions would not accept 'a minority relationship' with Labour.[204]

Nevertheless, the weight of the 'Blair effect' was reflected in the row over Clause Four.

Back to the pre-1918 era?

Though adopted to head off revolution,[205] Clause Four also represented a break with the Liberal Party. In 1995 it symbolised what remained in

Labour of the idea of socialism. Of course, the Party had largely ignored Clause Four and by 1995 had dropped commitments to renationalise any industry. Ambiguous about the railways, the only firm nationalisation target was private prisons 'when their contracts expire'.[206] Yet contracts could then last up to 25 years.

Blair wanted new Labour 'liberated from our history', replacing socialism with 'social-ism'. Clause Four represented 'a party born out of the trade unions and formed largely to represent people at work'. Blair insisted this was 'too narrow… I want Labour to be a party which has in its membership the self employed and the unemployed, small business people and their customers, managers and workers'.[207] Blair summarised his alternative in these terms: 'Socialism…is not about class or trade unions, or capitalism versus socialism. It is about a belief in working together'.[208] One Blairite put the abolition argument more crudely: 'We are dealing with a rump of people suffering final withdrawal symptoms, who have not yet come to terms with the fact that we are a social democratic party'.[209]

New Labour was in fact very old, pre-1918 Labour. But abolition of Clause Four did not simply return the Party to its past. At that time Labour was led by convinced reformists who feared including socialism in the constitution because most workers were still wedded to Liberalism. By the mid-1990s this was reversed: a leadership which had abandoned reformism and was attempting to stifle such aspirations in a working class wedded to reformism. It is true that, when in office, Labour's practice had been as right wing as as it became under Blair. At such times it was, in effect, the prisoner of the ruling class. Blair's Labour Party was different. It had moved dramatically to the right in opposition. Moreover, Labour Prime Ministers tried to excuse their betrayal of policies by pointing to special circumstances—the 'bankers' ramp' of 1931, the 'gnomes of Zurich' in the 1960s, or IMF in the I970s. By contrast Blair revelled in following openly capitalist policies.

So scrapping Clause Four was not updating the Party image, but an attempt to ideologically break with reformism. Blair's campaign coincided with Thatcher's aim as divulged to the *Sunday Times* in 1994: 'her ultimate ambition was to destroy a socialist Labour Party and replace it with a British-style Democratic Party. Britain would then have two parties committed to the success of capitalism: the Tories in the anti-state role of the American Republicans, opposed by a Labour Party backed by the unions but free of left wing dogma'.[210] In terms of ideology Arthur Scargill's comment was deadly accurate: 'Clause Four is what marks out the Labour Party from the other major political parties in Britain. Without Clause Four the Labour Party is indistinguishable from the Liberal Democrats and the Tories.'[211]

Blair's new clause promoted: 'A dynamic economy...in which the enterprise of the market and the rigour of competition are joined with the forces of partnership and co-operation to produce the wealth the nation needs.'[212] Market enterprise and rigour meant a world in which 820 million people, 30 percent of humanity, were idle (according to the ILO), in which children starved in the midst of plenty. It meant the untrammelled power of a tiny minority and their grotesque wealth over the exploited and oppressed majority. Yet the new clause was adopted at Labour's Special Conference on 29 April 1995 by 65 percent.

A full 90 percent of constituencies were in favour, but only 54.6 percent of the unions. In analysing these results we are beset with contradictions. The first indications, in a *Tribune* poll of constituencies, was that 60 out of 62 had decided against scrapping Clause Four.[213] These decisions were made by activists. A typical viewpoint was reported in the *Independent*: 'Our party leader's nickname—Tory Blair, is now looking less like a joke.'[214] On the other hand, in the 500 constituencies which had postal ballots, just 3 voted to retain Clause Four.[215] The average vote per constituency was just 200 people, or 47 percent of the full membership.[216]

The distinction between passivity and activism was shown in Blair's own Sedgefield constituency, where 25 voted to amend the Clause yet 200 turned up to hear Scargill defend it. A survey by Seyd and Whiteley compared their 1990 findings with 1992 data. The proportion of members rejecting the idea that 'the production of goods and services is best left to the free market' was rising (from 60 to 63 percent), while the number wanting more privatisation was static at just 2 percent.[217] A survey of new members published in *Red Pepper* showed the following ambiguous picture:

Survey of new Labour members[218]	*Yes*	*No*	*Don't know*
Should Labour set a rate for the minimum wage before the next election?	57	40	3
Do you feel positive towards the left wing of the party?	34	12	54
Do you think unions should be more active in the party?	30	26	44
Did you support the change to Clause Four?	67	33	–

The unions told a similar story. Blair's special conference preceded those of all Labour's affiliated unions except USDAW. The 9–1 pro-abolition ballot in the UCW union was conducted by sending out forms with the union journal; 83 percent did not vote. A random sample of 4,000 AEEU members yielded an 11–1 result.[219] The Transport and General, however, conducted its own consultative exercise, and at a preliminary meeting only 7 out of 75 delegates backed Blair. Unison cast its 11 percent for Clause Four.[220] The press made much of the difference between unions which used postal ballots and those which decided at meetings. But what shaped the decisions of each? In the former, the chief source of information and advice came from the likes of the Murdoch press. By contrast, union meetings involved informed discussion.

What of the public? Again the evidence was paradoxical. Opinion polls were moving against the market and privatisation. When Tory plans to levy full VAT on fuel were beaten (December 1994), Labour had an average 32 percent lead. The start of the Clause Four debate caused this lead to plummet 14 points.[221] Blair's plan seemed a vote loser. At the same time most people said their vote would not be influenced by scrapping Clause Four, though 24 percent (three quarters of them Tories) said they would look on Labour more favourably.[222]

When newspaper calls for abolishing Clause Four grew to a frenzy, Blair's move gained support (though when it was explained what the clause meant, opinions were less favourable). The eternal refrain was heard—Labour must move right to be electable. Left winger Diane Abbott described the atmosphere—Blair's new version was 'a lot of tosh', but 'if the leadership asked for a vote on the healing powers of cabbage it would get it'.[223]

The Clause Four issue reveals the contradictions of Blairism. Other events pointed the same way—the poor showing of some modernisers in NEC and Shadow Cabinet elections, and the disgust at Blair and Harman flouting education policy. Both Blair's biographers pinpoint the phenomenon in the same terms. Rentoul writes: 'Many Labour Party members voted for him because they thought he could win, not because they believed in what he was doing'.[224] Sopel agrees: 'There was a schizophrenia in the mind of many Labour activists that while they voted for Blair because they knew he stood a better chance than anyone else of winning the next election for Labour, they didn't actually like his approach to policy'.[225] Even Blair's inner circle recognised that new Labour 'is not yet a cohesive integrated political party sharing the same political ideology'.[226] A GMB delegate to the 1995 TUC put the situation very clearly:

> I know it sounds silly, but I often voted against the way I felt because I do believe there is a bigger issue of having to get a Labour government. I'm not sure about standing up to Blair. You may think I am a coward, but I can tell you I'm boiling angry at what this government has done. I'll support anyone who does fight. I'm itching to get Labour into Downing Street so we can begin piling on the pressure for more change than Blair is proposing.[227]

Firstly, there was intense hatred from vast sections of the population for the Tories' policies. This, above all, gave Labour consistent poll leads, in spite of Blair adopting these self same Tory policies. If 'New Labour' rode high in the polls, then this apparently confirmed Blair's indispensability. But 1992 was a warning. Blair may have grabbed disillusioned Tory voters while Labour supporters had no electoral alternative. Yet this was a short term, high risk strategy. If the Tories appeared to overcome their worst problems, then Tory voters would return to their natural home in droves. Blair treated his own party in such a cavalier fashion that it may have provoked splits. But even if the party stayed united until the election frustration was likely to explode afterwards.

This raises a second issue. If, as we have argued, Labour reflects the conflicting pressures of the ruling class and working class, and if there has been a modest revival in working class confidence and ideological shift to the left, then why did Labour not reflect this? The counter pressure of capitalism had also grown. Thatcher's direct offensive had to be abandoned after the poll tax but the ideological offensive was given added weight by the 'fall of Communism'. In previous times the Labour leadership attempted to balance the interests of workers and the system. Now this seemed an even more impossible task because of the void separating simple reformist demands (for a job, decent pay and conditions, and basic public services) and the system's insistence on higher exploitation and cost cutting at all levels.

Thirdly, Labour's structures, sclerotic at the best of times, were now even less responsive to working class pressure due to weaker union links and an anaesthetised membership. The ideological gulf between the Party leadership and the day to day experience of supporters was much wider. Although not a fully representative sample, compare Blair's vision of New Labour ('one nationism', tilted as much towards small business and managers as workers) with candidates for the various parties in 1992 (see table below).

Distribution of selected occupations of 1992 election candidates[228]

	Tory	*Labour*	*LibDem*
Company executives	148	21	90
Legal profession	114	37	37
Company directors	67	1	20
Farmers	25	2	8
Armed services	17	0	2
Teachers	50	189	162
White collar workers	20	100	70
Skilled workers	4	70	15
Miners	1	13	0
Semi/unskilled	0	8	1
Total number of candidates	634	634	632

Unlike the other two parties, 356 of Labour's candidates were union sponsored. It is such facts which explain why, in spite of any number of prawn cocktail offensives, £500-a-head banquets and pro-business lunches, Labour remained the second eleven team for British capitalism.

Thus despite all the changes since 1988 Labour was still regarded as a working class party (despite its record). In March 1995 the Tories reached a record low point in the polls. When MORI asked if Labour would 'help to improve your standard of living?' those in the poorest social groupings, C2s and D/E answered positively, scoring +16 points. By contrast groups A/B and C1 were −23 points against. Questioned about whether Labour would keep its promises the working class groupings showed +10, the upper groups polled −21 points.[229] These results have little to do with the reality of the Labour Party, but everything to do with its perception. For the moment the reality and the perception did not enter into direct conflict. A small incident showed this would not always be the case—the strong reaction in broad Labour circles to Harman's sending of her child to a selective grammar school.

Tension between Blair and the social reality of Labour's support was great, but the bonds of mutual dependence were also strong. Blair could not do without the votes of workers or the cash of the unions. On the other hand, many Labour supporters were convinced that Blair alone could win the next election. The strength of such bonds mean reformist alternatives to Labour faced major obstacles.

A similar situation defeated the ILP in the 1930s and Militant in the early 1990s. In the latter case, Leslie Mahmood's candidature in Eric Heffer's old seat of Walton, gained 6.5 percent. This was a good base for a revolutionary policy of intervention in the daily struggles of the working class. A reformist perspective demanded that the seat be won, and compared with the right wing Labour candidate's 53 percent the result was a disaster.

Announcing the formation of a Socialist Labour Party in early 1996, Scargill sensed the deep unease felt in broad Labour circles about Blair. This does not mean there was much room for a second reformist party in Britain. The SLP did save its deposit at the Hemsworth by election, but it is clear in this case too that the first past the post system hampered any challenge to Labour from the reformist left. Meanwhile, the wish to remove the Tories, shared by trade unionists from rank and file to bureaucracy, meant the unions were unlikely to support a competitor to this Party.

Many Labour supporters were extremely angry with what the modernisers had done to Labour policies, but it would take a change of circumstances to release this anger, when the hopes met the real New Labour party in head on collision.

Until that time the sharp edge of conflict between New Labour and the needs and aspirations of workers was more likely to be found on the industrial scene. Those workers who do not accept a revolutionary alternative to electoral politics would wait for the election of a Labour government, even though there was rising anger over the way Blair was behaving on education, the minimum wage and much more. However, the immediate problems of the workplace cannot be ignored for long and here the battle was joined between a union bureaucracy which was anxious to do nothing to rock the boat for Labour, and the needs of ordinary workers in their day to day defence of jobs, pay and conditions. The effect of New Labour is seen here at its clearest.

Prospects for a Blair government

The ability of Labour to speak left when it suits should never be underestimated. But even in these circumstances, Labour was unlikely to be different in national rather than local government. Twelve years of Labour rule in Australia produced a drop in real wages of 30 percent, along with the most savage union busting operation in the country's history against building workers. In Spain the government of Felipe Gonzales, the Blair of his day, produced 20 percent unemployment, the highest in Europe. Only one third of those unemployed received state benefits. New Zealand, where the Labour government embraced the 'rigours of competition', alone outstripped Britain in terms of wealth inequality.

British Labour, before the 1997 election, only announced what policies it had abandoned. Blair said he had 'the guts, the decency, the honesty to tell it to people how it really is, to not make promises we can't deliver'.[231] We know 'how it really is'—mass unemployment, poverty and decaying services. But Blair's Labour was 'liberated from particular policy prescriptions'[232] and so how he would deal with this reality was left unsaid. Some papers drew their own conclusions. The *Independent* commented: 'So Blair—a Labour leader—seeks to inherit the radical mantle that Margaret Thatcher's Tory successor let drop'.[233] The *Financial Times* agreed that the next Labour government would be a 'third Tory party' offering 'policies any One Nation Tory could support with a strong heart and a clear conscience'.[234]

How would Labour relate to the key social groups? Blair told the TUC: 'We have an obligation to listen, as we do to the employers. You have the right to persuade, as they do'.[235] He gave a clue as to which he would find most persuasive. Blair's government would encourage 'a true meritocracy'[236] since, 'the country needs entrepreneurs and people who can go out and make an awful lot of money',[237] while the rest would face: 'Ever more intense competition, ever more creative innovations and ever more advanced skills have made insecurity at work a permanent feature of life'.[238]

If Blair's close ally Peter Mandelson was anything to go by, the sort of policies that would be followed could include:

> coalition with the Lib Dems;...abolition of universal child benefit;... 'workfare' programmes for the unemployed and single mothers;... no-strike deals in the public sector;...major emphasis on private pensions...all schools to be free of local authority control.[239]

A favourite theory of Labour lefts like Ken Livingstone was that rapid disillusionment with a Blair government would lead to a dramatic swing to the left in the party such as occurred in 1931 and 1979. However, it is important to notice how short term these swings were. The longer term effect was quite the opposite—a major shift to the right caused by disillusionment and the desire to win back office at any cost.

Stakeholding

By the end of 1995 it seemed Labour and Tories had mimicked each other to a Parliamentary standstill. *The Economist* was amazed to witness that 'Blair went so far as to steal the Tories ancient ace, the patriotic card... By the end Mr Blair's colleagues were not the only ones who must have been wondering what the Tories had left to throw at them'.[240] Austin Mitchell, MP, warned that the electorate will be furious to discover that 'Tory Tweedledum' has merely been replaced by 'Labour Tweedledee'. He added: 'To come to power with not an idea in our head on how to face the crisis which will hit us is to invite disaster'.[241]

Labour needed an idea of its own and came up with 'stakeholding' which Blair set out in Singapore in January 1995. Stakeholding, said Will Hutton, whose book *The State We're In* seemed to be the idea's source, put 'red water' between Labour and the Conservatives.[242] Its redness was doubtful. Hutton's argument was for a modernised Keynesianism which made no pretence at being socialist. In his chapter entitled 'Stakeholder capitalism' Hutton said 'the object is to keep the merits of private ownership while reshaping the way it works'.[243]

In fact, like Labour confronting Keynesianism in 1931, whenever Labour was pressed to back the stakeholder theory with detail it ran for cover. The CBI asked for assurances that the new slogan would not strengthen workers' rights. Labour rushed to agree. The party had already promised to introduce the European Social Chapter (including some rights to union recognition) and a minimum wage so nothing had been added by the stakeholding policy, since 'all the history shows, if you pass rules and regulations to try and force someone to change their culture, it doesn't work'.[244]

Blair's choice of Singapore as a venue was not accidental. He had come to study a country where 'there are restrictions on individual rights, the banning of labour organisations, tight controls on the press and the subordination of citizens rights to internal security'.[245] The political system of the so called Asian tiger economies has been aptly described as 'Happy face fascism'. South Korea, for example, locked up more trade union leaders than any other country. Blair showed particular interest in Singapore's welfare system which he said 'has certainly done the job'. *The Guardian* noted 'the irony of British politicians coming back to study a savings system first conceived by Singaporean British colonial rulers [which is] designed to look after the needs of the workers when they retire in a [society] that offers no social security benefits or subsidised health service'.[246] *The Economist* thought 'There is indeed much to be said for such a system, which amount to abolishing the universal state pension, but it wonders if 'Mr Blair could convince his party that scrapping Britain's biggest universal benefit was what they meant by social cohesion and the stakeholding economy'.[247]

Blair's stakeholding was based on faith in 'a cohesive society, one nation'.[248] He had made the 'moral assertion that individuals are interdependent, that they owe duties to one another as well as themselves...the belief that only by recognising their interdependence will individuals flourish, because the good of each does depend on the good of all, that the good society backs up the efforts of the individuals within it'.[249] This exciting new idea turned out to be strangely reminiscent of the speeches of Lord Salisbury, who, in 1880, professed his belief in:

> a homogeneous people. It is only a people who in the main are agreed—who upon deep questions that concern a community think with each other, who have sympathy with each other, and havc common interests...it is only people who have these conditions of united action who can have any prospect of prosperity and success.[250]

Lord Salisbury was a Victorian Tory Prime Minister, a 'self-proclaimed enemy of democracy' who described socialists as 'looters'.[251] Blair's New Labour reeked of very old one nation Toryism.

None of this solved the basic contradiction that faced Blair when he was elected. What would happen when the millions who for years have been gritting their teeth and containing their pent up anger, found Blair carrying on with more or less the same policies as the Tories? How would they feel when the massive gap between rich and poor grew under market conditions, when people still died because there were no available NHS beds, the school roof continued to leak, and the boss still treated them with contempt?

18

New Labour in government

How new was New Labour?

The Labour governments of 1997 to 2010 form a remarkable phase in the Party's history. In 1997 the Party won the biggest parliamentary majority since 1935, gaining a record 419 MPs. The Tories had 'not been smashed so thoroughly since the Great Reform Act of 1832'.[1] That was just the start. When Labour finally fell from office, Blair could claim 'I won three general elections. Up to then, Labour had never even won two successive full terms. The longest Labour government had lasted six years. This lasted thirteen'.[2]

There is another perspective. Between 1980-84 Britain occupied the lowest band of social inequality among 30 EU and OECD countries. Under New Labour it joined an exclusive club at the top, alongside Latvia, Lithuania, Portugal, Romania and the US.[3] Britain and the US also shared bottom place for social mobility.[4] Therefore, 'on all measures of income inequality, the situation worsened somewhat under Labour'.[5] Even the *Financial Times* noted 'the very rich have grown richer at double the pace of most Britons...'[6] As early as 2001, Liz Davies, a left-wing member of Labour's NEC, decided to quit because: 'Taken as a whole, its record on asylum, civil liberties, privatisation, cuts in welfare provision, its attacks on the poor, its subservience to big business, and its willingness to bomb people in other countries had made [standing] impossible...'[7]

There is a common view that these electoral triumphs (and betrayals) happened because 'New Labour' was, as it claimed, a break from all that came before. When asked for her greatest achievement Thatcher declared: 'Tony Blair and New Labour'.[8] From the opposite end of the spectrum Davies saw something 'qualitatively different from the old broad alliance that used to make up the Labour Party. The argument within the labour movement used to be over how effectively, and at what speed, the Labour government was taking steps to ameliorate the worst excesses of capitalism. It was taken for granted that there should be some progress towards greater equality and redistribution. That is no longer the case'.[9]

An alternative is to see New Labour as the ultimate vindication of Ralph Miliband's argument, made as far back as 1961: 'Of political parties claiming socialism to be their aim, the Labour Party has always been one of the most dogmatic—not about socialism, but about the parliamentary system. Empirical and flexible about all else, its leaders have always made devotion to that system their fixed point of reference and the conditioning factor of their political behaviour...'[10] This stresses continuity and would see New Labour emanating from the Party's fundamental outlook. Which is correct?

'The most popular government ever!'[11]

Alastair Campbell, Blair's spin doctor, based this judgement on polls in *The Sun* and *Telegraph*.[12] In isolation the parliamentary arithmetic looks impressive. However, further analysis is revealing. Labour's strong polling (from a 7 percent deficit to a 30 percent lead over the Tories) followed sterling's plunge in value on Black Wednesday, September 1992.[13] With their economic reputation destroyed the Tories scored 29 percent in the June 1994 Euro elections, their lowest vote share ever in a national contest.[14] This was a month *before* Blair became Labour leader.

New Labour was not embraced enthusiastically. The Party's share of votes in 1997 was 'lower than it had achieved in all elections from 1945 to 1966, including the three it lost in a row in the 1950s,' because Labour's heartlands 'were distinctly lukewarm'.[15] At 71 percent, turnout was the poorest since WWII, and *worse* in typical Labour seats than in Conservative ones. Only 31 percent of the total electorate voted for Blair.[16] His spectacular win was helped by Tory collapse, tactical voting, and the peculiarities of the first-past-the-post system.[17] If New Labour made a difference it was that support now rested on shakier foundations. Turnout fell most sharply 'among the trade unionists, working-class council tenants and the unemployed', while 'one third of Labour's 1997 support was drawn from people who had not voted for the party in 1992'[18] and could readily desert.

In the 2001 election Labour's majority fell by only 14 seats. But underlying this was the loss of 3 million votes, 'a far bigger drop than that suffered by any of the Conservative governments elected between 1983 and 1992... At 42 percent Labour's share of the British vote was less than that secured by any other post-war government bar the two administrations formed by Labour in 1974'.[19] Equally striking was the 59 percent turnout—the lowest since 1918 (the 'Khaki Election' when millions of servicemen were abroad and so were excluded).[20] Turnout was again lower in Labour areas than Tory ones.[21] Labour won because the Tories again did so badly.

2005 saw turnout rise marginally because a close result was expected and the Iraq war provided a focus, but Labour's majority fell to 66, and vote share declined further. With Blair 'an election liability' and 'his credibility battered', fewer than 21.5 percent of the overall electorate voted Labour.[22] Britain's electoral system still masked fundamental New Labour weaknesses.

When Tony Blair stepped down, his Chancellor, Gordon Brown, took over and lost the 2010 election. Blair stated the Party could have 'gone on longer, had it not abandoned New Labour'.[23] He was hinting at the notorious conflict over when he would relinquish the premiership, wittily described by Rawnsley as the 'TB/GBs'. Blair's 2002 Conference speech and Brown's riposte were symptomatic. Blair bragged of his readiness to ditch left policies, telling delegates: 'We're at our best when we're at our boldest'.[24] In 2009 Brown's punchline was: 'This Labour Party, best when we're united—best when we are Labour'.[25] If their lengthy memoirs[26] are to be believed, TB represented New Labour while GB's heart held traditional Labour's values.

Unfortunately, Brown's premiership bore all the hallmarks of its predecessor. He too invited Thatcher to 10 Downing Street. His 'government of all the talents' included a former director of the CBI and former head of the Navy. Lib Dem MPs took on projects and Tory MPs acted as advisers.[27] 'Labour politicians—and not only predictable Blairites—began...to wonder if his 13-year campaign to become Prime Minister had more to do with just being Prime Minister rather than for what he would do once he had the office'.[28] His first Conference speech as PM confirmed suspicions: 'In the 1990s Tony and I asked you to change policy to meet new challenges. We are and will always be a pro-enterprise, pro-business and pro-competition government... And we pay special tribute to the heroism of our armed forces...in Iraq and in Afghanistan'.[29]

Brown's disgraced spin doctor, Damian McBride, explains that while that 'angry, bitter soap opera-style rivalry...continued, it was the only political story that mattered. No one else, least of all the Conservative Party could get a look in'. It was akin to the Cola Wars: 'Coke vs Pepsi remains the only real choice there is, despite being—to the undiscerning palate—essentially the same product'.[30] Thus Brown oversaw 2010's defeat flying New Labour colours. Five million voters had abandoned Labour since 1997.[31]

The myth was touted that New Labour was 'clutching at every opinion-poll straw in the wind and prepared to ditch policies at the slightest hint of disapproval'.[32] In fact its abject subservience to big business (such as with privatisation) and US imperialism ran directly counter to majority opinion. Claims to be a brilliant vote-winning machine were therefore largely a fraud. The Tories were already in trouble beforehand, and New Labour's right-wing policies undermined its future. But within the Party the con-trick worked because 'victory at the ballot box had always been [New Labour's] trump card, and its answer to all criticisms'.[33]

New Labour and class

Hitherto this book has shown that once in office running the system usually takes precedence over Labour's reformist promises. New Labour was different. Two years *before* 1997 Kinnock, whose 'New Realism' had shifted the Party rightwards, was exasperated that Blair had 'sold out before he's even got there... Tax, health, education, unions, full employment, race, immigration... It won't matter if we win, the bankers and stockbrokers have got us already, by the fucking balls, laughing their heads off'.[34] The accusation was accurate. Blair's memoir says: 'Thatcher had done the right thing in liberating enterprise and industry... Above all we had to divest power away from the dominant interest groups, unions and associations,' by which he meant diminishing the strength of the organised working class in favour of the bosses.[35] Privately Blair said, after meeting the Unison leader, 'they can just fuck off', while Transport Union officials were 'stupid and they are malevolent'.[36]

Campbell recounts that regarding the promised minimum wage, Blair: 'was amazed that the Low Pay Commission was recommending from £3.50 to £3.75. He was off on one, ranting that they were all going native and not understanding the bigger picture and have they thought of the effect on business?... He said just because we have some superhumanly mad people running the unions does not mean we are obliged to meet them halfway in their madness. [One of Blair's advisors] slipped me a note—"Has he been seeing Thatcher again?"'[37] Over the commitment to amend anti-union laws Blair told *The Sun*: 'The changes that we do propose would leave British law the most restrictive on trade unions in the Western World.' This prompted *The Independent* to comment on 'how extraordinary this historic settlement is. Here is the leader of a party founded by the trade unions, who still hold 50 percent of the votes in Labour's policy-making conference and who still pour millions into party coffers, striking a balance...in favour of the right of managers to manage'.[38] New Labour's paltry concessions did nothing to loosen the anti-union legal straitjacket and union membership fell by half a million by 2010. Even so Blair complained about unions resisting, telling an audience of bosses 'I bear the scars on my back'.[39]

Such contempt led Brendan Barber, head of the TUC, to conclude the Party 'didn't want them around, didn't want the link at all'.[40] The GMB leader warned he might 'have to look for a political partner that would advance the interests of people we represent'.[41] The Communication Workers Union Deputy General Secretary declared: 'If you asked our members how much they want to give to Labour at the moment I reckon that from the 200,000 of them you'd get £5. That's not £5 each—it's £5 between them'.[42] Bill Morris of the Transport Union complained that by 'describing trade unionists as wreckers and dinosaurs Labour is creating a dangerous divide between the party and its natural supporters'.[43]

While the majority of unions cut their financial contributions, the TSSA (white collar rail union) and CWU resolved to disaffiliate, though the votes were not binding. In the end, only the RMT (a founding union of the Party), and the FBU (whose 2002 strike was demonised and defeated by the government) did so.[44] Notwithstanding a number of left leaning general secretaries being elected (collectively known as 'the awkward squad'), the link was not broken. Transport Union leader Tony Woodley typified the approach: 'I don't support breakaways from Labour, there is just no sense in it. So we need a real change of leadership to one that remembers the roots of the trade unions and Labour Party. There are people like Gordon Brown, but there are others'.[45]

Faced with organising mass industrial action or relying on Labour, the majority of bureaucrats always tended towards the latter course. They were under little pressure to do otherwise. As one writer pointed out in 2015, 'In *every* year since 1991 the number of strikes has been lower than the number of strikes in *any* year prior to 1991'.[46] This does not excuse the leaders' quiescence, however. Observing matters from within Labour's NEC, Davies wrote: 'The trade union representatives were the only people at the meetings with a real chance to challenge New Labour's agenda...[But with few exceptions] none of the other trade union representatives uttered so much as a whisper of protest at privatisation, cuts to public sector workers, the low level of the minimum wage, or the government's pensions policy. Yet nearly all of them represent unions opposed to privatisation, and in favour of an index-linked minimum wage, and restoring the link between pensions and earnings…'[47]

The contrast between the way New Labour treated unions and capitalists could not have been sharper. An arena where the two mingled was Labour Conference. In 1995 the union bloc vote at Conference was cut to 50 percent. In 1998 trade unions (and constituency parties) lost the right to submit motions. Meanwhile, that year 'out of 20,000 people attending Conference, only 1,500 were Party or trade union delegates. 18,500 were lobbyists, business representatives or journalists. For £700, a corporate executive could purchase breakfast with government ministers, a ringside seat to watch the Prime Minister deliver his speech to Conference and attendance at an evening cocktail party to meet cabinet ministers. Donors who had given more than £25,000 to the Party were treated to a free private lunch with cabinet ministers before Blair's speech, and tea with the Prime Minister immediately after he had delivered his speech.'[48]

These exorbitant sums reflected New Labour's plan to wean the Party off union finance. For the first time 'high value donors' matched contributions from workers. With tainted money came sleaze, an accusation Labour had eagerly thrown at Major's government. Blair described himself as 'a pretty straight sort of guy',[49] but when Formula One's Bernie Ecclestone, the Tory tycoon, gave Labour £1 million (in what *The Guardian* called 'an astonishing political u-turn')[50] racing was mysteriously exempted from a ban on tobacco advertising.

Later many were surprised the government decided to maintain an unelected House of Lords despite its 'modernising' constitutional changes, such as Scottish and Welsh devolution, and Northern Ireland's Good Friday Agreement (that ended armed conflict but left sectarianism entrenched). There was a reason. Blair created more peerages than any previous PM[51] and all but one of the £1 million-plus donors to Labour was a recipient. Here Blair emulated Lloyd George, who sought an independent financial basis within a fractured Liberal Party.[52] Allegations of 'cash for honours' led to Blair becoming the first serving PM interviewed by police in a criminal investigation.[53]

New Labour's fawning extended to newspaper editors of whatever political stripe. Blair's 'lavished attention' on Rupert Murdoch (News International) and Paul Dacre (*Daily Mail*), while *The Mirror*'s Piers Morgan was astonished to receive hospitality amounting to '22 lunches, 6 dinners, 6 interviews, 24 further one-to-one chats over tea and biscuits, and numerous phone calls.'[54]

Many commentators assume the government's approach was attributable to Blair. He is rightly described as a 'non-political Conservative implicitly accepting the assumptions and values of a typical middle-class English Conservative'.[55] But New Labour outlived Blair and was embraced by numerous figures with impeccable Labour backgrounds. For example, Employment Minister Alan Johnson, himself a former CWU general secretary said of the 'awkward squad': 'The TUC left Planet Zog 20-odd years ago, but a few union leaders go back for the occasional day trip'.[56] Peter Mandelson, grandson of a Minister in Attlee's government, told US executives that New Labour was 'intensely relaxed about people getting filthy rich,' but he disdained 'blue-collar, working-class, north, horny-handed, dirtly-overalled people'.[57]

As Chancellor, Gordon Brown took responsibility for overall economic policy. His view was that elected representatives had no business interfering with capitalism. Their duty was merely to provide a stable environment for it. His first measures—cutting corporation tax to its lowest rate[58] and having the Bank of England independently setting interest rates—exemplified the approach. The latter policy had been advocated by recent Tory Chancellors, but Thatcher and Major wanted to retain the politicians' ability to influence the economy.[59] Brown's move saw shares surging to levels unknown for years.[60]

His vision was set out in a 1999 lecture promising 'for the first time in this generation—a sound and credible platform for long term stability for the British economy.' Labour was already committed to 'eye-wateringly tight'[61] Tory spending plans for its first two years, and Brown promised: 'We will not make the old mistake of relaxing our fiscal discipline the moment the economy starts to grow. The same tough grip will continue'.[62]

The lecture's main subject was full employment—a traditional Labour theme. Context, however, is everything. Full employment can mean people finding the work they want, or capitalists exploiting the maximum number possible. That Brown wanted the latter was shown by his 'New Deal which offers opportunities to work but demands obligations to do so'. Referring to 1.2 million claimants and one million vacancies, he implied a mass of poor people were too lazy to work. For those already in work 'wage responsibility...is a price worth paying to achieve jobs now and prosperity in the long term.' Whose prosperity? Under Thatcher and Major real household disposable income rose on average 3.1 percent per year. Under New Labour, even before the 2008 Crash, income growth dropped to 2 percent per year.[63] 'Wage responsibility' did not extend to the bosses: 'From 1996 to 2003, the highest paid directors of stock-market listed companies had double-figure percentage pay rises each and every year. In 2001 *Management Today* found that the average salary of the chief executives of British companies was £509,000—up by one third on 1999. They were the best-paid bosses in Europe. The only executives to earn more were American executives. British salaries were 33 percent above French chief executives, who were the next highest paid on £382,128. Swedish executives had to get by on £311,400, while the Germans, at the bottom of the pay pile were close to beggary with £298,223'.[64]

Taking the classic neoliberal line Brown saw capitalism as a self-regulating mechanism best left undisturbed. Therefore, he would end the 'fifty years of endless and sterile divisions between capital and labour, between state and market, and between public and private sectors...' Then came his fateful, and oft-repeated claim: there would be no 'returning to the boom and bust of the past'.[65] The Iron Chancellor's public speeches may have been more elegant than Blair's private rantings against organised workers, but in class terms they amounted to exactly the same.

New Labour was lucky at first. Rising exploitation and increasing personal debt (by 2005 private household debt equalled 102 percent of GDP),[66] a bubble in house prices, cheap money from Asia, and non-inflationary growth, helped Britain's GDP rise a third before the 2008 crash.[67] This was ahead of the other G6 countries (Germany, US, France, Japan and Italy)[68] and provided ideal conditions for a genuine reformist programme. New Labour could watch the wealth gap widen, keep to promises of no income tax rises, and still spend money in a consistently progressive direction. But that was not to be.

Public spending

Initially the increase in public spending was cautious—1.4 percent more between 1997 and 2001, while tax revenues rose 4 percent.[69] Later funding for the flagships of the NHS and education more than doubled in real terms,[70] while benefits for those with children rose by half.[71] Unfortunately, the policies were laced with poison.

The New Deal was typical of their duplicitous nature. It was touted as helping the unemployed find jobs—'from a hand-out to a hand-up'—with £3.6 billion investment from a windfall tax on utilities.[72] Whatever the immediate benefit to the 400,000 covered, long-term it reoriented the welfare system towards policing the working class: 'the sanctions attached to the New Deal would be tough'[73] said Brown. Single parents' benefits were cut if they did not seek work because, as *The Guardian* noted: 'Blair has put "moral" on the masthead... Moral means to him what it did to Octavia Hill in the 1880s: the evils of poor people fornicating'.[74]

Working family tax credits were similar. Families gained, but so did low-wage employers, and the sub-text was to stigmatise claimants—'Work now pays—now go to work'.[75] The aim was to force people into low-paid jobs, which is the real meaning behind Brown's statement: 'The more our welfare to work reforms allow the long-term unemployed to re-enter the active labour market, the more it will be possible to reduce unemployment without increasing inflationary pressures'.[76] When coupled with reduction in the value of unemployment benefit (compared to earnings),[77] and a low minimum wage, 'the overall impact in the period from 1999 to 2007 was to shift a sizeable minority of households from workless to in-work poverty'.[78]

Another double-edged policy concerned the NHS. Between 1997 and 2007 funding grew by 5.9 percent per year compared to 3.2 percent for 1975-1996.[79] Its share of national income rose by a third[80] lifting the UK to around the OECD average. Waiting times for treatment were slashed, in-patient or day case treatments grew by a third,[81] cancer deaths fell 22 percent, and so on.[82] The problem was the conditions attached.

One was partial privatisation. Between 2006 and 2011 the NHS spent 55 percent more on non-NHS care.[83] A 76 percent increase in secondary care funding was explained 'almost entirely by spending on independent sector providers'.[84] Blair also introduced foundation hospitals as a 'breach in the wall of the monolith...to be followed by choice, by the introduction of the private sector...'[85] He and Health Minister, Alan Milburn, wanted all hospitals to take this path, but Brown resisted.[86] The Chancellor's opposition was not on principle. He feared the Exchequer would pick up the tab for self-managing institutions going bust.[87] In Labour's last six years the business agenda meant health manager numbers rose at double the rate of nurses.[88]

Education tells a similar story. In New Labour's final decade spending increased from 4.5 percent to 6.4 percent of GDP,[89] and class sizes fell.[90] However, under the cloak of 'increasing choice and diversity' Labour expanded Tory specialist schools fivefold.[91] University maintenance grants were abolished and tuition fees introduced. Performance-related pay for teachers was brought in. Then came academies which give control to businesses and individual entrepreneurs within the public education system. Labour continued with Tory school performance tables. In 1997 18 schools were 'named and shamed'. By 2008, 683 faced closure if they did not 'improve'.[92] By 2010 the education of one in twenty children was under private supervision.[93] One study concludes that 'there was a good deal of continuity with the reforms of the Thatcher and Major governments in the sense that education continued to be defined as a servant of economic growth and international competitiveness and positioned as a private rather than a public good...'[94]

That one in five pupils studied in brand new or refurbished buildings[95] highlights another facet of Labour's spending—the Private Finance Initiative (PFI), a Tory policy from 1992.[96] Instead of the government building schools, hospitals and other infrastructure this would be done privately, and the public would pay for their use—typically over 25 to 30 years. Major's government signed 21 deals, Blair's—850.[97] In 2007-8 alone 55 deals were struck worth £5.5bn. The frenzy ended with the Crash. In 2016 Cameron's government only signed one deal[98] due to 'concerns about cost efficiency and value for money'.[99] Spending £53bn on PFI meant it cost £25bn more than if the state had carried out the building itself.[100] and the public sector will be saddled with £199 billion debt (£7.7 billion per year) until the 2040s.[101] PFI typified New Labour's devious approach—eye-catching spending figures now, but a shift to privatisation in the long-term.

The New Labour vision was that: 'We've put together economic prosperity and social justice' (John Prescott, Deputy PM); [102] 'We need vision and values—uniting economic prosperity to social justice.' (Tony Blair).[103] A Blairite MP neatly described 'the prospectus on which the New Labour project had been founded—that it was possible to combine economic efficiency with social justice in a viable political and electoral strategy'.[104] This prospectus was a fantasy. A system built on exploitation was bound to deliver both economic and social injustice.

The Home Office

In venerating capitalism New Labour inevitably also reflected its attitude towards the poor. Bosses see themselves as 'the wealth creators', not the reason for poverty and social problems. To do otherwise would be to condemn themselves. So if people are poor this must be self-inflicted. The core theory dates back to the 1834 Poor Law Reform Act, and was neatly expressed in the 1909 Majority Report on the Poor Law: 'where there is a failure of social self-maintenance there is a defect in the citizen character'.[105] Fundamental to the concept was targeting welfare based on a distinction between the 'deserving' (who due to unavoidable factors require help) and the 'undeserving' (whose defective character necessitates coercion). Thus Campbell was instructed to 'push the line that there was bad welfare spending and good welfare spending, we were dealing with one and expanding the other'.[106]

By contrast Labour's 1945 welfare state provided universal benefits, accepting arguments from people like Beatrice Webb. A founder of the Party, she was no revolutionary, but her 1909 Minority Report located the source of social problems in society, not individual failings.[107] Brown explicitly rejected that: 'some will always argue that all benefits should be universal, but I am in no doubt that the real challenge is to explain and popularise the more progressive policy (!) of doing more to help those who need help most'.[108]

A punitive approach was extended from single parents and the unemployed to the working class generally. Home Secretary, David Blunkett thought: 'those committed to a 21st century welfare state have to cease paternalistic and well meaning indulgence of thuggery, noise, nuisance and anti-social behaviour'.[109] Young and old were reproached: 'Where there is a problem, it is all too often because parents claim not to have the time, because they have disengaged... With such a lack of expectation [reinforcing] generations of disadvantage...it is the poverty of expectation and dedication which is the deciding factor.[110] Anti-Social Behaviour Orders followed, Blair suggesting that 'Twelve year old children should not be on the street at night'.[111] There were even curfews.

Criminalising the 'undeserving' working class fitted Blair's agenda of outdoing the Tories on law and order: 'There's no excuse for crime. None'.[112] So between 1997 and 2003 the government enacted 661 different crime bills, including ending jury trials for some cases.[113] Spending on police grew by a third.[114] Some stalwart Labour MPs were appalled. Hattersley blasted 'the Blairite Revolution', which like the 'Victorians of 1834 believed the poor were guilty of an offence. They had failed to maintain themselves.' 'Poverty', insisted Hattersley, 'is not a crime'.[115]

New Labour philosophy was applied to race and immigration. There were deserving migrants, useful to the economy, and those against whom the race card could usefully be played to outflank the Tories. In 2003 Blunkett affirmed that without legal migration 'growth would stall, economic flexibility and productivity would reduce'.[116] At the very same time the Home Office was bringing in 'tough reforms to reduce asylum claims'.[117] This included 14 years jail for bringing anyone labelled 'illegal immigrant' into the UK. Nick Cohen highlighted the hypocrisy. The crackdown began after Blair's first significant war—Kosovo. Labour's Immigration and Asylum Bill's 'unstated aim was to make it impossible for a refugee...to reach Britain legally. In all but rare circumstances, they would be forced to turn to criminal gangs and therefore, by definition, become "illegal immigrants", who were no better than criminals'.[118] Another Home Secretary, Jack Straw, insisted that refugees 'come in principally to claim cash benefits'.[119] Preventing them from working and providing assistance through a miserly voucher scheme ensured the demarcation between 'good' and 'bad' migrants was obvious to everyone. His Immigration Act also outlawed 'bogus marriages'.[120]

With Blair's wars generating ever larger numbers in flight, coupled with the accession of new countries to the EU, the PM became worried that 'The Tories had one good issue to beat us with: immigration'.[121] Not for nothing had he declared Enoch Powell, the notorious racist Conservative MP, to be 'one of the great figures of 20th-century British politics, gifted with a brilliant mind'.[122] So shortly before the 2005 election the PM proposed limiting all immigration using the Australian points system. Yet, as was pointed out at the time: 'it wasn't immigration that ripped the guts out of working-class Britain, white and non-white. It was the closure of whole industries, the run-down of manufacturing and council housing, the assault on trade unions, the huge transfer of resources to the wealthy, the deregulation of the labour market, and the unconstrained impact of neoliberal globalisation...'[123]

Each time Labour made concessions on the race issue it assisted the right. While those fleeing oppression and misery suffered, one beneficiary was the neo-Nazi British National Party, whose leader, Nick Griffin, noted: 'The asylum-seeker issue has been great for us... This issue legitimates us'.[124] Its vote rose from 45,000 in 2001 to 192,000 in 2005.[125] As PM, Brown went as far as using the BNP slogan 'British jobs for British workers'.[126] In 2009 two BNP members were elected as MEPs.

The legitimacy Griffin referred to was revealed by polling. In 1997 immigration did not even figure as one of the public's twelve key election issues.[127] By 2001 it was in ninth place.[128] In 2005, with Labour's manifesto saying 'It's not racist to impose limits on immigration', polls found 58 percent thought laws should be much tougher[129] and 'the salience of immigration rose to levels not witnessed in British politics for more than 25 years'.[130] By the time Labour lost, in 2010, immigration was in second place.[131] Ironically, the thanks New Labour got for pandering to racism rather than denouncing it was that when people were asked 'Who does Labour most want to help?' the answer given tended to be 'immigrants and non-whites'.[132]

Closely connected to this evolution of attitudes were issues of war and terrorism.

War—at home and abroad

Blair wants to be remembered for Labour's longest period of rule, but will always be reviled as Tony B*liar,* cheerleader for US President George Bush's 'war on terrorism'. The media focussed on a 'dodgy dossier' manipulating intelligence data about Saddam Hussein's non-existent weapons of mass destruction, and breaches of international law. The fallout included the alleged suicide of a government scientist, resignation by the BBC's Director General, and three enquiries (the last—led by Chilcot—took seven years to deliver the largest report ever produced). Unfortunately, the official narrative ignores the key issue of imperialism. Chilcot, for example, wrote that although there was no threat from Saddam, 'Military action might have been necessary at some point...'[133]

Nonetheless, his enquiry usefully summarises the scale of the disaster: a minimum of 134,000 Iraqi civilians killed, with *The Lancet* estimating 600,000; 3.9 million refugees, 2 million of whom fled the country, the rest being internally displaced; 4,806 military personnel of the invading Coalition dead; and a cost to the UK of £9.6 billion.[134] The ramifications continue. In July 2018 Iraqi demonstrators were killed for protesting that: 'Since the fall of Saddam in 2003...we still drink filthy water and forgot what air conditioning means during summer'.[135]

Blair, as an individual, played a key role in British involvement. No less central a figure than Gordon Brown entitles a chapter of his memoir 'Iraq: How we were all misled'.[136] It is peppered with phrases like: 'As we were later to discover...'[137] He writes: 'I did not know until after I left office of the Blair-Bush telephone call in December 2001 in which Tony appeared to agree in principle to support the American-led intervention in Iraq'.[138] It is notable that Blair's strongest self-criticism is reserved for the 'blunder' of the 2001 Freedom of Information Act: 'You idiot. You naive, foolish, irresponsible nincompoop...'[139]

However, the PM's warmongering tendencies were no secret. Coming after engagements in Kosovo and Sierra Leone (1999), and Afghanistan (2001) Iraq meant 'he had sent British forces to fight and die in more theatres than any other Prime Minister since Churchill...'[140] Two years before the Iraq invasion, during the fight with Serbia's Milosevic, he laid out the exact programme he would follow. In the post-Cold War era of globalisation (which 'is not just economic, it is also a political and security phenomenon') Kosovo could not 'be seen in isolation...we are now in a new world. We need new rules...' The targets were already identified: 'Many of our problems have been caused by two dangerous and ruthless men—Saddam Hussein and Slobodan Milosevic'. Blair asked: 'how do we decide when and whether to intervene?' His tests included: 'are there military operations we can sensibly and prudently undertake?' and, 'do we have national interests involved?' To the US he said: 'You are the most powerful country in the world, and the richest. You are a great nation. You have so much to give and to teach the world...' Therefore Britain and its EU partners must execute a 'real step-change in working more closely together' with America.[141]

Blair did not invent Britain's 'special relationship' with the US, although he enthusiastically embodied it, as evidenced by his grovelling to Bush when a microphone was inadvertently switched on. Bush began with 'Yo Blair. How are you doin?' after which the PM humbly offered himself as US envoy to the Middle East. The President replied his Secretary of State covered that role. 'Well,' said Blair, 'it's only if, I mean, you know, if she needs the ground prepared as it were. Because obviously if she goes out, she's got to succeed, whereas I can go out and just talk'.[142]

Whatever his personal inclinations, Blair reflected British state interests as he saw them. The collapse of the Soviet Union had discredited state economic intervention (including its Keynesian western variant) and underpinned New Labour's craven submission to market forces at home and abroad. On the level of inter-state relations a relatively stable system with two superpowers and their satellites, had given way to a disordered unipolar world offering opportunities for the US to step in. Whether it was President Bill Clinton's subtler version, or the 'neocon' Project for a New American Century and 'full spectrum dominance'.[143] New Labour politicians then dressed this up under the term 'globalisation', presented as a sort of natural and inevitable phenomenon, like weather.

Britain's imperial decline made it a junior partner to the US in exerting influence. As *International Socialism* put it: 'Far from being an aberration, Blair was the culmination of the Labour Party's post-1945 commitment to the American alliance'.[144] Hog-tying British foreign policy in the Middle East to the US was the geopolitical equivalent of handing economic levers over to the Bank of England. Blair's wars were therefore not proof of personal subservience but 'the maintenance of a transatlantic-bridge strategy, designed as a means to enhance and project British power and influence on the world stage by positioning Britain as a pivotal power between Europe and America'.[145]

Campbell's diaries reveal it was often Blair, rather than Clinton or Bush, who urged immediate action against Iraq. In February 1998 the PM 'was worried that we were overdoing the diplomatic rather than military'.[146] In November 'Clinton wanted a 24-hour delay [to bombing Iraq]. I immediately redrafted the statement to say TB had authorised the use of force... But the US did not want to refer to the authorisation of force... TB said he understood why Bill did it, but our general view was that we should have gone ahead without the pause...'[147] We cannot know what interventions might have happened had Blair not resigned, but this statement gives a clue: 'why we don't get rid of Mugabe, why not the Burmese lot. Yes, let's get rid of them all. I don't because I can't, but when you can, you should'.[148]

Brown would be equally committed to imperialism, writing: 'during all my time in government, whether as chancellor or prime minister, I never engaged in public criticism of Tony'.[149] While military defeat in Basra led him as PM to withdraw from Iraq on the advice of British commanders,[150] he threw money and extra troops at Afghanistan, and 'bent over backwards to meet every request for new equipment...'[151] His general view was expressed to an African audience: 'the days of Britain having to apologise for its colonial history are over... We should celebrate much of our past rather than apologise for it'.[152]

In 2001 Bush suggested invading Iraq was a necessary part of his 'war on terror', based on a straightforward lie—that Saddam was connected to the 11 September terrorist attack. Perversely, intervention stimulated the very terrorism it was supposed to suppress. Ken Livingstone (expelled from Labour for standing as London Mayor) pointed out the US National Intelligence Committee considered 'Iraq has become a breeding ground for terrorists that previously did not exist',[153] though it was a shame that after readmission he denied the link.[154] Even fervent British supporters of intervention like General Charles Guthrie recognised that Blair's condoning of 'Western use of torture to counter terror has been a propaganda coup for al-Qaeda and a recruiting sergeant for its global jihad'.[155] However, the PM now had a justification for domestic war on Muslims and civil liberties in line with New Labour's authoritarianism and targeting of those fleeing its wars.

A classic expression of this came from Straw, Home Secretary and MP for Blackburn's many Muslim constituents. He had no problem with murderous invasions but felt 'uncomfortable' when meeting someone wearing the veil: 'So I decided that I wouldn't just sit there the next time a lady turned up to see me in a full veil, and I haven't... I explain that this is a country built on freedoms... I thought a lot about raising this matter... But if not me, who? My concerns could be misplaced. But I think there is an issue here'.[156] Soon polls suggested Britons were 'more suspicious of Muslims than are Americans or citizens of any other major Western European country'.[157]

Straw's outburst coincided with failed attempts to enforce indefinite detention without trial for terror suspects, and Labour's first Commons defeat (for proposing 90 days' detention without trial).[158] A compromise of 28 days was ironed out—still the longest detention without charge in the Western world.[159] Later Brown extended it to 49 days, though like Blair previously, clinching the vote depended on non-Labour MPs, in this case the Democratic Unionist Party.[160]

New Labour's segregating 'good' and 'bad' welfare claimants, good and bad migrants, or good and bad Muslims, always fell apart. Injury to one was indeed injury to all. After a major expansion in deployment of armed police a Brazilian, wrongly identified as a terrorist, was shot dead. Blair 'felt desperately sorry for the officers involved who were acting in good faith'.[161] In 2006 preparatory legislation for ID cards was passed, and, as Rawnsley puts it: 'Britain became the most watched society on the planet. It had a fifth of the earth's CCTV cameras covering less than one hundredth of the world population. The number of organisations permitted to legally use invasive surveillance grew from nine in 2000 when the legislation was first passed to nearly 800 by 2009... In the meantime it built the largest DNA database in the world, far larger than its American equivalent'.[162] The former head of MI5 accused the government of making people feel 'we live in fear and under a police state',[163] while one historian noted: 'Not since the rule of Lord Liverpool, who served as prime minister between 1812 and 1827, had there been so comprehensive an attack on civil liberties...'[164]

Despite massive popular opposition (discussed below) Britain invaded Iraq, only to see its official excuse—the presence of weapons of mass destruction—completely disproved. In the 2005 election turnout increased marginally due to 'a generally increased determination to vote against the government'.[165] Iraq cost Labour around 3 percent of votes, but it survived due to factors that produced previous victories, and extra spending on public services.

Blair then infuriated Brown by hinting he would serve another full term, but his eventual decision to quit had little to do with the 'TB/GBs'. In 2006 the Israeli state killed up to 1,300 Lebanese (compared to 165 on its side). The PM refused to condemn the Israeli government because 'the occupation of Palestinian land may be an injustice, depending on your viewpoint, but this is a region with plenty of injustices'.[166] For even staunch New Labour MPs Lebanon was the last straw and they called for Blair to go. A Number 10 insider realised they were not the usual malcontents, commenting 'who'd be impressed if Jeremy Corbyn was a signatory.'

Quitting office in 2007 Blair continued his love affair with the rich and powerful by becoming the highest paid public speaker in the world, and through his various financial strategems (such as Tony Blair Associates) fostering links with dictatorial regimes under the pretext of 'giving advice.' With Blair gone Brown, not to be outdone, became the first British PM to address the Israeli Knesset.[167]

The 'no more boom and bust' prime minister

Even before his accession, Brown wielded considerable power. He even kept his Budget plans from Blair until just before they were announced[168] and, as Chancellor controlling the purse strings, determined economic policy and social services spending. Brown left his colleagues 'in no doubt that we had to embrace markets, competition and the essential role of the private sector in achieving economic growth...'[169] This was not rhetoric. 'I did promote some difficult privatisations... So where I thought competition, liberalisation, privatisation or tax incentives to be in the public interest, I would be not just supportive but leading the charge'.[170] He claimed this could 'deliver both a strong economy and a fair society...prosperity and social justice were not at odds with each other but inextricably bound together'.[171]

Brown's last speech as Chancellor on 21 March 2007 promised 'we will never return to the old boom and bust'.[172] On 14 September 2007 long queues stood outside Northern Rock bank in a panic.

Yet even earlier the hollowness of his conception was obvious. Between 2004 and 2006 'incomes fell for the poorest third of households, including skilled manual workers, unskilled workers and the out of work poor.' For middle incomes growth had 'been agonisingly weak since 2001'—15 percent above inflation until 2001 but only 4 percent in the following 5 years.[173] Disposable income fell 15 percent in the year before the crisis was felt.[174] Brown's policies played a direct part. After large cash injections helped buy election victory in 2005, he 'halved the growth rate of public spending' and began cutting the public sector workforce.[175] His final budget as Chancellor abolished the 10 pence starting rate for income tax, hitting 3 million of the poorest earners.

Nonetheless, 2008's Crash was a step change. Brown portrays himself as an innocent victim: 'It is true we were not prepared for what was happening... No one was.'[176] It did not require close reading of Marx's *Capital* to know 'no more boom and bust' was nonsense. Keynesian economists like Will Hutton poured scorn on the notion when it was first proclaimed: 'the whole point of the economics in which left-of-centre politics is rooted is that capitalism is definitionally unstable and its workings inequitable. There are vicious and virtuous cycles; credit booms and busts...'[177]

Brown was proud that by driving government spending to its lowest level since the late 1950s, and 'holding firm against demands for additional spending, we moved deficit into surplus.'[178] But with the City of London a major centre of world credit and finance, it made little difference that the Iron Chancellor's 'prudence' left Britain with 'lower debt than any other major country.'[179] The scale of casino capitalism here meant the UK suffered a 4 percent decline in GDP—the EU average.[180] This was not supposed to happen, since 'globalisation—sourcing capital from all over the world—had spread the risk and...reduced the risk.' As champion of 'the most pro-competition policy in the world...'[181] he had actively promoted the banking sector's innovative methods. New Labour, as Mandelson said in 1998, wanted an 'enterprise-orientated, risk-taking, failure-tolerant business culture...' Brown's last Mansion House speech as Chancellor announced 'a new Golden Age' had dawned. The City was making Britain 'a new world leader [by using] the most modern instruments of finance.'[182] He eventually admitted his beloved safeguards were in fact 'the driving force for disastrous contagion.'[183]

Afterwards Brown wrote that financial failure 'was the fallout from years of greed'[184] and 'rogue bankers should be jailed for running risks with other people's money.'[185] But in 2008 prudence, tough sanctions for anti-social behaviour, and stigmatising people who 'come in principally for cash payments', were unceremoniously thrown aside. Bank

CEOs were invited to the Treasury and offered £50 billion: 'They were shocked by the amount...and tried to halve it'.[186] Generosity incarnate, Brown and his Chancellor, Alistair Darling, announced £50 billion recapitalisation would go ahead, 'together with £250 billion credit guarantee for banks issuing debt and £200 billion of extra liquidity'.[187] Eventually the banks were nationalised (until safe to hand back). This Damascene conversion to government intervention did not indicate a long-term return to Keynesian policies. It was simply emergency surgery to save the life of capitalism, and the blood transfusion would come from ordinary people. £500 billion went to the rich, while Brown promised to 'cut costs, cut inefficiencies, cut unnecessary programmes and cut lower-priority budgets' for everyone else.[188]

The patient showed its gratitude for the multi-billion bailout by abandoning Labour at the 2010 election. 51 companies donated to the Tories £7m pot. Labour had three and once again relied on union donations which formed 66 percent of its £5m fund.[189] *The Sun* led the return of the national press to the Tories. Brown's plan to celebrate Britishness with the rabidly right-wing *Daily Mail* editor, Paul Dacre, also ended in tears.[190] In 2001 papers with a 71 percent share of circulation were for voting Labour. In 2010 the figure was 13 percent.[191]

Labour had lost its advantage over the Tories on economic competence. Moreover, when polled 63 percent of those asked felt Labour used to care for them, but only 19 percent felt it did so now, with the Party seen as caring more for 'welfare shirkers and immigrants'.[192] Brown fell victim to having pushed the political agenda rightwards. He laid the groundwork in his first speech to Labour conference as leader referring to 'Britain', 'British' or 'country' 112 times. It ended: 'I will stand up for British values. I will stand up for a strong Britain. And I will always stand up for you'.[193] The most notable incident of his election campaign was when he was overheard describing a Labour-supporting woman who complained about immigration as a 'bigot'. That 'the last glimmer of hope was extinguished' at Labour's campaign HQ (according to Rawnsley)[194] speaks volumes about how New Labour had convinced the public and itself that the movement of people was a central problem.

At the 2010 election the 'longest Labour government' had dragged the Party's vote share to 30 percent paralleling 1931—the highest drop for any ruling party between two elections.[195] Yet the debacle was not due to keenness for the Conservatives. The combined Labour/Tory vote was just two thirds of all those cast, a figure not seen for 90 years.[196] For that reason the election produced a coalition.

Brown was mocked for claiming his actions during the Crash had 'saved the world'. While establishing the interventionist template that other countries followed *had* saved world capitalism[197] ordinary people faced years of austerity, cuts and stagnant or declining living standards.

Inside and outside Labour

What of the government's relationship with the wider Party? Hattersley saw New Labour as 'a Cuckoo in the nest'.[198] A recent history says: 'Ensconced in Millbank Tower, the inner leadership formed a party within a party, autonomous and highly centralised'.[199] This argument carries weight.

Blair and co brought in an army of special advisers which not only alarmed the traditional civil service, but provided an apparatus independent of the Party with exceptional freedom of movement. The government projected itself directly through people like Alistair Campbell (for Tony Blair) and Damian McBride (for Gordon Brown) via the bourgeois media. Close relationships with people like Rupert Murdoch and business tycoons also exerted a powerful influence. Bypassing internal channels and activists Philip Gould's polling and focus groups provided an upward information flow.

We have already seen New Labour deliberately distanced itself from the trade unions, and the same applied to the Party. Previous governments had often ignored internal decision-making, as developed by Labour's annual conferences and the National Executive Committee, but any pretence was now abandoned. In their place was a National Policy Forum.[200] From the inside Davies reported: 'meeting in secret its deliberations are not open to the media or to party members (unlike annual conferences)...' Local parties were to hold forums on topics determined by Millbank, but 'No votes were taken at the forums. No motions were considered... There was no mechanism of any kind whereby local parties or individual members could chase up their input... Thus the body that was supposed to inform government policy with the views of Party members was dominated by the very people who were making and implementing government policy in the first place'.[201] Constituency parties' selection of prospective MPs now came from a list issued centrally.[202]

The impact on individual membership was devastating. Starting in 1992 Labour recruited an additional 150,000, reaching over 400,000 in total by 1997.[203] Blair's Sedgefield constituency saw a fivefold increase.[204] The total did not match the one million plus members of Attlee's era, but it now exceeded that of the Tories.[205] Yet after 1997 the decline was relentless. Numbers halved by the end of 2003, and were just 160,000 when Brown's government ended.[206]

The mood of the survivors was grim. In 1997 35 percent of members thought the leadership paid them little attention; by 1999 it was 53 percent.[207] One London activist wrote about 'sorrowful anger at the machinations, dishonesty, nepotism, vapid statements [and] sheer arrogance' of New Labour.[208] Blair was especially resented by members and described in 2001 as 'a man we believe to be the slipperiest, most profoundly disliked politician to hold the office of prime minister in our lifetime'.[209] By then: 'On the ground, across most of the country, the Party barely functioned. Most election activity was carried out by paid Party staff, the candidates and their families. Accounts of de-selection of popular councillors or Party officers after Millbank intervention were rife'.[210] In 2006 an MP confirmed 'the Party has disappeared. There are no local parties. There's nothing to campaign with. It's all top down and instructed from Party headquarters'.[211] One study concludes 'the United Kingdom offered the lowest level' of party membership as a proportion of the electorate in Europe.[212]

Those who clung on felt disengaged. In 2000 successful candidates for the NEC needed only half the votes required in 1997.[213] The impact was visible at Conference. By 2001 a third of constituency parties did not bother to send delegates since 'proceedings are of so little significance that the hall is half-empty, even for ministerial set pieces... And the delegates themselves have changed. It is rare to see anyone who is not dressed to the nines, often at some expense'.[214]

As already noted, a similar disillusion developed among the trade union bureaucracy. The government's centralised approach demoralised local councillors thus marking a 'continuing retreat from the municipal tradition that had sustained the movement since the 1920s'.[215] Even the Parliamentary Labour Party was alienated. In 1997 there was just one rebellion when 47 Labour MPs opposed cuts in benefit to single parents.[216] By 2003 there were 19 rebellions with a cumulative total of 925 Labour MP votes.[217] Brown's honeymoon period was brief and in his last two years as PM Labour MPs were rebelling in one in three votes.[218] This was the highest rate for any post-war Parliament.[219]

Is all this evidence of a political or ideological rift between the New Labour government (acting as a 'party within a party') and the members, trade unionists, councillors and backbench MPs in the movement? The evidence is complex.

The trend regarding individual members is revealed by their voting for the NEC. Of seven places available the left secured two in 1994 and three the following year. After Ken Livingstone beat Mandelson in 1997[220] the rules were changed to exclude MPs from the constituency section, and its seats were cut to six. The newly-formed left-wing Grassroots Alliance then took four seats, despite spending only £3,000 as against the hundreds of thousands paid by Millbank.[221] Impressive though this was, the advance was not sustained. Soon afterwards the Alliance's vote fell from 47 percent to 40 percent.[222] Disgruntled trade union leaders were easily bought off by the 2004 Warwick Agreement, which included provisions such as not selling off the Royal Mail (though Mandelson attempted to do just that in 2008).

Despite the numerous rebellions of MPs in the voting lobby, the left was in a parlous state. A good example was when Blair stepped down. That neither John McDonnell nor Michael Meacher were able to gather the 45 nominations needed to challenge Brown 'was a signal indication of the emasculation of the Labour left in Parliament'.[223] Union funding backed John Cruddas (centre-left) for Deputy Leader, but he still came third. The left Labour Representation Committee concluded 'we do not have a Party of Labour, the task is to build one'.[224]

The picture was entirely different beyond the narrow confines of Labour's internal world and parliament. There was an explosion of challenges and protests against New Labour showing the real strength of left-wing ideas in the country. This appeared at many levels. Though Labour MP Dennis Canavan was expelled for standing in the 1999 Scottish Parliamentary election, he won the largest majority of any MSP. At that same election Tommy Sheridan, another Labour expellee, was elected as Scottish Socialist Party MSP and joined by five others at the next poll. Millbank blocked Ken Livingstone from standing as Mayor of London and put up Frank Dobson. Members wanted Livingstone over Dobson 6/4, and the unions 7/3, but the MPs 87 percent for Dobson clinched it.[225] In London's mayoral vote Livingstone romped home with 200,000 votes more than Dobson, who was in third place, after what Davies described as the 'most solid strike by Labour's foot soldiers ever seen'.[226] In 2005 George Galloway, who was expelled for his stand over Iraq, overturned a 10,000 Labour majority to take Bethnal Green for the Respect Party.

The anti-globalisation movement was another channel for anger inspired by mass demonstrations in Seattle (1999) and Genoa (2001), but it was above all the anti-war campaign that expressed the mood. The impetus came from outside Westminster, though it led to the largest rebellions 'by MPs of any governing party—Labour, Conservative or Liberal—on any type of policy since modern British party politics began.' On 26 February 2003 121 Labour MPs voted against their government. On 18 March it was 139. These 'shattered all existing records... To find a larger rebellion than Iraq, you have to go back to the rebellion by Sir Robert Peel's MPs over Corn Laws' in 1846.[227] Significantly, those Parliamentary votes came *after* the largest demonstration in British history when, on 15 February, some 2 million people marched behind the banner of Stop the War. The previous Westminster vote on Iraq (November 2002) only attracted 30 rebels.[228] Over the key question of the moment the rebel MPs were led by the masses.

Inside Westminster Foreign Secretary Robin Cook resigned, but Blair was bolstered by Clare Short (International Development) failing to do so. Left-wingers like Diane Abbott, George Galloway and McDonnell were derided by their colleagues. However, outside, with polls showing 75 percent of the public against intervention in Iraq,[229] these MPs played a crucial role in the Stop the War Coalition, whose ranks included a vast number of Labour voters, sympathisers and (former) activists. Jeremy Corbyn deserves special mention here. He participated in founding the Coalition,[230] spoke at its first demonstration in 2001,[231] and helped expose the 'dodgy dossier'.[232] For him, 'being an activist in the anti-war movement and a Member of Parliament [was] akin to inhabiting parallel universes.' On 18 March he 'made several journeys through the police cordon to the warmth of the protest and then back to the cynicism of the tea room—two worlds 200 yards apart'.[233] Tony Benn was of a similar opinion: 'I live in two quite different worlds'[234] and his decision to leave parliament 'to devote more time to politics',[235] though tough in cheek, was revealing.

What the contradictory evidence regarding Party members, unions and MPs reveals, is that while Party supporters at all levels detested New Labour's unfair treatment of individuals and the practical consequences of its policies, this was not matched by widespread rejection of the belief that 'it was possible to combine economic efficiency [ie, capitalism] with social justice in a viable political and electoral strategy'.[236] Without this political alternative the left remained perilously weak.

Conclusion

This chapter began by asking whether or not the New Labour governments were an alien imposition on the Labour Party. Luxemburg, a

Marxist who analysed reformism at its inception, perfectly encapsulated the process at work in her 1900 formulation: 'people who pronounce themselves in favour of the method of legislative reform *in place and in contradistinction to* the conquest of political power and social revolution do not really choose a more tranquil, calmer and slower road to the *same* goal, but a *different* goal'.[237] The determination to ditch progressive reforms *even before* being elected, to attack the legacy of 1945 and their own supporters, while being 'intensely relaxed' about the 'filthy rich' *was new*, but was *also* a continuation down the road towards that 'different goal' from socialism. This signified the Blair/Brown governments were afflicted with more than an obsession with parliament. The ending of the Cold War and neoliberal turn of contemporary capitalism meant they lost even the basis for the sort of reformist ideology that underpinned the Attlee years.

So Thatcher was mistaken in claiming New Labour as her achievement. Attempting to square the needs of the mass of ordinary women and men with a system that oppresses and exploits them is bound to end in failure, though how this manifests itself varies according to the circumstances. It is true New Labour's ascendancy within the Party was secured by success on the electoral front (however ephemeral its roots were), but the trajectory was dictated by logic of reformism as it operates under capitalism. Yet the 1997-2010 period also revealed a parallel universe of politics outside of Westminster that could engage the enthusiasm and activity of millions, in a way that ticking a box once every five years could not.

19

From Miliband to Corbyn

GORDON BROWN resigned as Labour leader and then prime minister a few days after the 2010 election. The brothers David and Ed Miliband—sons of the Marxist writer Ralph Miliband—soon emerged as front runners for the leadership, with David seen as the favourite to win. There was much talk of the 'sibling rivalry', but there was political basis to their contest. David was the choice of the Blairites, and they identified Brown's failure to win the election as a result of deviation from the true cause of defending the bankers and celebrating imperialist adventures. David said he would be different to the Tories but would share their determination to slash the deficit. His pitch was to 'build our own story of political economy that embraces neither the masochism of [Tory chancellor] Osborne nor the denial of economic reality'.[1]

Ed said he was ready to make the break from New Labour and to question Blairism. 'It is my rejection of this New Labour nostalgia that makes me the modernising candidate at this election,' he said.[2] However, he added that, 'The New Labour model of minimally regulated markets combined with redistribution of income and wealth achieved significant progressive gains' and 'there is no escaping the need to make significant savings across government'.[3] There were other candidates—Ed Balls, Andy Burnham and left winger Diane Abbott, although Abbott managed to reach the ballot paper only through the support of right wingers who wanted it to be seen that there was a 'fair contest'.

Ed Miliband's partial move away from New Labour was enough to secure the backing of the three biggest unions—Unison, Unite and GMB—and this was to prove crucial. When the votes were counted, David had won narrowly among MPs and Labour members, but Ed had swept the union section by 60 percent to 40 percent, enough to secure his wafer-thin victory.[4] This marked the return of the union bureaucracy as a key influence within Labour following the brutal rejection of the Party by big business (despite all New Labour's wooing). The right-wing press and the hard Blairites reacted with fury to 'red Ed's' election. The man they had decided was the safest possible defender of the New Labour legacy had been defeated, and by trade unionists' votes. *The Sun* carried a cartoon which had Ed Miliband as a creature from another planet surrounded by trade unionists as little green men wearing cloth caps and chanting 'Shoot to Kill'. 'New Labour is dead,' lamented the *Daily Telegraph*, denouncing Ed Miliband's 'doctrinaire socialism'. 'Last rites for New Labour,' agreed the *Mail*.

Ed Miliband's victory reflected, in weak form, a growing disenchantment with pro-market policies and veneration of the gods of finance, particularly as the economic crisis was developing. He was the 'acceptable' and 'electable' face of a break from Blairism. Many Labour supporters wanted to move away from New Labour but not to embrace a clear socialist alternative. Just seven MPs backed Abbott. She came third in the members' vote in her own constituency.

Miliband made one important shift in a conference speech just after his election when he condemned the war in Iraq. He said, 'I do believe that we were wrong. Wrong to take Britain to war and we need to be honest about that.' There was nervous applause. He was saying the unsayable, that Blair and Brown had presided over a terrible mistake about Saddam Hussein's supposed weapons of mass destruction or, worse, had known the truth about the Iraqi regime but had backed the US anyway. However, Miliband's speech showed the limits of his critique of imperialism when he was strongly in support of continuing the occupation in Afghanistan.

Throughout his time as leader Miliband tried to mediate between those who wanted an end to Blairism and those on the right of the party. But trying to balance in practice meant that the pro-market, conservative forces won the ideological battle—and he was blocked from encouraging real resistance to the Tories. In the same speech where he said the Iraq war was wrong, he backed 'responsible trade unionism' but then said, 'I have no truck with overblown rhetoric about waves of irresponsible strikes. The public won't support them. I won't support them. And you shouldn't support them either.' He said, 'There will be cuts and there would have been if we had been in government. I won't oppose every cut the coalition proposes.' To those who had dubbed him 'Red Ed' he said, 'Come off it.' This conference balancing act was now to come into contact with reality.

Miliband and the resistance to austerity

Miliband was elected just as struggle against austerity was on the rise, in Britain and internationally. Most significant was a wave of revolutions across the Arab world. The end of 2010 saw Tunisia's dictator Ben Ali removed by popular revolt. In January Egypt exploded in rebellion. Within three weeks the dictator Hosni Mubarak has been forced out. In the Spanish state an anti-austerity movement focused on occupation of city squares began in May and soon drew in hundreds of thousands of people who were not just against a particular economic policy but were questioning the entire political establishment. In Greece the revolt against austerity saw a rising tide of strikes, street protests and student agitation. This would prepare the way for the virtual elimination of the social democratic party Pasok and the rise of the left-wing Syriza.

The year 2011 saw the curve of resistance turn upwards in most parts of the world. In Britain the Tory-Lib Dem government of David Cameron was determined to make working class people pay for the bailout of the bankers. But there was instantly a fightback. One of the governing coalition's earliest measures was to propose trebling university tuition fees to £9,000 a year. It was a total betrayal of a pledge that the Lib Dems had made at the election not to raise fees at all (Lib Dem leader Nick Clegg was later to apologise—for making the pledge, not putting up fees).

On 10 November more than 50,000 students and workers from universities and colleges across Britain marched in London against the fees and the wider marketisation of education in the biggest and angriest protest that had taken place against the new government. The demonstration was young, confident and furious. Activists blocked roads, hurled eggs at the Treasury and held an angry protest outside the business department. Then thousands laid siege to Millbank Tower, which now housed the Tory headquarters (since Labour could not afford the rent). Some occupied the building and around 50 got onto the roof—to deafening cheers from the protesters below. The day sent a clear and defiant message to the government—students won't stand for your attacks and we will fight alongside other groups to crack austerity. The protests spread to include large numbers of sixth form and other school students.

The 'violent' protest at Millbank was denounced initially by the leaders of the NUS student union, and the UCU lecturers' union. But not by Miliband. Labour leaders are sometimes aware enough to recognise when there is a great movement on the wing. In general Labour leaders will come down firmly against most strikers and protesters, especially those accused of violence—think of Neil Kinnock during the great 1984-5 miners' strike or deputy leader Roy Hattersley calling for 'exemplary sentences' for poll tax rioters in 1990. But while Miliband never did anything to build the student revolts, still less to spread them wider, he knew that there was a chance to grab large numbers of votes from the Lib Dems, and he grasped the opportunity. Protest was popular enough to avoid his denunciation.

Miliband's instincts were correct. An article in the *Daily Star* newspaper in the immediate aftermath of the 10 November march began, 'David Cameron has warned that anarchists behind London's student riots would be hunted down and prosecuted with the "full force of the law".' But hidden away at the bottom was the sentence '*Daily Star* readers remained split last night over whether the students were right to riot, with 54 percent saying yes and 46 percent saying no.' A clear majority of the paper's readers, far from demanding the 'full force of the law' against protesters, believed they were 'right to riot'. In the *Sunday Times* an opinion poll asked if people supported VIOLENT (their capitals) protests in a democracy—even though the student protest was not violent. One in five people signed up for violence. The same poll found that 77 percent supported increasing taxation on the very rich to reduce the gap in earnings between the richest and the poorest.

After another demonstration on 24 November Miliband said, 'I was quite tempted to go out and talk to them [the protesters]. Peaceful demonstrations are part of our society. As Labour leader I am willing to talk to people who are part of them'.[5] Following the riots in England in August 2011, he denounced the 'irresponsibility' of the looters and their 'law breaking'. But he also insisted society had 'to avoid simplistic answers'. Miliband spoke of an irresponsibility that applied not only to the people involved in the riots, but 'wherever we find it in our society. We've seen in the past few years...MPs' expenses, what happened in the banks'. And he admitted that Labour had not done enough to tackle what he called 'deep-rooted moral problems' during its 13 years in power. 'I deeply regret that inequality wasn't reduced under the last Labour government,' he told BBC Radio 4's *Today* programme.[6]

Miliband's real test came over mass workers' protests and strikes. On 26 March 2011 the biggest trade union demonstration in British history saw 500,000 take to the streets. Miliband spoke to it and echoed some of the anti-austerity feeling. 'They say we are all in this together. But how can it be right that while children's centres close, it is business as usual for the bankers? How can it be right that while the cost of living goes up for everyone else, the government gives the banks a tax cut?' But he was also very careful not to frighten the bosses, adding, 'There is a need for difficult choices, and some cuts... We do need to cut the deficit'.[7] The monster demonstration was followed by two big rounds of strikes on 30 June (involving 750,000 people) and 30 November (2 million) over the government's assault on public sector pensions. These were an opportunity for Labour to identify with workers' struggles. Had the party done so, and encouraged the trade unions to unite in more extended strikes, it would have boosted further the level of resistance and could potentially have snuffed out the coalition's austerity policies at birth. The pattern of long-term decline in strike days and lack of mass industrial resistance was not inevitable. Indeed, November's strike was the biggest single day's stoppage since the 1926 General Strike. However, the fate of this upsurge did not just depend on the anger welling up from below, but the leadership—both political and trade union—that it was offered.

Ed Miliband had won his position because, unlike his brother, he was conscious of the need to restore Labour's reformist credentials after the decimating impact of the New Labour years. However, a choice between voicing the aspirations of the working class and the norms of behaviour for those within the capitalist institution of parliament was now unavoidable. Unfortunately Miliband was terrified to be seen as a red who supports strikes—even though he was leader only because of the vote of trade unionists.

During the 30 June strikes he appeared on the BBC robotically to distance himself from the action. The *New Statesman* reported:

> No matter what question the interviewer asked, Miliband began his answer with: 'These strikes are wrong.' He doesn't seem to have just learnt his brief, he appears to have swallowed it whole. His first answer is delivered with all the spontaneity of a six-year-old in a school play. Had he been asked his favourite colour or whether he is enjoying married life, his response would have been a monotonous: 'These strikes are wrong'.[8]

His condemnation of the strikes was met by anger across the labour movement. Mary Bousted, the moderate ATL general secretary, summed up the mood. 'The response of Ed Miliband has been a disgrace—he should be ashamed of himself,' she said at the London strike rally. 'If our strike is a mistake, what has he done to oppose this devastating attack on our pensions? If the opposition will not defend our pensions, we will.' A YouGov poll found that 47 percent of Labour voters thought Miliband handled the strikes badly, compared to only 24 percent who thought he handled them well. The poll also found that 70 percent of Labour voters thought unions acted 'reasonably' in the strike. At the TUC conference in September Miliband repeated, 'I do believe it was a mistake for strikes to happen. I continue to believe that.' This led to shouts of 'Shame' and heckling from the audience—an extraordinary thing to happen among the generally loyalist ranks of TUC delegates when a Labour leader is addressing them.[9]

By the time of the millions-strong mass strike on 30 November, Miliband was under even more pressure. On the day of the strikes he said he would refuse to 'demonise the dinner lady, the cleaner or the nurse, people who earn in a week what the Chancellor pays for his annual skiing holiday' and later that 'I am proud that millions of hard-working people in this country support the Labour Party—better that than millions from Lord Ashcroft.'[10] But he still did not support the strikes—indeed he crossed a picket line on his way into Parliament. It underlined how Labour continued to shy away from serious struggle and backed the bosses in key strikes. And the fact that most of the trade union leaders involved agreed to kill off the strike campaign after just one (highly successful) day emphasises the links between the union bureaucracy and Labour leadership.

Labour also rides to the rescue of the British state when it is under threat. The 2014 referendum on Scottish independence was not a mortal threat to capitalism. But it did offer a focus for those searching for a rejection of austerity and posed a challenge to the power of the imperialist state. The Yes campaign created a vibrant social movement of activists in workplaces and housing schemes. Labour, however, never had any doubt it would fight on the side of the existing state.

As the opinion polls narrowed, the leaders of the British state panicked. Two days before the referendum, Miliband joined fellow party leaders Cameron and Clegg to pledge 'extensive new powers' for the Scottish parliament if there was a No vote. But figures such as the British party leaders were not an effective force. Indeed there was a fear that their presence in Scotland would shovel votes to the Yes camp. Instead former prime minister Gordon Brown was hastily employed to make a speech about the benefits of the union. He spoke about the welfare state and the NHS, of a vision of Scotland of 'comradeship and community' and, less attractively, that, 'We fought two world wars together. And there is not a cemetery in Europe that does not have Scots, English, Welsh, and Irish lying side-by-side.'[11] Brown, usually excoriated by the media, was praised to the skies for his unionist rhetoric.[12]

Had Labour not joined with the Tories in the Better Together campaign and instead backed Yes, it is highly likely that Scotland would now be independent. Labour saved the British state, but its jigging about with the Union Jack alienated a vast swathe of people, especially young people. Many of them joined the SNP after the vote.[13] Not for the first time were there disastrous consequences for Labour, a party seemingly obsessed with electoralism, of siding with the system against the instincts of many of its working class supporters. Labour had 41 Scottish MPs before the independence referendum. In 2015's general election that fell to just one, and the damage endures. In 2017 it came third, gaining fewer seats than the Tories, a situation last seen in Scotland in 1955.

Miliband and immigration

Instead of backing a fightback that united workers, Miliband accepted falsehoods which divided them. One of the toxic ways that a ruling class seeks to divert attention from its own crimes is to seek to persuade workers that their enemies are groups at the bottom of society rather than those at the top. As the Tories attacked migrants and benefit claimants Labour shamefully went along with many of their lies, weakening the working class and smoothing the path for the rise of the United Kingdom Independence Party.

In June 2012 Miliband said New Labour had 'got it wrong' on immigration when in government. He attacked Blair and Brown for allowing 'uncontrolled immigration' from new EU states in 2004.[14] Disgustingly he said that a Labour government would force employers to declare if more than a quarter of the workforce was foreign-born.[15] He parroted all the myths about low-paid workers having their wages cut by migration, and Labour went along with inhumane Tory proposals to break up or deport UK-migrant families on less than average incomes. In an echo of his statement during Blair's premiership, the fascist British National Party leader Nick Griffin said Miliband's attitude was a 'legitimation of our message' and hailed the Labour leader as a 'BNP recruiting sergeant'.

Labour MP John McDonnell was about the only prominent voice featured in the media to hold fast to basic anti-racist principles and declined to join the immigrant-bashing bandwagon. He was right to criticise Miliband for producing 'a nuanced version of blaming the migrants for the jobs and housing crisis'. Later Miliband chose *The Sun* newspaper to announce that a future Labour government would not offer a 'soft touch' to foreigners. 'The Labour Party I lead will listen to people's worries and we will talk about immigration... We know low-skill immigration has been too high and it should come down,' he wrote. By the time of the 2015 general election, Labour made 'controls of immigration' one of its key pledges and then infamously produced a mug featuring the pledge. Diane Abbott said, 'This shameful mug is an embarrassment. But the real problem is that immigration controls are one of the five pledges at all.'[16] The anti-immigration pledge also appeared on the 'Ed stone', a two-tonne slab of limestone, with Labour's policies carved into its surface.

None of these compromises and retreats aided Labour. Miliband saw his poll ratings rise when he offered some hope of change—an end to the non-domicile status that enabled billionaires to avoid tax, a higher tax rate for those grabbing over £150,000 a year and a mansion tax. But the glimmers of progress and class politics were battered aside by the clunking fist of financial 'iron discipline', 'not a penny more' of borrowing, and 'cuts in the deficit every year'. When the votes were counted, despite five years of brutal austerity, mass strikes, riots and a student revolt, Labour ended up with 26 seats fewer than 2010 the Conservatives, only 800,000 votes more than the 1983 election that had been regarded as an historic low, and the Conservatives grabbed an unexpected majority.

It's not surprising that people were not inspired by a programme of more attacks on public services, more wage curbs, more jobs lost and a squeeze on health and education. Labour's leaders ludicrously ended up attacking Cameron for 'unfunded promises' to spend more on the NHS. In contrast the Scottish National Party (SNP) went from six seats to 56 seats. This wholly unprecedented shift happened because the SNP was able to portray itself as left of Labour. Its leaders spoke out against austerity, Trident nuclear missiles, recent imperial wars and much else. Labour's shadow foreign secretary Douglas Alexander acknowledged, 'Scotland has voted to oppose the Tories, but hasn't trusted Labour to do so.' The stage was set for the most extraordinary development in Labour politics for decades.

Miliband had failed to solve the conundrum that haunted social democratic leaders everywhere. With capitalism suffering a long-term decline in profit and demanding increasing sacrifices from the working class, these parties found it ever harder to satisfy both sides. The general tendency was to back the former even at the expense of losing the votes of the latter. Less red than claimed, Ed ended up electorally dead as a consequence.

Jeremy Corbyn and the earthquake in Labour

Ed Miliband resigned immediately as leader following his defeat. Every commentator expected the next party leader to be even more right wing than the man who had lost the election. *The Guardian* came out for Yvette Cooper, the *Mirror* for Andy Burnham. Absolutely nobody, including Corbyn himself, thought that he could win.

Yet he won the election for Labour leader by a landslide. When he was announced as leader on 12 September 2015, he had won almost 60 percent of the vote. This was a higher percentage than when Tony Blair took over Labour in 1994. Corbyn won 251,000 votes—nearly twice the number of Tory party members. The detailed breakdown demonstrated Corbyn's broad appeal inside the party. He won the votes of half the full party members, 84 percent of those who had paid £3 to be a supporter, and 58 percent of trade unionists and other affiliates. To underline the transformation, in 2010 Diane Abbott won 9,314 votes in the members section of the leadership ballot. In 2015 Corbyn secured 121,751.

His success was based on reflecting global political developments and the revolt against austerity, changes in the way Labour elected its leader—plus extraordinary luck. Corbyn's win can be understood only as part of a broader phenomenon. He became the focus of a political insurrection inside the Labour Party driven by young people and the former Labour members who had been alienated or left during the Blair years but now rejoined or registered to vote.

The financial crisis that broke in 2007-8 led to grinding attacks on the working class everywhere as the bosses and bankers were bailed out and ordinary people handed the bills. There was bitter anger against endless austerity and the unaccountable elites who dominate politics. Sometimes such feeling can be partly captured by the right—the fascist Front National in France and the Lega party in Italy for example. But it has also fuelled the left—Syriza in Greece, Podemos in the Spanish state, People Before Profit in Ireland. There are echoes of it in the Bernie Sanders campaign and the growth of the Democratic Socialists of America in the US, and the rise of the Economic Freedom Fighters in South Africa. In Britain this feeling was one of the factors behind the rise of the Scottish National Party. And then far more spectacularly it found a home in Corbyn's campaign.

Even establishment commentators recognised that Corbyn was an expression of this insurgent feeling. In an article attacking Corbyn, the

Financial Times' chief political commentator Philip Stephens wrote, 'In another age, the 2008 crash might have triggered a revolution. Instead, Mr Corbyn and his fellow travellers are now capturing the seething popular resentment.' He added, 'The brand of unbridled capitalism that hands all the gains of open markets and economic integration to the top 1 percent, while piling austerity and insecurity on to the rest, is politically unsustainable'.[17]

Simon Schama noted, 'A spectre is haunting the liberal democracies—the spectre of populism—and the political times have the insurrectionary feel of 1848 when Karl Marx wrote that sentence (with a significant difference at the end). From the stomping exhilaration and fervour greeting Senator Bernie Sanders, Hillary Clinton's challenger for the Democratic party's nomination, to Jeremy Corbyn's appearance among Labour's sinners as the cleanser of Blairite wickedness, politics has become passionate and the devotees have fire in their bellies and stars in their eyes'.[18]

Corbyn wasn't just an expression of such trends but also of campaigns and struggles. Until his triumph he was almost a complete outsider in the PLP, who only maintained a tenuous position there because he was an elected MP. It was this outside connection that enabled the most left-wing person in the Party's 115 year history to become leader. He survived the New Labour years by finding an outlet for his beliefs, involving himself deeply with movements outside of Parliament, against the Iraq war, for Palestine, and so on. This gave him a personal counter-weight to the dead hand of the 'most exclusive club in Europe'. It also meant that between 1997 and 2010 he defied the Party Whip or more occasions than any other of his colleagues.

Not only did this shape him, in turn he would not have won without the mood and networks created by the battles against the war, racism and austerity. In this sense his victory inside Labour was prepared and secured by activists outside Labour who had participated in many of these struggles and sometimes led them. His win was the property of the whole left.

But for any of this to happen he had to be on the ballot paper, and that required the support of 35 MPs. For much of the nomination period this looked unlikely, and the target was reached with just minutes to spare.[19] It involved John McDonnell literally going on his knees to beg MPs to nominate Corbyn 'in the interests of democracy'. Such arguments persuaded some very unlikely figures to back Corbyn, including Frank Field,[20] Margaret Beckett and Sadiq Khan. Beckett later agreed with an interviewer that she was a 'moron' and said of her decision, 'I probably regard it as one of the biggest political mistakes I've ever made'.[21]

Just appearing on the ballot paper made sections of the Labour right furious. John Mann MP said Corbyn's candidacy showed the party's desire never to win again. Jonathan Reynolds, a supporter of Liz Kendall, said it showed that Labour was not taking itself seriously. He added, 'If people think Jeremy is genuinely the man to win a parliamentary majority, then they are deluding themselves, and someone needs to say that,' he said. 'If Jeremy was leader, the Tories would win a majority of at least a 100, and possibly more'.[22]

But Corbyn's message of opposition to austerity, war and racism, his obvious estrangement from the stuffy conventions of established politics, and his record of campaigning proved hugely popular among Labour members. Having cut through the obstacles in the Labour Party rules to be able to stand, he soared away from the grey trinity of Cooper, Burnham and Liz Kendall. The Blairite Kendall, so right wing that at times she seemed to be running for the Tory party leadership, was eventually to receive just 4.5 percent of the vote.

An incident during the campaign underlined the differences. In July 2015 the Tories put forward in the Commons the second reading of the Welfare Reform and Work Bill. Its vicious attacks on some of the poorest people in Britain included reducing the household welfare cap from £26,000 to £23,000, abolishing legally binding child poverty targets, cuts to child tax credits, cuts to Employment and Support Allowance, and cuts to housing benefit for young people.

Over 180 Labour MPs did not oppose the bill. Out of the four leadership candidates, Cooper, Burnham, and Kendall all abstained. Corbyn voted against.

None of this this might have mattered had it not been for another factor—who was allowed to vote. In 2014 Labour implemented the Collins Review into how to elect its leader. The whole purpose was to slash trade union influence, block a left challenge, and seek to cover up the class questions in politics. The review said it wanted to achieve 'a simpler and more democratic process of selection' but in truth it hoped to make another shift towards a party more like the US Democrats.

The Collins Review authors had forgotten some of their party's history. Blairites might bemoan the residual class identification which goes with trade union influence in Labour, but at crucial moments in the past the trade unions have been used to break the challenge of the left. Weakening the union link made possible both a victory for more right-wing forces inside Labour but also created the possibility of a hectic surge of backing for left-wing candidates.

This was reinforced by allowing a vote in the leadership contest to non-members who paid £3 to register as Labour supporters. The idea was the 'ordinary people'—who were expected to be more right wing than activists—would keep Labour on a Blairite path. The party bureaucracy had fallen for its own myth-making propaganda—that almost everyone was a 'Middle Englander'. In fact the move proved a gift to Corbyn, a candidate who could appeal to radical people who didn't particularly want to join Labour but who were happy to spend £3 on expressing their desire for an alternative to the sterile mainstream politics. These '£3 members' voted 88,449 for Corbyn, 17,149 for all the other candidates combined. It was Corbyn's achievement to campaign as if he were founding a new party while actually standing for the leadership of an existing and very conservative one. His vision of change seemed, to many people, not only a total political break from all the Blairite drivel that had preceded it but also an organisational one—a fresh start.

In the context of this book the processes involved in Corbyn being able to stand in the first place, and then bring in new sources of support, seem outside the stream of Labour history—an accident. But, as the Russian Marxist Plekhanov explained: 'Accident is something relative. It appears only at the point of intersection of inevitable processes.[23]

Around 62,000 people joined the Labour Party in the immediate aftermath of Corbyn's election. More people joined the Labour Party in the five months after the general election than were members of the Conservatives. At the start of October Labour said 183,658 people had joined the party since 5 May, meaning membership had roughly doubled in the months since the party's loss. By July 2016 the membership was 515,000.

Labour HQ staff wore black on the day of Corbyn's election to mourn the party they had lost. But his victory was a massive boost to the whole of the left. For all the limitations of Labour, it demonstrated that socialist ideas could be popular with large swathes of people. As the news of Corbyn's victory was released, the Socialist Workers Party put out a statement saying, 'The Blairites are crying, we're cheering. The Socialist Workers Party congratulates Jeremy Corbyn on becoming Labour Party leader. His success is a clear sign of the feeling against austerity, racism and war. His victory is an utter rejection of the warmongering and veneration of big business that were the hallmarks of the Tony Blair eras.'[24]

Every left Labour figure is tested by their attitude to international policy. Throughout its history, many ordinary members of the Labour Party have been committed to peace. But at every key moment the party leadership has supported imperialism and war. Corbyn offered a challenge to this grim record. He had campaigned bravely and relentlessly against war, and in particular the Iraq war. This was a key issue for the Labour right. They could just about stomach some increased taxation of the rich or some gradual renationalisation of some industries, but 'disloyalty' to the British state was not up for debate. The question of whether to support British forces taking part in the bombing of Syria in the wake of the 13 November 2015 attacks in Paris accelerated all the splits inside Labour.

Corbyn opposed the airstrikes. The Labour right were appalled and saw an early chance to undermine him. Here was an issue where they could rely on the media to tear Corbyn apart and paint him as a sympathiser of terrorism. Such lies were to re-appear again and again. Most Labour leaders would have dealt with the impasse by backroom deals. But Corbyn went halfway towards using pressure outside parliament to bring Labour MPs into line. The pro-Corbyn group Momentum said that it was 'proud that we assisted over 30,000 people to email their MP asking them not to vote for bombing'. More importantly, thousands of people took part in street demonstrations. Campaigning shifted public opinion. Peter Kellner of pollsters YouGov said on 2 December that polls suggested that 'in just seven days, five million people have joined the ranks of those opposed to air strikes in Syria.'[25]

That didn't halt the opposition from the Labour right. Street movements could exert pressure while on the street, but afterwards the permanent existence of the PLP, the demands of capital and the structures of the state were still bearing down. Unless continuously conjured up, the forces that brought Corbyn into Labour's leadership would not be standing beside him as he confronted the threat of shadow cabinet resignations. He allowed Labour MPs to vote whatever way they felt was correct on the Syria issue. On the most crucial issue of war and peace, he prioritised the unity of Labour—and that meant conceding to the right. In the end most Labour MPs did vote against the bombing (sometimes using the excuse that Cameron was not going far enough because he had no plan for a serious military follow-up). But 66 Labour MPs openly defied him by voting for it bombing, led by Hilary Benn, the shadow foreign secretary. Benn was not sacked. Instead he was allowed to remain, plotting and organising to bring Corbyn down.

The European Union, Brexit and international capital

Tory David Cameron's unexpected outright win at the 2015 election meant that he had to implement his pledge to have a referendum on British membership of the European Union. It was disastrous for the Conservatives, but also posed problems for Labour. Labour's EU policy had shifted hugely during the 1980s. The 1983 manifesto called for a withdrawal from membership. The 1987 manifesto said virtually nothing on the issue, but by the 1989 European elections Labour was presenting itself as more pro-European than the Tories. In a process that also took part in the trade unions, after a series of defeats Labour had come to see the EU as protection from the ravages of Margaret Thatcher and multinational capital. But Corbyn had not backed such a shift. Throughout their time in parliament both Corbyn and McDonnell backed anti-EU motions. In this they were simply following the position of their political mentor, Tony Benn.

During the 1993 debate on the Maastricht treaty Corbyn said it 'takes away from national parliaments the power to set economic policy and hands it over to an unelected set of bankers who will impose the economic policies of price stability, deflation and high unemployment throughout the European Community'. Corbyn also said that he voted against the EU's predecessor, the Common Market, in 1975. Then during his battle for the Labour leadership, Corbyn hinted he might support leaving the EU. He said he had 'not closed his mind' to exit and was opposed to giving David Cameron a 'blank cheque'. At one hustings he said, 'I think we should be making demands—universal workers' rights, universal environmental protection, end the race to the bottom on corporate taxation, end the race to the bottom in wage protection'.

It turned out the way to make Corbyn back the EU was to elect him Labour leader. He compromised to keep at least some of the right vaguely on side. The reappointment of Pat McFadden as shadow minister for Europe was seen as the first victory for Labour's right under Corbyn's leadership. The announcement that the party would campaign to stay in the EU followed.

This ensured that the case against the EU would be dominated by reactionary forces. The left case against the EU received only marginal exposure. He could have said that the EU is an openly pro-capitalist institution which in recent years had shed any pretence of delivering social protection and instead has emerged as the enforcer of austerity across a continent. He could have added that the EU, through its Fortress Europe structures, acts to repel migrants and refugees from outside Europe. In addition the EU is part of the imperialist world order that, along with Nato, delivers important support for the United States and provides reliable partners in its murderous actions. Had he done so he could have claimed the legacy of the Leave vote rather than handing it to the Tory right and Nigel Farage.

The 52 percent vote to leave the EU was a bitter blow for the establishment, big business, the international financial institutions, the rich and the politicians. With only minor exceptions they had united to support a Remain vote. Remain had the support of most of the Tory leadership, Labour, the Scottish National Party, Plaid Cymru, the Lib Dems, the Greens and Sinn Féin, parties that make up 97 percent of the House of Commons. But Remain lost.

The central issue was that it was a revolt against the establishment. People who were generally forgotten, ignored or sneered at delivered a stunning blow against the people at the top of society. It was a rejection of the governing class.[26] But the laurels were stolen by rabid reactionaries like Boris Johnson and Michael Gove because the real motivation behind a substantial proportion of the vote had not been articulated by the Labour leadership, and those Labour MPs in favour of Remain chose to denigrate the outcome as purely racist and backward-looking. Each reinforced the other.

Far from pacifying his critics by backing Remain, Corbyn was then criticised for not hurling himself into the campaign—which he strongly denied. It was to be the trigger for a determined assault.

The 'chicken coup'

The rudderless Conservatives lurched from crisis to crisis after the Brexit referendum, with Cameron stepping down, and then a chaotic leadership election seeing a meltdown of the campaign by the expected successor Boris Johnson. It was the ideal moment for the Labour Party to redouble its opposition and to seek to sweep them out of office.

Instead the large majority of its MPs turned on Corbyn and directed all their energy to securing his resignation. A contemptible manoeuvre saw a carefully-orchestrated series of resignations from the shadow cabinet and other ministerial posts. Then 172 MPs supported a vote of no confidence in Corbyn's leadership. Why was the Labour right prepared to risk political suicide, to divide the Party and assist the Tories who were in disarray? The majority of Labour MPs may have been cynical opportunists who genuinely believed left-wing policies lost votes or honest believers that 'it was possible to combine economic efficiency with social justice'; but either way they reflected one wing of a capitalist workers' party. Their reformist acceptance of capitalism's 'rules of the game' co-existed with a rejection of the consequences of capitalism by the mass of Labour supporters.

When circumstances favour it this co-existence can be harmonious. In the Attlee period capital required state intervention to reconstruct basic infrastructure and services (health, education and so on) and this coincided with a mass desire for nationalisation and welfare. But in recent decades the gap between the two sides has grown ever wider, producing a lurch towards New Labour and then in the opposite direction to Corbyn. Unstable though this appears to be, co-existence was the key feature even if self-destructive civil war was the result after 2015.

Under intense pressure to quit, Corbyn was boosted by wider support. Most central was the surge of backing from the ordinary members and supporters of the party. They did not just sit passively as spectators of events. They came to large and enthusiastic meetings and demonstrated in the streets.

At just a few hours' notice up to 10,000 people rallied outside parliament to urge him to stay. Hundreds joined similar rallies in Newcastle and Manchester. Secondly nearly all the union leaders backed Corbyn. Corbyn's opponents had hoped he would step down, but faced with his defiance they had to launch a formal leadership challenge. After a series of hesitations, which had the move dubbed the 'chicken coup', the right united around the obscure Owen Smith as their candidate. His pitch was not to challenge Corbyn over his (highly popular) economic policies but to say that they should be presented in a more palatable manner. This utterly failed to destabilise Corbyn's supporters—in fact tens of thousands more people joined Labour in an effort to support him. Smith's team started phoning people who had recently stopped paying their Labour subs in the belief that they were disgusted by Corbyn and might be persuaded to rejoin. They frequently found themselves speaking to the relatives of people who had died.

Corbyn then held rallies and meetings around Britain which encouraged his supporters and demoralised the right. Jim Waterson writes, 'Over the course of the week following Hilary Benn's resignation pro-Corbyn meetings were organised in 35 locations across the country. There were meetings in major cities such as Manchester and Liverpool. Then there were shows of support in smaller towns like Penzance, Lincoln, and Ipswich. All were organised by local Momentum groups at short notice with no speakers or Jeremy Corbyn to address them. In that first week, Momentum claims, over 25,000 people came out to show their support—half the total who attended all of Corbyn's leadership events the previous year'.[27]

Far from smashing Corbyn, when the result of the leadership challenge was announced, Corbyn had won an even bigger victory than in his first election. He secured 62.5 percent of the vote and was thereafter immune from further leadership challenges—unless he proved an electoral disaster as the right believed he surely would.

A historically unique situation had been created inside Labour. The pattern has generally been that the party's ordinary members have been curbed and disciplined by the union leaders and the MPs, headed by the party leader. But now the members were supported not only by most union leaders (on however temporary a basis) but also by the party leader.

It also saw a big boost for Momentum, the group of Corbyn supporters who came together to support him after the 2015 election win. It had only about 4,000 members at the time of the leadership challenge. But its role in instantly mobilising to beat back the right greatly increased its allure. By the end of the year it had over 20,000 members. But this raised a question about its role. Was it there just to do the leadership's bidding or to organise for Corbyn, but also campaign and discuss ideas more widely, including with those outside Labour?

Almost as soon as Owen Smith had been defeated, Momentum leader Jon Lansman unveiled a new constitution for the group which concentrated power at the top, restricted membership to Labour Party members, and made it clear that those deemed 'entryists' were not welcome. It was the start of a process that would see Momentum move towards a role that at points undermined Corbyn rather than sustained him.

Momentum had been willing to act as a bridge between extra-parliamentary, extra-Labour movements or groups and the Labour Party proper. But it too was not immune to the central focus of political reformism, which is Parliament and the Party's role as a vehicle to winning office.

The 2017 election

It wasn't just the Labour right who thought that if Corbyn faced the voters he would preside over a historic defeat for Labour on the scale of 1983 or perhaps even 1931. In the middle of 2017 Tory prime minister Theresa May became convinced that she could strengthen her hand in the Brexit talks, weaken backbenchers' opportunities to pressure her, achieve her own mandate and go down in history as the conqueror of Labour. She called a snap election. But instead of the anticipated annihilation of Corbyn, a disastrous Tory campaign and an insurgent Labour one produced a wholly unexpected result. Labour in 2017 did not just win more votes than it did in the defeats under Miliband in 2015 and Brown in 2010. It took more votes than Tony Blair did in two of his three victories (2001 and 2005).

It was a shattering setback for May and the Tories. The results showed that Britain was not, in general, a right-wing country and that the left can win. Before the vote media pundits and right-wing Labour MPs all gave apocalyptic warnings of a landslide defeat caused by Corbyn's leadership. They said Corbyn's left-wing politics put Labour out of touch with most working class people who, they insisted, would support only right-wing policies. Instead Labour gained 30 seats and ten percentage points on its vote share, reaching 40 percent. It was the biggest increase in popular support during a campaign in British electoral history.

Corbyn's vision of Labour won a higher percentage share than in the two elections of 1974 and those of 1979, 1983, 1987, 1992, 2001, 2005, 2010 and 2015. Apart from Blair's first election in 1997, you would need to go back to Harold Wilson's landslide in 1966 to find Labour getting more votes at a general election. In fact, Labour got more votes than any party coming second at a general election since it lost the 1951 election. Labour overcame the lies and hostility of the media. *The Sun* newspaper declared that a vote for Corbyn would mean 'open immigration', 'nuclear surrender', 'puppet of unions', 'Marxist extremism' and more—and 30 percent its readers chose Labour in the polling booth.

The bosses' magazine the *Economist* lamented that, 'Chronic instability has taken hold of British politics," and it 'will be hard to suppress'. The political tumult, and the possibility of fundamental change, that had swept so many other parts of the world had now come to Britain. The *Financial Times*' star columnist Janan Ganesh wrote on the day after the general election, 'The stablest of democracies has become the Western world's box of surprises'.[28]

It was all a vindication of the policies that Corbyn had promoted during the election and the way that he and his supporters put the message across. At the campaign launch Corbyn attacked the rich—and pledged that Labour would 'overturn this rigged system'. He said Labour would announce policies aimed at taking the wealth off rich tax evaders and bankers and ending austerity and racist scapegoating. He said, 'It is the rigged economy the Tories are protecting that Labour is committed to challenging. 'If I were Southern Rail or if I was Philip Green, I'd be worried about a Labour government. If I were Mike Ashley or the CEO of a tax avoiding multinational corporation, I'd want to see a Tory victory, I really would. Why? Because those are the people who are monopolising the wealth that should be shared by each and every one of us in this country'.[29]

The manifesto included pledges to increase tax on the rich and corporations, more money for health and education, the abolition of university tuition fees and repealing the latest anti-union law.

In many ways this was not particularly radical. In 1980 the main economic resolution at the Labour conference, moved by the far from revolutionary David Basnett, leader of the GMB, demanded restrictions on the flight of capital, an 'extension of public ownership with industrial democracy', 'reflation of public service spending', 'a substantial cut in arms spending', a 'wealth tax', a 35 hour week without loss of pay and recognition that 'Britain's social and economic problems can only be resolved by socialist planning'. It was passed overwhelmingly with the leadership's support. This makes Corbyn's policies seem pallid by comparison.

But the 2017 manifesto came after years of austerity from the Tories and austerity-lite from Labour. It felt like an inspiring break. But perhaps more important was the way Labour campaigned. Instead of being imprisoned by stuffy conventions about how to win, Corbyn set off on a series of rallies. Mark L Thomas writes, 'The turning point came in mid-May when Corbyn addressed a crowd of 2,000 in York, hundreds in the small Yorkshire town of Hebden Bridge and then 3,000 in Leeds. A few days later Corbyn spoke to thousands on the beach at West Kirby on the Wirral and then was greeted ecstatically by a young crowd of thousands when he appeared on stage at a Libertines gig at Prenton Park stadium (where the "Oh, Jeremy Corbyn" chant that echoed through the summer's festivals and beyond was born). These mobilisations reached a crescendo with the huge 10,000-strong crowd Corbyn drew three days before the election in Gateshead...such mass rallies gave Labour supporters confidence and helped create a pole of attraction in society that boosted the idea that Corbyn and his programme were popular. Research by Alia Middleton at the London School of Economics suggests "Labour vote share rose by almost 19 percentage points in constituencies where Jeremy Corbyn had visited".[30]

Another crucial moment came after the appalling terror attack on a Manchester concert during the campaign which killed 22 people. Instead of ritualistically calling for a crackdown, Corbyn asked why it had happened. Alex Nunns quotes a Corbyn adviser saying 'There were people within our campaign team who were like, "Fuck, are you sure about doing this?" But the choice, as they saw it, was between getting out in front or passively waiting to be pummelled by the inevitable onslaught'.[31]

The Leader's Office could not find an MP willing to introduce Corbyn for the speech. But it went ahead with the key phrase, 'Many experts, including professionals in our intelligence and security services, have pointed out the connections between wars that we've been involved in or supported and fought in, in other countries such as Libya, and terrorism here at home.' He then moved on to attack May for cutting police numbers by 20,000 during her time as home secretary and saying that this was part of the austerity project.

But it was the 'risky' connection between Britain's wars abroad and bombs at home that proved the most popular element. An instant YouGov poll on 26 May found that 53 percent believed that 'wars the UK has supported or fought are responsible, at least in part, for terror attacks against the UK' while only 24 percent disagreed.

The 2017 election result destroyed the Blairites' central argument that Corbyn could never win an election. To their great dismay it had shown that the way to win votes was to move away from austerity, not embrace a slightly diluted version of it. Even before the votes were counted, Philip Collins, who was once Tony Blair's chief speechwriter, wrote that 'could have been Labour's worst week in years'. Why? 'Because the prevailing, unspoken, assumption among Labour MPs before this election began was that it would be a condensed education in political reality for their membership. The Tories would throw a lot of mud, most of which would stick. Mr Corbyn would collapse under pressure and the electorate would deliver a damning verdict.

'The surge has changed everything because it is now so much harder to argue that Mr Corbyn's brand of politics is not viable.'

But Corbyn's significant success in 2017 also had dangerous repercussions. Most trade union leaders, and many activists, were now convinced that the way to achieve progress was to 'wait for Jeremy'. Instead of using the election result to accelerate struggles, demonstrations were smaller and strikes less frequent. Corbyn was advised that his new persona as 'prime minister in waiting' meant he should appear less at protests and picket lines. The idea of 'social movement activism' called for by some Corbyn supporters was placed firmly second to appearing ready for office. Such a move was demobilising and damaging. Passivity does not encourage people to vote for radical alternatives. More importantly it weakens the working class in its struggles to improve its conditions.

Making compromises

The rise of Corbyn was welcome for all socialists. He deserved unstinting support when he was attacked by the Tories and the Labour right. His policies proved electorally more attractive than the dreary pro-market mantras from Labour-type parties elsewhere in Europe. The French Socialist Party saw its candidate come fifth in the 2017 presidential election and was forced to sell its historic Rue de Solferino headquarters in Paris to cover its debts. The German SPD hit an historic low in the 2017 federal elections. Its 21 percent vote share was the party's worst result since the Second World War and its vote has halved since 1989. The Dutch Labour Party went from junior partner in government to seventh place. These parties are paying the price for implementing austerity or offering only token opposition to it.

But Corbyn did not escape the pressures to retreat and compromise and there was an element of tragedy for someone with decades of principled campaigning behind him. This process began immediately he was leader. Labour right winger Luke Akehurst celebrated that 'During this first week Corbyn has made six main concessions to the PLP: Clarification that Labour will campaign for a Yes vote in the EU referendum. Clarification that he won't be seeking to take the UK out of NATO. Acceptance that he can't force MPs to vote against Trident renewal next year. Disavowal of proposals to bring back mandatory reselection of MPs. Appointment of moderates to all the key positions in the Shadow Foreign Affairs and Shadow Defence teams. Reappointment of the top team in the Whips' office'.[32]

A crucial reverse came over the renewal of Trident nuclear missiles. Corbyn has always opposed nuclear weapons, and enraged the right wing when, as leader, he declined to say that there was some point at which he would give the order to unleash nuclear armaggedon and potentially destroy the world. 'I am opposed to the use of nuclear weapons. I am opposed to the holding of nuclear weapons. I want to see a nuclear-free world. I believe it is possible,' he said soon after he was first elected leader. In the same interview he added, 'I don't think we should be spending £100 billion on renewing Trident'.[33]

Such a policy was not just unacceptable to the Tories and the military but also the Labour right and the trade union leaders. Using the wholly spurious claim that it was necessary to keep Trident to protect workers' jobs, Unite union leader Len McCluskey and GMB leader Paul Kenny jointly pressured Corbyn to retreat. By the 2016 Labour conference the shadow defence secretary Clive Lewis said, 'I am clear that our party has a policy for Trident renewal'.[34] And the 2017 election manifesto would have been wholly acceptable to Gordon Brown or Tony Blair. It said:

> Alongside our commitment to Nato, we will continue to work with the EU on a range of operational missions to promote and support global and regional security. The last Labour government consistently spent above the Nato benchmark of 2 percent of GDP. Conservative spending cuts have put Britain's security at risk...Labour's commitment to spending at least 2 percent of GDP on defence will guarantee that our Armed Forces have the necessary capabilities to fulfil the full range of obligations... Labour supports the renewal of the Trident nuclear deterrent.[35]

It is hardly possible to imagine policies that were more conventional, pro-imperialist or less in tune with radical change.

Corbyn also retreated over migration during the debate over the terms on which Britain might break from the EU. He abandoned the (partial) freedom of movement for workers allowed inside the EU and instead accepted as inevitable that a harsher series of migration laws would have to be enacted as a consequence of leaving. The general, and correct, understanding that migrants are not a problem was not translated into policy to tear up the anti-migrant and anti-refugee laws.

Compromises encourage the right wing. Having secured concessions they seek more, as was shown most graphically in the battle over alleged antisemitism in the Labour Party. Having failed to remove Corbyn from the leadership, and having witnessed the rise in the Labour vote at the 2017 general election, his opponents looked to other methods. One of the most determined assaults came by suggesting that Corbyn was antisemitic, or at least was a friend of antisemites who he protected and allowed to remain inside Labour. The baseless charge was particularly damaging because of Corbyn's reputation as a lifelong anti-racist campaigner.

But it was not just a thrust against Corbyn by the Labour right. It was also a concerted effort to reverse the acceleration of solidarity with Palestine and the growth of the Boycott, Divestment and Sanctions movement internationally. It was a campaign that went on for years.

In April 2016 Labour MP Naz Shah was suspended from the party over a series of social media posts about Israel. Former London mayor Ken Livingstone went on the radio to defend Shah but ended up claiming that Hitler supported Zionism. His remarks were ill-judged and historically suspect—some Zionists did end up accepting some of Hitler's actions, but very many did not and gave their lives fighting Hitler. But Livingstone has a strong anti-racist record and is not an antisemite. Nonetheless he was suspended by Labour.

The incident was used to suggest that Labour was infested with antisemites. It was a useful further prong to attack Corbyn as preparations were made to remove him after the EU referendum.

In October 2016 the Commons home affairs select committee accused Labour of incompetence in dealing with antisemitism and helping to create a safe space for people with 'vile attitudes towards Jewish people'. Right from the start Corbyn should have responded by insisting that although antisemitism was always unacceptable, it was far more common among the right, was a central theme of fascism, and that Labour would unstintingly continue to support the Palestinians.

Instead he made concessions to his critics, admitting that there needed to be a tougher line against antisemitic abuse. Then in March 2018 Corbyn had to concede he was wrong to have supported on social media a graffiti artist whose work, featuring several known antisemitic tropes, was scrubbed off a wall in London's East End. This obscure post had been dredged up to find a new way to attacks Corbyn. It was an opening to further assaults. Some Jewish community leaders published an open letter accusing him of 'siding with antisemites' and held a protest at Westminster supported by Tory and Labour MPs. Again Corbyn retreated. In May 2018 Ken Livingstone resigned from the party saying his suspension had become a distraction. It is inconceivable this wasn't discussed with Corbyn. Who would have thought that Corbyn's leadership would have seen Blair confident in his Labour membership while Livingstone was forced out.

In July 2018, as the pressure grew, Labour accepted the International Holocaust Remembrance Alliance's (IHRA) definition of antisemitism, but its national executive decided not to adopt all 11 examples given, arguing that, under one of them, legitimate criticism of Israel could be deemed antisemitic. Labour MP Margaret Hodge angrily confronted Corbyn, calling him a 'fucking racist and antisemite'. The *Jewish Chronicle*, *Jewish News* and *Jewish Telegraph* printed joint front-page editorials calling any potential Corbyn-led government an 'existential threat' to Jewish life in Britain. Corbyn's response was to apologise for the 'concerns and anxiety caused' after taking part in a 2010 event where the actions of Israel in Gaza were compared to the Nazis.

Each individual case seemed insignificant. But the overall trend was unmistakable—Corbyn allowed his critics to define the agenda and to push Labour away from solidarity with Palestine. It encouraged more attacks. In August 2018 Corbyn was excoriated for his presence four years previously at graves in Tunisia of Palestine Liberation Organisation figures who had been linked to the killing of 11 members of the Israeli Olympics team at the Munich 1972 Olympics.

Labour was now in full scale retreat. A critical role was played by the trade union leaders. We have seen how they backed 'red Ed' as leader in 2010, and Corbyn against the 'chicken coup' in 2016. But 2018 was different. As the Tories, supporters of Israel, the Labour right, practically the entire media and even Israeli leader Binyamin Netanyahu tore into Corbyn, the leaders of some of Britain's biggest unions also decided it was the moment to tell him to surrender. Tim Roache of the GMB, Dave Prentis of Unison, Paddy Lillis of Usdaw and Len McCluskey of Unite all counselled Labour to adopt the IHRA definition of antisemitism and all the examples. As a largely independent player with its own base operating inside the Labour Party, the trade union bureaucracy can exert a powerful influence, but it does so for its own reasons and with the same reformist limitations as the political wing. As a mediating layer between workers and capital it wants a Labour government because it is not prepared to fight for major working class advance outside of Parliament. Therefore, like its politician equivalent, it succumbs to what it believes is electorally expedient.

The final concession came in September 2018 as the national executive accepted all the IHRA examples including accepting that it is antisemitic to describe the state of Israel as 'a racist endeavour'. When Corbyn tried to introduce a statement blunting this he was abandoned by several trade union reps on the committee and many Momentum supporters. The 'pro-Corbyn' Momentum became 'anti-Corbyn'.

Obstacles to change

What would a Corbyn government look like? It would obviously be very different to one headed by Blair. But it would face massive obstacles to fundamental change. The first would be its own limited objectives. Its economic policies at the 2017 election were not a mortal threat to capitalist Britain. Secondly, the Labour right remains dominant among MPs. It was clear they would unhesitatingly vote against more radical measures even if they came from their own party.

But there are deeper issues. The experience of Greece has shown the limitations of parliamentary rule. At the start of 2015 the radical Syriza party won elections, a victory that saw celebrations across Europe. Alexis Tsipras came to office promising to roll back austerity measures imposed by the troika of international lenders—the European Commission, International Monetary Fund and European Central Bank.

This austerity programme had wrecked millions of lives. The economy had declined by a quarter since 2008. On average people's incomes had fallen by over a third, hurling many back to the living standards of their grandparents. Nearly 40 percent of the population was officially poor, a quarter has no job and half of young people were unemployed. Millions no longer had access to health care. The election result reflected this carnage and the confidence flowing from a very high level of resistance—general strikes, student movements, occupations of public squares and more.

But the bankers and the EU institutions had no interest in the views of an electorate. Instead the only negotiations they were prepared to have with Syriza were on continuing the policies of cuts. They began a policy of financial waterboarding to torture Greece into submission and to prevent the message running across the world that if you vote against austerity you can escape the bankers' regime. There was nothing especially Greek about this situation. Certainly there were features that are different to Britain such as the relatively small size of its economy and its pressing debts. But these are not fundamental. The French economy is almost exactly the same size as Britain's, as are its debts. But the bankers and bosses were able to block the very mild reforms from Socialist Party president Francois Hollande and then drive him to implement austerity. This is the experience of previous Labour governments in Britain. Harold Wilson encountered a similar situation in 1964 when, in his words, 'international speculators...forced [the Government] into the adoption of Tory policies to which it was fundamentally opposed'.[36]

In some ways the significance of Britain would make it even more important for the capitalists to confront a reforming Corbyn government than it was to take out Syriza. The wider inspiration from a successful battle to turn back austerity in Britain would be much greater than it happening in Greece. To that end, what counts as 'significant' debts can be manipulated by the bankers. According to the International Monetary Fund,[37] the United States has one of the highest ratios of gross government debt to GDP in the world. But there are no calls for emergency programmes or removing the administration. It is a question of power and politics.

Yanis Varoufakis, the Greek finance minister at the time, has given an insight into how his talks went. He said that Wolfgang Schäuble, Germany's finance minister and the architect of the deals Greece signed in 2010 and 2012, was 'consistent throughout'. 'His view was "I'm not discussing the programme—this was accepted by the previous [Greek] government and we can't possibly allow an election to change anything". So at that point I said, "Well perhaps we should simply not hold elections anymore for indebted countries", and there was no answer. The only interpretation I can give [of their view] is, "Yes, that would be a good idea, but it would be difficult. So you either sign on the dotted line or you are out".'

When Varoufakis put forward careful counter-proposals he says, 'There was point blank refusal to engage in economic arguments. Point blank. You put forward an argument that you've really worked on, to make sure it's logically coherent, and you're just faced with blank stares. It is as if you haven't spoken. What you say is independent of what they say. You might as well have sung the Swedish national anthem—you'd have got the same reply.'

This intransigence left Syriza with a massive problem. Eventually it put to the Greek people the demands of the troika. And the Greek people responded with a great Oxi (No) to these measures. The referendum in July saw 61 percent reject austerity. This was 25 percentage points higher than the vote for Syriza in January. But Syriza had no plan to continue the resistance. In fact it had already surrendered.

Varoufakis reflects:

> By the end of June my colleagues had already decided to give in, and in a sense the referendum was called to be lost. It was an escape route. The hope was that the Greek people would vote yes. And the Greek people voted no. The Greek people were not subdued. I was surprised. I had

> expected a whole week of closed banks would bend the Greek people to the troika's will. I was elated that night. It was one of the happiest moments of my life. Unfortunately my side, the Greek government, collapsed and surrendered.[38]

The price was terrible. As Greece exited the EU bailout scheme in 2018, one study found that over a third of Greek households existed on less than £8,000 a year, over half of households depended on pension income and unemployment was over 20 percent. Greece was required by its overlords to funnel at least 3.5 percent of economic output to debt servicing until 2022, and 2.2 percent until 2060—four decades more of austerity.

Syriza could not have moved forward without being more radical, and also breaking from the EU. Instead, fixated on parliament, negotiations with the powerful, and staying in the EU, it utterly crumbled. Within a week Tsipras declared he would implement a worse round of austerity than those imposed by his Tory predecessors. Electing a leader and a party with left-wing policies was not enough to stop the bosses' blackmail.

It could only have been different if Syriza had based itself on mass mobilisation. It would have had to advance measures such as nationalising banks under workers' control, seizing the wealth of the oligarchs, imposing controls on the bosses' ability to move money and assets and so on. This would have required an immense movement from the base of society and a deepening of democracy in the workplace and communities. In other words, to secure anti-austerity policies required genuine socialist policies and a socialist movement. This was possible, as the Oxi referendum showed. But Tsipras ran away from it.

After the 2012 elections, when it was clear Syriza could win the next election, the encouragement for struggle outside parliament stopped. There was no attempt to bring anti-austerity and anti-racist mobilisations into the centre of any plan for government. And after Syriza came to office in 2015 any sniff of resistance from below was regarded as at best a distraction and at worst disloyal.

Greece is not the only recent example. In France the presidency of the Socialist Party's Francis Hollande from 2012 saw continued implementation of austerity and racism, clearing the way for the growth of the fascist National Front and the electoral collapse of the Socialists. In an era of deep crisis reversing austerity and attacking racism and war requires far more than winning an election.

What if Corbyn was more determined? If bosses' economic strikes and pressure did not work, if the influence of the Labour right was insufficient, if Corbyn himself did not draw back, then physical repression would be possible. A senior serving British Army general told the *Sunday Times* that if Corbyn became prime minister, 'There would be mass resignations at all levels and you would face the very real prospect of an event which would effectively be a mutiny...You would see a major break in convention with senior generals directly and publicly challenging Corbyn over vital important policy decisions such as Trident, pulling out of Nato and any plans to emasculate and shrink the size of the armed forces.

'The Army just wouldn't stand for it. The general staff would not allow a prime minister to jeopardise the security of this country and I think people would use whatever means possible, fair or foul to prevent that.'

The *Sunday Times* added that 'intelligence chiefs' had also stated, 'The intelligence services will refuse to let Corbyn see information on live operations because of his sympathy towards some terrorists.' And then the paper quoted a senior intelligence source stating, 'None of the intelligence community—whether we're talking about the security services or the counter-terrorism police bosses—would give Corbyn, or any of his cabinet, information that they don't want to give. And any information that they do decide to give will be restricted and tailored to general stuff and provided against the clear backdrop of Corbyn's detestation of Britain's security services'.[39]

Action by the military may seem far-fetched. But we shouldn't rule it out if a Corbyn government saw a mass rise in workers' struggle. And there would certainly be a battery of financial measures similar to those launched against Syriza.

The real struggles will be fought in the streets and the workplaces.

20

Conclusion

THESE LINES are being written on the tenth anniversary of the collapse of Lehman Brothers, and instability continues. Gordon Brown, the 'no more boom and bust' PM of that time, now warns that although a new crash may be looming 'the international co-operation between central banks and governments to stem the crisis seen in 2008 would no longer be possible'.[1] This is being said even before most people's livelihoods have recovered from the last crisis. The waterboarding of Greece is just one example of how people have endured falling living standards, austerity and unemployment, while the rich get richer. The gap between the two has risen to grotesque levels. The top 1 percent of wealthiest individuals owned 33 percent of global total wealth in 2017, up from 28 percent in 1980.[2]

Such facts should help the left's case, but clearly some have been fooled into believing that the cause of their misery must be refugees, immigrants, Muslims or whatever scapegoats the capitalist-owned media finds convenient. There has been a widespread rise of populist nationalism, racism and fascism both electorally and in the emergence in places of violent street armies. Even in Sweden a re-branded Nazi party has made significant electoral gains while the Social Democrats, often seen as the model party of that type, have received their lowest vote in a century.

Finally, we have just lived through the hottest summer on record confirming the fear that global warming is making the very future of humankind unpredictable.

This snapshot of twenty-first century society underlines the urgent need to end the blind and ruthless pursuit of profit and its replacement by collective democratic control of the economy. Socialism or barbarism is the choice we face, but the former can only be brought about through the action of the mass of people in society, the working class who, in Britain, currently tend to vote Labour. But what sort of Party is it now?

Set against its first hundred years the last two decades seem highly unusual. There could be no greater contrast between Labour's governments of 1997-2010 and Corbyn's arrival as leader. Nonetheless, even these events still reflect facets of reformist politics. Thus the 1996 edition could accurately predict that under a Blair government the Party would be 'a reformist organisation that cannot deliver reforms, only destroy them. It is committed to electoralism but is reducing its base of committed voters, eliminating its activist cadre and more and becoming more dependent on grabbing votes and members by occupying Tory territory.'

However, it also went on to ask: 'Does this mean that Labour's reformism has no future?' and concluded: 'Far from it. Reformist consciousness—the ideas of the ruling class modified by the experience of exploitation and oppression—is not dependent on the actual prospect of winning reforms, of voting Labour or being a party member. So reformist beliefs continue. Despite Labour becoming increasingly less capable of channelling these aspirations it does not mean that other organisations can easily displace the party as the political expression of reformism. Although modified, Labour's unique relationship with the trade union bureaucracy continues and gives it an inherent stability. Similarly the very indirect, but nevertheless real link between [reformist] consciousness and the Labour vote guarantees the party's mass influence. Labour may temporarily attract right-wing support, but its core support is the working class, its most advanced section being overwhelmingly committed to Labourism.'

It is indeed remarkable how, in a time of extreme political volatility, so many shifting elements have been contained within the Labour Party rather being expressed through different competing parties (such as Syriza in Greece, or Podemos in Spain). The only exception to this pattern in the UK has been in Scotland, where the SNP out-manoeuvred Labour electorally by successfully posing as a reformist alternative. Labour's capacity to act as a broad church should not lead to ignoring the bitter civil war taking place today. It represents a fight for the very soul of the Party.

Before its establishment in 1900 the aspirations of the working class were not articulated within the parliamentary arena. Most working men (and it was only men at that time) cast their vote for the unashamedly pro-capitalist Liberals. The shift to Labour was therefore a major step forward. Writing in the 1860s about agitation for an Act of Parliament restricting working hours Marx suggested why such political action was important:

> This struggle...told indeed upon the great contest between the blind rule of the supply and demand laws which form the political economy of the middle class, and social production controlled by social foresight,

> which forms the political economy of the working class. Hence the Ten Hours' Bill was not only a great practical success; it was the victory of a principle; it was the first time that in broad daylight the political economy of the middle class succumbed to the political economy of the working class.[3]

Blair tried to overturn what the creation of the Party had achieved, but it is significant that he failed. New Labour was built on the myth that eagerly espousing capitalism brought electoral success. When millions of Labour voters begged to differ it lost the 2010 election and Corbyn became leader soon after. This is evidence of the limitations to rightward drift that Labour's electoral base imposed.

While Corbyn represents a welcome attempt to have Labour voice the discontent of ordinary people under capitalism, limits are appearing to the leftward trajectory. That is not just a feature of the many MPs from the New Labour era. Although Labour may express working class concerns, and indeed came into existence for this purpose (if mediated by the union bureaucracy), what it offers in practice is restricted because it accepts the framework set by capitalism.

Part of this framework is ideological. Labour has never had its own independent ideology, something that can only come from adopting a clear position for the working class and against the boss class and its institutions. Trying to straddle the divide means Labour borrows its ideas, whether it be the language of nation and national interest, or, at best, the economic and social theories of Liberals like Keynes and Beveridge.

Another part of the framework is political—the capitalist state, and an electoral system where individuals are atomised, voting on a constituency not a class basis, and so on. Running this political system whether at local or national level obstructs radical policies however well-intentioned their proponents may be.

For that reason Labour remains a 'capitalist workers' party' with all the good and bad sides that that represents: good that the workers have a distinct Party to vote for, bad insofar as it accepts the capitalist rules of the game and so disappoints its own supporters. Thus one day we may be campaigning against cuts imposed by Labour councillors, yet the next day be uniting with the same councillors in opposing attempts by fascists to march through our towns.

Consequently revolutionary socialists cannot afford to be indifferent to developments in the Labour Party, though our approach changes according to circumstances. Under New Labour the most radical forces in society operated almost entirely outside the Party, and indeed opposed its leader directly through movements such as Stop the War. Today the internal life of the Party is very important. We castigate the Labour right and their disgraceful efforts to smear and undermine Corbyn, a leader who, if given the opportunity, can inspire millions to vote left. We applaud his efforts and those of his supporters to transform Labour in a progressive direction.

Yet when the outcome of the internal fight becomes clear this may have to change again. And even getting Labour to commit itself to genuine reformism has always depended on looking beyond the narrow confines of internal Party structures and the ballot box. Clause Four, mass membership and Labour's eclipsing of the Liberal Party came about due to the impact of WWI and the Russian revolution. The Attlee government and the welfare state were made possible by a major shift in popular consciousness driven by the Depression and WWII. Corbyn's emergence as leader was assisted by his extra-parliamentary activities and the support of forces coming from beyond the PLP or party membership. Therefore, the internal life of the Labour Party must be understood as only one element of a wider struggle.

There is another issue. Even left-wing reformists no longer pretend they intend to fully abolish capitalism. Therefore, while socialists must back the efforts of the Labour left against the right, a revolutionary alternative is absolute necessary too. This requires an independent Marxist party that tries to take the struggle beyond the limits of reformism and its electoral focus, and emphasises the collective potential of the working class in action.

Our differences do not mean that genuine reformists and revolutionaries have nothing to do with each other. We both share a commitment to the working class even if we disagree about how its interests are best secured. A working relationship is not only possible, the need for working class unity means that the strategy of the united front is required to confront specific challenges, such as the threat of racism or war. This strategy, which combines a common class effort with continued debate on the best way forward, was described by Trotsky in the 1920s:

> We broke with the reformists and centrists in order to obtain complete freedom in criticising perfidy, betrayal, indecision and the half way spirit in the labour movement. For this reason any sort of organisational agreement which restricts our freedom of criticism and agitation is absolutely unacceptable to us. We participate in a united front but do

> not for a single moment become dissolved in it. It is precisely in the course of struggle that the broad masses must learn from experience that we fight better than the others, that we see more clearly than the others, that we are more audacious and resolute.[4]

The need of the moment is indeed for a course of struggle—against racism, fascism, sexism, imperialism, exploitation and so much more. Revolutionaries are ready to engage in this alongside those who look to parliamentary reform and the Labour Party to deliver improvements. We agree with Trotsky that in this fight the experience of struggle will decide, and all the history of Labour and the international experience today, reinforces the argument that a revolutionary socialist organisation is needed.

Notes

Chapter 1: The birth of reformism

1 J R MacDonald, *The Socialist Movement* (London no date), p235.
2 D Thompson, *The Chartists* (Aldershot 1984), p60.
3 Quoted in Thompson, *The Chartists*, p237.
4 Quoted in M Jenkins, *The General Strike of 1842* (London 1980), p37.
5 Thompson, *The Chartists*, pp284–85.
6 Quoted in J B Jeffreys, *The Story of the Engineers* (London 1945), p33.
7 T Rothstein, *From Chartism to Labourism* (London 1983), p202.
8 *Hansard*, House of Lords, 16 July 1867.
9 Marx and Engels, *On Britain* (Moscow 1953), p509.
10 Quoted in F Bealey and and H Pelling, *Labour and Politics 1900–1906* (London 1958), p148.
11 G M Wilson, Alexander MacDonald, *Leader of the Miners* (Aberdeen 1982), p175.
12 G D H Cole, *Working Class Politics* (London 1941), p72.
13 Cole, *Working Class Politics*, p72.
14 J Hinton, *Labour and Socialism* (Brighton 1983), p25.
15 For substantiation of this argument see H A Clegg, A Fox and A F Thompson, *A History of British Trade Unions Since 1889* (Oxford 1964), p89.
16 Marx and Engels, *On Britain*, p520.
17 F Hammill, in *Murray's Magazine*, vol 8 (1890), p124.
18 Marx to F Bolte, 23 November 1871, in Marx/Engels/Lenin, *Anarchism and Anarcho-Syndicalism* (USSR 1972), p57.
19 G Shipton, 'Trade Unionism, New and Old', in *Murray's Magazine* (June 1890), p725.
20 Shipton, in *Murray's Magazine*, p731.
21 T Mann and B Tillett, *The New Unionism* (London 1890), pp4–5.
22 *Justice*, 21 September 1889.
23 E and G Radice, *Thorne* (London 1974), p44. For a full account of this process see E Hobsbawm, *Labouring Men* (London 1964), pp179–203.
24 Quoted in Radices, *Thorne*, p46.
25 *Report from Great Britain and Ireland to the Delegates of the Brussels International Congress, 1891, Presented by the Gas Workers and General Labourers' Union; the Royal Eight Hours and International Labour League; the Bloomsbury Socialist Society; and the Battersea Labour League* (London 1891), p13.
26 *The Trade Unionist*, 20 June 1891.
27 Quoted in J Schneer, *Ben Tillett* (Kent 1982), p62.
28 Schneer, *Ben Tillett*, p62.
29 D Howell, *British Workers and the Independent Labour Party* (Manchester 1983), pp174 and 290.
30 For details, see *Workman's Times*, 27 February 1891 and 14 January 1893.
31 Quoted in Clegg and others, p184.
32 E P Thompson, 'Homage to Tom Maguire', in A Briggs and J Saville (eds), *Essays in Labour History* (London 1960), pp302–3.
33 *ILP 1893 Conference Report*, p3.
34 Undated press cutting from the Hardie Collection in the National Library of Scotland, Dep 176(2).
35 *1887 TUC Congress Report*, p31.
36 S Desmond, *Labour—Giant with Feet of Clay* (London 1921), pp55.
37 Quoted in Rothstein, p281.
38 P Snowden, *Autobiography*, vol 1 (London 1934), p80.
39 K Hardie, *After Twenty Years: All about the ILP* (no place of publication given 1913), p6.
40 Quoted in H M Drucker, *Doctrine and Ethos of the Labour Party* (London 1979), p24.
41 L Trotsky, *Writings on Britain* (London 1974), vol 1, p20.
42 P Snowden, 'The Christ that is to Be', quoted in C Cross, Philip Snowden (London 1966), p36.
43 'The Labour Party and the books that helped to make it', in *Review of Reviews*, June 1906.
44 E Hughes (ed), *Keir Hardie's Speeches and Writings* (Glasgow 1927), p119.

45 J R MacDonald, *Socialism and Society* (London 1905), p128.
46 P Snowden, *Socialism and Syndicalism* (London no date), pp15–16.
47 *Labour Leader*, 26 January 1895.
48 Hardie, *After Twenty Years*, p6.
49 Hardie, *After Twenty Years*, p950; L Thompson, *The Enthusiasts* (London 1971), p132.
50 L Thompson, *The Enthusiasts* (London 1971), p132.
51 K Hardie, *My Confession of Faith in the Labour Alliance* (London 1909), p112.
52 Quoted in *Forward*, 19 March 1927 (his emphasis).
53 Howell, *British Workers and the Independent Labour Party*, p218.
54 Howell, *British Workers and the Independent Labour Party*, p164.
55 *Nineteenth Century*, January 1899, p25.
56 *Nineteenth Century*, January 1899, p27.
57 B Webb, *Diaries*, vol 2 (London 1986) p66 (entry for 23 January 1895).
58 F Williams, *Fifty Years' March* (London 1950), p84.
59 A M McBriar, *Fabian Socialism and English Politics* (Cambridge 1962), p290.
60 B Webb, *Diaries*, vol 3, p269.
61 M Cole, *The Story of Fabian Socialism* (London 1961), p6.
62 B Webb, *Diaries*, vol 2, p23.
63 B Webb, *Diaries*, vol 3, p146.
64 B Webb, *Our Partnership* (London 1948), pp83–84.
65 B Webb, *Diaries*, vol 3, pp258 and 195.
66 B Webb, *Diaries*, pp151–52.
67 B Webb, *Our Partnership*, p45.
68 Sidney Ball, 'Fabian Tract' no 72, p5, quoted in G Stedman Jones, *Outcast London* (Oxford 1971), p333.
69 B Webb, *Our Partnership*, p51.
70 G B Shaw (ed), *Fabian Essays* (London 1889), p50.
71 Shaw (ed), *Fabian Essays*, p200.
72 Radices, *Thorne*, p295. This argument is contained in the Webbs' massive work, *Soviet Communism, A New Civilisation?* (London 1935).
73 Shaw (ed) *Fabian Essays*, p209.
74 Marx and Engels, *On Reformism* (Moscow 1984), p320.
75 R Blatchford, *Merrie England* (London 1908), p128.
76 R Blatchford, *My Eighty Years* (London 1931), p196.
77 K Hardie, 'Socialism', which is an extract from a larger work—*From Serfdom to Socialism* (no place no date), pp6–7.
78 J R MacDonald, *Socialism for Business Men*, a speech to Liverpool Rotarians, 1 October 1925 (no date or place) p5.
79 B Webb, *Our Partnership*, p117.
80 B Webb, *Our Partnership*, p72.
81 B Webb, *Our Partnership*, p132.

Chapter 2:
'Out of the bowels of the TUC'

1 H Pelling, *The Origins of the Labour Party* (London 1965), p229.
2 *1895 TUC Congress Report*, p28.
3 Pelling, p171.
4 *TUC 1889*, p57, and *TUC 1890*, p53.
5 *TUC 1893*, p46.
6 *TUC 1895*, p34.
7 *Labour Leader*, 27 October 1894.
8 *Labour Leader*, 24 April 1895.
9 *Labour Leader*, 5 February and 14 May 1898.
10 *Labour Party Conference Report 1902*, p12.
11 J O'Grady, in *TUC 1898*, p32.
12 S and B Webb, *A History Of Trade Unionism* (London 1920), pp577–8, and Clegg and others, p478.
13 Cole, *Working Class Politics*, p141 (emphasis added).
14 *ILP Conference 1896*, p5.
15 Keir Hardie in *Labour Leader*, 25 April 1899.
16 *TUC 1899*, p65.
17 *Labour Party Conference Report 1900*, p11.
18 *Labour Party Conference Report 1900*, p12.
19 *Labour Party Conference Report 1900*, p12.
20 Clegg and others, p326.
21 *Labour Leader*, 16 September 1899.
22 *The Times*, 1 March 1900, quoted in Pelling, p208.
23 Bealey and Pelling, pp37–8, and Brand, p13.
24 Bealey, p43.
25 See Cole, *Working Class Politics*, p164.
26 P Clarke, *Lancashire and the New Liberalism* (Cambridge 1971), p321.
27 Quoted in M Petter, 'The Progressive Alliance', in *History*, vol 5, no 192, February 1973, pp55–6.
28 Bealey, p163.
29 Howell, p80.
30 Clegg and others, p375.
31 *Labour Leader*, 23 November 1901.
32 The figures given refer to the respective high points of the January 1910 general election and the 1906 parliament. Full details are W D Muller, *'The Kept Men'?* (Hassocks 1977), p4.
33 TUC 1899, pp32 and 66.
34 J R Clynes, *Memoirs* (London 1937), p94.
35 *Infancy of Labour Party*, documents at the British Library of Political and Economic Science.
36 *The Miner*, July 1887.

37 Howell, p218.
38 Desmond, p137.
39 Pelling, Origins, p176.
40 R Gregory, *The Miner, and British Politics 1906–1914* (Oxford 1968), p189.
41 Gregory, pp114 and 139.
42 P Snowden, *The Game of Party Politics* (London 1914), p11.
43 Radices, *Thorne*, p58.
44 *Infancy of Labour Party*, documents.
45 Quoted in Bealey, p40
46 Quoted in I McLean, *Keir Hardie* (London 1975), p88.
47 *Labour Leader*, 7 March 1903.
48 Lord Beaverbrook, *Politicians and the War* (London 1960), p514.
49 T Wilson (ed), *The Political Diaries of C P Scott 1911–1928* (London 1970), p320 (entry for 16–19 December 1917).
50 *Daily Herald*, 4 June 1926.
51 Bealey, pp298–9.
52 *Labour Party Conference Report 1903*, p108.
53 Williams, *Fifty Years March* (London no date), p24, and Brand, p12.
54 Quoted in P Poirier, *The Advent of the Labour Party* (London 1958), p145.
55 A contemporary opinion quoted in R Moore, *The Emergence of the Labour Party* (Sevenoaks 1978), p90.
56 Cross, p75.
57 *Labour Party Conference Report 1929*, p150.
58 Cole, *Working Class Politics*, p184.
59 Thompson, *The Enthusiasts*, p145.
60 Quotations and story from J MacMillan, *The Way We Were* (London 1978), pp122–4.
61 Trotsky, *Writings on Britain*, vol 2, p15.
62 *Labour Party Conference Report 1902*, p65.
63 Desmond, p86.
64 Snowden, *Autobiography*, vol 1, p127.
65 J H Thomas, *My Story* (London 1937), p28.
66 Quoted in G Blaxland, *J H Thomas: A Life for Unity* (London 1984), p60.
67 D Kirkwood, *My Life of Revolt* (London 1935), pp201–2.
68 Snowden, *Autobiography*, p133.
69 Thompson, *Enthusiasts*, p150.
70 R T McKenzie, *British Political Parties* (London 1963), p12.
71 *Labour Party Conference Report 1907*, p15.
72 Quoted in J P Nettl, *Rosa Luxemburg* (Cambridge 1969), p101.
73 Nettl, p49.
74 Nettl, p49.
75 Snowden, *Autobiography*, vol 1, pp87–8.
76 Barker (ed), *The Political Writings of Ramsay MacDonald* (London 1972), p225.
77 *Labour Leader*, 8 February 1907.
78 *Labour Leader*, 15 February 1907.
79 *Labour Leader*, 22 May 1908.
80 See draft bill in *Infancy of Labour Party*, documents.
81 S Beer, *Modern British Politics* (London 1965), p125.
82 Bealey, p190.
83 Quoted in Gregory, p41.
84 Quoted in Barker, pp161–2.
85 MacDonald, *The Socialist Movement*, p235.
86 L Hall, J M McLachlan, C T Douthwaite and J H Belcher, *Let Us Reform the Labour Party* (Manchester no date), p10.
87 *Weekly Despatch*, 10 March 1912.
88 D Marquand, *Ramsay MacDonald* (London 1977), pp126 and 142.
89 ILP Conference 1914, p85.
90 R Miliband, *Parliamentary Socialism* (London 1972), p14.
91 For details see D Clark, *Labour's Lost Leader: Victor Grayson* (London 1985), and R Groves, *The Strange Case of Victor Grayson* (London 1975).
92 V Grayson, *The Appeal for Socialism* (no date or place), p10.
93 Hall and others, p1.
94 Quoted in Hall and others, p5.
95 *ILP conference 1909*, p47.
96 Cross, p157.
97 P Thompson, p156.
98 *Labour Leader*, 23 April 1909.
99 Lenin, *Collected Works* (Moscow), vol 16, p32.
100 Quoted in B Tillett, *Is the Parliamentary Labour Party a failure?* (London, no date), p7.
101 Local press, quoted in B Holton, *British Syndicalism 1900–1914* (London 1976), p100.
102 TUC 1912, p274.
103 Quoted in Holton, pp116–117.
104 *Weekly Despatch*, 10 March 1912.
105 Sidney Buxton, quoted in J H Winter, *Socialism and the Challenge of War* (London 1974), p25.
106 *Socialist Review*, May 1912, p163.
107 *Labour Leader*, 27 July 1912.
108 *Socialist Review*, May 1912, p164.
109 J B Glasier, *Socialism and Strikes* (reprinted London 1920), pp7 and 12.
110 *Socialist Review*, January 1914, p4.
111 *Manchester Guardian*, 26 January 1914.
112 A Bullock, *The Life and Times Of Ernest Bevin*, vol 1 (London 1960), p34.
113 *Socialist Review*, March 1912, pp97–103.
114 G McAllister, *James Maxton, Portrait of a Rebel* (London 1935), p163.
115 J R MacDonald, *Syndicalism* (London 1913), pp6 and 55.
116 *Socialist Review*, vol 9, pp215–6.
117 *Labour Leader*, 31 May 1912.
118 *Railway Review*, 13 October 1911.

119 *The Times*, 9 September 1911.
120 *TUC 1912*, p277.
121 *Labour Leader*, 9 July 1914.
122 Quoted in Holton, p37.
123 For details see K D Brown (ed), *The First Labour Party* (Kent 1985), pp4 and 182, and R I McKibbin, 'James Ramsay MacDonald and the Problem of the Independence of the Labour Party', in *Journal of Modern History*, vol 42 (1970), p221.

Chapter 3: War and reconstruction

1 Quoted in H Tiltman, *James Ramsay MacDonald* (London, no date) p104.
2 Quoted in Winter, pp236 and 235.
3 A Marwick, *The Deluge* (Harmondsworth 1965) p313.
4 M A Waters (ed), *Rosa Luxemburg Speaks* (New York 1970) pp261–2.
5 Quoted in Schneer, p192.
6 D Lloyd George, *War Memoirs* (London 1938) vol 2, p1141 (emphasis added).
7 Quoted in Clynes, p234.
8 Desmond, p68.
9 See Williams, p217.
10 Quoted in Lenin, *On Britain*, p96.
11 See Winter, p17.
12 E Hughes (ed) *Keir Hardie: Speeches and Writings* (Glasgow 1927), p155.
13 Quoted in J McNair, *James Maxton—the Beloved Rebel* (London 1955), pp43–4.
14 Quoted in McNair, p47.
15 Drucker, p18.
16 Drucker, p14.
17 Quoted in Clynes, p234.
18 Quoted in P Wyncoll, *The Nottingham Labour Movement* (London 1985), p182.
19 Schneer, p194.
20 Schneer, p194.
21 TUC 1916, p386.
22 R Dowse, *Left in the Centre* (London 1966), p30.
23 Dowse, p64.
24 Marwick, p86.
25 Quoted in T Cliff, *Lenin: All Power to the Soviets* (London 1976), pp45.
26 Warwick, p227.
27 Quoted in Marquand, p175.
28 Quoted in F Brockway, *Inside the Left* (London 1942) p45.
29 *Hansard*, 3 August 1914.
30 Brockway, p69.
31 *Forward*, 5 February.
32 Beveridge, quoted in I McLean, *The Legend of Red Clydeside* (Edinburgh 1983), p56.
33 Quoted in McNair, p61.
34 K Middlemas, *The Clydesiders* (London 1965), p68.
35 Kirkwood, p82.
36 Kirkwood, pp116–118.
37 E Shinwell, *Lead with the Left* (London 1981), p55.
38 Lenin, *On Britain*, pp282–3.
39 Quoted in P Stansky (ed) *The Left and War: The British Labour Party and World War i* (New York 1969), pp162–3.
40 Quoted in Tiltman, p110.
41 *The Left and War*, p164.
42 *TUC 1916*, p389.
43 Thomas, p45.
44 Quoted in Winter, p210.
45 Webbs, *History of Trade Unionism*, pp637–8.
46 Quoted in McKibbin, p105.
47 Quoted in Snowden, *Autobiography*, vol 1, p392.
48 B Webb, *Diaries*, p271 (entry for 8 December 1916).
49 The latter figure is for 1923; details in C L Mowat, *Britain between the Wars* (London 1968), p15.
50 R H Tawney, 'The Abolition of Economic Controls', in *Economic History Review* (1940), p273.
51 Marwick, p167.
52 *Hansard*, 30 March 1916.
53 *Labour Leader*, 27 May 1915.
54 Winter, p18.
55 Quoted in Winter, p239.
56 *British Labour and the Russian Revolution, The Leeds Convention: a report from the Daily Herald* (reprinted Nottingham no date), p22.
57 *British Labour and the Russian Revolution*, p29.
58 Quoted in K Coates, introduction to *British Labour and the Russian Revolution*, pp12–13.
59 Quoted in J M Winter, 'Arthur Henderson, the Russian Revolution and the Reconstruction of the Labour Party', in *The Historical Journal*, vol 15, no 4 (1972), p762.
60 *Historical Journal*, vol 15, no 4, p763.
61 Henderson, quoted in McKibbin, p6.
62 A Henderson, *The Aims of Labour* (London 1918), p57.
63 Henderson, p59.
64 Henderson, pp61–2 (emphasis added).
65 N Mackenzie (ed), *The Letters of Beatrice and SidneyWebb*, vol 3 (Cambridge 1978), p113.
66 See for example the entry in Tom Jones's diary from 10 September 1917, in T Jones, *Whitehall Diary* (London 1965), p36.
67 *Labour Party Conference Report 1918*, p15.
68 Jones, p45 (entry for 12 January 1918).

69 Quoted in Scott, p316 (entry for 11–12 December 1917).
70 *Labour Conference 1918*, p26.
71 F W S Craig (ed) *British General Election Manifestos 1900–1974* (London 1975), p41.
72 *Manifestoes*, pp34.
73 A summary of these debates can be found in McKenzie, pp465–71.
74 *Labour Leader*, 25 September 1908.
75 *Labour Conference 1918*, p44.
76 *Labour Conference 1918*, p44.
77 See *Labour Leader*, 31 January 1918.
78 *Labour Leader*, 4 April 1918.
79 E Wertheimer, *Portrait of the Labour Party* (London 1929), p14.
80 Hardie, Speeches and Writings, p33.
81 Quoted in G D H Cole, *A History of the Labour Party since 1914* (London 1948), p66.
82 K Marx, *Early Writings* (Harmondsworth 1974), p244.
83 Marx, *Early Writings*, p244.
84 P Snowden, *How to Nationalise the Mines* (Manchester no date), pp1 and 8.
85 *Labour Conference 1918*, p43.
86 *Labour Conference 1918*, p45.
87 *Labour Leader*, 9 October 1919.
88 *Labour Leader*, 27 March 1919.
89 Marx, *Surveys from Exile*, p176.

Chapter 4:
Riding the post-war storm

1 *Rosa Luxemburg Speaks*, p415.
2 *Theses, Resolutions and Manifestoes of the First Four Congresses of the Third International* (London 1980), p201 (emphasis added).
3 For details of the ferment in Britain after the end of the First World War, see C Rosenberg, *1919—Britain on the Brink of Revolution* (London 1987).
4 J Hinton, *Labour and Socialism* (Brighton 1983), p108.
5 *Hansard* 18 August 1918.
6 *Hansard* 7 November 1918.
7 Scott, *Diaries*, pp331–2 (entry for 30 January 1919).
8 Rosenberg, p83.
9 A Hutt, *A Post-War History of the British Working Class* (Wakefield 1972), p15.
10 Quoted in Hutt, p33.
11 *Hansard*, 29 May 1919.
12 Quoted in Cross, p173.
13 *Hansard*, 29 May 1919.
14 *Hansard*, 29 October 1919.
15 *Railway Review*, 20 June 1919.
16 *TUC 1919*, p48.
17 Desmond, p96.
18 For an explanation see Tony Cliff and Donny Gluckstein, *Marxism and Trade Union Struggle: The General Strike of 1926* (London 1986), pp81–92.
19 *ILP Conference Report 1919*, p72.
20 Bonar Law and Churchill, quoted in Rosenberg, p68.
21 R Smillie, *My Life for Labour* (London 1924), pp97–8.
22 Clegg and others, p50.
23 Quoted in A Bevan, *In Place of Fear* (London 1961), pp20–1.
24 Trotsky, *Writings on Britain*, vol 1, p33.
25 *Diaries*, pp335-6 (entry for 22 Feruary 1919).
26 *Daily Herald*, 11 July 1914.
27 E Barry, *Nationalisation in British Politics* (London 1965), p206 note.
28 *Railway Review*, 14 February 1919
29 Dowse, p65.
30 Smillie, *TUC 1919*, pp218–9.
31 *Labour Conference 1919*, p119.
32 *Labour Conference 1919*, p120.
33 *The Times*, 7 February 1919.
34 Clynes, in *Daily Herald*, 23 December 1918.
35 Thomas, *TUC 1919*, p294.
36 Clynes, *Labour Conference 1919*, p160.
37 Tom Shaw, *TUC 1919*, p291.
38 McGurk, *Labour Conference 1919*, p113.
39 *TUC 1920*, p88.
40 *Labour Conference 1920*, pp7–8.
41 Trotsky, *Writings on Britain*, vol 2, p137.
42 *Forward*, 6 May 1916.
43 *Socialist Review*, Summer 1916, p205.
44 For details see J Mahon, *Harry Pollitt* (London 1976), pp79–82.
45 Beatrice Webb's diary and *New Statesman*, quoted in S White, *Britain and the Bolshevik Revolution* (London 1979), pp49–50.
46 Quoted in Hutt, p39.
47 J R MacDonald, *Parliament and Revolution* (London 1919), p75.
48 MacDonald, *Socialism and Government* (1909) quoted in F Bealey, *The Social and Political Thought of the Labour Party* (London 1970), p69 (Emphasis added).
49 *The Communist*, 12 August 1920.
50 Quoted in White, p47.
51 Lenin, *On Britain*, p470.
52 *Socialist Review*, July–September 1920, p206.
53 Glasier in 1913, quoted in *Labour Leader*, 7 April 1921.
54 Lenin, *Collected Works*, vol 16, p32.
55 *Socialist Review*, October–December 1921, p299.
56 Selection of quotations from Cabinet meetings on 4 and 5 April 1921 in Jones, pp133–6.

57 *Socialist Review*, July–September 1921, p197.
58 *Socialist Review*, January–March 1921, p13.
59 *Labour Leader*, 7 July 1921.
60 Hinton, p90.
61 Dowse, pp74 and 76.
62 Williams, p203 (emphasis added).
63 See McKibbin.
64 *Labour Leader*, 6 October 1922.
65 *Labour Leader*, 13 October 1922.
66 See Clegg and others, p356.
67 Bevin in 1919, quoted in A Bullock, *The Life and Times of Ernest Bevin*, vol 1 (London 1960), p111.
68 Clegg and others, p379.

Chapter 5:
Proving Labour 'fit to govern': the 1924 administration

1 F Engels, *Anti-Dühring* (Peking 1976), p26.
2 Clynes, p17.
3 Thomas, p169.
4 Clynes, vol 2, p45
5 See for example the exchange of letters between Hankey and Jones, numbers one and two in the Cabinet Secretariat during September 1926, in Jones, pp73–75.
6 S W Roskill, *Hankey: Man of Secrets*, vol 1 (London 1942), p352.
7 See Jones, pp301 and 306.
8 Quoted in Marquand, p417.
9 *Labour Conference 1925*, p197.
10 Quoted in R W Lyman, *The First Labour Government* (London 1957), p106.
11 L MacNeill Weir, *The Tragedy of Ramsay MacDonald* (London 1938), p46.
12 A Morgan, *J Ramsay MacDonald* (Manchester 1987), p103.
13 Quoted in Lyman, p106.
14 H Nicolson, *George V* (London 1952), p384.
15 Nicolson, pp384–6.
16 B Webb, *Diaries*, vol 4, p10 (entry for 28 January 1924).
17 Thomas, p152.
18 Wertheimer, p88.
19 M A Hamilton, *Arthur Henderson* (London 1938), p242.
20 Clynes, p142; see also, p153.
21 MacNeill Weir, p146.
22 M Cowling, *The Impact of Labour* (Cambridge 1971), p369.
23 Quoted in *Workers' Weekly*, 29 February 1924.
24 S Webb, in *Political Quarterly* (1961), p23.
25 See Public Record Office document Cab 23/47.
26 PRO Cab 15/24, pp166–7; see also K Jeffery and P Hennessy, *States of Emergency* (London 1983).
27 S Webb, in *Political Quarterly* (1961), p23.
28 PRO Cabinet Paper 211/24.
29 T Shaw, *Can Labour Rule?*, number 3, p8 (no date or place).
30 *Hansard*, 23 June 1924.
31 *Daily Herald*, 18 February 1924 (emphasis added).
32 See R K Middlemas, *Politics in Industrial Society* (London 1979), p187.
33 PRO Cabinet Paper 204/24.
34 Quoted in V L Allen, *Trade Unions and the Government* (London 1960), p231.
35 Quoted in *Workers' Weekly*, 18 January 1924.
36 *Forward*, 16 August 1924.
37 *Hansard*, 12 February 1924 (emphasis added).
38 Snowden, *Socialism and Syndicalism*, p149.
39 Cross, p207.
40 *Hansard*, 1 May 1924.
41 Mowat, p176.
42 *Hansard*, 26 March 1924.
43 *Hansard*, 23 June 1924.
44 Clegg and others, p365.
45 Quoted in Cowling, p372.
46 Jones, p275 (diary entry for 9 April 1924); a sign of his personal difficulty was that his son, Oliver Baldwin, became a Labour MP.
47 *Hansard*, 13 February 1924.
48 *Hansard*, 13 February 1924.
49 *Hansard*, 19 February 1924; the actual debate concerned defence.
50 Quoted in *Workers Weekly*, 8 September 1924.
51 Lyman, p235.
52 Nicolson, p399.
53 Clynes, vol 1, p79.

Chapter 6:
Revolution or reform: the left in the 1920s

1 William McLaine speaking at the Second Comintern Congress, in *The Second Congress of the Communist International*, vol 2 (London 1978), p181.
2 *Communist Unity Convention*, London, 31 July 1920, pp39–40.
3 *The Socialist*, 6 May 1920.
4 Lenin, *On Britain*, pp462–3.
5 Lenin, *On Britain*, p461.
6 Lenin, *On Britain*, p450.
7 Lenin, *On Britain*, p424.
8 Lenin, *On Britain*, p399.
9 Lenin, *On Britain*, p449 (emphasis added).
10 *Labour Party National Executive Committee Minutes*, 30 June 1914.
11 Duncan Hallas, 'Revolutionaries and the Labour Party', *International Socialism* 2: 16 (Spring 1982), p4.

12 For an excellent discussion of this, see Duncan Hallas in *International Socialism* 2: 16.
13 V I Lenin, *On Britain*, (Moscow 1973), p398.
14 Lenin, p401.
15 Lenin, p415.
16 Lenin, p401.
17 This letter, dated 10 August 1920 and signed by Arthur MacManus and Albert Inkpin, Chairman and Secretary of the Communist Party respectively, is included in the Labour Party's *NEC Minutes*.
18 The votes at the last three were 3,086,000 to 261,000; 2,880,000 to 366,000 and 3,185,000 to 193,000 respectively.
19 Details in R Stewart, *Breaking the Fetters* (London 1967) pages 115–119, and J Klugmann, *History of the Communist Party of Great Britain*, vol 1 (London 1968), pp182–4.
20 *The Communist*, 12 August 1922.
21 Details from a letter by MacManus of 21 December 1923 to a provincial Communist which was intercepted by the Secret Services and cited in Report on Revolutionary Organisations in Cabinet Papers, Cab 24(165) CP 5(24).
22 *Workers' Weekly*, 8 February 1924.
23 B Webb, *Diaries*, vol 3, p46 (entry for 19 December 1924).
24 'Introduction' to the *Left Wing Programme* as adopted by the Second Annual Conference on 24–25 September 1927, in *Towards a Labour Government* (no place or date of publication), p15.
25 D Hallas, *The Comintern* (London 1985), p66.
26 *Report of the Seventh Congress of the CPGB*, 30 May–1 June 1925 (no place of publication).
27 *The Reds and the Labour Party: Towards a Left Wing Policy* (published by the Communist Party, London, no date), p19.
28 *The Reds and the Labour Party*, p23.
29 *Labour Monthly*, vol 7 (January–December 1925), p581.
30 *Communist International*, no 9, pp12–13.
31 There is no space here to discuss this point, but it has been dealt with in T Cliff and D Gluckstein, *Marxism and the Trade Union Struggle*, pp41–56.
32 Cliff and Glucksein, p145.
33 *Communist International*, no 9 (Summer 1925), p16.
34 *Communist International*, no 9, p13.
35 *Communist International*, no 9, p12.
36 *Labour Monthly*, vol 6 (July–December 1924), p662.
37 *Labour Monthly*, vol 7 (1925), p202.
38 *Tenth Communist Party Congress* (London 1929), p21.
39 Trotsky's *Writings on Britain*, vol 2 (London 1974), pp241–2.
40 Trotsky's *Writings on Britain*, vol 2, pp57–8.
41 Trotsky's *Writings on Britain*, vol 2, p248.
42 Trotsky's *Writings on Britain*, vol 2, pp118–9.
43 Trotsky's *Writings on Britain*, vol 2, p119.
44 Wertheimer, pp115–6.
45 Dowse, p115 (emphasis added).
46 Quoted in McKenzie, p371.
47 Joint Meeting of the Executive Committee of the Labour Party and the National Administrative Council of the ILP, 23 May 1925, in *Labour Party NEC Minutes*.
48 *Hansard*, 26 June 1924.
49 Kirkwood, pp191–2.
50 McAllister, p114.
51 Quoted in R Skidelsky, *Oswald Mosley* (London 1975), p169.
52 *ILP London Conference*, April 1923, p143.
53 Quoted in Middlemas, p129.
54 J A Hobson, 'The Ethics of Industrialism', in E Stanton Coit (ed), *Ethical Democracy* (London 1900), p106.
55 Quoted in *New Leader*, 1 October 1926.
56 *New Leader*, 24 December 1926.
57 *New Leader*, 28 May 1925.
58 *Forward*, 5 September 1925.
59 Quoted in *Forward*, 13 March 1926.
60 *Sunday Worker*, 21 June 1925.
61 Quoted in Howell, *A Lost Left* (Manchester 1986), p275.
62 Quoted in Howell, *A Lost Left*, p256.
63 Quoted in McAllister, pp191–2.
64 Quoted in Middlemas, p221.
65 J Paton, *Left Turn!* (London 1936), p303.
66 T Cliff, 'The Tragedy of A J Cook', in *International Socialism* 2: 31 (Spring 1986), pp100–101.
67 *Labour Monthly*, vol 2, January–June 1922, p388.
68 N Branson, *Poplarism*, 1919-1925 (London 1979), p102.
69 Quoted in Branson, p86.
70 Details in *East End News*, 23 May 1925, and E Lansbury, *Poplarism* (London 1924), p3.
71 *Theses Resolutions and Manifestos of the Four Congresses of the Third International* (London 1980), p101.
72 Cabinet Papers, CP 114(24).
73 Lansbury, p6.
74 Lansbury, p8.
75 Quoted in Branson, p215.
76 *East London Advertiser*, 13 June 1925.
77 Cabinet discussion quoted in Rosenberg, p31.

78 Wertheimer, p79.
79 I McLean, *The Legend of Red Clydeside* (Edinburgh 1983), p204.
80 J Scanlon, *The Decline and Fall of the Labour Party* (London 1932), pp92–3.
81 A Y Badayev, *The Bolsheviks in the Tsarist Duma* (London 1987), p35.
82 Quoted in Badayev, p155.

Chapter 7: General Strike and aftermath

1 N and J Mackenzie (eds) *The Letters of Sidney and Beatrice Webb*, vol 3 (Cambridge 1978), p264.
2 Blatchford's editorial in *Clarion*, 13 May 1892.
3 The description made by Robert Williams, president of the 1926 Labour Conference, and now a confirmed right-winger, see *Labour Conference 1926*, p38.
4 Quoted in Cliff and Gluckstein, p266.
5 *Socialist Review*, May 1926 p7.
6 See Jones, vol 1, pp326–8 and *Hansard*, 6 August 1925.
7 The phrase is MacNeill Weir's.
8 MacNeill Weir, p199.
9 See for example Cliff and Gluckstein, *Marxism and Trade Union Struggle*.
10 Quoted in Tiltman, p203.
11 Quoted in P Renshaw, *The General Strike* (London 1975,) p214.
12 MacKenzies (eds), *Letters*, pp265–6.
13 MacKenzies (eds), *Letters*, p176.
14 Paton, p246.
15 *London Labour Party Report*, 1925–6, p13.
16 Quoted in B Donoghue and G Jones, *Herbert Morrison: Portrait of a Politician* (London 1973), p80.
17 Dowse, p128.
18 *Forward*, 15 August 1925.
19 Details in Dowse, p128.
20 *Labour Leader*, 30 April 1926.
21 Paton, pp245–6.
22 *Daily Herald*, 20 May 1926.
23 Quoted in Cliff and Gluckstein, p262.
24 Cliff and Gluckstein, p270.
25 B Webb, *Diaries*, p77 (entry for 3 May 1926).
26 B Webb, *Diaries*, p95 (entry for 21 August 1926).
27 Quoted in R K Middlemas, *Politics in Industrial Society* (London 1979) p177.
28 *Forward*, 22 May 1926.
29 Snowden, *Autobiography*, vol 2, p725.
30 Thomas, p105.
31 Thomas, p108.
32 Clegg and others, p427.
33 *TUC Congress 1926*, p74.
34 Presidential address, *TUC Congress 1927*, p66.
35 *Daily Herald*, 31 May 1926.
36 *Labour Conference 1926*, p194.
37 Donoghue and Jones, p80.
38 *Socialist Review*, November 1926, p2.
39 'Report of meeting on 24 November 1926 between TUC General Council and Labour Party Executive' in *NEC Minutes*.
40 B Webb, *Diaries*, vol 4, p85 (entry for 12 June 1926).
41 *ILP Conference 1909*, pp47–8.
42 *Labour Conference 1922*, p177.
43 *Forward*, 8 January 1921.
44 *Labour Conference 1923*, p181.
45 For details of the Kelvingrove by-election, see letter of 11 May 1924 from Ben Shaw, secretary of the Scottish Labour Party, in *NEC Minutes*.
46 Report of sub-committee in *NEC Minutes*, 27 August 1924.
47 See L Chester, S Fay and H Young, *The Zinoviev Letter* (London 1967), p132.
48 Quoted in Tiltman, p133.
49 *Labour Conference 1924*, p130.
50 *Labour Magazine*, December 1924.
51 Quoted in *Sunday Worker*, 4 October 1925.
52 W Lawther, quoted in 'Report of Deputation Appointed by the National Executive of the Labour Party to enquire into the circumstances of the Kelvingrove by-election', *NEC Minutes*, 21 July 1924.
53 *Labour Conference 1925*, p181.
54 'Organisation Sub-Committee report', *NEC Minutes*, 26 July 1926.
55 The whip was withdrawn only in February 1927; see *NEC Minutes*, 8 February 1927.
56 *Sunday Worker*, 22 March 1925.
57 Chairman's address to Second Annual Left Wing Movement Conference, 1927.
58 *Sunday Worker*, 27 September 1925.
59 N Branson, *History of the Communist Party of Great Britain, 1927–1941* (London 1985), p5.
60 *Sunday Worker*, 17 October 1926.
61 *Sunday Worker*, 9 September 1928.
62 Will Crick in *Sunday Worker*, 23 September 1928.
63 Quoted in W Knox, *James Maxton* (Manchester 1987) p76.
64 *Forward*, 22 January 1927.
65 Lansbury's *Labour Weekly*, 19 December 1925.

Chapter 8: Reformists and the slump: the second Labour government

1 S Webb, 'What Happened in 1931', in *Political Quarterly* (1932), p1.
2 Quoted in R Bassett, *1931: Political Crisis* (London 1986), p424.
3 *Labour Conference 1928*, p100.

4 Wheatley, speaking at Labour Conference 1928, p212.
5 Knox, p83.
6 Quoted in *Daily Herald*, 7 June 1929.
7 Hugh Dalton quoted in Hutt, p196.
8 Robert Boothby, in *Hansard*, 4 July 1929.
9 J R Clynes, home secretary, in *Hansard*, 24 July 1929.
10 *Labour and the Nation*. (London 1928), p16 (emphasis added).
11 *Labour Conference 1930*, p173.
12 Mowat, p365.
13 For details see H Slesser, *Judgement Reserved* (London 1941), pp60 and 157.
14 *Labour Conference 1927*, p255.
15 Fenner Brockway, in *Hansard*, 26 May 1930.
16 R Skidelsky, *Politicians and the Slump* (Harmondsworth 1970), pp398–9.
17 S Lawrence, in *Labour Conference 1930*, p153.
18 Cab. 26(30), 8 May 1930.
19 J R Clynes Quoted in *Daily Herald*, 10 January 1931.
20 *Hansard*, 2 December 1929.
21 Speaking at the Oxford Union Society, 5 June 1930, quoted in W Hannington, *Unemployed Struggles* (London 1977), p211.
22 Quoted in Gross, p244.
23 Quoted in G Foote, *The Labour Party's Political Thought* (London 1986), p53.
24 *Hansard*, 31 March 1931.
25 Quoted in Jones, vol 2, p264 (entry for 4 June 1930).
26 Reported by Nicholson, p461.
27 Lansbury Papers, quoted in Skidelsky, *Politicians and the Slump*, p268.
28 *Hansard*, 11 February 1931.
29 *Daily Herald*, 17 February 1931.
30 Mowat, p379.
31 *Hansard*, 7 April 1931.
32 *Hansard*, 19 May 1931.
33 Quoted in R McKibbin, 'The Economic Policy of the Second Labour Government', in *Past and Present*, August 1976, p120.
34 B Webb, *Diaries*, vol 4, p252.
35 *Daily Herald*, 21 August 1931.
36 Reported by Nicholson, p459.
37 Cab. 43(31), 21 August 1931.
38 Johnston quoted in MacNeill Weir, p407.
39 B Webb, *Diaries*, vol 4 (entry for 23 August 1931).
40 Cab. 46(310), 23 August 1931.
41 Quoted in Nicolson, p464.
42 Kirkwood, p248.
43 Miliband, p185.
44 See Hannington, pp219–230, for a thrilling account of agitation.
45 *Daily Herald*, 21 February 1930.
46 *Daily Herald*, 15 October 1931.
47 *Daily Herald*, 3 October 1931.
48 C G Ammon quoted in *Daily Herald*, 23 September 1931.
49 Details in Clegg and others, p519, and A Ereira, *The Invergordon Mutiny* (London 1981).
50 Quoted in Bassett, p224.
51 Labour Conference, p155.
52 S Webb, in *Political Quarterly*, p1.
53 Quoted in Marquand, pp630–1.
54 Quoted in Snowden, vol 2, p957.
55 B Webb, *Diaries*, vol 4, p216 (entry for 19 May 1930).
56 *Hansard*, 16 April 1930.
57 *Hansard*, 11 February 1931.

Chapter 9:
From socialist dictatorship to National Unity: Labour in the 1930s

1 *Labour Conference 1933*, p166.
2 Quoted in W Golant, 'The emergence of C R Attlee as leader of the Parliamentary Labour Party in 1935', in *Historical Journal*, number 13 (1970), p320.
3 *New Clarion*, 17 December 1932, cited by Pimlott, 'The Socialist League: Intellectuals and the Labour Left in the 1930s', in *Journal of Contemporary History*, no 3 (1971).
4 *SSIP News*, August 1932, cited by Pimlott, in *Journal of Contemporary History*, no 3.
5 Donoghue and Jones, pp182–3.
6 See Donoghue and Jones, pp162–8.
7 R H Tawney, *The Choice before the Labour Party* (London 1932), p9.
8 P Williams, *Hugh Gaitskell* (London 1982), p47.
9 Quoted by Wheatley, in *Glasgow Evening Times*, 15 May 1930.
10 Miliband, p195.
11 A Cooke, *The Life of Richard Stafford Cripps* (London 1957), p127.
12 *Labour Conference 1931*, p205.
13 *New Nation*, September 1934.
14 *Daily Herald*, 5 November 1934.
15 *Manchester Guardian*, 8 January 1934.
16 *Manchester Guardian*, 28 May 1934.
17 S Cripps, 'Can Socialism Come by Constitutional Means?', in C Addison *Problems of Socialist Government* (London 1933), pp43, 46 and 66.
18 Cooke, pp159–60.
19 E Estorick, *Sir Stafford Cripps* (London 1949), pp122–3.
20 Quoted in B Pimlott, *Labour and the Left in the 1930s* (Cambridge 1977), p52.
21 P Seyd, 'Factionalism Within the Labour Party: The Socialist League 1932–37', in A Briggs and J Saville (eds), *Essays in Labour History 1918–1939* (London 1977).

22 *Labour Conference 1932*, pp182–94.
23 *Labour Conference 1932*, p204.
24 *Labour Conference 1932*, p205.
25 *Labour Conference 1933*, p159.
26 *For Socialism and Peace* (London 1934), p12.
27 B R Mitchell and P Deane, *Abstract of British Historical Statistics* (Cambridge 1971), pp68 and 71.
28 R Croucher, *Engineers at War* (London 1982), p26.
29 Croucher, p27.
30 Croucher, pp47–56.
31 Croucher, p364.
32 N Branson and M Heinemann, *Britain in the Nineteen Thirties* (London 1973), pp122–5.
33 J Stevenson and C Cook, *The Slump* (London 1977), p159.
34 J Saville, 'May Day 1937', in Briggs and Saville, p240.
35 Saville, in Briggs and Saville, p240.
36 Details in Stevenson and Cook, pp185–7.
37 Stevenson and Cook, pp185–7.
38 Stevenson and Cook, pp204–6.
39 *Labour Conference 1936*, pp228 and 230.
40 *Labour Conference 1934*, p18.
41 Branson and Heinemann, p318.
42 *Labour Conference 1936*, p164.
43 Saville, in Briggs and Saville, p241.
44 *Left News*, August 1937.
45 *Left News*, July 1938.
46 *Tribune*, 24 March 1939.
47 *Tribune*, 25 August 1939.
48 *Labour Conference 1935*, p153.
49 *Labour Conference 1935*, p177.
50 *Labour Conference 1935*, p193.
51 R Postgate, *The Life of George Lansbury* (London 1951), pp309–317.
52 *Labour Conference 1936*, p177.
53 *Labour Conference 1937*, pp212–5.
54 *Labour Conference 1937*, p15.
55 *Labour Conference 1939*, p6.
56 *Labour Conference 1933*, p186.
57 *Labour Conference 1934*, p178.
58 *Labour Conference 1934*, p140.
59 *Labour Conference 1934*, p142.
60 L Trotsky, *Whither France?* (New York 1936), p25.
61 *Labour Conference 1936*, p257.
62 *Daily Herald*, 15 February 1937.
63 *Labour Conference 1937*, p27.
64 *Labour Conference 1937*, p26.
65 *Tribune*, 21 May 1937.
66 Foot, *Bevan*, vol 1, p246.
67 *Labour Conference 1937*, p163.
68 *Labour Conference 1937*, p164.
69 *Manchester Guardian*, 6 October 1937.
70 *Tribune*, 14 April 1938.
71 *Tribune*, 23 September 1938.
72 *Labour Conference 1939*, p45.
73 *Daily Herald*, 22 February 1939, quoted in K Harris, *Attlee* (London 1984), p159. The Douglas Cole referred to is G D H Cole.
74 Foot, *Bevan*, vol 1, p291.
75 *Labour Conference 1939*, p236.
76 *Labour Conference 1939*, p299.
77 Pimlott, *Labour and the Left in the 1930s*, p181.
78 Estorick, p174.
79 Foot, *Bevan*, vol 1, pp291–2.
80 *Tribune*, 8 December 1939.
81 *Socialist League Annual Report 1933*.
82 *The Socialist*, September 1935.
83 *League of Youth Monthly Bulletin*, February 1931, in J Jupp, 'The Left In Britain 1931–41' (MSc Econ thesis, London 1956), p214.
84 *Labour Conference 1936*, p75.
85 *Labour Conference 1939*, p241.
86 *Labour Conference 1936*, p75.
87 *Labour Conference 1937*, p155.
88 *Labour Conference 1939*, p379.
89 *Labour Conference 1939*, p323.

Chapter 10: The Labour Party during the Second World War

1 *Hansard*, 22 May 1940.
2 'Legal Proceedings against Strikers under Order 1305', LAB 10/998.
3 Bullock, vol 2, pp300–1.
4 Bullock, vol 2, pp301–2.
5 *TUC 1944*, p216.
6 *TUC 1941*, p335.
7 *TUC 1941*, p336.
8 *Hansard*, 29 July 1942.
9 *Hansard*, 9 September 1941.
10 A Calder, *The People's War* (London 1971), p336.
11 *Hansard*, 8 October 1942.
12 *The Times*, 21 November 1942.
13 Calder, p354.
14 Foot, *Bevan*, vol 1, p404.
15 *Hansard*, 3 August 1943.
16 W Churchill, *The Second World War*, vol 6 (London 1954), p198.
17 *Hansard*, 8 December 1944.
18 Bullock, vol 2, p343, and *Labour Conference 1944*, p150.
19 S Orwell and I Angus (eds), *The Collected Essays, Journalism and Letters of George Orwell*, vol 2 (London 1968), pp351–2.
20 *New Statesman*, 1 June 1940.
21 H Thomas, *John Strachey* (London 1973), p207.
22 *Hansard*, 8 October 1940.
23 Cato, *Guilty Men* (London 1940), p18.
24 Cato, p19.
25 Cato, p124.

26 *Tribune*, 11 October 1940.
27 *Hansard*, 20 May 1943 (emphasis added).
28 *Tribune*, 3 January 1941.
29 *Tribune*, 1 August 1941.
30 G D H Cole, *Europe, Russia and the Future* (London 1941), p153.
31 *Tribune*, 14 March 1941.
32 *Tribune*, 2 February 1945.
33 *Tribune*, 16 February 1945.
34 *Tribune*, 6 February 1942.
35 Calder, p345.
36 *Hansard*, 2 July 1942.
37 *Hansard*, 9 September 1942.
38 R Luxemburg, *The Junius Pamphlet*, in *Rosa Luxemburg Speaks* (New York 1970), p262.
39 Calder, p293.
40 H M D Parker, *Manpower: A Study of Wartime Policy and Administration* (London 1957), p504.
41 Parker, p457.
42 Bullock, vol 2, p260.
43 R Page Arnot, *The Miners in Crisis and War* (London 1961), p396.
44 Foot, *Bevan*, vol 1, pp446–7.
45 *Hansard*, 28 April 1944.
46 *Hansard*, 28 April 1944.
47 *The Times*, 3 May 1944.
48 Foot, *Bevan*, vol 1, p459.
49 *The Times*, 17 and 18 May 1944.
50 *The Times*, 9 June 1944.
51 *Tribune*, 5 May 1944.
52 *The Times*, 18 June 1943.
53 *Tribune*, 3 March 1944.
54 P Addison, *The Road to 1945* (London 1975), pp154–5.
55 Addison, p226.
56 *Tribune*, 11 December 1942.
57 *Hansard*, 6 October 1944.
58 *Hansard*, 20 December 1944.
59 *Tribune*, 5 March 1943.
60 *Tribune*, 22 October 1943.
61 *Tribune*, 22 September 1944.
62 W K Hancock and M M Gowing, *The British War Economy* (London 1949), p297.
63 Quoted in H Thomas, *John Strachey*, p175.
64 Thomas, p178.
65 J Strachey, *A Programme for Progress* (London 1940), pp151–2.
66 A Crosland, *The Future of Socialism* (London 1956), p58.
67 Addison, pp232–3.
68 C R Attlee, *The Labour Party in Perspective* (London 1937), p15.
69 Attlee, p153.
70 Attlee, p145.
71 Calder, p616.
72 Addison, p262.
73 K Martin, *Harold Laski* (London 1969), p152.
74 *Hansard*, 21 June 1944.
75 J M Keynes, *The General Theory of Employment, Interest and Money* (New York 1964), p378.
76 *Hansard*, 23 June 1944.
77 V L Allen, *Trade Unions and the Government* (London 1960), p33.
78 W Citrine, *Two Careers* (London 1967), p28.
79 *TUC Congress Report 1946*, p269.
80 Quoted in Addison, p212.
81 Addison, p217.
82 Addison, p218.
83 Bullock, vol 2, p226.
84 See Calder, p613.

Chapter 11:
The Attlee government: zenith of reformism

1 *Hansard*, 23 April 1951.
2 E E Barry, *Nationalisation in British Politics* (London 1965), p375.
3 *Hansard*, 16 August 1945.
4 See R Eatwell, *The 1945–51 Labour Governments* (London 1978), p68.
5 Miliband, p290.
6 H Eckstein, *The English National Health Service* (Cambridge, Massachusetts 1960), ppix–x.
7 D N Chester, *Nationalisation of British Industry 1945-51* (London 1975) pp38 and following.
8 J Lee, *My Life with Nye* (London 1980), pp180–1.
9 K O Morgan, *Labour in Power 1945-51* (London 1984), p371.
10 Bevan, *In Place of Fear*, p98.
11 K Marx and F Engels, *The Communist Manifesto*, in *The Revolutions of 1848* (Harmondsworth 1973) p79.
12 *Manchester Guardian*, 19 February 1943, quoted in I Birchall, *Bailing out the System* (London 1986), p51.
13 Quoted in D Widgery, *Health in Danger* (London 1979) p24.
14 J Campbell, *Nye Bevan and the Mirage of British Socialism* (London 1987), p168.
15 Quoted in Morgan, p156.
16 *Hansard*, 9 February 1948, quoted in Foot, *Bevan*, vol 2, p186.
17 Campbell, p178.
18 Widgery, pp40–41.
19 D E Ashford, *Policy and Politics in Britain* (Oxford 1981) p200.
20 Lenin, *Collected Works*, ['What to Fight For'], vol 16, p170 and ['The Russian Bourgeoisie and Russian Reformism'], vol 19, p327.
21 A Cairncross, *Years of Recovery: British Economic Policy 1945–51* (London 1985), p500.

22 R Ovendale (ed), *The Foreign Policy of the British Labour Government 1945–51* (Leicester 1984), p3.
23 *News Chronicle*, 31 December 1946, quoted in H Pelling, *The Labour Government 1945–1* (London 1984), p165.
24 Morgan, p332.
25 H Dalton, *High Tide and After* (London 1962), p187.
26 Morgan, p340.
27 Morgan, p347.
28 *The Times*, 24 October 1947, quoted in Pelling, p184.
29 Morgan, p369.
30 *Hansard*, 24 October 1949.
31 Allen, p290.
32 Cairncross, pp405–6.
33 Allen, pp32–4.
34 PRO Cab 129/41 CP(50) 158, 5 July 1950.
35 Jeffery and Hennessy, p160.
36 PRO Cab 134/175.
37 PRO Cab 134/175, 1 May 1947.
38 PRO Cab 134/175, 23 June 1947.
39 PRO FREM 8/1290, 24 January 1950.
40 W Brome, *Aneurin Bevan* (London 1953), p194.
41 PRO FREM 8/673, 15 May 1947.
42 PRO Cab 128/10 CM 51 (47), 3 June 1947.
43 PRO Cab CP(50) 117, 26 May 1950.
44 G Ellen, 'Labour and strike-breaking 1945–1951', in *International Socialism* 2: 24 (Summer 1984), p45.
45 R A Butler, *The Art of the Possible* (London 1971) ,p146.
46 A Gamble, *The Conservative Nation* (London 1974), p44.
47 H Macmillan, *Tides of Fortune* (London 1969), p302.
48 *Economist*, 13 February 1954.
49 J Morgan (ed), *The Backbench Diaries of Richard Crossman* (London 1981), p30.
50 Eatwell, p116.
51 *Labour Conference 1948*, p122.
52 *Labour Conference 1948*, pp122–3.
53 *Labour Conference 1949*, p159.
54 *Labour Conference 1949*, p169.
55 Attlee, pp226–7.
56 *Labour Conference 1945*, p114.
57 *Evening News*, 26 July 1945.
58 *Hansard*, 20 August 1945.
59 A Eden, *Memoirs: Full Circle* (London 1960), p5.
60 J F Byrnes, *Speaking Frankly* (London 1947), p79.
61 R N Rosencrance, 'British Defense Strategy, 1945-1952', in R N Rosencrance (ed), *The Dispersion of Nuclear Weapons* (New York 1964), p69.
62 Field Marshal Viscount Montgomery of Alamein, *Memoirs* (London 1958).
63 PRO Cab 128/18, Cabinet conclusions 27 June 1950.
64 Pelling, p65.
65 I Davies, 'The Labour Commonwealth', in *New Left Review*, December 1963.
66 R Palme Dutt, *The Crisis of Britain and the British Empire* (London 1957), p199.
67 Quoted in A Campbell-Johnson, *Mission with Mountbatten* (London 1951).
68 Campbell-Johnson, pp199–200.
69 Morgan, p226.
70 Ovendale (ed), pp14–16.
71 M Gowing, *Independence and Deterrence*, vol 1 (London 1974), p21.
72 Gowing, pp19–20.
73 Martin, p218.
74 McKenzie, p525.
75 Martin, p218.
76 *Tribune*, 28 May 1948.
77 McKenzie, p512.
78 McKenzie, pp511–2.
79 *Labour Conference 1950*, p130.
80 *Hansard*, 5 July 1948.
81 *Daily Telegraph*, 15 July 1948, quoted in Gordon, p167.
82 *Hansard*, 23 January 1948.
83 *Labour Conference 1948*, p200.
84 *Tribune*, 26 November 1948.
85 *Tribune*, 9 April 1948.
86 *Tribune*, 28 October 1949.
87 *Tribune*, 25 June 1948.
88 *Tribune*, 15 July 1949.
89 *Tribune*, 13 February 1948.
90 *Tribune*, 1 June 1951.
91 *Tribune*, 6 January 1950.
92 *Tribune*, 19 March 1948.
93 *Tribune*, 30 November 1945.
94 *Tribune*, 18 March 1949.
95 *Hansard*, 14 May 1952.
96 *Hansard*, 12 May 1949.
97 *Tribune*, 28 October 1949.
98 Foot, *Bevan*, vol 2, pp227–8.
99 *Tribune*, 5 November 1948.
100 *Tribune*, 30 June 1950.
101 *Tribune*, 6 October 1950.
102 *Tribune*, 20 August 1948.
103 *Tribune*, 1 April 1949.
104 Foot, *Bevan*, vol 2, p299.
105 Foot, *Bevan*, vol 2, p234.
106 *Hansard*, 23 April 1951.
107 Foot, *Bevan*, vol 2, p332.

Chapter 12: 'Thirteen wasted years'

1 *Labour Conference 1951*, p92.
2 *Labour Conference 1951*, p75.
3 Gamble, pp61–2.
4 *TUC Report 1952*, p300.
5 Allen, p34.
6 Allen, p128.

7 Crosland, pp34–6.
8 Crosland, p505.
9 Crosland, p37.
10 Crosland, pp32–3.
11 Crosland, pp474–5.
12 Crosland, p468.
13 Crosland, p23.
14 Crosland, pp520–22.
15 Crosland, pp20–21.
16 Crosland, p76.
17 R J Jackson, *Rebels and Whips* (London 1968), p212.
18 Jackson, pp114, 152 and 175.
19 J Morgan (ed) *Crossman* (London 1981), pp185–6.
20 *Labour Conference 1954*, p108.
21 *Labour Conference 1952*, p113.
22 See the *Tribune* pamphlet *It Need Not Happen: The Alternative to German Rearmament* (London 1954).
23 D F Fleming, *The Cold War and Its Origins*, vol 2 (London 1981), p737.
24 P Duff, *Left, Left, Left* (London 1971), p46.
25 *Labour Conference 1977*, p80.
26 *Labour Weekly*, 28 September 1979.
27 *Tribune*, 5 October 1956.
28 M Harrison, *Trade Unions and the Labour Party since 1945* (London 1960), pp212–4.
29 Morgan, *Crossman*, pp47 and 53.
30 Lee, p217.
31 *Daily Telegraph*, 29 January 1953, quoted in M Jenkins, *Bevanism: Labour's High Tide* (Nottingham 1979), p180.
32 *Hansard*, 16 May 1956.
33 *The Economist*, 10 November 1956.
34 Maurice Edelman, *Labour Conference 1957*, p132.
35 *Labour Conference 1957*, p131.
36 *Labour Conference 1957*, p136.
37 *Labour Conference 1957*, p140.
38 *Tribune*, 23 August 1957.
39 Jackson, p163.
40 Jackson, pp181–2.
41 *New Statesman*, 12 October 1957.
42 Foot, *Bevan*, vol 2, p580.
43 Lee, p238.
44 Bevan, *In Place of Fear*, p46.
45 Quoted in Foote, p278.
46 *Forward*, 16 October 1959.
47 V Bogdanor, 'The Labour Party in Opposition, 1951–1964', in V Bogdanor and R Skidelsky (eds), *The Age of Affluence 1951–1964* (London 1970), p96.
48 D Butler and D Stokes, *Political Change in Britain* (London 1974), p350.
49 *Labour Conference 1959*, pp107-155.
50 Drucker, p38.
51 'Labour and the Bomb', *International Socialism* 1: 3, Winter 1960–1.
52 McKenzie, pp627–8.
53 *New Statesman*, 16 October 1960.
54 *New Statesman*, 10 February 1961.
55 Morgan, *Crossman*, p901.
56 *Socialist Review*, July 1983.
57 R Luxemburg, *Reform or Revolution*, in *Rosa Luxemburg Speaks*, p71.

Chapter 13:
The Wilson governments 1964–69

1 *Signposts for the Sixties*, p16.
2 P Foot, *The Politics of Harold Wilson* (London 1968), p135.
3 *Labour Conference 1963*, pp133–140.
4 Morgan, *Crossman*, p1026.
5 *New Statesman*, 6 March 1961, quoted in W Beckerman (ed) *The Labour Government's Economic Record: 1964–1970* (London 1972), p159.
6 G Brown, introduction to *The National Plan*, September 1965, Cmnd 2764.
7 F Engels, *Anti-Dühring* (Peking 1976) p352.
8 *The National Plan*, p4.
9 *The National Plan*, p55.
10 A Glyn and B Sutcliffe, 'The Collapse of UK Profits', in *New Left Review*, March/April 1971.
11 P Foot, p154.
12 H Wilson, *The Labour Government 1964–70* (London 1974), pp61–2.
13 M Stewart, *Politics and Economic Policy in the UK Since 1964* (London 1978), p33.
14 Wilson, p65.
15 Martin, p80.
16 Stewart, pp72–3.
17 R Opie, 'Economic Planning and Growth', in Beckerman, p170.
18 Stewart, pp88–9.
19 S Brittan, *The Steering of the Economy* (London 1971), p337.
20 *The Crossman Diaries 1964–70*, p211.
21 *The Observer*, 7 March 1966, quoted in K Coates, *The Crisis of British Socialism* (Nottingham 1971), p111.
22 *TUC Report 1962*, p244.
23 *Labour Conference 1963*, p189.
24 *The Economist*, 3 October 1964.
25 S Brittan, *The Treasury under the Tories 1951–1964* (Harmondsworth 1965), p276.
26 *The Crossman Diaries 1964–70*, pp187-8 (entries for 26 May 1966 and 14 June 1966).
27 Wilson, p300.
28 *Hansard*, 20 June 1966.
29 L Panitch, *Social Democracy and Industrial Democracy* (London 1976), pp109–10.
30 Joe Haines, in *Daily Mirror*, 1 August 1986.
31 *Employment and Productivity Gazette*.
32 T Cliff and C Barker, *Incomes Policy, Legislation and Shop Stewards* (London 1966), p135.

33 M Stewart and R Winsbury, *An Incomes Policy for Labour*, Fabian Tract 350, October 1963, p18.
34 *The Economist*, 5 June 1965.
35 *The Economist*, 4 September 1965.
36 *The Times*, 11 November 1969.
37 Cliff and Barker, p136.
38 For a details account, see C Harman, *The Fire Last Time: 1968 and After* (London 1988).
39 Cliff and Barker, p105.
40 Wertheimer, p91.
41 P Foot, p251.
42 Letter sent on Gaitskell's behalf by PLP Secretary, quoted in P Foot, p252.
43 *Hansard*, 27 November 1963, quoted in P Foot, p252.
44 *Hansard*, 27 November 1963, quoted in P Foot, p253.
45 P Foot, p254.
46 *The Crossman Diaries 1964–70*, pp67–8 (entry for 5 February 1965).
47 *The Crossman Diaries 1964–70*, p120 (entry for 2 April 1964).
48 Wilson, p664.
49 *Hansard*, 1 April 1965.
50 *Hansard*, 8 February 1966.
51 *The Crossman Diaries 1964–70*, p163.
52 R Crossman, *The Diaries of a Cabinet Minister*, vol 1 (London 1975), pp344 and 361.
53 P Foot, p272.
54 P Foot, pp275–6.
55 *The Crossman Diaries 1964–70*, p330.
56 *The Crossman Diaries 1964–70*, p331.
57 Wilson, p597.
58 P Foot, pp273–4.
59 D Seers and P Streeten, 'Overseas Development Policies', in Beckerman, p128.
60 L Minkin, *The Labour Party Conference* (Manchester 1978), pp237 and 326.
61 Minkin, p297.
62 Minkin, pp298 and 300.
63 *Labour Conference 1969*, p29.
64 P Jenkins, *The Battle of Downing Street* (London 1970), p79.
65 Cited in Jenkins, p119.
66 Jenkins, p154.
67 Panitch, p248.
68 *The Guardian*, 12 July 1967, quoted in Panitch, p138.
69 Panitch, p145.
70 *TUC Report 1968*, p354.
71 *TUC 1969*, p212.
72 Minkin, pp294–5 and 290.
73 *Sunday Times*, 31 May 1970, quoted in Minkin, p312.
74 Minkin, p314.
75 *Tribune*, 22 February 1963.
76 P Anderson, 'Critique of Wilsonism', in *New Left Review*, September–October 1964.
77 M Foot, *Harold Wilson: A Pictorial Biography* (Oxford 1964), p11.
78 *Tribune*, 22 February 1963.
79 *Tribune*, 4 December 1964.
80 *Tribune*, 8 January 1965.
81 *Tribune*, 10 December 1965.
82 *Tribune*, 16 September 1966.
83 *Tribune*, 23 September 1966.
84 *Tribune*, 28 October 1966.
85 *Tribune*, 2 May 1969.
86 C Cook and J Ramsden, By-*Elections in British Politics* (London 1973), p223.
87 D Butler and D Stokes, *Political Change in Britain* (London 1974), p206.
88 T Forrester, *The Labour Party and the Working Class* (London 1976), p24.
89 D Butler and M Pinto Duschinsky, *The British General Election of 1970* (London 1971), pXIV.
90 C Crouch, *Politics in a Technological Society* (London 1970), p18.
91 Butler and Pinto Duschinsky, p346.
92 Minkin, p290.
93 *Tribune*, 9 October 1970.
94 D McKie and C Cook (eds), *The Decade of Disillusion: Politics in the Sixties* (London 1972), p4.
95 Coates, pp181–2.
96 Labour Conference 1970, p171.
97 P Seyd and L Minkin, 'The Labour Party and Its Members', in *New Society*, 20 September 1979.
98 D Butler and D Kavanagh, *The British General Election of 1979* (London 1980), p2.

Chapter 14: The Labour Party under the Heath Government

1 M Silver, 'Recent British Strike Trends: A Factual Analysis', in *British Journal of Industrial Relations*, January 1973.
2 C Crouch, 'The Intensification of Industrial Conflict in the United Kingdom', in C Crouch and A Pizzomo (eds), *The Resurgence of Class Conflicts in Western Europe Since 1968* (London 1978), p253.
3 R Harrison, editor's introduction to *The Independent Collier* (Hassocks 1978), p1.
4 L Trotsky, *History of the Russian Revolution* (London 1977), p169.
5 *Socialist Worker*, 14 April 1973.
6 A Callinicos, 'The Rank and File Movement Today', in *International Socialism*, 2: 17, Autumn 1982.
7 E Heffer, *The Class Struggle in Parliament: a Socialist View of Industrial Relations* (London 1973), p232.

8 Heffer, p242.
9 *Labour Conference 1973*, pp128–9.
10 *Labour Conference 1973*, p301.
11 *Labour Conference 1970*, p176.
12 *Labour Conference 1970*, p176.
13 *Labour Conference 1971*, p342.
14 *Labour's Programme 1973* (emphasis added).
15 M Hatfield, *The House the Left Built* (London 1978), p210 (emphasis added).

Chapter 15:
The Labour government of 1974–79

1 T Cliff, 'Patterns of Mass Strike', in *International Socialism* 2: 29, Summer 1985, p48.
2 P Riddell, *The Thatcher Government* (London 1983) p59.
3 H Wilson, *Final Term: The Labour Government 1974–1976* (London 1979), pp267–8.
4 *Labour Conference 1976*, p188.
5 A Gamble, *Britain in Decline* (London 1981) p7.
6 Gamble, *Britain in Decline*, pp19–20.
7 Gamble, *Britain in Decline*, p21.
8 *The Times*, 15 May 1974.
9 P Whitehead, *The Writing on the Wall* (London 1985), p193.
10 Quoted in Whitehead, p131.
11 B Donoghue, *Prime Minister: The Conduct of Policy under Harold Wilson and James Callaghan* (London 1987), p149.
12 Donoghue, pp148–9.
13 *The Times*, 7 November 1975.
14 J Hughes, 'Public Expenditure: The Retreat from Keynes', in K Coates (ed), *What Went Wrong* (Nottingham 1979), p105.
15 This section is based on Chanie Rosenberg's article, 'Labour and the Fight against Fascism', in *International Socialism* 2: 39 (Summer 1988).
16 R Eatwell, *Whatever Happened to Britain?* (London 1982), p119
17 *The Times*, 12 July 1975.
18 W W Daniel and N Millward, *Workplace Industrial Relations in Britain* (London 1983), p37.
19 *Financial Times*, 7 May 1975.
20 *Comment*, 5 August 1978 (emphasis added).
21 *National Income and Expenditure*, May 1979.
22 Calculated from D Jackson, H A Turner and F Wilkinson, *Do Trade Unions Cause Inflation?* (second edition, Cambridge 1975), p66.
23 L Panitch, *Working Class Politics in Crisis* (London 1986), pp118–9.
24 F Field, 'How the Poor Fared', in Coates (ed), *What Went Wrong*.
25 *The Observer*, 1 May 1977.
26 *Financial Times*, 29 November 1977.
27 *Labour Research*, no 9, 1976.
28 M Walker, *The National Front* (London 1977), p196.
29 *The Times*, 19 May 1976.
30 *Socialist Worker*, 4 October 1986.
31 *The Times*, 17 August 1977.
32 *Morning Star*, 17 August 1977, quoted in *International Socialism* 1: 101, September 1977.
33 *Labour Conference 1977*, p314.
34 *Labour Conference 1977*, pp310–11.
35 *Socialist Review*, 2 May 1978.
36 L Trotsky, *The First Five Years of the Communist International*, vol 2 (London 1974), p93.
37 Trotsky, *First Five Years*, pp94–5.
38 *Labour Conference 1972*, p221.
39 *Labour Conference 1973*, pp301, 312.
40 G Bell, *Troublesome Business: The Labour Party and the Irish Question* (London 1982), p82.
41 Quoted in Bell, p119.
42 *The Times*, 6 May 1981, quoted in Bell, p145.
43 Minkin, pp349 and 359.
44 G Bish, 'Working Relations Between Government and Party', in Coates (ed), *What Went Wrong*, p163.
45 *Labour Conference 1977*, p347.
46 J Haines, *The Politics of Power* (London 1977), p13.
47 P Norton, *Dissension in the House of Commons* (Oxford 1980), p428.
48 Norton, pp438–440.
49 Norton, p437.
50 Norton, p431.
51 Norton, p428.
52 *Tribune*, 29 March 1974.
53 Haines, p66.
54 Haines, p28.
55 Haines, p31.
56 Haines, p27.
57 B Castle, *The Castle Diaries 1974–76* (London 1980), p205.
58 Wilson, *Final Term*, pp60–1.
59 Castle, p222.
60 Castle, p61.
61 Donoghue, p92.
62 See R Jenkins, *Tony Benn, A Political Biography* (London 1980), pp245–6.
63 *Labour Conference 1959*, p116.
64 A Taylor, *The Trade Unions and the Labour Party* (London 1987), pp104–5.

Chapter 16:
Labour under Thatcher

1 TUC 1983, p465.
2 A Callinicos and M Simons, *The Great Strike* (London 1985), p156.

3 Callinicos and Simons, Chapter 4
4 *Department of Employment Gazette*, July 1982, July 1983 and July 1984.
5 See T Cliff, 'Patterns of Mass Strike', in *International Socialism* 2: 29, pp48–50.
6 *Tribune*, 30 January 1981.
7 *Militant*, 30 January 1981.
8 *Socialist Challenge*, 29 January 1981.
9 *Morning Star*, 26 January 1981.
10 F Bealey, J Blondell, W P McCann, *Constituency Politics: A Study of Newcastle-under-Lyme* (London 1965), p283.
11 N Webb and R Wybrow, *The Gallup Poll* (London 1981), p30.
12 *Tribune*, 18/25 December 1987.
13 Minkin, p250.
14 Minkin, p249.
15 R H S Crossman, introduction to W Bagehot, *The English Constitution* (London 1963).
16 Adapted from A Mitchell, *Four Years in the Death of the Labour Party* (London 1983), p93.
17 Webb and Wybrow, p168, and Gallup Political Index, number 256, December 1981, p2.
18 *Guardian*, 23 June 1983.
19 A Przeworski, *Capitalism and Social Democracy* (Cambridge 1985), p331.
20 Przeworski, pp38–9.
21 *Financial Times*, 16 September 1987.
22 *Observer*, 21 June 1987.
23 Labour Conference 1983, pp193-200.
24 Labour Conference 1985, p209.
25 Labour Conference 1985, pp209 and 217.
26 Labour Conference 1985, p224.
27 *Guardian*, 1 October 1987.
28 *Guardian*, 26 September 1987.
29 *Observer*, 2 November 1986.
30 See N Kinnock, *Making Our Way* (London 1986), pp26 and 86–94.
31 *Financial Times*, 12 September 1986.
32 *Financial Times*, 16 September 1986.
33 Labour Conference 1984, p211.
34 *Tribune*, 14 February 1986.
35 Kinnock, *Making our Way*, p56.
36 *Daily Mirror*, 19 October 1986.
37 *Financial Times*, 23 July 1986.
38 Quoted in *New Statesman*, 29 August 1986.
39 *Hansard*, 28 April 1982.
40 *Socialist Review*, May–June 1982 and June–July 1982.
41 N Branson, *History of the CPGB 1927–41* (London 1985), p7.
42 *Membership Survey—Report of a sample survey of CPSA members* (London 1986), p10.
43 S McGregor, 'The History and Politics of Militant', in *International Socialism*, 2: 33, Autumn 1986.
44 Labour Conference 1983, p63.
45 *Tribune*, 11 October 1985.
46 Militant, 12 October 1985.
47 R Harris, *The Making of Neil Kinnock* (London 1984), p20.
48 *Hansard*, 14 February 1972.
49 Harris, p77.
50 *Tribune*, 7 January 1977.
51 *Hansard*, 17 March 1977.
52 Collated from Norton.
53 *Labour Conference 1983*, p80.
54 *Guardian*, 19 November 1986.
55 *Guardian*, 23 September 1987.
56 Report by Tony Milward, GLEB chairman, in *Tribune*, 24 July 1987.
57 Quoted in M Broddy, 'Local Economics and Employment Strategies', in M Broddy and C Fudge (eds) *Local Socialism* (London 1984), p185.
58 T Cliff, *Class Struggle and Women's Liberation* (London 1984), p187.
59 P Seyd, *The Rise and Fall of the Labour Left* (London 1987), p151.
60 The main thrust of Hobsbawm's argument is to be found in M Jacques and F Mulhern (eds), *The Forward March of Labour Halted?* (London 1981), and articles in *Marxism Today*, October 1982 and January 1983.
61 For an elaboration of this read the excellent article by Chris Harman, 'The Working Class After the Recession', in A Callinicos and C Harman, *The Changing Working Class* (London 1987).
62 *Financial Times*, 2 October 1987.
63 *Socialist Worker*, 10 October 1987.
64 *Social Trends*, no 17 (1987), p86.
65 *Guardian*, 1 September 1987.
66 *Social Trends*, no 17, pp99–100.
67 *Financial Times*, 5 November 1986.
68 See A Heath, R Jowell and J Curtice, *How Britain Votes* (Oxford 1985).
69 Heath and others, pp20–22.
70 Heath and others, p49.
71 Heath and others, p38.
72 Heath and others, pp14–15.
73 A Callinicos, 'The "New Middle Class"', in Callinicos and Harman, pp87–8.
74 See J Westergaard, 'The once and future class', in J Curran (ed), *The Future of the Left* (London 1984), p81.
75 C Harman, 'How the working class votes', Callinicos and Harman, p37.
76 J Kelly, *Labour and the Unions* (London 1987), p11.
77 J MacInnes, *Thatchersim at Work* (Milton Keynes 1987), p99.
78 MacInnes, p100.
79 MacInnes, p136.
80 MacInnes, p82.

81 J Curtice, 'Interim Report: Party Politics', in R Jowell, S Witherspoon and I Brook, *British Social Attitudes: The 1987 Report* (Aldershot 1987), p174.
82 A Heath and P Topf, 'Political Culture', in Jowell and others, pp60.
83 Heath and Topf, in Jowell and others, p60.
84 P Taylor-Gooby, 'Citizenship and Welfare', in Jowell and others, pp2, 3 and 16.
85 M Collins, 'Business and Industry', in *British Social Attitudes, 1987*, p84.
86 Collins, *British Social Attitudes, 1987*, p35–6.
87 Heath and Topf, in Jowell, 1987, p63.
88 D Butler and D Stokes, *Political Change in Britain: Forces Shaping Electoral Choice* (Harmondsworth 1971), p121.
89 D Gluckstein, 'Class struggle and the Labour vote', *Socialist Worker Review*, June 1987.
90 Heath and Topf, in Jowell, p51.
91 *Hansard*, 22 April 1986.
92 Ibid, 6 May 1986.
93 Ibid, 19 June 1986.
94 Ibid, 24 June 1986.
95 *The Independent*, 29 September 1987.
96 *Financial Times*, 2 July 1987.
97 *Independent*, 7 October 1987.
98 Ibid, 30 September 1987.
99 Ibid, 3 October 1987.
100 Ibid, 16 November 1987.

Chapter 17:
New Labour

1 Tricia Davies and David Green in *Marxism Today*, February 1989.
2 B Anderson in *New Statesman and Society*, 3 May 1991.
3 Stuart Hall and Martin Jacques, *Marxism Today*, quoted in *Socialist Review*, December 1990.
4 Blair's speech to News International Management, quoted in *Independent*, 17 July 1995.
5 W Hutton, *The State We're In* (London 1995), p18.
6 G Elliott, *Labourism and the English Genius: The Strange Death of Labour England?* (London 1993), pp116, 118.
7 *Guardian*, 6 September 1995.
8 It is true that the Tories were, and are, hopelessly split over Europe but Thatcher had been flexible enough in her approach to sanction entry into the European Exchange Rate Mechanism and to sign the Maastricht Treaty, both important steps towards the sort of European Union she so detested. Equally her successor survived Tory internal divisions on the issue.
9 *Tribune*, 17 June 1988.
10 *Tribune*, 5 February 1988.
11 D Blunkett, Labour's local government spokesperson in *Tribune*, 7 April 1989.
12 D Butler and D Kavanagh, *The British General Election of 1992* (Basingstoke 1992), p318.
13 Heffernan and Marqusee, *Defeat from the Jaws of Victory* (London 1992), pp265–77. Labour's memory is long. Five years after the demise of the poll tax it is still deselecting candidates such as Liz Davies in Leeds North East, who had connections with non-payment. One local voter commented: 'I like the fact that she especially went the whole hog against the poll tax. Without people like her we'd still be paying it.' *Independent*, 17 July 1995.
14 *Tribune*, 23 February 1990.
15 Our emphasis, *Tribune*, March 1990.
16 According to Seyd and Whiteley, p92. A larger number, 42 percent, agreed that the 'Labour Party should support individuals who refuse to pay the Poll Tax, though 44 percent disagreed.' Seyd and Whiteley, p231.
17 *Hansard*, 2 April 1990.
18 Butler and Kavanagh, p10.
19 *Report of Ninetieth Labour Party Conference 1991*, pp211–213.
20 Brian Weddell, Lothian Regional Councillor in *Tribune*, 21 September 1990.
21 *Guardian*, 5 February 1992.
22 *Independent on Sunday*, 22 January 1995.
23 Heffernan and Marqusee, p314.
24 Butler and Kavanagh, 1992, p10.
25 Reported in *New Statesman and Society*, 18 January 1991.
26 The only debate in opposition time between December 1990 and the war's end in February 1991 was SNP initiated. R Heffernan and M Marqusee, p192.
27 *Hansard*, 15 January 1991.
28 *Hansard*, 17 January 1991 and 21 January 1991.
29 Reported in *Tribune*, 22 February 1991.
30 Heffernan and Marqusee, p201.
31 The highest vote against the government on a procedure motion was 57 MPs. Heffernan and Marqusee, p193.
32 *New Statesman and Society*, 25 January 1991.
33 *Socialist Review*, February 1991.
34 *Tribune*, 22 February 1991.
35 Heffernan and Marqusee, p136.
36 Heffernan and Marqusee, p194.
37 Speech to 1988 Labour Conference quoted in C Hughes and P Wintour, *Labour Rebuilt, The New Model Party* (London 1990).
38 Hughes and Wintour, p195.

39 *Tribune*, 15 June 1990.
40 Butler and Kavanagh, p269.
41 Hughes and Wintour, p54.
42 Hughes and Wintour, p183.
43 Hughes and Wintour, p195.
44 Butler and Kavanagh, p275.
45 Butler and Kavanagh, p249.
46 *Guardian*, 11 April 1992.
47 Butler and Kavanagh, p177.
48 Details in Butler and Kavanagh, p136.
49 Heffernan and Marqusee p312.
50 A Heath, R Jowell and J Curtice, *Labour's Last Chance? The 1992 Election and Beyond* (Aldershot 1994), p285 and p14.
51 Source, MORI, quoted in *New Statesman and Society*, 17 April 1992.
52 *Labour's Last Chance?*, p287.
53 *Labour's Last Chance?*, p292.
54 See Heffernan and Marqusee, p103.
55 Ibid, p386.
56 *Sun*, 17 October 1995.
57 *New Statesman and Society*, 17 July 1992.
58 *Panorama*, Monday, 2 November 1992.
59 Quoted in *Socialist Worker*, 7 November 1990.
60 J Pilger in *New Statesman and Society*, 17/31 December 1993.
61 *New Statesman and Society*, 11 June 1993.
62 *New Statesman and Society*, 11 June 1993.
63 *Independent* 14 July 1995.
64 Quoted in *Socialist Worker*, 2 October 1993.
65 *Fabian Review*, July 1992.
66 J Sopel, *Tony Blair: The Moderniser* (London 1995), p111.
67 Our emphasis. J Rentoul, *Tony Blair* (London 1995), pp206–7.
68 Ibid.
69 Rentoul, p252.
70 Quoted in *Socialist Worker*, 13 May 1995.
71 *New Statesman and Society*, 4 September 1992.
72 *Labour's Last Chance*, p285.
73 *Tribune*, 7 October 1988.
74 *New Statesman and Society*, 17 July 1992.
75 *Tribune*, 17 September 1993.
76 *Tribune*, 4 June 1993.
77 *Tribune*, 30 July 1993.
78 Quoted in Rentoul p332.
79 Rentoul, p339.
80 See the *New Statesman and Society* poll in S Platt and N Mann, 'Chipping away at the block vote', *New Statesman and Society*, 4 September 1992. Interestingly it was some of the larger unions that perhaps feel less dependent on Labour that were most resistant to OMOV, like the T&G and GMB.
81 Tom Sawyer, quoted in *Independent*, 2 June 1992.
82 Heffeman and Marqusee, p155.
83 P Seyd and P Whiteley, *Labour's Grass Roots* (Oxford 1992), p198.
84 *Tribune*, 6 May 1990.
85 *Guardian*, 24 March 1990.
86 Seyd and Whiteley, p89.
87 Elliott, p144.
88 Seyd and Whiteley p73.
89 Seyd and Whiteley, p39.
90 Seyd and Whiteley, p46–7.
91 Seyd and Whiteley, p89.
92 *New Statesman and Society*, 28 April 1995.
93 Peter Coleman, Labour Party Director of Organisation in *Tribune*, 31 March 1995.
94 *New Statesman and Society*, 28 April 1995.
95 BBC TV, *On the Record*, 18 December 1994.
96 *Financial Times*, 22 May 1995.
97 *New Statesman and Society*, 28 April 1995.
98 Hughes and Wintour, p92.
99 Seyd and Whiteley, p24.
100 Heffernan and Marqusee, p135.
101 *Tribune*, 19 August 1994
102 *Tribune*, 8 April 1994.
103 *New Statesman and Society*, 31 July 1992.
104 *New Statesman and Society*, 27 May 1994.
105 P Hain, *Ayes to the Left* (London 1995), p234.
106 *Tribune*, 3 September 1993.
107 *Tribune*, 14 October 1994.
108 *Guardian*, 18 February 1996.
109 Our emphasis, *Tribune*, 16 June 1995.
110 Hain quoting Ralph Miliband approvingly, p219.
111 Our emphasis. Hain p239.
112 *Tribune*, 21 October 1994.
113 See pp368–70. [ch 16]
114 *Labour's Last Chance*, p285.
115 *Labour's Last Chance*, p196.
116 See p376. [ch 16]
117 David Clark, Labour's defence spokesperson in *New Statesman and Society*, 12 November 1993.
118 *New Statesman and Society*, 29 July 1994.
119 *New Statesman and Society*, 24 February 1995.
120 J Straw, *Ninetieth Labour Conference*, p58.
121 *Tribune*, 21 October 1994.
122 Rentoul, p419–420.
123 Sopel, p279.
124 Blunkett, *Tribune*, 23 June 1995.
125 Margaret Hodge, in *Tribune*, 29 July 1994.
126 Reported in *Guardian*, 19 December 1994.
127 *Independent*, 22 June 1995. An example of current 'policy-making' procedure is illustrated by the fate of one mild proposal—VAT on private school fees. When Blunkett mentioned this agreed position Blair 'read the riot act' and Blunkett was accused of 'making policy

on the hoof', *Guardian*, 3 January 1995. In fact, Brown as shadow Chancellor had abandoned the idea and not bothered telling the education spokesperson.

128 Radio 4's summary of the situation, 5pm *News*, 6 January 1996.
129 T Blair, 'Why crime is a socialist issue', in *New Statesman and Society*, 29 January 1993.
130 Sopel, p164.
131 Ibid.
132 Ibid.
133 Sopel, p158.
134 *Sunday Times Magazine*, 10 April 1994.
135 BBC TV, *Panorama*, 9 May 1994.
136 Sopel, p166.
137 Quoted *Socialist Worker*, 23 April 1994.
138 *Guardian*, 23 June 1994.
139 *New Statesman and Society*, 7 July 1995.
140 *Ninetieth Labour Conference, 1991*, p134.
141 Hain, p95.
142 *Independent*, 30 June 1995.
143 Times, 19 September 1995.
144 *Eighty-ninth Conference, 1990*, p64.
145 *New Statesman and Society*, 31 January 1992.
146 Hain, p83.
147 *New Statesman and Society*, 5 February 1993.
148 *Tribune*, 22 January 1993.
149 *Independent*, 30 October 1994.
150 *Socialist Worker*, 4 June 1994.
151 *Times*, 24 November 1995.
152 *Socialist Worker*, 4 June 1994.
153 *Independent*, 7 September 1995.
154 Quoted in *Socialist Worker*, 16 September 1995.
155 *Financial Times*, 19 July 1995.
156 *Guardian*, 3 March 1995.
157 *Guardian*, 16 July, 1995.
158 *Financial Times*, 19 July 1995.
159 Our emphasis. G Brown, 'Harnessing the Workforce', *New Statesman and Society*, May 1993.
160 *New Statesman and Society*, 15 July 1994.
161 *Eighty-ninth Annual Conference of the Labour Party*, p29.
162 S Jenkins, *Winners and Losers, A Portrait of income distribution during the 1980s* (Rowntree Foundation), 1995.
163 Quoted in *New Statesman and Society*, 20 August 1993.
164 Our emphasis. *New Statesman and Society*, 15 July 1994.
165 *News of the World*, 28 August 1994.
166 Times, 20 November 1995.
167 Times, 21 November 1995.
168 Phrase used by Gould, *Tribune*, 7 May 1993.
169 *Tribune*, 7 May 1993.
170 I Aitken, 'Labour's Chance to Score' in *New Statesman and Society*, 17/31 December 1993.
171 Quoted in *New Statesman and Society*, 9 June 1995.
172 Quoted in P Anderson, 'Safety First', *New Statesman and Society*, 9 June 1995.
173 I Aitken, 'Killer Instincts', in *New Statesman and Society*, 15 October 1993.
174 Quoted in J Sopel, p55.
175 *Labour and Trade Union Review*, December 1989. Quoted in Rentoul, p395.
176 Quoted in *Independent*, 13 September 1995.
177 BBC1, *Morning News*, 18 January 1996.
178 *Socialist Worker*, 11 March 1995.
179 *Guardian*, 17 January 1996.
180 Our pp1–2. [Introduction]
181 Sopel, p3.
182 Quoted in Rentoul, p163.
183 *Daily Telegraph*, 13 January 1995.
184 Rentoul, p231.
185 Sopel, p239.
186 Quoted in *Tribune*, 5/12 August 1994.
187 Quoted in *Tribune*, 11/18 August 1994.
188 Quoted in *New Statesman and Society*, 17 June 1994.
189 *Economist*, 21 May 1994.
190 *Economist*, 29 April 1995.
191 *Tribune*, 5/12 August 1994.
192 Rentoul, p276.
193 Quoted in Sopel, p144.
194 *Sun*, 3 March 1993.
195 Sopel, p143.
196 *Independent*, 17 July 1995.
197 Quoted Rentoul, p453.
198 Quoted Sopel, p208.
199 *Sunday Times*, 23 April 1995.
200 Interview in *New Statesman and Society*, 15 July 1994.
201 T Blair, *Let Us Face the Future—the 1945 Anniversary Lecture*, Fabian Society pamphlet no 571 (London 1995), p14.
202 Details in Rentoul, p404.
203 *New Statesman and Society*, 11 August 1995.
204 *Financial Times*, 11 July 1995.
205 See our pp75–78 [ch 3].
206 *Guardian*, 8 March 1995.
207 Blair, *Let Us Face the Future*, pp12–13.
208 Rentoul, p424.
209 Quoted in *Socialist Review*, February 1995.
210 Quoted in Hain, p41.
211 Quoted in *Socialist Worker*, 25 February 1995.
212 Rentoul, p461.
213 Reported in *Socialist Review*, February 1995.
214 *Independent*, 13 September 1995.
215 Sopel, p297.
216 *Socialist Worker*, 29 April 1995.

217 *New Statesman and Society*, 9 December 1994.
218 *Red Pepper*, February 1996.
219 *Economist*, 13 January 1995.
220 *Socialist Worker*, 25 February 1995.
221 *Guardian*, 18 January 1995.
222 *Sunday Times*, 15 January 1995.
223 *Observer*, 30 April 1995.
224 Rentoul, p402.
225 Sopel, p271.
226 Leaked memo by Philip Gould in *Guardian*, 12 September 1995.
227 Quoted in *Socialist Worker*, 23 September 1995.
228 Figures from Butler and Kavanagh, p226.
229 *Times*, 23 March 1995.
230 K Milne, *New Statesman and Society*, 4 February 1994.
231 *Independent*, 13 September 1995.
232 Quoted in Rentoul, p400.
233 Ibid.
234 *Financial Times*, 27 June 1995.
235 *Independent*, 13 September 1995.
236 *Independent*, 17 July 1995.
237 *Times*, 18 September 1995.
238 *Independent*, 17 July 1995.
239 This is an outline of a book Mandelson was writing, as summarised in *The Observer*, 24 December 1995.
240 *Economist*, 7–13 October 1995.
241 *Guardian*, 29 December 1995.
242 *Guardian*, 17 January 1996.
243 Hutton, p298.
244 Alistair Darling, quoted in *Guardian*, 18 January 1996.
245 Walden Bello of the Centre for the South, summarised in *New Statesman and Society*, 10 March 1995.
246 *Guardian*, 8 January 1996.
247 *Economist*, 13 January 1995.
248 Singapore speech, quoted in *Economist*, 13 January 1995.
249 Blair, *Let Us Face the Future*, p12.
250 Quoted in M Pearce & G Stewart, *British Political History, 1867–1990*, p90.
251 Ibid, p84.

Chapter 18:
New Labour in government

1 A Rawnsley, *Servants of the People* (Penguin, London 2001), p12.
2 T Blair, *A Journey* (Arrow Books, London 2011), pXLIX.
3 I G Toth, *GINI Policy Paper No 3*, September 2013—https://www.researchgate.net/publication/269101804_Income_Distribution_Inequality_Perceptions_and_Redistributive_Preferences_in_European_Countries, p13.
4 S Milne, *The Revenge of History* (Verso, London 2013), p100.
5 http://www.smith-institute.org.uk/wp-content/uploads/2015/10/From-the-poor-law-to-welfare-to-work.pdf, p66.
6 This was in 2008. Quoted in http://www.smith-institute.org.uk/wp-content/uploads/2015/10/From-the-poor-law-to-welfare-to-work.pdf, p67.
7 L Davies, *Through the Looking Glass* (Verso, London 2001), p131.
8 http://conservativehome.blogs.com/centreright/2008/04/making-history.html.
9 Davies, p186.
10 R Miliband, *Parliamentary Socialism*, quoted in J Saville—'Parliamentary Socialism Revisited.' https://socialistregister.com/index.php/srv/article/download/5659/2557.
11 A Campbell, *The Alastair Campbell Diaries*, vol 2 (Arrow Books, London 2011), p24.
12 Campbell, p49.
13 D Butler and D Kavanagh, *The British General Election of 1997* (Macmillan Houndmills 1997), p12.
14 Butler and Kavanagh (1997), p13.
15 Butler and Kavanagh (1997), p299.
16 Butler and Kavanagh (1997), p295.
17 Butler and Kavanagh (1997), p251.
18 D Butler and D Kavanagh, *The British General Election of 2001* (Palgrave, Houndmills 2002), p23-4.
19 Butler and Kavanagh (2002), p305.
20 Butler and Kavanagh (2002), p305.
21 Butler and Kavanagh (2002), p311.
22 A Geddes and J Tonge (eds), *Britain Decides: The UK General Election 2005*, (Palgrave Macmillan 2005), p1.
23 T Blair, *A Journey* (Arrow Books, London 2011), pXLIX.
24 https://www.theguardian.com/uk/2002/oct/01/labourconference.labour.
25 https://www.theguardian.com/politics/2009/sep/29/gordon-brown-labour-conference-speech-in-full.
26 Blair's runs to 718 pages, and Brown's to 500—and the sub-text for both is the TB/GB conflict.
27 See G Brown, *My Life, Our Times* (Bodley Head, London 2017), p204.
28 D Kavanagh and P Cowley, *The British General Election of 2010* (Palgrave Macmillan, Houndmills 2010), p50-51.
29 2007 Labour conference speech http://news.bbc.co.uk/2/hi/uk_news/politics/7010664.stm.
30 D McBride, *Power Trip* (Biteback, London 2013), pp180-181.

31 S Hannah, *A Party with Socialists In It* (Pluto, London 2018), p212.
32 Milne, p84.
33 Davies, p93.
34 Quoted in M Pugh, *Speak for Britain!* (Vintage, London 2011), p394.
35 Blair, p288.
36 Quoted in Pugh, p393.
37 Campbell, p281-2.
38 https://www.independent.co.uk/voices/leading-article-a-modest-victory-for-the-workers-1158009.html.
39 Quoted in Rawnsley (2001), p298.
40 Campbell, p148.
41 Quoted in Pugh, p398.
42 Quoted in M Smith, *The Awkward Squad* (SWP, London 2003), p5.
43 Hannah, p212.
44 Hannah, p207.
45 Quoted in Smith, p5.
46 S Joyce, 'Why are there so few strikes?' *International Socialism*, 145, Winter 2015, p120.
47 Davies, pp174-5.
48 Davies, p52.
49 https://www.independent.co.uk/news/blair-i-think-im-a-pretty-straight-sort-of-guy-1294593.html.
50 https://www.theguardian.com/politics/2000/sep/20/labour.labour1997to99.
51 Kavanagh and Cowley, p23.
52 Pugh, p401.
53 Kavanagh and Cowley, p25.
54 A Rawnsley, *The End of the Party* (Penguin, London 2010), p127.
55 Pugh, p391.
56 Quoted in Smith, p2.
57 Quoted in http://www.socialismtoday.org/35/mandelson35.html.
58 Brown, p48.
59 Brown, p37. See also A Fisher, *The Failed Experiment* (Radical Read, London 2014), p60.
60 Rawnsley (2001), p37.
61 Rawnsley (2001), p38. The phrase was used by the previous Tory Chancellor, Ken Clarke, to describe his own plans.
62 G Brown's 1999 Mais Lecture, http://webarchive.nationalarchives.gov.uk/20100407174407/http://www.hm-treasury.gov.uk/speech_chex_191099.htm.
63 Figures calculated from http://www.telegraph.co.uk/finance/economics/8414447/How-UK-incomes-have-risen-and-fallen-since-1948.html.
64 N Cohen, *Pretty Straight Guys* (Faber and Faber, London 2003), p234.
65 G Brown's 1999 Mais Lecture, http://webarchive.nationalarchives.gov.uk/20100407174407/http://www.hm-treasury.gov.uk/speech_chex_191099.htm. See also 2006 budget speech https://www.theguardian.com/uk/2006/mar/22/budget2006.budget.
66 Geddes and Tonge (eds), p237.
67 Rawnsley (2010), p479.
68 http://cep.lse.ac.uk/pubs/download/cp366.pdf.
69 Butler and Kavanagh (2002), p4. Afterwards it rose considerably—from 40 to 48 percent of GDP. Kavanagh and Cowley, p34.
70 http://www.smith-institute.org.uk/wp content/uploads/2015/10/From-the-poor-law-to-welfare-to-work.pdf, p66.
71 The figure is for 2003. http://www.smith-institute.org.uk/wp-content/uploads/2015/10/From-the-poor-law-to-welfare-to-work.pdf, p63.
72 Quoted in S Fielding, *The Labour Party. Continuity and Change in the Making of New Labour* (Palgrave Macmillan, Houndmills 2003), p188.
73 Brown, p128.
74 https://www.theguardian.com/politics/1999/sep/06/labourconference.labour—'Blair Bounces Back, 6 September 1999.
75 M Lavalette and G Mooney, p39.
76 G Brown's 1999 Mais Lecture, http://webarchive.nationalarchives.gov.uk/20100407174407/http://www.hm-treasury.gov.uk/speech_chex_191099.htm.
77 researchbriefings.files.parliament.uk/documents/.../SN06762.pdf, p7.
78 http://www.smith-institute.org.uk/wp-content/uploads/2015/10/From-the-poor-law-to-welfare-to-work.pdf, p64.
79 https://www.nuffieldtrust.org.uk/.../public-payment-and-private-provision-web-final, IFS/Nuffield Trust—Public Pay and Private Provision, p6.
80 https://www.nuffieldtrust.org.uk/.../public-payment-and-private-provision-web-final, IFS/Nuffield Trust—Public Pay and Private Provision, p4.
81 https://www.nuffieldtrust.org.uk/.../public-payment-and-private-provision-web-final, IFS/Nuffield Trust—Public Pay and Private Provision, p6.
82 Brown, p231.
83 Figures calculated from https://www.nuffieldtrust.org.uk/.../public-payment-and-private-provision-web-final, IFS/Nuffield Trust—Public Pay and Private Provision, p4.

84 This is for 2006/7 to 2011/12. https://www.nuffieldtrust.org.uk/.../public-payment-and-private-provision-web-final, IFS/Nuffield Trust—Public Pay and Private Provision, p14.
85 Blair, p491.
86 See for example, Geddes and Tonge (eds), p31; and Rawnsley (2001), p77 and p81.
87 Geddes and Tonge (eds), p31.
88 The increases were 16 percent and 8 percent respectively. Calculated from https://www.nuffieldtrust.org.uk/resource/nhs-in-numbers#workforce.
89 https://www.ifs.org.uk/bns/bn121.pdf, p1.
90 Pupils' access to teachers increased from one teacher per 16.7 pupils in 1997 to one per 15.7 in 2010. https://www.trustforlondon.org.uk/publications/labours-record-education-policy-spending-and-outcomes-1997-2010/ p31.
91 From 200 in 1997 to 1000 in 2002. https://www.trustforlondon.org.uk/publications/labours-record-education-policy-spending-and-outcomes-1997-2010/ p10.
92 https://www.trustforlondon.org.uk/publications/labours-record-education-policy-spending-and-outcomes-1997-2010/p11.
93 https://www.trustforlondon.org.uk/publications/labours-record-education-policy-spending-and-outcomes-1997-2010/ p31.
94 https://www.trustforlondon.org.uk/publications/labours-record-education-policy-spending-and-outcomes-1997-2010/p14.
95 https://www.trustforlondon.org.uk/publications/labours-record-education-policy-spending-and-outcomes-1997-2010/, p31.
96 https://www.nao.org.uk/wp-content/uploads/2018/01/PFI-and-PF2.pdf, PFI and PF2. *Report by the Comptroller and Auditor General*, National Audit Office, p8.
97 Fisher, p32.
98 https://www.nao.org.uk/wp-content/uploads/2018/01/PFI-and-PF2.pdf, PFI and PF2. *Report by the Comptroller and Auditor General*, National Audit Office, p23-4.
99 https://www.nao.org.uk/wp-content/uploads/2018/01/PFI-and-PF2.pdf, PFI and PF2. *Report by the Comptroller and Auditor General*, National Audit Office, p23.
100 Milne, pxv.
101 https://www.nao.org.uk/wp-content/uploads/2018/01/PFI-and-PF2.pdf, PFI and PF2. *Report by the Comptroller and Auditor General*, National Audit Office, p23.
102 Quoted in Davies, p166.
103 Quoted in Davies, p166.
104 T Wright MP, 'The candidate: Tony Wright' in Geddes and Tonge (eds), p94.
105 Helen Bosanquet of the Charity Organisation Society, quoted in https://www.fabians.org.uk/wp-content/uploads/2012/04/FromWorkhousetoWelfare.pdf, p17.
106 Campbell, p455.
107 See T Horton, 'A Short Guide to the Minority Report, pp11-12 in E Wallis (ed), *From the Workhouse to Welfare What Beatrice Webb's 1909 Minority Report Can Teach us Today*, https://www.fabians.org.uk/wp-content/uploads/2012/04/FromWorkhousetoWelfare.pdf, pp11-12.
108 Brown, p152.
109 M Lavalette and G Mooney, p31.
110 M Lavalette and G Mooney, p33.
111 M Lavalette and G Mooney, p32.
112 Quoted in Cohen, p14.
113 Cohen, pp22, 37.
114 https://www.ifs.org.uk/uploads/publications/bns/BN179.pdf, p1 and the prison population rose from 41,000 to 73,000. Cohen, p36.
115 https://www.fabians.org.uk/wp-content/uploads/2012/04/FromWorkhousetoWelfare.pdf, pp22, 23.
116 David Blunkett quoted in https://www.theguardian.com/politics/2003/nov/13/immigrationpolicy.immigration.
117 Beverley Hughes, quoted in Cohen, p80.
118 Cohen, p67.
119 Jack Straw, quoted in Cohen, p76.
120 T Bower, *Broken Vows* (Faber and Faber, London 2016), p88.
121 Blair, p523.
122 *The Independent*, 9 February 1998.
123 Milne, p105.
124 Quoted in Cohen, p96.
125 A Geddes and J Tonge (eds), p289.
126 Quoted in Rawnsley (2010), p321, 2007, http://news.bbc.co.uk/2/hi/uk_news/politics/7010664.stm.
127 Butler and Kavanagh (1997), p220.
128 Butler and Kavanagh (2002), p237.
129 Geddes and Tonge (eds), p284.
130 Geddes and Tonge (eds), p250.
131 Kavanagh and Cowley, p337.
132 Kavanagh and Cowley, p342.
133 https://www.independent.co.uk/news/uk/politics/chilcot-report-the-seven-most-important-lines-from-the-iraq-war-inquiry-a7122646.html.

134 Figures given in https://www.independent.co.uk/news/uk/politics/chilcot-report-the-iraq-war-in-numbers-a7119336.html.
135 Usama Abbas, 25, an unemployed college graduate in Basra, quoted in //www.reuters.com/article/us-mideast-crisis-iraq-protests/two-protesters-killed-in-clashes-with-iraqi-police-as-unrest-spreads-in-south-idUSKBN1K507A.
136 Brown, pp247-265.
137 Brown, p254.
138 Brown, p251.
139 Blair, p516.
140 Rawnsley (2010), p173.
141 https://www.globalpolicy.org/component/content/article/154/26026.html.
142 Quoted in Rawnsley (2001), p381.
143 Milne, pXVIII.
144 J Newsinger, "When old Labour went to war,' *International Socialism*, Spring 2008, p120.
145 S Kettell, *Dirty Politics: New Labour, British Democracy and the Invasion of Iraq* (Zed Books, London 2006), p25.
146 Campbell, p298.
147 Campbell, p562.
148 Quoted in S Kettell, p95.
149 Brown, p260. Rawnsley was given this eye-witness account of a Cabinet discussion: 'Everyone realised that Gordon Brown was still at that stage the one person who could have stopped it.' When it came down to it, Brown did not have a fundamental disagreement in principle about Iraq...in the words of one of his closest aides: He was totally coloured by his fervent Atlanticism. His overriding position was that we can't afford to be seen as anti-American.' Rawnsley (2010), p162.
150 Pugh, p407.
151 Brown, pp277, 280.
152 http://www.dailymail.co.uk/news/article-334208/Its-time-celebrate-Empire-says-Brown.html. He shared this sentiment with Blair who, at the handover of Hong Kong to China 'still felt a tug, not of regret, but of nostalgia for the old British Empire'. Blair, p126.
153 A Murray and L German, *Stop the War* (Bookmarks, London 2005), p253.
154 Milne, p128.
155 Quoted in Rawnsley (2010), p260.
156 https://www.theguardian.com/commentisfree/2006/oct/06/politics.uk.
157 Milne, p132.
158 Blair, p583.
159 Rawnsley (2010), p341.
160 Rawnsley (2010), p548.
161 Blair, p567.
162 Rawnsley (2010), p338.
163 https://www.theguardian.com/uk/2009/feb/17/government-exploiting-terrorism-fear.
164 Pugh, p409.
165 Geddes and Tonge (eds), p12.
166 T Blair, *A Journey*, Arrow Books, London 2011 p597.
167 Brown, p243.
168 See for example Rawnsley's discussion of the 2007 budget, in Rawnsley (2010), p439.
169 Brown, p439.
170 Brown, p440.
171 Brown, p25.
172 Quoted in Fisher, p6.
173 IFS reports quoted in *International Socialism* 120, Autumn 2008, p8.
174 *International Socialism*, 120, Autumn 2008, p8.
175 Brown, pp350, 355.
176 Brown, p296.
177 Quoted in A Callinicos, *New Labour or Socialism?* (Bookmarks, London 1996), p6. See also Milne, pXIV.
178 Brown, p132.
179 In 2007 it was 51 percent of GDP compared to 77 percent for the US, 68 percent in Germany, 77 percent in France, 115 percent in Italy and 174 percent in Japan. Brown, p355.
180 https://www.statista.com/statistics/281734/gdp-growth-in-the-united-kingdom-uk/.
181 Quoted in Fielding, p160.
182 Quoted in Rawnsley (2010), p476.
183 Brown, p298.
184 Brown, p320.
185 https://www.thesun.co.uk/news/4804915/gordon-brown-bankers-rbs-fred-goodwin-jail/.
186 Brown, p315.
187 Brown, p316.
188 Quoted in Milne, p163. Brown's speech at 2009 TUC Conference.
189 Electoral Commission. https://docs.google.com/spreadsheets/d/1ABH72dKr2cXoYGJEyM_V9V7-RiO6xGVjuGIhnS-GDYw/edit#gid=0.
190 McBride,, p209.
191 Kavanagh and Cowley, p281.
192 Kavanagh and Cowley, p61.
193 2007 Labour conference speech, http://news.bbc.co.uk/2/hi/uk_news/politics/7010664.stm.
194 Rawnsley (2010), p733.
195 Kavanagh and Cowley, p385.
196 Kavanagh and Cowley, p385.

197 For example, according to Paul Krugman, Nobel prize-winner: 'Brown and Alistair Darling have defined the character of the worldwide rescue effort, with other wealthy nations playing catch-up.' https://www.theguardian.com/commentisfree/2012/feb/06/gordon-brown-save-world-uk.
198 Hannah, p201.
199 Hannah, p199.
200 See Fielding, p130.
201 Davies, p80.
202 Fielding, p141.
203 Kavanagh and Cowley, p58, H R Pemberton and M Wickham-Jones, 'Labour's lost grassroots: The rise and fall of party membership', *British Politics*, vol 8, no 2, p11. https://research-information.bristol.ac.uk/files/8434495/Labour_s_Lost_Grassroots_BP_FINAL.pdf.
204 Pugh, p397.
205 Kavanagh and Cowley, p58.
206 Butler and Kavanagh (2002); and Kavanagh and Cowley, p61.
207 Figures from Patrick Seyd and Paul Whiteley in *The Guardian*, 11 October 1999, quoted in Fielding, p136.
208 Quoted in L German, 'How Labour lost its roots' in *International Socialism*, 87, Summer 2000, p4.
209 Quoted in Butler and Kavanagh (2002), p33.
210 Davies, p69.
211 Quoted in Hannah, p212.
212 https://research-information.bristol.ac.uk/files/8434495/Labour_s_Lost_Grassroots_BP_FINAL.pdf, p3.
213 *What Next? Marxist Discussion Journal*, 2000, p8.
214 Davies, p179.
215 Pugh, p404.
216 Rawnsley (2001), pp112, 114.
217 Calculated from https://www.parliament.uk/documents/commons/lib/research/briefings/snpc-03038.pdf.
218 https://www.telegraph.co.uk/news/politics/6466127/Gordon-Brown-suffers-backbench-rebellions-as-he-struggles-to-control-party.html.Gordon Brown suffers backbench rebellions as he struggles to control party.
219 https://www.tandfonline.com/doi/abs/10.1080/13619462.2013.794694. In the Brown Stuff?: Labour Backbench Dissent Under Gordon Brown, 2007–10, Philip Cowley and Mark Stuart.
220 Davies, pp9-10.
221 Davies, p20.
222 *What Next? Marxist Discussion Journal*, 2000, p8.
223 Pugh, p411.
224 Hannah, p216.
225 Davies, p137.
226 Davies, p150.
227 P Cowley and M Stuart, *Dissension amongst the Parliamentary Labour Party, 2001-2005*, p1. http://revolts.co.uk/DissensionamongstthePLP.pdf.
228 https://www.parliament.uk/documents/commons/lib/research/briefings/snpc-03038.pdf.
229 Murray and German, p94.
230 Murray and German, p47.
231 Murray and German, p70.
232 Murray and German, p79.
233 Murray and German, p204.
234 T Benn, *Free Radical* (Continuum, London, 2001), p50.
235 Benn, p62.
236 Tony Wright, MP in Geddes and Tonge (eds), p94.
237 R Luxemburg, *Reform or Revolution*, in https://www.marxists.org/archive/luxemburg/1900/reform-revolution/ch08.htm.

Chapter 19:
From Miliband to Corbyn

1 Fabian Society, The Labour Leadership, 2010, p45. https://fabians.org.uk/wp-content/uploads/2010/08/TheLabourLeadership.pdf.
2 Ibid, p55.
3 Ibid, p64.
4 For all the figures go to https://en.wikipedia.org/wiki/Labour_Party_(UK)_leadership_election,_2010.
5 https://www.theguardian.com/uk/2010/nov/26/student-protests-police-under-fire.
6 https://www.bbc.co.uk/news/uk-politics-14503023.
7 https://www.newstatesman.com/blogs/the-staggers/2011/03/ed-miliband-hyde-park-speech.
8 www.newstatesman.com/blogs/the-staggers/2011/06/strikes-miliband-wrong.
9 www.bbc.co.uk/news/uk-politics-14890680.
10 https://publications.parliament.uk/pa/cm201011/cmhansrd/cm111130/debtext/111130-0001.htm.
11 https://www.mirror.co.uk/news/uk-news/gordon-brown-scottish-referendum-speech-4276089.
12 He was also celebrated as a hero when he attacked Corbyn's Labour over antisemitism in 2018.
13 SNP membership trebled in the two weeks after the referendum. https://www.dailyrecord.co.uk/news/politics/snp-membership-trebles-following-no-4359259.

14 https://www.bbc.co.uk/news/uk-politics-18539472.

15 In October 2016 Tory home secretary Amber Rudd proposed that companies should be forced disclose how many foreign workers they employ. The plan was near-universally derided, but was quite similar to Labour's in 2012.

16 https://www.theguardian.com/politics/2015/mar/29/diane-abbott-labour-immigration-controls-mugs-shameful.

17 *Financial Times*, 10 September 2015.

18 *Financial Times*, 28 August 2015. Marx's spectre was, of course, communism.

19 In the end Corbyn was nominated by 36 MPs—his supporters had miscounted how many he had achieved!

20 Field resigned the Labour whip in August 2018 in protest at Corbyn's leadership.

21 https://www.redpepper.org.uk/the-seconds-that-changed-labour-history/.

22 https://www.theguardian.com/politics/2015/jun/15/labour-leadership-contest-jeremy-corbyn.

23 https://www.marxists.org/archive/plekhanov/1898/xx/individual.html.

24 https://socialistworker.co.uk/art/41297/SWP+statement+on+election+of+ Jeremy+Corbyn+as+Labour+Party+leader.

25 https://yougov.co.uk/news/2015/12/02/analysis-sharp-fall-support-air-strikes-syria/.

26 For a full analysis see Charlie Kimber 'Why did Britain vote Leave?' *International Socialism*, 152, Autumn 2016 http://isj.org.uk/why-did-britain-vote-leave/.

27 https://www.buzzfeed.com/jimwaterson/the-corbyn-supremacy.

28 https://www.ft.com/content/cf7321b4-4c61-11e7-919a-1e14ce4af89b.

29 https://labourlist.org/2017/04/corbyn-comes-out-swinging-against-the-city-but-needs-an-urgent-answer-for-tv-on-labours-painful-polling/.

30 http://isj.org.uk/after-the-surge-corbyn-and-the-road-ahead/.

31 https://www.redpepper.org.uk/corbyn-and-the-manchester-speech/.

32 https://labourlist.org/2015/09/whats-going-to-happen-to-a-corbyn-led-labour-party/.

33 https://www.theguardian.com/politics/2015/sep/30/corbyn-i-would-never-use-nuclear-weapons-if-i-was-pm.

34 https://www.theguardian.com/commentisfree/2016/sep/26/labour-opposing trident playing politics-clive-lewis-theresa-may.

35 https://labour.org.uk/manifesto/a-global-britain/#third.

36 https://www.marxists.org/archive/cliff/works/1988/labour/13-wilson.html.

37 https://en.wikipedia.org/wiki/List_of_countries_by_public_debt.

38 https://www.theguardian.com/world/2015/oct/24/eu-referendum-yanis-varoufakis-says-britons-should-vote-to-stay-in-union.

39 https://www.rt.com/uk/316039-british-army-coup-corbyn/.

Chapter 20:
Conclusion

1 https://www.telegraph.co.uk/business/2018/09/13/gordon-brown-says-world-could-sleepwalking-financial-crisis/.

2 World Inequality Report. https://wir2018.wid.world/part-4.html.

3 https://www.marxists.org/archive/marx/works/1864/10/27.htm.

4 L Trotsky, *The First Five Years of the Communist International*, vol 2, p96.

Index

About the authors

The authors were or are all members of the Socialist Workers Party in Britain.

TONY CLIFF, a founding member of the Socialist Workers Party and its predecessors the Socialist Review Group and the International Socialists, was an active revolutionary for over 50 years in Palestine and in Britain. He was the author of many previous books, including the classic *State Capitalism in Russia*, a three volume biography of Lenin and a four volume biography of Leon Trotsky.

DONNY GLUCKSTEIN is a history lecturer in Edinburgh and the author of *The Western Soviets: Workers Councils 1915–20*, *The Nazis, Capitalism and the Working Class*, *A People's History of the Second World War*, and *The Paris Commune: A Revolution in Democracy.*

Together they wrote *Marxism and Trade Union Struggle* (1986), which is a study of the British General Strike of 1926.

CHARLIE KIMBER is the editor of *Socialist Worker* and the author of *Jeremy Corbyn, Labour and Fight for Socialism*, *Immigration: The Myths Sent to Divide Us*, and *Arguments for Revolution: The Case for the Socialist Workers Party* (with Joseph Choonara).

The Labour Party: A Marxist History